COMMUNICATION

Principles for a Lifetime

COMMUNICATION

Principles for a Lifetime

Eighth Edition

Global Edition

Steven A. Beebe
Texas State University

Susan J. Beebe
Texas State University

Diana K. Ivy
Texas A&M University–Corpus Christi

Harlow, England • London • New York • Boston • San Francisco • Toronto • Sydney • Dubai • Singapore • Hong Kong
Tokyo • Seoul • Taipei • New Delhi • Cape Town • Sao Paulo • Mexico City • Madrid • Amsterdam • Munich • Paris • Milan

Credits and acknowledgments borrowed from other sources and reproduced, with permission, in this textbook appear on the appropriate page of appearance or in the Credits on pages 451–454

Please contact https://support.pearson.com/getsupport/s/contactsupport with any queries on this content.

Cover image by bsaje/123rf.com.

Pearson Education Limited
KAO Two
KAO Park
Hockham Way
Harlow
Essex
CM17 9SR
United Kingdom

and Associated Companies throughout the world

Visit us on the World Wide Web at: www.pearsonglobaleditions.com

© Pearson Education Limited, 2022

The rights of Steven A. Beebe, Susan J. Beebe, and Diana K. Ivy, to be identified as the authors of this work have been asserted by them in accordance with the Copyright, Designs and Patents Act 1988.

Authorized adaptation from the United States edition, entitled *Communication: Principles for a Lifetime*, 8th Edition, ISBN 978-0-13-696792-7 by Steven A. Beebe, Susan J. Beebe, and Diana K. Ivy, published by Pearson Education © 2022.

All rights reserved. No part of this publication may be reproduced, stored in a retrieval system, or transmitted in any form or by any means, electronic, mechanical, photocopying, recording or otherwise, without either the prior written permission of the publisher or a license permitting restricted copying in the United Kingdom issued by the Copyright Licensing Agency Ltd, Saffron House, 6–10 Kirby Street, London EC1N 8TS.

PEARSON, ALWAYS LEARNING, and REVEL are exclusive trademarks owned by Pearson Education, Inc. or its affiliates in the U.S. and/or other countries.

All trademarks used herein are the property of their respective owners. The use of any trademark in this text does not vest in the author or publisher any trademark ownership rights in such trademarks, nor does the use of such trademarks imply any affiliation with or endorsement of this book by such owners. For information regarding permissions, request forms, and the appropriate contacts within the Pearson Education Global Rights and Permissions department, please visit www.pearsoned.com/permissions/.

ISBN 10: 1-292-35201-9
ISBN 13: 978-1-292-35201-5

British Library Cataloguing-in-Publication Data
A catalogue record for this book is available from the British Library

1   22

Typeset in Palatino LT Pro by Integra Software Services Pvt. Ltd.
Printed and bound by Neografia, Slovakia

For our teachers . . . and our students

Brief Contents

UNIT I PRINCIPLES OF COMMUNICATION

1. Identifying Foundations of Human Communication — 31
2. Exploring Self-Awareness and Communication — 57
3. Understanding Verbal Messages — 77
4. Understanding Nonverbal Messages — 96
5. Listening and Responding — 117
6. Adapting to Others: Diversity and Communication — 143

UNIT II INTERPERSONAL COMMUNICATION

7. Understanding Interpersonal Communication — 174
8. Enhancing Relationships — 193

UNIT III COMMUNICATING IN GROUPS AND TEAMS

9. Understanding Group and Team Performance — 216
10. Enhancing Group and Team Performance — 237

UNIT IV PUBLIC SPEAKING

11. Developing Your Speech — 268
12. Organizing and Outlining Your Speech — 295
13. Delivering Your Speech — 313
14. Speaking to Inform — 336
15. Speaking to Persuade — 354
A. Interviewing — 379
B. Sample Speeches for Discussion and Evaluation — 401

Contents

Preface 17

UNIT I PRINCIPLES OF COMMUNICATION

1 Identifying Foundations of Human Communication 31

Why Study Communication? 32
   To Improve Your Employability 33
   To Improve Your Relationships 34
   To Improve Your Health 35
The Communication Process 35
   Communication Defined 36
   Communication Characteristics 37
Communication Models 39
   Communication as Action: Message Transfer 39
   Communication as Interaction: Message Exchange 41
   Communication as Transaction: Message Creation 42
Critical/Cultural Perspectives & Communication: What's Your Position? 43
Communication Competence 44
   The Message Should Be Understood 44
   The Message Should Achieve Its Intended Effect 44
   The Message Should Be Ethical 45
Ethics & Communication: Is There a Universal Ethical Code? 45
Communication in the Twenty-First Century 46
   Immediate Communication 46
   Frequent Communication 47
   Communication That Meets Our Needs 47
Social Media & Communication: Facebook versus TikTok: Connecting on Social Media 48
   Comfortable Communication 48
Communication Contexts 49
   Interpersonal Communication 49
   Group Communication 49
   Presentational Communication 50
   Organizational and Health Communication 50
Communication Principles for a Lifetime 50
   Principle One: Be Aware of Your Communication with Yourself and Others 51
Diversity & Communication: Communication Principles for a Lifetime: Principles for All Cultures? 52
   Principle Two: Effectively Use and Interpret Verbal Messages 52
   Principle Three: Effectively Use and Interpret Nonverbal Messages 53
   Principle Four: Listen and Respond Thoughtfully to Others 54
   Principle Five: Appropriately Adapt Messages to Others 54
STUDY GUIDE: *Principles for a Lifetime* 55
Principle Points • *Principle* Terms • *Principle* Skills

2 Exploring Self-Awareness and Communication 57

Self-Awareness: How Well Do You Know Yourself? 58
Self-Concept: Who Are You? 60
   Self-Concept Components 60
   One or Many Selves? 60
   How the Self-Concept Develops 62
Diversity & Communication: Self-Concept among Students in Malaysia 62
Self-Esteem: What's Your Value? 64
   Gender 64
   Social Comparisons 65
Social Media & Communication: Fitspiration: Friend or Foe? 65
   Self-Fulfilling Prophecy 66
Communication and the Enhancement of Self-Esteem 66
   Engage in Positive Self-Talk 66
   Visualize 66
Ethics & Communication: Are Students Narcissistic? 67
   Reframe 67
   Develop Honest Relationships 68
   Surround Yourself with Positive People 68
   Lose Your Baggage 68
The Perception Process 69
   Stage One: Attention and Selection 69
   Stage Two: Organization 70
   Stage Three: Interpretation 71
   When Perceptions Vary 71
Communicate to Enhance Your Powers of Perception 72

Increase Your Awareness	72
Avoid Stereotypes	72
Check Your Perceptions	73
Critical/Cultural Perspectives & Communication: Stereotypes Are Lazy	73
STUDY GUIDE: *Principles for a Lifetime*	74
Principle Points • *Principle* Terms • *Principle* Skills	

3 Understanding Verbal Messages 77

Why Focus on Language?	79
The Nature of Language	80
People Use Words as Symbols	80
People Attach Meanings to Words	80
People Create Denotative and Connotative Meanings for Words	81
People Convey Concrete and Abstract Meanings through Words	81
Meanings Are Culture Bound	81
Meanings Are Context Bound	82
The Power of Words	82
Social Media & Communication: E-Thai	83
Confronting Bias in Language	84
Biased Language: Race, Ethnicity, Nationality, and Religion	84
Critical/Cultural Perspectives & Communication: Black Lives Matter vs. All Lives Matter	85
Biased Language: Sex, Gender, and Sexual Orientation	86
Diversity & Communication: Gender Bias in Malay Language	87
Ethics & Communication: France May Ban Gender Neutral Words	88
Biased Language: Age, Class, and Ability	89
Using Words to Establish Supportive Relationships	90
Describe Your Own Feelings Rather Than Evaluate Others	91
Solve Problems Rather Than Control Others	91
Empathize Rather Than Remain Detached from Others	91
Be Flexible Rather Than Rigid toward Others	92
Present Yourself as Equal Rather Than Superior	92
Avoid Gunny-Sacking	93
STUDY GUIDE: *Principles for a Lifetime*	93
Principle Points • *Principle* Terms • *Principle* Skills	

4 Understanding Nonverbal Messages 96

Why Focus on Nonverbal Communication?	98
Nonverbal Messages Communicate Feelings and Attitudes	98
Nonverbal Messages Are More Believable Than Verbal Ones	99
Nonverbal Messages Are Critical to Successful Relationships	99
Ethics & Communication: Do We Have a Rhythm or Are You Just Mimicking Me?	100
Nonverbal Messages Serve Multiple Functions	100
The Nature of Nonverbal Communication	101
The Culture-Bound Nature of Nonverbal Communication	101
The Rule-Governed Nature of Nonverbal Communication	101
The Ambiguous Nature of Nonverbal Communication	102
Diversity & Communication: Lessons from a Student in a Wheelchair	102
The Continuous Nature of Nonverbal Communication	103
The Nonlinguistic Nature of Nonverbal Communication	103
The Multi-channeled Nature of Nonverbal Communication	103
Codes of Nonverbal Communication	104
Appearance	104
Critical/Cultural Perspectives & Communication: How Powerful Is Beauty?	105
Body Movement, Gestures, and Posture	105
Social Media & Communication: Social Media Pressure: Do Comparisons Have Consequences?	106
Eye Contact	106
Facial Expressions	107
Touch	108
The Voice	109
Physical Environment, Space, and Territory	110
How to Interpret Nonverbal Cues More Accurately	112
An Application of Nonverbal Communication Research: Detecting Deception	113
STUDY GUIDE: *Principles for a Lifetime*	114
Principle Points • *Principle* Terms • *Principle* Skills	

5 Listening and Responding 117

The Importance of Listening and Responding Skills	118
Listening Enhances Our Relationships with Others	119
Listening Helps Us Work Collaboratively with Others	119
Listening Links Speaker and Audience	120
How We Listen	120
Selecting	121
Attending	121
Understanding	121
Remembering	121
Responding	121
Listening Styles	122
Relational Listening Style	122
Analytical Listening Style	122
Critical Listening Style	123
Task-Oriented Listening Style	123
The Benefits of Understanding Your Listening Style	123
Listening Barriers	125
Self Barriers	125
Information-Processing Barriers	126
Diversity & Communication: Does Your Gender Influence Your Listening Style?	128

Critical/Cultural Perspectives & Communication: What Are Your Listening Expectations and Assumptions?	129
Context Barriers	129
Listening Skills	**130**
Stop: Turn Off Competing Messages	130
Look: Listen with Your Eyes	131
Listen: Understand Both Details and Major Ideas	132
Responding Skills	**135**
Respond to Clarify and Confirm Understanding	135
Respond to Empathize with Others	137
Social Media & Communication: Keep Social Media Social	**137**
Ethics & Communication: Paraphrase Properly	**139**
Respond to Provide Social Support	140
STUDY GUIDE: Principles for a Lifetime	**141**
Principle Points • *Principle* Terms • *Principle* Skills	

6 Adapting to Others: Diversity and Communication — 143

Diversity and Communication	**145**
Sex and Gender	145
Gender Identity and Sexual Orientation	146
Age	148
Race and Ethnicity	150
Social Class	151
Intersectionality: A Combination of Differences	151
Culture and Communication	**152**
Defining Culture	152
Diversity & Communication: Malaysian Diversity Almanac	**153**
Cultural Contexts	154
Cultural Values	154
Social Media & Communication: Adapting to Differences When Making E-Connections	**156**
Critical/Cultural Perspectives & Communication: Do You Have Power?	**158**
Barriers to Adapting to Others	**160**
Assuming Superiority	160
Assuming Similarity	161
Assuming Differences	162
Stereotyping and Prejudice	163
Ethics & Communication: Can Stereotyping Others Ever Be a Good Idea?	**163**
Strategies for Adapting to Others	**164**
Aim for Intercultural Communication Competence	164
Be Motivated: Develop Positive Attitudes toward Those Who Are Different from Yourself	165
Develop Knowledge about Those Who Are Different from Yourself	166
Develop Skills: Engage in Behaviors That Enhance Understanding	167
STUDY GUIDE: Principles for a Lifetime	**171**
Principle Points • *Principle* Terms • *Principle* Skills	

UNIT II INTERPERSONAL COMMUNICATION

7 Understanding Interpersonal Communication — 174

What Is Interpersonal Communication?	**175**
Initiating Relationships	**176**
Interpersonal Attraction: Why We Like Whom We Like	177
Diversity & Communication: Unconscious Bias in Asian Business Leadership	**178**
Communicating Our Attraction	179
Social Media & Communication: Flirtmoji	**181**
Initiating Relationships	181
Maintaining Relationships	**185**
Ethics & Communication: Identity Theft and Social Media	**186**
Self-Disclosure: Revealing Yourself to Others	186
Properties of Self-Disclosure	187
Two Models of Self-Disclosure	188
Expressing Emotions	189
Critical/Cultural Perspectives & Communication: Where You Stand Affects How You Sway	**190**
STUDY GUIDE: Principles for a Lifetime	**191**
Principle Points • *Principle* Terms • *Principle* Skills	

8 Enhancing Relationships — 193

The Importance of Relationships: Friends, Family, and Colleagues	**194**
Friendship Matters	194
Family Matters	195
Colleagues Matter	195
Social Media & Communication: Video Chat during the COVID-19 Pandemic	**196**
Your Relationships and the Five Communication Principles for a Lifetime	196
Stages of Relationship Development	**198**
Relational Escalation	199
Relational De-Escalation	200
Relationship Dissolution (a.k.a. the Breakup)	**201**
Best Practices in Breaking Up	201
Ethics & Communication: Cyber Infidelity: Is It Cheating If You Don't Actually Touch?	**203**
After the Breakup: Communicating with an Ex	203
Tensions in Relationships: The Dialectical Perspective	**204**
Managing Interpersonal Conflict	**205**

Critical/Cultural Perspectives & Communication: Power to the Partners	206	Diversity & Communication: Hofstede, Culture, and Saudi Arabia	208
Constructive versus Destructive Conflict	206	Conflict Management Skills	209
Types of Conflict	207	**STUDY GUIDE: *Principles for a Lifetime***	**212**
Conflict Management Styles	208	*Principle* Points • *Principle* Terms • *Principle* Skills	

UNIT III COMMUNICATING IN GROUPS AND TEAMS

9 Understanding Group and Team Performance — 216

Groups and Teams Defined	218
Communicating in Small Groups	218
Social Media & Communication: Keep Your Phone Out of Sight During Meetings	220
Communicating in Teams	220
Ethics & Communication: How Far Would You Go to Achieve a Team Goal?	221
When Not to Collaborate in Groups and Teams	222
Group and Team Dynamics	222
Roles	222
Rules	225
Norms	226
Status	227
Power	228
Cohesiveness	229
Critical/Cultural Perspectives & Communication: Should You Form an Alliance with Others?	231
Group and Team Development	231
Orientation	231
Conflict	232
Emergence	233
Diversity & Communication: The Lewis Model	233
Reinforcement	234
The Process Nature of Group Phases	234
STUDY GUIDE: *Principles for a Lifetime*	**235**
Principle Points • *Principle* Terms • *Principle* Skills	

10 Enhancing Group and Team Performance — 237

What Effective Group and Team Members Do	239
Identify a Clear, Elevating Goal	239
Develop a Results-Driven Structure	239
Gather and Share Appropriate Information	240
Develop Options	240
Evaluate Ideas	241
Develop Sensitivity toward Others	241
Develop a Positive Personal Style	242
Structuring Group and Team Problem Solving	243
Step 1: Identify and Define the Problem	244
Step 2: Analyze the Problem	245
Step 3: Generate Creative Solutions	246
Step 4: Select the Best Solution	248
Ethics & Communication: What If Someone Can't Stop Judging?	248
Step 5: Take Action	250
Enhancing Group and Team Leadership	251
Trait Approach	251
Functional Approach	252
Styles Approach	253
Situational Approach	254
Social Media & Communication: Do We Still Need Face To Face Meetings?	255
Diversity & Communication: Deep and Surface Diversity: Which Differences Make a Difference?	256
Transformational Leadership	256
Enhancing Group and Team Meetings	257
Manage Meeting Structure	258
Manage Meeting Interaction	260
Critical/Cultural Perspectives & Communication: Who Controls the Agenda?	260
STUDY GUIDE: *Principles for a Lifetime*	**266**
Principle Points • *Principle* Terms • *Principle* Skills	

UNIT IV PUBLIC SPEAKING

11 Developing Your Speech — 268

Critical/Cultural Perspectives & Communication: Using Public Advocacy to Address Positions of Power	269
Overviewing the Public Speaking Process	270
Developing Your Speech Step By Step: Considering Your Audience	270
Building Your Confidence	271
Understand Public Speaking Anxiety	272
Know How to Develop a Speech	272
Be Prepared	272
Give Yourself a Mental Pep Talk	273
Use Deep-Breathing Techniques	273
Focus on Your Audience	273
Focus on Your Message	273
Take Advantage of Opportunities to Speak	273
Explore Additional Resources	273

Selecting and Narrowing Your Topic	274
Who Is the Audience?	274
What Is the Occasion?	274
What Are My Interests and Experiences?	274
Conducting Silent Brainstorming	275
Scanning Web Directories and Web Pages	275
Listening and Reading for Topic Ideas	275
Developing Your Speech Step By Step: Selecting and Narrowing Your Topic	**276**
Identifying Your Purpose	277
General Purpose	277
Ethics & Communication: Is It Ethical to Buy a Speech?	**277**
Specific Purpose	278
Developing Your Speech Step By Step: Identifying Your Purpose	**279**
Developing Your Central Idea	279
Developing Your Speech Step By Step: Developing Your Central Idea	**280**
An Audience-Centered Idea	280
A Single Idea	280
A Complete Declarative Sentence	281
Direct, Specific Language	281
Generating Main Ideas	282
Does the Central Idea Have *Logical Divisions*?	282
Can You Think of Several *Reasons* the Central Idea Is True?	282
Developing Your Speech Step By Step: Generating Your Main Ideas	**283**
Can You Support the Central Idea with a Series of *Steps* or a *Chronological Sequence*?	283
Gathering Supporting Material	284
Sources of Supporting Material	284
Social Media & Communication: Why do people share disinformation?	**286**
Types of Supporting Material	287
Developing Your Speech Step By Step: Gathering Supporting Material	**287**
Acknowledgment of Supporting Material	291
Diversity & Communication: Global English	**291**
STUDY GUIDE: *Principles for a Lifetime*	**292**
Principle Points • *Principle* Terms • *Principle* Skills	

12 Organizing and Outlining Your Speech — 295

Organizing Your Main Ideas	296
Organizing Ideas Topically	296
Social Media & Communication: Your Speech as a "Content Sandwich"	**296**
Organizing Ideas Chronologically	297
Organizing Ideas Spatially	298
Organizing Ideas to Show Cause and Effect	298
Organizing Ideas by Problem and Solution	298
Diversity & Communication: Public Speaking – The Cultural Diversity Question	**299**
Organizing Your Supporting Material	299
Ethics & Communication: The Ethics of Primacy and Recency	**300**
Signposting: Organizing Your Speech for the Ears of Others	300
Previews	301
Verbal and Nonverbal Transitions	301
Critical/Cultural Perspectives & Communication: Structures for Effecting Change	**301**
Summaries	302
Introducing and Concluding Your Speech	303
Introductions	303
Conclusions	305
Outlining Your Speech	306
Preparation Outline	306
Sample Preparation Outline	308
Speaking Notes	310
STUDY GUIDE: *Principles for a Lifetime*	**311**
Principle Points • *Principle* Terms • *Principle* Skills	

13 Delivering Your Speech — 313

Methods of Delivery	314
Manuscript Speaking	315
Memorized Speaking	315
Impromptu Speaking	316
Extemporaneous Speaking	316
Effective Verbal Delivery	317
Using Words Clearly	317
Using Words Accurately	318
Critical/Cultural Perspectives & Communication: Words Constitute Meaning	**318**
Crafting Memorable Word Structures	319
Social Media & Communication: Coded Language on Social Media	**321**
Effective Nonverbal Delivery	321
Eye Contact	321
Diversity & Communication: The Academic Quarter	**322**
Physical Delivery	322
Facial Expression	324
Vocal Delivery	324
Developing Your Speech Step By Step: Rehearsing Your Speech	**325**
Appearance	326
Effective Presentation Aids	326
Types of Presentation Aids	327
Ethics & Communication: Profanity in an Audio Presentation Aid	**330**
Additional Guidelines for Preparing and Using Presentation Aids	330
Some Final Tips for Rehearsing and Delivering Your Speech	332
Developing Your Speech Step By Step: Delivering Your Speech	**333**
Criteria for Evaluating Speeches	334
STUDY GUIDE: *Principles for a Lifetime*	**334**
Principle Points • *Principle* Terms • *Principle* Skills	

14 Speaking to Inform — 336

Types of Informative Speeches — 337
- Speeches about Objects — 337
- Speeches about Procedures — 337
- Speeches about People — 338

Ethics & Communication: Confidential or Potentially Dangerous Information — 339
- Speeches about Events — 339
- Speeches about Ideas — 340

Strategies for Organizing Your Informative Speech — 340
- Organizing Speeches about Objects — 340
- Organizing Speeches about Procedures — 341
- Organizing Speeches about People — 341
- Organizing Speeches about Events — 341
- Organizing Speeches about Ideas — 342

Strategies for Making Your Informative Speech Clear — 343
- Simplify Ideas — 343

Diversity & Communication: Using an Interpreter — 343
- Pace Your Information Flow — 344
- Relate New Information to Old — 344

Strategies for Making Your Informative Speech Interesting — 344
- Relate to Your Listeners' Interests — 344
- Use Attention-Getting Supporting Material — 345
- Establish a Motive for Your Audience to Listen to You — 345
- Use Word Pictures — 346
- Create Interesting Presentation Aids — 346

Social Media & Communication: Informative Speaking via Zoom for a Baseball Season Cut Short — 347
- Use Humor — 347

Strategies for Making Your Informative Speech Memorable — 348
- Build in Redundancy — 348
- Use Adult Learning Principles — 348
- Reinforce Key Ideas Verbally — 349
- Reinforce Key Ideas Nonverbally — 349

Critical/Cultural Perspectives & Communication: What Makes Fake News Fake — 349

Sample Informative Speech: "Elvis," by Angelitta Armijo — 350

STUDY GUIDE: *Principles for a Lifetime* — 352
Principle Points • *Principle* Terms • *Principle* Skills

15 Speaking to Persuade — 354

Understanding Persuasion — 355
- Persuasion Defined — 355
- The Psychology of Persuasion — 355

Ethics & Communication: More Than Just A Customer Loyalty Card — 356

Developing Your Audience-Centered Persuasive Speech — 359
- Narrowing Your Topic — 359
- Identifying Your Purpose — 359
- Developing Your Central Idea as a Persuasive Proposition — 360

Supporting Your Persuasive Message with Credibility, Logic, and Emotion — 361
- Ethos: Establishing Your Credibility — 361
- Logos: Using Evidence and Reasoning — 363

Diversity & Communication: "Elementary Reasoning, My Dear Watson" — 364
- Pathos: Using Emotion — 366

Organizing Your Persuasive Message — 366
- Problem–Solution — 366
- Cause and Effect — 367
- Refutation — 368
- The Motivated Sequence — 368

Social Media & Communication: Influencers and Social Media Houses — 368

Adapting Ideas to People and People to Ideas — 371
- The Receptive Audience — 371

Critical/Cultural Perspectives & Communication: Persuasion as Dialogue: The Power of Listening and Responding — 371
- The Neutral Audience — 372
- The Unreceptive Audience — 372

Sample Persuasive Speech: "Private Ambulances," by Blake Bergeron — 373

STUDY GUIDE: *Principles for a Lifetime* — 376
Principle Points • *Principle* Terms • *Principle* Skills

A Interviewing — 379

Interview Types — 380
- Information-Gathering Interview — 381
- Appraisal Interview — 381
- Problem-Solving Interview — 381
- Persuasion Interview — 381
- Job Interview — 382

Interview Phases — 382
- The Opening — 382
- The Body: Asking Questions — 383
- The Conclusion — 386

How to Be Interviewed for a Job — 386
- Be Aware of Your Skills and Abilities — 387
- Prepare Your Resume — 387

Sample Resume — 390
- Identify the Needs of Your Potential Employer — 391
- Look and Communicate Your Best — 391
- Polish Your Online Appearance — 392

Social Media & Communication: Putting Your Best Facebook Image Forward — 393
- Listen, Respond, and Ask Appropriate Questions — 393
- Follow Up after the Interview — 395

How to Be Interviewed in an Information-Gathering Interview — 395
- Prepare for the Interview — 396

Listen Effectively	396	**B**	Sample Speeches for Discussion and Evaluation	401
Respond Appropriately	396			

Interviewer Responsibilities 397

    Adapt to an Interviewee's Behavior 397

Informative Speech: "Recuperandos," by Manuel Reyes 401

    Deal Wisely with Sensitive Content 397

    Listen Effectively 397

Persuasive Speech: "Queers of the Court," by Caleb Newton 403

    Record Information 397

Critical/Cultural Perspectives & Communication: Becoming an Unbiased Person of Conscience 398

Endnotes 406

Credits 451

    Ask Appropriate Questions 398

Index 455

STUDY GUIDE: *Principles for a Lifetime* **399**

Principle Points • *Principle* Terms • *Principle* Skills

Preface

Communication is essential for life. The purpose of this text is to document this claim by presenting fundamental principles of human communication that enhance the quality of our communication with others as well as the quality of our own lives. Most students who read this text will take only one communication course during their entire college career. We want students to view this course on communication as a vital, life-enriching one that will help them enhance their communication with others—not just as another course in a string of curricular requirements. Because communication is an essential element of living, we want students to remember essential communication principles and skills for the rest of their lives. To remember and apply these essential communication principles, we believe students need a digest of classic and contemporary research and practice that will help them with both the mundane and the magnificent, the everyday and the ever-important communication experiences that constitute the fabric of their lives. In this edition, as in the seven that preceded it, we strive to create a highly appealing, easy-to-use text that is more effective than ever in helping students understand and use the five vital principles of communication.

What's New to the Eighth Edition?

Reviewers, instructors, and our students have given us feedback about the seven previous editions. This feedback has helped us make this new edition the best possible teaching and learning resource. We listened and responded (Principle Four) to their suggestions. Our commitment to providing a digest of essentials that does not overwhelm students has also led us to make some changes.

We have included the following new features in every chapter:

- New Critical/Cultural Perspectives & Communication feature boxes appear in each chapter and explore various communication topics from a critical/cultural communication perspective, focusing on messages about power, resistance, suppression, marginalization, and culture.
- The chapter-end Study Guide has been revised for this edition. Learning objectives, review summaries, key terms, and apply and assess questions are now called *Principle* Points, *Principle* Terms, and *Principle* Skills to call attention to the five *Principles for a Lifetime* we highlight throughout the text.
- In each chapter we've provided updated and expanded research that incorporates the latest findings about the principles and skills of human communication.
- We've added fresh, contemporary examples and illustrations to which students can relate.
- New photos and illustrations amplify the content of our message.

CRITICAL/CULTURAL PERSPECTIVES & COMMUNICATION

Stereotypes Are Lazy

Probably every person reading this text has felt the sting of a stereotype being applied to them in some way or another. Perhaps you were tagged as a nerd or geek growing up, simply because you enjoyed school, worked hard, and made good grades. Maybe you were a good athlete and somebody called you a "dumb jock," as though athleticism and intelligence could not co-reside in one person. Maybe the stereotype went deeper, into identity factors such as your sex or gender, sexual orientation, race, ethnicity, religion, or ability level. Maybe you moved from one part of the country to another and the stereotype emerged in your new locale.

What motivates someone to talk in stereotypes or to inflict stereotypical language onto other people? Is it laziness? Could it be power? Sometimes people feel insecure or in competition with others; sometimes people are simply ignorant about various forms of diversity. People also use labels to downgrade or diminish others in order to minimize a perceived disparity between them. It can be a tactic to make oneself seem more powerful and to project an air of superiority when you're in the outgroup, not the ingroup.[70]

We encourage you to inventory your attitudes about others and the language you use. Purge your language of stereotypes. No one wants to be treated like a category rather than a unique individual.

> **STUDY GUIDE: *PRINCIPLES FOR A LIFETIME***   CHAPTER 2
>
> **Self-Awareness: How Well Do You Know Yourself?**
>
> **2.1** Discuss the importance of self-awareness in the process of improving one's communication skills.
>
> **PRINCIPLE POINTS:** Self-awareness is the ability to develop and communicate a representation of yourself to others.
>
> **PRINCIPLE TERMS:**
> self-awareness   symbolic self-awareness
>
> **PRINCIPLE SKILLS:**
> 1. Describe an example of how you or someone you know progressed through Maslow's levels of competence. What skill did you or the other person develop? What behaviors did you or the other person demonstrate at each level?
>
> self, the social self, and the spiritual self. Our self-concept develops through our communication with others, our association with various groups, the roles we assume in our lives, and the labels we use to describe ourselves. Our avowed identity is assigned by ourselves, whereas our ascribed identity involves characteristics other people assign or attribute to us.
>
> **PRINCIPLE TERMS:**
> self   social self
> self-concept   spiritual self
> attitudes   avowed identity
> beliefs   ascribed identity
> values   self-reflexiveness
> material self
>
> **PRINCIPLE SKILLS:**
> 1. How has communication with family, friends, teachers, or others influenced your self-concept, either in the

- Appendix B includes two new student speeches that model the best practices in public speaking.

We've also updated popular continuing features that appear throughout the text, including the following:

- Revised Diversity & Communication feature boxes complement and expand discussions of new applications of research about diversity throughout the text.
- Revised Ethics & Communication feature boxes reinforce the importance of being an ethical communicator and may spark discussion of ethical questions.
- Revised Social Media & Communication feature boxes explore ways to effectively use social media as an important communication tool.

We've made many other specific changes to chapter content throughout the text. Here's a list of selected major revisions, changes, and additions that we've made to each chapter:

Chapter 1: Identifying Foundations of Human Communication

A new Critical/Cultural Perspectives & Communication feature box entitled "Where Are You Standing?" explains how a person's perceived power and ability to influence others can impact how he or she makes sense of the world and shares that sense with others. Additional research on the benefits of strong interpersonal relationships, how we use technology to make human connections, and mediated communication has also been added to the chapter. The Social Media & Communication feature box, "Facebook versus TikTok: Connecting on Social Media," discusses data on the popularity of various social media platforms. Our discussion about context has been expanded to include explanations of physical, historical, psychological, and cultural communication environments. We have clarified the difference between the word *communication* and *communications* (with the "s"). Revel features new videos and accompanying self-checks on interpersonal communication models and the benefits of studying communication. There is also a new journal prompt encouraging students to think about their career goals and how they relate to the study of communication.

Chapter 2: Exploring Self-Awareness and Communication

The new Critical/Cultural Perspectives & Communication box entitled "Stereotypes Are Lazy" discusses stereotypical language and encourages students to inventory their attitudes about others and the language they use. A new Diversity & Communication box talks about self-concept development among Malaysian vocational students. The various pros and cons of the "fitspiration" social media movement are covered in a new Social Media & Communication box. The chapter also includes new research on the connection between self-esteem and physical attractiveness, as well as the relationship between self-esteem and social media use. In Revel, there are new videos on how social media can affect our self-esteem, the accuracy of our perceptions, and why the Internet perpetuates gender stereotypes. A new journal prompt asks students if they have ever experienced self-esteem loss from comparing themselves to others and a new shared writing prompt encourages students to provide self-labels to describe their own attitudes, beliefs, values, and actions.

Chapter 3: Understanding Verbal Messages A new Critical/Cultural Perspectives & Communication box entitled "Black Lives Matter vs. All Lives Matter" explains why it's important to inventory and interrogate our use of language. The Social Media & Communication box in this chapter looks at the impact of "Netspeak". New examples and research have been added to the discussions about symbols, neologisms, the power of words, biased language, and empathy. Our discussion of transphobia and transphobic language has been expanded. Revel features new videos with accompanying self-checks about how people create meanings for language and how social media has changed the way news is communicated. New journal prompts ask students to consider the power of words and think about the ways words can communicate feelings.

Chapter 4: Understanding Nonverbal Messages To capture students' interest, we've added new nonverbal communication examples, including how the use of touch, eye contact, and physical space have changed as a result of the COVID-19 pandemic. A new discussion about the power and influence of physical beauty is included in the Critical/Cultural Perspectives & Communication box. New research findings about the multi-channeled nature of nonverbal communication, appearance, and affectionate touch have also been added to the chapter. A new video in Revel with an accompanying self-check explains why nonverbal communication is just as important as verbal communication. Another new video discusses why some people find lying much easier than others. A new journal prompt asks students to think of someone they know and to consider the nonverbal dominance cues they associate with that person.

Chapter 5: Listening and Responding The discussion of empathic listening has been significantly revised and updated with new examples and research. We have added a definition of closeness communication bias to the chapter. A new Critical/Cultural Perspectives & Communication feature box discusses listening expectations and assumptions. New research on meditation techniques, interrupters, asking relevant questions, emotional intelligence, and supportive messages has been added to the chapter. In Revel, new journal prompts ask students to consider a time when they may have experienced closeness communication bias and when they found their mind wandering while trying to listen. A new shared writing prompt encourages students to consider their most challenging barrier to listening.

Chapter 6: Adapting to Others: Diversity and Communication An introduction to and a discussion of the concept of intersectionality is now included in the chapter. Accompanying this discussion is a new Critical/Cultural Perspectives & Communication box entitled "Do You Have Power?", which explains why it's important to be aware of your own perceived power and your positionality, as well as the power others are perceived to have in order to be an effective communicator. Our coverage of sex, gender, gender identity, sexual orientation, race, ethnicity, and social class has been revised and updated with new research and examples. A discussion about gender expression has been added to the chapter. Research on Generation Z has been added to Table 6.1 and to the coverage of generational characteristics within the text. In Revel, a new journal prompt asks students to consider how their race, class, gender, and sexuality impact their social identity.

Chapter 7: Understanding Interpersonal Communication A new Critical/Cultural Perspectives & Communication feature box asks students to think about where they stand, in terms of privilege, power, and influence, in comparison to others. New research on flirting, online dating, and pickup lines has been added to the chapter. In Revel, new videos and video self-checks discuss strategies for maintaining long-distance friendships and the pros and cons of online dating. A new shared writing prompt asks students to consider the topic of social attraction.

Chapter 8: Enhancing Relationships The discussion of assertive and aggressive communication has been revised and updated. A new Critical/Cultural Perspectives & Communication feature box discusses interpersonal power and how it impacts our relationships with others. Additional research on college friendships, the global pandemic's impact on families, cheating, ghosting, and conflict has been added to the chapter. Revel includes two new videos and accompanying self-checks on apologies and family conflicts. We have also added a new journal prompt about breakups and a new shared writing prompt about ghosting.

Chapter 9: Understanding Group and Team Performance A new Critical/Cultural Perspectives & Communication box discusses how joining forces with others who hold similar views can help you gain more influence. A new discussion about information power has been added to the chapter. In Revel, we've added new videos on why it's important to study small group communication, how technology has changed the way we communicate in small groups, how to improve communication in virtual groups, and what makes a group a team. A new journal prompt asks students to think about what constitutes a group or team.

Chapter 10: Enhancing Group and Team Performance A new Critical/Cultural Perspectives & Communication box entitled "Who Controls the Agenda?" discusses how to assess who holds the most power in a meeting. In addition, a new Social Media & Communication feature box discusses the importance of virtual and face-to-face meetings. New research has been added to the chapter on the following topics: risk-taking within groups, the use of technology in helping groups stay on task, high-performing group practices, substantive conflict within groups and teams, transformational leadership, and virtual groups. In Revel, we've added a number of new videos on topics such as how to plan more productive meetings, problem-solving strategies for groups and teams, how to use collaborative apps to connect virtually with team members, obstacles that virtual groups face, small group leadership, how diversity contributes to group creativity, and the dangers of groupthink.

Chapter 11: Developing Your Speech To capture student interest, new speech examples have been added throughout the chapter on topics such as parental leave policies, pollution by the U.S. military, child slavery, Michigan's COVID-19 reopening policy, deaths in U.S. jails and prisons, domestic violence, and 3D printed guns. Figures 11.4 (Brainstorming a Topic), 11.5 (Possible Topics from a Web Directory Search), 11.6 (Narrowing a Broad Topic), and 11.10 (The central idea should be a complete declarative sentence) have been revised and updated with new examples. A new Critical/Cultural Perspectives & Communication feature box discusses public advocacy, and a new Social Media & Communication box discusses issues with disinformation on social media. In Revel, we have added new videos about the fear of public speaking, audience analysis, choosing the right speech topic, selecting the right sources, and plagiarism.

Chapter 12: Organizing and Outlining Your Speech To assist in student understanding, five new figures (12.1, 12.2, 12.3, 12.4, and 12.5) have been added to the chapter to visually present how topics can be organized topically, chronologically, spatially, to show cause and effect, and by problem and solution. A new Critical/Cultural

Perspectives & Communication box discusses how logically organizing your persuasive speech can help you effect positive change. To increase student interest, we've added new excerpts from speeches on overcrowded animal shelters, universal health care, bees, body brokering, and opioid abuse. In Revel, new videos have been added on the following speech topics: signposting, introductions, conclusions, outlines, and structure. A new journal prompt asks students to write an introduction for a speech on what "defunding the police" could mean for communities.

Chapter 13: Delivering Your Speech A new Critical/Cultural Perspectives & Communication feature box explains why words *constitute* rather than *transfer* meaning, and a new Social Media & Communication box discusses how the meaning of certain words can change over time, as evidenced by the evolution of the term *boogaloo*. To capture student interest, Figures 13.7 (Chart) and 13.8 (Three Types of Graphs) have been redrawn using U.S. COVID-19 data from the summer of 2020. We've also added a new word cloud illustration that visualizes the frequency with which activist Greta Thunberg used various words in her speech at the 2019 United Nations Climate Action Summit. In Revel, new videos discuss how Abraham Lincoln, John F. Kennedy, and Barbara Jordan used language in their most famous speeches, and how the typefaces in your presentation aids can influence your audience's impression of your speech. A new journal prompt encourages students to think about ways they could more effectively use presentation aids. A new shared writing prompt asks students to identify three examples of figurative language used in Martin Luther King Jr.'s famous "Dream" speech.

Chapter 14: Speaking to Inform In this chapter, we have provided new lists of sample subjects for speeches about people and events. A new Critical/Cultural Perspectives & Communication box discusses what makes "fake news" fake, and a new Social Media & Communication box shares an example of how informative speaking has moved online in response to the COVID-19 pandemic. In Revel, a new video discusses how good storytelling can make speeches more engaging and powerful. In addition, a new journal prompt asks students to provide ideas for attention-catching supporting material they could use for a speech about the most recent U.S. presidential election.

Chapter 15: Speaking to Persuade We've added a new figure (15.7) to visually present eight common logical fallacies so students can more easily identify them. A new Critical/Cultural Perspectives & Communication box explains why persuasion must be a dialogue, with both speaker and listener sharing responsibility for the outcome, and a new Social Media & Communication box discusses online influencers and the trend of social media houses in Los Angeles. In Revel, new journal prompts ask students to share a time when they were indirectly persuaded by a speech or an advertisement, and to come up with an emotion-arousing illustration or description for a speech about the importance of registering to vote.

Appendix A: Interviewing A new introduction to this appendix highlights how much the job application process has changed over time. A new Critical/Cultural Perspectives & Communication feature box discusses how to make unbiased, ethical, and legal hiring decisions. In Revel, a new video discusses how to have a successful job interview. A new journal prompt asks students to think about a question they had trouble answering in a past job interview and to consider how they would answer the same questions today.

Appendix B: Sample Speeches for Discussion and Evaluation This appendix features two new student speeches, including one about an alternative methodology of incarceration and rehabilitation in Brazil and another about the discrimination that queer defendants face in the U.S. justice system.

What Stays the Same in This Edition?

In our eighth edition of *Communication: Principles for a Lifetime*, our goal remains the same as in the first edition: to provide a cogent presentation of what is essential about human communication by organizing the study of communication around five fundamental communication principles that are inherent in the process of communicating with others.

Our Integrated Approach Remains Unchanged

To help students remember and integrate essential communication principles, we've organized the study of human communication around five fundamental communication principles:

Principle One: Be aware of your communication with yourself and others.
Principle Two: Effectively use and interpret verbal messages.
Principle Three: Effectively use and interpret nonverbal messages.
Principle Four: Listen and respond thoughtfully to others.
Principle Five: Appropriately adapt messages to others.

We don't claim that everything you need to know about communication is embedded in our five communication principles. These principles do, however, synthesize essential research and wisdom about communication. They are designed to help students in an introductory communication course see the "big picture" of the role and importance of communication, both as they sit in the classroom and as they live their lives.

The problem with many introduction to communication courses is that there is often too much of a good thing. An introductory course covers a vast terrain of communication concepts, principles, and skills. Besides learning about several theories of communication, students are also presented with what may appear to them to be miniature courses in interpersonal communication, group communication, and public speaking.

At the end of a typical hybrid or introductory communication fundamentals course, both students and instructors have made a breathless dash through an astounding amount of information and number of skills. The barrage of ideas, contexts, and theories can leave students and instructors feeling overwhelmed by a seemingly unrelated hodgepodge of information. Students may end up viewing communication as a fragmented area of study that includes a bushel basket full of concepts and applications, but they have little understanding of what is truly fundamental about how we make sense out of the world and share that sense with others. Rather than seeing communication as a crazy quilt of unrelated ideas and skills, we want students to see a unified fabric of common principles that they will remember long after the course is over. The five fundamental principles provide a framework for understanding the importance of communication in our lives.

Our pentagon model illustrates the relationships among the five communication principles that provide the overarching structure of the text. As a principle is being introduced or discussed, the appropriate part of the model is highlighted. In most texts, communication principles are typically presented in the first third of the text and then abandoned, as material about interpersonal, group, and public communication is presented. We don't use a "hit-and-run" approach. Instead, using examples and illustrations to which students can relate, we carefully discuss each principle early in the text. Throughout the latter two-thirds of the text we gently remind students of how these principles relate to interpersonal relationships, group and team discussions, and public presentations.

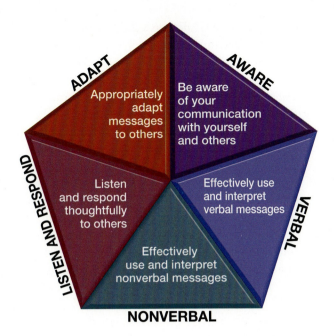

We link the five communication principles with specific content by using a margin icon to indicate that a discussion in the text of a skill, concept, or idea is related to one or more of the five communication principles. The icons, described in Chapter 1 and illustrated here, first appear in the margin in Chapter 7, "Understanding Interpersonal Communication," which is the first context chapter of the text. The icons help students see the many applications our five communication principles have to their lives as they read about interpersonal communication, group and team communication, and public speaking.

A subtext for these five principles is the importance of communicating ethically with others. Throughout the text we invite students to consider the ethical implications of how they communicate with others, through the use of probes and questions. As we discuss in Chapter 1, we believe that in order to be effective, a communication message must achieve three goals: (1) It must be understood; (2) it must achieve its intended effect; and (3) it must be ethical. Our five Communication Principles for a Lifetime are designed to help students achieve these three goals.

The Successful Structure of the Text Stays the Same

This eighth edition retains the overall structure of the seven previous editions and is organized into four units.

Unit I introduces the five principles (Chapter 1), and then each principle is explained in a separate chapter (Chapters 2 through 6). Each communication principle is discussed and illustrated to help students see its value and centrality in their lives. Chapter 2 discusses the principle of being self-aware. Chapter 3 focuses on using and interpreting verbal messages, and Chapter 4 focuses on using and interpreting nonverbal messages. Chapter 5 includes a discussion of the interrelated processes of listening and responding, giving special attention to the importance of being other-oriented and empathic. The final principle, appropriately adapting to others, is presented in Chapter 6; we use this principle to illustrate the importance of adapting one's behavior to culture and gender differences among people.

Unit II applies the five communication principles to interpersonal relationships. Unlike many treatments of interpersonal communication, our discussion links the concepts and strategies for understanding interpersonal communication with our five Communication Principles for a Lifetime. Chapter 7 presents information to help students better understand the nature and function of communication in relationships. Chapter 8 identifies communication strategies that can enhance the quality of interpersonal relationships.

Unit III discusses how the five communication principles can help students understand and enhance communication in small groups and teams. Chapter 9 explains how groups and teams work. We offer practical strategies for collaboratively solving problems, leading groups and teams, and running and participating in meetings in Chapter 10.

Finally, Unit IV presents classic content to help students design and deliver a speech, referring to contemporary research and using the latest technology. Based on our popular audience-centered approach to developing a speech, we emphasize the importance of adapting to listeners while also being an ethically vigilant communicator. Chapters 11 through 15 offer information and tips for developing speech ideas, organizing and outlining speeches, delivering a speech (including using presentational and multimedia aids), crafting effective informative speeches, and developing ethical persuasive messages.

We conclude the text with two appendices designed to supplement our instruction about communication fundamentals. Appendix A includes practical strategies for being interviewed and for interviewing others. We relate our discussion of interviewing to the five Communication Principles for a Lifetime. Appendix B includes two examples of recent student presentations to illustrate what effective, well-planned speeches look like.

Our Partnership with Students to Help Them Learn Stays the Same

A textbook is essentially a "distance learning" tool. As we write each chapter, we are separated from the learner by both time and space. To help lessen the distance between author and reader, we've incorporated a variety of learning resources and pedagogical features to engage students in the learning process. As we note in the text, information alone is not communication. Communication occurs when the receiver of information responds to it. Our special features help turn information into a responsive communication message that has an effect on students' lives.

Principles Model and Icons Our pentagon model and margin icons help students see connections between the various communication concepts and skills we present. Throughout the text we provide an integrated framework to reinforce what is fundamental about human communication. Long after students may have forgotten the lists they memorized for an exam, we want them to remember the five fundamental principles we highlight throughout the text. Remembering these principles can also help them remember strategies and concepts to enhance their interpersonal relationships, improve group and team meetings, and design and deliver effective presentations.

Critical/Cultural Perspectives & Communication These new Critical/Cultural Perspectives & Communication boxes appear in every chapter and explore various communication topics from a critical/cultural communication perspective, focusing on messages about power, resistance, suppression, marginalization, and culture. Students are invited to question and challenge traditional power structures, positions of influence, and historically marginalized, oppressed, or privileged individuals and groups due to a variety of intersecting factors including culture, sex, gender identity, race, ethnicity, disability, and social class.

Ethics & Communication To help students consider the ethical dimensions of human communication, in each chapter we provide a special boxed feature called Ethics & Communication. Students are asked to consider a case study or to ponder their responses to ethical questions. The cases and questions we pose are designed to be thought-provoking, to spark insightful class discussion, or to be used in combination with a journal assignment or other learning method to help students see connections between ethics and communication.

Social Media & Communication Because of the importance of social media in our lives, in each chapter we include special material about social media and communication to help students become sensitive to the sometimes mindboggling impact that social media platforms like Facebook, Twitter, Instagram, and TikTok have on our communication with others. We also discuss the importance and role of social media in several chapters throughout the text. The prevalence of social media in students' lives offers powerful teachable moments to help students learn and apply communication principles.

Diversity & Communication Each chapter includes a Diversity & Communication box designed to help students see the importance of diversity in their lives. Yet we don't relegate discussions of diversity only to a boxed feature. Because we believe diversity is such an important communication topic in contemporary society, we discuss diversity not only in relation to our fifth principle of communication (appropriately adapt messages to others) in Chapter 6, but throughout the text.

Comprehensive Pedagogical Learning Tools To help students master the material, we've built in a wealth of study aids:

- Learning objectives provide a compass to help students know where they are headed, which they can check at key points throughout each chapter.
- Chapter outlines preview key concepts.
- Concise and highly praised Recap boxes distill essential content.
- Key terms in boldface with marginal glossary or pop-up definitions in Revel help students master essential terms.
- Chapter-end Study Guides offer "*Principle* Points" narrative summaries and "*Principle* Terms" lists.
- Chapter-end "*Principle* Skills" questions and collaborative learning activities guide students to think critically about how they can apply chapter concepts to their lives and relationships.

Our Partnership with Instructors Stays Strong

As authors, we view our job as providing resources that instructors can use to bring communication principles and skills to life. A text is only one tool to help teachers teach and learners learn. As part of our partnership with instructors to facilitate learning, we offer an array of resources to help teachers do what they do best: teach. In addition to the vast array of learning resources we've built into the text, we offer a dazzling package of additional resources to help instructors generate both intellectual and emotional connections with their students.

Key instructor resources include an Instructor's Manual, TestBank, and PowerPoint Presentation Package. These supplements are available on the catalog page for this text on www.pearsonglobaleditions.com (instructor login required). For a complete list of the instructor and student resources available with the text, please visit the Pearson Communication catalog, at www.pearson.com/communication.

Inspire Engagement through Active Learning

Available separately for purchase in select regions is Revel®, a platform that provides an engaging learning experience to prepare students for class. The seamless blend of digital text, media, and assessment based on learning science provides one continuous experience—learning anytime, anywhere, and on any device.

Revel® improves results by empowering students to actively participate in learning. More than a digital textbook, Revel delivers an engaging blend of author content, media, and assessment.

With Revel, students read and practice in one continuous experience. Interactive content and assessments integrated throughout the narrative provide opportunities for students to explore and apply concepts. And Revel is mobile and user-friendly, so students can learn on the go—anytime, anywhere, on any device.

Special Features for Communication Students

Our communication authors have reimagined their content for Revel, embedding interactives throughout the narrative that bring the discipline to life. For example, when reading about public speaking anxiety, students are prompted to complete a self-assessment to gauge their own communication style, and explore ways to improve upon their skills. Or when students read about John F. Kennedy's famed Inaugural Address, they can also watch a video of the speech. By empowering students to actively participate in learning, Revel boosts engagement and improves results.

Dynamic content brings concepts to life

- **Videos and interactives** integrated directly into the narrative get students learning actively, making it more likely that they'll retain what they've read.
- Embedded **assessments** afford students regular opportunities to check their understanding. The results enable instructors to gauge student comprehension and provide timely feedback to address learning gaps along the way.
- **Writing assignments**—such as journaling prompts, shared writing activities, and essays—enable educators to foster and assess critical thinking without significantly impacting their grading burden.
- **Video quizzes** offer students opportunities to further their knowledge by applying concepts and testing their understanding. Instructors can share videos accompanied by time-stamped multiple-choice questions.
- **Shared multimedia assignments** make it easy for instructors and students to post and respond to videos and other media. Students can also record and upload their own presentations for grading, comments, or peer review.
- The Revel® **mobile app** lets students read and practice anywhere, anytime, on any device—online and off. It syncs work across all registered devices automatically, allowing learners to toggle between phone, tablet, and laptop as they move through their day.
- The **audio playlist** lets students listen and learn as they go.

Actionable insights help improve results

- The **educator dashboard** offers an at-a-glance look at overall class performance. It helps instructors identify and contact struggling and low-activity students, ensuring that the class stays on pace.
- The **enhanced grades view** provides detailed insights on student performance, from specific assignments to individual student scores.

- **LMS integration** provides institutions, instructors, and students easy access to their Revel courses via Blackboard Learn™, Canvas™, Brightspace by D2L™, and Moodle™. Single sign-on lets students access Revel on their first day.

For more information about all of the tools and resources in Revel and access to your own Revel account for the *Communication: Principles for a Lifetime,* Eighth Edition, Global Edition, go to www.pearson.com/revel.

MediaShare

MediaShare integration makes it easier than ever for students and instructors to share and comment on speeches, as well as other videos, documents, images, and more. Users can upload original content for peer and instructor feedback or embed YouTube content with just a few clicks. Having these share-and-comment tools available directly within Revel™ makes for an even more interactive learning experience.

Acknowledgments

Although our three names appear on the cover as authors, in reality hundreds of people have been instrumental in making this text possible.

Communication scholars who have dedicated their lives to researching the importance of communication principles, theories, and skills provide the fuel for this text. We thank each author we reference in our voluminous endnotes for the research conclusions that have brought us to our contemporary understanding of communication principles. We thank our students who have trusted us to be their guides in their study of human communication. They continue to enrich our lives with their enthusiasm and curiosity. They have inspired us to be more creative by their honest, quizzical looks and challenged us to go beyond "textbook" answers with their thought-provoking questions. We are most appreciative of the outstanding editorial support we continue to receive from our colleagues and friends at Pearson. We would like to thank Emily Edling for all her work on this edition. We also thank Joe Opiela for helping us keep this project moving forward when we wondered if the world needed another communication text. Our former editor, Karon Bowers, has continued to provide valued support and encouragement. Our exceptionally thoughtful and talented development editor, Ellen Keohane, helped us polish and prune our words and gave us a wealth of ideas and suggestions. We acknowledge and appreciate the ideas and suggestions from Mark Redmond, a valued friend, gifted teacher, and skilled writer at Iowa State University. His coauthorship with us on *Interpersonal Communication: Relating to Others* significantly influenced our ideas about communication, especially interpersonal communication.

We are grateful to the many educators who read the manuscript and both encouraged and challenged us. We thank the following people for drawing on their teaching skill, expertise, and vast experience to make this a much better text:

Reviewers of the First Edition: Michael Bruner, University of North Texas; Diana O. Cassagrande, West Chester University; Dan B. Curtis, Central Missouri State University; Terrence A. Doyle, Northern Virginia Community College; Julia F. Fennell, Community College of Allegheny County, South Campus; Phil Hoke, The University of Texas at San Antonio; Stephen Hunt, Illinois State University; Carol L. Hunter, Brookdale Community College; Dorothy W. Ige, Indiana University Northwest; A. Elizabeth Lindsey, The New Mexico State University; Robert E. Mild, Jr., Fairmont State College; Timothy P. Mottet, Texas State University–San Marcos; Alfred G. Mueller II, Pennsylvania State University, Mont Alto Campus; Kay Neal, University of

Wisconsin–Oshkosh; Kathleen Perri, Valencia Community College; Beth M. Waggenspack, Virginia Tech University; Gretchen Aggert Weber, Horry-Georgetown Technical College; Kathy Werking, Eastern Kentucky University; Andrew F. Wood, San Jose State University.

Reviewers of the Second Edition: Lawrence Albert, Morehead State University; Leonard Assante, Volunteer State Community College; Dennis Dufer, St. Louis Community College; Annette Folwell, University of Idaho; Mike Hemphill, University of Arkansas at Little Rock; Teri Higginbotham, University of Central Arkansas; Lawrence Hugenberg, Youngstown State University; Timothy P. Mottet, Texas State University–San Marcos; Penny O'Connor, University of Northern Iowa; Evelyn Plummer, Seton Hall University; Charlotte C. Toguchi, Kapi'olani Community College; Debra Sue Wyatt, South Texas Community College.

Reviewers of the Third Edition: Dom Bongiorni, Kingwood College; Jo Anne Bryant, Troy University; Cherie Cannon, Miami–Dade College; Thomas Green, Cape Fear Community College; Gretchen Harries, Austin Community College; Xin-An Lu, Shippensburg University of Pennsylvania; Sara L. Nalley, Columbia College; Kristi Schaller, University of Hawaii; David Shuhy, Salisbury University; John Tapia, Missouri Western State College.

Reviewers of the Fourth Edition: Ellen B. Bremen, Highline Community College; Patricia A. Cutspec, East Tennessee State University; Edgar D. Johnson III, Augusta State University; Peter S. Lee, California State University, Fullerton; Kelly Aikin Petcus, Austin Community College; Natalia Rybas, Bowling Green State University; Sarah Stout, Kellogg Community College.

Reviewers of the Fifth Edition: Leonard Assante, Volunteer State Community College; Sandra Bein, South Suburban College; Robert Dixon, St. Louis Community College; Glynis Holm Strause, Coastal Bend College; Linda Kalfayan, Westchester Community College; Barbara Maxwell, Linn State Technical College; Kay Neal, University of Wisconsin Oshkosh; Jeff Pomeroy, Southwest Texas Junior College.

Reviewers of the Sixth Edition: Kevin Clark, Austin Community College; Cynthia Brown El, Macomb Community College; Diane Ferrero-Paluzzi, Iona College; Gary Kuhn, Chemeketa Community College; Travice Obas, Georgia Highlands College; John Parrish, Tarrant County College; Daniel Paulnock, Saint Paul College; Shannon Proctor, Highline Community College; Kimberly Schaefer, Baker University; Katie Stevens, Austin Community College; Jayne Violette, Eastern Kentucky University.

Reviewers of the Seventh Edition: Tasha Davis, Austin Community College; Thomas Damp, Central New Mexico Community College; Kevin Clark, Austin Community College; Tila Maceira-Klever, Chemeketa Community College; Narissra Punyanunt-Carter, Texas Tech University; John Parrish, Tarrant County College; James Lohrey, Mercyhurst College.

Reviewers of the Eighth Edition: Christopher Deal, Louisiana Tech University; Janette Douglas, Louisiana Tech University; Cindy Garraway, Rio Salado College; Joel A. Garza, University of Texas Rio Grande Valley; Karley A. Goen, Tarleton State University; Valentin Guerra, University of Texas Rio Grande Valley; Abby Arnold Lackey, Jackson State Community College; Amy Lionberger, Louisiana Tech University; Michael Sollitto, Texas A&M University–Corpus Christi.

We have each been influenced by colleagues, friends, and teachers who have offered support and inspiration for this project. Happily, colleagues, friends, and teachers are virtually indistinguishable for us. We are each blessed with people with whom we work who offer strong support. Steve and Sue thank their colleagues at Texas State University for their insights and ideas that helped shape key concepts in this text. Cathy Fleuriet and Tom Burkholder, who served as basic course directors at Texas State, influenced our work. Tim Mottet, also a former basic course director at Texas State and now President of Colorado State University–Pueblo, is a valued, inspirational friend, coauthor, and colleague who is always there to listen and freely share his ideas and experience. Marian Houser, a former basic course director at Texas State, is a wonderful friend and provides important insight and support. Kristen LeBlanc Farris, also a former Director of Texas State's award-winning basic communication course, is a valued friend and continues to offer generous support. We thank Mark Paz, the current basic course director, for his invaluable suggestions and comments. Elizabeth Eger, Roseann Mandziuk, and Michael Burns, valued Texas State friends and colleagues, also offered excellent feedback and suggestions. Long-time friend Kosta Tovstiadi, University of Colorado, and communication student Gabriela Bidwell, Texas A&M University–Corpus Christi, provided skilled research assistance to help us draw upon the most contemporary communication research. Michael Hennessy, Patricia Margerison, and Daniel Lochman are Texas State English faculty who have been especially supportive of Sue's work. Finally, Steve thanks his skilled and dedicated administrative support team at Texas State: administrative assistant Sue Hall, a cherished friend and colleague, and Bob Hanna provided exceptional support and assistance for this project and many others.

Ivy is grateful to her students, colleagues, and friends at Texas A&M University–Corpus Christi, for their patience and unwavering support for her continued involvement in this project. In particular, President Kelly Miller, Associate Provost Amy Aldridge Sanford, Dean Mark Hartlaub, and Chair David Gurney constantly reaffirm the value of a well-written, carefully crafted text—one that speaks to students' lives. Their support of Ivy's research efforts, along with constant fueling from her wonderful students, always make this project a joy. Ivy's deepest thanks also go to Steve and Sue Beebe for their generosity in bringing her into this project, and for their extraordinary friendship.

Finally, we express our appreciation to our families. Ivy thanks her ever-supportive sister Karen Black, nephew, niece, and grandnieces, Brian, Sumitra, Mackenzie, and Sidney Black. They have been constant and generous with their praise for her writing accomplishments. Ivy will always be especially grateful to her late parents, Carol and Herschel Ivy, for lovingly offering many lessons about living the highly ethical life.

Sue and Steve especially thank their parents, Herb and Jane Dye, and Russell and Muriel Beebe, who taught them much about communication and ethics that truly are principles for a lifetime. They also thank their sons and daughters-in-law, Mark and Amanda Beebe, and Matthew and Kara Beebe; and their granddaughter, Mary Jensen; for teaching them life lessons about giving and receiving love that will remain with them forever.

Steven A. Beebe
Susan J. Beebe
Diana K. Ivy

Global Edition Acknowledgments

Pearson would like to thank and acknowledge the following people for their contributions to the Global Edition.

Contributor
Jon Sutherland

Reviewers
Elaine Ang Hwee Chin, Multimedia University, Malaysia
Matthew Lickiss, University of Reading
Fiona McManus, University of Lincoln
Sheila Yvonne Jayasainan, Taylor's College, Malaysia

UNIT I PRINCIPLES OF COMMUNICATION

CHAPTER 1

IDENTIFYING FOUNDATIONS OF HUMAN COMMUNICATION

There is no pleasure to me without communication. —MICHELE DE MONTAIGNE

Ammentorp/123RF

CHAPTER OUTLINE

- Why Study Communication?
- The Communication Process
- Communication Models
- Communication Competence
- Communication in the Twenty-First Century
- Communication Contexts
- Communication Principles for a Lifetime
- Study Guide: *Principles for a Lifetime*

LEARNING OBJECTIVES

1.1 Explain why it is important to study communication.

1.2 Define communication and describe five characteristics of the communication process.

1.3 Explain three communication models.

1.4 Describe three criteria that can be used to determine whether communication is competent.

1.5 Describe the nature of communication in the twenty-first century.

1.6 Identify and explain three communication contexts.

1.7 List and explain five fundamental principles of communication.

Like life-sustaining breath, communication is ever-present in our lives. That makes understanding and improving how we communicate with others a basic life skill.

Communication is an inescapable and fundamental aspect of being human. Consider the number of times you have purposefully communicated with someone today as you worked, ate, studied, shopped, or went about your daily duties. With the constant presence of social media in our lives, you are likely to be connected to others day and night. Most people spend between 80 and 90 percent of their waking hours communicating with others.[1] Even if you live in isolation, you talk to yourself through your thoughts. It is through the process of communication that we convey who we are, both to ourselves and to others; it is our primary tool for making our way in the world.

In the course of our study of human communication, we will discuss myriad skills, ideas, concepts, and contexts. To help you stitch together the barrage of ideas and information, we will organize our study around five fundamental communication principles:

Principle One:	Be aware of your communication with yourself and others.
Principle Two:	Effectively use and interpret verbal messages.
Principle Three:	Effectively use and interpret nonverbal messages.
Principle Four:	Listen and respond thoughtfully to others.
Principle Five:	Appropriately adapt messages to others.

We don't claim that everything you need to know about communication is covered by these five principles. They do, however, summarize decades of research, as well as the wisdom of those who have taught communication over the years, about what constitutes effective and ethical communication.

Before elaborating on the five fundamental communication principles, we will first provide some background for our study of communication. We will discuss why it is important to study communication, define communication, examine various models of—or perspectives on—communication, and identify characteristics of human communication.[2] Having offered this prelude, we will then discuss the five foundational principles of human communication, which we will use throughout this text to help you organize the concepts, skills, and ideas presented in our discussion of interpersonal, group, and presentational speaking situations.

Why Study Communication?

1.1 Explain why it is important to study communication.

Why are you here? No, we don't mean "Why do you exist?" or "Why do you live where you do?" What we mean is "Why are you taking a college course about communication?" Perhaps the short answer is "It's required." Or maybe your advisor, parent, or friend encouraged you to take the course. But required or not, what can a systematic study of human communication do for you?

Communication touches every aspect of our lives. To be able to express yourself to other people is a basic requirement for living in a modern society. From a practical standpoint, it's very likely that you will make your living with your mind rather than your hands.[3] Even if you do physical labor, you will need communication skills to work with others. When you study communication, you are also developing leadership skills. "The art of communication," says author James Humes, "is the language of leadership."[4] Although the value of being a competent communicator is virtually undisputed, there is evidence that many people struggle to express themselves clearly or to accurately understand messages from others.

- One study estimated that one-fifth of the students in the United States were not successful with even elementary communication tasks; in addition, more than 60 percent of the students could not give clear oral directions for someone else to follow.[5]
- When leaders in major corporations were asked to specify the most important skills for workers to have, 80 percent said listening was the most important work skill; 78 percent identified interpersonal communication skill as the next most important. However, the same leaders said only 28 percent of their employees had good listening skills and only 27 percent possessed effective interpersonal communication skills.[6]
- Another national study found that adults listen with only 25 percent accuracy.[7]
- The majority of adults in the United States are fearful of speaking in public and about 20 percent of the population is *highly* apprehensive.[8]

Aren't some people just born to be better communicators than others? If so, why should you work to develop your communication skill? Just as some people have more innate musical talent than others, there is evidence that some people may have an inborn biological ability to communicate with others.[9] This does not mean you should not work to develop your communication ability. Throughout this text, we will offer ample evidence that if you work to improve your skill, you will be rewarded by enjoying the benefits of enhanced communication competence. What are these benefits? Read on.

To Improve Your Employability

Regardless of your specific title or job description, the essence of what you do when working at any job is to communicate; you talk, listen, relate, read, and write. People who can communicate effectively with others are in high demand. As noted by John H. McConnell, former CEO of Worthington Industries, "Take all the speech and communication courses you can because the world turns on communication."[10] McConnell's advice is supported by research as well as by personal observations. Warren Buffett, one of the wealthiest persons in the world, attributes his success to developing communication skills. If you were to visit his office in Omaha, you would see a 1952 award certificate from his Dale Carnegie public speaking training proudly displayed, but not his undergraduate diploma from the University of Nebraska or his master's degree from Columbia University.[11] Buffett says, "Invest in yourself. The one easy way to become worth 50 percent more than you are now at least is to hone your communication skills—both written and verbal."[12] Taking this course is an investment in yourself.

▼ Warren Buffett, whose savvy investing has made him one of the richest people on the planet, agrees with many other leaders about the importance of communication skills at work. In one televised interview, Buffet declared, "If you improve your communication skills, I guarantee you that you will earn 50 percent more money over your lifetime!"[13]
Nati Harnik/AP/Shutterstock

Based on a survey of employers, here's a ranking of the top factors in obtaining employment immediately after college:[14]

1. Oral communication
2. Teamwork skills in diverse groups
3. Written communication
4. Critical thinking and analytic reasoning
5. Complex problem solving
6. Information literacy
7. Innovation and creativity
8. Technological skills
9. Quantitative reasoning

We're sure you know why we cited this survey. Communication skills were valued more highly than all of the other skills. And this survey isn't the only one that reached the same conclusion; several other research studies have shown that communication skills are the most sought-after skills in the workplace.[15] Whether you are communicating face-to-face or online, communication skills are highly valued. Increasingly, you will communicate with others on the job via text, video chat, and social media. If you are searching for a job, perhaps you have a LinkedIn account to showcase your skills and talents.[16] Being able to effectively communicate with others, either in person or via an electronic means, enhances your employability.[17]

What are your career options if you decide to major or minor in communication? Many! Students who major in communication or communication studies pursue successful careers in business, management, sales, marketing, public relations, customer service, public advocacy, public service, media, education, the ministry, law, or any career that emphasizes "people skills" such as speaking, listening, and relating to others.[18] At its essence, studying communication helps you manage people and ideas. *Research has consistently found that communication skills, including interpersonal and teamwork skills, continue to be the most valued skills on the planet.*[19]

To Improve Your Relationships

We don't choose our biological families, but we do choose our friends. For unmarried people, developing friendships and falling in love are the top-rated sources of satisfaction and happiness in life.[20] Conversely, losing a relationship is among life's most stressful events. Most people between the ages of 19 and 24 report that they have had five to six romantic relationships and have been "in love" once or twice.[21] Understanding the role and function of communication can help unravel some of the mysteries of human relationships. At the heart of a good relationship is good communication.[22]

Virginia Satir, a pioneer in family enrichment, described family communication as "the largest single factor determining the kinds of relationships [we make] with others."[23] Learning principles and skills of communication can give us insight into why we relate to other family members as we do. Our early communication with our parents had a profound effect on our self-concept and self-worth. According to Satir, people are "made" in families. Our communication with family members has shaped how we interact with others today.

Many of us will spend as much or more time interacting with people in our places of work as we do at home. And although we choose our friends and lovers, we don't always have the same flexibility in choosing those with whom, or for whom, we work. Increasing our understanding of the role and importance of human communication with our colleagues can help us better manage stress on the job as well as enhance our work success.

To Improve Your Health

Life is stressful. Research has clearly documented that the lack or loss of close relationships can lead to ill health and even death.[24] One study found that people who have strong interpersonal relationships with others are 50 percent less likely to die prematurely compared to those who have poor interpersonal relationships.[25] Having a social support system—good friends and supportive family members—seems to make a difference in our overall health and quality of life. Good friends and intimate relationships with others help us manage stress and contribute to both physical and emotional health. Physicians have noted that patients who are widowed or divorced experience more medical problems, such as heart disease, cancer, pneumonia, and diabetes, than do married people.[26] Grief-stricken spouses are more likely than others to die prematurely, especially around the time of the departed spouse's birthday or near their wedding anniversary.[27] Terminally ill patients with a limited number of friends or little social support die sooner than those with stronger ties.[28] Without companions and close friends, our opportunities for intimacy and stress-managing communication are diminished. Loneliness contributes to heart disease, high blood pressure, stroke, depression, lower-quality sleep, and impaired judgment.[29] Studying how to enrich the quality of our communication with others can make life more enjoyable and enhance our overall well-being. Because of Snapchat, Twitter, and other social networks, we are increasingly involved in relationships with others even when we are not interacting face-to-face. Relating to others, whether online or in person, occurs through communication.[30]

So again, we ask the question: Why are you here? We think the evidence is clear: People who are effective communicators are more likely to get the jobs they want; have better-quality relationships with friends, family, and colleagues; and even enjoy a healthier quality of life.

The Communication Process

1.2 Define communication and describe five characteristics of the communication process.

Communication is one of those words that seems so basic you may wonder why it needs to be formally defined. Yet scholars who devote their lives to studying communication don't always agree on its definition. One research team counted more than 126 published definitions.[31] In this section, we'll examine our definition of communication, the characteristics shared by all communication, major models that researchers and theorists have used to explain and study communication, and the three general contexts in which communication happens.

Communication Defined

In its broadest sense, **communication** is the process of acting on information.[32] Someone does or says something, and others think or do something in response to the action or the words as they understand them. Communication is not unique to humans; researchers study communication in other species, as well as between species. For example, you communicate with your pet dog if the dog sits in response to your spoken command, or if you respond to your dog's begging gaze by giving him a treat.

Some people confuse the word *communication* with the word *communications*—they add an "s." Adding an "s" narrows the meaning. **Communications** (with the "s") emphasizes the channel or method of distributing messages. Your phone, cable, or Internet provider are communications companies. Communication (no "s") focuses on the *process* of communicating rather than the *method* of sending messages. When you study communication you study the process of communicating rather than just focusing on how messages are dispersed.

The focus of this text is **human communication**, *the process of making sense out of the world and sharing that sense with others by creating meaning through the use of verbal and nonverbal messages.*[33] Let's look at the key components of this definition.

Making Sense *Communication is about making sense.* We make sense out of what we experience when we identify meaningful patterns and structure in what we see, hear, touch, smell, and taste. Although we often think that "making sense out of something" means rationally and logically interpreting what we experience, we also make sense through intuition, feelings, and emotions.[34]

Sharing Sense *Communication is about sharing sense.* We share what we experience by expressing to others and to ourselves what we experience. We typically use words to communicate our thoughts, but we also use facial expressions and gestures, or music, art, clothing, and a host of other means to convey what we are thinking and feeling to others.

Creating Meaning *Communication is about creating meaning.* As we will discuss later in this chapter, it's more appropriate to say that meaning is *created* through communication rather than sent or transmitted. To say that we send or transmit messages is to imply that what we send is what is received. However, presenting information to others does not mean communication has occurred: "But I told you what to do!" "It's there in the memo. Why didn't you do what I asked?" "It's in the syllabus." These exasperated communicators assumed that if they sent a message, someone would receive it. However, communication does not operate in a simple, linear, what-you-send-is-what-is-received process. *Information is not communication.* In fact, what is expressed by one person is rarely interpreted by another person precisely as intended.

Messages *Communication is about verbal and nonverbal messages.* We communicate messages—the written, spoken, or unspoken elements to which we assign meaning—by using **symbols**,

communication
The process of acting on information.

communications
The methods of distributing messages to others through various channels.

human communication
The process of making sense out of the world and sharing that sense with others by creating meaning through verbal and nonverbal messages.

symbol
A word, sound, gesture, or visual image that represents a thought, concept, object, or experience.

▼ Signs are usually carefully crafted examples of symbolic communication. What are the creators of this sign trying to communicate?
Patrick Strattner/AGE Fotostock

words, sounds, gestures, or visual images that represent thoughts, concepts, objects, or experiences. The words on this page are symbols you use to derive meaning that makes sense to you. Not all symbols are verbal; some are nonverbal. You use gestures, posture, facial expressions, tone of voice, clothing, and jewelry to express ideas, attitudes, and feelings. Nonverbal messages primarily communicate emotions, such as our likes and dislikes, whether we're interested or uninterested, and our feelings of power or lack of power.

Some scholars assert that *all* human behavior is really communication. When you cross your arms while listening to your friend describe her day, she may conclude that you're not interested in what she's talking about. But it could just be that you're chilly. While all human expression has the potential to communicate a message (someone may act or respond to the information they receive from you), it does not mean that you are *intentionally* expressing an idea or emotion. People don't always accurately interpret the messages we express—and this unprofound observation has profound implications.

Because of the ever-present potential for misunderstanding, communication should be *other-oriented*—it should acknowledge the perspective of others, not just that of the creator of the message. Communication that does not consider the needs, background, and culture of the receiver is more likely to be misunderstood than other-oriented communication. We'll emphasize the importance of considering others or considering your audience throughout the book. Knowing something about the experiences of the person or persons you're speaking to can help you communicate more effectively and appropriately.

Communication Characteristics

The following characteristics are evident any time communication occurs: Communication is inescapable, irreversible, and complicated; it emphasizes content and relationships; and it is governed by rules.

Communication Is Inescapable Opportunities to communicate are everywhere. We spend most of our waking hours sending messages to others or interpreting messages from others.[35] Many of our messages are not verbalized. As you silently stand in a supermarket checkout line, for example, your lack of eye contact with others waiting in line suggests you're not interested in striking up a conversation. Your unspoken messages may provide cues to which others respond. As we noted earlier, some communication scholars question whether it is possible to communicate with someone unintentionally. However, even when you don't intend to express a particular idea or feeling, others may try to make sense out of what you are doing—or not doing. Remember: People judge you by your behavior, not your intent.

Communication Is Irreversible "Disregard that last statement made by the witness," instructs the judge. Yet the clever lawyer knows that, once the witness has said something, he or she cannot really "take back" the message. In conversation, we may try to modify the meaning of a spoken message by saying something like "Oh, I really didn't mean it." But in most cases, the damage has been done. Once created, communication has the physical property of matter; it can't be uncreated. As the spiral shown in Figure 1.1 suggests, once communication begins, it never loops back on itself. Instead, it continues to be shaped by the events, experiences, and thoughts of the communication partners. A Russian proverb nicely summarizes this point: "Once a word goes out of your mouth, you can never swallow it again."

Communication Is Complicated Communicating with others is not simple. If it were, we would know how to dramatically reduce the number of misunderstandings and conflicts in our world. In addition, this text would be able to offer you a list of simple

FIGURE 1.1 Helical Model of Communication

Interpersonal communication is irreversible. Like the spiral shown here, communication never loops back on itself. Once it begins, it expands infinitely as the communication partners contribute their thoughts and experiences to the exchange.

Adapted from the model by F. E. X. Dance in *Human Communication Theory* (Holt, Rinehart and Winston, 1967), 294.

techniques and strategies for blissful management of communication hassles in all of your relationships. But you won't find that list in this book or any other credible book, because human communication is complicated by the number of variables and unknown factors involved when people interact.

To illustrate the complexity of the process, communication scholar Dean Barnlund has suggested that whenever we communicate with another person, at least six "people" are really involved:

1. Who you think you are
2. Who you think the other person is
3. Who you think the other person thinks you are
4. Who the other person thinks he or she is
5. Who the other person thinks you are
6. Who the other person thinks you think he or she is.[36]

Whew! And when you add more people to the conversation, it becomes even more complicated.

Life is not only complicated but also uncertain. There are many things we do not know. We seek information about such everyday things as the weather or about such questions as what others think about us. Several communication theorists suggest that we attempt to manage our uncertainty through communication.[37] In times of high uncertainty (when there are many things we do not know), we will communicate more actively and purposefully by asking questions and seeking information to help manage our uncertainty.

Adding to the complexity of communication and the problem of our own uncertainty is that messages are not always interpreted as we intend them. Osmo Wiio, a Scandinavian communication scholar, points out the challenges of communicating with others in the following maxims:

1. If communication can fail, it will.
2. If a message can be understood in different ways, it will be understood in just the way that does the most harm.
3. There is always somebody who knows better than you what you meant by your message.
4. The more communication there is, the more difficult it is for communication to succeed.[38]

Although we are not as pessimistic as Wiio, we do acknowledge that the task of understanding each other is challenging.

Communication Emphasizes Content and Relationships What you say—your words—and how you say it—your tone of voice, amount of eye contact, facial expression, and posture—combine to reveal much about the true meaning of your message. The **content dimension** of communication messages refers to the new information, ideas, or suggested actions the speaker wishes to express. When you tell your roommate you want the room cleaned, you convey an intentional message that you want a tidier room.

The **relationship dimension** of a communication message is usually less explicit; it offers cues about the emotions, attitudes, and amount of power and control the speaker directs toward others.[39] If one of your roommates loudly and abruptly bellows, "HEY, DORK! CLEAN THIS ROOM!" and another roommate uses the same verbal message but more gently and playfully suggests, with a smile, "Hey, dork. Clean this room," both are communicating the same message content, aimed at achieving the same outcome. But the two messages have very different relationship cues. Your use of emojis in text

---

content dimension
The new information, ideas, or suggested actions that a communicator wishes to express; *what* is said.

relationship dimension
The aspect of a communication message that offers cues about the emotions, attitudes, and amount of power and control the speaker directs toward others; *how* something is said.

messages is another way of expressing relational meaning. One study found that emojis were especially helpful in communicating sarcasm in a message.⁴⁰

Another way to distinguish between the content and relationship dimensions of communication is to consider that the content of a message refers to *what* is said. In contrast, *how* the message is communicated provides the relationship cues. For example, reading a transcript of what someone said may result in a different meaning than if you actually heard that person's words.

Communication Is Governed by Rules According to communication researcher Susan Shimanoff, a **rule** is a "followable prescription that indicates what behavior is obligated, preferred, or prohibited in certain contexts."⁴¹ When you play Monopoly, you know there are rules about how to get out of jail, buy Boardwalk, and collect $200 after passing "Go." The rules that help define appropriate and inappropriate communication in any given situation may be explicit or implicit. The rules of Monopoly are explicit; they are even written down. For a class, explicit rules are probably spelled out in your syllabus.

However, your instructor has other rules that are more implicit. They are not written or verbalized because you learned them long ago: Only one person speaks at a time; you raise your hand to be called on; you do not send text messages during class. Similarly, you may follow implicit rules when you play Monopoly with certain friends or family members, such as "always let Grandpa buy Boardwalk." Communication rules are developed by those involved in the interaction and by the culture in which the individuals are communicating. Most people learn communication rules from experience, by observing and interacting with others.

▲ During the COVID-19 pandemic, many stores had explicit rules about wearing masks before entering.
Steklo/123RF

rule
A followable prescription that indicates what behavior is required or preferred and what behavior is prohibited in a specific situation.

Communication Models

1.3 Explain three communication models.

Communication researchers have spent considerable time trying to understand precisely how communication takes place. In the course of their study, they have developed visual models that graphically illustrate the communication process. These **communication models** provide visual depictions or descriptions of the major elements included in the communication process. By reviewing the development of these models, you can see how our understanding of communication has evolved over the past century.

communication models
Visual depictions or descriptions of the major elements included in the communication process.

Communication as Action: Message Transfer

"Did you get my message?" This simple question summarizes the earliest, communication-as-action approach to human communication. These early models viewed communication as a transfer or exchange of information; communication takes place when a message is sent and received. Period. Communication is a way of transferring meaning from sender to receiver. In 1948, Harold Lasswell described the process as follows:

Who (sender)

Says what (message)

In what channel

To whom (receiver)

With what effect[42]

Figure 1.2 shows a simplified representation of the communication process developed by communication pioneers Claude Shannon and Warren Weaver, who viewed communication as a linear input/output process. Today, although researchers view the process as more complex, they still define most of the key components in this model in basically the same way that Shannon and Weaver did.

Source The **source** of communication is the originator of a thought or an emotion. As the developer of that thought or emotion, the source puts a message into a code that can be understood by a receiver.

- **Encoding** is the process of translating ideas, feelings, and thoughts into a code. Vocalizing a word, gesturing, and establishing eye contact are means of encoding our thoughts into a message that can be decoded by someone.
- **Decoding** is the opposite of encoding. A message is decoded when the words or unspoken signals are interpreted by the receiver.

Receiver The **receiver** is the person who decodes the signal and attempts to make sense of what the source encoded. Think of a radio station as a source broadcasting to a receiver (your radio) that picks up the station's signal. In human communication, however, there is something between the source and the receiver: We filter messages through past experiences, attitudes, beliefs, values, prejudices, and biases.

Message Messages are the written, spoken, and unspoken elements of communication to which we assign meaning. As we have noted, you can send a message intentionally (talking to a friend before class) or unintentionally (falling asleep during class); verbally ("Hi. What's up?"), nonverbally (a smile and a handshake), or in written form (this text); or through any number of electronic channels.

Channel A message is communicated from sender to receiver via some pathway called a **channel**. With today's technological advances, we receive messages through a variety of channels, including print, cable, TV and radio signals, and wireless Internet. Ultimately, however, communication channels correspond to your senses. When you

source
The originator of a thought or emotion who puts it into a code that can be understood by a receiver.

encoding
The process of translating ideas, feelings, and thoughts into a code.

decoding
The process of interpreting ideas, feelings, and thoughts that have been translated into a code.

receiver
The person who decodes a message and attempts to make sense of what the source has encoded.

message
Written, spoken, and unspoken elements of communication to which people assign meaning.

channel
The pathway through which messages are sent.

FIGURE 1.2 A Model of Communication as Action

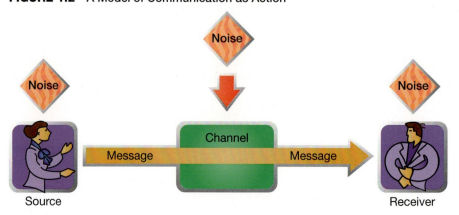

call your mother, the message is conveyed via an electronic channel that activates auditory cues. When you talk with your mother face-to-face, the channels are many. You see her: the visual channel. You hear her: the auditory channel. You may smell her perfume: the olfactory channel. You may hug her: the tactile channel.

Noise   Noise is interference. Noise keeps a message from being understood and achieving its intended effect. Without noise, all our messages would be communicated with considerable accuracy. But noise is always present. It can be literal—the obnoxious roar of a lawn mower—or it can be psychological, such as competing thoughts, worries, and feelings that capture our attention. Instead of concentrating on your teacher's lecture, you may start thinking about the chores you need to finish before the end of the day. Whichever kind it is, noise gets in the way of the message and may even distort it. Communicating accurate messages involves minimizing both literal and psychological noise.

> **noise**
> Interference, either literal or psychological, that hinders the accurate encoding or decoding of a message.

The communication-as-action approach was simple and straightforward, but human communication rarely, if ever, is as simple a matter as "what we put in is what we get out." Other people may not automatically know what you mean, even if the meaning seems very clear to *you*.

Communication as Interaction: Message Exchange

To take into account some of the complexities of actual communication, the early action model evolved to include a more interactive, give-and-take approach. The communication-as-interaction model, shown in Figure 1.3, uses the same elements as the action model but adds two new ones: feedback and context.

Feedback is the response to a message. Without feedback, communication is less likely to be effective. When you order a pepperoni pizza and the server responds, "That's a pepperoni pizza, right?" he has provided feedback to ensure that he decoded the message correctly.

> **feedback**
> The response to a message.

Feedback can be intentional (applause at the conclusion of a symphony) or unintentional (a yawn as you listen to your uncle tell his story about bears again); or it can be verbal ("That's two burgers and fries, right?") or nonverbal (blushing after being asked out on a date).

FIGURE 1.3   A Model of Communication as Interaction

Interaction models of communication include feedback as a response to a message sent by a communication source and place the process in a context.

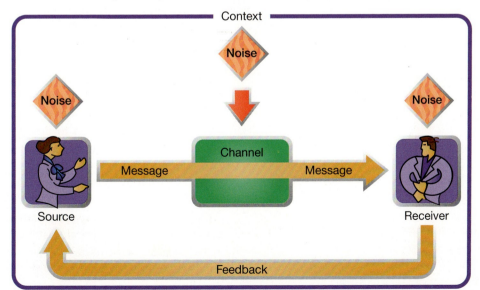

context
The physical, historical, psychological, and cultural environment that influences the nature of communication.

As the cliché goes, "Everyone has to be somewhere." All communication takes place in some **context**, which can include the following elements of the communication environment:

- *Physical context* is the place where the communication occurs. A conversation with your good friend on the beach would likely differ from one the two of you might have in a funeral home.
- *Historical context* is the influence of the past on present and future communication. How you communicate with your family members who have known you since birth is different than what you might say to someone you've just met.
- *Psychological context* is the influence of one's mental and emotional state on communication. Your personality, your mood, and the personality and mood of others has an effect on how you express and interpret messages at any given moment.
- *Cultural context* includes our identification with groups and society, as well as our level of perceived power and position. Power, influence, and perceived social standing are cultural elements that affect who we communicate with and what may be perceived as appropriate or inappropriate communication based on cultural expectations and norms.

The cultural context of communication has fostered the development of a critical lens through which we can examine all human communication. A **critical/cultural approach to communication**, which reflects part of the cultural communication context, focuses on messages about power, resistance, suppression, and culture.[43] This approach encourages questions and invites challenges to traditional power structures, positions of influence, and historically marginalized, oppressed, or privileged individuals and groups due to a variety of intersecting factors including culture, sex, gender identity, race, ethnicity, disability, and social class.[44] We will explore the range of these human differences in Chapter 6 and suggest strategies to increase our awareness of how these elements influence our communication with others. In each chapter, we have included a feature called *Critical/Cultural Perspectives on Communication* in which we explore the multiple ways power, culture, social class, roles, and norms influence our expression and interpretation of messages.

critical/cultural approach to communication
A communication perspective that focuses on messages about power, resistance, and culture; an approach that encourages questions and invites challenges to issues related to position, influence, power, social class, and historically marginalized, oppressed, or privileged role expectations.

Communication as Transaction: Message Creation

Although it emphasizes feedback and context, the interaction model of communication still views communication as a linear, step-by-step process. But in many communication situations, both the source and the receiver send and receive messages *at the same time*. The communication-as-transaction perspective, which evolved in the 1960s, acknowledges that when we communicate with another, we are constantly reacting to what our partner is saying and expressing. Most scholars today view this perspective as the most realistic model of communication. Although this model uses such concepts as action and interaction to describe communication, as Figure 1.4 indicates, all communication is simultaneous. Even as we talk, we are also interpreting our partner's nonverbal and verbal responses. Transactive communication also occurs within physical, historical, psychological, and cultural contexts. In addition, noise can interfere with the quality and accuracy of our encoding and decoding of messages.

RECAP
Components of the Human Communication Process

Term	Definition
Source	Originator of an idea or emotion
Receiver	Person or group who decodes a message and attempts to make sense of what the source has encoded
Message	Written, spoken, and unspoken elements of communication to which we assign meaning
Channel	Pathway through which messages are sent
Noise	Any literal or psychological interference that hinders the accurate encoding or decoding of a message
Encoding	Translation of ideas, feelings, and thoughts into a code
Decoding	Interpretation of ideas, feelings, and thoughts that have been translated into a code
Context	Physical, historical, psychological, and cultural communication environment
Feedback	Verbal and nonverbal responses to a message

CRITICAL/CULTURAL PERSPECTIVES & COMMUNICATION

What's Your Position?

In his novel *The Magician's Nephew*, C. S. Lewis wrote, "For what you see and hear depends a good deal on where you are standing: it also depends on what sort of person you are."[45] Lewis wisely suggests that how you make sense of the world and share that sense with others depends upon your vantage point. A critical/cultural perspective of communication reflects Lewis's sentiments: You can better understand your communication and the communication of others if you consider where you are standing—which includes your perceived power and ability to influence others based on a variety of factors including your sex, gender, race, ethnicity, social class, and cultural background.[46] Where do you stand in terms of privilege? Based on others' perceptions of you or your perception of others, do you come from a high or low position of privilege, or a more central or marginalized position? Do you enjoy certain privileges and freedoms that others do not? Are you aware of whether, due to an intersecting combination of your culture, history, race, ethnicity, age, sex, gender, sexual orientation, (dis)ability, sexual identity, and sexual expression, you do or do not have power to influence others? A critical/cultural perspective of communication invites you to consider, question, and challenge your position, role, or the communication expectations that others have about you or you have about others. To be critical is to be thoughtful, analytical, and assertive in challenging assumptions about power, influence, and social standing. Throughout this text we will ask questions inviting reflections about "Where are you standing?" and "Where are others expecting you to stand?" to increase your awareness of your cultural context, cultural position, perceived power, and the perspective others may have about you, and that you have about others.

For example, you ask a friend out for coffee but you're not sure if she really wants to go with you. As you're talking to her, you carefully observe her reactions to determine whether she's genuinely interested in your invitation. If you'd really like her company but you sense she'd rather not go, you may try harder, using your best persuasive pitch to get her to join you. During each communication transaction you have with another person, you look for information about how your message is being received even before you finish talking.

In a communication transaction, the meaning of a message is *co-created* by the individuals who are involved in the communication process. Meaning is created in the hearts and minds of both the message source and the message receiver, based on such things as the characteristics of the message, the situation, and the perceptions and background of the communicators. By drawing on our own experiences while attempting to make sense of a message, we actually shape the meaning of that message. As one research team puts it, communication is "the coordinated management of meaning" through episodes during which the message of one person influences the message of another.[47] Technically, only the sender and receiver of those messages can determine where one episode ends and another begins. We make sense out of our world in ways that are unique to each of us.

FIGURE 1.4 A Model of Communication as Transaction

The source and the receiver of a message experience communication simultaneously.

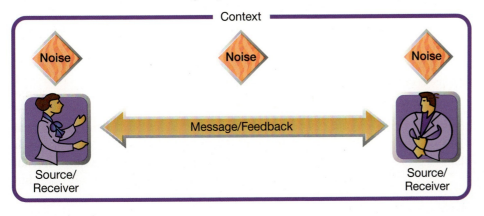

RECAP

An Evolving Model of Human Communication

Human Communication as Action
Human communication is linear, with meaning sent or transferred from source to receiver.

Human Communication as Interaction
Human communication occurs as the receiver of the message responds to the source through feedback. This interactive model views communication as a linear sequence of actions and reactions.

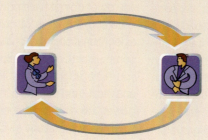

Human Communication as Transaction
Human communication is simultaneously interactive. Meaning is created on the basis of mutual, concurrent sharing of ideas and feelings. This transactive model most accurately describes human communication.

communication competence
The ability to communicate appropriately and successfully.

Communication Competence

1.4 Describe three criteria that can be used to determine whether communication is competent.

What does it mean to communicate competently? Being a competent communicator is more than just being well liked, glib, adept at giving polished presentations, or able to interact smoothly with individual people or in groups and teams. Although it is difficult to identify core criteria that define competent communication in all situations, we believe that certain goals of communication serve as measures of **communication competence**, or the ability to communicate appropriately and successfully, regardless of the setting. We suggest the following three criteria:[48]

- The message should be understood as the communicator intended it to be understood.
- The message should achieve the communicator's intended effect.
- The message should be ethical.

The Message Should Be Understood

A primary goal of any effective communication transaction is to develop a common understanding of the message from both the sender's and the receiver's perspectives.[49] You'll note how the words *common* and *communication* resemble each other. One of the aims of the principles we discuss in this text is to create clarity of expression and a common understanding.

Message clarity is missing in the following headlines, which have appeared in local U.S. newspapers:

> **Panda Mating Fails: Veterinarian Takes Over**
> **Drunks Get Nine Months in Violin Case**
> **Include Your Children When Baking Cookies**
> **Police Begin Campaign to Run Down Jaywalkers**
> **Local High School Dropouts Cut in Half**

Sometimes the placement of a mere comma can change our understanding of a message, such as the difference between the phrases "Let's eat, Grandma" and "Let's eat Grandma." Meanings are fragile, and messages can be misunderstood. An effective message is one that the receiver accurately understands.

The Message Should Achieve Its Intended Effect

When you communicate intentionally with others, you do so for a specific purpose: to achieve a goal or to accomplish something. Because different purposes require different strategies for success, being aware of your purpose can enhance your probability of achieving it.

We often use specific types of communication to achieve certain goals:

- The goal of *public speaking* may be to inform, to persuade, or to entertain.
- In *small groups*, our goals are often to solve problems and make decisions.
- In our *interpersonal relationships*, our goals may be to build trust, develop intimacy, or just enjoy someone's company.

The Message Should Be Ethical

A message that is understood and achieves its intended effect but that manipulates listeners, unfairly restricts their choices, or uses false information may be effective, but it is not appropriate or ethical. **Ethics** are the beliefs, values, and moral principles by which we determine what is right or wrong. Ethics and ethical behavior have long been considered critical components of human behavior in a given culture.

Philosophers have debated for centuries whether there is such a thing as a universal moral and ethical code.[50] British author and scholar C. S. Lewis argued that the teachings of cultures throughout the world and through time support the existence of a shared ethical code that serves as the basis for interpreting the "goodness" or "badness" of human behavior.[51] In their book *Communication Ethics and Universal Values,* communication scholars Clifford Christians and Michael Traber claim that "Every culture depends for its existence on norms that order human relationships and social institutions."[52] They suggest there are three universal cultural norms: (1) the value of truth, (2) respect for another person's dignity, and (3) the expectation that innocent people should not suffer harm.[53] As represented in the Ethics & Communication box, the world's major religions appear to share a common moral code for how people should treat others.[54]

ethics
The beliefs, values, and moral principles by which we determine what is right or wrong.

ETHICS & COMMUNICATION

Is There a Universal Ethical Code?

Most religions of the world emphasize a common spiritual theme, which is known in Christianity as the Golden Rule: Do unto others what you would have others do unto you.[55] This "rule" is also perceived as the basis for most ethical codes throughout the world.

Hinduism	Do nothing to others which would cause pain if done to you.
Buddhism	One should seek for others the happiness one desires for oneself.
Taoism	Regard your neighbor's gain as your own gain, and your neighbor's loss as your loss.
Confucianism	Is there one principle which ought to be acted upon throughout one's whole life? Surely it is the principle of lovingkindness: do not unto others what you would not have them do unto you.
Zoroastrianism	The nature alone is good which refrains from doing unto another whatsoever is not good for itself.
Judaism	What is hateful to you, do not do to others. That is the entire law: all the rest is but commentary.
Islam	No one of you is a believer until he desires for his brother that which he desires for himself.
Christianity	Do unto others what you would have others do unto you.

Does the fact that virtually all religions appear to have a common theme of valuing others as yourself provide evidence that there are universal human ethical standards?

Our purpose is not to prescribe a specific religious or philosophical ethical code, but rather to suggest that humans from a variety of cultures and traditions have sought to develop ethical principles that guide their interactions with others. Having an ethical code does not always mean that people follow the code, however. Scholars and philosophers who suggest that a universal code of ethics exists do not claim that people always behave in ways that are true to these universal standards.

Philosophy and religion are not the only realms that focus on ethical behavior. Most professions, such as medicine, law, and journalism, have explicit codes of ethics that identify appropriate and inappropriate behavior. The National Communication Association has developed a Credo for Communication Ethics to emphasize the importance of being an ethical communicator:

> Ethical communication is fundamental to responsible thinking, decision making, and the development of relationships and communities within and across contexts, cultures, channels, and media. Moreover, ethical communication enhances human worth and dignity by fostering truthfulness, fairness, responsibility, personal integrity, and respect for self and others.[56]

For most people, being ethical means being sensitive to others' needs, giving people choices rather than forcing them to behave in a certain way, respecting others' privacy, not intentionally decreasing others' feelings of self-worth, and being honest in presenting information. Unethical communication does just the opposite: It forces views on others and demeans their integrity. Echoing the wisdom offered by others, we suggest that competent communication is grounded in an ethical perspective that is respectful to others.

Communication in the Twenty-First Century

1.5 Describe the nature of communication in the twenty-first century.

We live in a technological age and we use technology to make human connections with others. Reportedly 57 million people use the Tinder dating app each year to connect with someone.[57] Over 20 billion matches have been made since Tinder launched in 2012.[58] About one-third of people in the United States have used at least one dating app, with people between 18 and 29 making up almost half of all users.[59] In addition, 55 percent of individuals who identify as gay, lesbian, or bisexual report using a dating app compared with 28 percent of straight users.[60] Whether you're seeking to meet new people or connecting with friends and family, it is increasingly important to use technology competently when communicating in the twenty-first century.

Mediated communication occurs when you use a medium such as a smartphone or the Internet to relay your message. Some physical media, such as a cable or router, transfers the message between sender and receiver. Face-to-face communication is considered unmediated because there are no media channels, other than light and sound waves, that carry messages between you and the other person. People have been using mediated communication for centuries—sending letters and other written messages is a long-standing human practice. In fact, a printed or digital textbook is a form of mediated "distance learning."

Mass communication occurs when a mediated message is sent to many people at the same time. A TV or radio broadcast is an example of mass communication. Although mass communication is important, our focus in this book is primarily on unmediated and mediated interpersonal, group, and presentational communication.

Immediate Communication

What's new today is that there are so many different ways of *immediately* connecting with someone whether *synchronously* (in actual time, such as a phone

---

mediated communication
Any communication that is carried out using some channel other than those used in face-to-face communication.

mass communication
Communication accomplished through a mediated message that is sent to many people at the same time.

conversation) or *asynchronously* (where there is a time delay between sending and receiving a message, such as with email).[61] Zoom, FaceTime, Skype, Facebook, Snapchat, Twitter, Instagram, and other contemporary methods of communicating with others are relatively recent inventions when we consider the entire spectrum of human history.

Frequent Communication

We spend a lot of time online. North Americans spend more than two hours a day online while people from South America and Africa spend more than three hours a day online.[62] Switching between face-to-face and mediated communication is a normal, seamless way of communicating with others, especially if you're a frequent user of computers or mobile devices. If you're under the age of 30, these technological tools have probably always seemed to be part of your life; you are, for example, much more likely to text friends than to phone them.[63]

In addition to frequently using our phones, there is evidence that we increasingly multitask as we connect with others, such as when we check messages on our phones while visiting with a friend or sitting through a meeting. Or we may participate in multiple text or Snapchat conversations at once. One research team suggests that excessive multitasking may be a reflection of our personality. Frequent multitasking may also be a symptom of attention-deficit/hyperactivity disorder (ADHD)—we may simply have difficulty focusing on one thing at a time for a sustained period of time. Or, multitasking may suggest a desire to always be "on" and connected due to a high need for social assurance, especially prominent among females according to one research study.[64]

If you are attending a college or university away from family, friends, and loved ones, you may have found that sending text messages, using FaceTime, or connecting on Facebook or Instagram can help you stay in touch with others who are important to you. During the COVID-19 pandemic, both faculty and students had to learn new ways to teach and learn when campuses closed and online instruction swiftly replaced face-to-face classes. The Social Media & Communication box discusses many of the ways we use social media to stay connected.

Communication That Meets Our Needs

Some researchers have wondered whether spending a lot of time online reduces people's need for face-to-face interactions. A team of researchers led by Robert Kraut and Sara Kiesler made headlines when they published the results of their study, which concluded that the more people use the Internet, the less they interact with people in person.[65] These researchers also found a relationship between people who said they were lonely and those who used the Internet. Another review of several research studies also found a positive relationship between extensive social media use and loneliness.[66]

SOCIAL MEDIA & COMMUNICATION

Facebook versus TikTok: Connecting on Social Media

With 4.57 billion people having access to the Internet, and in 2020 alone 346 million new users coming online, Facebook was the first social networking company to reach one billion registered users. In addition to acquiring Instagram in 2021 and WhatsApp in 2014, with a collective monthly user base of 3.3 billion, by the end of 2020, Facebook had over 2.74 billion monthly active users.[67] Facebook and Instagram are particularly effective for marketing products and services to millennials and Gen Z consumers.[68] However, the new contender for top social media platform is TikTok, which only launched in 2016, but already has in excess of 800 million monthly users. It is a short-form video sharing platform developed by the Chinese company, ByteDance.[69] According to the *Digital 2020: October Global Statshot*, social media has reached 4.14 billion monthly users (around 53 percent of the world's population) and this equates to 89 percent of all Internet users with 2 million people joining a social media network every day.[70]

While Facebook and its acquired companies are collectively the most used mobile apps, in terms of downloads, TikTok tops the list, indicating potential changes in terms of market dominance.[71] At the same time there are changes in the popularity of social media platforms for teens. Here's the ranking of the social media platforms (by percentage of users) three years apart:[72]

Rank	Platform	2017	Platform	2020
1	Snapchat	47 percent	Snapchat	34 percent
2	Instagram	24 percent	TikTok	29 percent
3	Facebook	9 percent	Instagram	25 percent
4	Twitter	7 percent	Twitter	3 percent

While Facebook users are falling in both Europe and North America, 40 percent of Facebook's users are in China and India is its largest single market.[73] Globally, Facebook is still the third most visited after Google and YouTube.[74] A typical user each month likes 12 posts, comments on 5 of these, shares one post, and clicks on 12 advertisements.[75]

However, while its user count is still high, Facebook's engagement is dropping. Of the average 3 hours spent on social media each day, Facebook users spend 35 minutes on the site. Statistics suggests that Facebook is becoming "an old people's app"; unlike younger users, older users are not migrating over to newer social media alternatives.[76]

▲ Can an overreliance on mediated communication lead to increased loneliness and social isolation?
Yulia Grogoryeva/123rf.com

Yet, research results have not been consistent. Three studies found that people who use the Internet are *more* likely to have a large number of friends; they are *more* involved with community activities; and overall have *greater* levels of trust in other people.[77]

Additional follow-up research suggests that for some people—those who are already prone to being shy or introverted—there may be a link between Internet use and loneliness or feelings of social isolation. This link might exist, however, because shy and introverted people are simply less likely to make contact with others in any way, not because they use the Internet a lot. For people who are generally outgoing and who like to interact with others, in contrast, the Internet is another tool with which to reach out to others.

Whether communicating face-to-face or using social media, we express ourselves to meet our need for human interaction.

Comfortable Communication

Cyberspace can be a more comfortable place to communicate with others if you are apprehensive about talking in face-to-face situations or even on the phone. And during the COVID-19 pandemic when people practiced social distancing, it was also a *safer* place to communicate. People who spend a lot of time online may not be lonelier; rather, they may just feel more comfortable having the ability to control the timing of how they interact with others. One study suggests that many of us may prefer to use a less immediate communication channel when we are feeling some apprehension or relationship uncertainty. Researchers also found that you are more likely to call a romantic partner on your cell phone when the relationship is going well versus when it isn't.[78]

Another concern is dishonest communication. In a digital world, it is easy to send messages and provide feedback anonymously. Because of this anonymity, it's easier to be deceitful. For example, in 2020 Facebook estimated that at any given moment more than 116 million of its accounts were fake.[79] Personal appearance plays less of a role in shaping initial impressions when using only text messages, unless we add photos or videos. Even then, especially with photos, we can more easily manipulate our image (for example, by sharing a photo of when we were younger or thinner).

Our recommendation? Your method of communication should fit well with your communication goal. Although connecting to others via the Internet is a normal way to communicate for a significant and growing percentage of the world's population, at times relating to someone live and in person is best—especially when expressing feelings and emotions. In other situations, the ease and speed of mediated communication make it preferable to face-to-face communication.

Communication Contexts

1.6 Identify and explain three communication contexts.

Communication takes place in a variety of situations. As we've discussed, a great deal of the communication in our lives today is mediated. In this section, we'll describe the three classic, face-to-face contexts of human communication studied by researchers: interpersonal communication, group communication, and presentational communication. All three contexts are part of communication in organizational and health settings.

Interpersonal Communication

Interpersonal communication is a special form of human communication that occurs when we interact simultaneously with another person and attempt to mutually influence each other, usually for the purpose of managing relationships. To relate to someone is to give and take, listen and respond, act and react. When we talk about a good or positive relationship with someone, we often mean that we are "together" or "in sync." Interpersonal communication reflects the characteristics of the transactional model of communication discussed earlier. It is a dialogue in the sense that all communicators influence each other and create meaning simultaneously.[80] At the heart of this definition is the role of communication in developing unique relationships with other people.[81] We will discuss interpersonal communication in more detail in Chapters 7 and 8.

In contrast to interpersonal communication, **impersonal communication** occurs when we treat people as objects, or when we respond to their roles rather than to who they are as unique people. For example, asking a server for a glass of water at a restaurant is impersonal rather than interpersonal communication. However, if you strike up a conversation with the server—say you discover that it's her birthday or that you both know the same people—your conversation changes from impersonal to interpersonal. We're not suggesting that impersonal communication is unimportant or necessarily inferior or bad. Competent communicators are able to interact with others in a variety of situations.

Group Communication

Human beings are social, collaborative creatures. We do most of our work and play in groups. One focus of this book is the

interpersonal communication
Communication that occurs simultaneously between two people who attempt to mutually influence each other, usually for the purpose of managing relationships.

impersonal communication
Communication that treats people as objects or that responds only to their roles rather than to who they are as unique people.

▼ We engage in interpersonal communication when we interact with another person.
Cathy Yeulet/123RF

communication that occurs in groups—how we make sense of our participation in groups and share that sense with others. We define **small group communication** as the verbal and nonverbal message transactions that occur among three to about fifteen people who share a common goal, feel a sense of belonging to the group, and exert influence on one another.[82] Today's globe-shrinking technology, such as Zoom, FaceTime, and GoToMeeting software, makes it possible for people to be linked with others in *virtual groups* even when they are in different physical locations.[83] In Chapters 9 and 10, we will discuss groups and teams, both in-person and virtual, more thoroughly.

small group communication
The transactive process of creating meaning among three to about fifteen people who share a common purpose, feel a sense of belonging to the group, and exert influence on one another.

Presentational Communication

For many people, speaking in public is a major source of anxiety. **Presentational communication** occurs when a speaker addresses a gathering of people to inform, persuade, or entertain. In this text, we will focus on applying the principles of communication when informing and persuading listeners. In Chapters 11 through 15, we present basic strategies for designing and delivering a speech to others. Effective public speakers are aware of their communication and how they interact with their audience. They also effectively use, interpret, and understand verbal and nonverbal messages; listen and respond to their audience; and adapt their message to their listeners.

presentational communication
Communication that occurs when a speaker addresses a gathering of people to inform, persuade, or entertain them.

Of the three contexts in which the principles we present in this text are applied, public speaking has the distinction of being the one that has been formally studied the longest. In 333 BCE, Aristotle wrote his famous *Rhetoric*, the first fully developed treatment of the study of speech to convince an audience. He defined **rhetoric** as the process of discovering the available means of persuasion in a given situation. In essence, persuasion is the process of using symbols to persuade others. Although we have certainly advanced in our understanding of informing and persuading others in the past two millennia, much of what Aristotle taught has withstood the tests of both time and scholarly research.

rhetoric
The process of using symbols to influence or persuade others.

Organizational and Health Communication

Many researchers study the communication that occurs in organizations such as businesses, government agencies, and nonprofits such as the American Cancer Society and other charities. **Organizational communication** is the study of human communication as it occurs within organizations. Although organizational communication includes applications of interpersonal, group, and presentational communication, there are unique ways in which communication functions in contemporary organizations.

organizational communication
The study of human communication as it occurs within organizations.

Health communication, a growing area of communication study, examines the role and importance of communication that has an effect on our health. Health communication researchers study the interaction between health care workers (such as physicians, physician's assistants, and nurses) and patients. One study found that doctors who take the time to talk and listen to their patients had a profound and positive effect on their patients' health.[84] Health communication scholars also study how to best design campaigns to encourage healthy habits, such as messages about getting fit, losing weight, avoiding sexually transmitted diseases, or quitting smoking.

health communication
The study of communication that has an effect on human health.

Communication Principles for a Lifetime

1.7 List and explain five fundamental principles of communication.

As we noted at the beginning of this chapter, underlying our description of human communication are five principles that provide the foundation for all effective communication, whether we are communicating with others one on one, in groups or teams, or by presenting a public speech to an audience. Throughout this book, we will emphasize how these principles are woven into the fabric of each communication context. We provide a brief introduction to these five Communication Principles for a Lifetime here. Then, in the next five chapters, we will present a more comprehensive discussion of their scope and power.

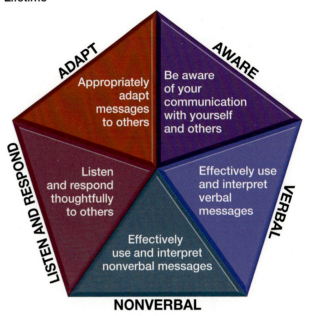

FIGURE 1.5 Communication Principles for a Lifetime

Principle One:	Be aware of your communication with yourself and others.
Principle Two:	Effectively use and interpret verbal messages.
Principle Three:	Effectively use and interpret nonverbal messages.
Principle Four:	Listen and respond thoughtfully to others.
Principle Five:	Appropriately adapt messages to others.

These five principles operate together rather than independently to form the basis of the fundamental processes that enhance communication effectiveness. The model in Figure 1.5 illustrates how the principles interrelate. Moving around the model clockwise, the first principle, being aware of your communication with yourself and others, is followed by the two principles that focus on communication messages, verbal messages (Principle Two) and nonverbal messages (Principle Three). The fourth principle, listening and responding, is followed by appropriately adapting messages to others (Principle Five). Together, these five principles can help explain why communication can be either effective or ineffective. A violation of any one principle can result in inappropriate or poor communication.

Throughout this text, we will remind you of how these principles can be used to organize the theory, concepts, and skills we offer as fundamental to human communication. Chapters 2 through 6 will each be devoted to a single principle. Chapters 7 through 15 will apply these principles to the most prevalent communication situations we experience each day: communicating with others interpersonally, in groups and teams, and when giving a talk or presentation.

To help you see relationships among the five communication principles and the various skills and content we will present in Chapters 7 through 15, we will place in the margin a small version of the model presented in Figure 1.5, like the one that appears here. We will also label which principle or principles we are discussing. Refer to Figure 1.5 as we introduce each of these principles.

Principle One: Be Aware of Your Communication with Yourself and Others

The first foundation principle is to be aware of your communication with yourself and others. Effective communicators are conscious, or "present," when communicating. Ineffective communicators mindlessly or thoughtlessly say and do things that they may later regret. Being aware of your communication includes being conscious not only of the present moment but also of who you are, your self-concept, your self-worth, and your perceptions of yourself and others. Being aware of your typical communication style is also part of this foundation principle. For example, some people realize that their communication style is to be emotional when interacting with others. Others may be shy.

As has been noted, self-awareness includes being conscious of your intrapersonal communication messages. By **intrapersonal communication**, we mean the communication

intrapersonal communication
Communication that occurs within yourself, including your thoughts and emotions.

DIVERSITY & COMMUNICATION

Communication Principles for a Lifetime: Principles for All Cultures?

Are the five Principles for a Lifetime applicable to all human communication, across a variety of cultures? Culture is the learned system of knowledge, behavior, attitudes, beliefs, values, and norms that is shared by a group of people. Is it true that people of all cultures should be aware of their communication, use and interpret verbal and nonverbal messages, listen and respond thoughtfully, and appropriately adapt their messages to others?

We suggest that these five fundamental principles may provide a common framework for talking about communication in a variety of cultures. We're not suggesting that all cultures use each principle the same way. There are obvious differences from one culture to another in language and in the use of nonverbal cues (Principles Two and Three), for example. But in all cultures, the use and interpretation of verbal and nonverbal messages are important in determining whether communication is effective.

There are also clear cultural differences in the way people choose to adapt messages to others (Principle Five), but people in all cultures may adapt messages to others in some way, even though adaptations vary from culture to culture.

Do you agree or disagree with our position? In your communication class, there are undoubtedly people from a variety of cultural backgrounds. Respond to the following questions, and then compare your answers with those of your fellow students.

1. How applicable are the five communication principles to your cultural experience?
2. Do any of the communication principles *not* apply in your culture?
3. Can you think of another fundamental communication principle that you believe should be added to our list of five? If so, what is it?
4. Do you agree that these communication principles apply to all people?

that occurs within yourself, including your thoughts, your emotions, and your perceptions of yourself and others. Talking to yourself is an example of intrapersonal communication. While our intrapersonal messages are often the focus of psychologists, they also form the basis of our communication with others.[85]

Earlier in this chapter, we noted that human communication is the process of making sense out of the world and sharing that sense with others. Being aware of who we are and how we perceive, or "make sense of," what we observe is a fundamental principle that helps explain both effective and ineffective communication.

Principle One also involves being aware of not just your own communication but also of what others do and say. We are more effective communicators if we are aware of how other people communicate. In Chapter 2, we discuss the principle of being aware of self and others in greater depth. We also describe how this principle relates to a variety of communication situations.

Principle Two: Effectively Use and Interpret Verbal Messages

The second principle we introduce here and elaborate on in Chapter 3 is to use and interpret verbal messages effectively. Verbal messages are created with language. A **language** consists of symbols and a system of rules (grammar) that make it possible for people to understand one another.

As we noted earlier, a symbol is a word, sound, gesture, or visual image that represents a thought, concept, object, or experience. When you read the words on this page or on your screen, you are looking at symbols that trigger meaning. The word is not the thing it represents; it simply symbolizes the thing or idea.

Your reading skill permits you to make sense out of symbols. The word *tree*, for example, may trigger a thought of the tree in your own yard or the great sequoia you saw on your family vacation in Yosemite National Park. Author Daniel Quinn once commented, "No story is devoid of meaning, if you know how to look for it. This is

language
The system of symbols (words or vocabulary) structured by rules (grammar) that makes it possible for people to understand one another.

as true of nursery rhymes and daydreams as it is of epic poems."[86] Meaning is created when people have a common or shared understanding.

The effective communicator both encodes and decodes messages accurately; he or she selects appropriate symbols to form a message and carefully interprets the messages of others. The process of using and interpreting symbols is the essence of how we make sense out of the world and share that sense with others. Some people feared that greater use of texting would lead to lower skills in language use and overall literacy. Research doesn't support that supposition, however: People who send and receive numerous text messages show no deterioration of language and literacy skills.[87]

Words have power. Any good advertising copywriter knows how to use words to create a need or desire for a product. Political consultants tell politicians how to craft sound bites that will create just the right audience response. And words can hurt us. As author Robert Fulghum wisely noted, "Sticks and stones may break our bones, but words break our hearts."[88] Words have the ability to offend and create stress. For example, derogatory words about someone's gender or ethnicity can do considerable harm. Throughout this book, we will present strategies and suggestions for selecting the best word or symbol to enhance your listeners' understanding.

Principle Three: Effectively Use and Interpret Nonverbal Messages

Messages are also nonverbal. **Nonverbal communication** is communication by means other than written or spoken language that creates meaning for someone. Nonverbal messages can communicate powerful ideas or express emotions with greater impact than mere words alone. An optimistic hitchhiker's extended thumb and an irate driver's extended finger are nonverbal symbols with clear and intentional meanings. But not all nonverbal symbols are clearly interpreted or even consciously expressed. You may not be aware of your frown when someone asks whether he or she may sit next to you in a vacant seat in a restaurant. Or your son may excitedly be telling you about his field trip to the fire station while you stare at your smartphone. You have no intention of telling your son he is not important, but your lack of nonverbal responsiveness speaks volumes. Our nonverbal messages communicate how we feel toward others.

When there is a contradiction between what you say and what you do, your nonverbal message is more believable than your verbal message. When asked how your meal is, you may tell your server "great," but your nonverbal message—facial expression and flat tone of voice—clearly communicates your unhappiness with the cuisine. As was noted earlier, when we discussed the concept of content and relationship messages, our nonverbal cues often tell people how to interpret what we are saying.

Effective communicators develop skill in interpreting the nonverbal messages of others. They also monitor their own messages to avoid unintentionally sending contradictory verbal and nonverbal messages. It's sometimes hard to interpret nonverbal messages because they don't have a neat beginning and ending point—the flow of information is continuous. It might not be clear where one gesture stops and another begins. Cultural differences, combined with the fact that so many different nonverbal channels (such as eye contact, facial expression, gestures, posture) can be used at the same time, make it tricky to "read" someone's nonverbal message accurately. We provide an expanded discussion of the power of nonverbal messages in Chapter 4.

nonverbal communication
Communication by means other than written or spoken language that creates meaning for someone.

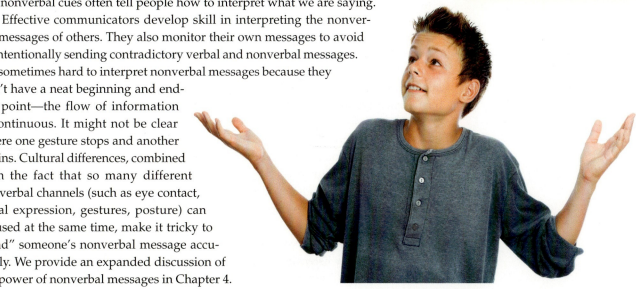

▼ Your gestures, facial expressions, and other nonverbal cues communicate your emotions, often more honestly than your words do. Is this person telling the truth?
Karelnoppe/Shutterstock

Principle Four: Listen and Respond Thoughtfully to Others

So far, our list of principles may appear to place much of the burden of achieving communication success on the person sending the message. But effective communication with others also places considerable responsibility on the listener. Because communication is a transactional process—both senders and receivers are mutually and usually simultaneously expressing and responding to symbols—listening to words with sensitivity and "listening between the lines" to nonverbal messages join our list of fundamental principles.

Listening can be hard because it looks easy. You spend more time listening than you do performing any other communication activity—probably more than any other thing you do except sleep.[89] But research suggests that many, if not most, of us do not always listen effectively. Both psychological, or internal, noise (our own thoughts, needs, and emotions) and external distractions (noise in the surroundings in which we listen) can create barriers to effective listening.

A widespread perception that listening is a passive rather than an active task also makes listening and accurately interpreting information a challenge. Effective listening is *not* a passive task at all; the effective and sensitive listener works hard to stay on task and focus mindfully on a sender's message. Effective listening requires you to develop an orientation or sensitivity to others when you listen and respond. When you are **other-oriented**, you consider the needs, motives, desires, and goals of your communication partners while still maintaining your own integrity. The choices you make in both forming the message and selecting when to share it should take into consideration your partner's thoughts and feelings. People who are skilled communicators both listen and respond with sensitivity; they are other-oriented, rather than self-focused.

other-oriented
Being focused on the needs and concerns of others while maintaining one's personal integrity.

adapt
To adjust both what is communicated and how a message is communicated; to make choices about how best to formulate a message and respond to others to achieve your communication goals.

Principle Five: Appropriately Adapt Messages to Others

It is not enough to be sensitive and to accurately understand others; you must use the information you gather to modify the messages you construct. It is important to **adapt** your response appropriately to your listener. When you adapt a message, you make choices about how best to formulate both your message content and delivery, and how to respond to someone, in order to ethically achieve your communication goals. Adapting to a listener does *not* mean that you tell a listener only what he or she wants to hear. That would be unethical. Adapting involves appropriately editing and shaping your responses so that others accurately understand your messages and so that you achieve your goal without coercing or using false information or other unethical methods.

One of the elements of a message that you can adapt when communicating with others is the structure or organization of what you say. Informal interpersonal conversations typically do not follow a rigid, outlined structure. Conversation has a more interactive, give-and-take flow as it freely bounces from one topic to another.[90] In contrast, formal speeches delivered in North America are usually expected to have a more explicit structure—an introduction, a body, and a conclusion—with clearly identified major ideas. Other cultures, such as those in the Middle East, expect a greater use of stories, examples, and illustrations, rather than a clearly structured, outlined presentation. Knowing your audience's expectations can help you adapt your message so that it will be listened to and understood. In Chapter 6, we will discuss this principle in greater detail by discussing the diverse nature of potential listeners and how to adapt to them. Adapting to differences in culture and gender, for example, may mean the difference between a message that is well received and one that creates hostility. Effective communicators not only listen and respond with sensitivity; they use the information they gather to shape the message and delivery of their responses to others.

STUDY GUIDE: PRINCIPLES FOR A LIFETIME

Why Study Communication?

1.1 Explain why it is important to study communication.

PRINCIPLE POINTS: Communication is essential for life. It is important to learn about communication because being a skilled communicator can help you obtain a good job, enhance the quality of your relationships, and improve your physical and emotional health.

PRINCIPLE SKILLS:

1. Why are you taking this class? What skills do you hope to develop or what questions do you want to answer?
2. Keep a communication log for one day. Note the amount of time you read, write, speak, and listen.

The Communication Process

1.2 Define communication and describe five characteristics of the communication process.

PRINCIPLE POINTS: At its most basic level, communication is the process of acting on information. Human communication is the process of making sense out of the world and sharing that sense with others by creating meaning through verbal and nonverbal messages. Communication is inescapable, irreversible, complicated, and governed by rules. It also emphasizes content and relationships.

PRINCIPLE TERMS:

communication	content dimension
communications	relationship dimension
human communication	rule
symbol	

PRINCIPLE SKILLS:

1. List the implicit and explicit communication rules for a situation you are in regularly, such as a particular class, a regular group or team meeting, or a line at a deli or coffee shop on campus.
2. How effectively can you identify the content and relational messages when interacting with others? After you conclude a conversation with a friend or acquaintance today, take a moment to write down the content of the message (the essence of what was said) and the relational message (how positive or negative, pleasant or unpleasant the interaction was). Were you aware of which specific behaviors led you to perceive the conversation as pleasant or unpleasant?

Communication Models

1.3 Explain three communication models.

PRINCIPLE POINTS: Early models viewed human communication as a simple message-transfer process. Later models evolved to view communication as interaction and then as simultaneous transaction. Key components of communication include source, receiver, message, channel, noise, context, and feedback.

PRINCIPLE TERMS:

communication models	channel
source	noise
encoding	feedback
decoding	context
receiver	critical/cultural approach
message	to communication

PRINCIPLE SKILLS:

1. In your own words, provide an example of a communication transaction in which all parties are sending and receiving information at the same time.
2. Reflect on a recent conflict you had with another person. Analyze this conflict by identifying the key components in the exchange (such as source, receiver, message, channel, etc.). What could or should have been changed to enhance the quality of communication?

Communication Competence

1.4 Describe three criteria that can be used to determine whether communication is competent.

PRINCIPLE POINTS: To be both effective and appropriate, a communication message should be understood as the communicator intended it to be understood, achieve the communicator's intended effect, and be ethical.

PRINCIPLE TERMS:

communication competence	ethics

PRINCIPLE SKILLS:

1. Identify recent communication situations in which you felt competent and those in which you felt incompetent. What factors determined whether you felt competent or incompetent?
2. Based on the description of communication competence in this chapter, think about the communication you typically have with your instructor for this course. How would you assess your communication competence with him or her?

Communication in the Twenty-First Century

1.5 Describe the nature of communication in the twenty-first century.

PRINCIPLE POINTS: Today, we commonly use various forms of media to communicate, either asynchronously or synchronously. Mediated communication is usually more anonymous than face-to-face communication and places less emphasis on a person's physical appearance. Shy or introverted people may prefer mediated to in-person communication, as do people who feel some relationship uncertainty.

PRINCIPLE TERMS:

mediated communication   mass communication

PRINCIPLE SKILLS:

1. How much time do you spend using technology to communicate with others? Keep a log for a specific period of time (such as six hours, twelve hours, or a day) noting how often you use your phone, computer, and other devices to read, write, speak, and listen.
2. Overall, consider how effectively you use technology to communicate with others. Do you, for example, glance at your phone when talking with others? Do you multitask and perhaps miss some messages because you are trying to do several things at once?

Communication Contexts

1.6 Identify and explain three communication contexts.

PRINCIPLE POINTS: The three classic contexts of in-person communication that researchers have studied are (1) interpersonal communication, which occurs simultaneously between two people who attempt to mutually influence each other, usually for the purpose of managing relationships; (2) small group communication, which is the transactive process of creating meaning among three to about fifteen people who share a common purpose, feel a sense of belonging to the group, and exert influence on one another; and (3) presentational communication, which occurs when a speaker addresses a gathering of people to inform, persuade, or entertain them. Communication in organizational and healthcare settings involves all three contexts.

PRINCIPLE TERMS:

interpersonal communication
impersonal communication
small group communication
presentational communication
rhetoric
organizational communication
health communication

PRINCIPLE SKILLS:

1. Which contexts of in-person communication have you experienced so far today? Have you communicated interpersonally or in small groups? Have you listened to or given a presentation?
2. In which of the three contexts of in-person communication do you have the strongest skills? Which area(s) do you want to improve, and what skills would you like to develop?

Communication Principles for a Lifetime

1.7 List and explain five fundamental principles of communication.

PRINCIPLE POINTS: The following five principles are fundamental to good communication.

1. Be aware of your communication with yourself and others. Being mindful of your communication helps you become a more effective communicator.
2. Effectively use and interpret verbal messages. Words are powerful and influence our thoughts, actions, and relationships with others.
3. Effectively use and interpret nonverbal messages. Unspoken cues provide important information about our emotions, feelings, and attitudes.
4. Listen and respond thoughtfully to others. Being able to interpret the messages of others accurately enhances comprehension and relational empathy.
5. Appropriately adapt messages to others. It is important to adapt messages to others to enhance both understanding and empathy.

PRINCIPLE TERMS:

intrapersonal communication
language
nonverbal communication
other-oriented
adapt

PRINCIPLE SKILLS:

1. As we noted at the beginning of this chapter, the five principles described in Figure 1.5 and throughout this text may not tell you everything you need to know about communication. What additional communication principle(s) would you suggest adding to the list?
2. Which communication principle or principles do you perform well? Which principles do you need to improve?

CHAPTER 2

EXPLORING SELF-AWARENESS AND COMMUNICATION

Don't compromise yourself. You are all you've got. —JANIS JOPLIN

saltodemata/Shutterstock

CHAPTER OUTLINE

- Self-Awareness: How Well Do You Know Yourself?
- Self-Concept: Who Are You?
- Self-Esteem: What's Your Value?
- Communication and the Enhancement of Self-Esteem
- The Perception Process
- Communicate to Enhance Your Powers of Perception
- Study Guide: *Principles for a Lifetime*

LEARNING OBJECTIVES

2.1 Discuss the importance of self-awareness in the process of improving one's communication skills.

2.2 Describe the components of the self-concept and major influences on self-concept development.

2.3 Describe how gender, social comparisons, and self-fulfilling prophecies affect one's self-esteem.

2.4 Practice six communication strategies for enhancing one's self-esteem.

2.5 Explain the three stages of perception and why people differ in their perceptions of people and events.

2.6 Summarize three communication strategies that can improve one's powers of perception.

Consistently for a few years now, college students' top three preferred social media sites have been Instagram, Snapchat, and Facebook, primarily because these platforms allow users to post, view, and comment on photos and videos.[1] Facebook has been waning in popularity among students in recent years because many don't want to post to a site their parents use. The Pew Research Center indicates that college students use social networking sites from 1 to 10 hours per day, with heavier use on weekends.

Do you think much about your choices when you use social media? Do you pause to consider who will see your post, photo, or video? Do you wonder who might comment on it and how you'll deal with people's responses? Some people regularly change their photos on social media platforms, while others leave the same ones up for years. Is your profile photo current or is it from another time, perhaps when you felt you looked better? What about your privacy settings—what information do you share and what do you keep private? Developing an engaging and appropriate social media presence relies on a central, important element: self-awareness.

Stephen Covey, author of *The Seven Habits of Highly Effective People*, describes self-awareness as a characteristic that "enables us to stand apart and examine even the way we 'see' ourselves."[2] Interpersonal communication scholar David Johnson points out the importance of self-awareness: "Self-awareness is the key to self-knowledge, self-understanding, and self-disclosure. Being open with another person begins with being aware of who you are and what you are like. To disclose your feelings and reactions, you must be aware of them."[3]

Figure 2.1 is the Communication Principles for a Lifetime model introduced in Chapter 1. The five principles provide the foundation for effective communication in various contexts you may encounter throughout your life. In this chapter, we explore the first principle: *Be aware of your communication with yourself and others.* Developing self-awareness involves being conscious not only of the present moment, but also of who you are, your values, and your perception of yourself and others.

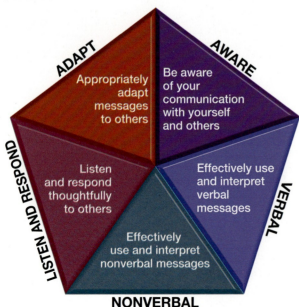

FIGURE 2.1 Communication Principles for a Lifetime

Self-Awareness: How Well Do You Know Yourself?

2.1 Discuss the importance of self-awareness in the process of improving one's communication skills.

Benjamin Franklin once said, "There are three things extremely hard: steel, a diamond, and to know oneself."[4] Knowing oneself is a lifelong process; we never reach a point at which we have maxed out our self-awareness. But it is also true that many of us experience phases of heightened self-awareness in life, perhaps in moments or periods when we're acutely aware that we're learning something important—something that will change us in some profound way. (College years can be full of these moments.) In this chapter, we deal with all forms of awareness—the simple and the profound, the casual and the dramatic—because any kind of awareness influences how we communicate and respond to communication from others.

By one definition, **self-awareness** is "the capacity to observe and reflect upon one's own mental states."[5] A related view holds that self-awareness, sometimes referred to as **symbolic self-awareness**, is the unique human ability to develop a representation of oneself and communicate that representation to others through language.[6]

The better we understand the complex, multilayered nature of the self, the more aware we will become of our own being; this awareness is critical to effective communication. Research shows that people who are highly self-aware are better able to anticipate others' opinions of themselves, take others' perspectives, and communicate empathy.[7] A framework attributed to Abraham Maslow helps explain the process of becoming self-aware. The same framework has also been used to explain our attainment of communication skill. It suggests that people operate at one of four levels:

1. *Unconscious incompetence.* We are unaware of our own incompetence. We don't know what we don't know.
2. *Conscious incompetence.* At this level, we become aware or conscious that we are not competent; we know what we don't know.
3. *Conscious competence.* We are aware that we know or can do something, but it has not yet become an integrated skill or habit.
4. *Unconscious competence.* At this level, skills become second nature. We know or can do something but don't have to concentrate to be able to act on that knowledge or draw on that skill.

self-awareness
The ability to see and reflect upon one's own state of mind.

symbolic self-awareness
A unique human ability to develop and communicate a representation of oneself to others through language.

To illustrate this framework, let's look at an example. Your coworker, Stella, sometimes says inappropriate things; she just doesn't seem to know how to talk to people in a way that doesn't make her come across like she was raised by wolves. Stella is at Maslow's level 1 when it comes to communication: She doesn't know that she communicates poorly. Eventually, customers and coworkers complain to Stella's supervisor. The supervisor calls Stella into the office, reprimands her for her poor communication skills, and requires her to enroll in communication training so that she can improve. Now Stella is at level 2 because she has become conscious of her own incompetence as a communicator. Stella embraces her communication training and, once back on the job, actively works to improve how she relates to coworkers, bosses, and customers. Her hard work pays off when her colleagues notice the changes she's making and provide positive feedback. Stella achieves level 3, in which she is conscious of her own competence as a communicator. If Stella continues to progress over time, at some point she may reach level 4. At that level, communication effectiveness would be incorporated into her style and self-concept and would no longer be something she would need to make a conscious effort to achieve.

Almost any communication skill can be described in terms of these four levels. It is also possible to be at one level with one skill and at a different level with another skill. For instance, you may skillfully meet new people but poorly manage conflict with a close personal friend. Someone may be very engaging when conversing with friends, but she or he would rather have a spinal tap than give a presentation.

Reading a text like this one and taking a communication course like the one you're enrolled in can spark periods of heightened self-awareness. You'll no doubt be challenged to inventory what you believe about yourself and how such aspects of identity as gender, ethnicity, nationality, sexual orientation, and social class contribute to your view of self. You'll be encouraged to go a step further to consider how you communicate that view of self to others. But the key beginning point is awareness. As Phil McGraw (a.k.a. Dr. Phil) says, "You can't change what you don't acknowledge."

Self-Concept: Who Are You?

2.2 Describe the components of the self-concept and major influences on self-concept development.

If someone asked you, "Who are you?" would you respond with basic demographic information, such as your age and where you're from? Or would you describe yourself in relation to groups and organizations to which you belong? Or might you talk about the various roles you assume, such as "I'm a student at State" or "I'm so-and-so's daughter (or son)"? Whatever answer you give will be incomplete because you can't really convey the totality of who you are to others.

Psychologist Karen Horney defines **self** as "that central inner force, common to all human beings and yet unique in each which is the deep source of growth."[8] Your "Who are you?" responses are part of your **self-concept**—your interior identity or subjective description of who you think you are, which remains relatively stable despite the changing world in which you live.[9] The self-concept is the way you consistently describe yourself to others; it is deeply rooted and slow to change.[10]

self
The sum of who you are as a person; your central inner force.

self-concept
Your interior identity or subjective description of who you think you are.

Self-Concept Components

The self-concept contains many components, but three critical ones are your **attitudes**, **beliefs**, and **values**. Table 2.1 describes each of these components in more detail. Of these three aspects, attitudes are the most superficial and likely to change, whereas values are more fundamental to a person and least likely to change.

attitudes
Learned predispositions to respond to a person, object, or idea in a favorable or unfavorable way.

beliefs
Ways in which you structure your understanding of reality—what is true and what is false.

values
Enduring concepts of good and bad or right and wrong.

One or Many Selves?

"I'm just not myself this morning," sighs Yasmin, as she drags herself out the door to head to class. If she isn't herself, *who is she?* Does each of us have just one self? Is there a more "real" self buried somewhere within?

One of the most enduring and widely accepted frameworks for understanding the self was developed by philosopher William James. He identified three components of the self: the material self, the social self, and the spiritual self.[11]

The Material Self Perhaps you've heard the statement "You are what you eat." The material self goes a step further than that by suggesting "You are what you have." The **material self** is a total of all the tangible things you feel ownership over: your body, your possessions, your home.

material self
The element of the self reflected in all the tangible things you own.

One element of the material self receives considerable attention in our culture: the body. Do you like the way you look? Most of us would like to change something about our appearance. Studies have determined that in the United States, women and girls tend to experience more negative feelings about their bodies than men and boys, which affects how women and girls view themselves.[12] However, research also shows that men and boys increasingly experience weight problems and body dissatisfaction from

TABLE 2.1 Self-Concept Components

Component	Definition	Dimensions	Example
Attitudes	Learned predispositions to respond favorably or unfavorably toward something	Likes–Dislikes	You like ice cream, video games, and posting photos on social media.
Beliefs	Ways in which you structure reality	True–False	You believe your parents love you.
Values	Enduring concepts of right and wrong	Good–Bad	You value honesty and truth.

comparing themselves with ideal muscular male bodies displayed in media (including video game characters). Increasingly, men and boys are becoming more concerned about what others want and expect them to look like.[13]

When there is a discrepancy between our desired material self and our self-concept, we may respond to eliminate the discrepancy. We may try to lose weight, buy new clothes, or even have a nose job. A recent study found that college students reported significantly higher levels of self-esteem after wearing a temporary tattoo for two weeks.[14] The connection between physical attractiveness and self-esteem may have led developers of the videoconferencing platform Zoom to offer a "Touch Up My Appearance" setting.[15]

The Social Self Your **social self** is the part of you that interacts with others. William James believed that you have as many social selves as you have people who recognize you, and that you change who you are depending on the people with whom you interact. For example, when you talk to your best friend, you're willing to "let your hair down" and reveal more thoughts and feelings than you might with your professor, parents, or boss. Each relationship you have with another person is unique because you bring to it a unique social self. This doesn't mean that you're false with people. Rather, you're multifaceted because you have different selves in relation to different people.

Have you ever been in an important relationship that changed your self-concept? As we said, the self-concept remains fairly stable over time; however, research has explored the topic of "when 'we' changes 'me.'"[16] When people are in relationships (particularly romantic or intimate ones) that are supportive, accommodating, and forgiving (when the need for forgiveness arises), their self-concepts tend to improve and expand. Conversely, when people are in relationships that are not supportive and involve such attributes as jealousy, revenge seeking, and threats of breakups, their self-concepts tend to degrade.

social self
Your concept of self as developed through your personal, social interactions with others.

The Spiritual Self Your **spiritual self** is a mixture of your beliefs and your sense of who you are in relationship to other forces in the universe. Notice that this aspect of the self is termed "spiritual," not "religious." The term *religious* implies adherence to a specific religion or faith, typically accompanied by a belief in a supreme being or creator. However, people who see themselves as spiritual often don't subscribe to any one religion, preferring to develop their views from an array of philosophies and belief systems. From William James's perspective, the spiritual self contains all your internal thoughts and introspections about your values and moral standards. It's not dependent on what you own or with whom you talk; it's the essence of who you *think* you are and how you *feel* about yourself. It's your attempt to understand your inner essence, whether you view that essence as consciousness, spirit, or soul. Your spiritual self is the part of you that attempts to answer the question "Why am I here?"

spiritual self
Your concept of self based on your beliefs and your sense of who you are in relation to other forces in the universe; also includes your thoughts and introspections about your values and moral standards.

RECAP

William James's Dimensions of Self

Dimension	Definition	Examples
Material Self	The component of self derived from physical elements that reflect who you are	The self you reveal through your body, clothes, car, phone
Social Self	The variety of selves that appear in different situations and roles, reflected in interactions with others	Your informal self interacting with friends; your formal self interacting with your professors
Spiritual Self	The component of self based on introspection about values, morals, and beliefs	Belief or disbelief in a supreme being or force; regard for life in all its forms

DIVERSITY & COMMUNICATION

Self-Concept among Students in Malaysia

Research papers published in 2020, funded by the Malaysian Ministry of Higher Education focused on the relationship between self-concept, career counselling and readiness for work among nearly 600 17- to 19-year-old students studying in industrial training institutes in Malaysia. The researchers found that career counselling for students provide a vital link between self-concept and work readiness. This direct and positive link was seen as instrumental in helping to prepare the students for future work opportunities. Because the students valued the career counselling, their career awareness improved and their work readiness was enhanced as a result. The researchers suggested that the students had a more concrete self-concept due to improved and resilience when looking at their respective possible careers.[17]

A study from 2010, which also focused on Malaysian 16- to 17-year-old students used Principal Component Analysis (PCA) to uncover factors that influenced the students' perceptions of self-concept. Three things were identified: academic self-concept, physical self-concept and social self-concept.[18] These were defined, respectively, as relating to the performance and achievement during the secondary phase of education, the students' views of their body image and how students regard their standing among their peers.

Another study from 2002 that looked at the self-concept of Malaysian students studying in a Malaysian university identified five "selves". These were the psychological self, the social self, the sexual self, the family self, and the physical self. The study noted that these could have marked impact on the success of these students, which could include exhibited behaviors and attitudes showing a significant relationship to how they might perceive their personal worth, their physical self, and their relationships with peers and families.[19]

All these studies note the impact of factors affecting students' concept of self is important to be aware of as they appear to also have an impact on future success, resilience, behaviors, and attitudes.

How the Self-Concept Develops

Research suggests we address the question "Who am I?" through four basic means: (1) our communication with other people, (2) our association with groups, (3) the roles we assume, and (4) our self-labels.

Communication with Others A valued colleague of ours often says, when he teaches communication courses, that every time you lose a relationship you lose an opportunity to see yourself. What he means is that we don't come to know and understand ourselves in a vacuum. We learn who we are by communicating with others, receiving their feedback, making sense out of it, and internalizing or rejecting all or part of it, such that we are altered by the experience. For example, let's say you like to think of yourself as a comedian. Now think about it for a moment: How would you know you were funny if not for the people who laugh at the humorous things you say or do?

In 1902, scholar Charles Horton Cooley first advanced the notion that we form our self-concepts by seeing ourselves in a figurative looking glass: We learn who we are by interacting with others, much as we look into a mirror and see our reflection.[20] Like Cooley, theorist George Herbert Mead also believed that our sense of self develops as a consequence of our past and present relationships with others.[21] Contemporary research confirms this idea. Results from a study of self-concept development in adolescents reinforced the important role parents play in developing a strong sense of self in their children. When parents, both generally and through daily conversations, affirmed their adolescents' sense of self and challenged them to realize their greater potential, the effect on self-concept development was powerful.[22]

We each have two components to our identity. Your **avowed identity** is one you personally assign to yourself and portray, such as student, athlete, or friend. Your **ascribed identity** involves characteristics others attribute or assign to you, which you may or may not agree with. For example, you may think you're a shy person (avowed identity), but others perceive your shyness as being aloof or conceited (ascribed identity). When contradictions emerge, you can enhance your self-awareness by processing your ascribed identity. Take it in, contemplate why people see you the way they do, and consider whether you need to make any changes in the way you relate to others. Avowed and ascribed identities aren't static; they shift and are negotiated through interactions with others.[23]

▲ Although identities change along with our circumstances and relationships, messages we receive early in life can have a long-lasting influence on our identities. How might an experience like this one shape this person's later views of herself?
Triloks/E+/Getty Images

Association with Groups I'm a native New Yorker. I'm a soccer player. I'm a rabbi. I'm a real estate agent. Politically, I'm an independent. Each of these self-descriptive statements answers the "Who am I?" question by citing identification with a group or organization. Our awareness of who we are is often linked to those with whom we associate. Some groups we're born into; others we choose on our own. Either way, group associations are significant parts of our identities.[24]

Assumed Roles A large part of most people's answers to the "Who am I?" question reflects roles they assume in their lives. Mother, aunt, brother, manager, salesperson, teacher, partner, and student are labels that imply certain expectations for behavior, and they are important in shaping the self-concept.

Sex (biological) and gender (psychological and cultural) assert a powerful influence on the self-concept from birth on. As soon as many parents learn the sex of their child, they begin socializing their child according to cultural roles. They give their children sex-stereotypical toys, such as baseball mitts, train sets, and guns for boys, and dolls, tea sets, and dress-up kits for girls. These practices are based on cultural expectations and traditions, and they play a major role in shaping our self-concept and behavior.[25] By the time we reach adulthood, our self-concepts are quite distinguishable by sex, with men describing themselves more in terms of giftedness, power, and invulnerability, and women viewing themselves in terms of likability and morality.[26]

Self-Labels Although our self-concept is deeply affected by others, we aren't blank slates they can write on. The labels we use to describe our own attitudes, beliefs, values, and actions also play a role in shaping our self-concept.[27] Where do our labels come from? We interpret what we experience; we are self-reflexive. **Self-reflexiveness** is the human ability to think about what we're doing while we're doing it. We talk to ourselves about ourselves. We are both participants and observers in all that we do.[28] This dual role encourages us to use labels to describe who we are.

avowed identity
An identity you assign to yourself and portray.

ascribed identity
An identity assigned to you by others.

self-reflexiveness
The human ability to think about what you are doing while you are doing it.

RECAP

How the Self-Concept Develops

Communication with Others	The self-concept develops as we communicate with others, receive their feedback, make sense out of it, and internalize or reject all or part of it.
Association with Groups	We develop our self-concept partly through our identification with groups or organizations.
Assumed Roles	The self-concept is affected by roles we assume, such as son or daughter, employee, parent, spouse, or student.
Self-Labels	The words we use to describe our attitudes, beliefs, values, and actions that play a role in shaping the self-concept.

Self-Esteem: What's Your Value?

2.3 Describe how gender, social comparisons, and self-fulfilling prophecies affect one's self-esteem.

self-esteem
Your assessment of your worth or value as reflected in your perception of such things as your skills, abilities, talents, and appearance.

It may sound crass to consider your *value*, but you do this every day. Your assessment of your value is termed **self-esteem**. This *evaluation* of who you are is closely related to your self-concept, or your *description* of who you are.[29] Feminist author Gloria Steinem explains that, "It's a feeling of 'clicking in' when that self is recognized, valued, discovered, *esteemed*—as if we literally plug into an inner energy that is ours alone, yet connects us to everything else."[30] While self-concept focuses on who you are, self-esteem centers on how you *feel* about who you are.

While the self-concept pertains to your enduring identity, self-esteem pertains more to your current state of mind or view of self. But are the two aspects of the self related? Researchers continue to explore that very question, focusing on the notion of **self-concept clarity**, defined as the extent to which beliefs about oneself are clearly and confidently identified and stable over time.[31] This doesn't mean that your view of yourself doesn't change; we know people evolve as they mature and experience new things. Self-concept clarity relates to the stability associated with having a clear sense of who you are and feeling confident about that. Researchers have determined that people who suffer from low self-esteem also tend to have a less clearly defined sense of self; in other words, they tend to have more questions about who they are.[32]

self-concept clarity
The extent to which beliefs about oneself are clearly and confidently identified and stable over time.

Self-esteem can fluctuate because of relatively minor events, such as getting a high grade on a paper, or major upheavals, such as the breakup of an important relationship.[33] College graduates who struggle to land a job related to their field of study may suffer a downturn in self-esteem.[34] Self-esteem can rise or fall within the course of a day; sometimes just a look from someone (or being ignored) can send you into a tailspin and make you feel devalued. A certain level of self-esteem can also last for a while—you may have a series of months or even years that you look back on and think, "I felt pretty lousy about myself in those days. Glad that period is over." Three factors provide clues about the nature of self-esteem: gender, social comparisons, and the self-fulfilling prophecy.

Gender

gender
A cultural construction that includes one's biological sex, psychological and emotional characteristics, attitudes about the sexes, and sexual orientation.

Your **gender** is a complex cultural construction that includes your biological sex; psychological and emotional characteristics that cause you to be masculine, feminine, or androgynous (a combination of feminine and masculine traits); your attitudes about appropriate roles and behavior for the sexes in society; and your sexual orientation (to whom you are sexually attracted).[35] We discuss sex and gender in more depth in Chapter 6, but for now, just realize that all of these elements of gender affect your self-esteem.

Research documents ways that boys' self-esteem develops differently from girls' during childhood and adolescence. Even though women have made great strides in recent decades, the United States is still considered a patriarchal (male-dominated) culture. In such a culture, women and girls suffer loss of self-esteem to a greater degree than men and boys. This trend continues into adulthood.[36] Several prominent women have written books addressing the problem of American women's general lack of self-esteem and confidence. Katty Kay and Claire Shipman's *The Confidence Code*, Sheryl Sandberg's *Lean In*, and Mika Brzezinski's *Knowing Your Value* all speak to women's general lack of belief in their own worth and how such a deficit impedes their progress, both professionally and personally.[37]

Social Comparisons

One way we become more aware of ourselves and derive our sense of self-worth is by measuring ourselves against others, a process called **social comparison**.[38] I'm good at basketball (because I'm part of a winning team); I can't cook (others cook better than I do); I'm good at meeting people (whereas many people are uncomfortable interacting with people they've just met); I'm not handy (but my dad can fix anything). Each of these statements implies a judgment about how you perform certain tasks in comparison to others.

Social media use may also contribute to self-esteem fluctuations since it offers people ample opportunities for social comparison. According to research on social media use, Facebook is still the most popular social networking site in the United States, with 69 percent of all adults reporting that they use the platform.[39] Given social media's consistent growth and expansion across the globe, researchers have continued to examine how people socially compare themselves to others online.

Some researchers find that social media usage enhances self-esteem, especially when users interact primarily with online close friends.[40] However, other studies suggest that comparing oneself to others online can be a self-esteem downer. We generally want to hear positive or good news from online close friends, but we can be deeply affected if we receive criticism or negative information from them, causing our self-esteem to suffer. We may also experience self-esteem loss when we read about what others have achieved, as revealed in their posts and profiles. We may also feel loneliness and envy (even depression) when we see others' posts, photos, or videos, suggesting that they are more beautiful or healthier than we are, they have more fun, or they have more impressive friends or a larger social network. In general, online social comparison can be a risky business for your self-esteem.[41]

▲ High-school student Galia Slayen built this life-size Barbie doll to show how unrealistic standards for physical attractiveness can damage the self-esteem of girls and women. According to Slayen, if Barbie were a real woman, she would stand six feet tall and have an 18-inch waist.
CB2/ZOB/WENN.com/Newscom

social comparison
Process of comparing oneself to others to measure one's worth.

SOCIAL MEDIA & COMMUNICATION

Fitspiration: Friend or Foe?

Let's get real: A lot of us tire of reading online posts about others' health, beauty, and fitness miracles. That may sound petty, but it's a safe bet you've at least once let out a big sigh upon reading yet another post or seeing another image of someone accomplishing a fitness or weight goal. Are you tired of seeing yet another photo of someone's incredibly healthy dinner? Posts like "I'm back in my old size 10s," "That last mile was hard but I was determined to finish," and "Down 35 pounds as of today!" can get downright annoying.

Equally irritating can be people's attempts at inspiring others, using motivational slogans like "Be your best self!" or "Live your best life!" (attributed to Oprah). These forms of online messages and images are so prevalent that there's now a term for them: fitspirations (a combination of the words *fitness* and *inspiration*). As reflected by the millions of posts with the hashtags #fitspiration and #fitspo, this form of communication on social media appears to have spurred a movement.[42] This "fitness community" is especially active on Instagram because of the site's focus on images.[43] Many people find this form of communication motivating and enjoy the support that comes from connecting with other like-minded, active people. But research has also examined some negative outcomes of such online activity, primarily a loss of self-esteem through constant comparison. Other concerns include exercise addiction and disordered eating.[44]

If fitspirations offer you encouragement and motivation, plus a sense of community, the impact on your self-esteem is likely positive. However, if you find yourself constantly comparing your accomplishments to others' and either feeling superior to them or like you don't measure up, perhaps you should inventory your consumption of such online material. Maybe it's time to seek other sources for that self-esteem upper we all desire?

> **RECAP**
>
> **Factors Affecting Self-Esteem**
>
> | | |
> |---|---|
> | Gender | In male-dominated cultures, girls and women suffer self-esteem loss to a much greater degree than boys and men. |
> | Social Comparisons | Judgments about how well or poorly you can perform certain tasks as compared to others can be self-defeating and can cause self-esteem to suffer. |
> | Self-Fulfilling Prophecies | What you believe about yourself often comes true because you expect it to come true. |

Self-Fulfilling Prophecy

A **self-fulfilling prophecy** is the idea that what you believe about yourself often comes true because you expect it to come true.[45] If you think you'll fail a math quiz because you've labeled yourself inept at math, then you must overcome not only your math deficiency but also your low expectations of yourself when it comes to math. If you hold the self-perception that you're pretty good at conversation, then you're likely to act on that assumption when you talk with someone. Your conversations, true to form, will go well, thus reinforcing your belief in yourself as a good conversationalist.

self-fulfilling prophecy
The notion that predictions about one's future are likely to come true because one believes that they will come true.

Communication and the Enhancement of Self-Esteem

2.4 Practice six communication strategies for enhancing one's self-esteem.

We know the damage low self-esteem can do: It can limit our ability to develop and maintain satisfying relationships, to experience career successes and advancement, and to create a generally happy and contented life. Experts suggest that many societal problems stem from our collective feelings of low self-esteem. Our feelings of low self-worth may contribute to our choosing the wrong partners; becoming addicted to drugs, alcohol, sex, food, online activities, or gambling; and opting, in too many cases, for death over life. So we owe it to society, as well as ourselves, to develop and work to maintain a healthy sense of self-esteem, as an integral part of the process of becoming more self-aware.

Now is the *prime time* to develop a healthy self-esteem! Although there is no simple list of tricks that can easily make someone with low self-esteem feel valued and appreciated, it is possible to improve how you think about yourself. One thing is clear from research about the process of building and maintaining self-esteem: Communication is essential.[46]

Engage in Positive Self-Talk

intrapersonal communication
How you take in information and make sense of it; also, thoughts and ideas you say to yourself.

self-talk
Inner speech; communication with the self.

Intrapersonal communication refers to how you take in information and make sense of it.[47] It also involves communication within yourself—**self-talk**, or what some scholars term "inner speech."[48] Your self-concept and level of self-esteem influence the way you talk to yourself about your abilities and skills. The reverse is also true, in that your inner dialogue has an effect on both your self-concept and your level of self-esteem. Athletes use positive self-talk to motivate themselves to play better, especially if they're struggling on the court or field of play. Some also talk to themselves negatively when they perform poorly. Research shows, however, that athletes who engage in negative inner dialogue usually do nothing to improve their performance.[49]

Visualize

visualization
The technique of imagining that you are performing a particular task in a certain way; a method of enhancing self-esteem.

Visualization—imagining oneself behaving in a certain way—takes the notion of self-talk one step further. Besides just telling yourself that you can achieve your goal, you actually try to "see" yourself conversing effectively with others, performing well on a project, or exhibiting some other desirable behavior.[50] Because the United States has such a visual culture, most of us have no trouble visualizing elaborate scenarios in our heads.

Research suggests that an apprehensive public speaker can manage her or his fears by visualizing positive results.[51] In fact, visualization reduces anxiety as well as

ETHICS & COMMUNICATION

Are Students Narcissistic?

Research suggests that students are relying on Facebook as an integral part of their social interactions and persona. A study shows that from a sample of 50 female students, 88 percent stated they were a "person of worth" and 96 percent that they had many good qualities.[52] In addition, 56 percent liked being the center of attention and 48 percent thought they were special compared to others. The study concluded that the sample had healthy self-esteem and only mild narcissistic characteristics.

In 2017, another survey looked at self-esteem and narcissistic personality self-reports of 200 Instagram users (male and female, aged 18 to 25 years) from Saudi Arabia and Kuwait. The researchers used five Instagram elements to assess how self-promoting each individual was—biography section, profile picture, first 20 pictures, frequency of uploads, and picture captions. The study suggested that the individuals are unlikely to use filters and self-promoting adjectives.[53]

Broader studies covering the Middle East suggest that collectivism is instrumental in defining individuals (tribe, family, lineage, and country). Sharing of information on social media is therefore linked to an individual's reputation, an integral element in collectivist societies.[54] As online behavior is in accordance with what is regarded as acceptable, many students seem to avoid posting revealing information. Interestingly, research into Twitter suggests that users are uncomfortable revealing personal information on social media. What is shared does not reveal true identities or personal experiences.[55]

Commercially, marketers have accepted that self-esteem is a strong driver for Saudi consumers on Instagram; they use this platform as a secure and private shopping tool.[56] Some may focus more on the image they would like to present on their social networks, but there are other experiential and personality variables that impact their behaviors.[57]

---

negative self-talk or the number of debilitating thoughts that can enter a speaker's consciousness.[58] If you're one of the many people who fear making presentations, try visualizing yourself walking to the front of the room, taking out your well-prepared notes, delivering a well-rehearsed and interesting presentation, and returning to your seat to the sound of applause. This visualization of positive results enhances confidence and speaking skill. The same technique can be used to boost your sense of self-worth about other tasks or skills.

reframing
The process of redefining events and experiences from a different point of view.

Reframe

The process of redefining events and experiences, of looking at something from a different point of view, is called **reframing**. When a movie director gets different "takes" or shots of the same scene, she or he is striving to get the best work possible. A director may alter small details, like camera angles or actor movements, to get yet another look or vision for a scene. Just like a movie director, you can reframe your "take" on events or circumstances that cause you to lose self-esteem.[59]

For example, your supervisor says you should improve an area of your performance, but instead of engaging in self-talk about how you're terrible at your job, you reframe the event within a larger context. You tell yourself that one negative comment doesn't mean you're a bad employee.

▼ Positive self-talk can motivate us to do our best in challenging situations. Are there situations in which you could make your own self-talk more encouraging?
Iakov Filimonov/123RF

Develop Honest Relationships

The suggestion that you develop honest relationships may sound like the latest advice from some self-help website, but it's actually harder to accomplish than it sounds. Think about it: How many people in your life really give you the straight scoop about yourself? Most of us can count the number of those people on one hand.

Having at least one relationship with someone who will give you honest feedback and help you objectively reflect on your virtues and vices can be extremely beneficial in fostering healthy, positive self-esteem. As we noted earlier, other people play a major role in shaping our self-concept and self-esteem. You don't want to find yourself at a point where you're oblivious to the feedback of others. That kind of attitude can make you narcissistic, unrealistic, and rigid—unable to adjust to life's changing circumstances. Most people who reject or overlook others' honest and objective feedback end up isolated and with low self-esteem.

Another benefit of having trusting, honest relationships is that you will feel more comfortable telling others about your feelings of low self-esteem. Conversations in which people can divulge their weaknesses can be very affirming. Yet some people have learned bravado, an ability to communicate a strong, confident air and work their way through challenges or situations in which their self-esteem may suffer.[60] But *everyone*, at some time or another, suffers a lack of self-esteem about *something*. Whether you reveal that fact and to whom you reveal it are important decisions.

Surround Yourself with Positive People

Related to the development of honest relationships is a suggestion about the people you choose to associate with the most in your life. If you want to improve your self-esteem and develop a more positive mood or outlook, it's better to surround yourself with people with good self-esteem rather than "Debbie Downers."[61]

Granted, sometimes you don't have a choice; you get assigned a roommate in college, your instructor pairs you with a lab or study partner, and you rarely get to choose the people you work with. So we're not suggesting that you disassociate yourself from people who have low self-esteem, because that's unrealistic. What we *are* saying is that people with low self-esteem need to be around uplifting people—those whose positive self-regard will rub off on them.

▼ One way to improve your self-esteem is to surround yourself with uplifting people.
Shutterstock

Lose Your Baggage

Not making the team. Getting passed over for a key promotion at work. Seeing a long-term relationship end. Feeling like a failure. We've all had experiences we would like to undo or get a second chance at, so we could do them differently or so we could *be* different. We all carry around experiential or psychological baggage, but the key question is, how much space does that baggage take up within your self-concept? To phrase this another way, how negatively is your self-esteem affected by your baggage?

People with low self-esteem tend to lock onto events and experiences that happened years ago and refuse to let go of, or move past, them. Looking back at what we can't change only reinforces a sense of helplessness. Constantly replaying negative experiences only serves to make our sense of self-worth more difficult to repair. Take a mental inventory of experiences in your past and then decide to let go of your baggage and move past those experiences that cause your present-day self-esteem to suffer.[62]

The Perception Process

2.5 Explain the three stages of perception and why people differ in their perceptions of people and events.

This chapter focuses on Principle One of our Communication Principles for a Lifetime: Be aware of your communication with yourself and others. Awareness involves developing greater understanding and skill by becoming more cognizant of yourself, others, and communication. Awareness includes exploring how we perceive ourselves and our communication with others, as well as the many ways in which we perceive other people and their communication. But just what is perception?

RECAP	
Strategies for Enhancing Self-Esteem	
Engage in Positive Self-Talk	If you want positive results, talk positively to yourself. If you are self-critical and negative, you may set yourself up for failure.
Visualize	In anticipation of a significant event, picture how you want the event to go, as a mental rehearsal. If you feel anxious or nervous, visualize success instead of failure.
Reframe	Try to look at experiences and events, especially those that can cause you to lose self-esteem, from a different point of view. Keep the larger picture in mind rather than focusing on one isolated negative incident.
Develop Honest Relationships	Cultivate friends whom you can confide in and who will give you honest feedback. Accept that feedback in the spirit of enhancing your self-esteem and making yourself a wiser, better person.
Surround Yourself with Positive People	Associating with people with high self-esteem can help you enhance your own self-esteem and develop a more positive outlook.
Lose Your Baggage	Dump your psychological and experiential baggage: Work to move beyond the negatives of your past so that you focus on the present and relieve your self-esteem of the burden of things you cannot change.

On the most basic level, **perception** is the arousal of any of our senses. A sound travels through the air, vibrates in the eardrum, activates the nerves, and sends a signal to the brain. A similar sequence of events takes place when we see, smell, feel, or taste something. So perception begins with the process of attending to stimuli in the environment. The process of perception also includes structuring and making sense of information provided by the senses. You come out of a building and see wet pavement and puddles of water, hear thunder, smell a fresh odor in the air, and feel a few drops of water on your head. You integrate all those bits of information and conclude that it's raining and has been for a while.

perception
The arousal of any of your senses.

Perceiving people, however, goes beyond the simple processing of sensory information. We try to decide what people are like by making judgments about their personalities and giving meaning to their actions by drawing inferences from what we observe.[63] When you meet someone new, you notice basic things like her or his physical appearance, the sound of the person's voice, whether or not he or she smiles, and so forth. You also attend to specific details that the person verbally and nonverbally communicates. Once you've chosen these stimuli to pay attention to, you then categorize the information into some sort of structure that works for you. Finally, you attempt to make sense of your structured perceptions; you assign meaning to what you have perceived. Let's more closely examine each of these three stages in the perception process.

Stage One: Attention and Selection

You're watching a group of parents at a playground with their children. The kids are playing, running around, laughing, and squealing, as children will do. You view the activity, hear the noise, feel the heat of the day on your skin, and smell hot dogs cooking on a grill. They smell so good you can almost taste them. A moment later,

▲ Because we cannot process every stimulus in our environment, we need to select which ones will get our attention. When you communicate in a noisy, distracting setting, how can you focus your attention to improve your powers of perception?
People Images/istock/Getty Images

attention
The act of perceiving stimuli in your environment.

selection
The act of choosing specific stimuli in your environment on which to focus.

organization
Converting information into convenient, understandable, and efficient patterns that allow us to make sense of what we have observed.

closure
The perceptual process of filling in missing information.

FIGURE 2.2 What Do You See?

a parent jumps up and runs over to comfort a crying child who has fallen. You were watching the action but didn't see the particular incident and didn't register the child's cry amidst all the noise. But the child's parent did. How did this happen?

The ability of parents to discern their own child's voice from a chorus of voices is a mystery of human nature, but it also exemplifies the first stage of perception. Our human senses simply cannot process all of the available stimuli at any given moment, so we select which sensations make it through to the level of awareness and ignore or filter out the rest. The activities of **attention** and **selection** constitute the first stage of the perception process.

Selectivity can also cause us to fail to perceive important information.[64] A professor may be so focused on teaching the material that she or he doesn't realize that students are lost and not following the lecture. By selecting certain stimuli, we sometimes miss other important clues that might help us better understand what is happening and determine how to respond.

Stage Two: Organization

After we select stimuli to attend to and process, we start to convert the information into convenient, understandable, and efficient patterns that allow us to make sense of what we've observed. This activity, termed **organization**, makes it easier for us to process complex information because it allows us to impose the familiar onto the unfamiliar and because we can easily store and recall simple patterns.

Look at the three items in Figure 2.2. What does each of them mean to you? If you're like most people, you'll perceive item A as a horseshoe, item B as the word *communication*, and item C as a circle. Strictly speaking, none of those perceptions is correct. For item A, you see a pattern of dots that you label a horseshoe because a horseshoe is a concept you know and to which you attach various meanings. Rather than processing a set of dots, it's much easier to organize the dots in a way that refers to something familiar. For some people, a more familiar pattern than a horseshoe might be an inverted U. For similar reasons, we organize patterns of stars in the sky into various constellations like the Big and Little Dippers.

In Figure 2.2, items B and C also reveal our inclination to superimpose structure and consistency on what we observe. This tendency leads us to create a familiar word from the meaningless assemblage of letters in item B and to label the figure in item C a circle, even though a circle is a continuous line without any gaps. The process of filling in missing information is called **closure**, and it applies to our perceptions of people as well. When we have an incomplete picture of another human being, we impose a pattern or structure, classify the person on the basis of the information we do have, and fill in the gaps.

Have you ever shown up early to class or to a public gathering, watched other people arriving, and tried to guess what they did for a living, what their personalities were like, or what their backgrounds were? As you looked at people's clothing and saw how they walked or behaved, you made inferences about them. You superimposed some structure by using a general

Item A	Item B	Item C

OMMUNICATION

label and filling in the gaps in your information. Such perceptions affect how you will communicate with those people.

Stage Three: Interpretation

Once we have organized stimuli, we are ready to assign meaning, a process termed **interpretation**. We attach meaning to what we observe to complete the perception process. In some cases, the meanings are fairly standardized, as they are for language. But others are much more personalized. If you meet someone whose cologne is too heavy and has a scent you don't like, what's your impression of that person? What if the person also has a great handshake and a warm smile? Does that change your interpretation of events and your impression of the person?

Our interpretations can be off-base; we may perceive a situation one way when in fact something entirely different is occurring.[65] Maybe you've been in a club or at a party and thought someone was flirting with you, only to discover the person was focused on someone behind or near you. Embarrassing? Yes, but inaccurate interpretations of our perceptions are commonplace.

RECAP		
The Perception Process		
Term	Explanation	Example
Perception	The arousal of any of our senses	Hearing the sound of laughter
Attention and Selection	The first stage in the perception process, in which we perceive stimuli and choose which ones to focus our awareness on	Watching TV while hearing giggling and laughter coming from another room and ignoring the TV show to eavesdrop on the giggler
Organization	The second stage in the perception process, in which we structure stimuli into convenient and efficient patterns	Realizing that the laughter is coming from your younger sister, who is on the phone
Interpretation	The final stage in the perception process, in which we assign meaning to what we have perceived	Deciding that your sister is talking on the phone to her boyfriend because she only laughs like that when she talks to him

interpretation
Attaching meaning to what is attended to, selected, and organized.

When Perceptions Vary

George and Martha have been married for, well, forever. They know each other very well, and each knows how the other thinks. So you would think their perceptions of things, events, and people would line up, right? Wrong. George and Martha are driving home from a party, chatting about the evening. George believes that everyone had a good time; that the house was filled with interesting, pleasant, relatively good-looking people; and that he received positive responses from everyone he talked to. Martha saw the party differently. She tells George that the reason people looked good was that most of them had cosmetic surgery, were Botoxed beyond all recognition, or were younger "replacement" partners for all the divorced people there. Many people at the party disliked each other so intensely that they stayed on opposite sides of the room all night. Martha's interpretation of events is based not on prior or external knowledge, but on her perceptions from observing and interacting with people at the party. And what about George's perception that everyone at the party liked him? Martha says, "Think again." She tells George that as soon as he walked away after having a conversation with one group of men, they nonverbally signaled to one another indicating that they thought George was a doofus. What's going on here? Who's right, George or Martha?

Neither is right and both are right. This example illustrates two differing perceptions of the same reality. There is no "truth" to be found, only different "takes" on the same people and set of events. Both sets of perceptions are valid even though they differ, because varying perceptions are the norm in life. You know this to be true in your own life experience—even people you are very similar to and know quite well can differ from you dramatically in their perceptions of people and events. Your life experiences, how you were raised, and how you developed contribute a great deal to how you perceive things, events, and people in your life. These elements create a filter through which you observe and process the world around you.

Communicate to Enhance Your Powers of Perception

2.6 Summarize three communication strategies that can improve one's powers of perception.

Has anyone told you that she or he formed a perception about you the first time you met, but changed that perception over time? On occasion, people who are shy, serious, or simply have a quieter communication style than others are perceived as being conceited, aloof, or cocky. Outgoing, extroverted people may be viewed as overbearing when they really just enjoy the company of others.

Sometimes our powers of perception are sharp, but other times we miss the mark.[66] Because our communication is affected by our perceptions of others, it is important to work toward forming the most accurate perceptions you can, because then you have better, more reliable information on which to act. How can you improve your ability to form accurate perceptions? Here are three suggestions: Increase your awareness, avoid stereotypes, and check your perceptions directly or indirectly.

Increase Your Awareness

We've made this topic—awareness—our first of five Communication Principles for a Lifetime for a reason. Exercise your senses, especially your sense of hearing. Work at really listening to people—*fully* listening, without interrupting them to put in your two cents' worth. Try to be more verbally and nonverbally aware; monitor how you communicate with others and how people respond to you. If you don't like the responses you're getting from people, it may be time for a change in *your* behavior, not theirs. You will also want to monitor the verbal and nonverbal cues others exhibit. Pay attention to contextual cues, such as where an interaction is taking place, the time of day, the perceived moods of those interacting, and any physical or psychological barriers that impede the communication exchange. Learn from your mistakes, rather than repeating them.

Avoid Stereotypes

"She's a snob." "He's a nerd." "They're a bunch of dumb jocks." These statements reflect **stereotypes**, or generalizations we apply to individuals because we perceive them to have attributes common to a particular group.[67]

What comes to mind when you hear the term *homeless*? Do you associate the word with someone begging on the street, people living in shelters or their cars, or "bums" or "bag ladies" in parks, alleys, or subway stations? If these images came to mind, you've just invoked a stereotype. What may not have come to mind are the many families who are homeless because of an economic downturn, home foreclosure, or other societal factors. Research shows that many of us hold unfortunate stereotypes about homeless people and homelessness in general.[68]

Some positive or functional aspects of stereotypes emerge from our human nature to simplify and categorize stimuli in our environment. Stereotypes serve as a baseline of information. If you know nothing else about a person other than she or he is a surfer, for instance, then you can think about commonly held characteristics of other people you have met who surf and go from there. But as social psychologist Douglas Kenrick and his colleagues point out, "Stereotyping is a cognitively inexpensive way of understanding others: By presuming that people are like other members of their groups, we avoid the effortful process of learning about them as individuals."[69]

Have you ever taken a class and, from day one, felt that the teacher pegged you a certain way? The instructor may have perceived you to be a slacker (on the negative side) or a future PhD candidate (on the positive side). The bottom line is that no one likes to be treated as a stereotype because it's limiting, impersonal, and linguistically

stereotype
A generalization applied to persons perceived to have attributes common to a particular group.

lazy. You can also feel pressure to try to live up to a stereotype, such as "all Asian students are exceptionally bright." Stereotypes are often degrading, as in age-old references to dumb blondes and dirty old men. Many of the worst stereotypes are related to gender, race, ethnicity, age, and physical appearance.[70]

Often we try to inhibit or suppress stereotypical thoughts before they have a chance to affect our behavior.[71] For example, if you grew up hearing family members invoke stereotypes about different ethnic groups, you may decide as an adult that you will not follow suit—that assigning ethnic stereotypes is inappropriate and often harmful. However, because it is part of your upbringing and ingrained in you, your first thoughts may be stereotypical when you encounter someone from an ethnic group other than your own. You have to assert mental control to suppress the stereotypical thoughts and adjust your communication.

Remember that there's nothing inherently wrong with a stereotype as a baseline of information. But the rigid way we enforce a stereotype, the expectations we form on the basis of the stereotype, and our ensuing communication with the stereotyped person are problematic.

Check Your Perceptions

By checking the accuracy of your perceptions and attributions, you can improve your ability to perceive things and people and respond to them effectively. **Indirect perception checking** involves an intensification of your own perceptual powers. You seek additional information to confirm, refute, or expand your interpretations of someone's behavior. If you suspect that your romantic partner wants to end your relationship, you are likely to look for cues in his or her tone of voice, eye contact, and body movements to confirm your suspicion. You will probably also listen more intently and pay closer attention to the language your partner chooses to use. The information you gain is "checked" against your original perceptions.

Direct perception checking involves asking straight out whether your interpretations of a perception are correct. You can accomplish this in two ways: asking people directly for their interpretations of their own actions or asking other observers for their take on a situation (going to a third or outside party). Asking people directly is often more difficult than asking a third party for an interpretation. For one thing, we don't

indirect perception checking
Using your own perceptual abilities to seek additional information to confirm or refute your interpretations of someone's behavior.

direct perception checking
Asking someone else whether your interpretations of what you perceive are correct.

CRITICAL/CULTURAL PERSPECTIVES & COMMUNICATION

Stereotypes Are Lazy

Probably every person reading this text has felt the sting of a stereotype being applied to them in some way or another. Perhaps you were tagged as a nerd or geek growing up, simply because you enjoyed school, worked hard, and made good grades. Maybe you were a good athlete and somebody called you a "dumb jock," as though athleticism and intelligence could not co-reside in one person. Maybe the stereotype went deeper, into identity factors such as your sex or gender, sexual orientation, race, ethnicity, religion, or ability level. Maybe you moved from one part of the country to another and the stereotype emerged in your new locale.

What motivates someone to talk in stereotypes or to inflict stereotypical language onto other people? Is it laziness? Could it be power? Sometimes people feel insecure or in competition with others; sometimes people are simply ignorant about various forms of diversity. People also use labels to downgrade or diminish others in order to minimize a perceived disparity between them. It can be a tactic to make oneself seem more powerful and to project an air of superiority when you're in the outgroup, not the ingroup.[72]

We encourage you to inventory your attitudes about others and the language you use. Purge your language of stereotypes. No one wants to be treated like a category rather than a unique individual.

like to admit uncertainty or suspicions to others; we might not trust that they will respond honestly. And if our interpretations are wrong, we might suffer embarrassment or anger. But asking someone to confirm a perception shows that you are committed to gaining a better understanding.

Perception checking with colleagues, as well as with family members and trusted friends, is an invaluable tool, particularly when emotions are involved. It can be very helpful to discuss situations with other people and get their input as to what happened, why it happened, how they would feel about it if it happened to them, and what you might do about it. This is especially advisable in work settings, when the wisdom of someone else's perceptions can save you professional embarrassment or prevent you from losing your job. The "Can I run something by you?" strategy gives you a broader perspective and a basis of comparison.[73]

STUDY GUIDE: PRINCIPLES FOR A LIFETIME — CHAPTER 2

Self-Awareness: How Well Do You Know Yourself?

2.1 Discuss the importance of self-awareness in the process of improving one's communication skills.

PRINCIPLE POINTS: Self-awareness is the ability to develop and communicate a representation of yourself to others.

PRINCIPLE TERMS:

self-awareness   symbolic self-awareness

PRINCIPLE SKILLS:

1. Describe an example of how you or someone you know progressed through Maslow's levels of competence. What skill did you or the other person develop? What behaviors did you or the other person demonstrate at each level?
2. How well do you know yourself? If you have an Instagram, Twitter, or other social media account, look at it with a critical eye. Does it reflect who you think you are?

Self-Concept: Who Are You?

2.2 Describe the components of the self-concept and major influences on self-concept development.

PRINCIPLE POINTS: Your self-concept is your interior identity or subjective description of who you think you are. Your self-image is your view of yourself in a particular situation. The self-concept contains three components: attitudes, beliefs, and values. Philosopher William James believed that three "selves" exist in each of us: the material self, the social self, and the spiritual self. Our self-concept develops through our communication with others, our association with various groups, the roles we assume in our lives, and the labels we use to describe ourselves. Our avowed identity is assigned by ourselves, whereas our ascribed identity involves characteristics other people assign or attribute to us.

PRINCIPLE TERMS:

self   social self
self-concept   spiritual self
attitudes   avowed identity
beliefs   ascribed identity
values   self-reflexiveness
material self

PRINCIPLE SKILLS:

1. How has communication with family, friends, teachers, or others influenced your self-concept, either in the past or present?
2. Write down five words or phrases that best describe you, at this point in time. Analyze your list. How many of the five entries are nouns? How many are adjectives? How many entries imply or reflect your relationships with others? Why did you put the first entry first? If you had to remove one entry, which one would it be and why?

Self-Esteem: What's Your Value?

2.3 Describe how gender, social comparisons, and self-fulfilling prophecies affect one's self-esteem.

PRINCIPLE POINTS: Your assessment of your worth as a person in terms of skills, abilities, talents, and appearance constitutes your level of self-esteem. Self-esteem is affected by many factors, but primary among them are your gender, your comparisons of yourself to others, and your self-fulfilling prophecies.

PRINCIPLE TERMS:

self-esteem
self-concept clarity
gender
social comparison
self-fulfilling prophecy

PRINCIPLE SKILLS:

1. In addition to self-comparisons sparked by social media, what situations or stimuli tend to make people engage in more self-comparisons?

2. **Rosenberg Self-Esteem Scale**

One of the most widely used scales to measure a person's self-esteem is the Rosenberg Self-Esteem Scale, developed in the 1960s by Dr. Morris Rosenberg, a sociologist. Respond to items on the scale using the following system: SA = Strongly Agree, A = Agree, D = Disagree, and SD = Strongly Disagree. Scoring information follows the scale.

1. I feel that I'm a person of worth, at least on an equal plane with others. SA A D SD
2. I feel that I have a number of good qualities. SA A D SD
3. All in all, I am inclined to feel that I am a failure. SA A D SD
4. I am able to do things as well as most other people. SA A D SD
5. I feel I do not have much to be proud of. SA A D SD
6. I take a positive attitude toward myself. SA A D SD
7. On the whole, I am satisfied with myself. SA A D SD
8. I wish I could have more respect for myself. SA A D SD
9. I certainly feel useless at times. SA A D SD
10. At times, I think I am no good at all. SA A D SD

Scoring Instructions

To score the scale, assign a value to each of the ten items as follows and total the values:

For items 1, 2, 4, 6, and 7: Strongly Agree = 3, Agree = 2, Disagree = 1, Strongly Disagree = 0.

For items 3, 5, 8, 9, and 10: Strongly Agree = 0, Agree = 1, Disagree = 2, Strongly Disagree = 3.

Scores on the scale range from 0 to 30, with 30 indicating the highest score possible, or the highest level of self-esteem the scale can measure. If you score on the low end of the scale, we suggest that you reread and perhaps try the suggestions in the section of this chapter on self-esteem enhancement.

Source: M. Rosenberg, *Society and the Adolescent Self-Image* rev. ed. (Middletown, CT: Wesleyan University Press, 1989). Reprinted with permission; retrieved from www.bsos.umd.edu.

3. **Inventory Your Self-Esteem**

One way to begin to improve your self-esteem is to take an honest measure of how you feel about yourself *right at this very point in time*. Take some time to think about yourself—who you used to be, who you were only a short time ago, and who you have developed into at this moment in time. Ponder the relationships that had the greatest effect on your development and maturation, and think about the events that caused you to change in some profound way. Then use the columns below to inventory where you stand and to reveal where you may need to put some energy into making change happen for yourself.

Things I Like About Myself	Things I Don't Like About Myself	How to Make Some Changes

Communication and the Enhancement of Self-Esteem

2.4 Practice six communication strategies for enhancing one's self-esteem.

PRINCIPLE POINTS: Because enhanced self-esteem is a goal for most of us, we recommend the following six means of improving the way you feel about yourself: (1) Engage in positive self-talk; (2) visualize the behavior you want to enact or the attributes you wish to acquire; (3) reframe, meaning redefine events and experiences from a different point of view; (4) develop honest relationships, ones in which people tell you the truth about yourself so you can reflect on and grow from their feedback; (5) surround yourself with positive people, not "Debbie Downers;" and (6) lose your baggage, meaning let go of the past and those experiences that can cause your self-esteem to suffer.

PRINCIPLE **TERMS:**

intrapersonal communication
self-talk
visualization
narcissism
reframing

PRINCIPLE **SKILLS:**

1. Describe a situation or event in your life for which it would be—or already has been—helpful to use positive self-talk or visualization to enhance your self-esteem.
2. Read or reread the Ethics & Communication feature box in this chapter. Do your own experiences correspond to the research conclusions? Have you noticed high or increasing narcissism in yourself or people you know? What do you see as the consequences of the narcissism for the individuals, for people they know, and for society?

The Perception Process

2.5 Explain the three stages of perception and why people differ in their perceptions of people and events.

PRINCIPLE **POINTS:** Perception, the process of receiving information from your senses, involves three stages:

1. Attention and selection, when you notice and choose stimuli in your environment on which to focus
2. Organization, when you convert stimuli into understandable information
3. Interpretation, when you attach meaning to what you have attended to, selected, and organized

People often differ in their perceptions of things, events, and other people. Your life experiences, how you were raised, and how you developed contribute a great deal to how you perceive the world around you.

PRINCIPLE **TERMS:**

perception
attention
selection
organization
closure
interpretation

PRINCIPLE **SKILLS:**

1. In addition to the example given in this chapter of mistakenly thinking a person was flirting with you, what experiences have you had with misperceiving other people's communication?
2. Rate yourself in terms of your powers of perception. Are you a 10, meaning you think of yourself as highly perceptive about people, communication, and events? Or are you closer to a 1 or 2, meaning that your perception often does not match the reality of a situation?

Communicate to Enhance Your Powers of Perception

2.6 Summarize three communication strategies that can improve one's powers of perception.

PRINCIPLE **POINTS:** If you want to enhance your perceptual accuracy, we recommend you first increase your awareness by fully listening, observing, and paying attention to your surroundings and other people. Secondly, avoid stereotypes or generalizations about people. And finally, check your perceptions—indirectly and directly—to confirm or refute your interpretations of events or someone's behavior.

PRINCIPLE **TERMS:**

stereotype
indirect perception checking
direct perception checking

PRINCIPLE **SKILLS:**

1. What are some stereotypes held by people you know? Have you had a stereotype negatively inflicted on you? How did it affect your relationship with the person who used the stereotype? How did it affect your communication?
2. Generate statements that reveal common stereotypes about people in the following groups. Try to think of stereotypes that reflect positive as well as negative perceptions. We've provided a couple of examples to get you started. Then focus on the damage that stereotypes can do to someone's self-esteem. How might your communication with someone from each group be affected by these stereotypes?

Group	Positive Stereotype	Negative Stereotype
elderly	Old people are wise.	Old people can't fend for themselves.
women	Women are naturally loving and nurturing.	Women are terrible drivers.
men		
straight-A students		
blondes		
fundamentalist Christians		
bodybuilders		
southerners		
overweight people		
athletes		
police officers		
video gamers		

CHAPTER 3

UNDERSTANDING VERBAL MESSAGES

Words form the thread on which we string our experiences. —Aldous Huxley

Ampyang/Shutterstock

CHAPTER OUTLINE

- Why Focus on Language?
- The Nature of Language
- The Power of Words
- Confronting Bias in Language
- Using Words to Establish Supportive Relationships
- Study Guide: *Principles for a Lifetime*

LEARNING OBJECTIVES

3.1 List two reasons why it is important to study verbal communication.

3.2 Summarize how words are used as symbols that have denotative, connotative, concrete, and abstract meanings and are bound by culture and context.

3.3 Identify five primary ways in which words have power.

3.4 Describe the major ways in which language reveals bias about race, ethnicity, nationality, religion, gender, sexual orientation, age, class, and ability.

3.5 Explain how language helps create supportive or defensive communication climates.

---

ttyl
j/k
wfh
by4now

Many students are familiar with and comfortable using abbreviated messages, known as *textisms*, in their texts and emails. You probably deciphered the above textisms as shorthand for "talk to you later," "just kidding," "work from home," and "bye for now." But don't assume everyone decodes textisms with equal skill. For example, some people may think that texting "BTW" (uppercase) means "between," when it really means "by the way." Textisms and acronyms (using the first letters of words to form a new word) make texting, messaging, and emailing faster. These adaptations of the English language are becoming more popular in everyday communication, especially communication mediated by technology.[1] A persistent use of slang may be fine when texting, posting, or talking with friends, but when it becomes such a habit that it slips into other written or oral communication—especially at inappropriate moments (like calling a potential boss at a job interview "dude")—you've got a problem. The key is to be able to develop **code-switching** abilities, as bilingual speakers often exhibit when they shift from one language to another. Code switching helps you adapt to listeners. Be sure to use standard or formal language for college papers, professional resumes, and job interviews. Relegate the shortcuts and "slanguage" to informal texting, posting, and conversing with friends who can accurately translate.[2]

code switching
Changing seamlessly from one form of language use to another form.

Figure 3.1 depicts our five core Communication Principles for a Lifetime. In Chapter 2 we explored Principle One, which involves becoming more aware of yourself and your perceptions of things and people. An important step in this process of coming to know and understand yourself better is an honest, insightful examination of how you talk.

Consider this: *What you say is who you are*. That may sound like a strong statement, but the words you use reveal who you are. Granted, you communicate with more than your words. Your background, culture, values, experiences, and the way you express yourself nonverbally reveal who you are as well. But every time we use language, we reveal our thoughts, our very selves to others—no matter how inane, superficial, or emotion-laden the conversation. In addition to their tremendous potential to reveal the self, our words also carry the power to make and break relationships and careers and to shape cultures. Because of the immense power of words, we've chosen to make verbal communication the second of our five key Communication Principles for a Lifetime.

FIGURE 3.1 Communication Principles for a Lifetime

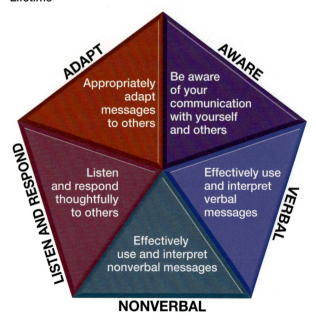

Why Focus on Language?

3.1 **List two reasons why it is important to study verbal communication.**

Take an inventory of your use of language as you read this chapter. Do you use language with other people that accurately and effectively represents who you are? Do some areas need improvement? How do you come across when meeting someone new? When talking with your best friends? What kind of communicator do your closest friends and family members *think* you are?

On occasion, we do stop to consider the effects of our language on others—usually when we are attempting to persuade or when we have said something that has injured or angered someone else. We have all been in situations that made us wish we could get a conversational second chance. The first reason we study verbal communication relates to one of our main messages in this chapter: *Words are powerful.* They affect your emotions, thoughts, actions, and relationships. They also affect how you are perceived by others. As we stated in Chapter 1, communication is irreversible. Once your words are "out there," they cannot be reversed or unspoken, much as we might like to try to take them back.

A recent Job Outlook Survey conducted by the National Association of Colleges and Employers (NACE) produced a list of key attributes employers want to see on college graduates' resumes. Written communication skills were fifth on the list of twenty; verbal communication skills were seventh. The top two attributes were problem-solving skills and team building—both of which involve verbal and nonverbal communication ability.[3] Another research team analyzed job advertisements also in an effort to determine the most critical twenty-first century workplace skills.[4] First in their findings was collaboration, second was problem-solving, and third was communication. Based on both sets of research results, it is clear that by gaining a better understanding of the nature and power of language, attending to your use of language, and working to use words with forethought and skill, you can expand your chances of landing a great job, as well as exerting influence and enhancing your relationships.

The second reason we study verbal communication relates to this reality: *We choose language.* We do not use language as an involuntary reflex to a stimulus, in the way our knee might jerk when rapped with a doctor's mallet. We choose the language we use—even if we make that choice in the split second it takes our brain to select a symbol (word) to communicate our thoughts or impulses. At times we go into "default mode," choosing language we have used before. We are prone to patterns in our language because, as humans, we prefer regularity. We also choose particular words because we like them, they have worked well for us in the past, or we grew up with those words and have used them for many years. But pattern and history can breed too much comfort, preventing us from asking ourselves, "Is this the best way to say this? Should I say this another way?" We have an incredible wealth of words from which to choose and the power to make choices that allow us to communicate who we are to others in the most effective way possible.

The Nature of Language

3.2 Summarize how words are used as symbols that have denotative, connotative, concrete, and abstract meanings and are bound by culture and context.

language
A system of symbols (words or vocabulary) structured by rules (grammar) and patterns (syntax) common to a community of people.

A **language** is a system of symbols (words or vocabulary) structured by grammar (rules and standards) and syntax (patterns in the arrangement of words) common to a community of people. Two language researchers, Edward Sapir and Benjamin Lee Whorf, developed what has come to be known as the Sapir–Whorf Hypothesis.[5] This hypothesis suggests that human language and thought are so interrelated that thought is actually rooted in and controlled by language. One implication of this supposition is that you cannot conceive of something for which you have no word. As a quick illustration of what we mean by this, think about colors. A woman describes her new dress to her friend using the term *puce*, but if the friend does not have the term *puce* (a brilliant purplish-red) in her frame of reference, she will be unable to conceive of the color her friend mentions.

The Sapir–Whorf Hypothesis provides further evidence of the *power* of language. When you choose words, you reveal how you think and what you think about. In essence, the quality of your language reflects the quality of your thought. The more extensive your vocabulary, the more options you have to communicate your ideas to others and to understand theirs. The connection between language and thought strengthens the argument in favor of learning more than one language; some ideas, emotions, or impulses may be better captured by words in a different language than your native one. Learning other languages, in turn, expands your thinking.

People Use Words as Symbols

symbol
A word, sound, gesture, or visual image that represents a thought, concept, object, or experience.

As we noted in Chapter 1, words are **symbols** that represent something else. Just as a flag is a symbol of a country, words are symbols that trigger thoughts, concepts, or feelings. For instance, what comes to mind when you see or hear the word *peace*? Perhaps you think historically, remembering what you studied about hippies in the 1960s and "peace and love" protests on college campuses. Or maybe you envision something a bit closer to home, like your need for peace and quiet when you're tired of your roommates making noise.

People Attach Meanings to Words

meaning
A person's interpretation of a symbol.

Now imagine using the word *peace* in a conversation, in an effort to convey to the other person the concept or image in your mind. You know what you are thinking when you say the word; the challenge is for the other person to understand your thoughts behind your word choice. In communication terms, this is the process of creating **meaning**. The meaning of a word is a person's interpretation of that symbol—it is how the person makes sense of the symbol. Meanings do not reside in the words themselves but in the ways in which communicators use the words. You attach a meaning to the word *peace*, the symbol you choose in conversation; your listener creates meaning for the word when he or she attempts to interpret what you have said. Words are not the culprits in communication problems; the meanings people create for words lead to successful or problematic communication.

bypassing
A communication problem that arises when the same words mean different things to different people.

Sometimes speakers' and receivers' meanings do not correspond because the same words mean different things to different people; the term for this communication problem is **bypassing**. Using the *peace* example, think about a couple in a long-term romantic relationship. If one partner says to the other, "I need more peace in this relationship," what might that mean? It might mean that the partner wants things to cool down a bit, because the relationship is struggling through a period of conflict. But it might also mean that the partner is feeling a lack of *peace* about even being in a relationship. If the partner is using *peace* in this latter sense, the relationship may soon be over. Some issues in relationships can be boiled down to a simple difference in the meaning of the words that get exchanged.

People Create Denotative and Connotative Meanings for Words

Symbol sharing through language is not just a simple process of uttering a word and having its meaning clearly understood by another. People create meanings for language on two levels: the denotative and the connotative.[6]

The **denotative meaning** of a word conveys content. Denotation is the restrictive, or literal, meaning of a word. For example, one dictionary defines *apartment* as "a room or suite of rooms used as a residence."[7] This definition is a literal, or denotative, definition of the word *apartment*; it describes what the word means in American culture.

By contrast, the **connotative meaning** of a word conveys feelings; people create personal and subjective meanings for words.[8] To you, the word *apartment* might mean a comfortable place where you can relax at the end of the day or a setting where you can entertain friends. To others, though, the word *apartment* might engender feelings of guilt (if the apartment hasn't been cleaned in a while) or feelings of dread (if rent is draining the wallet or relationships with roommates leave something to be desired). Clearly, the connotative level of language is more individual. While the denotative or objective meaning of the word *apartment* can be found in any dictionary, your subjective response to the word is probably not contained there.

People Convey Concrete and Abstract Meanings through Words

Meanings for words can be placed along a continuum from concrete to abstract.[9] A word's meaning is **concrete** if we can experience what the word refers to (the referent) with one of our senses; if we can see it, touch it, smell it, taste it, or hear it, it is concrete. If we cannot do these things, the word's meaning is **abstract**. In general, the more concrete the language, the easier it is for others to understand and retain. For example, the word *patriotism* is abstract because we cannot hear or taste patriotism. But a word that suggests a demonstration of patriotism, such as *voting*, is more concrete, because we can physically perform the act of voting. Minimize the use of abstract words when you're trying to clarify a message. Concrete terms help make a message clearer and more memorable.[10]

Meanings Are Culture Bound

Culture is a learned system of knowledge, behavior, attitudes,

denotative meaning
The restrictive, or literal, meaning of a word.

connotative meaning
The personal and subjective meaning of a word.

concrete meaning
Meaning that refers to something that can be perceived with one of the senses.

abstract meaning
Meaning that refers to something that cannot be perceived or experienced with one of the senses.

culture
A learned system of knowledge, behavior, attitudes, beliefs, values, rules, and norms that is shared by a group of people and shaped from one generation to the next.

▼ Because different people can attach different meanings to the same word, it is easy to get confused. What can you do to help clarify your own meaning so that others understand you?
Christopher Robbins/Photodisc/Getty Images

co-culture
A culture that exists within a larger cultural context.

beliefs, values, rules, and norms that is shared by a group of people and shaped from one generation to the next.[11] The meaning of a word, just like the meaning of any symbol, can change from culture to culture and across **co-cultures** (cultural groups that exist within a larger culture). To a European, for example, a *Yankee* is someone from the United States; to a player on the Boston Red Sox baseball team, a *Yankee* is an opponent; and to an American from the South, a *Yankee* is someone from the North. Some years ago, General Motors sold a car called a *Nova*. In English, *nova* means "bright star," and in Latin, *nova* means "new"—both appropriate connotations for a car. In Spanish, however, the spoken word *nova* sounds like the words *no va*, which translate to "It does not go." As you can imagine, this name was not a great choice for the Spanish-speaking market.

Sometimes members of a cultural group will have a need for a completely new word or combination of words because some phenomenon emerges without language to capture or communicate it. New terms introduced into a language are called **neologisms**. One example is *Ms.*, a term popularized by Sheila Michaels in the 1960s, who sought "a title for a woman who did not 'belong' to a man."[12] Michaels' work inspired the name of *Ms.* magazine. Before this neologism, women were "marked" by whether or not they were married to a man; their only choices of titles were Miss or Mrs. A more recent example of a newly popularized title is "Mx.," defined by Merriam-Webster as "a gender-neutral honorific for those who do not wish to be identified by gender."[13] It is pronounced like "mix" and was introduced to the English language in the 1970s, but only very recently began to be used in print as a non-binary neologism. Other attempts at adding new words to the English language have not been as successful, such as efforts in the 1970s to persuade English speakers to use "tay" or "gen" as non-sex-specific pronouns, as in "If a student wants to be successful, *tay* should not get behind in assigned reading."[14]

neologism
A new term introduced into a language.

Meanings Are Context Bound

Politicians often claim that the media "takes them out of context," causing the intended meanings of their words to be lost or distorted. Many times, the politicians are right. In an effort to deliver a speedy, pithy sound bite to an audience, reporters may edit politicians' comments, deleting context and sometimes changing the intended message.

Context plays a central role in how accurately our communication is interpreted by receivers. The context includes all of our words, plus ever-present nonverbal elements, like the setting in which the communication occurs as well as people's facial expressions, tone of voice, and other nonverbal cues that accompany a verbal message and help us decode it. Removing words from their context distorts their meaning.

> **RECAP**
>
> **The Nature of Language**
>
> - People use words as *symbols:* Symbols represent something else.
> - People create *meanings* for words: Meaning is a person's interpretation of a symbol.
> - Words have both *denotative* and *connotative* meanings: The denotative meaning is a restrictive, or literal, meaning; the connotation is a personal and subjective meaning.
> - People convey *concrete* and *abstract* meanings through words: A word's meaning is concrete if we can experience what the word refers to with one of our senses; if not, the meaning is abstract.
> - Meanings are *culture bound:* The meaning of a word can change from culture to culture.
> - Meanings are *context bound:* The situation or context for communication aids people as they attach meanings to symbols.

The Power of Words

3.3 Identify five primary ways in which words have power.

No doubt you've heard the old schoolyard chant, "Sticks and stones may break my bones, but words can never hurt me." We don't know who first came up with that statement, but we imagine it was someone who never experienced the sting of name calling, the harmful effects of being labeled "math challenged," or the legacy of an unfortunate family nickname. Words *do* hurt. With constant news stories about the tragic consequences of bullying, teasing, and harassment, it is important to consider the damage language can do.[15]

SOCIAL MEDIA & COMMUNICATION

E-Thai

Ten years ago, the impact of "Netspeak" (words, abbreviations and phrases used on the Internet) on languages was beginning to be noticed and researched.[16] In 2020, a major study of the impact of social media on Thai education was undertaken, with an emphasis on whether Facebook, Twitter, blogs, YouTube, Instagram, and other social media enhanced learning. This related to the problem of managing and controlling what was being read and whether it was a reliable source. There were also concerns about the impact of a globalized social media on the Thai language.[17]

The key concerns regarding the deterioration of the Thai language are broad, and perhaps irreversible and inevitable. Thai students can be confused by words that are pronounced and spelt in different ways, by some characters in a particular order having a specific meaning, and some popular English words having different meanings.

The spread of Netspeak is seen as rather unavoidable given that there are four major dialects in Thailand, with Central or Bangkok Thai being used in the media and taught in schools. However, English is taught across Thailand which gives Thais a positive advantage when facing the impact of Netspeak on their language.

Jakkrit "Tom" Yompayorm, a Thai language teacher, noted that Thai language used in social media is a useful hybrid to help younger Thais communicate. Back in 2015, he had around 90,000 followers and became known as the teacher that makes grammatical corrections. Perhaps his fun approach to correcting mistakes is the best way forward to protect languages from the pervasive influences of the Internet.[18]

Words have the power to evoke a wide range of emotions in listeners. But words can also heal, inspire, and transform the human spirit, which is another reason why one of our five Communication Principles for a Lifetime is about the effective use and interpretation of verbal messages. Let's explore five powers of words.

- *The Power to Create and Label Experience.* Alzheimer's, Parkinson's, Tourette syndrome—each of these afflictions is named after the person who discovered the condition. The name of a phenomenon has the power to label the experience and make it more real.[19] One humorous addition to the English language is the term *mansplaining*, which the Merriam-Webster dictionary defines as the activity of "explaining something to a woman in a condescending way that assumes she has no knowledge about the topic."[20]

- *The Power to Communicate Feelings.* Words help communicate your moods and emotional states, giving labels to feelings that otherwise would be hard to convey.[21] Staff writers at *New York* magazine generated new words and definitions for 78 emotions that many people experience but do not have the language to specifically identify. Some of our favorites are "jealoushy," defined as "the feeling of being jealous of someone while also having a crush on them"; "ventastic," a "fabulous and exhausting feeling right after a particularly animated and energetic venting session"; and "creatifiphoria," the "heady certainty that what you're making is brilliant."[22] The emotional power of words is not limited to expressing your feelings; your words and corresponding outlook may also have the power to affect your emotional, mental, and physical health.

- *The Power to Affect Thoughts and Actions.* A few decades ago, a weight-loss product called Ayds came on the market. Ayds were small, brown, chewy squares that manufacturers claimed would help reduce appetite.

▼ This woman's strong reaction to a text shows the power of words to convey our emotions and to affect other people's thoughts and feelings. What steps help you to consider others' feelings when choosing your words?
Olena Zaskochenko/123RF

> **RECAP**
>
> **The Power of Words to . . .**
>
> - *Create and Label Experience.* New experiences may lead to new words.
> - *Communicate Feelings.* Words help create and communicate our moods and emotional states.
> - *Affect Thoughts and Actions.* Words influence how we think and behave.
> - *Shape and Reflect Culture.* Cultures change; language both creates and reflects the changing nature of culture.
> - *Make and Break Relationships.* Verbal communication creates opportunities for us to know others and be known by them. It also helps establish and deepen relationships; sometimes it causes them to end.

Sales significantly declined for this appetite suppressant during the AIDS epidemic of the 1980s. The product was eventually discontinued. Advertisers have long known that the way a product is labeled greatly affects the likelihood consumers will buy it, because words affect the way we think about and react to things.

- *The Power to Shape and Reflect Culture.* International students often puzzle over English slang and ask such questions as "What does it mean to 'cowboy up'?" (Translation: When things get tough, you have to get up, dust yourself off, and get back to it—whatever "it" is.) Here's another one: "What is a 'back burner relationship'?" (This metaphor is about stoves with front and back burners. Some communication scholars study the back burner relationship, which refers to keeping in contact with potential romantic partners in case one's current relationship ends.)[23] Cultures and co-cultural groups within them develop unique languages as a way to forge connections and enhance solidarity. The language you use both shapes and reflects your culture.

- *The Power to Make and Break Relationships.* You have probably used words to draw people to you and to maintain all sorts of relationships. But you have probably also had the experience of saying something you regret, or being too blunt and offending someone. If you've ever said something so inappropriate that it cost you a romance or friendship, you know firsthand the power of words to make and break relationships.

Confronting Bias in Language

3.4 Describe the major ways in which language reveals bias about race, ethnicity, nationality, religion, gender, sexual orientation, age, class, and ability.

For all of us, our language could use a bit of reflection, and then some refreshing. Improving your linguistic choices is not about conforming to some societal standard of how you should talk; it's about using the best language adapted for your listeners. It is also about using language that shows you're a highly educated person with excellent communication skills. Insensitive or stereotypical language use often arises out of ignorance or a lack of education. But even well-meaning, educated people can communicate bias through the language they choose to use. Words that reflect bias toward members of other cultures or groups can create barriers for listeners. In addition, such language ignores the fact that the world is constantly changing. In the following section, we explore a few categories of language that illustrate the constant evolution of verbal communication. As you read this information, think to yourself: Do I have some "refreshing" to do?

Biased Language: Race, Ethnicity, Nationality, and Religion

Think about whether you have ever said or overheard someone say the following:

> "Work on your resume so that you're not handicapped at your job interview."
>
> "Drive faster; you're driving like a geezer."
>
> "I met some new students at the university who are illegal aliens."
>
> "That divorce settlement gypped me out of what's rightfully mine!"

The language used in each of these examples demonstrates an insensitivity to members of different cultural and social groups. (The last statement tends to puzzle people more than the others. It includes the term *gypped*, which is derived from the word *gypsies*, a derogatory name for the nomadic Romani people who primarily live in Europe. The stereotype relates to being suckered or cheated out of what one is due.) Each of these statements contains a word barrier known as **allness**, which occurs when words reflect unqualified, often untrue generalizations that deny individual differences or variations.

Terms pertaining to racial and ethnic groups continue to change over time. Refer to Table 3.1, which provides many of the racial categories that appeared as options in the U.S. censuses of 1970, 1980, 1990, 2000, 2010, and 2020. Not all cultural groups' terms are represented in the table, but you will see how our language has become more specific over time in an attempt to better communicate racial and ethnic identity in this country.

Sometimes it is a challenge to keep pace as language changes over time, but try not to get lazy with language. It is important to inventory and revolutionize your language with regard to the racial, ethnic, national, and religious affiliations of people. After all, the language you choose to use is your primary tool for creating the reality of your existence. It reveals how you think. It is also how you are known by others, and how you know others.[24]

allness
A word barrier created through the use of language that reflects unqualified, often untrue generalizations that deny individual differences or variations.

TABLE 3.1 U.S. Census Racial Categories

1970	1980	1990	2000	2010	2020
White	White	White	White	White	White
Negro or Black	Negro	Black	Black or African American	Black, African American, or Negro	Black or African American
Indian (American)	Indian (American)	Indian (American)	American Indian or Alaska Native (specify tribe)	American Indian or Alaska Native	American Indian or Alaska Native

SOURCES: Table based on information from M. Anderson and S. Feinberg, 2000, "Race and Ethnicity and the Controversy over the U.S. Census," *Current Sociology* 48.3: 87–110; National Research Council, *Measuring Racial Discrimination* (Washington, DC: National Academies Press, 2004); U.S. Census Bureau, 2001, "Population by Race and Hispanic or Latino Origin for All Ages and for 18 Years and Over for the United States: 2000," www.census.gov/PressRelease/www/2001/tables/st00_1.pdf; U.S. Census Bureau, 2010, *Questionnaire Reference Book* (Washington, DC: U.S. Department of Commerce, Bureau of the Census, Washington DC), retrieved from 2010census.gov.; American Community Survey 2020, www.census.gov (accessed June 6, 2020).

CRITICAL/CULTURAL PERSPECTIVES & COMMUNICATION

Black Lives Matter vs. All Lives Matter

Language has power. It can convey status and dominance; it can unite or divide. It is important to inventory and interrogate our use of language because it is the primary tool we use to communicate who we are to others, and who they are to us.

According to the movement's website, #BlackLivesMatter was founded in 2013 in response to the acquittal of Florida teen Trayvon Martin's murderer. As a global organization, their mission is to raise awareness of racism and assist local communities in their fight against racially motivated violence against Black people.[25] Many members and supporters of the movement are active users of social media. Traffic on sites like Facebook, Instagram, and Twitter was heightened in the spring of 2020, after the killing of George Floyd by the Minneapolis police.

Some controversy arose when the movement first began to grow and gain media attention. At protests and gatherings, some critics reacted to chants of "Black lives matter" by shouting "All lives matter." Likely no one can disagree with the sentiment that "all lives matter," so what was the problem?

Actor Ice-T explains it best: "When I say, 'Black lives matter,' and you say 'All lives matter,' that's like you saying, 'women's rights,' and I say 'human rights.' It dilutes what you're saying."[26] Both statements about "lives that matter" may be true and justified, but the language of "all lives" detracts from the important piece of language that conveys the movement's core message. The language a movement chooses to use sends a powerful message.

Biased Language: Sex, Gender, and Sexual Orientation

sexist (exclusive) language
Language that reveals bias in favor of one sex and against others.

Language that reveals bias in favor of one sex and against others, termed **sexist (exclusive) language**, is more prevalent than you might think. Decades of effort, spurred by the women's liberation movement in the 1960s, have raised the consciousness of American culture regarding exclusive language. But even in this day and age of heightened awareness about sex and gender issues, many people still do not use gender-fair verbal communication.

Language and the Sexes Even though women now constitute 50 percent of the U.S. population, to listen to the language of some people, you would think it was still a man's world. Sexist language can reflect stereotypical attitudes or describe roles in exclusive terms, ignoring others' experiences.[27] Research indicates that exclusive language usage does the following: (1) maintains sex-biased perceptions, (2) shapes people's attitudes about careers that are appropriate for one sex but not others, (3) causes some people to believe that certain jobs and roles are not attainable, (4) contributes to the belief that men deserve more status in society than other people do, and (5) mutes the voices of many people, because the words and norms formed by the dominant group do not allow for the articulation of others' experiences.[28]

generic language
General terms that stand for all persons or things within a given category.

The most common form of sexism in language is the use of **generic language**, using a masculine term to describe all people. There are two primary ways in which masculine-as-generic language typically appears in written and oral communication: pronoun usage and man-linked terminology.[29]

Consistent evidence from research on sexist language shows that people—particularly in American culture—simply do not tend to think in neuter. When we hear the term "policeman," we do not think of some amorphous sex-less person. Instead, we tend to picture a male police officer. Likewise, we do not tend to think of living entities as *it*, and we rarely use that pronoun to refer to them. When most people read or hear the word *he*, they think of a masculine person, not a sexless person.[30] Using generic masculine language, in essence, turns all persons into male persons. For example, one of our students gave a speech on how to project a winning, confident style in a job interview. He said, "When you greet the boss for the first time, be sure to look him straight in the eye, give him a firm handshake, and let him know you're interested in the job." The student's exclusive language choice only allowed for the possibility of a male boss, not a female or transgender boss. A recent study of American university undergraduates found that students used masculine labels much more frequently than feminine ones in everyday conversation.[31]

We don't know what you were taught in high school or in other college classes about generic language, but most current publishing standards require the use of nonsexist language, which means that masculine terms cannot stand for all persons.[32] Note our use of inclusive language in this text—because it reflects our value system and because our publisher requires it.

The solution to the problem of sexist language is not to replace each *he* with *she* but to use terms that include all sexes so that your language reflects the contemporary world. If you want to refer to a person of any sex, the clearest, most grammatical, and nonsexist way to do that is to use *she or he*, *he/she*, or *s/he*.[33] Some people may wish to be referred to as a singular *they*, choosing to reject pronouns that restrict them to binary choices. Other options for avoiding gender-specific pronouns include (1) omitting a pronoun altogether, either by rewording

▼ The gender-neutral term *firefighter* describes both of these people, whereas the sexist term *fireman* excludes the person on the left.
Shutterstock

a message or by substituting an article (*a, an,* or *the*) for the pronoun; (2) using *you* or variations of the indefinite pronoun *one;* or (3) using the plural pronoun *they.*[34] The third option is becoming much more popular and grammatically acceptable than in times past because of its common conversational usage and the changing times. In 2016, *The Washington Post* became one of the first newspapers to adopt a singular "they" into its style standards.[35] It is less likely now that your English teacher will correct such a statement as this: "If a person wants to be successful in life, they must work hard."

What form of gender-fair language, particularly pronouns, should be used with people who are transgender? An increasingly common practice for people of all sexes and genders is to clearly communicate their preferred pronouns so that others can comfortably use sensitive and accurate language.[36] Some people include their preferred pronouns in their signature file, information automatically inserted at the end of every outgoing email message. Some transgender students contact their professors if their legal names on class rosters reflect their biological sex, rather than their transgender identities. In general, transgender people prefer pronouns related to the sex they are transitioning to. For example, some trans men (those transitioning from biological female to a male or masculine transgender identity) may prefer "he," "his," and "himself" as pronouns, while other transgender people may prefer "they," "their," and "themselves" because no sex or gender is indicated. It's wise to be aware of these different options and take cues from others, so that our language keeps pace and reflects sensitivity.

Consciously remembering to use nonsexist, inclusive language brings the following benefits:[37]

- Inclusive language reflects inclusive attitudes. Monitoring your verbal communication for sexist remarks will make you aware of any sexist attitudes or assumptions you may hold.
- Using inclusive language helps you become more other-oriented, which will have a positive effect on your relationships. Consciously purging sexist language from your vocabulary reflects your awareness of others and their sensitivities.

DIVERSITY & COMMUNICATION

Gender Bias in Malay Language

There have been several studies focused on English, Chinese, and European languages to identify and suggest alternatives to words and phrases that could be considered as sexist or suggestive of a gender bias. Many male-orientated terms, phrases, and even proverbs are not gender-neutral and they reveal biases that have been passed down the generations without being contested.[38]

A study of Malay proverbs revealed deep-rooted gender bias. While the proverbs suggest traditional and popular wisdom, many related to women and conveyed a sense of negativity towards them.[39] It was found that the proverbs fell into one of the following four categories:

- Proverbs that used women to symbolize or represent a negative trait—Berteras ke hujung dahan (holding onto the tip of a branch) refers to a husband being henpecked by his wife.
- Proverbs that contain stereotypes of women—Ada wang abang sayang, tak ada wang abang Melayang (a man with money is loved by a woman, but a penniless man will be abandoned) suggests that a woman's love for a man is dependent on the man's wealth.
- Proverbs that are not overtly directed at women, but still use a negative female reference—Timur beralih sebelah barat (the east has moved to the west) refers to a man who follows the instructions of a woman.
- Proverbs that contain an irrelevant reference to women—Baik jadi ayam betina supaya selamat (it is better to behave like a hen in order to be safe) suggests that it is foolish to appear courageous as you will put yourself in danger, so it is better to behave in a female way (the hen being female).

A 2013 study looked at how gender bias is often reinforced in the most unexpected ways in English language textbooks used in schools. Five textbooks and two literature readings were examined for their depictions of gender through vocabulary, social norms, and pictures. Many common nouns and pronouns were male dominated and male identities were more common than female ones.[40]

A study into subliminal sexism in certain school textbooks noted the frequency of stereotypes. Males dominated stories and were seen as strong, creative, and powerful, while women were often depicted as passive and conventional. The study recommends more effective gender edits.[41]

- Inclusive language makes your communication more contemporary and unambiguous. If you say *he*, for example, how is a listener to know whether you are referring to a male person or to just any person?
- Using nonsexist language strengthens your communication style and demonstrates a sensitivity that can empower others. By eliminating sexist bias from your communication, you affirm the value of all individuals with whom you interact.[42]

Language, Sexual Orientation, and Gender Identity We realize that sexual orientation is one of the more difficult topics to discuss, mainly because people tend to hold strong opinions about it. But no matter your views about sexuality, it's vital to use sensitive, appropriate communication with whomever you encounter.

Insensitivity or intolerance toward persons who are gay, lesbian, bisexual, or queer (a term of liberation from labels about gender identity and sexual orientation) is often reflected in **homophobic language**.[43] Homophobic language denigrates people of non-heterosexual orientations and may arise out of a fear of being labeled gay, lesbian, or queer (homophobia). Sometimes homophobic language is obvious, such as calling someone a derogatory term that we've heard all too often. But homophobic language is often subtle, sometimes cloaked in an attempt at humor. Examples include blithe references to a lesbian as "wearing the pants in the family" or a gay man as being "light in the loafers." Both subtle and overt homophobic language reveals insensitive attitudes and a rigid communication style.

Transphobia is defined as a resistance to transgender identity, and as a fear of or antagonism toward people who are transgender.[44] Thus it follows that **transphobic language** is verbal communication that conveys resistance, fear, and antagonism toward transgender people. On June 15, 2020, the U.S. Supreme Court ruled in a six to three decision that gay, lesbian, and transgender workers were protected from job discrimination, under an expanded view of the Civil Rights Act of 1964. The decision was seen by

homophobic language
Language that overtly denigrates persons of non-heterosexual orientations, usually arising out of a fear of being labeled gay, lesbian, or queer.

transphobia
A resistance to transgenderism or antagonism toward transgender people.

transphobic language
Language that conveys resistance and antagonism toward transgender people.

ETHICS & COMMUNICATION

France May Ban Gender Neutral Words

Sexual orientation and identity impacts on language use in a variety of ways. For languages that have engendered nouns, should these remain as they are or should they be replaced with gender inclusive words?

In February 2021, around 60 members of the French National Assembly announced that they would be introducing legislation to ban what they believed were confusing gender inclusive words. They argued that the use of gender inclusive nouns threatened the very future of French as an international language as it made learning French more complicated.[45]

French grammar dictates that all nouns, pronouns, and adjectives carry the gender of the person or the object they refer to. This means that words such as "they" are not gender neutral. In the case of a group of French women, they would be referred to using the feminine form. However, if just one man joins the group, because the masculine form is dominant in the plural, the gender would switch to the masculine form. For many years, there has been pressure to make French more gender neutral so that it no longer prolongs the use of heterosexist language and is supportive of diversity. However, intended legislation aiming to ban the use of gender-neutral text across the government is supported by the ruling LREM party and the opposition Les Républicains.[46]

In 2015, the French High Council for Gender Equality released a guide for communications avoiding the use of gender stereotyping. The suggestion was that someone's job title, for example, has the gender of the person in that role, such as Madam Mayor.[47] This was dropped in 2019. The masculinization of the French language can be traced back to the 17th century when many feminine names were eradicated and replaced with masculine ones.[48] Whether this marginalizes inclusivity and sexual diversity or not is worthy of further discussion.

In April 2021, France's neighbor Belgium announced that it would be moving in the opposite direction and was switching to a more gender-neutral language. A prime example is the move from using the phrase "good house father" or "family man" to "prudent and reasonable person". This follows a Belgian trend to reduce the influence of patriarchal terms and associations.[49] This may well be the beginning of a move away from what can be perceived as heterosexist language by removing gender assumptions within what has been commonly-used language.

many people in the country and around the world as a major step forward for diversity and inclusion, especially because the ruling pertained to workers identifying as queer or transgender.[50]

Another way to communicate bias is through the use of **heterosexist language**, language that reflects an assumption that the world is (or should be) heterosexual, as if romantic and sexual attraction other than heterosexual is not possible or acceptable. Consider one public speaking student who started a speech like this: "How many of you ladies have trouble getting your boyfriend to go shopping with you?" In a mixed-sex/gender audience, what are some possible interpretations of this speech introduction? One take is that the speaker is addressing only those women in the audience who he or she believes to be straight and in possession of a boyfriend and is excluding all others. Another interpretation is that the use of the term "ladies" is derogatory and intended to include some of the men in the audience, particularly the gay men who might have boyfriends. Either way, such an introduction shows a speaker's biased assumptions as well as his or her poor choice of language.

Heterosexist language is often more subtle than homophobic language. It may emerge through *omission*, meaning what *is not* said, rather than *commission*, or what *is* said. One form of heterosexist language surrounds people's level of comfort with using "husband" and "wife" to refer to the married partners of gays and lesbians. Some people hold religious views or notions from their upbringing that preclude them from acknowledging same-sex marriage and the language that goes with it, but because same-sex marriage has been the law of the land since 2015, our language should, at the very least, reflect the changing times.[51]

heterosexist language
Language that reveals an assumption that the world is heterosexual, as if other orientations did not exist.

▼ People sometimes use the word *retarded* in casual conversation to refer to occasions when someone does something foolish or incorrectly. Publicity campaigns help curb the use of this biased language, as has increased visibility of celebrities with Down syndrome, such as Jamie Brewer, a member of the cast of *American Horror Story*.
2013 HPA/Hutchins Photo/Newscom

Biased Language: Age, Class, and Ability

"Just turn the car, grandpa!" Ever heard a driver say something like this in irritation or said it yourself? Ever call an elderly person a "geezer" or an "old-timer"? Just as some people contend that Americans are hung up on gender and racial diversity, many believe that Americans are hung up on age. We live in a culture that glorifies youth and tends to put its elders out to pasture.[52] Age discrimination is a very real problem in the workforce—so much so that laws have been enacted to guard against someone's being denied professional opportunities because of age. In contrast, people may also hold stereotypes about young people and speak to them as though their youth exempts them from intelligence or responsible action. We recommend that you inventory your language for any terms that either show disrespect for elders or are patronizing or condescending to younger people.

Another factor influencing language is socioeconomic class.[53] Class distinctions are typically revealed in derogatory references to "blue-collar workers," "manual laborers," "welfare recipients," or "one percenters" (the wealthiest one percent of Americans). Another class slur is "white trash." In the late 1990s, when Paula Jones filed a sexual harassment lawsuit against then-president Bill Clinton, she was ridiculed and called "white trash" and "trailer trash" in the press. Inventory your language so that you rid it of references that reveal a condescending or disrespectful attitude toward someone's education (or lack of it) and socioeconomic status. You don't want to come off as an entitled, insensitive college student.

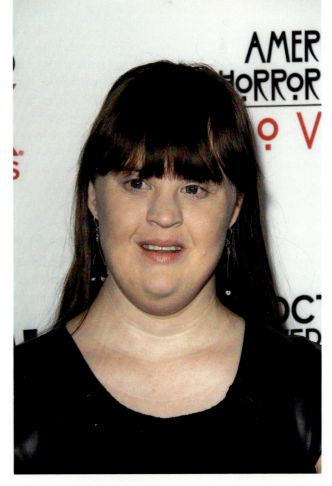

> **RECAP**
>
> **Confronting Bias in Language**
>
> Inventory your language for subtle and not-so-subtle indications of bias in several areas:
>
> - *Race, Ethnicity, and Nationality.* Avoid language that denigrates members of a racial or ethnic group; be careful not to "mark" a person by misusing adjectives referring to national origin, as in "that Oriental student in my class."
> - *Religion.* Watch for stereotypical language pertaining to religious affiliation.
> - *Gender.* Include all sexes and genders in your language, especially in your use of pronouns; avoid masculine generic pronouns and male-linked terms that exclude others. Try to stay current in your use of language, even if terms for sex and gender identity change quickly.
> - *Sexual Orientation and Gender Identity.* Be alert to the potential for heterosexism in your language—the assumption that everyone is heterosexual or that heterosexuality is the only legitimate orientation. Eliminate homophobic and transphobic language that degrades and stereotypes LGBTQ+ individuals.
> - *Age.* Avoid calling too much attention to a person's age in your verbal communication. Be especially vigilant not to label or stereotype the elderly or to condescend to or glorify youth.
> - *Class.* Monitor references to socioeconomic differences, such as distinctions between blue-collar and white-collar workers.
> - *Ability.* Avoid verbal communication that draws attention to a person's physical, mental, or learning ability.

Finally, an area of bias in language relates to ability. Some years ago, Helen Keller was described as "deaf, dumb, and blind." Nowadays, the term "dumb" is considered offensive and is no longer used to describe people who are speech impaired. Be careful that your language doesn't make fun of or draw attention to someone's physical, mental, or learning disability, such as calling someone a "gimp," "retard," or "slow reader" or describing someone as having an "ADD moment." Research has found that when people with disabilities are called demeaning names, they're perceived as less trustworthy, competent, persuasive, and sociable than when they're described in positive terms.[54] However, just as some people have reclaimed the word "queer" as a pride term, once-derogatory language like "crip communication" and "crip identity" have also been reclaimed to signal a point of pride and to emphasize solidarity among persons with disabilities.[55]

Using Words to Establish Supportive Relationships

3.5 Explain how language helps create supportive or defensive communication climates.

For more than five decades, communication scholar Jack Gibb's research has been used as a framework for both describing and prescribing verbal behaviors that contribute to feelings of either supportiveness or defensiveness.[56] Gibb spent several years listening to and observing groups of individuals in meetings and conversations, noting that some exchanges created a supportive climate whereas others created a defensive one. Gibb defined **supportive communication** as language used to create a climate of trust, caring, and acceptance. The language used in **defensive communication**, in contrast, creates a climate of hostility and mistrust. When someone gets defensive, communication is seriously impaired.

Two specific word barriers tend to engender negative reactions and defensiveness in most of us and can damage even the most secure of relationships.

- **Polarization** occurs when we describe things in extremes or opposites without any middle ground. One romantic partner might say to the other, "You either love me or you don't." Pronouncements of this kind can be interpreted as ultimatums with no compromise position. It's wise to avoid language that creates a false or forced choice for people, making them feel controlled, hemmed in, or manipulated.[57]

  In our current political climate, polarizing language is not hard to find, as people with divergent views may resort to heated terms in defense of entrenched positions. Lynn H. Turner, a former president of the National Communication Association, warned readers against using polarizing speech in a column in the association's newsletter:

  > Using inflammatory language and demonizing people who espouse a perspective other than your own encourages us to see things as opposites and obscures any

supportive communication
Language that creates a climate of trust, caring, and acceptance.

defensive communication
Language that creates a climate of hostility and mistrust.

polarization
The tendency to describe things in extremes, as though no middle ground existed.

search for common ground. We won't be heard if our language instantly puts others on the defensive. We don't have the luxury of indulging ourselves in invectives and pushing each other into opposing camps. Our knowledge of good communication practices should help us pull together now when we need it most. "You cut the cake, I choose the slice" might just be the type of technique we could really use right now.[58]

- **Trigger words** arouse our emotions. Travis, a former student, described in class a word his wife used during arguments that really irked him more than anything else. When Travis would make a point that would frustrate his wife—one for which she had no comeback—she would look at him, toss her hand in the air, and say, "Whatever." Perhaps this word triggers you too, because it punctuates a conversation; it dismisses the other person and her or his point. Language can make us feel accepted and appreciated or disrespected and hostile.[59]

trigger words
Forms of language that arouse strong emotions in listeners.

Think about times when your words made someone defensive and how hard you had to work to get the person to let those defenses down. In the following section, we suggest six ways to use verbal communication to create a supportive rather than an antagonistic climate.

Describe Your Own Feelings Rather Than Evaluate Others

Most of us don't like to be judged. One way to avoid evaluating others is to use "I" statements instead of accusatory "you" statements. A statement like, "You always say you'll call, but you never do" attacks a person's sense of self-worth and usually results in a defensive reaction. Instead, use the word *I* to describe your own feelings and thoughts about a situation or event: "I find it hard to believe you when you say you'll call." When you describe your own feelings instead of berating the receiver of the message, you take ownership of the problem. This approach leads to greater openness and trust because your listener is less likely to feel rejected or as if you are trying to control him or her.

Solve Problems Rather Than Control Others

When you were younger, your parents gave you rules to keep you safe. Even if you resented their control, you needed to know that the stovetop was hot, when not to cross the street, and how dangerous it was to stick your finger in a light socket. Now that you're an adult, when people treat you like a child, it often means they're trying to control your behavior and take away your options.

Most of us don't like to be controlled. Someone who presumes to tell us what is good for us instead of helping us puzzle through issues and problems to arrive at our own solutions or higher understanding is likely to engender defensiveness. In truth, we have little or no control over others. Open-ended questions such as "What's going on?" or "How can we deal with this issue?" create a more supportive climate than critical comments such as "Here's where you are wrong" or "You know what your problem is?" or commands like "Don't do that!"

Empathize Rather Than Remain Detached from Others

Empathy, one of the hallmarks of supportive relationships, is the ability to understand and actually feel or approximate the feelings of others, and to communicate accordingly.[60] Empathy doesn't require you to have had the same experience as someone else; empathy means feeling what another person feels to the best of your ability. Maybe you haven't had a parent pass away, but you've felt sadness and loss in your life. You can communicate empathy to someone going through a loss because you know what

empathy
The ability to understand and feel what another person is feeling.

▲ Being genuine and showing empathy for others' feelings are two ways to help establish supportive relationships. What words can help convey your empathy when a friend is troubled?
Juanmonino/E+/Getty Images

loss *feels* like. When expressing empathy, use language that conveys the emotions you feel, connects with others, and provides support. Empathy is a building block of a supportive relationship; it may come naturally to some people, but most of us have to work at it, just like many other skills we can develop with a bit of effort.[61]

The opposite of empathy is neutrality, which is indifference or apathy toward others. A statement that epitomizes neutrality is "I don't love you or hate you; I just *don't* you." Such language generates defensiveness in most people.

Be Flexible Rather Than Rigid toward Others

Some people are just *always* right, aren't they? (These people spend a lot of time alone, too.) Most people don't like people who always seem certain that they are right, because such a stance creates a defensive climate. This does not mean that you should avoid sharing your opinions and go through life passively agreeing to everything. And it doesn't mean that there isn't a clear-cut right and wrong in many situations. But instead of making rigid pronouncements, at times you may want to qualify your language by using phrases such as "I may be wrong, but it seems to me . . ." or "Here's something you might want to consider." Conditional, provisional, and flexible language gives your opinions a softer edge that allows room for others to express a point of view; it opens the door for alternatives. Declarations tend to shut the door.

Present Yourself as Equal Rather Than Superior

You can antagonize others by letting them know that you view yourself as better than they are. You may be gifted and extraordinarily intelligent, but it's not necessary to announce or publicize it. Ever hear of the humblebrag? It's language that, at first glance, makes a person sound humble, but upon further inspection, it's a way to tell others about your achievements.[62] Examples include "When I bought my Mercedes, no one told me I'd get pulled over all the time" and this one from comedian Dane Cook: "Being famous and having a fender bender is weird. You want to be upset, but the other driver's just thrilled and giddy that it's you." This subtle style of bragging doesn't typically engender supportiveness in conversations with others; even the humblebrag will eventually be interpreted as pompous and can create defensiveness in listeners.

Avoid using "highfalutin" (unnecessarily complicated) words just to posture, impress others, or project some image. Sometimes referred to as "bafflegab," this kind of language can come in the form of words, phrases, or verbal shorthand that people use but no one understands. People with a particular expertise may use abbreviated terms or acronyms. The military is notorious for its use of language that doesn't easily translate outside of military circles. It's better to use informal language appropriate to the situation and your listeners than to attempt to talk over the heads of everyone in the room.

Avoid Gunny-Sacking

Gunny-sacking involves dredging up someone's past mistakes or problems and linking them to a current situation. Suppose your best friend has just been dumped by his "one true love," but you—being the good friend that you are—remind him that the last three people he dated were also his "one true love," at least at the time. Your friend wants empathy, but you respond by highlighting his tendency to turn "Ms. Right" into "Ms. Right Now." Such an approach will likely make him feel criticized and engender defensive reactions in him.

> **RECAP**
>
> **Using Words to Create a Supportive Climate**
>
> - Describe your own feelings instead of evaluating the point of view or behavior of others.
> - Keep the focus on problem solving rather than controlling others.
> - Instead of ignoring someone's feelings or staying neutral, try to empathize.
> - Use conditional language and demonstrate flexibility rather than rigidity in your communication.
> - Present yourself as an equal rather than a superior. Speaking like a know-it-all and talking over the heads of listeners usually breeds defensiveness.
> - Avoid gunny-sacking, or reminding someone of past mistakes or issues.

STUDY GUIDE: PRINCIPLES FOR A LIFETIME — CHAPTER 3

Why Focus on Language?

3.1 List two reasons why it is important to study verbal communication.

PRINCIPLE POINTS: Words are powerful; they affect your emotions, thoughts, actions, and relationships, as well as how you are perceived by others. The language you use also impacts your relationships.

PRINCIPLE TERM:
code switching

PRINCIPLE SKILLS:

1. In taking a mental inventory of your use of language, what did you notice that you can change to improve the effectiveness of your communication?
2. How much of a challenge is it for you to change your language, in ways both large and small? Recall a time when you became acutely aware that you needed to "watch your language." How successful were you at making changes?

The Nature of Language

3.2 Summarize how words are used as symbols that have denotative, connotative, concrete, and abstract meanings and are bound by culture and context.

PRINCIPLE POINTS: Language is a system of symbols (words or vocabulary) structured by grammar (rules and standards) and syntax (patterns in the arrangement of words) common to a community of people. The Sapir–Whorf Hypothesis suggests that language and thought are so interrelated that thought is rooted in and controlled by language. The limits of your language may be the limits of your thought. Six important aspects of language are (1) people use words as symbols (something that represents something else); (2) people attach meanings to words, and sometimes meanings differ (bypassing); (3) people use denotative and connotative meanings for words; (4) people convey concrete and abstract meanings through words; (5) meanings are culture bound; and (6) meanings are context bound.

PRINCIPLE TERMS:

language	concrete meaning
symbol	abstract meaning
meaning	culture
bypassing	co-culture
denotative meaning	neologism
connotative meaning	

PRINCIPLE SKILLS:

1. Do you find that people's verbal communication seems to accurately reflect the quality of their thoughts? Have you ever met anyone whose verbal skills did not seem to match his or her thinking skills?

2. **Practicing Denotation and Connotation**

   Below we review the differences between denotative and connotative meanings of words and provide examples.

Level	Definition	Example
Denotative	Literal, restrictive definition of a word	*Teacher:* the person primarily responsible for providing your education
Connotative	Personal, subjective reaction to a word	*Teacher:* the warm, supportive person who fostered a climate in which you could learn or the cold taskmaster who drilled lessons into you and made you feel inferior

For each of the following terms, provide a denotative, or dictionary-type, definition; then generate connotative meanings of your own.

Term	Denotative Definition	Connotative Meanings
work		
parent		
infidelity		
professionalism		
loyalty		

The Power of Words

3.3 Identify five primary ways in which words have power.

PRINCIPLE POINTS: Words are extremely powerful. They can create and label our experiences, communicate our feelings, affect our thoughts and actions, shape and reflect our culture, and make and break our relationships.

PRINCIPLE TERM:

allness

PRINCIPLE SKILLS:

1. Give an example of a time when you became acutely aware of the power of words because someone said something that either worked miracles or turned out badly for everyone involved.
2. Do your words have power, meaning do you use verbal language in a way that corresponds to any of the five primary ways words have power? Assess whether you tend to use words to create or label an experience, to communicate your attitudes and feelings, and so forth. Work through the five ways words have power.

Confronting Bias in Language

3.4 Describe the major ways in which language reveals bias about race, ethnicity, nationality, religion, gender, sexual orientation, age, class, and ability.

PRINCIPLE POINTS: Our language often reveals our biases. Monitor your language to avoid bias in these categories: (1) race, ethnicity, nationality, and religion; (2) sex, gender, and sexual orientation; and (3) age, class, and ability.

PRINCIPLE TERMS:

sexist (exclusive) language   transphobia
generic language   transphobic language
homophobic language   heterosexist language

PRINCIPLE SKILLS:

1. What do you do when someone makes a biased remark around you or to you? How can you effectively respond to show that you don't accept such language?
2. **Your Bias Is Showing**

   Here's an activity to illustrate how people reveal their biases through their use of language. Generate a list of stereotypical terms, both positive and negative, often associated with each word below. For example, if you think about the word *Democrat*, you might think of positive and negative terms like "liberal," "tax and spend," "big government," "antiwar," "environmentalist," and "populist."

Term	Positive Stereotypical Language	Negative Stereotypical Language
conservatives		
liberals		
hipsters		
homeless people		
churchgoers		
movie stars		
athletes		

Using Words to Establish Supportive Relationships

3.5 Explain how language helps create supportive or defensive communication climates.

PRINCIPLE POINTS: Supportive communication creates a climate of trust, caring, and acceptance; defensive communication creates a climate of hostility and mistrust. Two uses of language that breed hostility and mistrust are polarization and trigger words. Here are six tips for developing a supportive communication climate: (1) Describe your own feelings rather than evaluate others; (2) solve problems rather than control others; (3) empathize rather than remain detached from others; (4) be flexible rather than rigid toward others; (5) present yourself as equal rather than superior; and (6) stick to the present situation and avoid gunny-sacking (dredging up the past).

PRINCIPLE TERMS:

supportive communication
defensive communication
polarization
trigger words
empathy

PRINCIPLE SKILLS:

1. Think of language you have used or someone has used toward you that reflects polarization, as though there was no common ground. What effect did such language have on you or your listener?

2. What are your trigger words? Think about experiences related to these words and ponder how they came to trigger your emotions and attitudes. How might you react more effectively when these forms of language are directed at you in the future?

CHAPTER 4

UNDERSTANDING NONVERBAL MESSAGES

Over the years your bodies become walking autobiographies, telling friends and strangers alike of the minor and major stresses of your life. —MARILYN FERGUSON

Anna Karwowska/Shutterstock

CHAPTER OUTLINE

- Why Focus on Nonverbal Communication?
- The Nature of Nonverbal Communication
- Codes of Nonverbal Communication
- How to Interpret Nonverbal Cues More Accurately
- An Application of Nonverbal Communication Research: Detecting Deception
- Study Guide: *Principles for a Lifetime*

LEARNING OBJECTIVES

4.1 Provide four reasons for studying nonverbal communication.

4.2 Discuss six elements that reveal the nature of nonverbal communication.

4.3 Identify and explain the seven nonverbal communication codes.

4.4 Explain Mehrabian's three-part framework for interpreting nonverbal cues.

4.5 Describe the primary nonverbal cues associated with deception.

PROFESSOR: You okay? You looked a bit tense during the exam.

STUDENT: Yeah, I have test anxiety. What was I doing that made you notice me?

PROFESSOR: Nothing strange or out of the norm—just fidgeting with your hair, shifting in your seat, and staring off into space, like you were trying to recall material you studied or something. This kind of thing is quite common when students take exams.

STUDENT: Hmmm, that's interesting. I'm aware of how I twirl my hair when I'm tense, but I didn't realize others would notice.

PROFESSOR: It's no big deal. Just do what you need to do, because test anxiety is a real thing that happens to a lot of students.

The comments in the above example all center on *nonverbal communication*, a form of human communication that occurs without words. In this conversation, comments about eye gaze, body shifts, and habitual movement all relate to nonverbal elements that have a profound effect on how we interact with one another. As we explained in Chapter 1, **nonverbal communication** is communication other than written or spoken language that creates meaning for someone. An exception to this definition is sign language. For people who have no hearing impediments, sign language appears to be nonverbal communication. However, to people who are deaf, sign language is verbal communication; certain movements, signs, and facial expressions convey words, phrases, and emphasis.[1]

We know you're becoming familiar with our five-sided model of Communication Principles for a Lifetime, shown in Figure 4.1, but let's do a quick recap. In Chapter 2, we explored ways to become more aware of yourself and your perceptions of things and people with whom you come into contact. An important step in this process of coming to know and understand yourself better is an honest, insightful examination of how you talk. In Chapter 3, we challenged you to consider the power of words, to take inventory of your use of language, and to think about ways to improve your verbal communication so that you extend yourself to others and respond to them in an appropriate, effective manner.

Now we get to what most people consider an even greater challenge: understanding and evaluating your own nonverbal communication and improving your ability to interpret the nonverbal behavior of others. Nonverbal communication is of great importance; a person who can read others' nonverbal communication with sensitivity and skill makes a memorable impression on other people. Because of the power of nonverbal communication to complement verbal communication, to further reveal the self (particularly in situations when talking is inappropriate, impossible, or inadequate), and to affect how you connect with others as you initiate and build

nonverbal communication
Communication other than written or spoken language that creates meaning for someone.

FIGURE 4.1 Communication Principles for a Lifetime

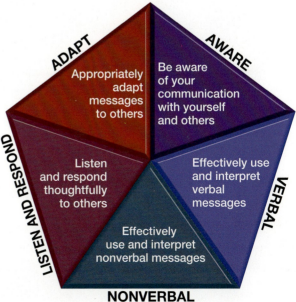

relationships, we've chosen to make this the third of our five key Communication Principles for a Lifetime.

We have two primary goals in this chapter:

* To help you become more aware of your own nonverbal communication and
* To enhance your nonverbal receiving skills, or your ability to detect and interpret the nonverbal cues of others more accurately.

Why Focus on Nonverbal Communication?

4.1 Provide four reasons for studying nonverbal communication.

Have you ever watched a person interact with someone else and thought, "That person just doesn't have a clue"? We've all seen or met people who appear not to pick up on the communication clues of others. Maybe you have a few minutes before class and you just want some time to yourself to check your email or Twitter feed, or get some work done. A classmate approaches to chat and doesn't notice your lack of nonverbal responsiveness (you avoid eye contact and do not turn your body or face toward the person). This person is oblivious, but your nonverbal cues are screaming "Please, leave me be!"

We all have times when we can't "catch a clue," even if we consider ourselves to be fairly perceptive people. Certain people, places, moods, or topics of conversation may impede our ability to give and receive nonverbal communication effectively. But we don't want to be clueless. We want to be able to exhibit effective nonverbal communication and to read and interpret the clues others give us more sensitively and accurately.

No one can become a perfect interpreter of the nonverbal communication of others, because human beings are unique, complicated, and ever-changing creatures. Although we encourage you to deepen your understanding of nonverbal communication, sharpen your powers of observation, and develop greater skill in interpreting the meanings behind others' nonverbal actions, we also suggest that you remain keenly aware of the idiosyncratic and complex nature of nonverbal communication. To begin our exploration of this topic, let's look at four reasons for studying nonverbal communication.

▼ How aware are you of the power of your nonverbal communication with others? Think about confrontations you've had in the past. In your opinion, which communicates emotions most effectively: the volume, pitch, and intensity of the voice; nonverbal gestures, facial expressions, and body positions; or the meaning of the actual words spoken?
Hybrid Images/Image Source/Alamy Stock Photo

Nonverbal Messages Communicate Feelings and Attitudes

Nonverbal communication is a primary tool for conveying our feelings and attitudes and for detecting the emotional states of others.[2] Nonverbal communication scholar Albert Mehrabian suggests that the most significant source of emotional information is the face, which can channel as much as 55 percent of our meaning. Vocal cues such as volume, pitch, and intensity convey another 38 percent of our emotional meaning. In all, we communicate approximately

93 percent of our emotional meaning nonverbally; as little as 7 percent of the emotional meaning is communicated through explicit verbal channels.[3]

Did the COVID-19 pandemic that ravaged the globe in 2020 and 2021 make nonverbal communication more or less important, compared to verbal communication? Debates about that question continue, but we contend that the changes the pandemic brought about—like practicing social distancing, refraining from shaking hands, and wearing face coverings, which mask some cues of emotion—haven't taken away the power of nonverbal communication. Rather, these changes have heightened its importance. When you have fewer cues at your disposal or circumstances cause those cues to be altered, emphasized, or replaced, nonverbal communication skill becomes even more central to successful communication.

Nonverbal Messages Are More Believable Than Verbal Ones

JONAS: Hey—are you mad or something?

DANITA: (Big sigh.) Oh, no. I'm not mad. (Said in a subdued tone of voice and without making eye contact.)

JONAS: You sure? Because you're acting funny, like you're ticked off. (One more try and then Jonas will likely give up.)

DANITA: I SAID I'M NOT MAD, OKAY? WILL YOU LEAVE IT ALONE PLEASE?

Despite Danita's claim to the contrary, the real story is—she's mad. The reason the phrase "Actions speak louder than words" has become a cliché is because nonverbal communication is more believable than verbal communication. Verbal communication is a conscious activity; it involves the translation of thoughts and impulses into symbols. Some nonverbal communication is conscious, but a great deal of it is generated subconsciously, as we act and react to stimuli in our environment. It's easier to control your words than to control a quiver in your voice when you're angry, the heat and flush in your face when you talk to someone you're attracted to, or shaky knees when you're nervous.

When a person's verbal and nonverbal communication contradict, as in Danita's case, which should an astute observer believe? The nonverbal actions carry the truer message most of the time.

Nonverbal Messages Are Critical to Successful Relationships

One researcher suggests that as much as 65 percent of the way we convey messages is through nonverbal channels.[4] Of course, the message others receive from our behavior may not be the one we intended. But we begin making judgments about people just a fraction of a second after meeting them, based on nonverbal information.[5] We may decide whether a date is going to be pleasant or dull during the first thirty seconds of meeting the person, before he or she has had time to utter more than "Hello."[6]

In April of 2020, medical expert Dr. Anthony Fauci suggested that the handshake, as a ritual in American culture, might be a thing of the past because of its potential to spread viruses.[7] We're not so sure, because handshakes convey powerful nonverbal messages, especially in professional settings. Once the public is safe from viral spread, will the handshake return? William Chaplin and his colleagues examined the judgments Americans make about someone's personality based on a handshake and determined that the most positive handshake was strong (but not so strong as to cut off blood supply), vigorous, not too brief or too long, and complete (meaning people gripped each other's hands fully, with palms touching).[8] We form more favorable first impressions of people with good handshakes than of those with lousy ones. So if and when this simple nonverbal ritual returns, remember that your handshake can have a definite and long-lasting impact on how others perceive you.[9]

ETHICS & COMMUNICATION

Do We Have a Rhythm or Are You Just Mimicking Me?

People often talk about being "out of synch" with others or having "timing problems" that cause some relationships to end. Many of us are sensitive to the rhythm of relationships and communication with key people in our lives.

In research, this rhythm phenomenon is termed **interactive synchrony** (sometimes called the "chameleon effect," "contagion," or "interpersonal coordination"). It refers to the coordination of speech and body movement between at least two speakers.[10] People can get so in synch that they mirror each other's movements unintentionally, a fascinating phenomenon to observe and experience. Sometimes relationships in conflict or decline will show a lack of synchrony, as though partners "can't get a rhythm." Not having rhythm with another person can be an early signal that a relationship is in trouble.

In some cases, we may choose to purposely mirror our conversational partners by matching someone's speed or cadence of speech. Intentional mirroring is called **mimicry**, which can be an effective sales or persuasive technique.[11] Is mimicry ethical or is it taking synchrony too far? At times, mimicry may merely reflect the skill of effectively adapting our communication. Adaptation is our fifth Principle for a Lifetime, and we discuss it fully in Chapter 6. A good deal of our ability to adapt our communication involves nonverbal awareness and sensitivity to how we and others nonverbally communicate.

---

interactive synchrony
Coordination of speech and body movements between at least two speakers.

mimicry
Intentional mirroring of another person's verbal and nonverbal communication.

Nonverbal cues are important not only in the early stages of relationships, but also as we maintain, deepen, and sometimes terminate those relationships. In fact, the more intimate the relationship, the more we use and understand the nonverbal cues of our partners. We also use nonverbal cues to signal changes in the level of satisfaction with a relationship. When we want to cool things off, we may start using a less vibrant tone of voice and cut back on eye contact and physical contact with our partner.

Nonverbal Messages Serve Multiple Functions

Nonverbal messages function in a variety of ways:

- Nonverbal cues can *substitute for* verbal messages. Raising your index and middle fingers in the air can mean "peace" or "V" for victory, or it can simply be someone's way of ordering two of something in a noisy, crowded environment where it's hard to be heard.

- Nonverbal cues delivered simultaneously with verbal messages *complement*, clarify, or extend the meaning of the verbal cues, conveying more information and allowing for a more accurate interpretation. When someone waves, makes eye contact, and says "Hello," the hand gesture and eye contact are nonverbal complements to the verbal greeting, providing context and revealing emotions and attitudes.

- Sometimes our nonverbal cues *contradict* our verbal cues. In our earlier example, Danita said she wasn't mad but her nonverbal cues revealed her true emotional state. In most instances when verbal and nonverbal cues contradict each other, the nonverbal message is the one we should believe.

- We use nonverbal messages to *repeat* our verbal messages. You and a friend head in different directions after class. You yell, "See you at the dorm at 4," but your friend can't hear you over the hall noise, so he makes a face as though he's confused. You point in the direction of the dorm and then raise four fingers in the air, to which your friend nods his head up and down, signaling that he understands your message. In such a situation, the verbal message comes first, but the nonverbal cues repeat the message to create greater understanding.

RECAP

Why Focus on Nonverbal Communication?

- Nonverbal communication is our primary means of communicating feelings and attitudes toward others.
- Nonverbal messages are usually more believable than verbal messages.
- Nonverbal communication is critical in the initiation, development, and termination of relationships.
- Nonverbal messages function to substitute for, complement, contradict, repeat, regulate, and accent verbal messages.

- Nonverbal cues *regulate* our participation in conversation. When talking with people, we rely on such nonverbal cues as eye contact, facial expressions, audible intakes of breath, vocalizations such as "um," shifts in posture or seating position, and movements closer to or farther away from others.
- We may use nonverbal cues to *accent* or reinforce a verbal message. "We simply must do something about this problem or we will all bear the blame," bellows the mayor. When the mayor says the word *must*, she pounds the podium and increases her volume for emphasis. Such a vocalization and gesture serve to accent or add intensity to the verbal message.

The Nature of Nonverbal Communication

4.2 Discuss six elements that reveal the nature of nonverbal communication.

While the benefits of studying and improving one's facility with nonverbal communication are clear, deciphering unspoken messages can be tricky. Dictionaries help us interpret words, but no handy reference book exists to help decode nonverbal cues. Below are some of the challenges inherent in the interpretation of nonverbal communication.

The Culture-Bound Nature of Nonverbal Communication

Some evidence suggests that humans from every culture smile when they are happy and frown when they are unhappy.[12] They also all tend to raise or flash their eyebrows when meeting or greeting others, and young children in many cultures wave to signal that they want their parents, raise their arms to be picked up, and suck their thumbs for comfort. These trends indicate some underlying commonality in human emotion. Yet each culture tends to develop unique rules for displaying and interpreting the expression of emotion.[13]

Nonverbal behavior is culture bound. If you don't situate nonverbal actions within a cultural context, you'll make critical errors in communicating nonverbally and in attempting to interpret the nonverbal behavior of others. Intercultural communication scholars teach us that one culture's friendly or polite action may be another culture's obscene gesture.[14]

The Rule-Governed Nature of Nonverbal Communication

You operate according to many rules in your nonverbal communication. You may be unaware that you function according to these rules, but when your rules are violated, you definitely know it. During the COVID-19 pandemic, some people had very strict rules about social distancing, touching, and mask wearing. Yet others came and went in public spaces without wearing masks or gloves as casually as before the health crisis occurred.[15]

Communication scholar Judee Burgoon created a theory of how nonverbal communication functions, termed **expectancy violations theory**.[16] The theory suggests that we develop expectations for appropriate nonverbal behavior in ourselves and others, based on our cultural backgrounds, personal experiences, and knowledge of those with whom

▲ We're usually uncomfortable when someone breaks our unwritten rules for nonverbal communication. President Lyndon Johnson, for example, was known for standing too close when he talked to people, giving listeners what came to be called "the Johnson treatment." In this 1966 conversation, civil rights leader Whitney Young seemed to be so uncomfortable with President Johnson's space invasion that he closed his eyes. How do you typically respond when someone violates your nonverbal communication expectations?
Yoichi Okamoto/White House Photo Office/Lyndon B. Johnson Presidential Library

expectancy violations theory
A theory suggesting that we develop rules or expectations for appropriate nonverbal behavior and react when those expectations are violated.

we interact. When those expectations (or rules) are violated, we experience heightened arousal (we become more interested or engaged in what's happening), and the nature of our interpersonal relationship with the other person becomes a critical factor as we attempt to interpret and respond to the situation. For example, if someone stands too close to you in conversation, the way you'll react may depend on the credibility, status, and attractiveness of the person who's violating your space. Depending on these factors, you may decide not to move away or to step back. Only rarely do most of us resort to a verbal response.

The Ambiguous Nature of Nonverbal Communication

Most words are given meaning by people within a culture who speak the same language. But the intended meaning of a nonverbal message is known only to the person displaying it. The person may not mean to convey the meaning that an observer interprets from it. In fact, the person may not intend for the behavior to have any meaning at all.

Some people have difficulty expressing their emotions nonverbally. They may have frozen facial expressions or monotone voices. Often it's a challenge to draw meaningful conclusions about these people's behavior, even if we know them quite well. One strategy that helps us interpret others' nonverbal cues is called **perception checking**, as we mentioned in Chapter 2 in our discussion of self-awareness. Jonas, whom we read about earlier in this chapter, was trying to check Danita's perceptions when he asked whether she was mad. To check your own perceptions, observe in detail the nonverbal cues, make your own interpretation, and then do one (or both) of two things: (1) Ask the people you're observing how they feel or what's going on, and/or (2) run your interpretation by another observer to get a second opinion or more input before you draw a conclusion.

perception checking
The skill of asking other observers or the person being observed whether your interpretation of his or her nonverbal behavior is accurate.

DIVERSITY & COMMUNICATION

Lessons from a Student in a Wheelchair

When many people think of cultural diversity, they may only think about nationalities and customs in other countries. But it's important to consider other forms of cultural diversity that may relate to physical or learning ability, sex and gender identity, racial and ethnic diversity, and so forth.[17]

The following is an important lesson about nonverbal communication and cultural sensitivity. With his permission, we tell our student Kurt's story: Kurt has been in a wheelchair for most of his life as a result of having a condition from birth called osteogenesis imperfecta (OI). This condition causes a person's bones to become brittle and break easily. Some people with OI are ambulatory on their own. But many others, like Kurt, use wheelchairs to facilitate their lives. One day we were discussing nonverbal cues and awareness in class, and Kurt recounted a situation he had experienced multiple times. Recently, in a crowded elevator on campus, another student rested his hand on one of Kurt's grips—the handles on the back of most wheelchairs. Kurt recognized the extra weight on his chair, so he gently reached over his shoulder and slid the person's hand off. Yet this person was so oblivious and engrossed in conversation that he put his hand back on the grip. Kurt said he realized that some people don't understand that "his wheelchair feels like part of his body," so the touch on the chair was a nonverbal violation. He didn't make a big deal out of it at the time, but revealed that he has commented on these forms of intrusion in the past. Kurt hopes to educate people that, for him, when people touch his wheelchair (usually out of ignorance or a lack of awareness), it's an uninvited touch on his body.

As you think about nonverbal communication and its link to culture, we encourage you to broaden your view of what constitutes "culture." It's important that we all continue to be enlightened about *many* forms of diversity, so that we can become more appropriate and sensitive communicators.

The Continuous Nature of Nonverbal Communication

Words have a beginning and an end. You can point to the first word in this sentence and underline the last one. Our nonverbal behaviors are not as easily dissected because they're continuous. Imagine you're standing in the hallway after class, talking to a classmate. You both make eye contact as you talk, and your facial expressions coordinate with what you're saying. You stand a certain distance apart, move and change your posture as the conversation flows, add a hand gesture or two to emphasize what you're saying, and change your pitch, volume, and rate of speaking to further make yourself understood. Your classmate's cell phone rings. Your classmate apologizes, answers the phone, and makes eye contact with you once again, along with a facial expression of apology. Your classmate then signals to you with a hand gesture that she or he has to go, and you understand that your conversation is over. You wave goodbye, break eye contact, and go your separate ways, and your nonverbal behaviors go with you. In this simple example, the nonverbal cues are flying faster than the verbal ones, but they're essential in getting the message across. The sheer volume and continuous flow of nonverbal cues—not to mention complications such as culture and emotion—make accurate interpretation a challenge.

The Nonlinguistic Nature of Nonverbal Communication

Even though some writers in the 1960s and 1970s tried to make readers think otherwise, there is no "language of the body." Julius Fast, author of the 1970 book *Body Language*, believed that nonverbal communication was a language with pattern and grammar, just like verbal communication.[18] He suggested that if you were savvy and observant enough, you could quickly and easily interpret certain nonverbal behaviors to mean certain things—in any case, at any time. For example, Fast contended that if a woman sat cross-legged and pumped her foot up and down while talking to a man, that was a clear-cut sign of her romantic interest in him. If someone didn't make eye contact, then she or he should automatically be considered dishonest and untrustworthy. If people crossed their arms in front of them, that indicated hostility.

The problem is that Fast's theories about body language didn't take into account the complexities of individual, contextual, and cultural differences. Pumping the foot up and down might be an indication of nervousness, impatience, or habit, not attraction. Some people are shy; others come from a culture in which making direct eye contact is considered rude. It's important to remember that nonverbal communication doesn't conform to the patterns of a language.

The Multi-channeled Nature of Nonverbal Communication

The "second screen" phenomenon is becoming a norm in the United States and globally. Many people consume media content through the use of multiple devices.

> **RE**CAP
>
> **The Nature of Nonverbal Communication**
>
> - *Nonverbal communication is culture bound.* Nonverbal behaviors vary widely across cultural and co-cultural groups. Interpret nonverbal cues within a cultural context.
> - *Nonverbal communication is rule governed.* We develop rules or expectations for appropriate nonverbal behavior in ourselves and others.
> - *Nonverbal communication is ambiguous.* Nonverbal behavior is difficult to interpret accurately because the meanings for different actions vary from person to person.
> - *Nonverbal communication is continuous.* Unlike the stop-start nature of verbal communication, nonverbal messages flow from one situation to the next.
> - *Nonverbal communication is nonlinguistic.* Nonverbal communication does not have the regularities of vocabulary, grammar, and pattern that language has.
> - *Nonverbal communication is multi-channeled.* Nonverbal cues register on our senses from a variety of sources simultaneously, but we can actually attend to only one nonverbal cue at a time.

According to 2016 research, 47 million adults in the United States watched or listened to TV while simultaneously accessing the Internet on a second device like a smartphone, tablet, or laptop. By 2021, that figure is expected to grow to more than 55 million. Besides searching for information related to what is watched or heard on TV, people use social media, such as Twitter, Instagram, and Facebook, to comment about TV programming or to connect with other people during "down time."[19] But even with your powers of multitasking and an ability to switch your attention rapidly, you can really focus on only one medium at a time.

Nonverbal communication works the same way; nonverbal cues are communicated in multiples or clusters, but we process the cues individually. However, before you try to interpret the meaning of a single nonverbal behavior, look for clusters of corroborating nonverbal cues, in conjunction with verbal behavior, to get the most complete picture possible.

Codes of Nonverbal Communication

4.3 Identify and explain the seven nonverbal communication codes.

Many researchers and theorists have long been fascinated with nonverbal communication, but two who have made perhaps the greatest contributions to our understanding are Paul Ekman and Wallace Friesen—they are sometimes referred to as the "great classifiers" of nonverbal behavior.[20] Next, we introduce and explain these classifications or codes and then provide a few research findings to illustrate how we can apply knowledge of nonverbal communication to further our understanding of human behavior.

Appearance

Many cultures around the world place a high value on appearance—body size and shape, skin color and texture, hairstyle, and clothing—but it seems like Americans *really* emphasize this one nonverbal cue. In 2019, Americans spent nearly $8.2 billion on cosmetic procedures. Women outpaced men in seeking body modifications, with breast augmentation still being the most prevalent surgical procedure. The practice of injecting substances like Botox into the face and other parts of the body remains the most common nonsurgical procedure—its popularity increased by 17.8 percent between 2015 and 2019.[21]

We put such pressure on ourselves and others to be physically attractive that our self-esteem may decline when we realize we cannot match up with some perceived ideal.[22] Whether they deserve it or not, we tend to put highly physically attractive people on a pedestal. We often attach all sorts of desirable qualities to them, a phenomenon known as the **halo effect**.[23] Research shows that we tend to think physically attractive people are more credible, extraverted, happy, popular, socially skilled, prosperous, employable, persuasive, honest, poised, strong, kind, outgoing, and sexually warm than other people.[24] And studies have shown that college students perceive physically

halo effect
Attaching positive qualities to people who we deem highly physically attractive.

CRITICAL/CULTURAL PERSPECTIVES & COMMUNICATION

How Powerful Is Beauty?

In U.S. culture, as well as many other cultures around the world, physical beauty is power. You might not like or agree with that statement, but we can probably all agree that beautiful people are perceived to have influence over others. People deemed highly physically attractive are often thought of as more persuasive than others and as having greater ability to control other people and their perceptions of them.[25] Sometimes beautiful people do ruthless things to try to protect and hold onto the power they believe they possess.

How affected are you by physical beauty? When in the presence of someone you perceive to be highly physically attractive (based on whatever standards your culture imposes), do you stumble for words or feel self-conscious? Are you concerned about not impressing or measuring up to that person? How is your view of your own level of attractiveness affected when in the presence of someone you perceive as more attractive than you? Although you may find this discussion superficial or distasteful, these questions are important to consider, especially within the field of communication studies. Do you change your communication style when in the presence of a beautiful person? What influence or power does that person have over you?

---

attractive teachers to be more approachable than other teachers and give them higher evaluation scores.[26]

Another aspect of physical appearance is clothing, which serves many functions. Chief among them are keeping the body warm and protected; preserving a person's modesty and a society's sense of decency; conveying one's personality, status, and culture; demonstrating one's sexuality; and communicating identification with a group, such as wearing one's university's logo on a T-shirt.[27] **Artifacts** such as jewelry, tattoos, piercings, makeup, cologne, and eyeglasses are also displays of culture and personality. These nonverbal elements of appearance affect how we feel about ourselves and how we are perceived by others.[28]

artifact
Clothing or another element of appearance (e.g., jewelry, tattoos, piercings, makeup, cologne).

Body Movement, Gestures, and Posture

Kinesics is the study of human body movements, gestures, and posture, all of which are affected by your self-esteem and emotional state.[29] For example, when you're feeling upbeat and confident, you're likely to carry yourself more upright and possibly exhibit a "spring in your step." Conversely, if you're having a bad day, your posture might be more slumped over or stooped.

kinesics
Study of human body movements, gestures, and posture.

One component of kinesics is gestures, which are culture bound, context bound, and rule governed.[30] Most gestures are specific to a culture's history and traditions. However, some have cross-cultural, widely understood meanings, such as the pointing gesture and the "come here" and "stay away" gestures accomplished with the placement of the palms and motion of the hands and arms. But here's our repeated warning about nonverbal cues: *Don't assume.* Don't assume a universal interpretation applies to a gesture you've grown up using in your home culture. These forms of nonverbal communication are complicated; some take centuries to develop within a culture.

▼ Texting or talking on your phone while walking slows you down and makes you a dangerous, inefficient walker.
Cathy Yeulet/123RF

Another component of kinesics is how you carry yourself, and more specifically, how you walk. Have you ever thought about how you walk? Each person has a unique walk that can become easily recognizable with even a brief amount of observation.[31] But technology is affecting this phenomenon. Anyone on a college campus has seen this: people staring down at their smartphones, reading or responding to texts, but certainly not watching where they're walking. They meander and weave, almost running into you or inanimate objects. We get it: Smartphones are

SOCIAL MEDIA & COMMUNICATION

Social Media Pressure: Do Comparisons Have Consequences?

We've all seen them—photos and posts on social media by a friend or acquaintance whose life looks infinitely more successful or fun than ours. As we discussed in the Chapter 2 Social Media & Communication box, many people love to post about their physical fitness activities and accomplishments and who can blame them?[32] But what impact, if any, does viewing these posts have on you? Do comparisons prompted by social media affect you negatively? Do they make you competitive? Do they cause your self-esteem to drop, even temporarily?

Two communication scholars, Analisa Arroyo and Steven Brunner, explored online friends' responses to others' social media posts.[33] They found that posts focused on fitness achievements or weight loss successes generate negative body talk, especially from individuals who tend to compare themselves to others. Examples of such responses include, "Wow, congrats on finishing the marathon; I sure couldn't do that. I'd keel over at the second mile" and "Glad you lost weight. Now I'm eating for both of us!"

It's understandable to want to communicate online about our physicality, since it's a powerful nonverbal cue. It's also understandable that we may want to share exciting or unusual experiences with others. All we caution here is to think about the receivers of your online messages (just as we encourage you in this text to become more other-oriented in all of your communication). Might someone suffer self-esteem loss or body image issues because of your posts and photos on social media? Do you have a responsibility here?

---

mesmerizing. But here's something you may not know: Just like talking or texting on your phone makes you a dangerous driver, it also makes you a dangerous, inefficient *walker*.

Eric Lamberg and Lisa Muratori, professors at Stony Brook University in New York, studied the effects of cell phone use on walking behavior.[34] Their results weren't surprising: Like drivers who slow down when using their phones, students who walked across campus while talking or texting walked more slowly than those not using their phones. In addition, cell phone walkers evidenced significant "lateral deviation," straying by as much as 61 percent from a straight path as they walked toward their destination. Although both talking and texting caused walking problems, texters were worse at walking than talkers.

We know students are going to use their smartphones on campus—that's not going to change. But we encourage you to try to be more aware when using your phone. Notice your own nonverbal behavior, such as how you walk, how loudly you talk, and how little eye contact you make (preferring your phone over greeting people as they pass by). You may be motivated to make some changes that can make your life more efficient and productive (or at least keep you from walking into a professor or a wall).

Eye Contact

Do you agree that the eyes are the "windows to the soul"? What can people tell about you by looking into your eyes? Are you comfortable making eye contact with most people or only with people you know well? In 2020 when people started wearing face masks in public to help slow the spread of COVID-19, making eye contact and "smiling with your eyes" (a.k.a. Tyra Banks' "smizing") became even more critical than in pre-pandemic times.[35] When facial expressions are inhibited or covered, using one's eyes to nonverbally communicate becomes even more critical.

Eye behavior is extremely important in many cultures around the world. People judge others' trustworthiness, truthfulness, and sincerity based on eye contact, as well as the presence or absence of tears in the eyes.[36] Table 4.1 summarizes circumstances under which we're more or less likely to make eye contact with a conversational partner.[37]

How much eye contact do you make when speaking to others versus listening to them? In nonverbal communication research, this phenomenon is called the **visual dominance ratio**.[38] Romantic partners may feel agitated by an imbalance in this regard.

visual dominance ratio
Amount of eye contact made while speaking with others, versus listening to them.

TABLE 4.1 When Do We Make Eye Contact?

You are more likely to look at your conversational partner when you . . .	You are less likely to look at your conversational partner when you . . .
• are physically distant from the person. • are discussing impersonal topics. • have nothing else to look at. • are interested in your partner's reactions. • are romantically interested in or like your partner. • wish to dominate or influence your partner. • come from a culture that emphasizes visual contact in interaction. • are an extrovert. • are listening, rather than talking. • are female.	• are physically close to the person. • are discussing intimate topics. • have other objects, people, or backgrounds to look at. • aren't romantically interested in or dislike your partner. • come from a culture that doesn't value visual contact in interaction. • are an introvert. • are embarrassed, ashamed, sorrowful, sad, or submissive. • are trying to hide something. • are male.

For example, suppose you're the partner who maintains a lot of direct eye contact—no matter if you're speaking or listening. But when you start speaking, your partner turns her or his attention to a phone, other people, a computer or TV screen, or other distractions, which leaves you feeling unimportant and unheard. Some people may be unaware that they exhibit poor eye contact while listening, but for others, it's an intentional power move.

Facial Expressions

Actor/comedian Steve Carell has a very expressive face. Researchers suggest that the human face is capable of producing 250,000 different facial expressions.[39] Steve Carell can probably make them all.

As early as 1872, when Charles Darwin systematically studied the expression of emotion in both humans and animals, scientists realized that nonverbal cues are the primary ways humans communicate emotion.[40] As we stated earlier in this chapter, facial and eye expressions, along with posture, gestures, and body movements (such as how we walk) reveal our feelings.[41] Your face tends to express which *kind* of emotion you're feeling, whereas your body reveals the intensity or how *much* emotion you're feeling.

You've downloaded a new app on your phone and show it to your romantic partner or a friend. Or as an interviewer reads your résumé, you sit in silence across the desk from her or him. In both of these situations, you scan the other person's face, eagerly awaiting some reaction. To interpret someone's facial expressions accurately, you need to focus on what the other person may be thinking or feeling. It helps if you know the person well, can see her or his whole face, have plenty of time to observe, and understand the situation that prompted the reaction.[42]

Even if you don't know people well, you can still learn a lot from their facial expressions. For example, Oxford scholar Peter Collett analyzed the facial expressions of U.S. President Donald Trump during his 2016 campaign and the early stages of assuming the presidency.[43] Collett noted the "sheer variety" of "dramatic and over-stated" facial expressions that the president displayed. He then summarized these nonverbal cues into seven categories, including the "alpha face" (designed to communicate a macho personality by lowering the brows, narrowing the eyes, and firmly setting the mouth). Another category that Collett termed the "puckered chin" incorporated a "zipped smile." This facial expression is accomplished by pulling the chin in toward the chest and using a smile that doesn't reveal the teeth. According to Collett, this oft-used facial expression is in response to feeling threatened.

▲ You can learn a lot from people's facial expressions. On the left is what nonverbal communication expert Peter Collett calls U.S. President Donald Trump's "alpha face" and on the right is his "puckered chin" incorporating a "zipped smile."
Mike Pont/WireImage/Getty Images (left), Andy Katz/PACIFIC PRESS/Alamy Stock Photo (right)

How accurately do we interpret emotions expressed on the face? Researchers who have attempted to measure subjects' skill in identifying the emotional expressions of others have found it a tricky business. Ekman and Friesen determined that the human face universally exhibits six primary emotions: happiness, sadness, surprise, fear, anger, and disgust or contempt.[44] However, researchers at Ohio State University have documented people's abilities to consistently express twenty-one recognizable facial expressions that reflect combined, even contradictory or conflicting, emotions, such as "happily disgusted" or "sadly angry."[45]

Even though our faces provide a great deal of information about emotions, we quickly learn to control our facial expressions. One fascinating study examined children's facial expressions when they received either wonderful, new toys or broken, disappointing toys.[46] When they received the disappointing toys, the children showed a flash of disappointment on their faces, but then very quickly they masked their disappointment and changed their facial expressions to reveal a more positive, socially appropriate reaction. Even very young children learn to control the way an emotion registers on their face.

Touch

Touch is the most powerful form of nonverbal communication; it's also the most misunderstood and carries the potential for the most problems if ill-used. The COVID-19 pandemic may have caused you to reevaluate how and under what circumstances you touch your face, surfaces, and other people. Upon receiving recommendations from the Centers for Disease Control and Prevention (CDC) to avoid touching our eyes, nose, and mouth, how many of us realized *just how often we touch our faces*? Common habits such as chewing your nails or holding your chin in your hand while watching TV are now considered possible delivery systems for germs.[47] We've already discussed how we may, as a culture, need to change our views of the importance of the basic handshake, after receiving warnings to protect our health by limiting contact with other people.

Countless studies on touch, termed **haptics** in research, have shown that intimate human contact is vital to our personal development, well-being, and physical health.[48] Being deprived of affection tends to lead to psychological problems, but it also impacts how well we sleep and our ability to cope with physical pain.[49] As a culture, we may need to rethink our touch behavior, especially in light of the recent pandemic when isolation negatively impacted many people's physical and mental health.

haptics
The study of human touch.

Think about your role models and the lessons you learned about touch while growing up. If you grew up in a two-parent family, did your parents show each other affection in your presence? If not, you may have grown up believing that affectionate touching should not be done in front of others. As an adult, you may be uncomfortable with public displays of affection. If you grew up with parents or family members who were affectionate with each other and their children, your **touch ethic**—what you consider appropriate touching—as an adult is influenced by that experience.50 We don't mean to insinuate that a touch ethic that accepts public affection is somehow more psychologically healthy than one that reserves touching for private moments. But what if you date or partner with someone whose experiences growing up led to a very different touch ethic than yours? You may be headed for some conflict but, ideally, some compromise as well.

▲ Our views of appropriate touch, termed the *touch ethic*, are typically formed early in life, as we interact with family members. Andy Dean/123RF

touch ethic
A person's own guidelines or standards as to appropriate and inappropriate touch.

The amount of touch we need, initiate, tolerate, and receive also depends on our cultural background.51 Certain cultures are high contact—meaning that touching is quite commonplace—such as some European and Middle Eastern cultures in which men kiss each other on the cheek as a greeting and may even hold hands. Other cultures are low contact, such as some Asian cultures in which public demonstrations of affection are rare and considered inappropriate.52 A recent U.S. study examined Mexican Americans' and European (Caucasian) Americans' comfort with and beliefs about affectionate touch. Findings indicated that Mexican Americans believed affectionate touch to be more culturally acceptable than European Americans. Mexican American men and women alike were more comfortable with affectionate touch than European Americans, while Caucasian men were the least comfortable with and accepting of affectionate touch.53

The Voice

"We have nothing to fear but fear itself."

"Ask not what your country can do for you—ask what you can do for your country."

"I have a dream . . . I have a dream today."

"I am not a crook."

"Mr. Gorbachev, tear down this wall."

"There is not a black America or a white America or Latino America or Asian America— there's the United States of America."

If you recognize these statements as having been made by American leaders and you have heard them live or on recordings, you're likely to read them aloud (or hear them in your mind) using the same pauses and changes in pitch, volume, and emphasis as did the famous speakers. John F. Kennedy greatly emphasized the word *not*, as in "Ask NOT what your country. . . . " Martin Luther King Jr. used rising pitch and increased volume as he uttered the word *dream* over and over again in his speech. Barack Obama used a rapid rate of speech for the first part of his statement about America and diversity, then slowed down to emphasize his last six words. These leaders used the tremendous capacity and versatility of the voice to create memorable moments.

Like your face, your voice is a major vehicle for communicating your thoughts, your emotions, and the nature of your relationships with others. It also provides information about your self-confidence and influences how you're perceived.54 The pitch, rate, and

paralanguage (vocalics)
Nonverbal aspects of voice, such as pitch, rate, volume, or use of silence.

volume at which you speak and your use of silence—elements termed **paralanguage** or **vocalics**—all provide important communication clues. Most of us would conclude, as has research, that a speaker who mumbles, speaks very slowly and softly, continually mispronounces words, and uses "uh" and "um" is less credible and persuasive than one who speaks clearly, rapidly, fluently, and with appropriate volume.[55]

Sometimes it is surprising or jarring when a person's physical appearance doesn't seem to match her or his voice.[56] A famous example is former boxing champ Mike Tyson, whose high-pitched voice isn't what we tend to expect out of someone with such a muscular physique. Transgender people often struggle with voices that do not "match" their outward physical appearance.[57] In general, it is easier for trans men (biologically female persons who transition to male) to adjust their voices to be lower in pitch than trans women to raise their pitch, given that men typically have lower-pitched voices. Some trans men and trans women seek hormone treatments, speech therapy, and surgery of the larynx to alter their voices, but many believe that a transition can be complete enough without including vocal transformation.[58]

Physical Environment, Space, and Territory

Many college faculty and students experienced the challenge of shifting from face-to-face campus learning to online-only instruction during the COVID-19 pandemic. One of the changes that emerged was how students and professors were able to view each other's homes via video conferencing services like Zoom and Webex. Whereas Zoom offers a wide variety of virtual backgrounds you can use to mask your real environment and protect your privacy, not all services have this capacity.[59] As a student participating in virtual classes, what choices did you make about the personal space you shared on camera? One of your textbook coauthors decided to change it up a bit, moving her laptop to her piano, so she could start a lesson by playing the ominous opening notes of Beethoven's Ninth Symphony. That may not have been the best choice of music, but she feared students would tire of the same old background of her home office. What nonverbal messages do you think your classmates and instructors received about you from seeing part of your home environment? What messages did you receive about them?

You may be unused to looking at the environment as a form of nonverbal communication, but the miniworld you create for yourself reveals a good deal about you. Also, your preferred amount of space, the level of ownership you attach to that space, and your behavior as you delineate and protect that space are fascinating nonverbal elements that researchers continue to study.[60]

The Physical Environment   What's so great about a corner office with wall-to-wall windows? It's one of many indications in American culture of high status. In a working world increasingly structured into cubicles, an employee's work location serves as a symbol of importance.[61] The physical environment is important to the study of nonverbal communication in two ways:

- The choices we make about the environments in which we live and operate reveal a good deal about who we are; physical environments are extensions of our personalities.[62] We tend to put our "signature" on our environments by adorning the settings in which we work, study, and reside to make them unique and personal.
- Nonverbal behavior is altered by the various environments in which we communicate.[63] Formal settings may make our movements more restrained, our body posture more rigid, and our speech limited and whispered. Informal settings tend to cause us to expand and relax our nonverbal behaviors.

One of the more cutting-edge and interesting lines of research into the environment as a form of nonverbal communication surrounds designing spaces for people with disabilities.[64] Although those without physical disabilities might think this area pertains to building ramps and installing elevators in older buildings, design for disability means much more. Some examples include placing extensive Braille signage on campuses (not just in elevators), retrofitting computer labs to offer people with disabilities better access to technology, and providing furniture design in classrooms that assimilates into the environment and accommodates learners of all physical types.[65]

Space Imagine that you're sitting alone at a long, rectangular table in your campus library. As you sit dutifully with your head in a textbook, you're startled when a complete stranger sits directly across from you at the table. Because there are several empty chairs at the other end of the table, you may feel uncomfortable that this unknown individual has invaded *your* area.

Every culture has well-established ways of regulating spatial relations. How physically close we are willing to get to others relates to how well we know them, to considerations of power and status, and to our cultural background.[66]

A pioneer in helping us understand personal space was Edward T. Hall, who studied **proxemics**, or the distances that people allow between themselves and objects or other people. Hall identified four spatial zones, which are diagrammed in Figure 4.2:[67]

- *Intimate space.* The most personal communication occurs when people are from 0 to 1 ½ feet apart. Unless we're forced to stand in a crowded space, intimate space is open only to those with whom we are well acquainted.
- *Personal space.* Most of our conversations with family and friends occur when we are 1 ½ to 4 feet apart. We feel uncomfortable if someone we don't know well enters our personal space zone on purpose.
- *Social space.* The majority of formal group interactions and many of our professional relationships take place in the social space zone, which ranges from 4 to 12 feet.
- *Public space.* Many public speakers position themselves at least 12 feet away from their audiences, but interpersonal communication doesn't usually occur in the public space zone.

The specific space that you and others choose depends on several variables, most specifically your cultural background.[68] Generally, however, the more you like people, the closer you tend to stand next to them. Higher-status and larger people are afforded more space than lower-status and smaller people.[69] We also tend to stand closer to others in a large room than we do in a small room. In general, women tend to stand closer to others than men do.[70]

Territory The study of how people use space and objects to communicate occupancy or ownership of space is termed **territoriality**.[71] You assumed ownership of that part of the table in the library and the right to determine who sat with you. You may have reacted negatively not only because your sense of personal space was invaded, but also because the intrusive stranger broke a cultural rule governing territoriality.

You announce your ownership of space with **territorial markers**—things and actions that signify that an area has been claimed. If you arrive early to class, for example, you may put your book bag on a chair while you get up and go out into the hall to make a call on your cell phone. That book bag signifies temporary ownership of

proxemics
The study of how close or far away from people and objects we position ourselves.

territoriality
The study of how humans use space and objects to communicate occupancy or ownership of space.

territorial marker
A thing or action that signifies that an area has been claimed.

FIGURE 4.2 Edward T. Hall's Four Zones of Space

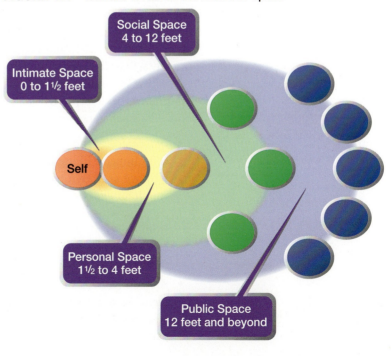

> **RE**CAP
>
> **Codes of Nonverbal Communication**
>
> | | |
> |---|---|
> | Appearance | Influences perceptions of credibility and attractiveness. |
> | Body Movement, Gestures, and Posture | Communicate information, status, warmth, credibility, interest in others, attitudes, and liking. |
> | Eye Contact | Conveys trustworthiness, sincerity, honesty, and interest. |
> | Facial Expressions | Reveal thoughts and express emotions and attitudes. |
> | Touch | Communicates intimacy, affection, and rejection. |
> | Voice | Communicates emotion and clarifies the meaning of messages through pitch, rate, and volume. |
> | Environment | Communicates information about the person who functions in that environment; provides context that alters behavior. |
> | Space | Provides information about status, power, and intimacy. |
> | Territory | Provides cues as to use, ownership, and occupancy of space. |

your seat. If you returned to find that someone had moved your stuff and was sitting in your seat, you would probably become indignant. The most common form of territorial marker is a lock. We lock our doors, windows, cars, offices, briefcases, TVs (using V-chips), and computers (using passwords) to keep out intruders.

While we traditionally think of space as a physical dimension, with increased accessibility and use of technology, we have begun to think of space differently.[72] With the ease of hacking into personal computers and smartphones these days, we all have to face the reality of someone violating our territory and gaining access to our personal information and communication with others. As hacking increases, more innovative methods of protecting private information continue to be developed, such as anti-skimming wallets and two-step authentication systems. It seems we are in a tug-of-war with regard to who wins the privacy–territory battle at any given point in time.

How to Interpret Nonverbal Cues More Accurately

4.4 Explain Mehrabian's three-part framework for interpreting nonverbal cues.

How do we make sense of all the nonverbal cues we receive from others? If you earnestly want to accurately interpret and sensitively respond to someone's nonverbal communication, you must be willing to spend time and effort to develop this skill. Enhancing your interpretive skills requires, first, an awareness of the importance of nonverbal elements in the communication process. A second requirement is the willingness and emotional maturity to make your own behavior secondary to that of someone else. If you're so wrapped up in yourself that you can think about and deal only with how *you're* feeling, what *you're* thinking, and what *you* want at a given moment, your ability to take in others' nonverbal cues, interpret them accurately, and respond appropriately will be hampered.

Albert Mehrabian provides a three-part framework that can help you improve your nonverbal interpretive skills. Mehrabian found that we synthesize and interpret nonverbal cues along three primary dimensions: immediacy, arousal, and dominance.[73]

immediacy
Nonverbal behaviors that communicate feelings of liking, pleasure, and closeness.

- *Immediacy.* Mehrabian contends that **immediacy**—nonverbal cues that communicate liking and engender feelings of pleasure and closeness—explains why we're drawn to some people but not others.[74] In U.S. social contexts, we watch for eye contact, smiling and other pleasant facial expressions, head nods, an open and relaxed posture, a body orientation toward us rather than away from us, close proximity, a rising intonation in the voice, and culture- and context-appropriate touch to find out whether someone likes us or views us favorably.[75]

arousal
Nonverbal behaviors that communicate feelings of interest and excitement.

- *Arousal.* Nonverbal cues of **arousal** communicate feelings of interest and excitement. As nonverbal scholar Peter Andersen puts it, arousal is "the degree to which a person is stimulated or activated."[76] Primary arousal cues include increased eye contact; closer conversational distances; increased touch; animated vocal expressions (such as laughing); more direct body orientation, smiling, and active facial expressions; and interactive synchrony (or mimicry, as discussed earlier in this chapter).[77]

- *Dominance.* The third dimension of Mehrabian's framework communicates the balance of power in a relationship. **Dominance** cues indicate status, position, and importance. People who are high in status tend to have a relaxed body posture, less direct body orientation toward lower-status people, a downward head tilt, and less direct eye contact, smiling, head nodding, and facial animation than lower-status people.[78] As we alluded to earlier, "power people" usually have more space around them; they have bigger offices and more barriers (human and nonhuman) protecting them. They may communicate their sense of power through clothing, possessions, and their use of time.

▲ Who is the most powerful person in this room? What nonverbal cues indicate that person's dominance?
Andre Andrade/Corbis/Getty Images

dominance
Nonverbal behaviors that communicate power, status, and control.

An Application of Nonverbal Communication Research: Detecting Deception

4.5 Describe the primary nonverbal cues associated with deception.

Communication research is incredibly practical and useful; we can apply it to our daily lives and see real results. However, one area of nonverbal communication research that is especially helpful is deception detection.[79] What nonverbal cues are reliable indicators of deceit? What do you need to look and listen for? What behaviors do you enact when you are being less than truthful? Granted, nonverbal cues can change depending on whether you're telling a "little white lie" ("No, that outfit does not make you look fat") versus a "big whopper" ("No, I did not cheat on you"). Cues can also change if someone has had time to prepare a lie, versus lying spontaneously, on the spur of the moment.

People intent on lying (or who lie easily, unconcerned with ethics or the impact of their actions) can learn commonly held beliefs about deception cues and can *change* these cues.[80] For instance, it used to be a commonly held belief that people could not look others in the eye and lie, straight to their faces. A lack of, or break in, eye contact was seen as a reliable deception cue. However, this is no longer the case! Once word got out about eye contact and lying, liars changed their behavior so they wouldn't get caught. The "best" liars now believe that successful deception is associated with keeping a steady, normal gaze when lying.

The most reliable, accurate nonverbal deception cues aren't visual, but auditory. Scholars contend that we should pay attention to people's voices, rather than trying to read their eyes, facial expressions, or body positioning.[81] Here's why: Vocal cues are the hardest to control because they are so connected to the body's physical state at the time of deception. Just like it's hard to control a shaking or cracking voice when you're nervous or a change in pitch when you're surprised, fearful, or excited, it's hard to regulate your voice (and the breathing that produces sound) when your body is activated by an act of deception.

response latency
How long it takes someone to respond to another person's communication.

message duration
How short or long someone's message is, typically in response to another person's communication.

A change in **response latency**, the amount of time it takes someone to respond to a question, can also be a sign of deception. For example, if someone responds more quickly to a question than normal, this vocal cue might indicate deception. Alternatively, if someone who usually responds quickly takes a longer than usual time to reply, that might also indicate deception.[82]

A change in **message duration** can also be a sign of deception. If someone typically gives brief responses to another person's communication, an exceptionally long response from that person might indicate deception. Alternatively, if a typically "chatty" and long-winded person starts answering questions with short, abrupt comments or one-word answers, this behavior might also imply deception. Other reliable vocal deception cues include disfluency (struggling for words, not having a normal rhythm to speech); speech errors (lapses in pronunciation or using incorrect words or word substitutions); filled pauses (short silences filled with utterances like "um," "er," or "ah"); and an unusual shift in volume, pitch, or rate of speaking.[83]

Most of us have extra energy or activation in our bodies when we choose to be deceptive, mainly because we were taught or we believe that deceiving others is wrong. This extra body activation has to go somewhere and for many of us, that energy is released through our extremities.[84] So if you observe someone making unusual foot movements or perhaps clutching their hands together or wringing them, those cues might also indicate deception.

Note that we keep saying "*might* be a cue of deception," because you can never know for certain. We've provided you with research findings on a number of nonverbal deception cues, but caution you not to apply these findings too liberally. You don't want to declare that people are lying to you when they aren't. Many factors must be taken into account when interpreting nonverbal cues as indications of deception.[85] Best look for a cluster of nonverbal cues, rather than only one. The safest approach is to have a baseline of information about a person. If you know how a person normally behaves, then you can look, listen, and evaluate cues more accurately.

When you attempt to interpret someone's nonverbal communication, realize that there's a good deal of room for error. Humans are complex, and they don't always send clear signals. But the more you learn about nonverbal communication and the more you become aware of your own nonverbal communication and the nonverbal cues of others, the greater your chances of accurately perceiving and interpreting someone's message.

STUDY GUIDE: PRINCIPLES FOR A LIFETIME — CHAPTER 4

Why Focus on Nonverbal Communication?

4.1 Provide four reasons for studying nonverbal communication.

PRINCIPLE POINTS: Nonverbal communication is communication other than written or spoken language that creates meaning for someone. It is important to become more aware of your own nonverbal communication and to enhance your ability to detect and interpret others' nonverbal cues more accurately. Nonverbal messages communicate our feelings and attitudes and are critical to successful relationships. They can substitute for, complement, contradict, repeat, regulate, and accent verbal messages. Nonverbal messages are also more believable than verbal messages.

PRINCIPLE TERMS:

nonverbal communication
interactive synchrony
mimicry

PRINCIPLE SKILLS:

1. Give an example of how you or someone you know has used nonverbal communication to substitute for, complement, contradict, repeat, regulate, or accent a verbal message.
2. Conduct an honest assessment of your skill level, as a nonverbal communicator. Do others have a hard time accurately interpreting your nonverbal cues? In other words, are you easy or hard to read? Do you wish to change any of your nonverbal cues? If you want to successfully incorporate new behaviors into your repertoire and rid yourself of unwanted past behaviors, how will you go about this?

The Nature of Nonverbal Communication

4.2 Discuss six elements that reveal the nature of nonverbal communication.

PRINCIPLE POINTS: Nonverbal communication is culture bound, rule governed, ambiguous, continuous, nonlinguistic, and multi-channeled.

PRINCIPLE TERMS:

expectancy violations theory
perception checking

1. In addition to the personal space rules described in the chapter, give an example of another nonverbal communication rule you hold and what happens when people violate it.
2. Think about how much you have traveled in your life, even within your own state or territory. Did you have any trouble understanding people's nonverbal communication in any area or place you visited? Did you feel that your own nonverbal cues were correctly interpreted?

Codes of Nonverbal Communication

4.3 Identify and explain the seven nonverbal communication codes.

PRINCIPLE POINTS: Ekman and Friesen identified the primary codes or categories of nonverbal behavior, which are enacted differently by people depending on their cultural background. Each code has been researched extensively and applied to different contexts and relationships. The primary codes include appearance, kinesics (body movement), eye contact, facial expressions, touch (haptics), the voice (paralanguage or vocalics), the physical environment, and how we interact with space (proxemics).

PRINCIPLE TERMS:

halo effect
artifact
kinesics
visual dominance ratio
haptics
touch ethic
paralanguage (vocalics)
proxemics
territoriality
territorial marker

PRINCIPLE SKILLS:

1. Think about the research findings regarding the various codes or categories of nonverbal communication presented in this chapter. Does your experience with nonverbal communication correspond to these findings?
2. Inventory your nonverbal communication according to the codes or categories provided in this section of the text. What nonverbal codes represent your strengths? Which areas are weaker for you and need improvement? How will you work to change those behaviors?
3. Provide examples of body movements or expressions that reveal each of the six primary emotions listed below. Then generate possible alternative meanings for the same movement. For example, having your arms crossed across your chest might reveal anger or that you're closed off and not open to conversation. It might also mean that you're just chilly. We've provided an example to get you started.

Emotion	Body Movements	Alternative Meaning of Movement
Embarrassment	Covering your face with your hands	Could also indicate deception
Happiness		
Anger		
Surprise		
Fear		
Disgust		
Sadness		

How to Interpret Nonverbal Cues More Accurately

4.4 Explain Mehrabian's three-part framework for interpreting nonverbal cues.

PRINCIPLE POINTS: It takes time and effort to develop our skills in detecting and accurately interpreting others' nonverbal communication. Albert Mehrabian's work suggests that nonverbal cues can communicate *immediacy* (liking and pleasure), *arousal* (excitement and interest), and *dominance* (status, position, and importance).

PRINCIPLE TERMS:

immediacy   dominance
arousal

PRINCIPLE SKILLS:

1. Find a quiet place (where you won't be noticed) to sit and observe people in casual conversation. Can you detect who likes who and who dislikes who (and by how much)? Who holds more status and power in the conversation, based on the nonverbal cues you observed?
2. Consider how you behave nonverbally when interacting with someone you are attracted to, someone you like (as a friend, acquaintance, or coworker), and someone you don't like. Would an observer be able to detect, from your nonverbal cues, how you feel about these people?

An Application of Nonverbal Communication Research: Detecting Deception

4.5 Describe the primary nonverbal cues associated with deception.

PRINCIPLE POINTS: While we cannot be certain someone is deceiving us based on their nonverbal communication, researchers have found some nonverbal cues that are reliably associated with deception. Vocal cues tend to be more reliable cues of deception than eye contact, facial expressions, and body movements, because the voice is affected by emotions and hard to control. To form a judgment about truthfulness, it helps to get a baseline of information about how a person behaves nonverbally and then compare "normal" behavior to behavior that is out of the norm.

PRINCIPLE TERMS:

response latency   message duration

PRINCIPLE SKILLS:

1. Which nonverbal cues do you believe are the most reliable when attempting to detect deception in others?
2. What nonverbal signals do you make when you are less than truthful in your communication with someone? Do your nonverbal cues align with research findings?

CHAPTER 5

LISTENING AND RESPONDING

Most people do not listen with the intent to understand; they listen with the intent to reply. —DR. STEPHEN R. COVEY

Mimagephotography/Shutterstock

CHAPTER OUTLINE

- The Importance of Listening and Responding Skills
- How We Listen
- Listening Styles
- Listening Barriers
- Listening Skills
- Responding Skills
- Study Guide: *Principles for a Lifetime*

LEARNING OBJECTIVES

5.1 Explain the principle of listening and responding thoughtfully to others.

5.2 Identify the elements of the listening process.

5.3 Describe four listening styles.

5.4 Identify and describe barriers that keep people from listening well.

5.5 Identify and use strategies that can improve your listening skills.

5.6 Identify and use appropriate responding skills.

You have heard about distracted driving—driving while texting, talking on your phone, or looking at your GPS instead of the road. But have you heard about distracted listening? Researchers have found that even the visible presence of a phone when you are face-to-face with someone distracts from the quality of the conversation.[1] Your tendency to periodically glance at the phone to see if someone has sent you a message results in distracted listening.

In this chapter, we focus on the principle of increasing your sensitivity to others—your awareness of and concern for them—by listening. Becoming sensitive to others includes more than just understanding and interpreting their words, thoughts, and ideas. It also involves understanding the emotions underlying the words and unspoken messages of others.[2] Increasing your skill in listening to others is one of the most productive ways to increase all these aspects of your communication sensitivity.

As shown in our familiar model of the Communication Principles for a Lifetime (Figure 5.1), effective communicators do more than absorb a message; they also provide an appropriate response to the speaker. We'll address both listening and responding to others in this chapter.

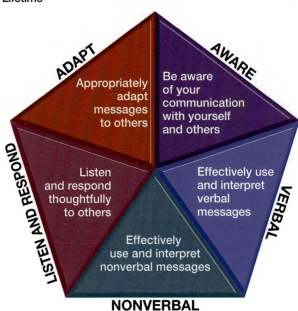

FIGURE 5.1 Communication Principles for a Lifetime

The Importance of Listening and Responding Skills

5.1 Explain the principle of listening and responding thoughtfully to others.

Some researchers suggest that because listening is the first communication skill we learn (we respond to sounds even while in our mother's womb), it's also the most important skill.[3] Listening and responding skills are vital as we develop relationships with others, collaborate, and listen to lectures and speeches.

You spend more time listening to others than almost anything else you do. Americans spend up to 90 percent of a typical day communicating with people, and spend more of that time listening to others than any other communication activity.[4] As Figure 5.2 shows, you spend the *least* amount of your communication time writing, yet you receive more training in writing than in any other communication skill.[5] Although these statistics are averages and vary from person to person, they give you an idea of the relationships among the various modes of communication.[6] Most people have not had any formal training at all in listening or responding.[7] Reading this chapter will provide you with the information and skills many people lack.

Listening Enhances Our Relationships with Others

Your skill as a listener has important implications for the relationships you establish with others.[8] In interpersonal communication situations, the essence of being a good conversationalist is being a good listener. Listening to others is a way to express your interest in, compassion for, and even your love for another.[9] We feel closer to other people when we sense they have truly listened to us.[10] Even when using social media, we expect our friends to "listen" to us when we post or tweet.[11] Listening also influences how others respond to us; when people are in the presence of someone whom they perceive to be a good listener, they are likely to respond with greater empathy and interest.[12] One research study found that a key difference between couples who remain married and those who divorce is the ability to listen to each other.[13] **Closeness communication bias** is a specific problem that occurs when listening to people we know well and love. This bias occurs because we *think* we know what the other person will say, so we don't focus on his or her message.[14] Partners in marriages that endure report that being a good listener is key to a satisfying marital relationship. As French author André Maurois put it, a happy marriage is ". . . a long conversation that always seems too short."[15]

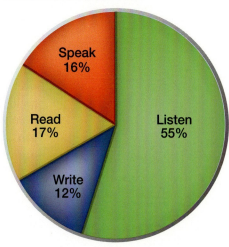

FIGURE 5.2 What You Do with Your Communication Time

closeness communication bias
A listening problem that occurs when people stop listening to a close friend or family member because they think they already know what the other person will say.

Listening Helps Us Work Collaboratively with Others

People who are perceived to be good listeners enjoy greater success in their jobs than those who are viewed to be poor listeners.[16] For example, physicians, nurses, and other healthcare professionals who are good listeners are perceived to be more competent and skilled than those who listen poorly.[17] Research has also found that workers who thought of their supervisors as "good listeners" reported being happier, more satisfied on the job, and more content with their work–life balance.[18] Research has also found that people rate organizations more favorably if they are perceived to "listen and respond," even via social media.[19]

One of the hallmarks of an effective leader is being a good listener.[20] Author Robert Caro, who has spent a lifetime studying U.S. President Lyndon B. Johnson, found that although Johnson was perceived as a persuasive and sometimes domineering speaker, he actually spent more time listening than speaking when in the presence of others. In transcribing Johnson's telephone recordings Caro concluded, "People think Johnson talks all the time. If you listen to these tapes, he often doesn't talk at all for the first few minutes . . . he's listening for what the guy really wants . . . ."[21] Effective listeners connect with those whom they lead and have a genuine interest in the needs of others.

One study found that being a good listener was the most important skill to have when working with others in groups and teams.[22] Your ability to listen and connect with others will affect your value to other group members whether you are the appointed or emerging leader of a group or a member.[23] Group members who verbally dominate meetings are not usually held in high esteem. Groups need people who can listen and connect conversational threads that often become tangled or dropped during group dialogue.

Listening Links Speaker and Audience

Without effective listening skills, you'll likely miss some messages in public speaking situations. Listening skills are especially important when you need to understand and retain spoken information.[24] There is evidence, for example, that listening skills correlate with academic ability. One study found that almost half of college students who had low scores on a listening test were on academic probation at the end of their first year in college. In comparison, just over 4 percent of the students who had high scores on the same listening test were on academic probation.[25] Improving your listening skills can improve your grade-point average.[26] Neuroscience research has also found that listening is enhanced when the brainwaves of speakers and listeners are in sync.[27] So being a good listener can literally help you make a positive neurological connection with a speaker.

Listening is not just for audience members; it is also important for speakers. Good speakers are audience-centered. They consider the needs of their listeners first. They understand what will hold listeners' attention. Many effective speakers acquire this knowledge by listening to audience members one on one before a talk or lecture. Effective speakers also listen to the feedback from their audiences and use that feedback to adjust their speeches while giving them.[28]

How We Listen

5.2 Identify the elements of the listening process.

Do you know someone who is interpersonally inert? Interpersonally inert people are those who just don't "get it." You can drop hints that it's late and you'd rather they head home instead of playing another hand of cards, but they don't pick up on your verbal and nonverbal cues. The physiological processes that let their ears translate sound waves into information in the brain may be working so they can *hear* you, but they certainly aren't listening; they are not making sense out of your symbols.

Hearing is the physiological process of decoding sounds. You hear when the sound waves reach your eardrum. Hearing and listening are two different processes.

Listening is the process we use to make sense out of what we hear; it is a complex process of receiving, constructing meaning from, and responding to verbal and nonverbal messages.[29] Listening involves five activities: (1) selecting, (2) attending, (3) understanding, (4) remembering, and—to confirm that listening has occurred—(5) responding. Understanding these five elements in the listening process can help you diagnose where you sometimes get off track when listening and figure out how to get back on track to increase your listening skill.[30]

hearing
The physiological process of decoding sounds.

listening
A complex process of receiving, constructing meaning from, and responding to verbal and nonverbal messages; involves selecting, attending, understanding, remembering, and responding.

Selecting

To listen, you must first **select**, or focus on, one sound among the myriad noises always competing for your attention. Even now, as you are reading this text, there are probably countless sounds within earshot. Stop reading for a moment. What sounds surround you? Do you hear music? Is a TV on? Can you hear traffic noises or birds? Maybe there is the tick of a clock, a whir of a computer, a whoosh of a furnace or an air conditioner. A listener who is sensitive to others selects the sound or nonverbal behavior that symbolizes meaning. The interpersonally inert person does not pick up on the same clues, because he or she is oblivious to the information.

select
To focus on one sound as you sort through the various sounds competing for your attention.

Attending

After selecting a sound, you attend to it. To **attend** is to maintain a *sustained* focus on a particular message. When you change channels on your TV, you first select the channel and then attend to the program you've selected. Just as you tune in to TV programs that reflect your taste in entertainment while you channel surf, you attend to the messages of others that satisfy your needs or whims. Attending to a message is vital to being a good listener, yet there is evidence that our attention span is decreasing.[31] A person who is skilled in maintaining sustained attention to a message (just listening without interrupting) is perceived as a better listener than someone with a "restless mind."[32]

attend
To maintain a sustained focus on a particular message.

Understanding

To **understand** is to assign meaning to messages—to interpret a message by making sense out of what you hear. You can select and attend to sounds and nonverbal cues but not interpret what you see and hear. Understanding occurs when you relate what you hear and see to your experiences or knowledge.[33] Perhaps you have heard the Montessori school philosophy (based on an old Chinese proverb): "I hear and I forget, I see and I remember, I do and I understand." It is when we can relate our experiences to what we hear, see, and do that we achieve understanding.

understand
To assign meaning to messages.

Remembering

To **remember** is to recall information. Remembering is considered part of the listening process because it is the primary way we determine whether a message was understood. But you can't actually retrieve or remember all the bits of information you experience; your eye is not a camera; your ear is not a microphone; your mind is not a hard drive. Sometimes, even though you were present, you have no recollection of what occurred in a particular situation. When we are not aware of our actions, our thoughts, or what we perceive—when we are mindless—our ability to remember what occurs plummets. We increase our ability to remember what we hear by being not only physically present, but also mentally present.

You tend to remember what is important to you (such as the time of a meeting mentioned in a voice message) or something you try to remember (like the information in this text for your next communication test). You tend to remember dramatic information (such as where you were when you heard extremely good news or bad news) or vital information (such as your phone number or your mom's birthday).

remember
To recall information.

Responding

As you learned in Chapter 1, communication is a transactive process, not a one-way, linear one. Communication involves responding to others as well as simply articulating messages. You **respond** to let people know that you understand their message. Your lack of response may signal that you didn't understand the message. Your predominant

respond
To confirm your understanding of a message.

response is often unspoken; direct eye contact and head nods let your partner know you're tuned in. An unmoving, glassy-eyed, frozen stupor may tell your communication partner that you are physically present yet mentally a thousand miles away.[34] As you'll discover in the next section, you likely have a certain style of listening and responding to others.

Listening Styles

5.3 **Describe four listening styles.**

Your **listening style** is your preferred way of making sense out of the messages you hear and see. Researchers have found that you tend to listen using one or more of four listening styles: relational, analytic, critical, and task-oriented.[35] The specific style you use depends on your personality, the specific listening situation, and your listening goal.[36]

listening style
A person's preferred way of making sense out of messages based on his or her personality, listening situation, and listening goal.

Relational Listening Style

Relational listeners tend to prefer listening to people's emotions and feelings. They are especially interested in hearing personal information from others. Perhaps for that reason, evidence suggests that relational-oriented listeners are less apprehensive than people with other listening styles when communicating in small groups and interpersonal situations, and especially when listening to just one other person.[37]

relational listeners
Those who prefer to focus on the emotions and feelings communicated by others verbally and nonverbally.

A person with a relational listening style searches for common interests and seeks to empathize with the feelings of others—she or he connects emotionally with the sentiments and passions others express.[38] Relational listeners seem to have greater skill than other listeners in empathizing with and understanding the thoughts and feelings of others.[39] One study found that jurors who are relational listeners are less likely to find a defendant at fault in a civil court trial, perhaps because of their tendency to empathize with others.[40]

Research also shows that relational listeners have a greater tendency than those with other listening styles to be sympathetic to the person to whom they are listening.[41] A sympathetic listener is more likely to voice concern about the other person's welfare when that person is sharing personal information or news about a stressful situation. A sympathetic listener says, for instance, "Oh, Pat, I'm so sorry to hear about your loss." They are also more likely to use a relational listening style when listening to others share personal information about themselves.[42]

Analytical Listening Style

analytical listeners
Those who withhold judgment, listen to all sides of an issue, and wait until they hear the facts before reaching a conclusion.

Analytical listeners listen for facts and tend to withhold judgment before reaching a specific conclusion. Analytical listeners would make good judges; they generally consider all sides of an issue before making a decision or reaching a conclusion. They tend to listen to an entire message before assessing the validity of the information they hear. To help them analyze information, they take the perspective of the person to whom they are listening, which helps them suspend judgment. Analytical listeners also like the information they hear to be well organized so that they can clearly and easily analyze it. While listening to a rambling personal story, the analytic listener focuses on the facts and details of the story rather than on the emotions being expressed. Analytical listeners prefer listening to rich message content and then finding ways of organizing or making sense of the information.

Critical Listening Style

Critical listeners are good at evaluating the information they hear. They are able to identify inconsistencies in what someone says. They are comfortable listening to detailed, complex information and focusing on the facts, yet they are especially adept at noting contradictions in the facts presented. Critical listeners are also likely to catch errors in the overall logic and reasoning being used to reach a conclusion. In addition, skilled critical listeners are able to effectively recognize patterns in what they hear, compare and contrast new information with previous knowledge, and re-evaluate prior knowledge based on the new information.[43]

▶ A task-oriented listener is interested in achieving a specific outcome.
Image Source Plus/Alamy Stock Photo

Critical listeners tend to be a bit more skeptical and demanding than relational listeners of the information they hear. Researchers call this skepticism **second guessing**—questioning the assumptions underlying a message.[44] It's called second guessing because critical listeners don't always assume that what they hear is accurate or relevant; they make a second guess about the accuracy of the information they hear. Accuracy of information is especially important to critical listeners because if they are going to use the information in some way, they want it to be valid.

critical listeners
Those who prefer to listen for the facts and evidence that support key ideas and an underlying logic; they also listen for errors, inconsistencies, and discrepancies.

second guessing
Questioning the assumptions underlying a message.

task-oriented listeners
Those who look at the overall structure of a message to see what action needs to be taken; they also prefer efficient, clear, and briefer messages.

Task-Oriented Listening Style

Task-oriented listeners are more interested in focusing on a specific outcome or task than on the communication relationship when listening to others. They emphasize completing a specific transaction such as solving a problem, taking action, or making a purchase. Task-oriented listeners focus on verbs—what needs to be done. Consequently, they don't like to listen to rambling, descriptive messages that don't seem to have a point. They appreciate efficient communicators who organize messages so that their listeners can focus on the outcomes—the "bottom line."

The Benefits of Understanding Your Listening Style

There are at least three reasons to think about your listening style and those of others: (1) to enhance your self-awareness, (2) to adapt your own listening style to different situations, and (3) to communicate more effectively.

Enhance Your Self-Awareness Understanding your preferred listening style can help you become more aware of how you behave in communication situations. Some research suggests that women are more likely to be relational listeners, whereas men have a tendency to assume one of the other listening styles.[45] Your listening style, however, may be less influenced by your sex than by the overall approach you take to interpreting and remembering the information you hear. Your cultural traditions, one research team suggests, may have a major influence on your particular listening style. People from a more individualistic, self-focused cultural perspective (such as the United States) tend to be more action-oriented listeners than people from other places. Relational listeners, according to research, are more likely to have collectivistic values, are group-oriented, or were raised in a collaborative cultural tradition (such as some Asian cultures).[46]

You may wonder, "Do I have just one listening style, or do I have more than one?" According to researchers Larry Barker and Kittie Watson, who have done extensive research into listening styles, about 40 percent of all listeners have one primary listening

RECAP

Listening Styles

Relational Listening Style — Listeners prefer to attend to feelings and emotions and to search for common areas of interest when listening to others.

Analytical Listening Style — Listeners prefer to withhold judgment, listen to all sides of an issue, and wait until they hear the facts before reaching a conclusion.

Critical Listening Style — Listeners are likely to listen for the facts and evidence that support key ideas and an underlying logic; they also listen for errors, inconsistencies, and discrepancies.

Task-Oriented Listening Style — Listeners are focused on accomplishing something and look at the overall structure of the message to see what action needs to be taken; they also like efficient, clear, and brief messages.

style that they use, especially if they are under stress. Another 40 percent of listeners use more than one style—for example, they may prefer to listen to evaluate (critical listening style), but they also want the information delivered in a short amount of time, and they want it focused on the task to be accomplished (task-oriented listening style).

About 20 percent of people do not have a specific listening style preference. These individuals may want to avoid listening altogether because they are shy and don't like to be around others in social situations, they may have receiver apprehension, or they may just have listener burnout—they are weary of listening to other people.[47] Or they may not have a predominant style because they are good at adapting to others.

Adapt to Different Listening Situations Knowing your preferred listening style can help you adapt and adjust your listening style to fit the specific listening situation you are experiencing. Evidence suggests that the occasion, time, and place all have an effect on the listening style or styles you adopt.[48] For example, if you tend to be a relational listener and you are listening to a message that has little information about people but lots of technical details, you will have to work harder than other types of listeners to stay tuned in to the message. Research has found that you sometimes adjust your listening style to fit your listening goal.[49] If you are listening to your communication professor tell you what will be covered on the next exam, you may shift to a task-oriented or critical listening style because you want to do well on the test. But when your roommate tells you about his frustrating day, you may adopt a more relational listening style.

Communicate Effectively Your awareness of others' listening styles can help you communicate messages that they are more likely to listen to. If you know that your spouse is an analytical listener, you should communicate a message that is rich in information because that's what your spouse prefers. Tell the analytical listener, "Here are three things I have to tell you," and then say those three things. The information preview tells your analytical listener that you are about to convey three pieces of information. There is evidence that telling a story, rather than just sharing unrelated bits of information, can help people enhance their listening skills; this is especially effective when talking to relational listeners.[50] It may be difficult to determine someone's listening style, especially if you don't know the person very well. But it is worth the time to try and determine what it is. Keep in mind that it is easier to consider the listening styles of people you do know well, such as your family members, coworkers, instructors, or boss.

Listening Barriers

5.4 **Identify and describe barriers that keep people from listening well.**

Although we spend almost half of our communication time listening, some say we don't use that time well. One day after hearing something, most people remember only about half of what was said. Two days later, our retention drops by another 50 percent. The result: Two days after hearing a lecture or speech, most of us remember only about 25 percent of what we heard.

Our listening deteriorates not only when we listen to speeches or lectures, but also when we interact interpersonally or in small groups. Even in the most intimate relationships (or perhaps we should say *especially* in the most intimate relationships), we tune out what others are saying. One study reported that we sometimes pay more attention to strangers than to our close friends or spouses. Married couples tend to interrupt each other more often than unmarried couples and are usually less polite to each other than are strangers involved in a simple decision-making task.[51]

What keeps us from listening well? The most critical elements are (1) self barriers—self-centered habits that work against listening well, (2) information-processing barriers—the way we mentally manage information, and (3) context barriers—the surroundings in which we listen.

Self Barriers

"We have met the enemy and he is us" is an oft-quoted line from the vintage comic strip *Pogo*. Evidence suggests that we are our own worst enemy when it comes to listening to others. We often attend to our own internal dialogues and diatribes instead of to others' messages, and when we do, our listening effectiveness plummets.

Self-Focus A self-focused communicator thinks about what he or she is going to say next rather than listening to the other person. Most of us are egocentric—self-focused—although we may develop a consciousness of others' needs as we grow and mature. Scholars of evolution might argue that it is good that we are self-focused; looking out for number one is what perpetuates the human race. Yet an *exclusive* focus on ourselves inhibits effective communication. While trying to listen, we may be carrying on an internal narration, one that is typically about us. "How long will I have to be here for this lecture?" "Wonder what's for dinner tonight?" "She's still talking—will we be out of here in ten minutes?" Focusing on such internal messages often keeps us from selecting and attending to the other person's message.

What can you do to regain your listening focus if you are focused on yourself rather than on the other person's message? Consider these suggestions:

- *Become aware of the problem.* Become consciously competent. Notice when you find yourself drifting off rather than concentrating on the speaker.
- *Concentrate.* Yes, some messages are boring, useless, and stupid. But even if you think you're listening to such a message, avoid mindlessly tuning it out. Developing a habit of quickly dismissing ideas and messages without making an effort to stay focused on them will degenerate your ability to listen well to other, more important messages.
- *Be active rather than passive.* The key to concentration is finding ways to be actively involved in the communication process. Taking notes when appropriate and providing nonverbal and even sometimes verbal feedback can help keep your focus

on the speaker rather than on yourself. If you don't understand something the speaker says, ask for clarification. Don't just sit there and "take it;" if you find your concentration waning, you'll more than likely "leave it."

Emotional Noise Emotions are powerful. What we see and hear affects our emotions. **Emotional noise** occurs when our emotional arousal interferes with communication effectiveness. Certain words or phrases can arouse emotions very quickly, and, of course, the same word may arouse different emotions in different people. You respond emotionally because of your personal experiences, cultural background, religious convictions, or political philosophy. Words that reflect negatively on your nationality, ethnic origin, or religion can trigger strong emotional reactions. Cursing and obscene language may also reduce your listening efficiency. If you grew up in a home in which R-rated language was never used, four-letter words may distract you.

The emotional state of the speaker may also affect your ability to understand and evaluate what you hear. Research has shown that if you are listening to someone who is emotionally distraught, you will be more likely to focus on his or her emotions than on the content of the message.[52] Another researcher advises that when you are communicating with someone who is emotionally excited, you should remain calm and focused and try simply to communicate your interest in the other person.[53]

Developing an awareness of the effect that emotions have on your listening ability (such as how you feel after reading this section) is a constructive first step to avoid being ruled by unchecked emotions. Becoming consciously aware of our emotions and then talking to ourselves about our feelings is a way to avoid emotional sidetracks and keep your attention focused on the message. When emotionally charged words or actions kick your internal dialogue into high gear, make an effort to quiet it down and steer back to the subject at hand. The principle of self-awareness gives you choice *and* control.

Criticism We usually associate the word *criticism* with negative judgments and attitudes. Although critiquing a message can provide positive as well as negative insights, most of us don't like to be criticized. The well-known advocate for the poor, the late Mother Teresa, once said, "If you judge people, you have no time to love them."[54] Being inappropriately critical of the speaker may distract us from focusing on the message.

There may be times when your intention is not to criticize, but your listening response indicates otherwise. What are some annoying listening behaviors that others might perceive as criticism? Here's a list:

- Interrupting
- Vague or incoherent responses
- Checking your phone
- Looking at your watch
- Searching for someone else as you look around the room
- Fidgeting (tapping, shifting, or fiddling)[55]

It would be unrealistic to suggest that you never share critical opinions about speakers and their messages. It is realistic, however, to monitor your internal critiques of speakers to make sure you are aware of your biases. Good listeners say to themselves, "Although this speaker may be distracting, I am simply not going to let appearance or mannerisms keep my attention from the message." Avoid using your mental energy to criticize a speaker unnecessarily; the longer your mental critique, the less you'll remember.

Information-Processing Barriers

In addition to self barriers that contribute to our loss of focus on messages, the way we process the information we hear may keep us from being good listeners.

---

emotional noise
A form of communication noise caused by emotional arousal.

Four information-processing listening barriers are (1) processing rate, (2) information overload, (3) receiver apprehension, and (4) shifting attention.

Processing Rate You can think faster than people speak. Most people speak 125 words per minute, give or take a few words. You have the tremendous ability, however, to process four to ten times that amount of information. Some people can listen to 600 to 800 words per minute and still make sense out of what a speaker is saying; another estimate puts the processing rate up to 1,200 words per minute. Yet another estimate claims that we think not just in words but also in images and sounds: We can process 2,000 bits of information per minute for short periods of time. This difference between the average speaking rate and your capacity to make sense out of words as they register in your cortical centers can cause trouble. You have extra time on your hands to tune in to your own thoughts rather than focusing on the speaker.[56]

▲ Remaining aware of the dangers of information overload can help you keep electronic messages from distracting you from conversations. It is much harder to give your full attention to another person while continually glancing at your phone for incoming messages.
Olena Yakobchuk/Shutterstock

You can use your information-processing rate to your advantage if you apply this extra time to mentally summarize what a speaker is saying. By periodically sprinkling in mental summaries during a conversation, you can dramatically improve your listening ability and make the speech-rate/thought-rate difference work to your advantage.

Information Overload One word to describe many beleaguered listeners is "weary." We spend 55 percent of our communication time listening, and the pace at which information zips toward us exhausts us. The millions of words we hear each year contribute to our fatigue. The pace has only increased now that much of that information is electronic. Incoming email, texts, voice messages, or social media updates can interrupt conversations and distract us from listening to others.

Again we recommend self-awareness. Be on the alert for drifting attention because of information overload. And when the encroaching information dulls your attentiveness, either take a break or consider conducting some *communication triage*—determining what's urgent and what's not—so that you can focus on the information that is most important.

Receiver Apprehension Just as some people are fearful of presenting a speech or speaking up during a meeting, research suggests that some people are fearful of receiving information. **Receiver apprehension** is fear of misunderstanding or misinterpreting the messages spoken by others or of not being able to adjust psychologically to messages expressed by others.[57] Some people may be fearful of receiving new information because they worry about being able to understand it. Or apprehension may be a characteristic of the way some people respond psychologically to information; they may not be able to make sense out of some of what they hear, which causes them to be anxious or fearful of listening to others.[58] There is evidence that if English is not your native language, you are likely to experience receiver apprehension when listening to someone speak English.[59] If you are fearful of receiving information, you'll remember less information.

receiver apprehension
The fear of misunderstanding or misinterpreting the messages spoken by others or of not being able to adjust psychologically to messages expressed by others.

If you know that you are fearful of listening to new information, you'll have to work harder than others to understand the information presented. Recording video or audio of a lecture may help you feel more comfortable and less anxious about trying to remember every point. Becoming actively involved in the listening experience by taking notes or mentally repeating information to yourself may also help.[60]

Shifting Attention Can you multitask? A few people can easily do two things at once, but our performance on at least one of the tasks suffers when most of us try it. Some evidence suggests that men who have a masculine listening style have a tendency to lock onto a message and are less adept at shifting between two or more simultaneous

DIVERSITY & COMMUNICATION

Does Your Gender Influence Your Listening Style?

Researchers have identified a number of different listening styles, including a feminine style (a more relational approach) and a masculine style (more task-oriented). These characterizations may vary based on a person's socially constructed gender and are not always based on one's biological sex as male or female. The following chart summarizes research conclusions from several studies about feminine and masculine listening styles.[61]

	Feminine Listening Style	Masculine Listening Style
Different Listening Focus	• Tends to search for existing relationships among separate pieces of information • Tends to identify individual facts • Tends to shift listening focus among people who may be speaking at the same time	• Tends to look for a new organizational pattern when listening • Tends to listen for the big picture • Tends to lock on to a specific message without shifting between two or more conversations
Different Listening Goals	• More likely to listen for new information to gain greater understanding • Tends to use information to develop relationships with listening partners • Tends to have greater motivation to provide supportive feedback[62]	• More likely to listen to new information to solve a problem • Tends to listen to reach a conclusion; shows less concern about relationship cues • Tends to have less motivation to provide supportive feedback

Listening experts Stephanie Sargent and James Weaver suggest that studies of listening style differences between men and women may simply be measuring listening stereotypes or a self-fulfilling prophecy:[63] Men and women assume that they *are* listening the way they think that they *should* listen.[64] Although we have noted some perceived differences between masculine and feminine listening styles, our intention is not to promote sex-based stereotypes. Listening differences reflect people's preferred listening styles and are not necessarily based on biological sex differences.

messages.[65] For example, when many men stream news or TV shows on their laptops, they seem lost in thought—oblivious to other voices around them. In contrast, those who have a feminine listening style are more likely to carry on a conversation with one person while also focusing on a message they hear nearby. This difference doesn't mean that women are more likely to eavesdrop intentionally, but it does mean that some women have a greater ability to listen to two things at once. What are the implications? If you have a feminine listening style, you may want to stop and focus on the messages of others rather than on either internal or external competing messages. And if you have a more masculine listening style, you may need to be sensitive to others who may want to speak to you rather than becoming fixated on your own internal message or on a single external message such as a TV program.

Cultural Differences   Different cultures place different emphases on the importance of listening. Some cultures are more source- or speaker-oriented, whereas others are more receiver or listener-oriented. North American communication, for example, often centers on the sender. Much emphasis is placed on how senders can formulate better messages, improve credibility, and polish their delivery skills. Recently, there has been increased interest in listening in the United States.[66] However, far more U.S. colleges and universities offer courses in speaking than provide courses in listening.

In contrast, East Asian cultures typically emphasize listening and interpretation. The Chinese culture, for example, places considerable emphasis on the listener. It's understood by both speaker and listener that the listener can make infinite interpretations of what has been said. A strategy called **anticipatory communication** is common

anticipatory communication
A listening process in which the listener guesses the speaker's needs and accommodates them so that the speaker does not have to say what he or she wants.

CRITICAL/CULTURAL PERSPECTIVES & COMMUNICATION

What Are Your Listening Expectations and Assumptions?

How you are expected to listen depends, in large part, on the listening context. For example, the listening role you are expected to assume when your angry roommate complains about keeping the kitchen tidy versus hanging out with friends at the beach is obviously different. With whom you are communicating has implications for how you listen. Does the person have power to influence you, such as your boss, or are *you* the one with the power? Because of the other person's power or position, is there an expectation that you will just politely listen and not respond? Or, if you are among equals during a meeting, are you expected to challenge ideas and be a critical listener? If you are the person in the room with the most power, do you use that power to listen to others and empower them, or do you use power to control them? Being aware of the listening context can help you become a more sensitive listener, which can help you assess when to confront listening assumptions or expectations. Sometimes it is appropriate to be assertive. But before you challenge your listening role, it is useful to first be aware of what those role expectations and assumptions are.

in Japan. Instead of having the speaker explicitly say or ask for what he or she wants, listeners guess and accommodate the speaker's needs, sparing him or her the embarrassment that could arise if the verbally expressed request could not be met.[67] Thus, foreign students from East Asia may be puzzled about why they are constantly being asked what they want when visiting American homes. In their home countries, a good communicator should anticipate what others want and act accordingly, so the host or hostess should not have to ask what is needed.[68]

Context Barriers

In addition to the barriers that relate to how you process information and those that occur when your emotions and thoughts crowd out a message, listening barriers can arise from the communication context or situation. **Noise** is anything that interferes with your ability to listen to a message. Although you may think of it as sounds you hear, noise can be processed by any one of your five senses. Not only sounds, but also sights, the feeling of something touching you, and even tastes and smells can affect your listening ability. Two factors that can increase interfering noise are *when* you listen and *where* you listen.[69]

noise
Anything that interferes with your ability to listen to a message.

Barriers of Time Are you a morning person or an evening person? Morning people are cheerfully and chirpily at their mental peak before lunch. Evening people find it easier to tackle major projects after dark; they are at their worst when they arise in the morning.

The time of day can affect your listening acuity. If you know you are sharper in the morning, schedule your key listening times then whenever possible. Evening listeners should try to shift heavy listening to the evening hours. Of course, that's not always practical. If you can't change the time of listening, you can increase your awareness of when you will need to listen with greater concentration.

Daily activities, such as work, can also cause timing issues. When a person wants to converse with you at a time when you're busy with other things, for example, it may be tempting to try to do two things at once. We have all tried to get away with a few "uh-huhs" and "mm-hmms" to indicate that we're listening to everything that's being said while, in fact, our attention was divided.

Respect the effect of timing on other people, too. Don't assume that because you are ready to talk, the other person is ready to listen. If your message is particularly sensitive

▼ Be sensitive to the timing of your message. Just because you're ready to talk, it doesn't mean your communication partner is ready to listen.
Antonio Guillem/123rf

> **RECAP**
>
> **Managing Listening Barriers**
>
> | Listening Barriers | What to Do |
> |---|---|
> | **Self Barriers** | |
> | Self-Focus | • Notice when you find yourself drifting off. |
> | | • Shift attention back to the speaker. |
> | | • Take notes. Ask for clarification. |
> | Emotional Noise | • Become consciously aware of your emotions. |
> | | • Remain calm and focused. |
> | | • Use self-talk to stay focused on the message. |
> | Criticism | • Be aware of your biases. |
> | | • Monitor your internal critiques. |
> | **Information-Processing Barriers** | |
> | Processing Rate | • Use the difference between speech rate and thought rate to mentally summarize the message. |
> | Information Overload | • Take a break. |
> | | • Determine what's urgent and what's not when listening. |
> | Receiver Apprehension | • Record the message and review it later. |
> | | • Take notes. |
> | | • Mentally repeat the information. |
> | Shifting Attention | • Make a conscious effort to stop and focus on one message. |
> | Cultural Differences | • Acknowledge that some cultures place greater emphasis on the listener than on the speaker. |
> | **Context Barriers** | |
> | Barriers of Time | • If possible, schedule your key listening times for when you're at your best. |
> | Barriers of Place | • Eliminate distracting noise. |

or important, you may want to ask your listening partner, "Is this a good time to talk?" Even if he or she says yes, look for eye contact and a responsive facial expression to make sure the positive response is genuine.

Barriers of Place Listening takes all the powers of concentration you can muster. A good listener seeks a quiet time and place to maximize listening comprehension. For most people, the best listening environment is one that offers as few distractions as possible.

When *you* want to talk to someone, pick a quiet time and place, especially if you plan to discuss a complex or potentially difficult topic. Even in your own home, it may be a challenge to find a quiet time to talk. Closing a door or window, turning off music or the TV, asking noisy or offensive talkers to converse more quietly or not at all, and simply moving to a less distracting location are steps you may need to take to manage noise.

Listening Skills

5.5 Identify and use strategies that can improve your listening skills.

At the heart of listening is developing sensitivity to focus on the messages of others rather than on your own thoughts. A skilled listener is attentive, friendly, and responsive to others. Good listeners also maintain the flow of the conversation and provide feedback indicating that the message was understood.[70] In this section, we discuss several specific underlying skills that will increase your sensitivity so you can be a good listener.

At first glance, the skills we present may look deceptively simple—as simple as the advice given to most elementary students about crossing the street: (1) stop, (2) look, and (3) listen. Despite the appearance of simplicity, these three words summarize decades of research and insight about how to avoid being interpersonally inert. Those steps may seem like common sense, but they are not common practice.[71] Let's consider each one separately.

Stop: Turn Off Competing Messages

As we noted earlier, while you are listening, you may also be talking to yourself, providing a commentary about the messages you hear. These internal, self-generated messages may distract you from giving your undivided attention to what others are saying. To stop and focus on a message, you need to (1) be aware of the competing messages, (2) stop the internal competing chatter and attend to the message, and (3) socially decenter to focus on the thoughts of others.

Be Aware of Competing Messages Becoming aware of your internal dialogue is the first step toward stopping your own running commentary about issues and ideas that are self-focused rather than other-focused.[72] To be aware of what you are doing is to be consciously mindful of what you are attending to.[73] If you aren't aware that you are talking to yourself, you will likely continue your internal monologue and miss a portion of the message from your listening and speaking partner.[74] How can you increase your awareness of competing messages? At any given moment, you are either on task or off task when listening. Periodically ask yourself, "Am I on task? Am I focused on the speaker or my own internal conversation? Am I aware of what I'm doing?"

Stop Internal Noise Two researchers conducted a study to identify the specific behaviors that good listeners perform when listening.[75] What they discovered supports our admonition that after becoming aware of whether you're on task, the next step is to stop focusing on your own mental messages. Specifically, you should try to become other-oriented by taking the following actions during what the researchers called the *preinteraction phase* of listening:

- Put your own thoughts aside.
- Be there mentally, not just physically.
- Make a conscious, mindful effort to listen.
- Take adequate time to listen; don't rush the speaker; be patient.
- Be open-minded.

▲ Some people find that yoga or quiet meditation helps dissolve the internal barriers that prevent effective listening. What strategies have you used to become more aware of your intrapersonal communication and any internal barriers to listening you may have experienced? What methods have you found helpful for making yourself more conscious of the way your own self-talk affects your ability to listen to and communicate with others?
PM Images/Stone/Getty Images

It may also help if you simply speak less. Members of some religious groups take a vow to be silent and not talk to anyone else. They believe the maxim, "You have been given two ears and one mouth so that you will listen more and talk less." We do not suggest that you stop talking entirely; rather, you should increase your awareness of how your own thoughts and talk can interfere with being a good listener. Meditation techniques such as focusing on your breathing and noting when thoughts scamper through your mind like a tree full of hyperactive monkeys (also known as "monkey mind") can help you become more aware of when you are "off task."[76] Stop—do your best to eliminate the distracting, chattering mental messages that keep you from listening well.

Socially Decenter After becoming aware of competing messages and stopping your internal chatter, try a process called social decentering. **Social decentering** is a cognitive process that involves stepping away from your own thoughts and attempting to experience the thoughts of another. Instead of making yourself the center of your focus, you *decenter*—you are not the center of the conversation. Instead, you place your focus on the other person. In essence, you ask yourself, "If I were the other person, what would I be thinking?" Although the goal is to focus on someone else, decentering first requires you to practice the first principle of communication—self-awareness. You need to become aware when your own thoughts keep you from focusing on another's message. Then you can focus on the other person.[77] Of course, we do not suggest that you forever repress your own ideas and internal dialogue; that would be both impossible and inappropriate. Instead, we suggest that you focus on the other person rather than on yourself and, while doing so, consider what the other person may be thinking as he or she communicates with you.

social decentering
Stepping away from your own thoughts and attempting to experience the thoughts of another.

Look: Listen with Your Eyes

Sensitive listeners use their eyes as well as their ears. As we discussed in Chapter 4, nonverbal messages are powerful, especially in communicating feelings, attitudes, and emotions.[78] A person's body movement and posture, for example, communicate the intensity of his or her feelings, whereas facial expression and the vocal cues that accompany spoken words provide clues about the specific emotion being expressed. A competent listener notices these cues; an incompetent listener attempts to decode a message based only on what is said rather than "listening between the lines." When there is a contradiction between the verbal message and the nonverbal message, we will almost always believe the unspoken one; nonverbal cues are more difficult to fake. How do you focus on nonverbal messages? We suggest two strategies: (1) attend to the meta-message, and (2) nonverbally communicate *your* interest in the other person.

Attend to the Meta-Message *Meta-communication* is communication about communication. By attending to your interpersonal partner's unspoken message, you are looking for the **meta-message**—the nonverbal message that helps you interpret the verbal message. Nonverbal cues provide information about the emotional and relational effect of what a speaker is expressing verbally. Accurately decoding unspoken meta-messages helps you understand what people really mean.

> **meta-message**
> The nonverbal message that helps you interpret the verbal message.

Often, a person will express a positive feeling with a nonverbal message, such as smiling, that matches a verbal message, such as "I'm happy to be here." Sometimes, though, the nonverbal communication contradicts the verbal message. Your friend may say, "Oh, that's just great," but may use an exaggerated, sarcastic tone of voice and a facial expression that communicates just the opposite of the verbal message. The sarcasm expressed by your friend's tone of voice and facial expression (relationship cues) modifies the meaning of the verbal message (the actual content of the message).[79] Sometimes these meta-messages are quite subtle, so you have to be a careful observer.

How can you clarify the meaning of a nonverbal meta-message? Ask. For example, when you detect a smirk or a grimace from your listening partner, you can seek information about the communication by asking, "Is what I'm saying bothering you?"

Nonverbally Communicate Your Interest in the Other Person A key aspect of the "look" step of good listening is to actually look at the person you are listening to—establish eye contact, which signals that you are focusing your attention on your partner. Even though mutual eye contact typically lasts only one to seven seconds, when you carry on an interpersonal conversation, your eye contact reveals how attentive and responsive you are to your listening partner.[80] If you look as if you are listening, you will also be more likely to listen. We usually have more eye contact with someone when we are listening than when we are talking.[81]

In addition to eye contact, other nonverbal cues signal whether you are on task and responsive to others' messages. Remaining focused, keeping your hands and feet still, and even leaning forward slightly communicate that you are listening. Appropriate head nods and verbal responses also signal that you are attending to the other person's message.[82]

Listen: Understand Both Details and Major Ideas

How do you improve your listening skill? Now that you've stopped your own internal dialogue, paused, and looked for nonverbal cues, it's time to listen. Here are six additional strategies for improving your listening skill.[83]

Identify Your Listening Goal You listen to other people for a variety of reasons. Knowing your listening goal can increase your self-awareness of the listening process and increase your skill. As we discussed earlier in this chapter, adapting your listening style to your listening goal can enhance your listening skill.[84] If you're listening to your Aunt Deonna talk about her recent trip to northern Minnesota for the annual bear hunt, you need not worry about taking extensive notes or trying to remember all the details of her expedition. But when your sociology professor tells a story to illustrate a particular theory, you should be more attuned to the point he or she is making; the theory may be on a test. At other times, you may need to be on your guard to evaluate a politician's message or a salesperson's pitch. Having a strong motivation to listen for specific kinds of information can enhance your listening effectiveness.[85] There are four primary listening goals: to enjoy, to learn, to evaluate, and to empathize.

- *Listening to enjoy.* Sometimes we listen just because it's fun. You might listen to music, watch TV, go to a movie, or visit with a friend. Because you know you won't be tested on Jimmy Fallon's monologue, you can relax and just enjoy the humor.
- *Listening to learn.* Nothing snaps a class to attention more quickly than a professor's proclamation, "This next point will be covered on the test." Another key reason we listen is to learn. But you don't have to be a college student to listen to learn. Phone calls and conversations with family and friends also often contain information that you will want to remember.
- *Listening to evaluate.* When you listen to evaluate, you try to determine whether the information you hear is valid, reliable, believable, or useful. One problem with this listening goal is that you may become so preoccupied with evaluating the message that you may not completely understand it. Yet you can be taught to improve your skill in critically listening to messages.[86]
- *Listening to empathize.* The word *empathy*, which we introduced in Chapter 3 and will discuss in more detail later in this chapter, comes from a Greek word for "passion" and the German word *Einfühlung*, meaning "to feel with." To empathize with someone is to try to feel what he or she is feeling rather than just thinking about or acknowledging those feelings.[87] Empathic listening serves an important therapeutic function; just having an empathic listener may help someone out. No, we are not empowering you to be a therapist, but we are suggesting that sometimes simply listening and acknowledging someone's feelings can help that person sort things out.

Mentally Summarize the Details of the Message Because you can process words more quickly than a person speaks, you can use this extra time to your advantage by periodically summarizing the names, dates, and facts embedded in a message. If a speaker is disorganized and rambling, use your tremendous mental ability to reorganize the speaker's information into categories or try to place events in chronological order. It is important to have a grasp of the details your communication partner presents. But remember that to listen is to do more than focus on facts. Research suggests that poor listeners are more likely than good listeners to focus *only* on facts and data, rather than on the overall point of the message.[88] If you listen too much for the details, you may miss the main point.

Link Message Details with the Major Ideas of the Message As we just pointed out, facts and data make the most sense when we can use them to support an idea or point. Mentally weave your summaries of the details into a focused major point or series of major ideas. Use facts to enhance your critical thinking as you analyze, synthesize, evaluate, and finally summarize the key points or ideas your partner makes.

Practice by Listening to Difficult or Challenging Material Learning any skill takes practice. Experts suggest that our listening skills deteriorate if we listen only to easy and entertaining material. Make an effort to listen to news or documentary programs. As you listen to a lecture that seems full of content, make a conscious effort to stay focused, concentrate, and summarize facts and major ideas.[89]

Work to Overcome Listening Barriers If you can avoid the listening barriers discussed earlier in this chapter, you will be well on your way to improving your listening skill. Avoid being self-focused, letting emotional noise

▼ Personal concerns and distractions, such as texts, are challenges to effective listening for many students. You can, however, make yourself a better listener by learning to overcome these and other barriers.
Southerlycourse/E+/Getty Images

distract you, or criticizing a message before you've understood it. Watch out for information overload. And, when possible, take steps to minimize external noise and provide an environment more conducive to listening.

Don't Interrupt If you want to be perceived as a good listener, do not interrupt a speaker when he or she is talking. When we interrupt someone, we are saying, "What I have to say is more important than what you have to say." This translates to the other person as, "I'm more important than you are." In addition to being rude, interrupting others also decreases your credibility and your ability to understand the other person.

When someone stops talking, we recommend that you pause briefly before responding. The pause should be brief; too long of a pause may be misinterpreted as disinterest or that you have nothing to say. Yet research has found that it is rare for people to pause and not immediately comment when someone stops speaking.[90] So for many, a brief pause may seem unnatural. But a brief, natural pause does three things. First, it ensures that the other person has finished talking. Second, a brief, natural pause signals that you are listening rather than rushing in to say what you want next. And finally, especially during a heated conflict, pausing for just a moment helps slow down the conversation and manage the emotional climate.

Do you want to make sure you *don't* get hired because of the impression you make during a job interview? Interrupt your interviewer and talk over him or her and you're less likely to get the job, according to one research study.[91] To listen without interrupting seems simple, but because thoughts are bouncing around in our heads, we sometimes blurt them out, or we think that we know what the other person is going to say (closeness communication bias), so we talk over her or him.[92] Resist these temptations. Not talking over someone is a nonverbal, meta-message that communicates *you* are listening.

Consider That You May Be Wrong During a heated argument it is important not only to understand what someone is saying, but also to be open to change. Listening is more than comprehending a message; it is being willing to thoughtfully reconsider your own perspective and whether you may be wrong. Neuroscience researchers have found that when you listen to information that challenges your ideas or contradicts your beliefs, your brain reacts the same way as if you were being chased by a bear![93] When emotions are heightened you are less likely to consider that your perspective may be flawed. To improve your listen skill during confrontational conversations, take time to breathe, be more mindful of your intense emotions, and think about how your ideas may be wrong.

Listen Actively Our suggestion that you listen actively is a distillation of the other recommendations we've offered. Active listeners are engaged listeners who listen with both their minds and their hearts. They are engaged physically and mentally in the listening process.[94] Active listeners are aware of what they are doing; they stop thinking about things that might take them off track.[95] They also maintain good eye contact with the speaker and communicate their interest with an intent facial expression and a slight forward lean.

By contrast, passive listeners are not involved listeners; they are detached and may fake attention with a frozen, blank facial expression or a single, unchanging expression that mimics interest. One listening research team noted that a passive listener receives information by being talked *to* rather than as an equal partner in a speaking–listening exchange.[96]

This same team described active listeners as people who do the following:

- Give full attention to others by mentally focusing on what is being said.
- Maintain appropriate eye contact.
- Expend considerable energy participating in the listening process.
- Have an alert posture, such as a slight forward lean.

Another research study found that listeners who offered person-centered comments (comments that acknowledge the feelings of others) and provided immediate nonverbal responses (eye contact, natural forward lean, appropriate head nods) were judged to be better listeners than those who did not.[97]

It seems that the best listeners are mentally alert, physically focused on the other person, and actively involved in seeking understanding. In short, they stop, they look, and they listen.

Responding Skills

5.6 Identify and use appropriate responding skills.

To respond is to provide feedback to another about his or her behavior or communication. Your response can be verbal or nonverbal, intentional or unintentional.

Responding—especially verbally—to others is one of the best things you can do to be perceived as a good listener.[98] Your thoughtful response serves several purposes. First, it tells a speaker how well you have understood his or her message. Second, your response lets a speaker know how the message affects you. It indicates whether you agree or disagree. Third, it provides feedback about statements or assumptions that you find vague, confusing, or wrong. It helps an individual keep the communication on target and purposeful. Finally, your response signals to the speaker that you are still "with" him or her—that you are still ready to receive messages. We respond to let others know that we understand what we have heard, to empathize with the feelings of others, and to provide support.

RECAP
How to Listen Well

What to Do	How to Do It
Identify your listening goal.	Decide whether you are listening to enjoy, learn, evaluate, or empathize. Your listening goal should determine the strategies you use to achieve it.
Mentally summarize the details of the message.	Every few minutes, take time to create your own mental recap of the key information presented. In just a few seconds, you can summarize much information.
Link message details with the major ideas of the message.	Consciously relate the bits of information you hear to the key points the speaker is developing rather than focusing only on facts and details or only on major points.
Practice by listening to difficult or challenging material.	Periodically make an effort to listen to material that is complex and richer in detail and information than what you typically listen to.
Work to overcome listening barriers.	Identify the key obstacles that keep you from listening at peak effectiveness (self barriers, information-processing barriers, or context barriers); make conscious efforts to overcome the underlying causes of these barriers.
Don't interrupt.	Increase your awareness of whether you interrupt others. Wait until the other person has finished speaking before you speak.
Consider that you may be wrong.	Be open to thoughtfully reconsidering your own perspective when hearing new information.
Listen actively.	Be engaged in the listening process by maintaining good eye contact with the speaker and an alert posture (slight forward lean, sitting up rather than slouching).

Respond to Clarify and Confirm Understanding

The skill of thoughtfully responding to others lets them know that you have understood their message and that they communicated clearly. Research has found that making a relevant, pertinent comment; answering questions; elaborating; offering opinions and perspectives; and asking relevant questions all contribute to perceptions of being an effective listener.[99] Active listening skills have also been shown to correlate with student success; active listeners learn better than students who are passive listeners.[100] There are several ways to ensure that your confirming responses are helpful.

Be Descriptive Although one listening goal is to evaluate and make critical judgments about messages, don't start your evaluation until you're sure you understand the speaker. Effective feedback describes rather than evaluates what you hear. We're not suggesting that it's easy to listen from a nonevaluative perspective or that you should refrain from ever evaluating messages and providing praise or negative comments. But feedback that first acts like a mirror to help the speaker understand what he or she has said is more useful than a barrage of critical comments. Describing your own reactions to what your partner has said rather than pronouncing a quick judgment on his or her message is also more likely to keep communication flowing. "I see that from a different point of view" often evokes more thoughtful responses than "You're wrong, I'm right."

If your partner thinks that your prime purpose in listening is to take potshots at the message or the messenger, the communication climate will cool quickly. Not surprisingly, listening researcher Eve-Anne Doohan found that when wives expressed negative emotions and critical evaluative comments to their listening husbands, the husbands were less satisfied with the overall quality of their relationships with their wives.[101]

Be Timely Feedback is usually most effective at the earliest opportunity after the behavior or message is presented, especially if the purpose is to teach. Waiting to provide a response after much time has elapsed invites confusion.

Now let us contradict our advice. Sometimes, especially if a person is already sensitive and upset about something, delaying feedback can be wise. Use your critical-thinking skills to analyze when feedback will do the most good. Rather than automatically offering an immediate correction, use the just-in-time approach. Provide feedback just before the person might make another mistake, just in time for the feedback to have the largest benefit.

Be Brief Less information can be more. Cutting down on the amount of your feedback can highlight the importance of what you do share. Don't overwhelm your listener with details that obscure the key point of your feedback. Brief is usually best.

Be Useful Perhaps you've heard this advice: "Never try to teach a pig to sing. It wastes your time, it doesn't sound pretty, and it annoys the pig." When you provide feedback to someone, be certain it is useful and relevant. Ask yourself, "If I were this person, how would I respond to this information? Is it information I can act on?" Immersing your partner in information that is irrelevant or potentially damaging to the relationship may make you feel better, but it may not enhance the quality of your relationship or improve understanding.

Ask Appropriate Questions As you listen for information and attempt to understand how another person is feeling, you may need to ask appropriate questions to help clarify your conclusions. A key word in this tip about responding skills is the word *appropriate*. Avoid grilling people or asking for more information in a way that seems intrusive. Think about the ways you like people to respond to you, then try and emulate that behavior as you respond appropriately to others.

Most of your questions will serve one of four purposes:

- To obtain additional information ("How long have you been living in Buckner?"),
- To find out how the person feels ("Are you frustrated because you didn't finish your project?"),
- To ask for clarification ("What do you mean when you say you want to telecommute?"), or
- To verify that you have reached an accurate conclusion about your partner's intent or feeling ("So are you saying you'd rather work at home than at the office?").

Another way to sort out details and get to the emotional heart of a dialogue is to ask questions to help you (and your communication partner) identify the sequence of events. Asking questions like "What happened first?" and "Then what did he do?" can help both you and your partner clarify a confusing event.

Paraphrase Message Content **Paraphrasing** is restating in your own words what you think a person is saying. Providing a brief summary of what you just heard confirms your understanding of the message. To paraphrase is not repeating something exactly as it was spoken; that would be parroting (and annoying). Paraphrase when you need to confirm your understanding of a murky message or to help the speaker sort out a

paraphrasing
Checking the accuracy of your understanding by restating your partner's message in your own words.

jumbled or confusing situation. Your paraphrase can summarize essential events, uncover a detail that was quickly glossed over, or highlight a key point. Typical lead-ins to a paraphrase include statements such as the following:

"So here is what seems to have happened...."

"Here's what I understand you to mean...."

"So let me see if I get what you are saying...."

"Are you saying...?"

Does paraphrasing a speaker's message really enhance the overall quality and accuracy of communication? Yes. Several researchers have found that checking your understanding of a message can enhance overall communication quality.[102] People are also more likely to feel listened to if you can describe what you just heard them say.[103]

Researcher Harry Weger and his colleagues found that listeners perceived people who skillfully used paraphrasing as more socially attractive than other people. That is, the listener liked a person who paraphrased more than a person who didn't.[104]

Imagine the Conversation You Anticipate Having with Someone Are there times when you know you are going to have a conversation with someone that may call upon your empathic responding skills? For example, perhaps a friend has lost a loved one or had a difficult day and needs someone to listen to him or her. Before approaching that person, imagine what the conversation will be like. One research team found that you can increase your empathic listening and responding skills if, prior to having a difficult or challenging conversation with someone, you imagine what that conversation might be like. Just thinking about how someone may respond can help you anticipate that person's emotions and enable you to be more supportive and empathic.[105]

Respond to Empathize with Others

Empathy, as we noted earlier in this chapter, is the process of feeling what another person is feeling. Empathizing is more than just acknowledging that another person feels a particular emotion. Being empathic involves making an effort to feel the same

SOCIAL MEDIA & COMMUNICATION

Keep Social Media Social

Does it happen often to you? You read a "friend's" tweet or Facebook post that you strongly disagree with. Whether an emotionally charged statement about politics, religion, or human rights, or a negative personal comment directed at someone you know, the message raises your blood pressure, and you consider firing back an angry response. Before quickly reacting with a negative, emotionally escalating response, just stop, take a breath, and consider the implications of what you may post. In all probability, the sender is not thinking about you but is merely expressing his or her opinion—you just happen to strongly disagree. Will hurling a reciprocal post or angry tweet change the other person's mind? Probably not. Make a conscious choice not to make someone's post personal.

Social media plays an important role in our relationships with others. How we "listen" and whether we thoughtfully respond can have serious consequences for our relationships.[106] Keep social media social.

Pause and think twice before firing off an angry message on social media. Chris Rout / Alamy Stock Photo

emotion yourself.[107] Henri Nouwen eloquently expressed both the challenge and the rewards of empathic listening:

> To listen is very hard, because it asks of us so much interior stability that we no longer need to prove ourselves by speeches, arguments, statements, or declarations. True listeners no longer have an inner need to make their presence known. They are free to receive, to welcome, to accept. . . . Listening is a form of spiritual hospitality by which you invite strangers to become friends, to get to know their inner selves more fully, and even to dare to be silent with you.[108]

As Nouwen notes, at the heart of empathic listening is the ability not only to know when to speak, but also to know when to be silent. It is no surprise that empathic listeners tend to have more satisfying relationships. Research has also found that highly empathic teachers receive fewer negative responses from their students.[109]

Psychologist Carl Rogers suggests that empathic listening is more than a technique; it's a "way of being."[110] Effective empathic listeners make empathy a natural and normal way of interacting with others. Yet, some people are simply better at being empathic than others. Just as you inherit physical qualities from your parents, there is evidence that you inherit communication traits as well.[111] Some people may have personality and communication traits that naturally make them more skilled empathic listeners.[112] This does not mean that if you are not naturally empathic, you can never develop empathic skills, but it does mean that you may have to work a bit harder than others to enhance these skills. Can people be taught to be more empathic? Research suggests that the answer is a clear "yes." One goal of this book is to enhance your skill in appropriately adapting to others; empathy is at the heart of focusing on the needs and emotions of others.[113]

Being empathic is not a single skill but several related skills that help you predict how others will respond.[114] Three strategies to help you respond empathically are to (1) understand your partner's feelings, (2) paraphrase his or her emotions, and (3) be emotionally intelligent.

Be Emotionally Intelligent To be emotionally intelligent is to understand and express emotion, interpret emotions in yourself and others, and regulate or manage emotions.[115] Emotional intelligence theorist Daniel Goleman summarizes the importance of emotions in developing empathy by quoting the French writer and poet Antoine de Saint-Exupéry: "It is only with the heart that one can see rightly; what is essential is invisible to the eye."[116] Researchers have found evidence supporting Goleman's ideas. Studies suggest that empathic listeners make better salespeople, teachers, counselors, and therapists; they also develop better relationships with others overall compared to nonempathic listeners.[117]

Evidence suggests that people who are emotionally intelligent—because of their skill in recognizing, expressing, and managing their emotions—are better listeners.[118] Being attuned to the emotions of your listening partner helps you discern the underlying, sometimes not explicitly expressed, meaning of a message.[119] For example, one simple yet powerful strategy to manage emotions when you are about to lose control is to take a deep breath. Yes, just breathe. Taking a deep, slow breath is a way of regaining control by calming down. It helps make you more conscious of your anger or frustration, much like the old technique of counting to ten.

Another strategy for managing emotions is to use the power of self-talk, a concept we discussed in Chapter 2. Tell yourself you won't get angry. Early detection of the emotions bubbling up inside you can help you assess and then manage them before your irrational, emotional impulses take control. And sometimes, of course, expressing your frustration is appropriate.

Understand Your Partner's Feelings If your goal is to empathize, or "feel with," your communication partner, you might begin by imagining how you would feel under the same circumstances. If your roommate comes home from a hassle-filled day at work or school, try to imagine what you might be thinking or feeling if you had had a stressful day. If a friend calls to tell you his mother died, consider how you would feel if the

ETHICS & COMMUNICATION

Paraphrase Properly

If used with wisdom, paraphrasing can help both you and your partner clarify message accuracy. The most essential guideline is to use your paraphrasing skills *only* if you are able to be open and accepting. If you try to color your paraphrased comments to achieve your own agenda, you aren't being ethical.

Also avoid the overuse of paraphrasing. Too much of it can slow down a conversation and make the other person uncomfortable or irritated. A sensitive communicator tries not to let his or her technique show.

Other guidelines to keep in mind when you ask questions and paraphrase content and feelings are the following:

- Use your own words—don't just repeat exactly what the other person says.
- Don't add to the information presented when paraphrasing.
- Be brief.
- Be specific.
- Be accurate.

---

situation were reversed. Even if you have not yet experienced the loss of your mother, you can imagine what it would be like to suffer such a loss. Of course, your reaction to life events is unlikely to be exactly like someone else's response. Empathy is not telepathically trying to become your communication partner.[120] But you do attempt to decenter—to consider what someone may be thinking—by putting yourself "in the other person's shoes" and imagining what he or she may be feeling. Considering how others might feel has been called the Platinum Rule—even more valuable than the Golden Rule ("Do unto others as you would have others do unto you."). **The Platinum Rule** invites you to treat others as *they* would like to be treated—not just as *you* would like to be treated.

the Platinum Rule
Treating others the way *they* would like to be treated rather than how *you* would like to be treated (the Golden Rule).

Paraphrase Emotions The bottom line in empathic responding is to make certain that you understand your communication partner's emotional state. You can paraphrase his or her feelings using common lead-in phrases, such as "So you feel . . .," "So now you feel . . .," and "Emotionally, you are feeling. . . ." Although active listening may not always solve a person's problem, there is evidence that listening and paraphrasing someone's emotions can provide emotional and social support to those in need of a friendly and supportive ear.[121]

Paraphrasing feelings (as well as content) can be especially useful in situations in which messages could escalate emotions or produce conflict, such as the following:

- Before you take an important action
- Before you argue or criticize
- When your partner has strong feelings
- When your partner just wants to talk
- When your partner is speaking "in code"—using unclear jargon or abbreviations you don't understand
- When your partner wants to understand your feelings and thoughts
- When you are talking to yourself (you can question and check your own emotional temperature)
- When you encounter new ideas[122]

As a final word on responding with empathy, realize that although we have discussed empathic responses and the active listening process using an orderly, step-by-step textbook approach, in practice the process won't be as neat and tidy. You may have to back up and clarify content, ask more questions, and rethink how you would feel before you summarize how your partner feels.[123] Or you may be able to summarize feelings without asking questions or summarizing the content of the message. Be sure to adapt the skills appropriately, and ethically, to each specific communication situation. The Ethics & Communication box offers more advice for when and how to paraphrase.

Respond to Provide Social Support

social support
Sensitive and empathic listening, followed by messages of comfort or confirmation, that lets a person know he or she is understood and valued.

Responding with empathy is especially important if you are listening to provide social support or encouragement to someone. You provide **social support** to someone when you sensitively and empathically listen to him or her and then offer messages of comfort or confirmation that let the person know that he or she is both understood and valued. Supportive messages are person-centered; responses should be customized to focus on the other person's specific needs.[124] Research has found that if you value listening as a means of showing social support, then it is more likely that you will be comforted by positive, supportive messages.[125] Supportive listening begets supportive responding. Providing social support does *not* mean trying to solve the issue or problem your communication partner has. Instead, it means communicating genuine concern rather than just going through the motions of pretending to listen.[126]

How to Provide Appropriate Social Support What's the best way to express your support? Tables 5.1 and 5.2 summarize research-based suggestions that can help you say the right thing and avoid saying the wrong thing when you are providing social support to others. Research suggests that following these guidelines as appropriate to the other person's situation can help you develop empathic and comforting messages that are likely to be appreciated by your listener.[127] The best types of supportive comments tend to be positive, customized, and person-centered.[128] Remember, however, that there are no magic words or phrases that will always ease someone's stress or anxiety.

Don't be discouraged if your initial attempts to use these skills seem awkward and uncomfortable. Learning to use any new set of skills well takes time. The instructions and samples you have seen in this chapter should serve as a guide rather than as hard-and-fast prescriptions to follow every time. Being an empathic listener can be rewarding in both your personal and your professional life.[129] And here's some encouraging news about listening and responding skills: These skills can be improved. People who have received listening training show overall improvement in their ability to listen to others.[130] Reading this chapter, listening to your instructor give you tips on enhancing your skills, and participating in skill-building activities are well worth your time.

How to Provide an Appropriate Level of Social Support What level or intensity of social support should you offer? One research study suggests that when we experience

TABLE 5.1 Suggestions for Providing Social Support

What to Do	What to Say
Clearly express that you want to provide support.	"I would really like to help you."
Appropriately communicate that you have positive feelings for the other person; explicitly tell the other person that you are her or his friend, that you care about her or him, or that you love her or him.	"You mean a lot to me." "I really care about you."
Express your concern about the situation the other person is in right now.	"I'm worried about you right now, because I know you're feeling ____ [stressed, overwhelmed, sad, etc.]."
Indicate that you are available to help, that you have time to support the person.	"I am here for you when you need me."
Let the other person know how much you support him or her.	"I'm completely with you on this." "I'm here for you, and I'll always be here for you because I care about you."
Acknowledge that the other person is in a difficult situation.	"This must be very difficult for you."
Paraphrase what the other person has told you about the issue or problem that is causing stress.	"So you became upset when she told you that she didn't want to see you again."
Consider asking open-ended questions to find out whether the other person wants to talk.	"How are you doing now?"
Use conversational continuers to let the other person know that you are listening and supportive.	"Yes—then what happened?" "Oh, I see." "Uh-huh."
After expressing your compassion, empathy, and concern, just listen.	Say nothing; just establish gentle eye contact and listen.

TABLE 5.2 What to Avoid When Providing Social Support

What Not to Do	What Not to Say
Don't criticize or negatively evaluate the other person. She or he needs support and validation, not judgmental comments.[131]	"Well, you never were the best judge of people. You should expect this kind of stress if you hang around with him."
Don't tell the other person to stop feeling what he or she is feeling.	"Oh, snap out of it!" "Don't be sad."
Don't immediately offer advice.	"So here's what you should do: Cut off all communication with her."
Don't tell the other person that all will necessarily be well.	"It's going to get better from here." "The worst is over."
Don't tell the other person that she or he really has nothing to worry about.	"Oh, it's no big deal." "Just think happy thoughts."
Don't tell the other person that the problem can be solved easily.	"You can always find another girlfriend."
Don't blame the other person for his or her problems.	"Well, if you didn't always drive so fast, you wouldn't have had the accident."
Don't tell the other person that her or his expression of feelings and emotion is wrong.	"You're just making yourself sick. Stop crying."

sadness, disappointment, or trauma, most of us prefer a "midlevel" intensity of social support. An intense, overly dramatic response or a tepid, mild response may create additional "noise" for the person you are trying to support. When providing social support, consider offering a moderate level of positive, genuine, and authentic supportive communication.[132] Although the women in the study preferred a slightly higher level of comforting than the men, most of the people studied didn't want over-the-top, melodramatic expressions of support. Neither did they like weak or timid expressions of support. When supporting others, a good place to begin is providing a thoughtful, personal, empathic, and yet not-too-dramatic response.

STUDY GUIDE: PRINCIPLES FOR A LIFETIME

CHAPTER

The Importance of Listening and Responding Skills

5.1 Explain the principle of listening and responding thoughtfully to others.

***PRINCIPLE* POINTS:** You spend more time listening than doing any other communication activity. Being a good listener and responding thoughtfully to others will help you enhance the quality of your interpersonal relationships, develop good collaboration skills, and forge a stronger link between speaker and audience.

***PRINCIPLE* TERM:**

closeness communication bias

***PRINCIPLE* SKILLS:**

1. Identify specific instances from your own experience in which poor listening skills resulted in a significant communication problem. How would using effective listening skills have diminished or eliminated the problem?
2. Keep a listening journal for one day. Keep track of your listening goals and how long you have listened. Review your journal and note when you were an effective listener and when you were less effective.

How We Listen

5.2 Identify the elements of the listening process.

***PRINCIPLE* POINTS:** Listening is a complex process of receiving, constructing meaning from, and responding to verbal and nonverbal messages. The five activities of listening are (1) selecting, (2) attending, (3) understanding, (4) remembering, and (5) responding.

PRINCIPLE TERMS:

hearing
listening
select
attend
understand
remember
respond

PRINCIPLE SKILLS: Which of the five activities of listening do you do well? Which need to be improved?

Listening Styles

5.3 Describe four listening styles.

PRINCIPLE POINTS: Each person develops a preferred listening style based on his or her personality, the listening situation, and the listening goal. The four listening styles are relational, analytical, critical, and task-oriented. Knowing your preferred listening style can help you adapt your listening approach for maximum listening effectiveness.

PRINCIPLE TERMS:

listening style
relational listeners
analytical listeners
critical listeners
second guessing
task-oriented listeners

PRINCIPLE SKILLS:

1. What is your usual listening style? Do you have more than one? How do you adapt your style depending upon your listening goal?
2. What listening situations are the most challenging for you? What strategies could you use to help yourself become a more flexible listener?

Listening Barriers

5.4 Identify and describe barriers that keep people from listening well.

PRINCIPLE POINTS: Many people struggle with the skill of listening. Barriers to effective listening include (1) self barriers: self-focus, emotional noise, and criticism; (2) information-processing barriers: processing rate, information overload, receiver apprehension, shifting attention, and cultural differences; and (3) context barriers: time barriers and place barriers.

PRINCIPLE TERMS:

emotional noise
receiver apprehension
anticipatory communication
noise

PRINCIPLE SKILLS: Identify your primary listening barriers. What are strategies you could use to overcome the most difficult listening barriers you experience?

Listening Skills

5.5 Identify and use strategies that can improve your listening skills.

PRINCIPLE POINTS: To become a better listener, consider three simple steps that may sound easy to do but are challenging to put into practice: stop, look, and listen. To stop means to be mindful of the message and to avoid focusing on your own distracting inner talk. To look is to listen with your eyes—to focus on nonverbal information. To listen involves the skill of capturing the details of a message while also linking those details to a major idea.

PRINCIPLE TERMS:

social decentering
meta-message

PRINCIPLE SKILLS:

1. Do you find yourself interrupting or getting interrupted often? What can you do—as a listener or a speaker—to avoid interruptions and deal with them if they happen?
2. Which of the skill steps (stop, look, listen) do you need to improve the most? What are specific strategies that can help you improve your listening skills?

Responding Skills

5.6 Identify and use appropriate responding skills.

PRINCIPLE POINTS: To respond thoughtfully means to consider the needs of the other person. Check the accuracy of your listening skills by reflecting on your understanding of what your partner has said. To respond effectively, be descriptive, timely, brief, and useful. Ask appropriate questions and paraphrase message content to check the accuracy of your understanding. To listen with empathy is to be emotionally intelligent, understand your partner's feelings, and paraphrase emotions. When you provide social support, offer messages of comfort and concern so your partner feels understood and valued.

PRINCIPLE TERMS:

paraphrasing
the Platinum Rule
social support

PRINCIPLE SKILLS:

1. Do you usually paraphrase when listening to others in everyday life? If so, how do you summarize messages in a helpful and natural-sounding way? If you don't paraphrase much, what kinds of phrases do you think would help you?
2. How would you assess your ability to empathize with others? What are specific strategies you could use to be more empathic?

CHAPTER 6

ADAPTING TO OTHERS: DIVERSITY AND COMMUNICATION

There are no ordinary people. —C. S. LEWIS

Rawpixel.com/Shutterstock

CHAPTER OUTLINE

- Diversity and Communication
- Culture and Communication
- Barriers to Adapting to Others
- Strategies for Adapting to Others
- Study Guide: *Principles for a Lifetime*

LEARNING OBJECTIVES

6.1 Describe how differences of gender, sexual orientation, age, ethnicity, and social class influence communication.

6.2 Define *culture*, and compare and contrast cultural contexts and cultural values.

6.3 Illustrate four barriers that inhibit communication between individuals.

6.4 Describe seven strategies that will help bridge differences between people and help them adapt to differences.

One of life's unprofound principles with profound implications for human communication is this: *We each have different backgrounds and experiences.*[1] Your employers, teachers, religious leaders, best friends, or romantic partners may not share the same ethnicity, culture, age, sexual orientation, or socioeconomic status as you. And the not-so-startling fact that people *are* different from one another provides the context for discussion of our final Communication Principle for a Lifetime: *Effective communicators appropriately adapt their messages to others.* Figure 6.1 presents our now-familiar model, which includes this final principle of appropriately adapting messages to others.

We introduce this principle last because often people learn how to adapt only after they have learned the other communication principles. The ability to adapt suggests that you already have a sense of who you are and a consciousness of the presence of others—self-awareness and other-awareness, the components of the first principle we presented.[2] Studies in developmental communication further suggest that the ability to appropriately adapt our behavior to others evolves after we have become aware that there is a "me," after we have learned to use verbal and nonverbal symbols to communicate, and after we have developed an ability to hear and listen to others. We begin to develop all of these skills as infants and refine them throughout our lives. The ability to adapt ethically to others requires maturity and an other-oriented perspective.

The goals of this chapter are to identify human differences that may inhibit communication with others and to suggest adaptive strategies that can improve the quality and effectiveness of our communication with others. To frame our discussion of diversity and communication, we'll note differences in gender identity, sexual orientation, ethnicity, age, and social class, and the implications these differences have for communication. These categories of difference represent a broad range of human diversity including, but not limited to, other factors such as religious views, political affiliations, and disability.

But simply understanding that there are a range of human differences is not enough to improve communication; it is important to learn how to use effective communication skills to first understand and then adapt to those differences. The ability to adapt is a quintessential communication principle that will serve you well for a lifetime.[3]

The goal of being able to appropriately adapt your communication to other people does not mean you have to abandon the traditions, preferences, orientations, and cultural elements that make you unique. Nor does it mean you only tell others what they want to hear. It does suggest that appropriately using communication strategies to understand and bridge differences that exist among people can enhance human understanding. So, we'll conclude the chapter by identifying strategies to establish equitable relationships with others by appropriately adapting to our differences.

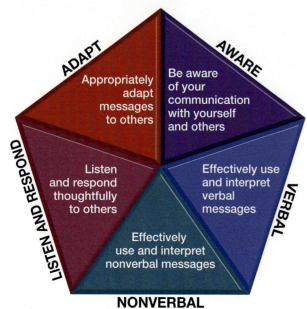

FIGURE 6.1 Communication Principles for a Lifetime

Diversity and Communication

6.1 Describe how differences of gender, sexual orientation, age, ethnicity, and social class influence communication.

Communication researchers have found that differences in our sex, gender, sexual orientation, ethnicity, age, and social class affect the way we interact with one another. Some of these differences among groups of people are learned, and some are based on biology—or, in the case of age differences, simply how long someone has lived—but they all have an effect on how we perceive and interact with others. As we study these group differences, however, keep in mind that groups are made up of individual people, and every single person has different experiences. As you read in Chapter 2, each of us perceives the world differently. To some degree, we are each estranged from others. Although you may have some things (such as your gender, age, skin color, where you grew up, or your language) in common with a larger group of people, you nonetheless are a unique individual. And so is everybody else. As C. S. Lewis observed in the quotation that opens this chapter, *there are no ordinary people*.

Sex and Gender

Perhaps the most obvious form of human diversity is biological sex. As we discussed in Chapter 2, a person's sex is driven by biology. In contrast, gender is a complex, culturally constructed and psychologically based perception of oneself. Gender includes your biological sex; your sexual orientation; your view of yourself relative to feminine, masculine, or **androgynous** (a blend of feminine and masculine) characteristics; and your attitudes about roles the sexes should play in society. Some people have an internal, personal sense that the sex assigned to them at birth is not their authentic self; they realize that they transcend the boundaries of conventional sex and gender and are **transgender**. Being transgender is not the same thing as being androgynous. It is a unique gender identity that is not confined by traditional notions of masculinity or femininity. It is independent of one's sexual orientation.[4] Gender identity is different than gender expression. **Gender expression** is a person's behavior and appearance that communicates that person's gender identity, including a broad range of masculine and feminine characteristics, to other people.

John Gray, author of the self-help book *Men Are from Mars, Women Are from Venus*, would have us believe that the sexes, based on our biology, are so different that we approach life from two distinct "planets," or spheres of perspective.[5] Although communication scholars have challenged several of Gray's conclusions because they are not supported by research, some research has documented differences in the ways men and women communicate.[6] Yet these differences are likely based on gender rather than sex. Deborah Tannen, author of several books on the behavior of the sexes, views men and women as distinctly different cultural groups.[7] She suggests that female (feminine)–male (masculine) communication is cross-cultural communication, with all the challenges inherent in exchanging messages with persons of very different backgrounds and value systems.

Perhaps these viewpoints are a bit extreme and the sexes are actually more alike than different. Research using multiple methods and originating in various disciplines

androgynous
Exhibiting both masculine and feminine characteristics.

transgender
A unique identity not confined by traditional notions of masculinity or femininity and independent of one's sexual orientation.

gender expression
A person's behavior and appearance that communicates an individual's gender identity, including a broad range of masculine and feminine characteristics, to other people.

▼ Have you ever been in a social situation like the one pictured here, in which coworkers, friends, relatives, or loved ones seem to self-segregate according to sex? What does this common social phenomenon reveal about the nature of sex, gender, and communication? How can you appropriately adapt messages to others across these lines?
Gmast3r/123RF

consistently shows that differences in men's and women's communication have more to do with *why* we communicate than with *how* we communicate. According to this research, those with a masculine style tend to approach communication from a content orientation; they view the purpose of communication as primarily goal oriented, with an emphasis on accomplishing something or completing a task. In contrast, people who have a feminine style tend to use communication to relate or connect to others, and to extend themselves to other people in order to know them and be known by them.[8] What you talk about is less important than the act of talking, because talking implies a relationship. One study found that when interrupted, those with a feminine style are sometimes more likely to simply smile, agree, politely nod, and laugh. According to researchers, these actions suggest a greater effort, even when interrupted, to maintain a positive relationship and facilitate the flow of conversation.[9]

To summarize this difference: *Those with a masculine style often communicate to report; those with a feminine style may communicate to establish rapport.*[10] So the point of difference isn't necessarily the way the sexes actually communicate but in the motivations or reasons for communicating.[11] Our instrumental and expressive orientations to the world translate into our communication behavior.

To bridge the gap, here's what we suggest you do:

- First, work to understand the differences that may exist.
- Second, make an insightful examination of your own behavior in light of the differences discussed and then determine how you conform to and differ from these descriptions.
- Third, be a gender researcher yourself. Note differences as well as similarities between you and those whose gender is different from yours. Be careful not to ascribe differences in communication only to a person's sex or gender. Consider the many other reasons for communication differences such as age, personality, or culture, too.
- Fourth, when in conversation with someone, try to assess the person's communication motivation. Does the other person just want you to listen? Sometimes it's wise to simply ask the person what he or she wants.
- Finally, make a conscious effort to adapt your behavior appropriately; be mindful of how you interact with others to enhance the quality of your relationships with them.

Just because you're female or identify more closely with a feminine gender doesn't mean that you have to or will take an expressive approach to every interaction. Likewise, just because you're male or view yourself as masculine doesn't mean that conversations are always about exchanging information. By developing the ability to take *both* content and relational approaches to communication, you broaden how you adapt to others. Your communication skill increases.

Gender Identity and Sexual Orientation

Lesbian, gay, bisexual, transgender, and queer (LGBTQ+) communities are important groups within the larger U.S. culture. Although we use the terms *lesbian, gay, bisexual, transgender*, and *queer* (a term that communicates a liberation from labels about sexual orientation), there are many more ways of describing one's gender identity

RECAP

Gender-Based Approaches to Communication

Masculine Style
- More instrumental; often characterized by assertiveness and getting things done
- Usually more emphasis on the content of messages and the information being exchanged (the *what*) rather than on relational elements (the *how*) in the message
- More attention given to verbal than nonverbal messages

Feminine Style
- More expressive; often characterized by an emphasis on connecting with others and fostering harmonious relationships
- Usually more emphasis on the relational elements of messages
- More attention given to nonverbal elements, such as *how* something is said rather than *what* is said

and sexual orientation. The plus sign in LGBTQ+ signifies that many additional gender identities exist, and some are yet to emerge. (See the discussion of gender complexity in the Chapter 3 Diversity & Communication box.) So rather than thinking about a person's gender identity or sexual orientation in terms of just a few rigid categories, it's more accurate to consider a wide range of orientations, identities, and expressions.

Perspectives on Sexual Orientation   Regardless of the label, sexual orientation has become a source of pride for some people but remains socially stigmatized for others. Although 92 percent of LGBTQ+ individuals surveyed said that society is becoming more accepting of them, there is evidence that LGBTQ+ individuals continue to be judged negatively solely on the basis of their sexual orientation.[12] As of 2020, more than 400 million people live in a country where being gay is punishable by death and 40 percent of the world's population live in a country where people can be prosecuted based on their sexual orientation[13] Yet, in 2020, the United States Supreme Court ruled that the Civil Rights Act of 1964 protects gay, lesbian, and transgender employees from discrimination in the workplace.[14]

Research has found that a heterosexual person who knows someone who is gay or a lesbian is more inclined to be accepting of gays or lesbians and more likely to support same-sex marriage. Still, about 40 percent of LGBTQ+ individuals report that at some point in their lives a family member or close friend rejected them because of their sexual orientation.[15] In addition, people who hold negative attitudes toward LGBTQ+ individuals are less likely to communicate with them than are those with more accepting views. Research further suggests that heterosexuals who have negative perceptions of LGBTQ+ people are more likely to have rigid views about gender roles and will assume that their peers also hold such rigid views and negative impressions of the LGBTQ+ community.[16] Perhaps related to such perceptions, **homophobia**, which is a fear of or aversion toward gay and lesbian people often accompanied by the fear of being labeled or perceived as LGBTQ+, continues to exist among many people.

Because of the persistence of these negative attitudes toward members of LGBTQ+ communities, as well as antigay violence and harassment, some LGBTQ+ individuals continue to live "in the closet," concealing their sexual orientations.[17] Research has found that LGBTQ+ individuals are frequent communicators via social media; 80 percent report that they have used Facebook or Twitter, compared to 58 percent of the general public. Yet only 16 percent of LGBTQ+ people indicate that they regularly discuss LGBTQ+ issues online.[18]

Enhancing Awareness   Drawing on the first Principle of Communication for a Lifetime, an effective and appropriate communicator is aware of, and sensitive to, issues and attitudes about sexual orientation in contemporary society. Just as you have been taught to avoid biased expressions that degrade someone's race or ethnicity, it is equally important to avoid using language that demeans a person's sexual orientation or gender identity. Telling stories and jokes whose point or punchline relies on ridiculing a person's gender identity or sexual orientation lowers perceptions of your credibility not only among LGBTQ+ people but also among people who dislike bias and support the LGBTQ+ community.

It's important to create a communication climate in which LGBTQ+ individuals can be themselves and comfortably talk about who they are without fearing rejection or discrimination. Creating a climate of openness and acceptance is important for any human relationship. Family members who have a gay, lesbian, bisexual, transgender, or queer member report more overall relational satisfaction if their family doesn't avoid a discussion of gender identity and sexual orientation. Many universities offer training courses, known as *ally training*, to help faculty and staff members create safe, accepting relationships. Participants are informed about LGBTQ+ culture and taught how to

homophobia
Fear of, aversion to, or discrimination against gays or lesbians.

provide appropriate support. A faculty or staff member who has completed ally training may post a sign on his or her door to indicate that it's safe to be yourself in that person's office or classroom.[19]

Sometimes we unintentionally offend someone through subtle use or misuse of language. For example, gays and lesbians typically prefer to be referred to as *gay* or *lesbian*, rather than as *homosexual*,[20] and the term *sexual orientation* is preferred over *sexual preference* in describing a person's sexual orientation. The key point is this: It is important to be aware of the range of human sexual expression and to be sensitively other-oriented as you interact with those whose sexual orientation and gender identity are different from your own.

Age

Because different generations have experienced different cultural and historical events, they often view life differently. If your grandparents or great-grandparents experienced the Great Depression of the 1930s, they may have different attitudes about bank savings accounts than you or even your parents do. Today's explicit song lyrics may shock older Americans who grew up with such racy lyrics as "makin' whoopee." The generation gap is real and has implications for how we communicate with others.

There is considerable evidence that people hold stereotypical views of others based on others' perceived age.[21] You may see someone with graying or thinning hair and wrinkles and make assumptions about that person's preferences in music, food, technology, or even politics. Similarly, older people who see a younger person with tattoos, piercings, and wildly colored hair may make stereotypical assumptions about a host of preferences of that person. (Even our example of old and young draws on stereotypes and runs the risk of reinforcing those stereotypical images.)

Regardless of the accuracy of the assumptions we make about others on the basis of perceived age, a person's age has an influence on his or her communication with others, including how messages are processed. For example, one study found that older adults have greater difficulty in accurately interpreting the nonverbal messages of others than do younger people.[22] Older adults don't like to be patronized or talked down to (who does?).[23] And younger people seem to value social support, empathic listening, and being mentored more than older people do.[24]

Generation Characteristics Authors Neil Howe and William Strauss, researchers who have investigated the role of age and generation in society, define a generation as "a society-wide peer group, born over a period roughly the same length as the passage from youth to adulthood, who collectively possess a common persona."[25] Table 6.1 summarizes five generational labels along with their characteristics and values.

Baby boomers is the label for the generation of people born between 1943 and 1960. Perhaps your parents or grandparents are "boomers." If you are not a boomer, you may experience some communication differences and conflicts with those who are because of differing values and perspectives.

Generation X is the term used for people born between 1961 and 1981. Of course, not all Generation Xers share all of the characteristics listed in Table 6.1, such as living with uncertainty, valuing a balanced life, or saving for the future. While these attributes provide a general overview, they vary from person to person.

Millennials are those born between 1982 and 1996. Researchers Howe and Strauss suggest that, as a group, "millennials are unlike any other youth generation in living memory. They are more numerous, more affluent, better educated, and more ethnically diverse." They also have a number of "positive social habits," including "a new focus on teamwork, achievement, modesty, and good conduct."[26] Not surprisingly, millennials are more comfortable with technology than people in older age groups because the Internet, cell phones, and personal computers have always been part of their lives.[27] According to research by the Pew Research Center, millennials are also less likely to

TABLE 6.1 Summary of Generation Characteristics[28]

Generation Name	Birth Years	Typical Characteristics
Baby boomers	1943–1960	• Value personal fulfillment and optimism • Crusade for causes • Buy now/pay later • Support equal rights for all • Work efficiently
Generation X	1961–1981	• Live with uncertainty • Consider balance important • Live for today • Save • Consider every job as a contract
Millennials	1982–1996	• Are close to their parents • Feel "special" • Are goal and team-oriented • Frequently use social media • Focus on achievement
Generation Z	1997–	• Understand that diversity is important, expected, and natural • Believe it's a challenge to achieve the "American Dream" • Are likely to have multiple jobs • Technology and social media are integral to their lives • Have some distrust of hierarchies

be tied to a specific religious institution and more likely to build their own personal networks using social media.

Generation Z are people born since 1997. Because Generation Z individuals are just emerging, there is less research examining the specific attributes of this generation. According to a Pew survey, 48 percent of Generation Z individuals are nonwhite and 35 percent know someone who prefers to use gender-neutral pronouns.[29] Generation Z individuals, who have always used technology to connect, view technology as an even more seamless means of interacting with others than do millennials.[30]

Implications for Communication Your generation of origin has important implications for communication, especially as you relate to others in both family and work situations. Each generation has developed its own set of values, anchored in social, economic, and cultural factors stemming from the times in which the generation has lived.

Our values—core conceptualizations of what is fundamentally good or bad and right or wrong—color our way of thinking about and responding to what we experience. Generational and age differences may create barriers and increase the potential for conflict and misunderstanding. For example, after investigating the role of generations in the workforce, one team of researchers found that Generation X workers are paradoxically both more individualistic (self-reliant) and more team-oriented than boomers.[31] In contrast, boomers are more likely to have a sense of loyalty to their employers, expect long-term employment, value a pension plan, and experience job burnout from overwork. Generation Xers, by contrast, seek a more balanced approach between work and personal life, expect to have more than one job or career, value working conditions over other job factors, and have a greater need to feel appreciated.[32] This research suggests that if you have a boomer boss and you are a Generation Xer, your boss may not understand why you want to take extra vacation time just to "clear your head" when there is a lot of work that needs to be done. The phrase "OK boomer" is sometimes used as a dismissive response to boomers' "old fashioned" ideas. Of course, these broad generalizations do not apply to all people in these categories.

Race and Ethnicity

Racial and ethnic differences are frequently discussed and sometimes debated. Although the terms *race* and *ethnicity* are often used interchangeably, race is a category that historically has been based on genetic or biological factors that are not clear-cut.[33] A person's race was traditionally based on visible, physical attributes called *phenotypes*, which include skin color, body type, hair color and texture, and other physical characteristics. Although it may seem easy to genetically classify individuals as belonging to one race or another, it's not quite that simple. Much more genetic variation has been documented *within* any given racial categories than *between* one race and another. That's why scholars now suggest that in addition to biological or genetic characteristics, **race** should include cultural, economic, social, geographic and historical elements.[34] Skin color and other physical characteristics continue to affect our responses to others and influence the way people of different races interact. Despite its continuing use as a descriptive term in the media and in casual conversation, race is a fuzzy and somewhat controversial way of classifying people.[35] Nonetheless, race continues to appear on surveys and the U.S. 2020 Census, which included 15 racial categories.

Racism or being racist consists of negative attitudes, beliefs, and behaviors expressed or unexpressed toward others based on the prejudiced view that someone of a different race is inferior. Structural or **systemic racism** takes many forms—it can consist of cultural elements, attitudes, beliefs, and behaviors enacted within groups, institutions, or societies that inherently and consistently, although not always consciously, negatively discriminate against a person's race due to historical and institutional practices. Racial disparities in healthcare, average income levels, arrests, and incarcerations, and racial profile differences reflected in housing, education, and positions of power provide additional evidence of the existence of systemic racism.

Ethnicity is a related term, yet scholars suggest it has a broader definition than race. Ethnicity is a *social classification* based on a variety of factors, such as nationality, religion, and language, as well as biological ancestral heritage, shared by a group of people with a common geographic origin. Simply stated, an ethnic group is a group of people who have identified themselves as such, based on a variety of factors that may or may not include ancestral heritage or biological characteristics such as skin color. Communication scholar Brenda Allen writes in her book *Difference Matters* that ethnicity refers to "a common origin or culture based on shared activities and identity related to some mixture of race, religion, language and/or ancestry."[36] Ethnicity fosters common bonds that affect communication patterns.

Discrimination is the unfair or inappropriate treatment of categories of people, based on their race, sex, age, gender, and ethnicity, as well as other group memberships.

race
A group of people with a common cultural history, nationality, or geographical location who may share some genetically transmitted physical attributes.

racism
Negative attitudes, beliefs, and behaviors expressed or unexpressed toward others based on the prejudiced view that someone of a different race is inferior.

systemic racism
Cultural elements, attitudes, beliefs, and behaviors enacted within groups, institutions, or societies that inherently and consistently, although not always consciously, negatively discriminate against a person's race due to historical and institutional practices.

ethnicity
A social classification based on factors such as nationality, religion, and language, as well as biological ancestral heritage, that are shared by a group of people with a common geographic origin.

discrimination
The unfair or inappropriate treatment of categories of people, based on their race, sex, age, gender, and ethnicity, as well as other group memberships.

Although different ethnic groups bring vitality and variety to American society, members of these groups often experience discrimination. One of the most significant problems stemming from attempts to classify people by racial or ethnic type is the tendency to discriminate and unfairly, inaccurately, or inappropriately ascribe stereotypes to racial or ethnic groups. One of the goals of learning about diversity and becoming aware of both differences and similarities among groups is to eliminate discrimination and stereotypes that cause people to rigidly and inappropriately prejudge others.

Social Class

Social class refers to the status, influence, authority, and power people are perceived to have based on economic factors, education, and family history. Social psychologist Michael Argyle suggests that the factors we use to identify social class distinctions are (1) way of life, (2) family, (3) job, (4) money, and (5) education.[37] Communication scholar Brenda Allen describes social class as encompassing " . . . a socially constructed category of identity that involves more than just economic factors; it includes an entire socialization process."[38] Virtually every group, community, and organization develops a hierarchy that makes status distinctions based on social class.

Socialization is the process of learning and reinforcing a role or position based on the norms of a group or society. When you join a new group or organization, you become socialized to its expectations of acceptable behavior. Social class influences who we talk with and even what we talk about, who we may invite to social gatherings, and who we choose as our friends and lovers. Members of a social class develop ways of communicating class differences to others by the way they dress, the cars they drive, the homes they live in, the schools they attend, and other visual "status symbols" that communicate influence and power. Although we tend to communicate most frequently with those within our own perceived social class, a person's social class can change through education, employment, and income.[39]

social class
The status, influence, and power people are perceived to have, based on their way of life, family, job, money, and education.

socialization
The process of learning and reinforcing a role or position based on the norms within a group or society.

Intersectionality: A Combination of Differences

So far, we have described several categories of human differences, including sex, gender, gender identity, gender expression, sexual orientation, race, ethnicity, age, and social class. Each person is a composite of all of these differences. Yet our description of diversity is incomplete; there are innumerable ways we are different, including our religious beliefs, body types, (dis)abilities, political affiliations, regional identities, and organizational and professional identities, as well as a host of other factors.

The concept of **intersectionality** describes how each person's multitude of characteristics interact to affect one's sense of oppression or power.[40] Your identity is socially constructed through communication based on a combination of differences, rather than only one of these factors. Communication scholar Gus Yep describes intersectionality as " . . . how race, class, gender, sexuality, the body, and nation, among other vectors of difference, come together simultaneously to produce social identities and experiences in the social world, from privilege to oppression."[41] The intersection, for example, of being lesbian, African American, low-income, and female results in a different social perception than being straight, African American, high-income, and female, or straight, white, high-income, and male. Intersectionality describes the simultaneous *combination of differences* that contribute to people's responses to the social world, which range from being oppressed to being privileged (Figure 6.2). The intersection of these multitude of factors and the way we communicate to socially construct our identities, contributes to the development of our self-identity, as discussed in Chapter 2.

intersectionality
The way in which various social and demographic elements such as ethnicity, gender, sex, social class, age, and other factors result in intersecting and dynamic social identities that affect one's sense of oppression or power.

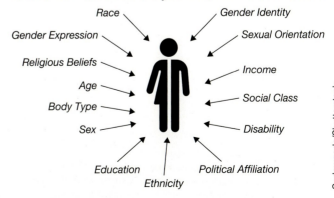

FIGURE 6.2 Intersectionality: A Combination of Differences

positionality
An individual's perceived level of influence, power, and status, ranging from being oppressed and marginalized to being privileged and powerful, within a group, community, or society based on a combination of social, demographic, and cultural elements such as age, gender, gender identity, race, ethnicity, and sexual orientation.

Positionality, a concept closely related to intersectionality, is your perceived level of influence, power, and status, which ranges from being oppressed to being privileged within the hierarchy of your group, community, and society. Your position of power or lack of power is based on the intersection of a combination of demographic, social, and cultural factors. Some groups and individuals have been and continue to be marginalized and oppressed due to being in the minority (such as being gay, lesbian, bisexual, transgender, or queer) or belonging to an ethnic or racial group that has experienced historical, systemic, stereotypical prejudices and discrimination. Just as some groups have been marginalized, others enjoy privileges because they are in a higher social class due to their income or education. For example, it is undisputed that the overwhelming majority of U.S. senators, U.S. presidents, university presidents, and corporate chief executive officers are white and male.[42]

It is important to be aware (principle one) of how various social and demographic elements interact (intersectionality) to affect a person's power (positionality) on a continuum ranging from being oppressed and marginalized to having privilege and power. Being aware of your perceived sense of power or lack thereof can give you insights into your patterns of communication with others. Although the goal is to communicate with others as equals, cultural, social, institutionalized, and systemic factors result in a range of power levels within a society. It is because of our differences that it is important to develop ways to communicate effectively with those who are different from ourselves as well as to ethically confront inequality, marginalization, and oppression. To assertively confront inequality or unjust attitudes and behavior draws upon all five of the Communication Principles for a Lifetime emphasized in this text. Civil rights activists Rosa Parks and Martin Luther King, Jr., South African leader Nelson Mandela, and gay rights leader Frank Kameny drew upon these principles when they used verbal and nonverbal messages to confront social injustice, racism, and homophobia.

Culture and Communication

6.2 Define *culture*, and compare and contrast cultural contexts and cultural values.

You need not travel the world to encounter people who are different from you; the world is traveling to you. The following Diversity & Communication feature documents how culturally diverse the United States is already and also provides evidence that the trend toward greater diversity will continue.[43]

globalization
The integration of economics and technology that is contributing to a worldwide, interconnected business environment.

Globalization, the integration of economics and technology that is contributing to a worldwide, interconnected business environment, is changing the way we work and relate to people around the world.[44] For example, when you call to get technical assistance with your computer or advice on fixing your TV, you may talk to someone in India rather than in Indiana. One statistician notes that if the world were a village of 1,000 people, the village would have 590 Asians, 122 Africans, 96 Europeans, 84 Latin Americans, 55 members of the former Soviet Union, and 53 North Americans.[45] Clearly, globalization has increased the probability that you will communicate with someone today who has a cultural background different from your own.[46] To ignore the range of human cultural differences is to ignore a significant factor, which can mean the difference between effective and ineffective communication.

Defining Culture

culture
A learned system of knowledge, behavior, attitudes, beliefs, values, and norms that is shared by a group of people and shaped from one generation to the next.

Culture is a learned system of knowledge, behavior, attitudes, beliefs, values, and norms that is shared by a group of people and shaped from one generation to the next.[47] Communication and culture, says anthropologist Edward T. Hall, are inseparable—you can't talk about one without the other.[48] Ample evidence documents the influence of

DIVERSITY & COMMUNICATION

Malaysian Diversity Almanac

1. In 2019, Bumiputera accounted for 69.3 percent of Malaysia's population and 22.8 percent were classified as ethnic Chinese.[49] According to Malaysia's Department of Statistics, there are 18 recognized ethnic groups in the country.[50]
2. The average Chinese household in Malaysia has an income around twice that of a Bumiputera household.[51] There are some signs of convergence in mean household incomes between the main ethnic groups.[52]
3. Malaysia is home to significant populations from over 15 nationalities with some 137 different languages spoken.[53]
4. Malaysia has seven major religions or faiths including Islam (61.3%), Buddhism (19.8%), Christianity (9.2%), and Hinduism (6.3%). The country's religious-freedom policy confers the right to practice different religions.
5. The most common languages spoken are Malay (Bahasa Malaysia), Chinese, Tamil, and English. Malay and English are the most used across the media.[54]
6. Nearly two-thirds of Malaysians believe employers favor employees who look, think, and act as they do. Around 55 percent think their careers have been limited by their gender, background, or age, and 50 percent feel they did not get a job due to their gender, family commitments, ethnicity, marital status, religion, or sexuality. However, 94% of companies in Malaysia are supportive of diversity and inclusion.[55]
7. The LGBT community can be tried in Islamic courts; the Shariah Courts (Criminal Jurisdiction) Act allows heavy penalties to be imposed on the LGBT community.[56]
8. In 2019, 415,000 female students were enrolled in public higher education institutions across Malaysia in comparison to the 291,000 male students. However, only 14 percent of board members are female.[57]
9. Millennials in Malaysia are the largest age group (some 29 percent of the population) and have a monthly disposable income of $327 million. They are smartphone and Internet dependent and spend up to 8 hours a day on social media. They are well educated and entrepreneurial and as consumers they are influential and independent.[58]
10. In 2020, Gen Z accounted for 40 percent of the Malaysian workforce, Millennials 21 percent, Baby Boomers 45 percent and Gen Xers 33 percent. Baby Boomers and Gen X groups prioritize better health and financial security, while Millennials and Gen Z prioritize job stability.[59]

---

culture on how we work and live.[60] In the broadest sense, culture includes how people think, what they do, and how they use things to sustain their lives. Researcher Geert Hofstede says culture is the "mental software" that helps us understand our world.[61] Like the software and operating system in a computer, our culture provides the framework within which we interpret the data and information that enter our lives.

Cultures are not static; they change as new information and new technologies modify them.[62] We no longer believe that bathing is unhealthy or that we should use leeches as the primary medical procedure to make us healthy. Through research, we have changed our cultural assumptions and values about personal hygiene and medical care.

Some groups of individuals can best be described as a **co-culture**—a cultural group within a larger culture. Examples of co-cultures include people with physical disabilities, different age groups, and various religious groups. Different Christian denominations, such as the Amish or members of the Church of Jesus Christ of Latter-day Saints (Mormons), have distinct traditions and cultural norms. A person's gender also places her or him in one of the co-cultures that researchers have used to analyze and investigate the influence of communication on our relationships with others. Gay, lesbian, bisexual, transgender, and queer people constitute other important co-cultures in our society.

Intercultural communication occurs when individuals or groups from different cultures communicate. The transactional process of communicating with people from different cultural backgrounds can be challenging; the greater the difference in culture between two people, the greater the potential for misunderstanding and mistrust. There is evidence that studying the role of culture in our lives can help us adapt when we encounter cultural differences—whether those differences occur in our hometown or when we are living in a culture different from our own.[63] Understanding the nature of culture and cultural differences helps us develop strategies to make connections and adapt to others with different "mental software."[64]

co-culture
A culture that exists within a larger cultural context.

intercultural communication
Communication between people or groups from different cultures.

culture shock

Feelings of confusion, loss, stress, and anxiety that a person may experience when encountering a culture different from his or her own.

When you encounter a culture that has little in common with your own, you may experience **culture shock**, a sense of confusion, anxiety, stress, and loss.[65] If you are visiting or actually living in the new culture, your uncertainty and stress may take time to subside as you learn the values and message systems that characterize the culture. Research has found that one of the ways we seek to adapt to a new culture is by using social media. International exchange students, for example, often use Zoom, WhatsApp, or Skype, as well as various social media platforms to help them feel closer to their friends and family back home and less stressed when in a new culture. Other research also found that students studying abroad were more likely to use Skype or other video messaging platforms to communicate with family and close friends.[66]

worldview

A perspective shared by a culture or group of people about key beliefs and issues, such as death, God, and the meaning of life, that influences interaction with others; the lens through which people in a given culture perceive the world around them.

Our culture and life experiences determine our **worldview**—the general cultural perspective that shapes how we perceive and respond to what happens to us. The intersection of various factors such as gender, sex, race, ethnicity, social class, and age that influence your positionality play an important role in influencing your worldview. A culture's worldview, according to intercultural communication scholar Carley Dodd, encompasses "how the culture perceives the role of various forces in explaining why events occur as they do in a social setting."[67] These beliefs shape our thoughts, language, and actions. Your worldview permeates all aspects of how you interact with society; it's like a lens through which you observe the world. Because, as we noted in Chapter 1, communication is how we make sense of the world and share that sense with others, our worldview is one of the primary filters that influence how we communicate. Two frameworks for describing how culture influences our worldview are cultural contexts and cultural values.

Cultural Contexts

cultural context

Additional information about a message that is communicated through nonverbal and environmental cues rather than through language.

The **cultural context** of any communication consists of the nonverbal cues that surround and give added meaning to the message. In this sense, *all* nonverbal cues are part of a cultural context. When interpreting the overall meaning of a message, some cultures give more weight to the surrounding nonverbal context than to the explicit verbal message. In contrast, other cultures place less emphasis on the nonverbal context and greater emphasis on what someone says.

For example, when you interview for a job, you may be scanning the face of your interviewer and looking for nonverbal messages to provide cues about the impression you are making on the interviewer. These contextual cues (in this case, the nonverbal messages) provide meaning to help you interpret your interviewer's message. Edward T. Hall helped us understand the importance of cultural context when he categorized cultures as either high- or low-context.[68]

high-context culture

A culture in which people derive much information from nonverbal and environmental cues and less information from the words of a message.

High-Context Cultures In **high-context cultures**, nonverbal cues are extremely important in interpreting messages. Communicators rely heavily on the context of subtle information such as facial expression, vocal cues, and even silence in interpreting messages—hence the term *high-context cultures*, to indicate the emphasis placed on the context. People from Asian, Arab, and southern European countries are more likely to draw on context for message interpretation.

low-context culture

A culture in which people derive much information from the words of a message and less information from nonverbal and environmental cues.

Low-Context Cultures People in **low-context cultures** rely more explicitly on language and the meaning of words and use fewer contextual cues to send and interpret information. Individuals from low-context cultures, such as North Americans, Germans, and Scandinavians, may sometimes perceive people from high-context cultures as less knowledgeable and trustworthy because they violate unspoken low-context cultural rules of conduct and communication. Individuals from low-context cultures often are less skilled in interpreting unspoken contextual messages.[69] Figure 6.3 describes differences in communication style between high-context and low-context cultures.

Cultural Values

Ancient Egyptians worshiped cats. The Druids of England believed they could tap into spiritual powers in the shadow of the mysterious rock circle of Stonehenge at the summer solstice. Some would say contemporary Americans place a high value on

FIGURE 6.3 A Scale of High-Context and Low-Context Cultures

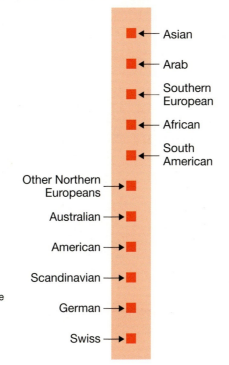

Low-Context Cultures
Place emphasis on words

- Are less aware of the nonverbal environment and situation
- Need detailed background information
- Tend to segment and compartmentalize information
- Control information and share it on a "need to know" basis
- Prefer explicit and careful directions from someone who "knows"
- Consider knowledge an important commodity

High-Context Cultures
Place emphasis on nonverbal expressions and surrounding context

- Consider nonverbal cues important
- Take into account the environment and situation
- Observe a communication partner's gestures, facial expressions, tone of voice, and overall mood
- Maintain extensive information networks

accumulating material possessions and making pilgrimages to sports arenas on weekends. By paying attention to what a culture values, we can get important clues about how to respond to communication messages, establish relationships, and avoid making embarrassing errors when interacting with people from a given culture. Identifying what a particular group of people values or appreciates can give us insight into the behavior of an individual raised within that culture.

Although there are considerable differences among the world's **cultural values**—clearly, not all cultures value the same things—Geert Hofstede has identified six categories for measuring values that are important in almost every culture.[70] These generalizations are based on several surveys that he developed and administered to more than 100,000 people. Even though much of his data were collected more than thirty-five years ago and sampled only employees (predominantly males) who worked at IBM—a large international company with branch offices in many countries—Hofstede's research remains one of the most data-based comprehensive studies cited in research to help us describe what people from a culture may value.[71]

According to Hofstede's research, every culture establishes values relating to (1) individualism versus collectivism, (2) distribution of power (either centralized or shared), (3) avoidance of uncertainty versus tolerance for uncertainty, (4) masculine or feminine cultural perspectives, (5) long-term and short-term orientation to time, and (6) expectations about happiness in terms of indulgence or restraint. An overview of Hofstede's research conclusions for several countries is included in Table 6.2 at the end of this section, but first we'll consider each of these six categories of values in more detail.

As we discuss these six cultural values, keep in mind that we are applying generalizations to a cultural group. There are vast differences *within* a culture as well as between cultural groups; certainly not all the people within a cultural group will hold the cultural values we will discuss. Think of these values as explaining cultural *group* differences viewed from an anthropological perspective rather than *individual* differences viewed from a psychological perspective.[72] Using Hofstede's six cultural values to describe a given culture or geographic region is a bit like flying over a country at 35,000 feet; at that height, you can't see the details and notice nuances of difference, but you can gain a broad overview of the landscape.

cultural values
Whatever a given group of people values or appreciates.

SOCIAL MEDIA & COMMUNICATION

Adapting to Differences When Making E-Connections

As we have noted, it is increasingly likely that you communicate with people who are far from where you work and live. It's not unusual to use Facebook, instant messages, email, or texts to contact people from other cultures. With the advent of social media, such as Instagram and Facebook, as well as Skype, Zoom, and other easy-to-use videoconference methods, it's also not surprising to see and hear the person you're talking with.[73]

A team of communication researchers points out that when we communicate via email, phone, or social media it takes a bit longer to interpret information about relationships, because often there are fewer nonverbal cues available.[74] Evidence also shows that, because of these limited cues, we are more likely to inaccurately stereotype others, especially on the basis of gender, when interacting via electronic channels than we are when communicating face to face.[75] Research has also confirmed that we are more interculturally sensitive when someone is standing in front of us than when we communicate via social media.[76]

With the growing importance and prevalence of social media and e-communication, there comes an increased potential for misunderstanding.[77] So how can you enhance the quality of your relationships online? Consider these suggestions:

- If you are using a "lean" communication channel, such as email or texting, to interact with a person who is from a high-context culture, you may need to provide more explicit references to your feelings and emotions by telling your partner how you feel or by using emoticons.

- Take time to get to know other team members personally, especially early in a group's formation.[78] High-performing groups and teams found that having high-quality social relationships resulted in better outcomes.[79]

- When appropriate, consider asking more questions to clarify meanings.

- Consciously make more small talk about the weather or other topics that may not directly be related to the task at hand. Such interaction helps connect you to others, makes the interaction less task oriented, and provides a balance of relational information that humanizes the communication.

- Use paraphrasing to confirm that you understand what others are saying.

- Finally, you may simply need to be more patient with others; relationships may take longer to develop because of the diminished nonverbal cues. Be mindful of the differences and consciously develop other-oriented skills.

collectivistic culture
A culture that places a high value on collaboration, teamwork, and group achievement.

individualistic culture
A culture that values individual achievement and personal accomplishments.

Individualistic and Collectivistic Cultural Values Which of the following two sayings better characterizes your culture: "All for one and one for all" or "I did it my way"? If you chose the first one, your culture is more likely to value group or team collaboration—it is what researchers call a **collectivistic culture**. Collectivistic cultures champion what people do together and reward group achievement. In contrast, the "I did it my way" phrase emphasizes the importance of the individual over the group.[80] A culture that celebrates individual achievement and in which individual recognition is important is an **individualistic culture**.

Traditionally, North Americans place a high value on individual achievement. The United States—with its Academy Awards, its reality TV shows in which contestants vie for the title of "American Ninja Warrior," and its community awards to volunteers for dedicated service—perhaps epitomizes the individualistic culture. Psychologist Alan Waterman summed up the American value system this way:

> Chief among the virtues claimed . . . is self-realization. Each person is viewed as having a unique set of talents and potentials. The translation of these potentials into actuality is considered the highest purpose to which one can devote one's life.[81]

People from Asian cultures are more likely to value collective or group achievement. In a collectivistic culture, people strive to accomplish goals for the benefit of the group rather than the individual. As one communication author describes, Kenya is another country with a culture that emphasizes group or team collaboration:

> Nobody is an isolated individual. Rather, his [or her] uniqueness is a secondary fact. . . . In this new system, group activities are dominant, responsibility is shared and

accountability is collective.... Because of the emphasis on collectivity, harmony and cooperation among the group tend to be emphasized more than individual function and responsibility.[82]

Some researchers believe that the values of individualism and collectivism are the most important values of any culture—they determine the essential nature of every other facet of how people behave.[83] Research has found that people from individualistic cultures especially value conversational communication skills, informative skills, effective listening, and the ability to tell a good story.[84] Other researchers, however, caution that cultures are complex and that it is dangerous to label an entire culture as individualistic or collectivistic.[85] We agree—as we've pointed out, not everyone in a given culture fits a single label. But in trying to understand the role of culture and its effect on human communication, we believe that Hofstede's concept of cultural values, with special emphasis on individualism and collectivism, can help to explain and predict how some people may send and interpret communication.[86]

▲ Awards for individual achievements are one indicator of how much North American cultures tend to value individualism.
FOX/Getty Images

Decentralized and Centralized Approaches to Power and Cultural Values Some cultures are more comfortable with a decentralized, broad distribution of power than other cultures. In cultures that value decentralized power, leadership is less likely to be vested in just one person. Decisions in cultures that value decentralized power distribution, as found in countries such as Australia and Ireland, are more likely to be made by collaborative consensus in a parliament or congress rather than by decree from a monarch or dictator.

Cultures that place a high value on centralized power, such as those found in Indonesia, India, and the Philippines, are more comfortable with a more structured form of government and with managerial styles that feature clear lines of authority. Hierarchical bureaucracies are common in these cultures, and the general assumption is that some people will have more power, control, and influence than others.

Uncertainty and Certainty and Cultural Values "Why don't they tell me what's going on?" exclaims an exasperated student. "I don't know what my grades are. I don't know when the test is. I'm in a complete fog." Many people like to know "what's going on." People from an uncertainty avoidance culture are more comfortable being able to predict what's going to happen. Too much uncertainty makes them uncomfortable. Cultures in which people need certainty to feel secure are likely to develop and enforce more rigid rules for behavior and establish more elaborate codes of conduct.

Other cultures tolerate more ambiguity and uncertainty. Those from an uncertainty tolerance culture have more relaxed, informal expectations for others; they accept that uncertainty and sometimes not knowing the outcome is normal. "It will sort itself out" and "Go with the flow" are phrases that characterize their attitudes.[87]

Again, we remind you that despite evidence for the existence of the general cultural value of uncertainty avoidance, not all people in a given culture or country find this cultural value equally important. Considerable variation exists within cultures as to how people respond to uncertainty.

CRITICAL/CULTURAL PERSPECTIVES & COMMUNICATION

Do You Have Power?

You have power if you can influence others. We have noted that some cultures place a high value on centralized power, or power residing in a single individual or group, compared with a more decentralized, equal distribution of power. To be an effective communicator it is useful to be aware of your own perceived power and your positionality, as well as the power others are perceived to have. How does your gender, age, ethnicity, socioeconomic status, sexual orientation, gender identity, and gender expression influence your perceived power? To be marginalized is to be perceived as less influential—to be on the margins means having less power and status versus being central or important. Having a realistic sense of your own ability to influence others, which unfortunately may be a result of stereotypes and systemic discrimination, can help you make decisions about how to respond to prejudice. *Being mindful of your influence, positionality, or marginalization doesn't mean you have to accept or be content with your perceived lack of influence.* It's also useful to understand if you are privileged, based on the intersection of several factors including your ethnicity, level of education, sex, or income. Increasing your awareness of your own power can help you understand the dynamics of your interactions with others and develop communication adaptation or assertiveness skills.

Masculine and Feminine Cultural Values Some cultures emphasize traditional "male" values such as getting things done and being assertive; other cultures place greater emphasis on traditional "female" values such as building relationships and seeking peace and harmony with others. These values are not really about biological sex differences but about general, gender-based assumptions that influence how we interact with others. People from **masculine cultures** tend to value more traditional roles for men and women. People (both men and women) from masculine cultures value achievement, heroism, material wealth, and making things happen. Men and women from **feminine cultures** tend to value such things as caring for the less fortunate, being sensitive toward others, and enhancing the overall quality of life.[88] Later in this chapter, we will discuss how gender contributes to the development of a culture, but for now it is enough to realize that whole cultures can be typified by whether they identify with or emphasize masculine or feminine values.

> **masculine culture**
> A culture that values achievement, assertiveness, heroism, material wealth, and traditional gender roles.
>
> **feminine culture**
> A culture that values being sensitive toward others and fostering harmonious personal relationships with others.

We caution you once more to avoid making sweeping generalizations about every person in any cultural group. Just as there are differences between and among cultures, there are differences within a cultural group. For centuries, most countries have emphasized masculine cultural values. Men and their conquests are featured in history books and all aspects of society more than women are. But today's cultural anthropologists see some shift in these values. There is some movement toward the middle, with greater equality between masculine and feminine roles.

Long-Term and Short-Term Time Orientation and Cultural Values A culture's orientation to time falls on a continuum between long-term and short-term.[89] People from a culture with a **long-term orientation** to time place an emphasis on the future and tend to value perseverance and thrift because these are virtues that pay off over a long period of time. A long-term time orientation also implies a greater willingness to subordinate oneself for a larger purpose, such as the good of society or the group.

> **long-term orientation**
> A cultural value that emphasizes the future and recognizes the importance of perseverance and working toward a long-term goal.
>
> **short-term orientation**
> A cultural value that emphasizes more immediate and short-term goals.

In contrast, a culture that tends to have a **short-term time orientation** values spending rather than saving (because of a focus on the immediate time rather than the future), tradition (because of the value placed on the past), and saving face (making sure that an individual is respected and that his or her dignity is upheld). A short-term time-oriented culture also has an expectation that results will soon follow the actions and effort expended on a task. In addition, short-term cultures place a high value on social and status obligations.

As shown in Table 6.2, cultures or societies with a long-term time orientation include many Asian cultures, such as China, Hong Kong, Taiwan, and Japan. Cultures with a short-term time orientation include Pakistan, the Czech Republic, Nigeria, Spain, and the Philippines. Both Canada and the United States are closer to the short-term time orientation than the long-term time orientation, which suggests an emphasis on valuing quick results from projects and greater pressure toward spending rather than saving, as well as a respect for tradition.[90]

Indulgent and Restrained Expectations about Happiness Do you expect to be happy? Embedded in the U.S. Constitution is the explicit quest for "life, liberty and the pursuit of happiness."[91] The newest cultural dimension added by Hofstede focuses on expectations about happiness.[92] According to Hofstede, some cultural values include the expectation that people should and will be happy.

Those who live in what Hofstede called an **indulgent culture** are more likely to have a greater desire and expectation for freedom and happiness. People from indulgent cultures tend to place a high value on freedom of speech, leisure activities, and sports. The United States, Canada, Mexico, Brazil, and Australia are examples of more indulgent cultures.

In contrast, a **restrained culture** is one in which people do not necessarily expect to achieve happiness by having all of their needs met. People from more restrained cultures are less likely to remember positive emotions of the past and have fewer expectations about being happy in the future. In general, they also participate less frequently in

indulgent culture
A cultural value that tends to place a high value on happiness and also values freedom of speech, leisure activities, and sports.

restrained culture
A cultural value that does not assume happiness is a right and that happiness should be expected, as evidenced by a more limited focus on leisure activities and sports.

TABLE 6.2 Six Categories of Cultural Values

Cultural Value	Countries Where People Scored Higher on This Cultural Value	Countries Where People Scored Lower on This Cultural Value
Individualism: Societies with higher individualism scores generally value individual accomplishment rather than the collective or collaborative achievement valued by societies with lower scores.	United States, Australia, Great Britain, Canada, Netherlands, New Zealand, Italy, Belgium, Denmark, Sweden, France	Guatemala, Ecuador, Panama, Venezuela, Colombia, Indonesia, Pakistan, Costa Rica, Peru, Taiwan, South Korea
Power Distribution: Societies with higher power distribution scores generally value greater power differences between people; they are generally more accepting of fewer people having authority and power than are those with lower scores on this cultural dimension.	Malaysia, Guatemala, Panama, Philippines, Mexico, Venezuela, Arab countries, Ecuador, Indonesia, India	Australia, Israel, Denmark, New Zealand, Ireland, Sweden, Norway, Finland, Switzerland, Great Britain
Uncertainty Avoidance: Societies with higher uncertainty avoidance scores generally prefer to avoid uncertainty; they like to know what will happen next. Societies with lower scores are more comfortable with uncertainty.	Greece, Portugal, Guatemala, Uruguay, Belgium, Japan, Peru, France	Singapore, Jamaica, Denmark, Sweden, Hong Kong, Ireland, Great Britain, Malaysia, India, Philippines, United States
Masculinity: Societies with higher masculinity scores value high achievement, men in more assertive roles, and more clearly differentiated sex roles than people with lower scores on this cultural dimension.	Japan, Australia, Venezuela, Italy, Switzerland, Mexico, Ireland, Jamaica, Great Britain	Sweden, Norway, Netherlands, Denmark, Costa Rica, Finland, Chile, Portugal, Thailand
Orientation to Time: Societies with higher scores have a longer-term orientation to time; they tend to value perseverance and thrift. Societies with lower scores have a shorter-term orientation to time; they value the past and present, respect for tradition, saving face, and spending rather than saving.	China, Hong Kong, Taiwan, Japan, Vietnam, South Korea, Brazil, India, Thailand, Hungary, Singapore, Denmark, Netherlands	Pakistan, Czech Republic, Nigeria, Spain, Philippines, Canada, Zimbabwe, Great Britain, United States, Portugal, New Zealand
Happiness: Societies with higher scores have a greater expectation of happiness as a right; they tend to value freedom of speech, leisure activities, and sports. Societies with lower scores are more restrained; they do not necessarily expect to have all of their needs met to achieve happiness.	United States, Canada, Mexico, Brazil, Australia	Russia, China, much of Eastern Europe

SOURCE: Adapted with permission from Geert Hofstede, Gert Jan Hofstede, and Michael Minkov, *Cultures and Organizations, Software of the Mind*, Third Revised Edition (New York: McGraw Hill, 2010). ISBN 0-07-166418-1 © Geert Hofstede BV.

RECAP

Cultural Values

Individualistic vs. Collectivistic	• Individualistic cultures value individual accomplishments and achievement. • Collectivistic cultures value group and team collaboration.
Decentralized vs. Centralized Power	• Centralized power cultures value having power in the hands of a smaller number of people. • Decentralized power cultures favor more equality and a more even distribution of power in government and organizations.
Uncertainty vs. Certainty	• Cultures that value certainty do not like ambiguity and value feeling secure. • Cultures with a greater tolerance for uncertainty are comfortable with ambiguity and less information.
Masculine vs. Feminine	• Masculine cultures value achievement, assertiveness, heroism, material wealth, and more traditional gender roles. • Feminine cultures value relationships, caring for the less fortunate, overall quality of life, and less traditional distinctions between gender roles.
Long-Term vs. Short-Term Orientation to Time	• Cultures with a long-term orientation to time tend to be future oriented and value perseverance and thrift. • Cultures with a short-term orientation to time tend to value the past and present, respecting tradition, saving face, and fulfilling social obligations.
Indulgent vs. Restrained Expectations about Happiness	• People from indulgent cultures tend to have a greater expectation of happiness as a right. • People from restrained cultures do not necessarily expect to achieve happiness by having all of their needs met.

leisure activities, including sports.[93] More restrained cultures include Russia, China, and much of Eastern Europe. Although less data supports this newest cultural dimension, Hofstede has been including it in his latest research results as yet another dimension of our mental software.[94]

Barriers to Adapting to Others

6.3 Illustrate four barriers that inhibit communication between individuals.

Now that we've identified some of the ways people are different from one another, let's identify barriers that *increase* the differences that exist between people. Differences, whether based in culture, age, ethnicity, sexual orientation, gender, or social class often breed misunderstanding, which can lead to feelings of distrust, suspicion, and even hostility. News headlines continue to chronicle the prevalence of terrorism, war, and conflict around the globe, which are due, in part, to different cultural perspectives.

Is it possible to develop effective relationships with people who are different from ourselves? The answer is "of course." Although almost every relationship experiences some degree of conflict, most of the world's people do not witness annihilating destruction each day. Bridging culture and gender differences is possible. To develop effective strategies to adapt to others who are different from ourselves, we'll examine some of the barriers that often separate us from one another.

Assuming Superiority

ethnocentrism
The belief that one's own cultural traditions and assumptions are superior to those of others.

One of the most powerful barriers to adapting to others is the belief that one's own culture or gender is better than that of others. **Ethnocentrism** is the attitude that our own cultural approaches are superior to those of other cultures.[95] Extreme ethnocentrism involves championing one's own "tribe" or cultural group over all others. It is the opposite of being other-oriented. When fans from two rival high schools at a Friday night football game scream, "We're number one!" at one another they are hardly establishing high-quality communication. Competition is, of course, expected in sports; but when the mind-set of unquestioned superiority is created through cultural or religious identification, the resulting mistrust and suspicion are breeding grounds for conflict. Ethnocentrism and cultural snobbery create a barrier that inhibits rather than enhances communication.

Most of us are more comfortable with people from our own culture and those who are like us. In fact, some degree of ethnocentrism can play a useful role in perpetuating our own cultural traditions; we form communities and groups based on common traditions, beliefs, and values. A problem occurs, however, if we become so extremely biased in favor of our own cultural traditions that we fail to recognize that people from other cultural traditions are just as comfortable with their approach to life as we are with ours. And when we mindlessly attack someone else's cultural traditions (which may be a prelude to physical aggression), we erect communication barriers.

Xenophobia is the fear and dislike of people simply because they are from a different country or culture. A person who is xenophobic is also likely to be ethnocentric because she or he is not only fearful of difference, but also assumes superiority over those who are from a different culture. In addition, those who are ethnocentric and xenophobic may seek greater power and control over others. Conflicts are often about power—who has it and who wants more of it. Differences in power are, therefore, breeding grounds for mistrust and conflict. Nineteenth-century British scholar Lord John Acton said that absolute power corrupts absolutely; although this may not always be the case, an ethnocentric or xenophobic mind-set that assumes superiority may add to the perception of assumed power over others. It's true that there are cultural differences in attitudes toward power (whether power is centralized or decentralized), but world history has taught us that people who are consistently pushed and pulled and pummeled eventually revolt and seek greater equity of power.

xenophobia
The fear and dislike of someone from a different culture or country.

Assuming Similarity

We've all done it. On meeting a new acquaintance, early in the conversation we usually explore what we may have in common. "Did you watch *Tiger King*?" "Oh, you're from Buckner. Do you know Mamie Smith?" The search for similarities helps us develop a common framework for communication. But even when we discover a few similarities, it's a mistake to make too many assumptions about our new friend's attitudes and perceptions. Because of our human tendency to develop categories and use words to label our experiences, we may lump people into a common category and assume similarity where no similarity exists. Even if they appear to be like you, people do not all behave the same way.[96] As an ancient Greek proverb tells us, "Every tale can be told in a different way."

Anthropologists Clyde Kluckhohn and Henry Murray have suggested that every person is, in some respects, (1) like all other people, (2) like some other people, and (3) like no other people.[97] Our challenge when meeting another person is to sort out how we are alike and how we are unique. Focusing on superficial factors such as appearance, clothing, and even a person's occupation can lead to false impressions. Instead, we must take time to explore the person's background and cultural values before we can determine what we really have in common.

Our cultural worldview has a profound effect on how we describe ourselves and people in other cultures. Each of us perceives the world through our own frame of reference. We not only see the world differently, but also express those differences in the way we talk, think, and interact with others. For example, research has found that English-speaking people tend to describe themselves and others by identifying individual personality traits ("Matt is friendly") rather than merely describing behavior ("Matt

brings snacks to the meeting").⁹⁸ If we fail to be mindful of others' cultural values and individual worldviews, we may take communication shortcuts, use unfamiliar words, and assume that our communication will be more effective than it is.

Assuming Differences

Although it may seem contradictory to say so, given what we just noted about assuming similarities, another barrier that may keep you from bridging differences between yourself and someone else is to automatically assume that the other person will be different from you. It can be just as detrimental to communication to assume that someone is essentially different from you as it is to assume that someone is just like you. The fact is, human beings *do* share common experiences and characteristics despite their differences.

If we don't seek to connect with those factors that make us all human, we may miss opportunities for bridging the real differences that exist. The words *communication* and *common* resemble each other. Identifying common cultural issues and similarities can also help you establish common ground with your listeners whether speaking before an audience or visiting with a friend or colleague.

How are we all alike? Cultural anthropologist Donald Brown has compiled a list of hundreds of "surface" universals of behavior.⁹⁹ According to Brown, people in all cultures:

- Have beliefs about death.
- Have a childhood fear of strangers.
- Have a division of labor by sex.
- Experience certain emotions and feelings, such as envy, pain, jealousy, shame, and pride.
- Use facial expressions to express emotions.
- Experience empathy.
- Value some degree of collaboration or cooperation.
- Experience conflict and seek to manage or mediate conflict.

▼ People from many different cultures similarly value close, happy families, but they may have different ideas about what makes a family close and happy. How can you discover similarities and differences in values when you communicate with someone from another culture?
Jane September/Shutterstock

Of course, not all cultures have the same beliefs about death or the same way of dividing labor according to sex, but all cultures address these issues.

Communication researcher David Kale believes that protecting the dignity and worth of the human spirit is another universal value. Therefore, he suggests that all people can identify with the struggle to enhance their own dignity and worth, although different cultures express it in different ways.¹⁰⁰ Another common value that Kale notes is world peace.

Intercultural communication scholars Larry Samovar and Richard Porter assert that there are other elements that cultures share.¹⁰¹ They note that people from all cultures seek physical, emotional, and psychological pleasure while avoiding personal harm. It's true that each culture and each person decides what is pleasurable or painful; nonetheless, Samovar and Porter argue, all people operate somewhere on this pleasure–pain continuum.

Another advocate for common human values was Oxford and Cambridge professor and widely read author C. S. Lewis. In his book *The Abolition of Man*, Lewis argued for the existence of universal, natural laws, which he called the Tao, that serve as benchmarks for all human values.[102] Lewis identified such common values as do not murder; be honest; hold parents, elders, and ancestors with special honor; be compassionate to those who are less fortunate; keep your promises; and honor the basic human rights of others.

What are the practical implications of trying to identify common human values or characteristics? If you find yourself disagreeing with another person about a particular issue, identifying a larger common value such as the importance of family or of peace and prosperity can help you find common ground so that the other person will at least listen to your ideas. Discovering how we are alike can provide a starting point for human understanding.

Communication effectiveness is diminished when we assume that we're all different from one another in every aspect, just as communication is hindered if we assume we're all alike. We're more complicated than that.

Stereotyping and Prejudice

Similar to ethnocentrism and feelings of cultural and gender superiority, making a rigid judgment against a class or type of people can also be a barrier to effective communication.

> All Russians like vodka.
>
> All men like to watch wrestling.
>
> All Asians are good at math.
>
> All women like to go shopping.

These statements are stereotypes. They are all inaccurate. To **stereotype** someone is to place him or her in an inflexible, all-encompassing category. The term *stereotype* started out as a printing term to describe a process in which a typesetter uses the same type to print text again and again. When we stereotype, we "print" the same judgment over and over again, failing to consider the uniqueness of individuals, groups, or

stereotype
To place a person or group of persons into an inflexible, all-encompassing category.

ETHICS & COMMUNICATION

Can Stereotyping Others Ever Be a Good Idea?

Reaching conclusions about someone before you get to know her or him can hinder communication and result in a dishonest relationship. Most people are taught not to be prejudiced toward others. Yet, might stereotypes sometimes serve a useful purpose, especially when a quick decision is needed and you have only partial information?

Imagine, for example, that you are driving your car late at night and have a flat tire in a neighborhood that's known to have a high crime rate. While wondering what to do, you see two people who have observed your plight and are moving toward you. Do you hop out of your car and seek their help? Or do you lock yourself inside the car and use your cell phone to call for assistance? Could a case be made that the ability to respond stereotypically may be useful in times of stress when quick thinking is needed?

What do you think? Is it ever appropriate to hold stereotypical views of others and to make judgments about them without knowing all the facts? Why or why not? When do stereotypical evaluations hinder communication? When is it preferable to avoid stereotypical decisions?

> **RE**CAP
>
> **Barriers to Bridging Differences and Adapting to Others**
>
> | | |
> |---|---|
> | Assuming Superiority | Becoming ethnocentric—assuming that one's own culture and cultural traditions are superior to those of others |
> | Assuming Similarity | Assuming that other people respond to situations as we respond; failing to acknowledge and consider differences in culture and background |
> | Assuming Differences | Assuming that other people are always different from ourselves; failing to explore common values and experiences that can serve as bridges to better understanding |
> | Stereotyping and Prejudice | Rigidly categorizing others and prejudging others on the basis of limited information |

events. Such a "hardening of the categories" becomes a barrier to effective communication and inhibits our ability to adapt to others. Evidence suggests that we are even more likely to stereotype others when viewing bits and pieces of someone's life on social media or via email.[103] Being aware of our tendency to stereotype other people, whether online or offline, is a first step to ensuring that stereotypes won't dominate the way we perceive others.

A related barrier, **prejudice**, is a judgment based on the assumption that we already have all the information we need to know about a person. To prejudge someone as inept, inferior, or incompetent on the basis of that person's ethnicity, race, country of origin, age, social class, culture, sexual orientation, sex, gender, or some other factor is a corrosive practice that can raise significant barriers to effective communication. As noted earlier, xenophobia is a fear or dislike of someone simply because that person is from another country or culture. Like xenophobia, misogyny is another form of prejudice. A **misogynist** is someone who holds negative attitudes toward women. Some prejudices are widespread. Although there are more women than men in the world, one study found that even when a man and a woman held the same type of job, the man's job was considered more prestigious than the woman's.[104] Even though it is illegal in the United States to negatively discriminate because of a person's sex, sexual orientation, gender identity, gender, race, or age in offering employment or promotions, women and members of minority groups, such as LBGTQ+ communities, continue to experience discrimination in the workplace.[105] Stereotyping and prejudice remain a formidable barrier to communicating effectively with others.

Mark Twain once said, "It is discouraging to try and penetrate a mind such as yours. You ought to get out and dance on it. That would take some of the rigidity out of it." Learning how to break rigid stereotypes and overcome prejudice is an important part of the process of learning how to adapt to others.

prejudice
A judgment based on the assumption that we already have all the information we need to know about a person.

misogynist
A person who holds negative attitudes toward women.

Strategies for Adapting to Others

6.4 Describe seven strategies that will help bridge differences between people and help them adapt to differences.

Eleanor Roosevelt once said, "We have to face the fact that either we, all of us, are going to die together or we are going to live together, and if we are to live together we have to talk."[106] In essence, she was saying that we need effective communication skills to overcome our differences. It is not enough just to point to the barriers we have identified and say, "Don't do that." Identifying the causes of misunderstanding is a good first step, but most people need more concrete advice with specific strategies to help them overcome these barriers.[107]

Aim for Intercultural Communication Competence

intercultural communication competence
The ability to adapt one's communication toward another person in ways that are appropriate to the other person's culture.

To have **intercultural communication competence** is to be able to adapt your communication toward another person in ways that are appropriate to the other person's culture. As we've stressed, intercultural competence involves more than merely being aware of what is appropriate or being sensitive to cultural differences.[108] An interculturally competent person *behaves* appropriately toward others.[109] Research has found that people who are interculturally competent do the following three things: (1) They prepare by doing things such as studying others' cultural traditions and learning their language, (2) they thoughtfully engage in conversations with others, and (3) they evaluate and periodically reflect on their interactions with others.[110]

To become competent at any task, you need three things: motivation, knowledge, and skill. The remaining portion of this chapter presents specific strategies to help you develop your intercultural communication competence:[111]

To motivate yourself to adapt when communicating with others who are different from you,

- Become mindful of differences.
- Develop positive attitudes about adapting to others who are different from yourself.
- Strive to tolerate ambiguity and uncertainty.

To increase your knowledge about others,

- Seek information about a culture.
- Ask questions and listen to the responses.

To develop your communication skill set,

- Become other-oriented: socially decenter and be empathic toward others.
- Learn appropriate ways to ethically adapt your communication.

Be Motivated: Develop Positive Attitudes toward Those Who Are Different from Yourself

The first step in becoming interculturally competent is to be motivated to relate to others in ways that are sensitive to their culture.[112] **Motivation** is an underlying willingness or desire to achieve a goal. Without motivation, it is less likely that you will become interculturally competent.[113] How do you cultivate a desire to be interculturally competent? Be aware of your existing attitudes, biases (including the discovery of unconscious bias) and work on developing positive, unbiased attitudes about adapting to others. Next, remind yourself of the benefits of effectively and appropriately adapting to others. And finally, accept, or at a minimum, tolerate those who are from a culture different from your own.

motivation
An underlying willingness or desire to achieve a goal.

Develop Mindfulness To be **mindful** is to be aware of how you communicate with others and the attitudes you hold toward those with whom you communicate. Are you conscious of your existing stereotypes and prejudices? Do you have a positive attitude toward people who are different from you? A mindful communicator puts into practice the first communication principle presented in this book: *Be aware of your communication with yourself and others*. To be a mindful communicator, constantly remind yourself that other people are not like you. Also, be aware that other people do not use different communication strategies to offend or be rude; they just have different culturally based strategies of interacting with others. Intercultural communication scholars William Gudykunst and Young Kim suggest that being mindful is one of the best ways to approach any new cultural encounter.[114] Mindfulness is a conscious state of mind, a realization of what is happening to you at a given moment. If you are not mindful, you are oblivious to the world around you. You are on mental cruise control.[115]

mindful
Being aware of what you are doing and how you are communicating with others.

One way you can become more mindful is through **self-talk**, something discussed earlier in this text. Self-talk consists of messages you tell yourself to help manage your discomfort, emotions, or negative thoughts about situations. For example, acknowledging cultural differences through self-talk, rather than emotionally and mindlessly becoming offended, can help you maintain your composure and

self-talk
Inner speech; communication with the self; the process of mentally verbalizing messages that help a person become more aware or mindful of how he or she is processing information and reacting to life situations.

communicate in a manner appropriate to the circumstances. Evidence suggests that mindfully reflecting on your different cultural experiences can also improve your intercultural competence.[116] As a tool to help you reflect, consider keeping a journal to document your thoughts about and reactions to the cultural differences you experience.

Develop Positive Attitudes   Although it's important to be aware of the attitudes, biases and feelings you hold toward others, evidence suggests that you will be a more effective communicator if you have positive regard for others, especially those who are different from you.[117] Be mindful and take inventory of your existing attitudes and feelings. If you harbor negative attitudes about other people or cultural groups (i.e., if you are xenophobic, homophobic, or misogynistic) you will be less likely to treat others fairly and equitably and to communicate in appropriate or effective ways.

Tolerate Ambiguity   An additional strategy for developing a positive motivation for being interculturally competent is to accept, or at a minimum, tolerate the uncertainty and ambiguity you feel when you meet people who are different from yourself. Many people become uncomfortable when faced with uncertainty and ambiguity—especially if they are from a low-context culture such as those in North America. As we discussed earlier in this chapter, people from low-context cultures prefer a more direct approach to getting information. North Americans, for example, often say things like "Tell it to me straight," "Don't beat around the bush," or "Just tell me what you want."

Communicating with someone from a culture that does not value such directness produces uncertainty. It may take time and several exchanges to clarify a message. If you are from a culture that is uncomfortable with uncertainty, you may have to acknowledge this cultural difference. Be patient. Don't rush to have all the details nailed down. Remind yourself that the other person does not have the same attitudes you do. To tolerate ambiguity is to be open and accepting of others who have different traditions, cultures, and ways of life.

Develop Knowledge about Those Who Are Different from Yourself

Learning about another culture's traditions, language, and values can help you adapt to cultural differences. By seeking information, asking questions, and listening, you can become more interculturally competent and more comfortable around people from cultures different from your own.

Seek Information   Philosopher André Gide said, "Understanding is the beginning of approving." Prejudice often is the result of ignorance. Learning about another person's values, beliefs, and culture can help you understand that person's messages and their meaning.[118] Researchers have found, not surprisingly, that if you have increased contact and experience interacting with someone from another culture, you will be more sensitive, mindful, and other-oriented when communicating with that person.[119] As you speak to a person from another culture, think of yourself as a detective, watching for implied, often unspoken messages that provide information about the values, norms, roles, and rules of that person's culture.

▼ A good way to understand people from other cultures is to learn all you can about their culture. If you were planning a visit to another country, how would you find out about its culture and people?
Image Source/Getty Images

You can also prepare yourself by studying other cultures. If you are going to another country, start by reading a travel guide or another general overview of the culture. You may then want to learn more detailed information by studying the history, art, or geography of the culture. The Internet offers a wealth of information about the cultures and traditions of others. In addition, talk to people from other cultures. If you are trying to communicate with someone closer to home who is from a different background, you can learn about the music, food, and other aspects of his or her culture. Given the inextricable link between language and culture, the more skilled you become at speaking another language, the better you will understand the traditions and customs of the culture where it is spoken.[120]

Ask Questions and Listen Communication, through the give-and-take process of listening, talking, and asking questions, helps reduce the uncertainty present in any relationship. When you meet people for the first time, you are typically not certain about their likes and dislikes, including whether they like or dislike you. When you communicate with a person from another culture or co-culture, the uncertainty level escalates. When you talk with people who are different from you, you may feel some discomfort and uncertainty. This is normal. We are more comfortable talking with people we know and who are like us. However, as you begin to talk with this person, you exchange information that helps you develop greater understanding. If you continue to ask questions, eventually you will feel less anxiety and uncertainty. You will become better able to predict how the other person will behave.

When you meet a person who is different from you, ask thoughtful questions and then pause to listen.[121] As we discussed in Chapter 5, the skills of stopping (focusing on the other person's message rather than your own thoughts), looking (observing nonverbal cues), listening (noting both details and major ideas), and responding thoughtfully will serve you well in enhancing communication with people from cultural traditions different from your own.

Develop Skills: Engage in Behaviors That Enhance Understanding

Becoming other-oriented involves several strategies that can enhance our understanding of those who are different from us. By putting ourselves in another person's mental and emotional frame of mind, we can increase our sensitivity to and understanding of others so that we can ethically and appropriately adapt our behavior.

Become Other-Oriented **Other-oriented communication** is communication in which we take into account the needs, motives, desires, and goals of our communication partners while still maintaining our own integrity by using listening and nonverbal awareness skills. Most of us are **egocentric**—focused on ourselves.[122] Our first inclination is to focus on meeting our own needs before addressing the needs of others.[123] Scholars of evolution might argue that our tendency to look out for number one is what ensures the continuation of the human race. But as we noted earlier, assuming superiority is a major barrier to communicating with others. If we focus exclusively on ourselves, it is very unlikely that we will be effective communicators.

We should consider the thoughts and feelings of others when forming messages and selecting the time and place to deliver them.[124] If we fail to adapt our message to listeners, especially listeners who are different from us (and isn't everyone different from you?), it is less likely that we will achieve our communication goal. As we noted earlier, adapting messages to others doesn't mean that we tell others only what they want to hear. That would be unethical, manipulative, and ineffective. Nor does being considerate of others mean we abandon all concern for our own interests.

How do you become other-oriented? We suggest a two-stage process, using skills discussed previously. The first stage, which we previewed in Chapter 5, is called social

other-oriented communication
Communication in which we focus on the needs and concerns of others while maintaining our personal integrity; achieved through the processes of socially decentering and being empathic.

egocentric
Focused on oneself and one's importance.

decentering—consciously *thinking* about another person's thoughts and feelings. The second stage is developing empathy, a set of skills we also discussed in Chapter 5. To empathize is to respond *emotionally* to someone else's feelings and actions. We'll discuss each of these two stages in more detail.

Socially Decenter Social decentering is a *cognitive process* through which we take into consideration another person's thoughts, values, background, and perspectives. It is seeing the world from the other person's point of view. To socially decenter is not to be a mind reader but to use past experiences and the ability to interpret the clues of others to understand what they may be thinking or how they may be perceiving issues or situations. According to Mark Redmond, a scholar who has extensively studied the process of social decentering, there are three ways to socially decenter.[125]

> **social decentering**
> A cognitive process through which we take into account another person's thoughts, values, background, and perspectives.

1. *Consider how you have responded in the past.* Develop an understanding of the other person based on how you have responded when something similar has happened to you.[126] For example, when someone you know says that he or she feels frazzled because he or she was late for a major meeting, you can think about what would be going through your mind if the same thing happened to you.

2. *Consider how the other person has responded in the past.* Base your understanding of what another person might be thinking on your knowledge of how that person has responded in similar situations. When communicating with someone who is different from you, the more direct experience you have interacting with that person, the better able you usually are to make predictions about how that person will react and respond. For example, suppose that you have never known a particular friend to be late for a meeting; you know that this friend is generally punctual. You can, therefore, guess that your friend would be quite frustrated by being late.

3. *Consider how most people respond to similar situations.* The more you can learn about other people's cultural or gender perspectives, the more accurate you can become in socially decentering. If your friend is from Germany and you have some general idea of the high value many Germans place on punctuality, your ideas about how most German people would react to being late for a meeting might help you understand how your friend feels. It is important, however, not to develop inaccurate, inflexible stereotypes and labels for others or to base your perceptions of others only on generalizations.

Develop Empathy Socially decentering involves attempting to understand what another person may be thinking. Developing **empathy**, a second strategy for becoming other-oriented, is feeling the *emotional* reaction that the other person may be experiencing. When we feel empathy, we feel what another person feels.

> **empathy**
> An emotional reaction that is similar to the reaction being experienced by another person.
>
> **sympathy**
> An acknowledgment that someone is feeling a certain emotion, often grief; compassion.

Empathy is different from **sympathy**. When you sympathize, you acknowledge someone's feelings or let the person know that you recognize the way he or she feels. When you empathize, however, you experience an emotional reaction that is similar to the other person's; as much as possible, you strive to feel what he or she feels. Emotional intelligence, which includes accurately assessing the emotions of others, is essential to both sympathy and empathy, which in turn help us establish high-quality relationships with others, especially when there are cultural differences.[127]

As we discussed in Chapter 5, you develop the ability to empathize by being sensitive to your own feelings, assessing how you feel during certain situations, and then projecting those feelings onto others.[128] The late author and theologian Henri J. M. Nouwen suggested that empathy lies at the heart of enhancing the quality of our relationships with others. As Nouwen phrased it, to bridge our differences, we need to "cross the road for one another":

> We become neighbors when we are willing to cross the road for one another. There is so much separation and segregation: between black people and white

people, between gay people and straight people, between young people and old people, between sick people and healthy people, between prisoners and free people, between Jews and Gentiles, Muslims and Christians, Protestants and Catholics, Greek Catholics and Latin Catholics.

There is a lot of road crossing to do. We are all very busy in our own circles. We have our own people to go to and our own affairs to take care of. But if we could cross the road once in a while and pay attention to what is happening on the other side, we might indeed become neighbors.[129]

Ethically Adapt to Others After you have thought about how you may be different from others and have identified your own potential barriers to communication, you reach this question: So now what do you *do*? What you do is appropriately and ethically adapt.

> **RE**CAP
> **How to Become Other-Oriented**
>
> Socially Decenter — View the world from another person's point of view.
> - Develop an understanding of someone based on your own past experiences.
> - Consider what someone may be thinking, based on your previous association with the person.
> - Consider how most people would respond to the situation at hand.
>
> Develop Empathy — Consider what another person may be feeling.
> - Stop: Avoid focusing only on your own ideas or emotions.
> - Look: Determine the emotional meaning of messages by observing nonverbal cues.
> - Listen: Focus on what the other person says.
> - Imagine: Consider how you would feel in a similar situation.

To **adapt** is to adjust your behavior in response to the other person or people you are communicating with. Adapting to others gets to the bottom line of this chapter. You don't just keep communicating in the same way you always did. Instead, make an effort to change how you communicate, to enhance the quality of your communication. Whether you are in an interpersonal interaction, a group, or a presentational speaking situation, adapting your message to others makes common sense. Even so, being sensitive to others and wisely adapting behaviors to others is often not common practice.

Communication accommodation theory suggests that effective communication occurs when we adapt to the communication style of our communication partner.[130] To maximize our understanding and to build a positive relationship with others, we accommodate—or adapt—the way we communicate. Adapting to others or accommodating our communication message does not mean that you do or say only what others expect or that your primary goal in life is always to please others. You don't have to abandon your own ethical principles and positions to adapt. In fact, it would be unethical to change your opinions and point of view just to avoid conflict and keep the peace—like a politician who tells audiences only what they want to hear.[131] As President Harry Truman said, "I wonder how far Moses would have gone if he'd taken a poll in Egypt?"[132] When we encourage you to adapt your messages to others, we are not recommending that you become a spineless jellyfish. We are suggesting that you be sensitive and mindful of how your comments may be received by others.

We do not advocate adapting communication in any way that is false or manipulative. You have a responsibility to *ethically* adapt your messages to others. To be ethical is to be truthful and honest while also observing the rights of others. Ethical communication is responsible, honest, and fair; enhances human dignity; and maintains listener options rather than coercing or forcing someone to behave against his or her will. Ideally, both (or all) parties' goals are met.

We adapt messages to others for several reasons: to enhance their understanding of the

adapt
To adjust behavior in response to someone else.

communication accommodation theory
A theory that suggests people adapt their style and approach to communicating with others in order to enhance the quality of the relationship and understanding.

▼ Today's technology can help you adapt your communication. For example, your phone can translate your words when you don't speak the local language or display a map. But you must still be aware of what adaptations are appropriate and ethical.
Image Source/Getty Images

message, to help us achieve the goal or intended effect of our communication, to ensure that we are ethical in our communication with others, and to establish and develop satisfying relationships. Your communication goal can help you choose from among the following adaptation strategies.

To...	You may need to...
Enhance understanding	• Slow down or speed up your normal rate of speech. • Use more examples. • Use appropriate examples or illustrations that your communication partner can easily identify. • Use simple, concrete words. • Speak in a very structured, organized way. • Stop to ask if your partner has any questions. • Make your message more redundant; preview and summarize key ideas. • Use pictures or other images to support your verbal message. • Be cautious when telling jokes because humor may not translate well from one culture to another.
Achieve your communication goals	• Present evidence that is most valuable to your listener; statistics may prove your point to some listeners, but others may be more moved by a story that poignantly illustrates your point. • Think about your specific communication goal and then clarify that goal with your communication partner. • Make sure you understand your partner's goal. • Identify areas in which your goal is similar to your partner's goal.
Ensure ethical communication	• Give your partner choices and identify options rather than coercing or making demands. • Tell the truth, without withholding information. • Give your partner a chance to respond. Use good listening skills. Rather than providing long stories or lengthy details, pause to see if your partner has questions or concerns about what you are sharing. • Give your communication partner an opportunity to ask questions. • Treat your partner how you believe your partner would like to be treated.
Establish and develop relationships	• Use communication that generates positive feelings. • Clearly express your positive regard for others. • Find areas of common interest. • Develop empathy: Stop, look, listen, and imagine how you would feel in similar situations. Ask questions. • Be aware of your own bias, stereotypes, and prejudices; set them aside and listen to the other person nonjudgmentally.

It is not possible to prescribe how to adapt to others in all situations, but you can draw on the other four Communication Principles for a Lifetime presented in this book:

1. *Be aware of your communication with yourself and others.* You will be more effective in adapting to others if you are aware of the intersection of differences that make you and others unique. Consider your own position, cultural traditions, and gender-related behavior and how they differ from those of other people.
2. *Effectively use and interpret verbal messages.* To be able to interpret spoken information accurately is a linchpin of competence in creating meaning when adapting to others.
3. *Effectively use and interpret nonverbal messages.* Being able to "listen with your eyes" to unspoken messages will increase your ability to understand relational and emotional messages, and then adapt and respond to others.

4. *Listen and respond to others thoughtfully.* The essential skills of listening and responding to others are key competencies in being able to adapt to others—to be oriented toward others.

Can the skills and principles we have suggested here make a difference in your ability to communicate with others? The answer is a resounding "yes."[133] Several research studies document the importance and value of skillfully being able to adapt your communication behavior.[134] Communication researcher Lori Carrell found, for example, that students who had been exposed to lessons in empathy as part of their study of interpersonal and intercultural communication improved their ability to empathize with others.[135] There is also evidence that if you master these principles and skills, you will be rewarded with greater ability to communicate with others who are different from you—which means everyone.[136]

RECAP
Adapting to Others

Develop Motivation

Develop Mindfulness	Be consciously aware of cultural differences rather than ignoring them.
Develop Positive Attitudes	Look for ways to affirm and support others.
Tolerate Ambiguity	Take your time and expect some uncertainty.

Develop Knowledge

Seek Information	Learn about a culture's worldview.
Ask Questions and Listen	Reduce uncertainty by asking for clarification and listening to the answer.

Develop Skill

Become Other-Oriented	Put yourself in the other person's mental and emotional frame of mind; socially decenter and develop empathy.
Ethically Adapt to Others	Listen and respond appropriately.

STUDY GUIDE: PRINCIPLES FOR A LIFETIME

CHAPTER 6

Diversity and Communication

6.1 Describe how differences of gender, sexual orientation, age, ethnicity, and social class influence communication.

PRINCIPLE POINTS: Human differences result in the potential for misunderstanding and miscommunication. Differences in gender, sexual orientation, age, and ethnicity contribute to the challenges of communicating with others. To overcome these challenges, you must employ our fifth Communication Principle for a Lifetime: effective communicators appropriately adapt their messages to others.

PRINCIPLE TERMS:

androgynous
transgender
gender expression
homophobia
race
racism
systemic racism
ethnicity
discrimination
social class
socialization
intersectionality
positionality

PRINCIPLE SKILLS:

1. In addition to the differences described in this chapter—gender, sexual orientation, age, ethnicity, social class, and culture—what are other differences among people that might affect the way we communicate with each other?
2. How would you assess your skill in adapting to those who differ from your gender identity, sexual orientation, age, social class, and ethnicity?

Culture and Communication

6.2 Define *culture*, and compare and contrast cultural contexts and cultural values.

PRINCIPLE POINTS: Culture is a system of knowledge that is shared by a group of people. Because of the powerful role culture plays in influencing our values, culture and communication are clearly linked. Cultural values reflect how individuals regard stereotypically masculine perspectives (such as achieving results and being productive) and stereotypically feminine perspectives (such as consideration for relationships), their tolerance of uncertainty or preference for certainty, their preference for centralized or decentralized power structures, the value they place on individual or collective accomplishment, their long-term or short-term orientation to time, and their expectation of happiness.

PRINCIPLE **TERMS:**

globalization
culture
co-culture
intercultural
   communication
culture shock
worldview
cultural context
high-context culture
low-context culture

cultural values
collectivistic culture
individualistic culture
masculine culture
feminine culture
long-term orientation
short-term orientation
indulgent culture
restrained culture

PRINCIPLE **SKILLS:**

1. Provide an example of a recent intercultural interaction you had with a person from a different culture than your own. Identify cultural similarities and differences between you and your intercultural communication partner.
2. Based on the descriptions of cultural values described in this chapter, use the scales below to evaluate your own cultural values. Place an X or other mark to indicate where your culture falls on each scale.

    Individualistic _ _ _ _ _ _ _ Collectivistic
    Decentralized _ _ _ _ _ _ _ Centralized
    Uncertainty _ _ _ _ _ _ _ Certainty
    Masculine _ _ _ _ _ _ _ Feminine
    Long Term _ _ _ _ _ _ _ Short Term
    Indulgent _ _ _ _ _ _ _ Restrained

After assessing your cultural values, think of a friend, teacher, classmate, family member, or colleague who may have a different cultural value profile than yourself. Based on the discussion of ways to enhance intercultural competence that you studied in this chapter, what specific strategies could you use to adapt to someone whose cultural values are different from your own?

Barriers to Adapting to Others

6.3 **Illustrate four barriers that inhibit communication between individuals.**

PRINCIPLE **POINTS:** By doing the following, we create barriers that inhibit our communication with others:

- *Assuming superiority.* When one culture or gender assumes superiority or when someone is ethnocentric or xenophobic, communication problems often occur.
- *Assuming similarity.* It is not productive when individuals or groups from different backgrounds or cultures assume that others should behave or respond in the same way they do.
- *Assuming differences.* Don't automatically assume that other people are different from you.
- *Stereotyping and prejudice.* We stereotype by placing a group or person into an inflexible, all-encompassing category. Stereotyping and prejudice can keep us from acknowledging others as unique individuals and, therefore, can hamper effective, open, and honest communication.

PRINCIPLE **TERMS:**

ethnocentrism
xenophobia
stereotype

prejudice
misogynist

PRINCIPLE **SKILLS:**

1. Describe a time when you experienced one of the barriers mentioned in this chapter. For example, have you tried to communicate with someone who assumed you were more like them than you actually are? Or did you ever assume someone was much more different from you than she or he actually turned out to be?
2. Consider the four barriers discussed in this chapter that inhibit effective communication. Now rank them in order from your "biggest barrier" to your "smallest barrier." How do these barriers impact your communication with others? What could you do to reduce or remove your biggest barriers?

Strategies for Adapting to Others

6.4 **Describe seven strategies that will help bridge differences between people and help them adapt to differences.**

PRINCIPLE **POINTS:** You develop intercultural communication competence when you are able to adapt your behavior toward another person in ways that are appropriate to the other person's culture. Specific strategies for becoming interculturally competent include the following: be mindful, develop positive attitudes, tolerate ambiguity, seek information, ask questions and listen, become other-oriented by socially decentering and empathizing with others, and appropriately and ethically adapt your communication to others.

PRINCIPLE TERMS:

intercultural communication competence
motivation
mindful
self-talk
other-oriented communication
egocentric
social decentering
empathy
sympathy
adapt
communication accommodation theory

PRINCIPLE SKILLS:

1. You've been assigned to work on a semester-long research project with a partner who has told you that his or her sexual orientation is different from your own. How could you use the skills in this section of the chapter to appropriately adapt your communication with your research partner?

2. **Assessing Your Intercultural Skill**

   This chapter presented seven specific strategies to help bridge differences between people. Rank these strategies in the order of what you need to improve the most to what you need to improve the least in your interactions with people from different backgrounds. For example, assign a rank of 1 to the skill that you need to develop the most, then assign a rank of 2 to the next area you feel you need to work on, and so on. Rank yourself on all seven strategies.

Be mindful	___
Develop positive attitudes	___
Tolerate ambiguity	___
Seek information	___
Ask questions and listen	___
Become other-oriented (socially decenter and empathize)	___
Appropriately and ethically adapt to others	___

UNIT II INTERPERSONAL COMMUNICATION

CHAPTER 7

UNDERSTANDING INTERPERSONAL COMMUNICATION

The best of life is conversation, and the greatest success is confidence, or perfect understanding between sincere people. —RALPH WALDO EMERSON

Digital Vision/Photodisc/Getty Images

CHAPTER OUTLINE

- What Is Interpersonal Communication?
- Initiating Relationships
- Maintaining Relationships
- Study Guide: *Principles for a Lifetime*

Chapter 7 Understanding Interpersonal Communication

LEARNING OBJECTIVES

7.1 Define interpersonal communication and discuss its three unique attributes.

7.2 Describe the roles of communication in revealing interpersonal attraction and initiating relationships.

7.3 Explain the roles of self-disclosure and emotional expression in maintaining face-to-face and online relationships.

"Hi. I'm ___. Nice to meet you." This simple statement can strike fear in the heart of even the most outgoing person. Yet we know that meeting and getting to know people, as well as becoming known by them, are some of the most rewarding experiences in life. If we cannot break out of our comfort zones to communicate with others, we likely will not survive.

Interpersonal communication is the form of communication we experience most often in our lives, and it involves all five of our Communication Principles for a Lifetime, shown in Figure 7.1. In the remaining chapters of the book, you'll see a small version of the communication principles model in the margin to highlight our reference to one or more of the communication principles.

Effective interpersonal communication begins with an *awareness* of oneself. To heighten your awareness as a communicator, pay attention to what works well and what doesn't when you interact with others. You learn from these experiences and develop a personal style of communication. The second and third principles involve the *effective use of verbal and nonverbal messages*. We experiment with verbal and nonverbal communication as we interact with people, develop relationships, and, in some cases, let go of those relationships. As we discussed in Chapter 5, a major element that enhances relationships is the ability to *listen and respond thoughtfully* to others, our fourth principle. Finally, few interpersonal relationships last without *adaptation*. We live in an increasingly diverse and complex world. If we want to be effective communicators, it is imperative to learn to adapt our communication to others' cultural backgrounds and values, personalities, communication styles, needs, and goals.

interpersonal communication
Communication that occurs between two people who simultaneously attempt to mutually influence each other, usually for the purpose of managing relationships.

mediated communication
Communication that is carried out using some channel other than those used in face-to-face encounters.

mediated interpersonal communication
Communication that occurs when two people attempt to mutually influence each other through the use of a mediated channel, usually for the purpose of managing relationships.

What Is Interpersonal Communication?

7.1 Define interpersonal communication and discuss its three unique attributes.

Interpersonal communication is a special form of human communication that occurs when two people interact simultaneously and attempt to mutually influence each other, usually for the purpose of managing relationships. Interpersonal communication research focuses both on face-to-face (FtF) encounters and mediated interactions, which occur through channels such as smartphones and computers.[1]

In Chapter 1, we defined **mediated communication** as communication carried out using some channel other than those used in face-to-face (FtF) encounters. It then follows that **mediated interpersonal communication** occurs when two people attempt to mutually influence each other through a mediated channel, usually for the purpose of managing relationships. In this chapter, we explore some similarities and differences between mediated interpersonal communication and FtF interpersonal communication.

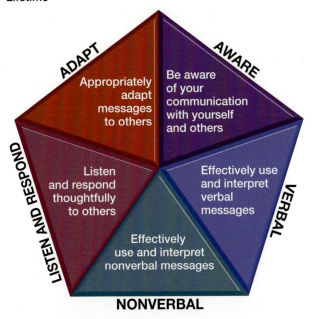

FIGURE 7.1 Communication Principles for a Lifetime

Let's begin by considering three attributes that help us better understand the nature of interpersonal communication:

- *Interpersonal communication involves quality.* If you're having dinner with a friend, let's hope that your communication with your friend is different from your communication with the wait staff. The quality of the communication makes the difference. Interpersonal communication occurs not just when we interact with someone, but when we treat a person as a unique human being. Conversely, **impersonal communication** occurs when we treat people as objects or respond to their roles rather than to who they are as unique people.[2] In terms of mediated interpersonal communication, emailing, texting, or direct messaging a friend is interpersonal communication; by contrast, responding to a mass text or email message, or to a Facebook post is impersonal communication because you likely don't know all the receivers of your message.

- *Interpersonal communication involves mutual influence.* We don't mean to imply that interpersonal communication exclusively involves persuasion—changing someone's mind or swaying someone's opinion. We simply mean that people who interact *affect* each other in some way. During that dinner with a friend, you might ask where your friend grew up. You have both been affected by this question—there's something you want to know and information your friend can provide. But what if your friend doesn't hear you because of a distracting noise in the restaurant? In this case, interpersonal communication has not really occurred because there was no mutual interaction; you have been affected by your attempt at communication, but your friend has not.

- *Interpersonal communication helps manage relationships.* **Relationships** are ongoing connections we make with others through interpersonal communication. For some people, the term *relationship* signals something serious and usually romantic, but we use the word in a much broader sense in this text. You probably have a wide variety of relationships, such as those with family members, coworkers, classmates, friends, and romantic interests. Some relationships are formed and maintained solely through mediated channels; others involve a combination of FtF and mediated interactions.

impersonal communication
Communication that treats people as objects or that responds only to their roles rather than to who they are as unique people.

relationship
An ongoing connection made with another person.

> **RECAP**
>
> **What Is Interpersonal Communication?**
>
> - High quality: Interpersonal communication is superior to impersonal communication.
> - Mutually influential: Both people in the relationship are affected.
> - Relationship managing: We use interpersonal communication to help start, maintain, and sometimes end our interpersonal relationships.

Initiating Relationships

7.2 Describe the roles of communication in revealing interpersonal attraction and initiating relationships.

Relationships form for different reasons. **Relationships of circumstance** form situationally, simply because our lives overlap with others' in some way or because a situation brings us into contact. Relationships with family members, teachers, classmates, and coworkers typically fall into this category. An online relationship of circumstance might be formed between members of a group, such as students enrolled in an online class. In contrast, relationships we seek and intentionally develop are termed **relationships of choice**. These relationships typically include those with friends, romantic partners, and spouses. Most of your online relationships are probably relationships of choice. Yet, these categories of relationships are not mutually exclusive. Relationships of circumstance can change into relationships of choice; your sister or brother can turn out to be your best friend.

Some people make relationships look easy; they just seem to meet people and make positive impressions effortlessly. For others, meeting and getting to know people is a huge challenge. We'll let you in on a little secret: Initiating relationships really isn't all that easy for anyone. Let's explore the nature of attraction—what draws us into a conversation in the first place.

relationship of circumstance
A relationship sought and intentionally developed.

relationship of choice
A relationship that forms situationally, simply because one life overlaps with another in some way.

Interpersonal Attraction: Why We Like Whom We Like

What does it mean to say you are attracted to another person? Most of the time, we tend to think of physical or sexual attraction. But there are many forms of attraction besides physical and sexual, including intellectual, spiritual, and personality attraction. **Attraction**, in general, is a motivational state that causes someone to think, feel, and behave in a positive manner toward another person.[3] **Interpersonal attraction** is the degree to which you desire to form and possibly maintain an interpersonal relationship with another person. More specifically, **social attraction** is your desire to develop a friendship with another person.[4] Several factors come into play when you decide to act on your attraction and establish a relationship.

▲ Attraction is fascinating to observe, as well as to feel for another person. How do you typically communicate the attraction you feel for someone? Do your nonverbal cues reveal your attraction, or do you use language to convey your feelings?
Cathy Yeulet/123RF

Physical and Sexual Attraction Volumes have been written about the role that physical and sexual attraction play in the formation of relationships.[5] While these forms of attraction are often lumped together or viewed as the same thing, actually they're different. In FtF situations, the degree to which we find another person's physical self appealing represents our **physical attraction** to that person, which is a powerful nonverbal cue. That appeal might be based on height, size, skin tone and texture, clothing, hairstyle, makeup, or vocal qualities. By this definition, even if you're heterosexual, you can still be attracted to a person of your own sex because you admire her or his physical attributes.

Is physical attraction a factor in establishing online relationships? Many online communicators find that the *lack* of emphasis on physical attractiveness is one of the most positive features of developing online relationships.[6] One set of researchers described the Internet as "a world where what you write, not how you look or sound, is who you are."[7]

However, because most online dating sites and apps like Bumble and Grindr require you to submit a photo when using their services, physical attractiveness plays a greater role in online relationship formation than in the past.[8] The popular dating app Tinder relies exclusively on physical attraction—users swipe right or left on their mobile phones to indicate interest.[9] Even if an online dating site or app doesn't require a photo, many people are suspicious about or turned off by those who won't post a picture of themselves to their online profile.

Sexual attraction has been defined as "the desire to engage in sexual activity with someone," a desire that "typically is accompanied by feelings of sexual arousal in the presence of the person."[10] You may be physically attracted to someone but not sexually attracted, as we stated before. But can you be sexually attracted but not physically attracted? We're not sure how to answer that question because the causes of attraction are unique for every individual. You may find another person's online communication sexually arousing even if you've never seen the person in the flesh. Suffice it to say that sexual and physical attraction usually operate in tandem, even though they represent different kinds of appeal.

Our perceptions about others' physical attractiveness affect relationship possibilities. In general, although we may be attracted to a range of people, we tend to seek out individuals who represent the same level of physical attractiveness we do.[11] In research, this tendency is termed the **matching hypothesis**.[12] Perhaps you perceive

attraction
A motivational state that causes someone to think, feel, and behave in a positive manner toward another person.

interpersonal attraction
The degree to which one desires to form or maintain an interpersonal relationship with another person.

social attraction
A desire to develop a friendship with another person.

physical attraction
The degree to which one finds another person's physical self appealing.

sexual attraction
The desire to have sexual contact with a certain person.

matching hypothesis
A tendency to seek out individuals who represent the same level of physical attractiveness as oneself.

DIVERSITY & COMMUNICATION

Unconscious Bias in Asian Business Leadership

There is a strong business case for increased diversity across the ASEAN region. Around 75 percent of businesses that tacked gender diversity reported profit increases, and 54 percent of these businesses saw improvements across innovation, creativity, and openness. Businesses where more than a third of the board members are women enjoy 1.5 times greater profits than those with fewer women. Thirty-seven percent of businesses stated that improved gender diversity had a positive impact on customer understanding. Across the ASEAN region, women account for 15 percent of board members and 25 percent of senior management in organizations.[13] The figures are between 20 and 30 percent in Thailand and 13 and 26 percent in Malaysia.[14]

Diversity and inclusion are major issues globally and around half of all organizations in Asia are prioritizing hiring of diverse talent but only 42 percent focus on measures to retain that talent. The main drivers in overcoming the unconscious bias include the creation of more collaborative teams, a fairer and unbiased means of hiring and promoting, promoting networking opportunities, encouraging employees to use flexible benefit packages, and ensuring compliance across the organization by setting targets and publishing diversity and inclusion data. The key barriers to achieving a diverse and inclusive environment are a lack of processes and accepted practices in the workplace like providing flexible career paths and packages of customizable benefits, dealing with an organizational culture that is often resistant to change, and failing to appoint an individual in the organization that is tasked with overseeing diversity and inclusion.[15]

How is diversity and inclusion handled in an organization that you are familiar with? How effective are the hiring, promotion, and retention processes?

---

yourself to be average looking, not model-beautiful but not unattractive. You may be physically or sexually attracted to extremely good-looking people; but if you're average looking, you're more likely to seek someone who is also average looking to date and even marry.

Similarity Opposites certainly do attract, and differences between people can be interesting. But we like to add another phrase to the "opposites attract" cliché: "Opposites attract, but dramatic opposites seldom last." People who are significantly different from each other in dispositions and preferences may intrigue and teach each other something in the short run, but similarity appears to be a more important factor in highly committed, long-term relationships than in short-term, noncommitted relationships.[16]

In general, you're attracted to people with whom you have **similarity**—those whose personality, values, upbringing, experiences, attitudes, or interests are similar to yours.[17] You may also be more attracted to people who are similar to you in age, intelligence, and life goals. The Internet allows people with similar interests to find one another much more easily than in the past and form online relationships.[18] In the initial stages of an online or FtF relationship, we try to emphasize positive information about ourselves to create a good first impression and an attractive image. We reveal those aspects of ourselves that we believe we have in common with the other person, and the other person does the same.[19]

similarity
The degree to which one's characteristics, values, attitudes, interests, or personality traits are like those of another person.

Proximity In a traditional sense, the principle of **proximity** in interpersonal relationships refers to the fact that you are more likely to be attracted to people who are nearer to you physically and geographically than to those who are farther away.[20] For example, you are more likely to form relationships with classmates sitting on either side of you than those at the opposite end of the room. Physical proximity increases our communication opportunities, and these opportunities to interact are likely to increase attraction.

proximity
The likelihood of being attracted to people who are physically close rather than to those who are farther away.

People in long-distance friendships and romantic relationships know firsthand that proximity plays an important role in whether a relationship will last or not.[21] Technological innovations, such as social networking and video chatting, are inexpensive and more readily accessible than ever, and they do help keep geographically-separated partners and friends in virtual proximity. However, particularly in romantic relationships, partners know that having the money and the time to travel to be physically with each other on weekends or vacations is extremely important when trying to keep a long-distance relationship going.[22]

Technology has turned the notion of proximity on its head by giving us virtual access to people around the globe in an instant. Those of you who are "digital natives" grew up in a world of computers where online information was always easily found at your fingertips. You have a different sense of boundaries, geographic limitations, and globalism than previous generations—the "digital immigrants" who discovered and adopted technology along the way.[23] People who have never met (and may never meet) in the physical world can come to feel a sense of proximity online and develop relationships with each other in the virtual world. In fact, some scholars contend that the instantaneous and pervasive nature of online communication bridges physical distance, creating a virtual closeness that FtF relationships might not achieve.[24]

▲ Video chats, Facebook usage, texts, and other technological innovations have redefined the meaning of proximity in attraction. How do your face-to-face relationships compare to your mediated ones in terms of proximity?
Alpa Prod/Shutterstock

Complementarity Although we tend to like people with whom we have much in common, most of us would not find it very exciting to spend the rest of our lives with someone who had identical attitudes, needs, and interests. We tend to be attracted to friends and romantic partners who are similar to us in important ways, such as having shared values, but when we consider less essential characteristics, we may be more interested in people with whom we share a **complementarity** of abilities and needs.[25] For example, if you are highly disorganized by nature (and that's fine by you), you might be attracted to someone who is very organized because you appreciate that person's sense of structure. Research has applied the concept of complementarity to other kinds of relationships where communication and rapport are extremely important, such as between therapists and clients.[26]

complementarity
The degree to which a person's different abilities, interests, and needs balance or round out one's own.

Communicating Our Attraction

According to research, we can size up a potential romantic partner or good future friend within the first three minutes of meeting the person.[27] That is impressive, but daunting. What kind of impression do *you* make in the first three minutes of meeting someone? What kind of vibe do you get from someone in the first three minutes that lets you know whether you would like to talk with the person further or whether there is a chance of something more meaningful developing?

When we are attracted to people, we use both verbal and nonverbal strategies to communicate our liking. Verbally, we ask questions to show interest and probe for details when others share information. We also listen responsively and refer to information shared in past interactions in an attempt to build a history

RECAP
Elements of Interpersonal Attraction

Physical Attraction	This form of attraction is based on a person's physical self.
Sexual Attraction	This form of attraction is based on the desire to have sexual contact with another person.
Similarity	Attraction increases if our characteristics, values, attitudes, interests, and personality traits are similar to those of another person.
Proximity	We are more likely to be interpersonally attracted to people who are physically close to us.
Complementarity	We may be attracted to someone whose abilities, interests, and needs differ from but balance or round out our own.

immediacy
Nonverbal cues, such as eye contact, a forward lean, touch, and open body orientation, that communicate feelings of liking, pleasure, and closeness.

with people. But we most often communicate our attraction nonverbally, through indirect cues referred to as **immediacy**. As described in Chapter 4, immediacy behaviors reduce the physical and psychological distance between people.[28] Studies have shed light on the connection between immediacy and perceptions of closeness and support in relationships, as well as the effects of immediacy on such contexts as the classroom, the workplace, and speed dating.[29] Some examples of nonverbal immediacy cues include the following:

- Sitting in closer proximity;
- Increasing our eye contact;
- Increasing our use of touch;
- Leaning forward;
- Keeping an open body orientation rather than a closed-off position;
- Using more vocal variety or animation;
- Using more facial animation, including smiling more often than we do normally; and
- Preening (adjusting clothing, playing with our hair) as a means of attracting attention.[30]

When thinking about physical or sexual attraction associated with romantic interests, most people don't think of immediacy—they think of flirtation.[31] Flirting involves verbal communication, such as the use of humor, but most often flirting is accomplished nonverbally.[32] Common nonverbal flirtation cues include surveying a room with our eyes; making prolonged, mutual eye contact; giving sidelong and darting glances at a person of interest; using more facial animation; and changing our tone of voice to reveal excitement.[33]

In the fall of 2019, the Pew Research Center surveyed approximately 5,000 U.S. adults about their use of online dating sites and apps. Thirty percent of respondents reported having used a dating site or app, up from 15 percent in 2016. Twenty-three percent indicated that they had gone on a FtF date with someone they met online and 12 percent said that they were in a committed relationship or marriage with someone they met online.[34] These statistics give rise to the question of how people convey attraction in an online or mediated context.[35] One study asked approximately 6,000 people how they flirt in person as well as online.[36] The majority of people in the study reported that flirting was accomplished online similarly to how it's done in person, meaning that people translate physical actions into text, such as typing an acronym like LOL or inserting emojis into texts, email messages, or posts. With the rise in video chatting, the more traditional nonverbal cues associated with flirtation can be effective, except, of course, cues that involve actual physical contact with another person.

▼ What nonverbal immediacy cues are these two people using to communicate that they like each other? What immediacy cues do you exhibit when you find yourself attracted to someone?
Siri Stafford/DigitalVision/Getty Images

SOCIAL MEDIA & COMMUNICATION

Flirtmoji

College students are great sources of information, especially about social media trends. A student recently educated her professor on the meaning behind "Netflix and chill." The professor thought that such a text or direct message meant, "Want to come over, watch something on Netflix, and relax?" Actually, Wikipedia describes the phrase as a "euphemism for sex, either between partners or casually, as a booty call."[37]

People's inclusion of emojis like the eggplant and pizza slice, used alone or with other images or words, can also indicate sexual interest. But now you can take it to another level: The flirtmoji can turn a text into a "sext." While we won't go into graphic detail describing these sexualized emojis, some of the tamer ones include a banana wearing a condom and the back hatch of an SUV opened to reveal two sets of bare legs.[38]

Initiating Relationships

How do we get a new relationship off the ground? Are you more comfortable initiating a relationship through online or mediated channels versus a face-to-face conversation?

In some ways, online interpersonal relationships have an advantage over FtF relationships in that they often develop out of conversation, meaning that online communication may be what launched the relationship in the first place.[39] Initial online interactions are critical in that they can make or break future exchanges. With repeated virtual contact, online topics of discussion often become personal and intimacy can develop at a more rapid pace than it typically does in FtF relationships. If rapport develops, it may lead to more personal texting, phone conversations, and FtF meetings.[40]

We understand that in FtF situations, the various steps of noticing someone interesting, realizing you're interested (physically, sexually, or interpersonally), finding a way to meet the person, and starting up a first conversation can all be nerve-racking.[41] Even though many people find communicating online easier than FtF interactions, we don't want to get rusty at having in-person conversations. Like any other skill, from playing a sport to improving our writing, conversation skills can diminish if unused. Sherry Turkle, author of *Reclaiming Conversation: The Power of Talk in a Digital Age*, suggests that flight from face-to-face conversation in our digital age can hamper our relationships, as well as our creativity and productivity.[42]

In FtF settings, once you realize you are attracted to someone, what do you do next? Research indicates that people who meet and have that all-important first conversation feel the enduring effects of that encounter even months later, no matter what direction the relationship took (if it took any direction at all).[43] We have some practical suggestions for how to approach those first conversations so that you feel confident and keep your self-esteem intact while communicating effectively.

Reducing Uncertainty Even though most of us like surprises from time to time, human beings are much more comfortable with certainty than with uncertainty. We prefer the known to the unknown, the predictable to the chaotic. Communicating in a new FtF or online relationship can involve *uncertainty*, or a fear of not knowing what to expect in a potential relationship. One communication research team developed an explanation called **uncertainty-reduction theory**, which focuses on how we use information to reduce our uncertainty, especially when communicating with people we don't know (or know well). Communication researchers Charles Berger, Richard Calabrese, and James Bradac contend that this driving motivation among humans to reduce our uncertainty prompts us to communicate.[44]

uncertainty-reduction theory
A driving motivation among humans to increase predictability by reducing the unknown in one's circumstances.

passive strategy
A noncommunicative strategy for reducing uncertainty by observing others and situations.

active strategy
A communicative strategy for reducing uncertainty by getting information from a third party.

interactive strategy
A strategy of communicating directly with the person who has the greatest potential to reduce one's uncertainty.

We typically respond to uncertainty in three ways:

- **Passive strategy**: We seek information by observing people and scoping out situations before more actively working to reduce uncertainty. Suppose you just started a new job, a transition that creates a level of uncertainty in most of us. One way to begin to reduce your uncertainty is to simply observe how your coworkers, supervisors, and clients interact. In an online context, you may read a person's tweets or check out photos on Instagram to get a sense of the person before communicating with her or him directly.

- **Active strategy**: After making passive observations, we might check our perceptions of things with a third party. You might ask a coworker about something associated with your new job or colleagues, for example. Finding out others' perceptions increases your knowledge, reduces your uncertainty, and helps you decide how to behave. People often network online in an attempt to learn more information from a third party before making a decision to contact a person directly. Some online daters conduct background checks on their online partners before considering more contact.

- **Interactive strategy**: The final strategy is going "straight to the horse's mouth," communicating directly with the person who has the most potential to reduce your uncertainty. At a new job, this person might be your boss, a coworker who has been on the job for a while, or perhaps someone in personnel or human relations. Online, many people reduce their uncertainty by directly asking a person for more information about himself or herself, a less risky exchange than a FtF meeting.

These strategies don't necessarily have to be used in order. You might bypass the active strategy and head to interactive, deeming it better to get information directly from the source. Also, you may not use all three strategies. In some cases, uncertainty can be reduced enough through passive and active strategies; there may be no cause for an interactive approach.[45]

Interactive strategies are frequently used in online relationships because starting up an online conversation or exchanging emails with someone tends to evoke less uncertainty than FtF first conversations. Online exchanges usually happen in private, with less potential for embarrassment than in FtF situations, when such factors as physical appearance and nervousness are in play. But one element can inject uncertainty into an online situation: the potential for deception. Because you stare at a computer monitor rather than into someone's eyes when you "meet" online, you really don't know to whom you're talking. Research has shown people's tendencies to give false information or to omit pertinent facts in their online communication.[46] Subjects in studies report lying about their age, weight, physical appearance, marital status, and even their sex or gender, meaning that some gender-bending experimentation occurs.

What Do You Say First? In some contexts, the first words you exchange with someone may be fairly scripted or expected. For example, in a job interview, introductions and ritualistic greetings typically take up the first few minutes. (See Appendix A for helpful information on communicating in interviews.) But what about situations in which there are no prescribed, explicit rules or expectations for behavior? Our students tell us that the official "date" is a dying institution—they just don't date much anymore. More common than dating is "hanging out," in which two people meet somewhere or a group of people gather together, many of whom are "talking," "seeing each other," or enjoying a special connection that goes beyond what they have with other people.

This first-conversation business used to be easier in the past, though perhaps not particularly satisfying. According to one 1980s study, many men reported being taught by their fathers or older brothers how to use opening or pickup lines to attract women, while women said they were schooled by their mothers or older sisters about how to respond (or ignore).[47] You might think such opening lines as "Come here often?"

"Haven't I met you before?" and (the 1960s all-time favorite) "What's your sign?" are relics of the past, but according to research, opening lines are surprisingly still effective at getting a conversation going.[48] While research on sexual minority relationships is increasing, it is still the case that most research on first conversations tends to focus on heterosexual interaction.[49] In one study on opening lines, researchers tested the effectiveness of the following categories of lines: (1) flippant and flirtatious, such as "You must be tired, because you've been running through my mind all day"; (2) direct and complimentary, such as "It took a lot of courage to approach you, so can I at least ask your name?"; and (3) innocuous, meaning that the line masked the man's interest, as in "What do you think of the band?" The women in the study liked the direct and complimentary lines the most,

believing they conveyed more trustworthiness and intelligence than other forms. Recent research examined a reverse situation to learn about men's perceptions of women's pickup lines; similar results were found, in that men preferred direct lines rather than flippant or innocuous ones.[50]

We do not recommend a one-size-fits-all approach to initiating first conversations with the use of stereotypical pickup lines. Instead, drawing on our fifth Communication Principle for a Lifetime, we encourage communicators to appropriately adapt their messages to others. Each situation and the unique qualities of each person you meet should dictate how you communicate.

The Art and Skill of Asking Great Questions   When students ask us, as they frequently do, "What makes someone a good conversationalist?" a variety of things come to mind. All five of our Communication Principles for a Lifetime could be reflected in our answer, but one important skill is the ability to ask another person a great question designed to initiate a meaningful exchange. However, this skill does not just magically appear. It takes time, maturity, and experience with a variety of people and relationships to develop fully.[51]

Social media doesn't exactly encourage people to develop their question-asking skills, because we tend to post more declarative statements than questions. Even though you may spend a lot of time on social media, try not to let your question-asking skills go to waste.[52]

What do we mean by "asking great questions"? We don't mean tossing rapid-fire, superficial questions at someone as though you were in the first five minutes of a job interview or gathering data for the census. Asking a great question means, first, tailoring the question to the other person as much as possible. Use what you have observed and learned from other sources to formulate your questions. Online, people typically ask for basic information just to break the ice, but too many "yes/no" questions or questions requiring one-word responses are unlikely to advance a conversation. Also, avoid questions that might be too personal or probing in the early stages of developing FtF and online relationships.

A second critical skill to develop is listening to a person's answers to your questions. It is important to fully listen, rather than formulating your next idea or looking for an opening to speak again. Pose follow-up questions based on the person's response to your previous question. You can offer your opinion, but opinions work best when

followed up with "Do you agree?" or "That's what I think, but what do you think?" Great conversationalists are great because they listen and then form responses that show they *are* listening—responses designed to draw other people out and let them shine.

Avoiding Self-Absorption   Too many people think the best way to be conversationally impressive is by talking glibly, smoothly, confidently, and virtually nonstop *about themselves*. In an online context, when one person's messages or posts consistently ramble on and on, it can be a turnoff. Some people use social media more frequently than others, constantly sharing photos and information about where they are, what fun things they're doing, who they're with, what they're eating and drinking, what new thing they just bought, what cute thing their dog just did, and so forth. Might these folks have narcissistic personalities and self-absorbed communication styles, or are they just avid users of social media? Some people worry that increased use of social media is contributing to a growing narcissism in our culture, given that most posts are about oneself.[53]

Researchers describe people who communicate like they are the center of the universe as having **conversational narcissism** or a **self-absorbed communicator style**. Some people who always (or predominantly) communicate this way have **trait conversational narcissism**; this type of narcissism may be an outgrowth of a personality trait in which oneself is the constant focus.[54] Other times, this kind of self-absorbed behavior reflects **state conversational narcissism**, which is a temporary style of interacting rather than a pervasive personal characteristic. We are all likely to be self-absorbed from time to time, but if this kind of communication continues and becomes a more permanent state, it is less likely that others will perceive us positively.

Some verbal indications of self-absorption include the number of times a person uses the pronoun *I* instead of *you* or *we*. Narcissistic communicators converse mostly about themselves and typically provide more detail in their narratives than necessary (perhaps because they enjoy the sound of their own voice).[55] They also talk more in statements than questions and constantly try to top someone's story or draw the topic of conversation toward themselves, as in "Oh, you think *you're* tired—let me tell you about the kind of day *I* had." No one's day is as bad, no one's opinion as valuable or information as correct as the self-absorbed communicator's. The person may feign empathy in a conversation: "Oh, I know exactly how you feel." This usually leads to "The same thing happened to me," followed by a long story that takes attention away from the original communicator. Another indication of self-absorption is talking ad nauseam on topics about which one has some particular knowledge or expertise but that may bore the socks off listeners. Although some people find the term offensive, "mansplaining" is when men talk at length or "hold court" in a condescending way, usually to women.[56] Many times, self-absorbed communicators are driven by insecurity and uncertainty rather than a belief that they truly are the center of the universe.

As for nonverbal cues, self-absorbed communicators tend to increase their speaking rate and volume, and assume dominant body postures in order to hold the floor and stave off interruptions from others. They may move closer to people to keep them in conversation, even to the extent of physically blocking a person from attempting to exit the scene. They are generally oblivious to others' nonverbal cues. People with self-absorbed personalities soon find themselves with a dwindling number of friends because few of us can tolerate such an out-of-balance relationship.

In sum, the best conversationalists aren't great talkers—they're great listeners and responders (as articulated in our fourth principle). In other words, it's not what *you* say, but how you respond to what *others* say that makes you a good conversationalist.

The Art and Skill of Giving and Receiving Compliments   Sometimes it seems as though people do not share feedback with one another unless it's to criticize. That's

---

conversational narcissism (self-absorbed communicator style)
A dominating communication style in which one focuses attention on oneself.

trait conversational narcissism
Habitual use of a narcissistic or self-absorbed communicator style in which one focuses attention on oneself.

state conversational narcissism
Occasional use of a narcissistic or self-absorbed communicator style in which one focuses attention on oneself.

unfortunate because positive reinforcement and support from others are central to our self-esteem. British linguistic scholar Janet Holmes calls compliments "social lubricants."[57] She explains that the most common purpose of a compliment is to make someone feel good by offering praise and encouragement, but an important by-product is a sense of increased goodwill and solidarity between the complimenter and the receiver. Research shows that compliments between romantic partners can enhance self-esteem and are viewed as a form of intimate talk. The sharing of positive feelings is also linked to how satisfied partners are with the relationship.[58]

However, giving compliments is a tricky business because some attempts at flattery can be interpreted in ways you do not intend. For example, many female professionals tire of receiving workplace compliments on their looks while their male coworkers are more often complimented on their work.[59] Some compliments are too personal and can make people feel uncomfortable. A pattern of personal compliments may be grounds for a claim of sexual harassment. But these are extreme examples. We encourage you to think about complimenting as a communication skill and a strategy that is particularly useful in first conversations, whether you're online or face-to-face. You don't want to come across as a phony or a predator, but a well-thought-out compliment can open the door to further conversation.

It's also important to know how to *receive* a compliment graciously—not by agreeing with the complimenter (and sounding cocky) or by disagreeing or attempting to talk the person out of his or her compliment, as in "You like this old outfit? I've had it for years—I just threw it on today." The best response is a simple "thank you" that acknowledges something nice was said about you.[60]

Maintaining Relationships

7.3 Explain the roles of self-disclosure and emotional expression in maintaining face-to-face and online relationships.

Not only do relationships bring us life's greatest joy, but they also dramatically improve our physical health. Research examining data from more than 300,000 people found that a lack of strong relationships increased one's risk of premature death by 50 percent. This statistic represents a health risk comparable to smoking up to fifteen cigarettes a day and a greater risk than obesity or physical inactivity.[61]

Once a relationship has been initiated, we rely on many forms of interpersonal communication (whether conveyed face-to-face, online, or both) to maintain the connection.[62] Relationship experts John Harvey and Ann Weber describe relationship maintenance as "minding." By "minding," they mean "thought and behavior patterns that interact to create stability and feelings of closeness in a relationship."[63]

A key maintenance decision surrounds the outing and defining of a relationship, both in FtF settings and on social media. For many partners—no matter gay, straight, bisexual, transgender, queer, etc.—a decision to go public with one's relationship status is a critical relationship maintenance moment. On Facebook, it's known as becoming "FBO" (Facebook official). Communication researchers have studied the reasons behind couples' decisions to go public or to keep their relationships private.[64] Often partners in relationships talk about the pros and cons of this decision and what terms they plan to use to define and explain their relationship to others. But what if one partner goes public, like FBO, but the other does not? If a decision is one-sided, it could be a potential source of conflict.

In this section, we explore two forms of communication that are most central to relationship maintenance: self-disclosure and emotional expression. These topics are among the most heavily researched in the communication discipline.

ETHICS & COMMUNICATION

Identity Theft and Social Media

In 2021, cybercrime across the world cost $6 trillion. The expectation is that it will grow at a rate of 15 percent each year until 2025 reaching a high of $10.5 trillion. Cybercrime encompasses many different threats from data theft and loss, theft of IP and data, fraud, hacking and other attacks and malicious breaches.[65]

Social media identity theft is one of the fastest growing trends with users of Facebook, Instagram and Snapchat facing a 46 percent higher risk than non-users. Active social media users are, on average around 30 percent more likely to be victims of identity theft. According to the 2020 Identity Fraud Report, released by Javelin Strategy & Research, around 5 percent of consumers were victims of identity theft in 2019.

Social media users are encouraged to share personal data with 45 percent sharing their full birth date, 63 percent sharing their schooling details, 18 percent sharing their phone number and 12 percent sharing the names of pets. Legally, if not ethically or morally, the social media platforms do allow users to hide or make private their personal details, but this often means that the user must go to the privacy setting to make changes. Often the default is to make these personal details public.

Users are also encouraged to use location tagging, which means that a public profile allows others to see that your home address is vulnerable if you are elsewhere. Many "friends" or contacts on social media have never been seen in real life which is another key security problem. There are also many fake accounts specifically set up to harvest personal data for identity theft attempts. There is also little clear advice about logging out (especially if you use social media on public networks) as well as poor use of passwords.

Common identity thefts often revolve around email phishing or contact via social media, increasingly the criminals will use fraudulent accounts to pose as government organizations. Hacked social media accounts are often used to access friends' accounts and broaden the scope of the identity thefts.[66]

Self-Disclosure: Revealing Yourself to Others

Have you ever had a doctor's appointment in which you didn't feel comfortable disclosing the real reason for your visit? Perhaps you didn't tell your doctor about a fear or concern until right before she or he exited the room? Research has actually studied this phenomenon—it's called *doorknob disclosure*.[67] Many patients feel powerless during medical appointments because they don't know what their doctor knows or because their doctor is in a position to tell them what may be happening in their own bodies. A medical visit is a fraught communication context. It may take some people time to "warm up" or summon the nerve to talk about an issue, so they wait to blurt out their concerns or questions until the doctor's hand is literally on the doorknob. This is a unique form of self-disclosure, a key form of communication in any relationship.

Self-disclosure, originally studied by psychologist Sidney Jourard, occurs when we voluntarily provide information to others that they would not learn unless we told them.[68] Communication scholar David Johnson provides eight reasons why people self-disclose:

- We begin and deepen a relationship by sharing reactions, feelings, personal information, and confidences.
- Self-disclosure improves the quality of relationships.
- Self-disclosure allows us to validate our perceptions of reality.
- Self-disclosure clarifies our understanding of ourselves.
- The expression of feelings and reactions is a freeing experience.
- Disclosing or withholding information about ourselves can be a means of social control.
- Self-disclosing is an important part of managing stress and adversity.
- Self-disclosure fulfills a human need to be known intimately and accepted.[69]

In Chapter 2 we discussed the notion of self-concept clarity, which is defined as the extent to which beliefs about oneself are clearly and confidently identified and stable

self-disclosure
Voluntarily providing information to others that they would not learn if one did not tell them.

over time. Research has determined that people high in self-concept clarity (meaning they know who they are and have known for some time) are more likely to self-disclose information to romantic partners. Self-concept clarity actually affects disclosure in relationships more than one's level of self-esteem.[70]

Properties of Self-Disclosure

Self-disclosure is a building block of intimacy, and greater intimacy generally leads to enhanced relationships, whether those relationships are developed face-to-face or online.[71] Because of the importance of self-disclosure, we need to understand three properties of this unique form of interpersonal communication.

- *Reciprocity*. When we share information about ourselves with others, we expect them to share information similar in risk or depth about themselves, that is, to provide **reciprocity**. Sharing information gives others a certain amount of power over you. If the other person reciprocates by disclosing similar information, it helps maintain a balance of power. Over time, unreciprocated self-disclosure may cause someone to end a relationship. The reciprocity aspect applies online as well. If someone does not respond to our social media posts or email messages with as much depth of disclosure as we would like, we may reduce or end our online communication with that person.[72]

- *Appropriateness*. It is sometimes hard to gauge what is appropriate to talk about and what is not while you are in the process of getting to know someone.[73] It may not feel right to share certain information during the early stages of a relationship, but it may be appropriate to disclose that same information at a later stage. People vary a good deal on this judgment. Unwanted disclosures may emerge because one person misjudges the nature of the relationship, assuming or wanting a greater level of intimacy than his or her partner. Be sensitive when you choose what and when to disclose; consider how the recipient of your disclosure will react to the information. Conversely, when someone reveals information to you, try to determine whether it's highly personal to her or him and respond appropriately.

- *Risk*. Self-disclosure can be extremely rewarding because of its potential to deepen a relationship and enhance trust. But self-disclosure is not without its risks. Some people find it de-stressing to vent about their relationships or to post something negative or judgmental about someone on social media. However, it's wise to avoid venting online because social media outlets are *public* sites.[74] The Internet has made the world smaller. In our increasingly open culture, protecting our privacy is a challenge.[75] For example, even in a society more accepting of homosexuality, bisexuality, and transgender and queer identities, coming out, as a form of self-disclosure, is still a risky prospect. Relationships with family members and friends can be hurt by the revelation, and the potential for rejection of, and hostility toward, the discloser is very real.[76] When we disclose, we make ourselves vulnerable and forfeit control of information. We might offend, hurt, or insult another person by our disclosure, thus damaging the relationship. In relationships, we typically seek a balance between the potential risks and rewards of disclosing personal information.

reciprocity
Sharing information about oneself with another person, with the expectation that the other person will share information that is similar in risk or depth.

> **RECAP**
>
> **Self-Disclosure**
>
> . . . is providing someone with information about yourself that she or he could not learn about you unless you revealed it.
>
> . . . is highly rewarding; it is a building block of relational intimacy.
>
> . . . should be reciprocal, meaning that the person you reveal something to should respond with information about himself or herself that is similar in depth. The frequency with which partners self-disclose should be reciprocal as well.
>
> . . . should be appropriate, meaning it can be a mistake to reveal information that is too personal too soon in the development of a relationship.
>
> . . . involves some risk, because knowledge is power. By revealing information to another person, you give that person a degree of power over you.

Two Models of Self-Disclosure

Research has explored the way in which self-disclosure works to move a relationship toward intimacy. Here we examine two of the more prominent models that illustrate the process by which this happens.

social penetration model
A model of self-disclosure that asserts that both the breadth and the depth of information shared with another person increase as the relationship develops.

The Social Penetration Model Irwin Altman and Dalmas Taylor developed the **social penetration model**, which illustrates how much and what kind of information we reveal in various stages of a relationship.[77] According to their theory, interpersonal communication in relationships moves gradually from the superficial to the more intimate. Two aspects of this communication increase: the breadth of the information (the variety of topics discussed) and the depth (the personal significance of what is discussed).

As shown in Figure 7.2, the Altman and Taylor model is a configuration of rings, or concentric circles. The outermost circle represents breadth, or all the potential information about yourself that you could disclose to someone—information about athletic activities, spirituality, family, school, recreational preferences, political attitudes and values, and fears. Then there are a series of inner circles, which represent the depth of information you could reveal about yourself. The innermost circle represents your most personal information.

As an online or FtF relational partner interacts with you, that interaction can be seen as a wedge that is at first narrow (few topics are discussed) and shallow (topics are fairly superficial). People who have just started hanging out might talk about commonalities (such as being students at the same college), hobbies, interests, and favorite activities. As the relationship progresses, the wedge becomes broader (as more topics are discussed) and deeper (as more personal topics are discussed). Over time and with more conversations, topics might turn more to values, such as the importance of family and friendships or attitudes about politics or social issues. Self-disclosure causes your layers to be penetrated as you penetrate the layers of the other person.

Each of your relationships exhibits a certain degree of social penetration, determined by the extent to which the other person has entered your concentric circles. Some relationships reflect a narrow, shallow wedge because they don't involve a great deal of personal disclosure. A few relationships represent almost complete social penetration, the kind you achieve in an intimate, well-developed relationship in which a large amount of in-depth self-disclosure has occurred. This model is a helpful way to assess your relationships in terms of whom you allow or encourage to get close to you and why.

FIGURE 7.2 Altman and Taylor's Model of Social Penetration

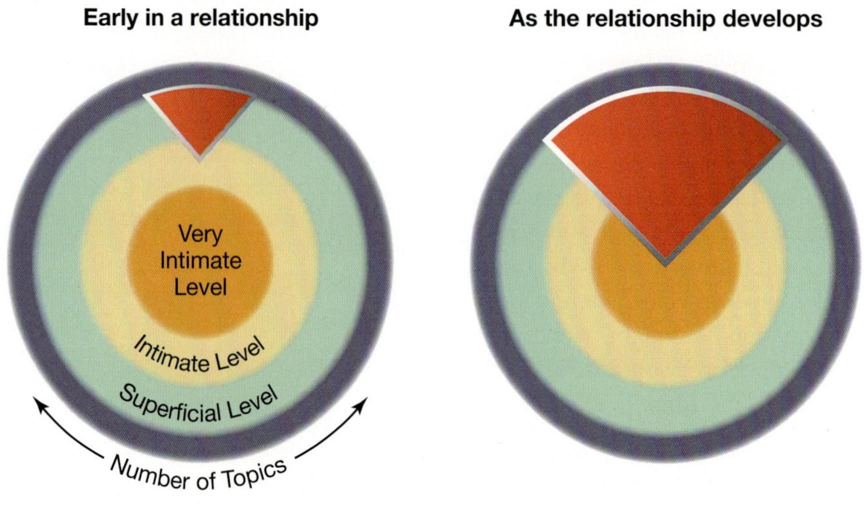

The Johari Window The **Johari Window** in Figure 7.3 is another model of how self-disclosure varies from relationship to relationship. It reflects various stages of relational development, degrees of self-awareness, and others' perceptions of us. The Johari Window is named for the two men who developed it (Joe Luft and Harry Ingham) and for its window-like appearance.[78] The large square window represents the self, which encompasses everything about you, including things you don't see or realize. A vertical line divides the square into what you have come to know about yourself and what you don't yet know about yourself. A horizontal line divides the square into what another person knows about you and doesn't know about you. The intersection of these lines divides the Johari Window into the following four quadrants:

Johari Window
A model that explains how self-disclosure varies from relationship to relationship; the model reflects various stages of relational development, degrees of self-awareness, and others' perceptions.

- *The Open quadrant.* The part of yourself that you know and have revealed to another person is the Open quadrant. As a relationship becomes more intimate, the Open quadrant grows larger.

- *The Blind quadrant.* Information that another person knows about you but that you fail to recognize is in your Blind quadrant. For example, your closest friends may be able to tell when you're attracted to someone even before you are aware of the attraction yourself. Before someone knows you well, the Blind quadrant is usually small; it grows larger as that person observes more information that's in your Unknown quadrant.

- *The Hidden quadrant.* Information that you know about yourself but haven't shared with another person makes up the Hidden quadrant. Initially fairly large, the Hidden quadrant shrinks and the Open quadrant grows as you disclose more and more.

- *The Unknown quadrant.* Information about yourself that you—as well as other people—have yet to discover or realize makes up the Unknown quadrant. People who aren't very introspective and don't have a very well-developed sense of self have larger Unknown areas than do those who've made a concerted effort to get to know themselves. This quadrant shrinks as you learn more about yourself or as others learn more about you.

Expressing Emotions

"Emotion is the fuel of human communication," says scholar Paul Bolls.[79] Expressing emotions is another powerful way we reveal ourselves to others and maintain our relationships. Such expression comes more easily to some people than others, but it is a skill that can be improved in both your online and FtF relationships.[80] However, keep in mind that culture affects the expression of emotions; many cultures designate particular emotions as appropriate for only some people to display in certain situations.[81] If you placed emotional expression on a continuum according to cultural groups, with an open approach to emotional display at one end and the suppression of emotional display at the other end, the United States would fall somewhere in the middle.[82]

The COVID-19 pandemic has no doubt had an effect on how people across the globe express their emotions in public settings and FtF interactions, mainly because masks block half of our faces. We use many nonverbal cues to convey emotion but without someone seeing our smile (or lack thereof) we may have to rely more on our eyes, gestures, voices, and words to communicate our feelings.[83]

Families teach children very specific rules about the appropriateness of emotional display, rules that often perpetuate sex and gender distinctions.[84] In the United States, many men are taught to contain

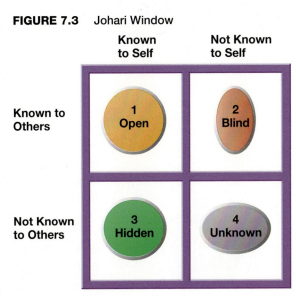

FIGURE 7.3 Johari Window

CRITICAL/CULTURAL PERSPECTIVES & COMMUNICATION

Where You Stand Affects How You Sway

As we explained in Chapter 1, a critical/cultural perspective invites us to consider where we stand, in terms of privilege, power, and influence, in comparison to others. How influential are you in your relationships? Are you likely to be the one to influence your friends and classmates? Think about your workplace relationships, too, because even if you are in a lower-status position, you can still be persuasive by using effective communication skills and principles to sway coworkers, supervisors, and clients.

Now shift to more intimate or romantic relationships, if you have such connections in your life. Do you perceive yourself as coming from a position of power and privilege in those relationships? If so, how does this position affect how you communicate with your relational partners? Or do you feel privileged by being a college or university student, even though you may have little power to influence important people? Many people believe that one of the most important factors in an intimate relationship is power, meaning being able to control or persuade a relational partner. Sometimes it comes down to an analysis of who influences more decisions about things large and small in the life of a relationship. Being aware of your power, both the power you assume and the power granted to you by others, helps you better understand your potential to sway others to your point of view.

▲ Many American men learn at an early age to mute most of their emotional expressions, whereas American women often learn to express a wide range of feelings. What were you taught about emotional expression that affects the way you communicate in relationships today?
IKO/Shutterstock

their emotions for fear that emotional expression may make them appear weak.[85] In fact, the male tendency to suppress emotion is so pronounced that it led Sidney Jourard (who first studied self-disclosure) to entitle one of his book chapters, "The Lethal Aspects of the Male Role."[86] Jourard found that men who had difficulty expressing their feelings had high levels of stress-related disease.

In American culture, it is socially acceptable for women to cry in most settings, whether prompted by sadness, fear, or joy. But many women receive negative reactions when they display anger. While these trends and expectations have changed somewhat with recent generations, there is still a significant tendency for men (as well as many women) to believe that emotional expression of any kind is more appropriate in women than in men.[87]

As relationships become more intimate, we have a greater expectation that our partner will disclose emotions openly. The amount of risk associated with such emotional disclosure varies from person to person.[88] Most of us are comfortable sharing the emotions of happiness and joy but are more reserved or hesitant about sharing fear, disappointment, and anger.

While emotional expression can sometimes be difficult to handle, we generally want to know how our close friends, family members, and intimate partners feel, even if their feelings are negative. As we first mentioned in Chapter 5, it is critical to successful relationship maintenance that we learn how to accurately identify and effectively respond to someone's expression of emotions and offer needed emotional support.[89] Research on emotional support has shown that this skill is important in relationships that rely mostly on face-to-face communication, but also for relationships maintained primarily through social media. Social media outlets are tremendous vehicles for offering emotional support.[90] For example, health challenges are often the subject of Facebook posts and Twitter comments. People who have experienced health problems themselves or have loved ones who are ill, often communicate support for a range of emotions associated with health concerns.[91]

In this chapter, we have explored several aspects of interpersonal communication, yet we have only scratched the surface of the complexities of relationships—those connections that give us life's greatest joys, as well as challenges. In the next chapter, we examine key aspects of communication that are critical to ongoing relationships, with regard to our five Communication Principles for a Lifetime.

STUDY GUIDE: PRINCIPLES FOR A LIFETIME

CHAPTER 7

What Is Interpersonal Communication?

7.1 Define interpersonal communication and discuss its three unique attributes.

PRINCIPLE POINTS: Interpersonal communication occurs when two people interact simultaneously and attempt to mutually influence each other, usually for the purpose of managing relationships. Interpersonal communication studies have traditionally focused on face-to-face relationships, but over the last few decades, researchers have investigated how online relationships are initiated and maintained through mediated interpersonal communication.

Interpersonal communication has three attributes:

- Interpersonal communication involves quality in contrast to impersonal communication, in which people are treated as objects or are communicated with based on the roles they hold.
- Interpersonal communication involves mutual influence.
- Interpersonal communication helps manage relationships of choice and circumstance.

PRINCIPLE TERMS:

interpersonal communication
mediated communication
mediated interpersonal communication
impersonal communication
relationship

PRINCIPLE SKILLS:

1. In your own life, have you experienced the mutual influence of interpersonal communication within the past 24 hours? Describe your experience.

2. Learning to Ask Great Questions

Because we think that learning to ask great questions is so important, we want to provide you with an opportunity to practice this art and skill. For each of the situations and snippets of conversation that follow, generate follow-up questions that would deepen and extend the conversation. We've provided an example to get you started.

Sample Situation and Conversation: The situation is a first conversation between two classmates who have never met before. They are seated in a classroom before class begins.

Bob: Hi. My name's Bob. What's yours?

Carmen: Hi. I'm Carmen.

Bob: I've never taken a philosophy course before, have you? What do you think this course will be like?

Carmen: Well, I've never taken one either, but I expect lots of reading. And I've heard the professor's tests are tough.

Bob: Oh, great! Is it too late to drop? When you say the tests are tough, tough in what way? Do you mean they cover lots of material, the professor's a hard grader, or what?

a. *Practice Situation:* At a fraternity/sorority mixer, a woman and a man are introduced to each other for the first time by other members of their organizations.

b. *Practice Situation:* After a staff meeting, two new coworkers who will be working on the same important project introduce themselves to each other.

Initiating Relationships

7.2 Describe the roles of communication in revealing interpersonal attraction and initiating relationships.

PRINCIPLE POINTS: We are drawn to other people because of physical, sexual, and interpersonal attraction; similarity; proximity; and complementarity. We use nonverbal immediacy cues to convey our attraction and communicate to reduce uncertainty as we initiate and develop relationships. Besides listening, adapting, and being sensitive to nonverbal cues, good interpersonal communicators ask great questions, avoid self-absorbed communication, and give and receive compliments graciously.

PRINCIPLE TERMS:

relationship of circumstance
relationship of choice
attraction
interpersonal attraction
social attraction
physical attraction
sexual attraction
matching hypothesis
similarity
proximity
complementarity
immediacy
uncertainty-reduction theory
passive strategy
active strategy
interactive strategy
conversational narcissism (self-absorbed communicator style)
trait conversational narcissism
state conversational narcissism

PRINCIPLE SKILLS:

1. Provide examples of when you have used passive, active, and interactive strategies to reduce your uncertainty in a new situation or when meeting a new person.
2. Think of someone you know who is either a trait or state conversational narcissist. How have you responded to that person's communication style? Has your relationship experienced distance because of this person's self-absorbed communication style? What do you think is the best way to respond to a self-absorbed communicator?

Maintaining Relationships

7.3 Explain the roles of self-disclosure and emotional expression in maintaining face-to-face and online relationships.

PRINCIPLE POINTS: An important communication skill is self-disclosure, or voluntarily providing information to others that they wouldn't learn if you didn't tell them. Self-disclosure is characterized by three aspects: (1) reciprocity, (2) appropriateness, and (3) risk. The social penetration model suggests that interpersonal communication in relationships moves gradually from the superficial to the more intimate. The breadth and depth of communication increase as intimacy increases in relationships. The Johari Window depicts various stages of relational development, degrees of self-awareness, and others' perceptions. Emotional expression is another powerful mechanism for revealing ourselves to others and deepening our relationships.

PRINCIPLE TERMS:

self-disclosure
reciprocity
social penetration model
Johari Window

PRINCIPLE SKILLS:

1. Consider how open a person you are. How comfortably and readily do you communicate information about yourself—such as your background, history, beliefs, views, and opinions? Do you have circles of friends who you are comfortable with and, thus, share more information with? How open are you with family members?

2. Too Private to Talk About—Unless It's Online?

For the following topics, check the column to indicate in which situation you would freely disclose the information to another person you were trying to get to know. Then analyze your answers. What information would you share anytime in any format? What information are you unlikely to reveal to anyone in either context?

Topic	Would Disclose FtF	Would Disclose Online
Weight		
Racial/ethnic background		
Sexual history		
Family details		
Relationship status		
Weaknesses/strengths		
Religious/spiritual beliefs		
Political views		

CHAPTER 8

ENHANCING RELATIONSHIPS

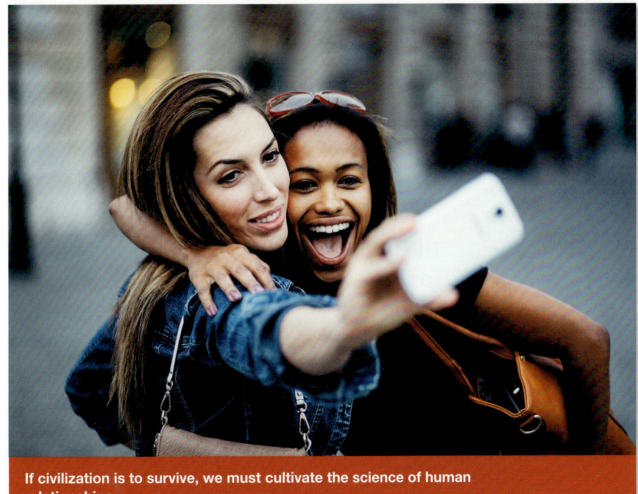

If civilization is to survive, we must cultivate the science of human relationships... —FRANKLIN D. ROOSEVELT

MinDof/Shutterstock

CHAPTER OUTLINE

- The Importance of Relationships: Friends, Family, and Colleagues
- Stages of Relationship Development
- Relationship Dissolution (a.k.a. the Breakup)
- Tensions in Relationships: The Dialectical Perspective
- Managing Interpersonal Conflict
- Study Guide: *Principles for a Lifetime*

LEARNING OBJECTIVES

8.1 Explain how the five Communication Principles for a Lifetime apply to interpersonal communication among friends, family members, and colleagues.

8.2 Identify and describe the stages of relational escalation and de-escalation.

8.3 Summarize research findings on relationship dissolution, including communication in the on-again/off-again relationship and the postdissolutional relationship.

8.4 Discuss relational dialectics and three primary tensions in relationships.

8.5 Summarize the seven types of interpersonal conflict, the key characteristics of conflict management, and the ways people can cooperate in conflict situations.

What makes you happy? Streaming a TV show on your computer? Working on a project for your job? Reading a great book? Playing a video game? Taking a long walk? Let's venture a guess: While any one of these things might bring some level of pleasure into your life, none of them could be considered *the* thing in life that gives you the most enjoyment. Probably most of us would answer that question with some response that involves other people or perhaps only one other person.

In Chapter 7, we examined some fundamental aspects of interpersonal communication that help us initiate and maintain online and face-to-face relationships. In this chapter, we discuss interpersonal communication as it occurs in ongoing, longer-term relationships, applying our five Communication Principles for a Lifetime.

The Importance of Relationships: Friends, Family, and Colleagues

8.1 Explain how the five Communication Principles for a Lifetime apply to interpersonal communication among friends, family members, and colleagues.

Our family members, friends, and coworkers are very important to us. We don't have to lecture students on the value of friendship. As for family, to some degree we all come from dysfunctional families—there is no such thing as a perfect family. No matter how imperfect our families are, how crazy our siblings still make us, or how far apart we may have grown, almost all of us would agree that family relationships are extremely important. On the job front, when people discuss what they like best about their jobs, most often they talk about the people they work with. So, disregarding the few true hermits out there, most of us are "people who need people."

Friendship Matters

One of the best definitions of a friend, attributed to Aristotle, is "a soul that resides in two bodies." A friend is someone we like and who likes us. We trust our friends and share good and bad times with them. We expect a certain level of sacrifice from our friends. For example, you know you've got a good friend when he or she gives up something (like a hot date) to help you through a tough time.

Researchers have examined some differences among friendships at four stages in life: childhood, adolescence, adulthood, and old age.[1] When we start to talk (around age two) and interact with others, our first friendships are typically superficial, self-centered, and fleeting because they are based on momentarily shared activities.[2] As we grow and mature, we develop more of a give-and-take in friendships. During adolescence we move away emotionally from relationships with parents, and peer relationships have more influence on our behavior.[3]

Adult friendships are among our most valued relationships, even though they may be few in number. Research has found that, on average, adults have ten to twenty casual friends, four to six close friends, and only one to two best friends.[4] Rather than progressing through a series of stages in which intimacy deepens, which is typical of romantic relationships, friendships often alternate between periods of development and deterioration.[5] The friendships you establish in college are some of the most important in your life, but how long these friendships last after graduation varies depending on the individuals.[6] For many Americans, our jobs are our lives, so we increasingly find that our coworkers become some of our closest friends.

Friendships are extremely important in old age.[7] During retirement, when many individuals have more time for socializing, friendships become increasingly critical. Older adults tend to rely on enduring friendships and maintain a small, highly valued network of friends.

Family Matters

Of all the relationships we experience in our lifetimes, none are more complicated than family relationships. Family life has certainly changed. Family units are dramatically different from what they were in the twentieth century, when the predominant profile was a two-parent, father-as-breadwinner, mother-as-homemaker arrangement.[8] In the 1980s, the New York Supreme Court provided a very broad definition of a family, stating, "The best description of a family is a continuing relationship of love and care, and an assumption of responsibility for some other person."[9] The most common profile of the American family in the twenty-first century is the stepfamily, or blended family, with rising rates of extended family or multigenerational arrangements. As of 2020, the average marriage in the United States lasted seven years, and over fifty percent of families consisted of remarried or recoupled parents.[10] After same-sex marriage became legal in the United States in 2015, we experienced another paradigm shift in our basic views of what constitutes a family.[11] More recently, the COVID-19 pandemic placed more emphasis on how families function, given that schools closed, people lost employment, and family members felt safest spending time at home as a family unit.[12]

Colleagues Matter

For many of us, our work is our livelihood, our most time-consuming activity. Many things make a job worthwhile and rewarding, but most people say that relationships with people at work make the difference between job satisfaction and dissatisfaction.

What are the most important skills people need to be successful on the job? Year after year, among the top ten skills employers look for in new hires is the ability to

▲ These two friends may have met just moments ago. Our earliest friendships are usually based on momentarily shared activities. How long does it take you now to decide someone is your friend? What influences that decision?
Thinkstock Images/Stockbyte/Getty Images

SOCIAL MEDIA & COMMUNICATION

Video Chat during the COVID-19 Pandemic

How has the COVID-19 pandemic impacted your communications? For many people, it enhanced relationships in ways face-to-face communications could never achieve. With work and everyday physical conversations being restricted, people were looking for solutions to communicate with family members, colleagues, and friends from the confines of their homes. As early as March 2020, rises in the use of video conferencing tools like Skype, Zoom, Slack, and Microsoft Teams were reported. In Deloitte's *2021 Global Marketing Trends*, a global audience was asked about experiences with video chat during the pandemic in comparison to traditional face-to-face communication. Approximately 55 percent thought it was an adequate experience and 42 percent rated it superior.[13] For corporations like Zoom, this is perhaps reflected in a rise in its share prices from $36 in 2019 to $68 in 2020 and then $340 in 2021.[14] In February 2020, there were fewer than 5 million active monthly users of Zoom in the United States, which increased to nearly 27 million in March 2020.[15]

A study by Bugsnag that identified the net impact on different apps concluded that during the pandemic some had thrived, were seemingly pandemic-proof, or had taken a big hit in popularity and use (but would probably bounce back in the future). The communication apps were pandemic-thrivers. Zoom was a big winner, with a global increase of 300 percent in its user base in March 2020 alone. While Zoom was the top ranked iPhone business app in just one market at the end of 2019, by March 2020 it was the top in 141 markets. The average number of daily meeting participants using Zoom went from 10 million to 200 million in three months.[16] The non-tech-savvy population faced either being left behind in communications or having to adapt quickly.

In the United Kingdom, the Office of Communications, commonly referred to as Ofcom, released its annual report, Online Nation, with figures suggesting that the average British adult was online daily for four hours and two minutes, up from three and half hours in September 2019. While TikTok and other social media apps were popular, the use of video-calling services grew with the Houseparty app rising from 175,000 users in January 2020 to 4 million by April. At the same time, Zoom had grown from 659,000 to 13 million. By May 2020, WhatsApp was being used by 49 percent of U.K. adults (from 20 percent in February 2020) and Facebook Messenger was up from 18 percent to 41 percent.[17]

In early 2021, Webhelp reported that the use of video conferencing tools in customer services had increased by 70 percent in Europe. The pandemic was bringing in some fundamental changes in consumer patterns as data revealed that 27 percent of European consumers would switch to a brand offering video chat options. In addition, around 40 percent of European consumers stated they would continue to use video chat after the pandemic and 14 percent thought they would use it more.[18]

communicate effectively with others, both orally and in writing.[19] You land your job through an interview; you keep your job on the basis of your ability to do the work and get along with coworkers, bosses, and clients, which usually involves a large amount of interpersonal interaction. The higher you go in an organization, the more your job will involve communicating with others, both online and in person.

Your Relationships and the Five Communication Principles for a Lifetime

Our familiar five Communication Principles for a Lifetime can help you enhance your relationships with friends, family, and colleagues.

- **Principle One: Be Aware of Your Communication with Yourself and Others**
  Awareness of ourselves as communicators is key to expanding our circle of friends and deepening our friendships. Awareness is also important as we grow up in families and begin to discover who we are and how we should communicate with others. Family members have more power to shape our self-concepts than other people do. Granted, at some point we may choose to lessen the effect family members have on our lives. But for most of us, those early messages we received as children remain in our psyches and affect who we are today. With regard to workplace relationships, awareness is a must if you want to be successful at your job. We need to figure out who is in the chain of command and which colleagues have the potential to develop into friends.[20] Perception checking with colleagues, supervisors, clients, and trainers also increases awareness.

- **Principles Two and Three: Effectively Use and Interpret Verbal and Nonverbal Messages** We use nonverbal immediacy cues to establish friendships—behaviors that reveal our liking of other people, such as leaning forward, moving closer, making eye contact, smiling, and nodding. As friendships develop, our verbal communication tends to become more frequent and deepens. Many of the ways we express ourselves verbally and nonverbally come from experiences with family members as we grew up and modeled our behavior after parents, siblings, and extended family members. Renowned family therapist Virginia Satir has conducted extensive research on family communication.[21] She suggests that the following elements are present in healthy families:

    - Self-worth of members is high.
    - Communication is direct and honest.
    - Rules are flexible.
    - People listen actively.
    - Family members look *at* one another, not *through* one another.
    - Family members treat children as people.
    - They touch one another affectionately regardless of age.
    - They openly discuss disappointments, fears, hurts, angers, and criticism, as well as joys and achievements.

  In a workplace setting, we interact with colleagues of varying status as well as with people external to the company, such as clients and customers. In these instances, we draw on our most effective verbal and nonverbal communication skills so that we make positive impressions on others. As we establish workplace relationships, verbal and nonverbal cues are often critical to our professional success.

- **Principle Four: Listen and Respond Thoughtfully to Others** Probably no other communication skill develops relationships more than the ability to listen and respond appropriately. Most of us don't stay friends with people who don't seem to listen to us or who listen but respond inappropriately. Healthy family relationships are built on foundations of trust, which involve listening to one another and responding helpfully. Many conflicts arise because family members don't listen well to one another and respond on the basis of that faulty listening.[22] In the workplace, it is important to listen patiently, fully, and nonjudgmentally to coworkers, supervisors, and clients. We need to exercise caution before responding to others at work so that we respond appropriately.

- **Principle Five: Appropriately Adapt Messages to Others** Our fifth principle about adaptation is critical to relationships of all types. We extend different parts of ourselves to various friends. Having a wide range of friends taps into different parts of our personality, which, in turn, helps us develop our skills of communication adaptation. Family relationships involve a good deal of adaptation, particularly when, as adults, we visit our parents. Sometimes our parents and extended family members talk a certain way mainly because they have always talked that way.[23]

But if you're the family member who has moved away, attended college, and adapted your communication to meet the changing times, relate to friends, and demonstrate professionalism at work, it can be quite awkward to be immersed once again in a family setting and realize how much you have changed. Reintegration into family patterns of communication can also be a challenge for military personnel who have served overseas and return to family life in the United States.[24] Finally, we will not be successful on the job if we communicate the same way to our boss as we do to our peers, subordinates, clients, and others in our life—including long-term friends, intimates, and family members.[25] This may seem obvious, but we find that people sometimes experience isolation on the job because they cannot get along with coworkers. They do not adapt to the situation, and it often costs them their jobs.

Stages of Relationship Development

8.2 Identify and describe the stages of relational escalation and de-escalation.

In this chapter, we explore aspects of communication that are critical to the successful functioning of ongoing, longer-term relationships, but it is helpful to first understand that relationships tend to develop in discernible stages.[26] Although the research on relational stages is most often applied to dating or romantic relationships, this information can also apply to other types of relationships.

Understanding relationship stages is important for two main reasons:

- Interpersonal communication is affected by the stage of a relationship. For instance, people in advanced stages discuss topics and display nonverbal behaviors that rarely appear in the early stages of a relationship.
- Interpersonal communication (both face-to-face and mediated) facilitates movement between the various stages.[27] Ongoing relationships change and are constantly renegotiated by those involved. Interpersonal communication moves a relationship forward—possibly from friends to romantic partners to marital or committed partners. Communication can also move a relationship back to a previous stage, although regressing a relationship or changing a relationship's definition can be difficult to accomplish.[28]

Think of relational stages as floors in a high-rise (see Figure 8.1). The bottom floor represents a first meeting; the penthouse is intimacy. Relational development is an elevator that stops at every floor. As you ascend, you might get off the elevator and wander around for a while before going to the next floor. Each time you get on the elevator, you don't know how many floors up it will take you or how long you'll stay at any given floor. If you fall head over heels in love, you might want to escalate quickly from floor to floor

FIGURE 8.1 Relationship Stages

SOURCE: Adapted from Steven A. Beebe, Susan J. Beebe, and Mark V. Redmond, *Interpersonal Communication: Relating to Others*, 9e. Reprinted and electronically reproduced by permission of Pearson Education, Inc., Hoboken, NJ. Copyright © 2020. Photograph: BJI/Blue Jean Images/Getty Images (top); MIXA/Getty Images (bottom)

Types of Relationships	Escalation Stages	De-Escalation Stages
Best Friend/ Lover/ Spouse	Intimacy	Turmoil or Stagnation
Close Friend	Intensification	De-Intensification
Friend	Exploration	Individualization
Acquaintance	Initiation	Separation
Stranger	Preinteraction Awareness	Post-Interaction

toward intimacy, possibly even skipping some floors. Other times, you stop at a particular floor and never get back on the elevator, electing instead to stay at a particular stage of relational development. This may represent stability or stagnation (which are not the same thing). Stagnation, which tends to have a negative connotation, is an indication that a relationship is flat and perhaps on the brink of de-escalation and termination. Stability may simply mean that a relationship has reached a comfortable point for both partners; it's not going up or down, but it's working. If one partner believes the relationship has stabilized and the other partner believes it has stagnated, dissatisfaction and conflict will often result.

The best approach to relationship development is to share this elevator with your partner or friend so that the two of you make decisions about how high to ride, how long to stay at each floor, and whether to take the elevator back down. But often partners do not share decisions about movement within the relationship. Sometimes one of the partners rides the elevator alone.

Relational Escalation

According to Mark Knapp and Anita Vangelisti, the two communication scholars who developed the model of developmental stages within relationships, relational escalation occurs in the following five stages:[29]

- **Pre-interaction awareness stage** is the first stage, one in which potential partners or friends observe each other and talk with other people about each other without having any direct interaction. If your impressions of a potential friend or relational partner aren't favorable or circumstances aren't right, you might not move beyond this first stage.
- In the **initiation stage**, first conversations occur between potential friends or romantic partners. Each person responds to the other's questions as both try to determine what they have in common. Nonverbal cues are important at this stage because they signal interest.
- The **exploration stage** occurs next as partners or friends begin to share more in-depth information. Minimal physical contact is typical, and the amount of time people spend together tends to be fairly limited as the relationship begins to build.
- If people proceed to the **intensification stage**, they start to depend on each other for self-confirmation, meaning each partner's or friend's opinions and feelings about the other weighs more heavily than the opinions of other people. Partners spend more time together in a wider variety of activities, adopt more intimate physical distance and contact, and personalize their language. The frequency and level of shared personal information increase, and the two people may decide to label their connection. Friends may move to "best friend" status; romantic partners may make a decision to publicize their relationship on social media, for example, deciding to become FBO ("Facebook official").[30]
- The top level of relationship escalation is the **intimacy stage**. At this stage, partners provide primary confirmation of each other's self-concept and communication is highly personalized and synchronized. Partners talk about anything and everything, and a commitment to maintaining a romantic relationship might even be formalized and socially recognized, such as with a decision to cohabitate or marry. Romantic partners share an understanding of each other's language and nonverbal cues and have a great deal of physical contact. Reaching this stage takes time—time to build trust, share highly personal information, observe each other in various situations, and create an emotional bond and commitment.

This is a nice and tidy model of what *may* happen as a relationship progresses, but we all know that relationships can be messier than this. Some people move through relational stages very quickly. We probably all know people whose relationships were

pre-interaction awareness stage
The first stage of relational escalation in which potential partners or friends observe each other without having any direct interaction.

initiation stage
The second stage of relational escalation in which first conversations occur between potential friends or romantic partners; usually characterized by asking and answering questions.

exploration stage
The stage of relational escalation that involves more in-depth interactions.

intensification stage
The stage of relational escalation in which partners begin to depend on each other for self-confirmation; characterized by more shared activities, more time spent together, more intimate physical distance and contact, and personalized language.

intimacy stage
The stage of relational escalation in which partners provide primary confirmation of each other's self-concept; characterized by highly personalized and synchronized verbal and nonverbal communication.

▲ At the intensification stage, a couple's relationship becomes the central focus of their lives.
Tetra Images/Getty Images

extremely physical and perhaps sexual from the very start. Are those relationships doomed because they didn't follow set or prescribed paths for development? No; some relationships may just proceed through stages faster than others. Extremely physical or sexual relationships may burn out quickly, however, because they lack the emotional foundation necessary to survive. Partners may have difficulty developing an emotional connection or finding things in common once the physical spark wanes.

Relational De-Escalation

Sometimes relationships begin to unravel, some to the point of termination. But as you may already know, a relationship in decline does not simply go down the same way it went up; it's not a mere reversal of the escalation process.[31] Relational de-escalation contains the following five stages:

- The **turmoil or stagnation stage** comes first in a relationship's decline and is characterized by increased conflict as partners find faults in each other.[32] The definition of the relationship loses clarity and mutual acceptance diminishes. Conversations are tense, difficult, and forced. The relationship loses its vitality and partners take each other for granted, perhaps feeling bored.[33] Communication and physical contact decrease. Partners or friends spend less time together but don't necessarily engage in conflict. People in a stagnating relationship go through the motions of an intimate relationship without the commitment or joy. But a stagnating relationship can be salvaged. People can repair, redefine, and revitalize their relationship.

- If turmoil or stagnation continues, friends or partners will likely experience the **de-intensification stage**, which involves decreased physical, emotional, and psychological closeness; significantly decreased interaction; and decreased dependence on each other for self-confirmation. Partners might discuss the definition of their relationship, question its future, and assess each other's level of dissatisfaction.

- After de-intensification, the **individualization stage** occurs, in which partners tend to define their lives more as individuals and less as a couple or unit. Interactions are limited; both partners tend to turn to others for self-concept confirmation. For romantic partners, physical intimacy is at an all-time low, maybe nonexistent, and nonverbal distance is easily detected.

turmoil or stagnation stage
The stage of relational de-escalation characterized by increased conflict, less mutual acceptance, a tense communication climate, and an unclear relationship definition that causes the relationship to lose its vitality. Partners begin to take each other for granted, and communication and physical contact decline.

de-intensification stage
The stage of relational de-escalation involving significantly decreased interaction, closeness, and dependence on one's partner for self-confirmation.

individualization stage
The stage of relational de-escalation in which partners define their lives more as individuals and less as a couple.

RECAP

Relational Escalation

Stage	Explanation
Pre-Interaction Awareness	You become aware of your attraction to someone and begin to observe that person.
Initiation	You initiate contact with the person with whom you want a relationship.
Exploration	Interactions deepen as questions and answers elicit more information from partners.
Intensification	Partners begin to depend on each other for confirmation of their self-concepts. They spend more time together, engage in more intimate touch, and personalize their language.
Intimacy	Partners provide primary confirmation of each other's self-concept. Verbally, language is highly personalized; nonverbal behaviors are synchronized.

- In the **separation stage**, individuals make an intentional decision to minimize or eliminate further interaction. Friends may feel awkward if they are also roommates or classmates, and they may take action to distance themselves on campus. If a married or romantic couple share custody of children, attend mutual family gatherings, or work at the same place, the nature of their interaction noticeably changes. They divide property, resources, and friends. Interactions in this stage are increasingly tense and difficult, especially if the relationship had been sexually intimate.

- The final level in de-escalation is the **post-interaction stage**. It represents the lasting effects the relationship has on the self and others. Relationships—even failed ones—are powerful experiences in our lives, so the effects continue even after the relationship has ended. In this stage, partners engage in "grave dressing," meaning that they create a public statement for people who ask why they broke up or are no longer friends.[34] Often people will employ social media to inform their social networks of a change in relationship status.[35] Sometimes self-esteem gets battered during the final stages of a relationship, so partners work to regain a healthy sense of self.[36]

RECAP
Relational De-Escalation

Stage	Explanation
Turmoil or Stagnation	Partners begin to take each other for granted and experience increased conflict. They exhibit less mutual acceptance, their communication climate is tense, and their relationship definition is unclear. The relationship loses its vitality; partners begin to take each other for granted and may experience boredom in the relationship. Communication and physical contact decline.
De-Intensification	Partners significantly decrease their interaction and their dependence on each other for self-confirmation; they increase their physical distance.
Individualization	Partners define their lives more as individuals and less as a couple.
Separation	Partners make an intentional decision to minimize or eliminate further interpersonal interaction.
Post-Interaction	This is the bottom or final level in relational de-escalation; it represents the lasting effects of a relationship on the individuals.

separation stage
The stage of relational de-escalation in which individuals make an intentional decision to minimize or eliminate further interpersonal interaction.

post-interaction stage
The bottom, or final, stage of relational de-escalation, which represents the lasting effects of a relationship on the self.

relationship dissolution
Ending a relationship.

Relationship Dissolution (a.k.a. the Breakup)

8.3 Summarize research findings on relationship dissolution, including communication in the on-again/off-again relationship and the postdissolutional relationship.

Friendships can fade away, marriages can end in divorce, and romantic partners can break up—we all know this. **Relationship dissolution** is the research term for relational endings, possibly preferred because "relationship termination" has connotations of death.[37] Since ending relationships is an inescapable part of everybody's life, let's take a moment to think about communication and breakups, as well as what happens to a relationship after a breakup.

▼ It's highly likely that you will have to break up with someone in your life, whether a friend or romantic partner.
Stefano Lunardi/123RF

Best Practices in Breaking Up

Friendships tend to end (or transition to a different level) more gradually than romantic relationships; sometimes friendships just fade away because of distance or changed circumstances or priorities. But it's bewildering when romantic relationships just fade away, a phenomenon known as "ghosting." People are left wondering what happened. Recent research indicates that ghosting tends to happen in shorter-term relationships that have minimal commitment. Although it has become a more common way of ending relationships, ghosting can cause serious distress to the person being ghosted.[38] In this section, let's focus on what research can teach us about appropriate romantic relationship endings, because our view of ghosting is that it's a cowardly way out.

With the popularity of texting and social media, you may know someone who was broken up with via social media or text message; perhaps you have been on the short end of that stick. Let's be clear (and blunt) about this too: *It is also a cowardly way to end a relationship.* We understand that it saves the "dumper" time and emotional angst, not having to witness in person the "dumpee's" reaction, but even in a superficial, short-term relationship, breaking up at a distance shows no respect for the other person. It also does not do your reputation any favors, because perpetrating a text or social media breakup reveals to others the kind of relational partner you are, even in short-term liaisons.[39]

One study examined college students' methods of delivering a breakup message.[40] Researchers found that 43 percent of subjects' breakups were accomplished face-to-face; 32 percent were handled through a phone call; 10 percent were conveyed through instant messaging via computer; 8 percent were done in an email message; 2 percent used a written letter; and another 2 percent used a third party, such as a friend, to be the bearer of the bad news. (Who would volunteer for *that* gig?) Some students used combinations of these methods. None said that they had broken up with someone via text, explaining that they would be even angrier and more upset if someone broke up with them that way. The takeaway from this study is that the predominant breakup method reported by these students was the good old-fashioned face-to-face conversation, which is also how they would prefer someone break up with them.

So on the basis of what research tells us, here is some advice on communication and breaking up, should you find yourself needing to end a romantic relationship someday (or processing how someone broke up with you):

- *Do not be a ghost.* Avoid ending a relationship by not calling someone back (ever), ignoring messages, unfriending or blocking him or her from your social networking sites, steering clear of places and situations where you might run into the person, and hoping the person will get the hint. These methods generate confusion and ambiguity, causing undue hurt to the target of the breakup.[41] Relational fuzziness can also keep both parties from moving on.

- *Give the other person a chance to respond.* Using a mediated channel to end a relationship may make it easier on the dumper but is terrible for the dumpee (and, some would argue, unethical). Without even a short conversation, the person is cut off from a full explanation, a chance at negotiation, and the opportunity to express her or his feelings.[42]

- *Do it face-to-face.* A face-to-face interaction offers a chance to exercise your communication skills. Although the "dreaded conversation" is rarely pleasant, resist the instinct to duck out or postpone. Force yourself to have a conversation with the person.[43] Thinking, "If I see so-and-so, I might not be able to go through with it" is no excuse to avoid or put off the inevitable. Both parties will retain more dignity and self-respect through a breakup conversation than by being denied the opportunity to talk.

- *Avoid the trite "let's still be friends" line.* For most people in the position of being dumped, the last thing they want to do or can even conceive of is being friends with a former romantic partner.[44] It's understandable for a dumper to try to soften the blow or retain some kind of connection to the dumpee, but it's selfish to expect the other person to adjust to a new relationship definition easily or quickly. Maybe, with time, something can be salvaged that works for both parties.[45]

- *Also avoid the dreaded and trite "It's not you—it's me" bit.* People getting dumped don't tend to believe that anyway. When someone says to us, "It's not you, it's me," most of us will think, "It's me." Granted, there are times when we may agree with the person—it really *is* them. But this line is overused, hurtful, and simply not believable in most circumstances. It does more damage than it saves hurt.

ETHICS & COMMUNICATION

Cyber Infidelity: Is It Cheating If You Don't Actually Touch?

What is your view of cyber or internet infidelity? Should technologically mediated liaisons outside of one's primary romantic relationship be viewed as breaches of ethics or morals, or simply as signs of the times?

We all know that technology and social media help us keep in touch with important people in our lives, including our romantic partners. But another use is to establish and maintain romantic connections with people *other* than our primary romantic partners.[46] As one source suggests, "Fueling our sexual freedom is our ability to pursue a fling without even opening the front door; we can simply open a laptop."[47] Such external liaisons may form through common interests and not begin as sexual relationships, but cyber relationships can quickly escalate. How many relationships have gone down in flames because one partner viewed another's browsing history, or checked text messages or voice mail on the other's phone and found evidence of infidelity?

Most people view in-person relational infidelity as a deal breaker.[48] Even people who haven't experienced it say that they would respond negatively to a partner's infidelity. However, in a recent survey of over 11,000 college students, two-thirds reported lying to a romantic partner, 44 percent reported cheating on a partner, and 16 percent said they had misrepresented their "body count" (number of previous sexual partners) to a romantic partner.[49] But some people view **cyber infidelity** (online sexual activity outside of one's monogamous relationship) differently than in-person relational infidelity because no physical consummation actually occurs. In this view, if the connection is virtual, it's not real; therefore, it's not cheating.[50] Do you find this argument persuasive?

What if the cybersex involves not just words (sexting) but also explicit photos? What about sexual activities via video chat? Does that now qualify as infidelity because people can see each other being sexual, whereas a text is just words that spark the imagination?

Researchers have asked people these questions.[51] One study found that 41 percent of respondents didn't believe online sexual activity was cheating on a partner under any circumstances. Some deemed it cheating only if a person engaged in cybersex repeatedly with the same person, if webcams were used, or if the online sex led to phone sex. Thirty-three percent believed that any form of online sex was cheating and that it was just as much an act of infidelity as in-person sex with someone other than one's partner. Where do you stand on this issue?

- *Don't use the infamous "timing" explanation either.* You may be tempted to trot out the classic line, "It's just not a good time for me right now to be in a relationship." Most of us don't believe that. Instead, most dumpees would prefer that the dumper be honest enough to tell them that the relationship just isn't what the dumper wants.

cyber (internet) infidelity
Online sexual activity outside of one's monogamous relationship.

After the Breakup: Communicating with an Ex

People may change the profile of their relationship, but that doesn't mean it can't change *again*. How many people do you know who "break up to make up"?

Research reveals a great deal about the **on-again/off-again relationship** (also called "cyclical" or "habitual"), which is quite common.[52] Communication scholar René Dailey conducts extensive research on this form of dating relationship, which occurs when people get back together with the same partner, sometimes over and over again. Some people return to a partner out of habit or because the relationship is comfortable or known, even if it's not great. Others experience turning points that cause breakups and reconciliations, such as key events like infidelity and the forgiveness that can come after a relational transgression.[53]

Other studies have focused on the ways people create or reinvent a connection once they have broken up. Yes, some people actually want to have a relationship of some form with an ex, as challenging as that may be. The **postdissolutional relationship** has been defined as "the relationship formed between dating partners after their romance terminates."[54] (The term typically doesn't apply to divorced couples who negotiate a connection once their marriage has ended.) Factors that may determine whether this form of relationship can be successful include how much the partners like each other,

on-again/off-again relationship
A relationship characterized by repeated breakups and reconciliations.

postdissolutional relationship
The relationship formed between dating partners after their romance terminates.

how long the partners were together romantically (the longer the romantic relationship, the less successful the post-relationship), and how much the partners hope they will get back together romantically.[55]

Tensions in Relationships: The Dialectical Perspective

8.4 Discuss relational dialectics and three primary tensions in relationships.

Relationships are living, breathing, evolving, dynamic entities; no two are the same. One way to view relationships is through **relational dialectics** or the dialectical perspective.[56] Developed by communication scholars Leslie Baxter and Barbara Montgomery, dialectics help us understand the messy, often illogical nature of interpersonal relationships. The theory describes tensions people in relationships commonly face, but by *tensions*, we don't mean to imply something negative. A dialectical perspective suggests that relationship issues are better understood in terms of push–pull dynamics.[57] Although tensions can occur in all sorts of relationships, they are arguably most revealing in romantic relationships.

Researchers have identified multiple tensions. We focus on three primary tensions that most relational partners face:

- **Integration–Separation: Autonomy versus Connection.** Although people want to be connected to others and feel like they are part of a couple or group, they also want to be self-sufficient and independent. The amount of autonomy partners desire varies widely, making this tension one of the most difficult to confront. Early on, relational partners tend to spend as much time together as possible. However, when a time-consuming activity or work intrudes, friends or family members demand some time, or one partner wants a night out without the other, an autonomy-versus-connection conflict can arise.[58] Partners can benefit from honest, open, and nondefensive communication about this tension. It is also best if they can proactively negotiate how much time they expect (and want) to spend together and apart. Even the amount of desired phone calling or texting may need to be negotiated between partners, as research shows that overuse of mobile phones between partners can heighten this tension.[59]

- **Stability–Change: Predictability versus Novelty.** Although people are drawn to stability and consistency in a relationship, we are also drawn to excitement and unpredictability. Becoming comfortable with a relationship's ebb and flow can be a challenge.[60] Typically, at the start of a relationship, people emphasize a partner's positive points and gloss over less-desirable personality traits or behaviors. Over time, however, people may have more difficulty accepting each other as they are; one partner may try to change the other. Being aware that this tension is likely to emerge at some point—or several points—within a relationship is key, because too many attempts to persuade or influence a partner often lead to less satisfaction with the relationship.

- **Expression–Privacy: Openness versus Closedness.** We all differ in how open we wish to be (or are comfortable being) and our need for privacy. If relational partners are dramatically different in this area, they will need to be proactive and work hard to manage this tension, or it might be a deal breaker. Couples, friends, even family members may feel a push–pull, with one person in the relationship wanting complete openness and equating openness with trust, while the other wants to retain a degree of privacy and connects privacy with individual identity.[61]

relational dialectics
A perspective that views interpersonal relationships as dynamic and constantly evolving, as they revolve around how relational partners manage tensions.

▼ As the novelty wears off in relationships, we may find that we are bored with the predictability of our partner. How can you balance stability and change in your own relationships?
Rido/Shutterstock

Managing Interpersonal Conflict

8.5 Summarize the seven types of interpersonal conflict, the key characteristics of conflict management, and the ways people can cooperate in conflict situations.

We live in a world full of conflict. Whether it is a political coup in a foreign country or a disturbance generated by extremist groups here at home, conflict seems inevitable. Developing an understanding of conflict and the effective communication skills needed to manage it begins one on one, in our day-to-day relationships. Conflict is rooted in interpersonal communication.

Interpersonal conflict is a struggle that occurs when people cannot agree on a way to meet their needs. If needs or goals are incompatible, if there are too few resources to satisfy them, or if individuals opt to compete rather than to cooperate to satisfy them, conflict occurs. The bedrock of conflict is differences—different goals, experiences, and expectations.[62]

It is surprising (and disconcerting) when people in relationships say, "We just get along so well. We belong together because we've never even had a fight." Conflict is a normal, inevitable element of relationships. Although we do not advocate staging or picking a fight with a partner as an experiment, we do believe that it is worrisome to commit to a person when you do not know how she or he handles conflict. If your partner or close friend is a screamer and you prefer to walk away from conflict in silent protest, your relationship is headed for very rough waters. One of the best ways to improve a relationship is to understand conflict—how it functions; how each person in a relationship approaches, processes, and responds to conflict; and how we can better manage conflict when it arises.[63]

Sometimes the emotion of a conflict can cause us to communicate aggressively when assertive communication would be preferable. You may think that assertive and aggressive communication are the same thing, but they are actually different. **Assertive communication** takes the other person's feelings and rights into account; **aggressive communication** does not. Let's say you experience a mix-up with a close friend over plans for the weekend. You get your signals crossed and don't end up getting together. When you next see your friend, you have the choice of expressing your frustration over the situation in a passive, assertive, or aggressive manner. You could be passive and say nothing, which some people choose to do even when they have been wronged, a phenomenon known as *self-silencing*.[64] The passive approach tends merely to internalize frustration, which may build into rage that erupts later.

Another option is to take a self-oriented approach and blow up at your friend in an aggressive way that does not take into account your friend's rights. Unfortunately, verbal aggression is the tactic of choice for some people, especially if they have anxiety and feel justified taking out their frustrations on others. An aggressive approach rarely achieves one's objectives.[65]

Clearly, an assertive approach to conflict is best—for ourselves and for the people we interact with. It is important to assert yourself and express your perception of a problem to the person who can best correct or clear it up, rather than blowing off steam to an innocent bystander or third party. Communicating assertively means that you explain your concerns or cause for disagreement in a direct and firm manner, staying in control of your emotions but not allowing yourself to be bullied or discounted, while also taking your receiver's rights into account.[66]

An assertive response to the mix-up with your friend might be something like this: "Hey, we were supposed to get together last weekend, but you never called. What happened?" In this response, you express your perception of the situation, but also ask the other person for her or his perception. If you communicate in this manner, you are far more likely to reach a positive resolution to any conflicts than if you behave passively or aggressively.[67]

interpersonal conflict
A struggle that occurs when people cannot agree on a way to meet their needs.

assertive communication
Communication that takes a listener's feelings and rights into account.

aggressive communication
Self-serving communication that does not take a listener's feelings and rights into account.

CRITICAL/CULTURAL PERSPECTIVES & COMMUNICATION

Power to the Partners

One of the most significant elements in interpersonal relationships is power.[68] We might not realize it, but the distribution of power between partners requires a lot of subtle negotiation. Without this negotiation, conflict can become rampant. Power has been defined in a variety of ways, but for our purposes, **interpersonal power** means the ability to influence another person in the direction we desire—to get someone to do what we want.[69] It also involves the ability to resist another person's influence on us.[70]

Conflict in a relationship has power dimensions, meaning when people argue, oftentimes there are winners and losers. Which best describes you when you experience conflict with someone? Do you approach conflict with a "power over" approach, in which your intent is to get your way or get others to see things your way? Or do you take more of an empowerment approach, in which you seek a compromise so all parties feel they have achieved something when the conflict is resolved?

A critical/cultural perspective helps us examine our own status, power, and privilege and how we express our sense of personal power to others. If you tend to be the one influenced by more forceful people most of the time, reflect on how that makes you feel and if you want to repeat that dynamic in future relationships.

interpersonal power
The ability to influence another person in the direction one desires; getting another person to do what one wants.

constructive conflict
Conflict characterized by cooperation in dealing with differences; helps build new insights and patterns in a relationship.

destructive conflict
Conflict characterized by a lack of cooperation in dealing with differences; dismantles relationships without restoring them.

Constructive versus Destructive Conflict

Although we usually think of conflict in its most negative, destructive sense, conflict can be constructive in a relationship.[71] To construct something is to build or make something new. When you engage in **constructive conflict**, you cooperate to deal with differences. This process can help identify which elements of a relationship need to change or be improved so that new patterns are established. Here's an example:

Jake: You know, I'm getting tired of always going to your parents' house on Sundays. It's like we're in a rut or something. Just one weekend, I'd like to have a Sunday with no schedule or agenda.

Nia: Jake, I thought you liked going over there, because my mom's such a good cook and you and Dad are working on that project together. Plus, it's one of the few times I get to spend time with my folks.

Jake: Well, I do like going over there, but not every weekend.

Nia: I didn't realize you were starting to resent it or feel like we were in a rut. Let's figure something out.

Notice that Nia transforms the issue of disagreement into a topic for discussion and relational adjustment. If Jake had not expressed his dissatisfaction, the issue might have taken on larger proportions. He might have expressed his feelings of being in a rut in a more hurtful way later on. A well-managed disagreement that includes expressing one's own needs or revising goals can lead people to examine and then revitalize their relationship. Constructive conflict enables both people to view a disagreement from different perspectives, even if the information shared seems negative at first.

A rapidly spiraling **destructive conflict** can do a great deal of damage. A conflict that starts over a seemingly small issue can increase in intensity as other issues and differences are brought into the discussion. Such destructive escalation blocks options for managing differences and makes a win–win solution more elusive. The primary characteristic of destructive conflict is a lack of flexibility in responding to others.[72] Combatants view their differences from a win–lose perspective rather than looking for solutions that allow each individual to benefit. This form of conflict dismantles relationships without restoring them. If both individuals are dissatisfied with the outcome of the conflict, it has been more destructive than constructive.

William Wilmot and Joyce Hocker are experts on communication and conflict. Below are their six hallmarks of constructive conflict:[73]

1. *People change.* In relationships, people are involved with each other. In conflict, people must work hard to *stay* involved with each other, because an interaction that escalates into conflict can pull people apart. Flexibility and a willingness to change are key.

2. *People interact with an intent to learn instead of an intent to protect themselves.* You can learn a great deal about yourself, your partner, and your relationship if you approach conflict as a learning experience—one that will take your relationship forward instead of allowing it to stagnate or regress. Protecting yourself against conflict does not help a relationship grow.

3. *People do not stay stuck in conflict when the conflict is constructive.* Destructive conflict can make you feel stuck in one place in a relationship. Constructive conflict is a dynamic process that emerges, plays out, and recedes.

4. *Constructive conflict enhances participants' self-esteem.* You probably do not associate conflict with enhanced self-esteem. However, constructive conflict brings energy and productivity to a relationship and provides partners with a more honest, complete picture of themselves.

5. *Constructive conflicts are characterized by a relationship focus instead of a purely individualistic focus.* If parties in a conflict focus on the relationship instead of themselves, the conflict will more likely be constructive than destructive. Participants should emphasize the "we" over the "I" so that conflict is seen as an experience that builds the relationship.

6. *Constructive conflict is primarily cooperative.* Conflict built on competition, power struggles, and self-interest will destroy a relationship. Conversely, a cooperative, win–win approach to conflict will open the door for greater growth.

Types of Conflict

Communication scholars Gerald Miller and Mark Steinberg have identified three types of conflict:[74]

- **Pseudoconflict** reflects a basic lack of understanding; one person misunderstands the meaning in a message.
- **Simple conflict** stems from differences in ideas, definitions, perceptions, or goals.
- **Ego conflict** occurs when conflict gets personal, such that people attack each other's self-esteem.

pseudoconflict
Conflict stemming from a lack of understanding.

simple conflict
Conflict over differences in ideas, definitions, perceptions, or goals.

ego conflict
Conflict based on personal issues in which people attack each other's self-esteem.

To help distinguish these three types of conflict, let's use an example that seems to be happening more and more in romantic relationships. As we mentioned before, conflict can arise over partners' mobile phone use. Let's say romantic partners have a simple misunderstanding (pseudoconflict) over what it means to watch a movie together. One partner is watching the film, but the other is frequently checking her or his mobile phone. This phenomenon is actually called "phubbing" (a combination of "phone" and "snubbing"), and it occurs when one or more communicators pay more attention to their phones than to the other people present.[75]

If the misunderstanding about spending time together escalates, they might argue over their varying perceptions of what "watching a movie together" means (simple conflict). If the disagreement degenerates and becomes personal, such as one person accusing the other of something deeper than mere misunderstanding (as in "You say you'll do something with just me, but then you're *always* on your phone with other people"), an ego conflict has erupted out of a simple conflict.

Two other types of conflict are worthy of note. First, people in ongoing relationships often have **serial arguments**, defined as "argumentative episodes focused on a given issue that occur at least twice."[76] How many times have you heard someone complain, "We have this same argument over and over"? Serial arguments typically involve repetitious, highly negative verbal communication (such as name calling) and negative nonverbal cues (yelling or aggressive movements). They usually spiral and are rarely productive. They engender mutual hostility in partners and create a pattern that is very hard to break. Over time, unchecked serial arguments have an adverse effect on relationships and can erode self-esteem.

Another form of conflict within interpersonal relationships is the **irresolvable or intractable conflict**, which occurs when one or both parties deem the conflict impossible to resolve.[77] A person who believes that an argument is irresolvable may not necessarily state that view out in the open, choosing simply to believe that compromise is impossible. She or he may adopt a "go along to get along" approach to appease the other person, or tolerate the situation rather than confronting the person and attempting to resolve it.

serial arguments
Argumentative episodes focused on the same issue that occur at least twice.

irresolvable (intractable) conflict
A conflict that one or both parties deem impossible to resolve.

Conflict Management Styles

Scholars in communication and other academic disciplines like to talk about conflict in terms of *management*, meaning that interpersonal communication can help people

DIVERSITY & COMMUNICATION

Hofstede, Culture, and Saudi Arabia

With a score of 25 on Hofstede's 6D model, Saudi Arabia is considered to be a collectivistic country. This is manifested in the importance of the extended family, family or business-based relationships and a more general sense of group membership. Loyalty is very important, and it supersedes formal rules and behaviors. There is an implicit notion of responsibility regarding group members. Honor and status are important, and many decision-making processes are based on strict moral codes.

In Saudi Arabia there is a strong tradition of favors, obligations, loyalty, and the nurturing of personal relationships across the wider family and in organizations. Family and friends, together with business connections are overriding factors in business activities. In most cases employment, recruitment and promotion is influenced by family or friend connections rather than the most qualified candidate. In some respects, the collectivist approach also means that performance related pay is unusual as it is contrary to the notion of group work and collective effort. In Saudi Arabia it is also customary to give feedback through a third party to avoid unnecessary conflict. Saudi Arabia favors a "we" rather than "I" approach and a focus on tradition and collaboration in all things.[78]

Individualistic Cultures	Collectivistic Cultures
1. The purpose of conflict is to air major differences and problems.	1. Conflict is damaging to self-respect and relational harmony; it should be avoided as much as possible.
2. Conflict can be either functional or dysfunctional.	2. For the most part, conflict is dysfunctional.
3. Repressed, unconfronted problems can lead to dysfunctional conflict.	3. Conflict signals emotional immaturity and a lack of self-discipline.
4. Functional conflict provides an opportunity for solving problems.	4. Conflict provides a testing ground for skillful negotiation and face-saving.
5. Substantive or informational issues should be handled separately from relational issues.	5. Substantive and relational issues are always intertwined.
6. Conflict should be handled directly and openly.	6. Conflict should be handled discreetly and subtly.
7. Effective conflict management should be a problem-solving activity with a win–win outcome.	7. Effective conflict management should be a face-saving negotiation game with a win–win outcome.

work through and resolve conflict so that something positive results.[79] What's your approach to managing interpersonal conflict: fight or flight? Do you tackle conflict head-on or seek ways to remove yourself from it? Most of us do not have a single way of dealing with disagreements, but we do have a tendency to manage conflict by following patterns we learned early in life and have used before. For many of us, our approach to conflict differs depending on the type of relationship we have with the other person, the importance we place on that relationship, and what is at stake.[80]

Researchers have attempted to identify different styles of conflict management. One widely accepted approach organizes conflict styles into three types: (1) nonconfrontational, (2) confrontational or controlling, and (3) cooperative (also known as a *solution orientation*).[81]

▲ People with a confrontational or win–lose approach to conflict may spend more effort trying to assign or avoid the blame for a problem than solving it.
Fizkes/123RF

Nonconfrontational Style   One conflict management style is to avoid conflict altogether, becoming aloof or giving in to the other person before or when a conflict emerges, which can have a chilling or silencing effect on a relationship.[82] Research shows that when conflict arises during problem-solving discussions, people who exhibit a **nonconfrontational style** are perceived as incompetent.[83] This dynamic often creates a lose–lose situation, where neither party feels the issue has been effectively addressed; instead, it has perhaps merely been postponed.

Confrontational Style   Each of us has some need to control others, but some people always want to dominate and make sure their objectives are achieved. In managing conflict, people with a **confrontational style** have a win–lose philosophy. They want to win at the expense of others, claim victory over their opponents, and control people and situations. They focus on themselves and usually ignore the needs of others. Confronters often resort to blaming or seeking a scapegoat rather than assuming responsibility for a conflict. For example, a confronter may claim, "I didn't do it," "Don't look at me," or "It's not my fault." If this strategy does not work, confronters may try hostile name calling, personal attacks, or threats.

Cooperative Style   Those who have a **cooperative style** of conflict management view conflict as a set of problems to be solved rather than as a competition in which one person wins and another loses. They work to foster a win–win climate by using the following techniques:[84]

- *Separate the people from the problem.* Leave personal grievances out of the discussion. Describe problems without making judgmental statements about personalities.
- *Focus on shared interests.* Emphasize common interests, values, and goals by asking such questions as, "What do we both want?" "What do we both value?" and "Where do we already agree?"
- *Generate many options to solve the problem.* Use brainstorming and other techniques to generate a range of solutions.
- *Base decisions on objective criteria.* Try to establish standards for an acceptable solution to a problem. These standards may involve costs, timing, effort, and other factors.

nonconfrontational style
A conflict management style that involves backing off, avoiding conflict, or giving in to the other person.

confrontational style
A win–lose approach to conflict management in which one person wants control and to win at the expense of the other.

cooperative style
A conflict management style in which conflict is viewed as a set of problems to be solved rather than as a competition in which one person wins and another loses.

Conflict Management Skills

As we saw in the previous section, nonconfrontational and confrontational styles of conflict management do not solve problems effectively, nor do they foster healthy relationships. Managing conflict, especially emotionally charged conflict, is not easy. Even with a fully developed set of skills, you should not expect to melt tensions and resolve disagreements instantaneously. However, the following skills that we touched on in our

RECAP

Conflict Management Styles

Nonconfrontational	A person avoids conflict and may become aloof or give in to another person just to stave off a conflict. This approach can be viewed as a lose–lose framework because issues aren't dealt with and conflict is likely to recur.
Confrontational	A person wants to manipulate others by blaming and making threats. This approach sets up a win–lose framework.
Cooperative	A person seeks mutually agreeable resolutions to manage differences and works within a win–win framework. This cooperative approach does the following: • Separates people from problems • Focuses on shared interests • Generates many options to solve problems • Bases decisions on objective criteria

discussion of the cooperative style can help you generate options that promote understanding and provide a framework for cooperation.[85]

Manage Emotions Suppose you have been working for weeks on a group project for an important class. The project has a firm deadline that your professor will no doubt enforce. You submitted your portion of the project to your group members two weeks ago. Today you check in with the group and discover that very little has been done since you completed your portion. Your grade is on the line; you feel angry and frustrated. How should you respond? Maybe you are tempted to scream at your classmates. Maybe you decide to go to the professor and complain. Here is our best advice at a moment like this: Try to avoid taking action when you are in an emotional state.[86] You may regret what you say, and you will probably escalate the situation into a heated conflict, making things worse.

The first sign that we are in a conflict situation may be a combination of anger, frustration, and fear that sweeps over us. In actuality, anger often is not the predominant emotion generated by conflict. Many of us are unprepared for the aching, lonely, sad, and forlorn feelings that can emerge in conflict.[87] As tall an order as it is, it is important to try to understand other people's feelings and take the emotion of the situation seriously.[88] Here are some specific strategies you can draw on when an intense emotional response to conflict clouds your judgment and decision-making skills:[89]

- *Select a mutually acceptable time and place to discuss a conflict.* If you are upset or tired (or really hungry), you are at risk for an emotion-charged confrontation. If you ambush someone with an angry attack, you cannot expect that person to be in a productive frame of mind. Give yourself time to cool off, rest, or have a meal before you try to resolve a conflict. In the case of the group project, you could call a meeting for later in the week. Take the intervening time to gain control of your feelings and think things through.

- *Plan your message.* If you approach someone to discuss a disagreement, take care to organize your message, perhaps even on paper. Identify your goal and determine what outcome you would like; do not barge in unprepared and dump your emotions on others.

- *Monitor nonverbal messages.* Nonverbal communication plays a key role in managing an emotional climate. Monitor your own and others' nonverbal cues to defuse an emotionally charged situation. Speak evenly, use direct eye contact, and maintain a calm facial expression and body position to signal that you wish to collaborate rather than control. Try to interact on the same physical plane as others. For example, it is unwise to tower over people (standing when others are sitting) because such a power move can exacerbate conflict.

- *Avoid personal attacks, name calling, profanity, and emotional overstatement.* Threats and bad language can turn a minor conflict into an all-out war. When people feel attacked, they usually respond defensively. Avoid exaggerating your emotions. If you say you are *irritated* or *annoyed* rather than *furious*, you can still communicate your feelings, but you will take the sting out of your description.

- *Use self-talk.* Instead of lashing out at someone, the better tactic is to pause, take a slow deep breath, and talk yourself down off your emotional ledge. You may think that talking to yourself is an eccentricity, but thoughts are directly linked to feelings. The messages we tell ourselves play a major role in how we feel and respond to others.[90]

Manage Information Because uncertainty, misinformation, and misunderstanding are often by-products of conflict and disagreement, skills that promote mutual understanding are important components of cooperative conflict management. The following skills help enhance the quality of communication during conflict:

- *Clearly describe the conflict-producing events.* Instead of blurting out complaints in a random order, try to deliver a brief, well-organized, chronological presentation. In the case of our group project example, you could offer your perspective on what created the conflict, sequencing the events and describing them dispassionately so that your fellow group members end up sharing your understanding of the problem.

- *"Own" your statements by using descriptive "I" language.* Use "I" language instead of "you" language to create a supportive climate. "I feel upset when it seems as if little is getting done and we're running the risk of not making our deadline" is an example of an "I" statement you could make to your group members. The statement describes your feelings as your own and keeps the issue manageable.
- *Use effective listening skills.* Managing information is a two-way process. Whether you are describing a conflict situation to someone or that individual is bringing a conflict to your attention, good listening and responding skills are invaluable. Give your complete attention to other speakers so that you can fully understand their perspectives, and then respond appropriately.

- *Check your understanding of what others say and do.* Checking perceptions is vital when emotions run high. If you are genuinely unsure about certain facts, issues, or major ideas addressed during a conflict, ask questions instead of barreling ahead with solutions. Then summarize your understanding of the information, checking key points to make sure that you comprehend the message.

Manage Goals Conflict is goal-driven; people involved in an interpersonal conflict want something, and for some reason—competitiveness, scarce resources, or a lack of understanding—their goals appear to be in conflict. To manage conflict, here are some techniques that will help you seek an accurate understanding of everyone's goals and identify where they overlap:

- *Identify everyone's goals.* Most goals can be phrased in terms of wants or desired outcomes. In the group project example, suppose you express your goal of turning the project in on time to your fellow group members. Next, it is useful to identify the goals of other people involved in the conflict. Use effective describing, listening, and responding skills to determine what each conflict partner wants. Obviously, if goals are kept hidden, it will be difficult to resolve the conflict.

- *Identify where your goals and everyone else's goals overlap.* Authorities on conflict negotiation stress the importance of focusing on shared goals in seeking to manage differences.[91] Suppose that after you explain your goal about the project deadline, another group member states that her or his goal is to make the project the best it can possibly be. These goals may be compatible, so you have identified a commonality that can help unify the group rather than keeping it splintered. But what if the goal of making the project the best it can be means that your group will have to ask the professor for an extension on the deadline? Now you may have

▲ When communicating to resolve a conflict, try to "own" your communication by using "I" language rather than accusatory "you" language.
Jack Hollingsworth/Photodisc/Getty Images

competing goals, but at least you have identified a central part of the problem. Framing the problem as "How can we achieve our mutual goal?" rather than arguing over differences of opinion moves the discussion to a more productive level.

Manage the Problem If you can view conflicts as problems to be solved rather than battles to be won or lost, you will better manage the issues that confront you in your relationships.[92] Of course, not all conflicts can be easily managed and resolved. But a rational, logical approach to conflict management is more effective than emotionally flinging accusations and opinions at someone. Structuring a disagreement as a problem to solve helps manage emotions that often erupt while also keeping the conversation focused on issues rather than personalities. As you apply a problem-solving approach to managing conflict, consider the following suggestions:

- *Define the problem before trying to solve it.* When a problem needs to be solved, we typically want to head directly for solutions. Resist that temptation, and make sure everyone fully understands the problem at hand before trying to fix it.
- *Think of lots of possible solutions.* The more possible solutions you identify and consider, the greater the likelihood that the conflict will be managed successfully. If you just bat around one or two solutions, you limit your options in managing the conflict.
- *Systematically discuss together the pros and the cons of each possible solution, arriving at the best decision.* After you have a list of possible solutions, honestly identify the advantages and disadvantages of each one. Determine which solution or combination of solutions best achieves the goals you and your feuding partners are trying to accomplish.

STUDY GUIDE: PRINCIPLES FOR A LIFETIME CHAPTER 8

The Importance of Relationships: Friends, Family, and Colleagues

8.1 Explain how the five Communication Principles for a Lifetime apply to interpersonal communication among friends, family members, and colleagues.

PRINCIPLE POINTS: Relationships of all types are important in our lives, but those with friends, family, and colleagues are most critical to our overall happiness. The five Communication Principles for a Lifetime can be applied to each form of relationship and can improve how we communicate interpersonally with others.

PRINCIPLE SKILLS:

1. How have your friendships changed since you were younger? How do you expect your long-term

friendships to develop as you get older? Has one of your family relationships, like with a sibling, turned into a friendship, as you have both gotten older?

2. Draw five concentric circles on a blank sheet of paper. (Concentric circles are circles within circles.) Write the word "me" in the center circle, representing the core of the model. Then think about all of your relationships—family members, friends, coworkers, acquaintances, bosses, etc. Place ten of these relationships at various spots within these circles. The people closest to you, in terms of intimacy or trustworthiness, get placed within the inner ring; others are placed farther out, depending on how close you perceive you are to those people. Finally, analyze the placements of these ten people; if you want someone to move closer in to the center (to *you*), what kind of communication is required to make that change?

Stages of Relationship Development

8.2 Identify and describe the stages of relational escalation and de-escalation.

PRINCIPLE **POINTS:** Research has determined that relationships, particularly intimate or romantic ones, tend to develop in stages of escalation and de-escalation. Interpersonal communication is affected by the stage of a relationship; in turn, movement through the stages is facilitated by interpersonal communication. The five stages of relational escalation are (1) pre-interaction awareness, (2) initiation, (3) exploration, (4) intensification, and (5) intimacy. The five stages of relational de-escalation are (1) turmoil or stagnation, (2) de-intensification, (3) individualization, (4) separation, and (5) post-interaction.

PRINCIPLE **TERMS:**

pre-interaction awareness stage
initiation stage
exploration stage
intensification stage
intimacy stage
turmoil or stagnation stage
de-intensification stage
individualization stage
separation stage
post-interaction stage

PRINCIPLE **SKILLS:**

1. How well does the description of relational escalation in this chapter match how your friendships and romantic relationships have developed? How did your process differ, if it did?
2. Review Figure 8.1 in this chapter (the model that depicts relational escalation and de-escalation). Assess a relationship using this model; it can be a friendship, intimate relationship, coworker, or so forth. Are both of you on the same level? Is the relationship escalating, stabilizing (meaning no movement upward or downward), or de-escalating? Do you think some communication changes are necessary to move this relationship upward or downward?

Relationship Dissolution (a.k.a. the Breakup)

8.3 Summarize research findings on relationship dissolution, including communication in the on-again/off-again relationship and the postdissolutional relationship.

PRINCIPLE **POINTS:** Not all relationships last, so communication skills are important when a romantic relationship, friendship, or other form of connection ends. Research shows that most people use and prefer a face-to-face channel of communication when being on both the sending and receiving end of relationship dissolution.

PRINCIPLE **TERMS:**

relationship dissolution
cyber (internet) infidelity
on-again/off-again relationship
postdissolutional relationship

PRINCIPLE **SKILLS:**

1. Imagine one of your friends wants to break up with a romantic partner. Using the advice in this chapter, what suggestions would you give your friend for accomplishing the breakup ethically and with as little pain as possible for both parties?
2. Think of three relationships in your past that have either faded away or ended abruptly. Consider childhood friends, neighbors, classmates, family members, or coworkers. Did these relationship endings involve some form of communication or did life circumstances change the status of these relationships?

Tensions in Relationships: The Dialectical Perspective

8.4 Discuss relational dialectics and three primary tensions in relationships.

PRINCIPLE **POINTS:** One approach to studying interpersonal communication in relationships is the relational dialectics perspective, which examines sets of tensions that emerge in ongoing relationships, especially romantic or intimate ones. Three tensions are particularly critical:

- Integration–separation: autonomy versus connection
- Stability–change: predictability versus novelty
- Expression–privacy: openness versus closeness

PRINCIPLE TERM:
relational dialectics

PRINCIPLE SKILLS:

1. Which of the three tensions described in this chapter have you experienced in your friendships or romantic relationships? How did you resolve the tension (if you have tension)? If you have not resolved the tension, how are you managing the relationship?

2. The three relationship tensions described in this chapter are listed as headings below. In the first column, write the name of someone you are currently in a relationship with—it can be a friendship, romantic relationship, family member, etc. Then assess on a 1-to-5 scale (1 = barely applies to us; 5 = always applies to us) how much your relationship reflects each tension. For example, if you write down the name of your best friend, is your handling of the Autonomy vs. Connection tension at a level 1 (we have no tension regarding time spent together versus apart), 2 (occasional tension), or all the way up to a 5 (constant tension)?

Person	Autonomy vs. Connection	Stability vs. Change	Expression vs. Privacy

Managing Interpersonal Conflict

8.5 Summarize the seven types of interpersonal conflict, the key characteristics of conflict management, and the ways people can cooperate in conflict situations.

PRINCIPLE POINTS: Interpersonal conflict occurs when people cannot agree on a way to meet their needs. Conflict can be constructive or destructive, and it occurs in multiple forms: pseudoconflict, simple conflict, ego conflict, serial arguments, and irresolvable (intractable) conflict. Conflict involves power, which may manifest itself in assertive or aggressive communication. Research has revealed three general styles of managing conflict: nonconfrontational, confrontational, and cooperative. In managing conflict, it is important to manage your emotions, the information surrounding the dispute at hand, competing goals, and the problem itself rather than the people involved.

PRINCIPLE TERMS:

interpersonal conflict
assertive communication
aggressive communication
interpersonal power
constructive conflict
destructive conflict
pseudoconflict
simple conflict
ego conflict
serial arguments
irresolvable (intractable) conflict
nonconfrontational style
confrontational style
cooperative style

PRINCIPLE SKILLS:

1. Have you experienced or witnessed a serial argument or intractable conflict in a relationship? What was the problem? How did the parties respond?

2. **Am I an Aggressive or an Assertive Communicator?** Sometimes it is hard to discern the difference between assertive and aggressive communication. To gain some practice, consider the following situations. For each one, first generate aggressive and inappropriate communication. Then rethink the situation and generate an assertive form of communication that would be more effective. We have provided an example to get you started.

   Sample Situation: You are expecting a raise at work but find out that a coworker, who has less time on the job than you, received a raise and you did not.

   Aggressive Communication: You interrupt a staff meeting that your boss is holding, storm about the room, and demand an explanation of why you did not receive the expected raise.

   Assertive Communication: You make an appointment with your boss for a meeting. At the meeting, you calmly ask the boss to assess your value to the company, leading up to the question of why you did not receive the expected raise.

   Situation: Two people have been in a monogamous dating relationship for several months when one partner finds out that the other person has cheated.

   Situation: A student receives a disappointing grade on a paper. After reading the papers of a few other classmates and finding that poorer-quality papers received higher grades, the student decides to confront the teacher about the grade.

3. **What's My Style?**
   In intimate relationships, in which a great deal is on the line, knowing how you usually tend to handle conflict, as well as how your partner handles it, can save you some major heartbreak. Below, we give you a sample situation along with examples of nonconfrontational, confrontational, and cooperative responses. Supply responses reflecting these three conflict management styles for the other two hypothetical conflict situations. (If you are really brave, pose these same situations to your relational partner and compare your responses to hers or his. This exercise can lead to a constructive, proactive discussion about how to handle conflict in your relationship.)

Conflict Situation 1: Your roommate is *wild*, partying every night, coming home late, and disrupting your study time and your sleep. This behavior is starting to affect your ability to get your schoolwork done and concentrate on your studies. You are not a fuddy-duddy, but you are not a nightly partier either. How do you communicate in response to this conflict situation?

Nonconfrontational Response: Ignore it. It's not my problem; it's my roommate's life to live as he (she) pleases. I would rather have more quiet time, but if I bring up my objections, the situation will escalate and get worse, and I'll regret mentioning anything in the first place.

Confrontational Response: I have rights; I live in this place and pay my fair share of the rent, so I should be able to have some peace and quiet so at least one of us doesn't flunk out of college. When my roommate comes home, I'm going to lay down the law on the late-night partying. If the problem persists, I'll threaten to move out.

Cooperative Response: My roommate and I both have rights because we both live in this apartment. When my roommate is sober and alone here at the apartment, not partying with a group of friends, I'll bring up the problem and ask for solutions we can both live with. I want to respect my friend's right to enjoy life, but I want to set limits so my goals can also be reached.

Conflict Situation 2: You work part time at a restaurant near campus. Thus far, the managers have been flexible and understanding about your class schedule and commitments at the university, but now—just when you've got three exams and two papers coming up—they decide to load you up with extra hours. You need this job and want to keep it, so how do you communicate to address the conflict between what you can do and what management wants you to do?

Nonconfrontational Response:

Confrontational Response:

Cooperative Response:

Conflict Situation 3: You have been dating someone fairly steadily for a few months but have recently developed a romantic interest in a classmate. You would like to keep dating your current relational partner but renegotiate your relationship so that you can start hanging out with other people, such as the attractive classmate. How do you communicate to manage this situation?

Nonconfrontational Response:

Confrontational Response:

Cooperative Response:

UNIT III COMMUNICATING IN GROUPS AND TEAMS

CHAPTER 9

UNDERSTANDING GROUP AND TEAM PERFORMANCE

It really boils down to this: that all life is interrelated. We are all caught in an inescapable network of mutuality, tied into a single garment of destiny. Whatever affects one directly, affects all indirectly. —MARTIN LUTHER KING, JR.[1]

Rawpixel.com/Shutterstock

CHAPTER OUTLINE

- Groups and Teams Defined
- Group and Team Dynamics
- Group and Team Development
- Study Guide: *Principles for a Lifetime*

LEARNING OBJECTIVES

9.1 Describe types of groups and teams, differences between groups and teams, and when participating in groups and teams should be avoided.

9.2 Identify and describe group and team dynamics, including roles, rules, norms, status, power, and cohesiveness.

9.3 Summarize the four stages of group and team development.

Do you like working with others in groups? Although you may be one of those people who relish working on team projects and going to meetings, many people don't like collaborating with others. Here are some typical sentiments people sometimes have about working in groups:

> To be effective, a committee should be made up of three people. But to get anything done, one member should be sick and another absent.

> A committee is a group of people who individually can do nothing and who collectively decide nothing can be done.

> A group task force is a collection of the unfit chosen from the unwilling by the incompetent to do the unnecessary.

Whether you are one of those people who likes group work or one who finds it frustrating and a waste of time, evidence suggests that groups are here to stay. Human beings collaborate.[2] We are raised in groups, educated in groups, and entertained in groups; we worship in groups and work in groups.

Today's technology makes it easier for us to collaborate in teams via Zoom, Skype, GoToMeeting software, and a variety of other technological applications, even when we're not meeting face to face.[3] There is evidence that you're likely to spend about one-third of your time on the job working in groups or teams and attending meetings or preparing for meetings. Increasingly, those meetings are happening online or via video conferencing.[4] And if you aspire to upper-management leadership positions, you'll spend up to two-thirds of your time in meetings.[5] One study found that more than 80 percent of organizations use teams to accomplish a major portion of the work.[6] Therefore, it is highly likely that your work will depend on that kindergarten skill called "getting along with others."

To help you with the group and team projects that will inevitably come your way, this chapter offers descriptions of how groups and teams work. In Chapter 10, we'll offer specific strategies for improving group and team performance. As we examine concepts and strategies of group skills and theories, we'll

▼ We are raised and educated in groups and continue to communicate in groups and teams throughout our lives, so strengthening your group communication skills now will provide lasting benefits.
Rawpixel/123RF

remind you how the core of group communication research can be discussed in terms of the five principles we've used to frame our presentation of human communication:

1. *Be aware of your communication with yourself and others.* Your awareness of your own behavior and other group members' roles is often the first step in understanding why you and other group members behave as you do and adjusting your behavior for improved group performance.

2. *Effectively use and interpret verbal messages.* The verbal messages you and other group members use are pivotal in shaping the roles you assume and how the group accomplishes its work.[7]

3. *Effectively use and interpret nonverbal messages.* The social climate of a group is influenced by the way group members behave nonverbally; eye contact, tone of voice, facial expression, and the use of space and time influence what it feels like to be in a group.

4. *Listen and respond thoughtfully to others.* How group members interact (or don't interact) is directly shaped by group members' skill in listening and responding to what others say and do. One survey found that effective listening was the skill most valued by those who work in groups and teams.[8]

5. *Appropriately adapt messages to others.* The ability to modify messages and adjust to the behavior of others is especially important when communicating with three or more people in a small group.

Groups and Teams Defined

9.1 Describe types of groups and teams, differences between groups and teams, and when participating in groups and teams should be avoided.

What makes a group a group? Is a collection of people waiting for an elevator a group? How about students assigned to a class project—do they meet the technical definition of a group? Is there a difference between a group and a team? By exploring these questions, you can better understand what groups and teams do and develop strategies for improving group and team performance.

Communicating in Small Groups

small group
Three to fifteen people who share a common purpose, feel a sense of belonging to the group, and exert influence on one another.

A **small group** consists of three to fifteen people who share a common purpose, feel a sense of belonging to the group, and exert influence on one another.[9] Let's look at this definition more closely.

A Group Consists of a Small Number of People A small group generally needs at least three people. Two people do not usually exhibit the characteristics of group behavior. A group is not *small* anymore when more than fifteen people meet together. In a larger group, it can become difficult for all members to participate, and a few members often will monopolize the discussion.[10] A large group frequently operates as a collection of subgroups rather than as a single body. Large groups need formal rules, such as parliamentary procedure, to provide structure to manage the group interaction. Without rules, it's unlikely a large group will stay focused on the task at hand.

A Group Has a Common Purpose To be a group, people need to be united by a common goal or purpose. Research has found that having a common group identity is a hallmark of group success.[11] Group members should all seek the same thing.[12] A collection of people waiting for an elevator may all want to go somewhere, but they probably haven't organized their efforts so that they all are going to the same place.[13] If an instructor assigns you to a class project, you and your classmates do have a common goal: to complete the project and earn a good grade. This class project group would meet our definition of a group.

primary group
A group, such as a family, that exists to fulfill basic human needs.

Groups can be classified according to their purposes into two general categories: primary and secondary. A **primary group** exists to fulfill basic human needs. It's called a primary group because the group meets a primary human need to socialize or just be together. Your family and many **social groups**—groups that provide opportunities for members to enjoy an activity with others—are primary groups.

Secondary groups are more focused on accomplishing a specific task or goal than are primary groups. Secondary groups include the following:

- **Study groups**, which exist to enhance learning;
- **Therapy groups**, which provide treatment, or mutual support, including those like Alcoholics Anonymous and WW (Weight Watchers);
- **Problem-solving groups**, which seek to solve a problem by overcoming one or more obstacles to achieve a goal; and
- **Focus groups**, which consist of people brought together to be interviewed so others can listen and learn from them in order to gather information and opinions.

Group Members Feel a Sense of Belonging   To be a group, the members must realize that they are part of the group. The people waiting for the elevator probably do not feel an obligation to others around them. In contrast, members of a group develop a sense of identity with their group. They know who is in their group and who is not.

Group Members Exert Influence on Others in the Group   When you are in a group, your presence and participation influence other people in the group. Group members are interdependent; what one group member says or does affects other group members. Your comments and even your silence help shape what the group does next. If you meet in person, your nonverbal messages have a powerful effect on personal relationships. Even silence, facial expressions, and eye contact (or lack of it) affect what the group does.

Group Members May Meet Face to Face or Virtually   If you are assigned to work on a class group project, it is likely that you will connect with other group members electronically (such as through instant messaging, email, Facebook, Skype, Zoom, text, or phone) as much or maybe even more than meeting face to face. You will meet virtually. A **virtual group or team** doesn't meet face to face but is instead connected via some electronic channel. Working as a virtual team has both advantages and disadvantages.[14]

The Advantages of Working in Virtual Teams

- A virtual team can save members travel time and expense.
- Virtual teams can develop the same degree of trust among members as face-to-face groups, especially if the team meets face to face before working virtually.[15]
- In computer-mediated meetings, ideas can be captured easily and recorded quickly and accurately.
- Technology can help structure a group's process and keep the group focused.
- Some team members may feel more comfortable sharing ideas electronically—or even anonymously—than they would in person.

The Disadvantages of Working in Virtual Teams

- Compared to in-person groups, developing trust among virtual group members can take longer.[16]
- When only some members participate virtually, a special effort must be made to integrate members who don't regularly meet in person into the fabric of the team.
- Cultural differences within a virtual group may result in less participation among group members.[17]
- The increased speed of information transfer can allow little time for reflection. Thus, technology may sometimes inadvertently help us make more mistakes, faster.
- When using computer-mediated technology, some group members do not thoroughly evaluate the pros and cons.
- The application of technology does not inherently result in better solutions and decisions. Problems are solved and decisions are made by people.[18]

social group
A group that exists to provide opportunities for group members to enjoy an activity in the company of others.

secondary group
A group formed to accomplish a specific task or goal.

study group
A group that exists to help its members learn new information and ideas.

therapy group
A group that provides treatment or mutual support.

problem-solving group
A group that meets to seek a solution to a problem and achieve a goal.

focus group
A group that is brought together to be interviewed so others can listen and learn from them in order to gather information and opinions.

virtual group or team
A group or team whose members are not in the same physical location but who are typically connected via some electronic channel.

SOCIAL MEDIA & COMMUNICATION

Keep Your Phone Out of Sight During Meetings

Have you ever been in a meeting and felt tempted to pull out your phone and quickly check your email messages, texts, or Instagram feed? You may want to control that impulse and leave your phone in your pocket. According to a research team's conclusions, using a phone during meetings is perceived as rude.[19] It gives the impression that you are not focused on what the group is doing and prefer to be elsewhere. One team of researchers found that men were almost twice as likely as women to think it was acceptable to use a phone during a meeting.[20]

If you can't resist pulling out your phone during a meeting, research has found that some behaviors are more offensive than others. Here is a list of the worst phone "sins" during meetings. At least 50 percent of study respondents found the following behaviors offensive:

- Writing and sending text or email messages
- Making or taking phone calls
- Browsing on the Internet
- Checking to see if you have received a message

About a third of all respondents felt the following behaviors were rude:

- Leaving the meeting to take a call
- Checking for incoming calls
- Frequently glancing at the time[21]

As we noted in Chapter 5, other researchers suggest that simply the presence of a phone during a conversation is distracting. With this in mind, you may want to consider keeping your phone out of sight during face-to-face meetings. Without a phone as a distraction, you may actually be able to pay attention to what's happening in the meeting!

---

small group communication
The transactive process of creating meaning among three to fifteen people who share a common purpose, feel a sense of belonging to a group, and exert influence on each other.

Small group communication is the transactive process of creating meaning among three to fifteen people who share a common purpose, feel a sense of belonging to the group, and exert influence on one another. Regardless of the type of group, communicating in small groups is sometimes a challenge because of the potential for misunderstanding. But don't assume that working in a group will inevitably be a frustrating experience. People accomplish a lot when working together. As anthropologist Margaret Mead said, "Never doubt that a small group of concerned citizens can change the world. Indeed, it's the only thing that ever has." In this chapter and the next, we'll provide concepts and strategies to enhance the quality of your collaborations with others.

Communicating in Teams

Most of us have participated on a sports team at some time. The goal of a sports team is to win the game or competition. A work team has some of the same characteristics as a sports team.[22] Instead of winning a game, the goal may be to get the contract, make a sale, or achieve some other objective. A **team** is a coordinated group of people organized to work together to achieve a specific, common goal.[23]

team
A coordinated group of people organized to work together to achieve a specific common goal.

Often the terms *team* and *group* are used interchangeably. Is there a difference? Yes. Given the increased importance teams have in today's workforce, it's important to know precisely how groups and teams differ from each other.[24] Although groups and teams are both made up of a small number of people who work together to achieve a goal, teams are often more coordinated and deliberately structured to achieve an explicit goal. Also, teams spend a great deal of time coordinating their efforts to accomplish the goal.[25] Every team is a group, but not every group is highly organized or coordinated enough to meet the definition of a team. Let's consider several specific characteristics of teams.

Teams Develop Clearly Defined Responsibilities for Team Members On a sports team, most team members have specifically assigned duties, such as shortstop, pitcher,

ETHICS & COMMUNICATION

How Far Would You Go to Achieve a Team Goal?

Without a clear goal, teams falter. But sometimes you may be part of a team whose goal or method of achieving the goal you don't support.

Assume you're a salesperson and part of a sales team. To get a raise in salary, everyone on the team has to meet the sales goal assigned to the team. To get the sales, one team member doesn't always tell the truth to customers about the company's product. That team member's sales success helps make the whole team look good in terms of sales, but bad in terms of ethics.

What would you do? Would you keep quiet and enjoy the benefits of being part of a "successful" sales team? Or would you bring the unethical behavior of the team member to the attention of your supervisor, even though it would place other team members in jeopardy for knowingly "going along to get along"? This raises the ethical question: Are team goals more important than individual ethical standards?

---

quarterback, or fullback. On a work team, team members' duties and roles are usually explicitly spelled out. Team members may perform more than one function or role, but they nonetheless have well-defined duties.[26]

Teams Have Clearly Defined Rules for Team Operation   Team members develop explicit rules for how the work should be done. A rule is a followable prescription for acceptable behavior.[27] Just as there are written rules in the game of *Monopoly,* there are usually explicit rules for how a team will function. For example, a team may establish a rule that a member who will be absent from a meeting must tell another team member beforehand. Team members know what the rules are and know how those rules affect the team.

Teams Develop Clear Goals   A third way to characterize a team is to look at the importance and specificity of the team goal.[28] A team goal is usually stated in such a way that the goal can be measured: to win the game, to sell more cornflakes than the competition, or to get to the North Pole before anyone else, for example.

Teams Develop a Way of Coordinating Their Efforts   Team members spend time discussing how to accomplish the goals of the team. Their work is coordinated to avoid duplication of effort.[29] A sports team spends considerable time practicing how to work together. Watching a sports team at work is like watching a choreographed dance. Team members have developed a system of working together rather than at cross-purposes. Just as a football team develops a list of the plays to get the ball down the field, a work team develops collaborative strategies to achieve its goal.

Although we have differentiated between groups and teams, don't get the idea that they are completely exclusive entities. Think of groups and teams as existing on a continuum. Some deliberations may more closely follow group behavior, whereas a more coordinated and

RECAP
Comparing Groups and Teams

	Groups	Teams
Roles and Responsibilities	Individual responsibilities of group members may not always be explicitly defined.	Expectations, roles, and responsibilities of team members are clearly developed and discussed.
Rules	Rules are often not written down or formally developed; rules evolve, depending on the group's needs.	Rules and operating procedures are clearly identified to help the team work efficiently and effectively.
Goals	Group goals may be discussed in general terms.	Clearly spelled-out goals are the focus of what the team does.
Methods	Group members may or may not decide to divide the work among its members.	Team members develop clear methods of collaborating and coordinating their efforts to achieve the team's goals.

structured process with clear rules and explicit goals may appear to be more team-like. Because every team is a small group, whenever we refer to a team, we are suggesting that it's a group as well.

When Not to Collaborate in Groups and Teams

Although we've just sung the praises of working in groups and teams, at times one head may be better than two or more. In what situations may it be best *not* to collaborate? The following are four situations in which it is better to work individually rather than collectively:[30]

▲ If conflicts among group members prevent thoughtful discussion, it's probably not a great idea to collaborate.
Fizkes/Shutterstock

- *When the group or team has limited time.* Sometimes you may not have time to gather a group together to discuss options; action may be needed immediately. If a very quick decision must be made, for example, in times of extreme crisis or emergency, it may be best to have a leader ready to provide some initial direction.

- *When an expert already has the answer.* If you want to know what the weather will be like tomorrow, ask a meteorologist. Don't collaboratively puzzle through questions that can be readily answered by someone else. You don't need a group to hash through the process of finding an answer if an individual can already provide one.

- *When the information is available from other research sources.* Using the power of the Internet, you can find vast amounts of information. Some groups find it useful for individual members to gather information and then meet with the rest of the group to analyze and discuss what they've found. But if you just need information and need it fast, click your mouse or use your smartphone.

- *When the group or team is entrenched in unmanageable conflict.* We don't suggest that you avoid group and team conversations just because they may arouse conflict and disagreement. In fact, it's normal for groups to experience some conflict. But if the conflict is so entrenched that group members can't listen and thoughtfully respond to each other, it may be advisable to take a break from group deliberations. If the conflict is so pervasive that no progress is likely, a more structured conversation, such as mediation or negotiation with a trained facilitator, may be needed to help sort things out.

Group and Team Dynamics

9.2 Identify and describe group and team dynamics, including roles, rules, norms, status, power, and cohesiveness.

Groups and teams are dynamic; their structure changes. As we study group dynamics we'll examine the roles, norms, status, power, and cohesiveness of groups. We'll also note how each of these concepts relates to the five Communication Principles for a Lifetime.

Roles

role
The consistent way a person communicates with others in a group.

Your **role** is the consistent way you communicate with others in a group. It is based on your expectations of yourself and the expectations others place on you. Do you often become a leader of a group, or are you more comfortable just blending in and taking directions from others? Or are you the one who makes sure the group gets the work done instead of just having a good time? There may also be group members who seem especially gifted at smoothing conflict and disagreement. Research has found that the roles you have assumed in previous groups will likely influence the roles you will occupy in future groups.[31] But what if there is no pattern to what you typically do in a group? Although you may be influenced by roles you have assumed in the past, your specific role depends on the group dynamics and who else is in the group.

Types of Roles   The following are three classic categories of group roles:

- **Task roles** are behaviors that help the group achieve its goal and accomplish its work, such as gathering and sharing research conclusions with the group, taking minutes of meetings, and writing ideas on a whiteboard.
- **Social roles** focus on behavior that manages relationships and affects the group climate; these roles help resolve conflict and enhance the flow of communication. Smoothing hurt feelings and helping the group celebrate its accomplishments are examples of social-role behavior.
- **Individual roles** focus attention on the individual rather than on the group. They do not help the group; they emphasize individual accomplishments and issues, not those of the entire group.[32] Dominating group discussions to talk about personal issues or concerns, telling frequent jokes that get the group off track, and constantly complaining or whining about how one's individual needs aren't being met are examples of individual roles.

task role
A role that helps a group achieve its goal and accomplish its work.

social role
A role that helps a group manage relationships and affects the group climate.

individual role
A role that focuses attention on the individual rather than on the group.

Leadership Roles   The role of leader, a person who influences others in the group, is a special kind of role, and more than one person can assume it. Some leaders focus on assisting with the team's task and, therefore, assume more task roles to get the job accomplished. Other leaders assume more social roles to help manage the quality of relationships in the group. Usually, a person who assumes an individual, self-focused role doesn't emerge as a natural leader. Being overly dominant or aggressive or blocking the team's progress may focus attention on an individual, but such self-focused behavior doesn't wear well over time, and people who focus on themselves rather than on the team aren't perceived as effective leaders.

Specific Roles   Helping to develop clear role expectations for yourself and other team members enhances overall performance.[33] Seventy-five years ago, group researchers Kenneth Benne and Paul Sheats came up with a list of group roles that remains a classic way of dividing up the roles that group and team members typically assume.[34] As you review these roles and their descriptions, as summarized in Table 9.1, note whether you usually assume roles in the task, social, or individual category. Or perhaps you'll see yourself in a variety of roles in all three categories.

As you look at the list of roles in Table 9.1, you may think, "Yes, that's what I usually do. That's the role I usually take." You can probably see roles that fit other group members. Most group members don't assume only one or two roles during group meetings. Most of us assume several roles when we interact in a group. A role is worked out jointly between us and the group, and the roles we assume change depending on which group we're in. Your personality and the personality characteristics of other team members also significantly influence role development within teams.[35] Effective group members adapt their behavior to what is happening or needed in the group. In some groups, your expertise may give you the confidence to share information and opinions freely. In other groups, your assumed role may be to maintain social harmony and peace.

TABLE 9.1 A Classification of Group Roles

Task Roles	Description	Example
Initiator/contributor	Offers new ideas or approaches to the group; suggests ways of getting the job done	"How about developing an agenda to help us organize our work?"
Information seeker	Asks for additional clarification, facts, or other information that helps the group with the issues at hand	"Can anyone tell me how many times the university has threatened to close the fraternities and sororities on campus because of problems with hazing?"
Opinion seeker	Asks group members to share opinions or express a personal point of view	"So what do you all think of the new dress code the school board is proposing?"
Information giver	Provides facts, examples, statistics, or other evidence that relates to the task confronting the group	"Within the past year, the vice president for student affairs has given a special award to three fraternities and one sorority for developing a program to combat underage drinking."
Opinion giver	Offers opinions or beliefs about what the group is discussing	"I think the new school dress code proposed for first graders is unworkable."
Elaborator	Provides comments or examples to extend or add to the comments of others	"Tom, that's a good point. I had the same thing happen to me when my children were attending a private school in New York last year."
Coordinator	Clarifies and notes relationships among the ideas and suggestions that have been offered by others	"Tyrone, your idea sounds a lot like Juanita's suggestion. Juanita, could you elaborate on your idea so Tyrone can decide whether he agrees or disagrees with you?"
Orienter	Summarizes what has occurred and seeks to keep the group focused on the task at hand	"I think we're getting a bit off track here. Let's go back to the issue on the agenda."
Evaluator/critic	Assesses the evidence and conclusions that the group is considering	"How recent are those statistics? I think there are newer figures for us to consider."
Procedural technician	Helps the group accomplish its goal by handling tasks such as distributing reports, writing ideas on a whiteboard, or performing other tasks	"I'll write your ideas on the board as you suggest them. After the meeting, I'll copy them and summarize them in an email message to each of you."
Recorder	Makes a written record of the group's progress by writing down specific comments, facts, or the minutes of the meeting	"I'll take the minutes for today's meeting."

Social Roles	Description	Example
Encourager	Offers praise and support and confirms the value of other people and the ideas they contribute	"You're doing a wonderful job."
Harmonizer	Manages conflict and mediates disputes among group members	"Tynesha, you and Mandy seem to be agreeing more than you are disagreeing. Both of you have the same goal. Let's brainstorm some strategies that can help you both get what you want."
Compromiser	Resolves conflicts by trying to find an acceptable solution; seeks new alternatives	"Jane, you want us to meet at 7:00 p.m., and Sue, you'd like us to start at 8:00. What if we started at 7:30? Would that work?"
Gatekeeper	Encourages people who talk too much to contribute less and invites those who are less talkative to participate	"Tim, we haven't heard what you think. What do you suggest we do?"
Follower	Goes along with the suggestions and ideas of other group members	"I can support that option. You have summarized the issues about the same way I see them."
Emotion expresser	Verbalizes how the group may be feeling about a specific issue or suggestion	"We seem to be frustrated that we are not making more progress."
Group observer	Summarizes the group's progress or lack of progress	"We are making great progress on all the issues except how much salary we should offer."
Tension reliever	Monitors stress within the group and offers suggestions for breaks, using humor or other appropriate strategies	"Hey, what we need is a good laugh. Here's a joke I saw on the Internet today."

Individual Roles	Description	Example
Aggressor	Deflates or disconfirms the status of other group members or tries to take credit for the work of others	"Lee, your idea is the pits. We all know that what I suggested two meetings ago is the only way to go."
Blocker	Is negative, stubborn, and disagreeable without an apparent reason	"I just don't like it. I don't have to tell you why. I just don't like it."
Recognition seeker	Seeks the spotlight by dwelling on his or her personal accomplishments; seeks the praise of others	"Don't you remember this was my idea? And say, did you see my picture in the paper? I won the grand prize at the science fair."
Self-confessor	Uses the group as a forum to disclose unnecessary personal feelings and personal problems unrelated to the group's task	"I can't deal with this stuff right now. My parents are being so unfair. They won't let me live off campus next year. They just don't understand me."
Joker	Wants to crack jokes, tell stories, and just have fun instead of focusing on the task or what the group needs	"Hey, let's forget this project and go to the mall. I'll tell you the gossip I heard about Professor Smith. What a kook!"
Dominator	Tries to take control of the group, talks too much, and uses flattery or aggression to push his or her ideas off on the group	"Now, here's what we're going to do: Marcie, you will take notes today; Phil, you go get us some pizza; and Russ, I want you to just sit there in case I need you to run an errand."
Special-interest pleader	Seeks to get the group to support a pet project or personal agenda	"My service club would like it if we would support the new downtown renovation project. I'll stand a good chance at club president if I can get you on board."
Help seeker	Seeks to evoke a sympathetic response from others; often expresses insecurity stemming from feelings of low self-worth	"I don't know if I can participate in this project. I'm not very good with people. I just feel like I don't relate well to others or have many friends."

Balancing Roles What are the best or worst roles to assume? We don't recommend that you assume any individual role; by definition, these roles focus attention on an individual rather than on the group. Every group needs a balance of task and social roles, instead of attention drawn to an individual. At the same time, however, don't ignore the contributions of your fellow group members. One study found that one of the most negative things a group member can do is ignore comments another member makes, isolating that member.[36]

What is the proper balance between task and social roles? Some experts recommend a 60–40 balance.[37] In general, more comments need to be about getting the work done than about having fun or managing the social climate, but it is also important to establish and maintain good working relationships among group members. If your group seems unduly focused on the task and members are insensitive to the harmony of group relationships, the group will not be as effective as it might be. Conversely, an out-of-balance group that focuses just on having a good time is not going to achieve its task goals.

Use two of the Communication Principles for a Lifetime to help you balance roles.

Principle 1: Be aware of your communication.	Monitor what roles are being assumed and not assumed in your group.
Principle 5: Adapt appropriately.	Adapt your behavior to the group's needs by helping meet a need or fill an unfilled role.

Rules

As we noted both in Chapter 1 and earlier in this chapter, *rules* are followable prescriptions that indicate what behavior is expected or preferred.[38] Rules also clearly specify what behavior is inappropriate. Leaders or members of groups and teams often develop rules that specify how people should behave.

team ground rules
The behaviors that are expected of team members, often spelled out in explicit rules developed by team members working together.

In particular, teams often develop ground rules that help them function more smoothly. Establishing **team ground rules** is a way for members to talk about expected behaviors. Rules are also needed to ensure that a team is both efficient and effective. They help manage uncertainty when working with others. Most informal groups do not develop explicit, written rules. But more formal, highly structured teams may take the time to develop rules such as everyone should attend all meetings, meetings will start on time, and each member should follow through on individual assignments. Making the rules explicit makes it easier to foster appropriate behavior and prevent inappropriate behavior. Research has found that when people are working in virtual teams, in which uncertainty is often high, clear rules help a team operate more efficiently.[39]

Norms

norms
Standards that determine what is appropriate and inappropriate behavior in a group.

Norms are general standards that determine what is appropriate and inappropriate behavior in a group. Although not all groups develop explicit rules, all groups and teams develop norms. As their name implies, norms reflect what's normal behavior in the group; they influence a variety of group member behaviors, such as the type of language that is acceptable, the casualness of members' clothing, or the acceptability of using first names. Is it normal for group members to raise their hands before speaking in your group? Is it acceptable to move around while the group is in session or to get a cup of coffee while someone is talking?

Norms and Rules How do norms differ from rules? Rules are more explicit. Group and team rules are written down or at least verbalized. Here's an example of a rule: Any member of this team who does not pay his or her dues on time will pay an extra $5 in dues. Norms are more general standards or expectations that are not as clearly spelled out. It may be a norm in your group that no one uses four-letter words; there's probably no written policy that prohibits expletives, and group members may never have said, "No one should ever use a curse word during our discussions," but even without such specific admonitions, members avoid using offensive or obscene words.

Sources of Norms Norms develop on the basis of what you and other team members have experienced in other groups as well as behavior that occurs naturally as group members interact. If after a couple of meetings no one utters a swear word, a norm has begun to gel.

The norms that emerge in a group are also strongly influenced by the larger cultural context in which group members live. Norms relating to how attentive the group is to deadlines and punctuality, for example, are anchored in overall cultural expectations. Some people approach time from a **monochronic time perspective**; they are more likely to develop norms to do only one thing at a time, to pay attention to deadlines and schedules, and to make plans to use time efficiently. Others prefer a **polychronic time perspective**; they do many things at a time, don't worry about deadlines and schedules, believe relationships are more important than work, change plans frequently, and are less concerned about deadlines than are monochronic individuals.[40] Many people from the United States and northern Europe tend to be monochronic; deadlines and timelines are valued.[41] People from Latin America, southern Europe, and the Middle East often tend to be polychronic; deadlines and strict adherence to schedules are less important.[42]

monochronic time perspective
Preferring to do one thing at a time, to pay attention to deadlines and schedules, and to use time efficiently.

polychronic time perspective
Preferring to do many things at once, to place less emphasis on deadlines and schedules, and to believe relationships are more important than work.

If you find yourself in a group whose members have cultural approaches to time or other norms that are different from yours, what should you do? Consider these suggestions:

- Take time to talk about those differences. Share your concerns and assumptions.
- Don't pounce on other team members and accuse them of being laggards or taskmasters.
- Make the issue a group concern rather than an issue between just one or two people.

Conversation and compromise can accomplish a lot when you find yourself facing cultural differences.

Enforcing Norms   Noticing when someone breaks a norm can help you spot a norm. If a member waltzes into a meeting twenty minutes late and several folks grimace and point toward the clock on the wall, that's a sure sign that a norm has been violated. The severity of the punishment for violating a norm corresponds to the significance of the norm.[43] Mild punishment is usually unspoken—such as silent glances or frowning stares. More serious punishment might include a negative comment about the behavior in front of other group members or even expulsion from the group.

You don't have to worry about whether your group will have norms or not; norms happen. You should, however, monitor group norms to ensure your behavior doesn't distract from the group's work and to notice the possible development of any unproductive group norms (such as spending too much time socializing) that the group should talk about.

Status

When she walks into the room, all eyes are fixed on *her*. Group members watch her every move. As the chairperson, she has much influence. Without her support, no new issues will come before the board. She has high status. **Status** refers to an individual's importance and prestige. Your status in a group influences to whom you talk, who talks to you, and even what you talk about. A variety of factors including education, income, expertise, and social status can affect your status. Cultural or demographic differences can also impact a person's status because of other members' perceptions or prejudices. Your perceived importance within a group affects both your verbal and your nonverbal messages. A person with high status typically

status
An individual's importance and prestige.

- Talks more than low-status members,
- Directs comments to other high-status group members,
- Has more influence on the decisions the group makes,
- Is listened to by group members, and
- Addresses more comments to the entire group than to individuals.[44]

Because high-status people enjoy more privileges, most people want to be in the "in-group"—the group with high status and influence. Being aware of status differences can help you predict who talks to whom. If you can discern status differences, you'll also be better able to predict how others in the group will interact and the types of messages they will communicate. Although some people underestimate their perceived level of status and influence in a group, research suggests that you are probably quite perceptive at knowing your own status level when communicating with others.[45]

But just because a person has status doesn't mean that his or her ideas are good. Some groups get into trouble because they automatically defer to the person with more status without reviewing the validity of the ideas presented. Don't let status differences influence your perceptions of, and critical thinking about, the merit of the ideas presented. Conversely, don't dismiss ideas simply because the person who suggested them doesn't have high status or prestige. Focus on the quality of the message, not on the messenger.

▲ Cultural norms about the use of time are just one source of diversity you may encounter when communicating in groups or teams. How can you initiate a discussion about group norms?
Fotos593/Shutterstock

Power

power
The ability to influence other people's behavior.

Status refers to perceived importance, whereas **power** is the ability to influence others' behavior. Although status and power often go hand in hand, a group member can have high status and still not be able to influence how others behave. People have power if they can affect what others do. Their power stems from the resources available to them to influence others. Power can also come from one's perceived cultural or social position within a group. Who does and doesn't have power in a group influences how people relate to one another.

A group in which the power is not balanced may have problems; when the "power people" dominate discussions, the group may lose other members' contributions and insights. People with less power tend to participate less in group discussions unless they're trying to gain power. A power struggle often creates ripples of conflict and contention through a group. Power struggles also tend to focus attention on individual group members rather than on the group as a whole. Research indicates that groups with equal power distribution usually have better-quality outcomes than other groups.[46]

According to classic studies of how individuals become powerful, there are six bases of power: legitimate, referent, expert, reward, coercive, and information power. These power bases explain why certain people have power and why others don't.[47]

legitimate power
Power that stems from being elected or appointed to a position of authority.

referent power
Power that stems from being liked.

expert power
Power derived from having expertise, skill, experience, and information.

reward power
Power that comes from the ability to provide rewards or favors.

Legitimate Power You have **legitimate power** if someone elected or appointed you to a position of power. Your power source comes from holding a position of responsibility. The president of your university or college has the legitimate power to establish and implement school policy. U.S. senators and your mayor are other examples of people who have legitimate power. A group or team member who has been elected chair or president of the group is given legitimate power to influence how the group operates.

Referent Power You have **referent power** if people like you. Put simply, people we like have more power over us than people we do not like. If you are working on a committee with your best friend, your friend exerts power over you in the sense that you will tend to give more credence to what your friend recommends than to other recommendations. Just the opposite occurs if you are working with someone you don't like. You will be more likely to ignore advice that comes from someone you don't admire than from someone you do, which means that person has less power to influence you.

Expert Power People who have **expert power** are perceived as skilled in performing important tasks, as well as experienced and knowledgeable. They have more influence in a group or team than do people who are perceived as unskilled, inexperienced, and uninformed. Suppose you are working with a group to develop strategies to clean up the river that runs through your town. Your colleague who is majoring in aquatic biology will probably have more power than other, less knowledgeable and skilled group members.

Reward Power People who can grant favors, money, or other rewards have more power than people who can't provide such rewards; those who can bestow rewards have **reward power**. People who have greater power to reward typically receive more positive, supportive messages than people who don't have the ability to reward others. Someone also has reward power if he or she can take away a punishment or other unpleasant experiences. But reward power is effective only if the person

"I've called this meeting because it's a big ego trip having the authority to call you all together whenever I want to."

Patrick Harden/Cartoon Stock

being rewarded finds the reward satisfying or useful. What is rewarding to one person may not be to someone else.

Coercive Power You have coercive power if you can punish others. **Coercive power** is the flip side of reward power. This influence comes from the ability to make others uncomfortable. If someone can cut your salary, lower your grade, demote you, put you in jail, or force you to do unpleasant jobs, that person has coercive power. This kind of power results from the perception that the person with the power will actually use the power. If a person has the authority to punish but group members perceive that the person will not use this power, there really is no coercive power.

coercive power
Power that stems from being able to punish others.

Information Power Information is power. You have **information power** if you know important information that is useful to the group and you are one of the only people who possesses that information.[48] If, for example, you are the only family member who has listened to the most recent weather report and you know there is a 90 percent chance of rain today, you have information power. You have the power to influence whether your family's reunion picnic will be held outdoors, as planned, or if it will need to be moved indoors. In most groups, once you have shared information that was known only to you, your power within the group diminishes. You only have information power when you have exclusive information that can be used to influence group outcomes or behavior.

information power
Power that results from having information that is important to the group that others do not have.

Even though we have categorized power into six different types, don't get the idea that group members may exert just one type of power. In reality, group or team members often have more than one type of power. For example, because a group member is the elected leader (legitimate power), he or she may also be able to offer rewards (reward power) or punishments (coercive power).

Cohesiveness

If you have ever read about the Three Musketeers or seen a movie about them, you know that their motto was "All for one, one for all." They were a cohesive group—they liked to be around one another. **Cohesiveness** is the degree of attraction that members of a group feel toward one another and the group.

cohesiveness
The degree of attraction group members feel toward one another and toward their group.

Characteristics of Cohesive Groups In a highly cohesive group, whether meeting face to face or virtually, members feel a high degree of loyalty to one another; the goal of the group is also the goal of the individual.[49] Cohesive group members listen to one another. Members of a cohesive group are more likely to use words and phrases that have a unique meaning to its members; they are also more likely to tell inside jokes—jokes that mean something only to them.[50] Groups that are cohesive generally are more effective than groups that are not.[51]

Groups become cohesive because of a variety of forces that attract people to the group and to one another. Shared goals, feelings of genuine liking, and similarity of backgrounds and culture are variables that influence group cohesiveness.

How to Enhance Group Cohesiveness Table 9.2 summarizes some strategies that enhance group cohesiveness and other strategies that make a group less cohesive. The common element in cohesive groups is the manner in which group members communicate with one another.

RECAP
Types of Power

Legitimate Power	Power that results from being elected, appointed, or ordained to lead or make decisions for a group or a team
Referent Power	Power that results from being popular and well-liked
Expert Power	Power that results from having expertise, skill, experience, or knowledge
Reward Power	Power that results from having the resources to bestow gifts, money, recognition, or other rewards that group members value
Coercive Power	Power that results from having the ability to punish others
Information Power	Power that results from having exclusive information that may be used to influence others

TABLE 9.2 Suggestions for Enhancing Group Cohesiveness[53]

Cohesive Groups	Incohesive Groups
Talk about the group in terms of "we" rather than "I"; stress teamwork and collaboration.	Emphasize the individual contributions of group members; stress individual accomplishment.
Reinforce good attendance at group meetings.	Make little effort to encourage group members to attend every meeting.
Establish and maintain group traditions.	Make little effort to develop group traditions.
Set clear short-term and long-term goals.	Avoid setting goals or establishing deadlines.
Encourage everyone in the group to participate in the group task.	Allow only the most talkative or high-status members to participate in the group task.
Celebrate when the group accomplishes either a short-term or a long-term goal.	Discourage group celebration; make sure group meetings are all work and little or no fun.

FIGURE 9.1 All-Channel Small Group Communication Network

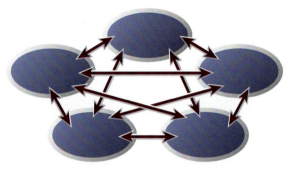

FIGURE 9.3 Wheel Small Group Communication Network

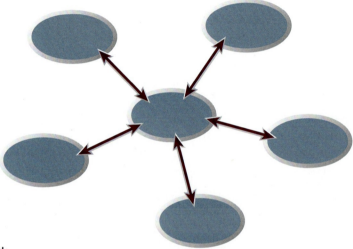

FIGURE 9.2 Chain Small Group Communication Network

Cohesiveness is more likely to occur if group members have the opportunity to talk with one another freely about a goal all members have in common and if this interaction increases group members' affection and liking for one another. Teams that have greater control over how they conduct their work are also more likely to be cohesive.[52]

Can a group be too cohesive? Yes. Although cohesiveness is usually a good thing, a group can have too much of a good thing. If group members are focused only on having fun and developing a positive, cohesive relationship to the exclusion of getting their work done, productivity can suffer. Strive for group cohesiveness, but balance it with concern for accomplishing the group's task.

A group's **communication interaction pattern** is the consistent pattern of who talks to whom. The all-channel network pattern shown in Figure 9.1, in which everyone talks to everyone else, is most likely to enhance group cohesiveness and productivity.[54] The chain interaction pattern in Figure 9.2 illustrates a form of group communication in which people convey a message to one person at a time rather than communicating with all group members at once. Groups in which a great deal of communication occurs within a **clique**, a smaller group of people within a group who form a common bond among themselves, are also usually less cohesive than groups with communication among all members.

communication interaction pattern
A consistent pattern of who talks to whom.

clique
A smaller, cohesive group within a group.

CRITICAL/CULTURAL PERSPECTIVES & COMMUNICATION

Should You Form an Alliance with Others?

If you have read the book or seen the movie *The Lord of the Rings* by J. R. R. Tolkien, then you know that rather than beginning his quest alone, Frodo forms an alliance with his fellow hobbits Sam, Merry, and Pippin. Like Frodo, sometimes you may find that you can gain greater influence if you form an alliance with other group members to accomplish a collective goal. Instead of acting alone, you can increase your influence by joining forces with other group members who hold similar views to your own. There is power in numbers. The civil rights, feminist, environmental, and Black Lives Matter movements gained power when many people banded together to give voice to being oppressed and marginalized. The goal of an alliance is to gain ethical influence within a group, not to bully or coerce others. As you seek ways to influence group and team outcomes, rather than "going it alone," consider how (1) identifying others with whom you have similar viewpoints and then (2) ethically collaborating with them on a common quest, can enhance your ability to influence group and team outcomes.

Sometimes, a great deal of communication is directed at the one person in the group who holds a different opinion than the rest of the group. This person is called a **group deviate**. Other group members may spend considerable time trying to change that person's opinion. The wheel interaction pattern, shown in Figure 9.3, occurs when one person is the focal point of communication with all other group members. The focal person in a wheel pattern is not always a group deviate; a quarterback speaking to other football team members is another example of the wheel pattern. However, the wheel pattern, like the chain pattern, is less likely than the all-channel pattern to foster group cohesiveness.

group deviate
A group member who holds an opinion, attitude, or belief that is different from that of other group members.

Group and Team Development

9.3 Summarize the four stages of group and team development.

Small group communication can be a disorganized, messy process, especially if the all-channel network is the predominant communication pattern. Although the free flow of ideas is generally a good thing, it may seem as though there is no order or structure to the way group members interact. But what may seem like chaotic talk may, in fact, be just a normal aspect of how groups behave.

Researchers have found that some groups go through certain phases or sequences of talk when they meet to solve a problem or make a decision.[55] Some researchers have found three phases; most have found four. One researcher labeled the four phases **forming** (the group sorts out its purpose), **storming** (disagreements occur), **norming** (norms are established), and **performing** (work is achieved).[56]

Communication researcher Aubrey Fisher developed one of the most descriptive four-phase models.[57] His model is particularly useful because his four labels describe the kind of communication occurring during each phase. His four phases of group talk are (1) orientation, (2) conflict, (3) emergence, and (4) reinforcement. Once you're able to identify and understand these four phases, you'll have the equivalent of a group map. By listening to what people are saying, you will be able to identify where the group is in the process of problem-solving or decision-making. We will describe these phases so you can identify them when they occur in your group.

Orientation

As you might suspect, when people first get together in a group, they enter the **orientation phase**. This is when the group forms. During this phase, they adjust to at least two things: who's in the group (group process) and what they will be doing (group task).

forming
The initial phase of group development during which the group determines its goal and roles begin to develop; also known as the *orientation phase*.

storming
The second phase of group development during which group members experience some disagreement due to differing points of view; also known as the *conflict phase*.

norming
The third phase of group development during which the group finds its rhythm, confirms norms, and begins to accomplish the task at hand; also known as the *emergence phase*.

performing
The fourth phase of group development during which the group accomplishes its goal and celebrates success; also known as the *reinforcement phase*.

orientation phase
The first phase of group interaction during which members become adjusted to one another and to the group's task; also known as the *forming phase*.

primary tension
Tension arising from the uncertainty and discomfort that occur when a group first meets.

conflict phase
The second phase of group interaction during which group members experience some degree of disagreement about social and task issues; also known as the *storming phase*.

task conflict
Conflict that occurs when a group disagrees about how to accomplish what it wants to achieve.

process conflict
Disagreement about the procedures or methods for accomplishing a task.

relational conflict
Conflict that becomes personal because group members do not like, value, or respect one another.

secondary tension
Conflict that occurs, after the members of a group have become acquainted with one another, over group norms, roles, leadership, and differences among member opinions.

▼ Taking a time-out might help to resolve this team's conflict. What other strategies have you found useful for dealing with conflict in groups?
Stockbyte/ Getty Images

Research on the orientation phase suggests that your earliest communication is directed at orienting yourself to others as well as to the group's task. What happens during this first phase is often referred to as **primary tension**. This tension results from the uncertainty and discomfort people experience when they meet for the first time.[58] Just as you may have some anxiety when giving a speech, some uncertainty and anxiety occur when group members try to figure out who is supposed to do what, who's in charge, and why they are there. Some group members who don't like uncertainty at all and are eager to start sorting things out will suggest an agenda: "Hello, my name is Steve. Let's each introduce ourselves." Other group members will be quite content to sit quietly in the background and let others take the lead. As people begin to become acquainted and start talking about the group's purpose, typical groups experience the second phase: conflict.

Conflict

As we have pointed out, people are different—and nowhere is that more evident than in a group discussion after the group gets down to business. As group members become more comfortable and oriented toward the task and one another, they start asserting opinions about what the group should be doing, how it should be done, and who should be doing it.[59] They have tested the water in the first phase and are now ready to jump in. This second phase, which is characterized by increased disagreement, is known as the **conflict phase**. Because of increased conflict it is also known as the *storming phase*.

Groups may experience **task conflict** in which they disagree about how to accomplish the task at hand, **process conflict** about the procedures and methods of working on the task, or **relational conflict**, in which conflicting opinions about who does what results in personal disagreement.[60] The relational conflict that arises in this phase is sometimes called **secondary tension**. This secondary tension or conflict occurs when there is a struggle for leadership or when the conflict becomes personal and group members disagree with one another. Research has found that the most dissenting group members are likely to receive more eye contact.[61]

Conflict isn't always bad—it occurs when people are honest about sharing their opinions. If there is no conflict, it usually means that people aren't honest about how they really feel.[62] As journalist Walter Lippmann once said, "When we all think alike, then no one is thinking." The conflict phase is necessary for solving problems and maintaining group relationships. When ideas aren't challenged and tested, groups are more likely

to make unwise decisions. We are not suggesting that you celebrate when you have conflict, only that you take some comfort in knowing that conflict is an expected part of group deliberations. The amount and intensity of the conflict will vary depending on how important the issues are to the group. The more important the issues are to group members, the greater the intensity of the conflict is likely to be.

Research indicates that when intense conflict arises in your group, especially conflict that results in heightened emotions and tension because of personal or cultural differences, it may be best to "cool it."[63] Taking time to back off rather than continuing to hash out issues verbally may be helpful in managing the tension. Regardless of the issue or trigger for the conflict, when emotions are aroused, rational discussion is hard to achieve. Especially if the group you're in includes people from a variety of cultural backgrounds, it may be best to let the group "breathe" rather than continuing to try to hammer out an agreement with more talk. We're not suggesting that all conflict should be managed by avoiding it. Rather, we are suggesting that when emotions become aroused, it's difficult to make headway on the issues. If you don't take a break, you'll likely expand the conflict rather than make progress.

When conflict in virtual groups and teams stems from differences in cultural values or perceptions, it's important that team members feel connected to the team and empowered to participate rather than feel marginalized or discounted. Research suggests that having virtual team members vote on decisions or on the value and importance of contributions is a useful way to keep them engaged with the team.[64]

Emergence

You know you are in the **emergence phase** when the group begins to solidify a common point of view. Decisions emerge, and conflict is reduced. Although conflict may be evident in this third phase, what sets the emergence phase apart from the conflict phase is the way in which group members manage conflict. During the emergence phase the group also settles on norms, which is why this is also referred to as the *norming phase*, and moves closer to agreement. Established norms, roles, and leadership patterns now help the group get work accomplished. The group begins to get a clearer glimpse of how issues will be resolved and what the group outcome will be.

Not all of what emerges may be productive. The group could decide that the conflict is so intense that the best decision is to disband the group, or an individual could decide to leave the group.

emergence phase
The third phase of group interaction during which conflict or disagreement is managed, decisions are made, and group problems begin to be solved or managed; also known as the *norming phase*.

DIVERSITY & COMMUNICATION

The Lewis Model

Hofstede's Culture Factor™ model considered collectivism vs. individualism alongside femininity vs. masculinity, uncertainty avoidance and power distance and long-term vs. short-term orientation Another model that has gained worldwide acclaim was developed by Richard Lewis in the late 1990s. Lewis' theory suggested that people belong to one of three categories: Linear-active, Multi-active, or Reactive. Lewis thought that categorizing people using a cross-cultural approach only resulted in complicated and confusing definitions and classifications. He was particularly critical of theorists who seemed to ignore the Asian mindset, which he categorized as Reactive. For his research, Lewis circulated over 150,000 questionnaires and gathered data from 50,000 executives attending residential courses, with the respondents being drawn from nearly 70 nationalities.[65]

The Reactive classification typifies individuals as good listeners who are reactive, polite, and indirect. They tend to conceal their feelings, are non-confrontational, and are keen not to lose face. A statement is considered to be a promise, and in complement to being diplomatic and patient, language and a reliance on connections in business activities is common. This Reactive group covers much of Asia, excepting the Indian sub-continent that Lewis categorized as being a hybrid area with characteristics of both Reactive and Multi-actives.

Lewis typifies Malaysians as Reactive based on characteristics which include gentleness, respect, courtesy, formality, trust, and compromise. As a result of these findings, Lewis suggests international businesses should interact with Malaysians in a courteous and gentle manner, should converse in a low and kind tone, and should have harmonious and balanced discussions during meetings. Problems should be referenced in an indirect manner to ensure that both sides save face, and compromises should be made.[66]

reinforcement phase
The fourth phase of group interaction during which group members express positive feelings toward one another and toward the group; also known as the *performing stage*.

Reinforcement

Group members become more unified in the **reinforcement phase**. During the orientation, conflict, and emergence phases, group members struggle through getting acquainted, developing cohesiveness, competing for status and prominence, puzzling over what action the group could take, and making decisions. The group eventually emerges from those struggles and develops a new sense of direction. At this stage the group is in high performance mode and members reinforce group accomplishment. This accomplishment results in a more positive feeling about the group. The group more clearly develops a sense of "we." In fact, one way you can identify the reinforcement phase is when group members use more collective pronouns (*we, us, our*) than personal pronouns (*I, me, my*) when talking about the group.

The Process Nature of Group Phases

Even though we have identified four distinct phases that groups can experience, don't get the idea that all groups progress neatly through these phases in exactly the same way. They don't.[67] Some researchers have found that only about one-third of all groups experience these distinct stages.[68] Other studies have had difficulty identifying four phases and found just one or two. Even if you have trouble identifying these phases in your group, you will probably see some elements of the four phases during your group meetings.

Some groups get stuck in one of the phases. For example, have you ever participated in a group that could never quite figure out what it was supposed to do? It was stuck in the orientation phase. Some groups remain in the conflict phase for long periods of time, perhaps bouncing between orientation and conflict. The group either seems torn by personal conflict between group members or just can't reach agreement or make a decision.

As we've noted, the group will eventually reach phase three, when something will emerge, even if it is not a wise decision or high-quality solution. The group may decide, for example, to disband and never meet again because it is so dysfunctional. Although this was not the original objective of the group, something emerged: The group members quit.

Reinforcement is likely to occur because we like to make sense out of what happens to us. Even if the group disbands, we are likely to celebrate its demise or reinforce the decision to disband. Because of our culture's emphasis on efficiency and productivity, many groups quickly gloss over the reinforcement aspects of group celebration. Wise group leaders and participants make sure that accomplishments are celebrated and both group and individual efforts are recognized. The cohesiveness and positive feelings that result from such celebrations will be helpful as the group prepares for its next task.

RECAP

A Map of Group Phases

Phase One: Orientation (Forming)	• What are we doing here?
	• What is our goal?
	• Who are these people?
	• What is my role?
Phase Two: Conflict (Storming)	• Who put that person in charge?
	• I see the goal differently.
	• I have different ideas.
	• I have different strategies.
Phase Three: Emergence (Norming)	• Something happens.
	• Decisions are made.
	• Issues are managed.
	• The group moves forward.
Phase Four: Reinforcement (Performing)	• The group is aware it is making progress.
	• Members seek to justify their actions.
	• Members reward others.
	• The team celebrates its success or rationalizes its failure.

STUDY GUIDE: PRINCIPLES FOR A LIFETIME

CHAPTER 9

Groups and Teams Defined

9.1 Describe types of groups and teams, differences between groups and teams, and when participating in groups and teams should be avoided.

PRINCIPLE **POINTS:** Small group communication is the transactive process of creating meaning among a small number (three to fifteen) of people who share a common purpose, feel a sense of belonging to the group, and exert influence on one another. Primary groups, such as family and social groups, exist to fulfill primary human needs to socialize and live together. Secondary groups form to achieve a specific goal. Secondary groups include study, therapy, focus, and problem-solving groups. Groups and teams are similar in that they are both made up of a small number of people who work together to achieve a goal. A team can be differentiated from a group in that it is more highly organized and the members' collaborative efforts are more coordinated to achieve the team goal.

PRINCIPLE **TERMS:**

- small group
- primary group
- social group
- secondary group
- study group
- therapy group
- problem-solving group
- focus group
- virtual group or team
- small group communication
- team

PRINCIPLE **SKILLS:**

1. What do you find most rewarding about working in groups and teams? What do you find most challenging?
2. Make a list of all of the groups and teams to which you belong. Analyze your list to determine which groups are most similar to this chapter's definition of a small group. Also identify those groups that function more like a team. Then on a scale of 1 to 10 (with 10 being the most effective and 1 the least effective), assess the effectiveness of each group or team using the criteria discussed in this chapter.

Group and Team Dynamics

9.2 Identify and describe group and team dynamics, including roles, rules, norms, status, power, and cohesiveness.

PRINCIPLE **POINTS:** A variety of factors influence the ever-changing nature of members' interactions in groups and teams. One factor is the role you assume in a group—the consistent way you communicate with others. There are three primary types of roles in small groups and teams: (1) task roles help the group do its work, (2) social roles help the group members relate to one another, and (3) individual roles inappropriately divert the group's focus to individual concerns rather than group concerns. Other factors that affect the dynamic nature of groups and teams include norms (standards of what is normal or expected), rules (explicit statements about appropriate and inappropriate behavior), status (a person's importance or prestige), power (the ability to influence others), and cohesiveness (the degree of loyalty and attraction the group members feel toward one another).

PRINCIPLE **TERMS:**

- role
- task role
- social role
- individual role
- team ground rules
- norms
- monochronic time perspective
- polychronic time perspective
- status
- power
- legitimate power
- referent power
- expert power
- reward power
- coercive power
- information power
- cohesiveness
- communication interaction pattern
- clique
- group deviate

PRINCIPLE **SKILLS:**

1. Identify the roles described in Table 9.1 that you fill most often in groups. Why do you think you usually take on these roles? Which roles would you like to fill more often?
2. Reflect upon your last group or team meeting. Evaluate the suggestions for enhancing group cohesiveness in Table 9.2 to assess how cohesive your group was. Based on your analysis, evaluate your group on a scale of 1 to 10 as highly cohesive (10) or not at all cohesive (1). What could you do to help your group or team become more cohesive?

Group and Team Development

9.3 Summarize the four stages of group and team development.

PRINCIPLE **POINTS:** The four stages of group and team development are (1) orientation (forming), (2) conflict (storming), (3) emergence (norming), and

(4) reinforcement (performing). During the orientation phase, group members get acquainted with both the task and one another. The second phase, conflict, occurs when group members recognize that they have differing ideas and opinions about both the group's task and its procedures for accomplishing the task. The third phase, emergence, is evident when the group begins to make decisions and starts to complete the task. The reinforcement phase occurs when the group has accomplished its task and takes some time to recognize and confirm the group's actions.

PRINCIPLE TERMS:

forming	task conflict
storming	process conflict
norming	relational conflict
performing	secondary tension
orientation phase	emergence phase
primary tension	reinforcement phase
conflict phase	

PRINCIPLE SKILLS:

1. Do you sometimes feel uncertain and uncomfortable when joining a new group? How do you typically try to resolve discomfort when you meet new group members? How successful is your method? What small group communication skills mentioned in the chapter can help make new group members feel part of the group?

2. Communication researchers Katherine Hawkins and Bryant Fillion surveyed personnel managers to find out what they considered the most important skills for successful groups and teams. The skills in the following list are among those that the personnel managers deemed most important. Rate each member of a group you are in on the following skills, using a scale from 1 to 5 (1 = not at all effective, 2 = generally not effective, 3 = uncertain, 4 = effective, and 5 = very effective). Then rate yourself.

Scoring Instructions

Total the score for each group member. A perfect score is 65; the lowest possible score is 13. Your instructor may invite you to share your ratings of other group members anonymously. If you don't share your ratings, simply note how you evaluated your own skills in comparison to other group members.

Skill	Group Member A	B	C	D	E
1. Listens effectively	___	___	___	___	___
2. Understands roles and responsibilities	___	___	___	___	___
3. Actively contributes to the group	___	___	___	___	___
4. Asks clear questions	___	___	___	___	___
5. Establishes and maintains rapport with others	___	___	___	___	___
6. Is sensitive to people with different cultural backgrounds	___	___	___	___	___
7. Uses clear, concise, accurate, and professional language	___	___	___	___	___
8. Communicates well with people who have different professional backgrounds	___	___	___	___	___
9. Gives clear and accurate instructions	___	___	___	___	___
10. Nonverbally presents a positive professional image (through appropriate grooming and attire)	___	___	___	___	___
11. Helps resolve conflicts	___	___	___	___	___
12. Accurately summarizes information for the group	___	___	___	___	___
13. Gives brief, clear, well-organized, and informative presentations to the group when appropriate	___	___	___	___	___
Total	___	___	___	___	___

CHAPTER 10

ENHANCING GROUP AND TEAM PERFORMANCE

Never doubt that a small group of concerned citizens can change the world; it's the only thing that ever has. —MARGARET MEAD

SDI Productions/E+/Getty Images

CHAPTER OUTLINE

- What Effective Group and Team Members Do
- Structuring Group and Team Problem Solving
- Enhancing Group and Team Leadership
- Enhancing Group and Team Meetings
- Study Guide: *Principles for a Lifetime*

LEARNING OBJECTIVES

10.1 Identify six functions that effective group members perform.

10.2 List and describe the five steps of group problem solving (reflective thinking).

10.3 Compare and contrast the trait, functional, styles, situational, and transformational approaches to understanding leadership.

10.4 Develop and use strategies to structure meetings appropriately, keep meetings on track, and promote appropriate dialogue and interaction.

What's so great about groups? Why does every organization, from the U.S. Congress to the local Parent Teacher Association, use groups, teams, and committees to get things done? The simple fact is: Groups work. Collaborating with other people produces clear benefits that just don't happen when a task is given to an individual. Research clearly supports the following conclusions:

- **Greater Creativity.** Groups and teams come up with more creative solutions to problems than a person does working alone.
- **Enhanced Comprehension.** Working with others in groups improves group members' understanding of the ideas presented.
- **Increased Satisfaction.** Group and team members are more satisfied with the group's conclusions and recommendations if they participated in the discussion than if they did not.
- **More Information.** Groups have access to more information when they tap into the experience of group members.[1]

All these advantages sound wonderful. But these benefits of collaboration don't occur automatically when people work in groups and teams. Sometimes there are significant disadvantages to working collaboratively:

- **Dominance by One Person.** Overly talkative or insensitive, overbearing people may speak too much.
- **Pressure to Conform.** Group members sometimes feel pressure to conform to what other members are doing and saying.
- **Take More Risks.** Groups sometimes make riskier decisions and take more extreme actions than individuals.[2]
- **Unequal Workload.** It may be easy for some people to loaf and not do their share of the work.
- **More Time.** Working in groups and teams takes more time than working individually.[3]

This chapter is designed to help you maximize the advantages of working in groups and minimize the disadvantages. We can't claim that if you follow all of the strategies we suggest, your life will be free of unpleasant and unproductive group experiences. (Although one study did find that taking an over-the-counter pain relief pill makes group work less painful.[4]) You don't, however, have to take pain medicine to make group work more tolerable; group members who both understand how groups work (see Chapter 9) and know principles and strategies for enhancing the quality of group work are much more likely to avoid the pitfalls and reap the benefits of working in groups.

Underpinning all the suggestions we offer in this chapter are the same five Communication Principles for a Lifetime that we introduced in Chapter 1 and have been discussing throughout the book. Effective group members are aware of what they are doing. They effectively use verbal and nonverbal messages, listen and respond, and then appropriately adapt their messages to others.

What Effective Group and Team Members Do

10.1 Identify six functions that effective group members perform.

"I hate groups," mutters an exasperated group member who has just finished a two-hour meeting in which nothing was accomplished. "Not me," chirps another group member. "Meetings and team projects are fun. I like the energy and productivity that occur when we work together." What does the second person know that the first one doesn't? As we noted at the start of this chapter, working in groups can have drawbacks, but you can reduce those disadvantages if you and other group members learn some fundamental ways to perform effectively.[5]

▼ Groups offer a lot of advantages in trying to solve problems, so it pays to learn how to overcome some of the challenges to effective group communication.
Rawpixel.com/Shutterstock

Identify a Clear, Elevating Goal

Among the first questions that a vigilant-thinking group asks itself relates to the group's goal: What are we trying to do?[6] According to one research team, the goal should be not only clear, but also *elevating*, or exciting to the group.[7] The group needs to know that it is pursuing a goal that is significant; the goal needs to be something more exciting and important than anything a group member could achieve individually. For example, a professional football team may see itself as a Super Bowl contender at the beginning of preseason. In addition to being exciting, a group's identified goal should also be clear and realistic, as it needs to drive all aspects of what the group does.[8] Without a goal and a results-driven structure to achieve it, group performance sputters. Research has found that it's important not only to set goals, but also to develop contingency plans in case a goal is not reached. Being able to react and adjust the group's plans to achieve a goal is especially important.[9]

Develop a Results-Driven Structure

A group or team may have a clear goal, such as winning the Super Bowl, getting an "A" on a group assignment, or selling more memberships than other groups in the company, but just having a clear, elevating goal doesn't mean the group will achieve what it wants to achieve. The group also has to carry out actions that contribute to reaching the goal. If you want to win the Super Bowl, you have to invest time in becoming physically fit and working on executing successful football plays. If you want to get an "A" on an assignment, you need to be doing what the instructor wants you to do rather than socializing and just having fun.

A group with a **results-driven structure** is organized around the action steps it needs to take to achieve its goal.[10] To be driven by results means "keeping your eyes on the prize" and then developing a group or team structure to secure that prize. Perhaps you've been part of a group or team that was quite busy but didn't seem to accomplish much; that kind of activity reflects a non-results-driven structure. Results-driven groups focus on verbs—action words—that provide the road map to success. Increasingly, using technology such as WhatsApp has proven to be useful in helping groups stay on task and make effective decisions.[11]

results-driven structure
A structure that causes a group to focus its efforts on the actions it needs to take to achieve its goals.

Gather and Share Appropriate Information

Another question that vigilant-thinking groups ask is, "Does something need to be changed?" To answer that question, high-performing groups and teams don't just rely on the unsupported opinions of group members. Instead, they gather information and analyze the situation.[12] Keep in mind that sharing information is just as important in virtual groups as it is in face-to-face groups.[13] To analyze an issue, an effective group should do at least three things: gather accurate information, share it with group members, and draw conclusions from that information.

Gather Accurate Information Computer programmers are familiar with the acronym GIGO: "Garbage in, garbage out." If you develop a computer program using bad information or a bad program command (garbage), you're likely to get low-quality output (more garbage). Information is the fuel that makes a group function well.[14]

Share Information Group members have a tendency to share information that everyone in the group already knows. Research has found that better decisions are made when group members make an effort to share information that others may *not* know.[15] So if you are uncertain whether other group members know what you know, don't hesitate to share that information with the entire group.[16]

Draw Accurate Conclusions from Shared Information Having too little evidence—or no evidence at all—is one reason groups sometimes fail to correctly analyze their current situation.[17] Even if group members have plenty of evidence, however, it may be bad evidence, or perhaps they have not tested the evidence to see whether it is true, accurate, or relevant.

Group members who use strong evidence to support their well-reasoned arguments are more likely to have their conclusions accepted by the entire group than members who do not.[18] Group members who don't gather and use information effectively are more likely to make bad and less creative decisions than others.[19] Here are some tips for gathering and using information effectively:

- In group deliberations, ask for expert advice sooner rather than later. Seeking expert advice results in better group outcomes.
- If you find that just a few people are doing the talking and sharing information, invite quieter group members to participate. Groups that have more equal participation among members are generally more effective than other groups.
- Don't rush to make a quick decision. To reach a better outcome, take your time and sift through the information you have.

Develop Options

Another hallmark of a vigilant-thinking group is that the members generate many ideas and potential solutions after gathering information and analyzing a situation. Effective groups don't just settle on one or two ideas and then move on. They come up with multiple creative approaches.

Sometimes groups get stuck, and ideas just don't flow. If that happens to your group, you may want to take a break from discussing difficult issues or problems rather than continuing to hammer away at them. Taking a break may give you the space you need to properly think through the issues. You may generate a breakthrough solution when you are not actively trying to; perhaps you've had a great idea come to you when you were taking a walk or driving. The principle of self-awareness operates here: As a group member, you have a responsibility to be aware of your group's ability to generate high-quality ideas. Be sensitive to the group's need to take a fresh look at the problem or issue.

Evaluate Ideas

High-performing groups know a good idea when they hear one. They are able to evaluate evidence, opinions, assumptions, and solutions to separate good ideas from bad ones. Low-performing groups are less discriminating. A group that does not critically evaluate ideas because members are too eager to come to a decision just so they can get a job done usually makes low-quality decisions. Research has also found that high-performing groups benefit from receiving useful evaluative feedback from their peers about their progress.[20]

As we've seen, a group of vigilant thinkers examines the advantages and disadvantages of an idea, issue, or opinion.[21] When zeroing in on a particular course of action, an effective group has at least one member who suggests, "Let's consider the positive and negative consequences of this decision." *Research reveals that it's especially important to talk about the negative consequences of a specific proposal.*[22] Some groups list pros and cons on a whiteboard or flipchart. Groups that do so are likely to come up with a better decision than groups that don't systematically evaluate the good and bad aspects of a potential solution or decision.

Not only is it a good idea to evaluate the conclusions of the group, but research suggests that it is useful to periodically evaluate the team's process and talk about how well team members coordinate the work. Don't wait until a project is finished to evaluate your team's process; discuss how well the team is achieving its goals as it works on a project.[23]

▲ Members of high-performing groups and teams are likely to enjoy spending time together. A good balance of social and task-based activities makes it more fun for group members to be together. How else can you make group membership more enjoyable for yourself and others?
Rawpixel.com/Shutterstock

Develop Sensitivity toward Others

Most of the functions we've described so far focus on getting work done effectively and efficiently, but group success is about more than just focusing on the task. Being solely task-oriented is not beneficial to the way a group functions. Effective group members need to balance concern for the task with concern for the feelings of others.[24]

Fostering a climate of fairness and supportiveness is essential to developing a well-functioning team.[25] How do you increase your sensitivity toward others?

- Be aware of how your comments might be perceived by others.
- Look for opportunities to confirm the value of others' contributions.
- Nonverbally show that you are genuinely interested in what others are saying.
- Listen to what each group member has to say—even members who hold a minority opinion.

One benefit of working in a group is that you can hear a variety of ideas. If some members' opinions are quickly dismissed because they are not what most other group members think or believe, the group loses the benefit of having many different points of view.

RECAP

What Effective Group and Team Members Do

Group Function	Description of Function
Identify a Clear, Elevating Goal	A clear, elevating, or important goal provides an anchor for group discussion.
Develop a Results-Driven Structure	Structure helps the group stay on task and do the things that will help it achieve its goal.
Gather and Share Appropriate Information	Effective teams conduct research, share information with all group members, and take steps to confirm that they have accurate information.
Develop Options	Effective groups generate a number of options before choosing a course of action.
Evaluate Ideas	Effective groups or teams examine the pros and cons of each option before implementing a strategy.
Develop Sensitivity Toward Others	Members of effective groups express sensitivity to the needs and concerns of group members by using appropriate verbal and nonverbal messages, listening, responding, and adapting messages to others.
Develop a Positive Personal Style	Effective group members have optimistic attitudes about the prospects for overall group success and use effective strategies to change ineffective member behavior.

A recent study found that one sign of a competent group is that group members simply like spending time with one another.[26] Another study explicitly noted the importance of trusting one another, clarifying misunderstandings by collaboratively defining important terms, listening effectively, consciously talking about what makes the group effective, sharing personal information, using humor, and laughing together.[27] Competent groups also treat new group members with respect.[28] In summary, competent group members are sensitive to how individual members relate to one another.

Develop a Positive Personal Style

You may have heard the story about a boy who awoke on the morning of his birthday to find only a large pile of manure where he'd hoped to find birthday presents. Undaunted, he smiled and said, "With this much horse manure, there's got to be a pony here somewhere!" Like that boy, effective team members are optimistic: Even in bad times, they find something to be positive about.

One thing effective team members are optimistic about is themselves. Researchers have found that effective teams and team members *believed* that they were effective, that they had the skills and resources to accomplish their task. Teams that were less effective *thought* that they were less effective.[29] Was the team effective due to a self-fulfilling prophecy—did its optimistic expectations cause the team to act effectively? Or did team members think they were effective because they really were a top-notch team? We're not quite sure what the precise cause-and-effect relationship is between self-perceptions of being effective and actually being effective. We do know, however, that teams that have a positive, can-do attitude perform better than teams whose members have doubts, worries, and uncertainties about whether they will get the job done. The bottom line is that optimism enhances effectiveness.

As we've seen, being driven by results makes group members more productive. Furthermore, perhaps not surprisingly, team members also like colleagues who are encouraging, patient, enthusiastic, and friendly. In contrast, *ineffective* team members tend to argue with others frequently, be intolerant and impatient, and cultivate skills that will help them win the "pain-in-the-neck" award. To be an effective team member, you need to find a way to deal with group members who may dominate, block, bully, or lack follow-through. Table 10.1 offers suggestions on how to collaborate with difficult members.

You may wonder whether these attributes of team effectiveness can be enhanced through study and training. There's good news: Evidence suggests that by learning more about teams and participating in training development courses, you can indeed improve your team skills.[30]

TABLE 10.1 How to Collaborate with Difficult Group Members

Problem	Suggestions
Dominator: A group member talks too much.	1. Consider giving the group member responsibility for a specific task. 2. Use gatekeeping skills to invite others to talk. 3. Privately ask the "oververbalizer" to give others an opportunity to talk. 4. If necessary, the group may collectively decide to confront the domineering member.
Blocker: A group member has a negative attitude and consistently insists that ideas can't be accomplished.	1. Consider defusing the tension with appropriate humor. 2. Ask the blocker to play devil's advocate, a role that gives the blocker permission to be negative at certain times rather than all the time. 3. Ask for evidence to support the blocker's claims. 4. Gently confront the blocker, noting how his or her negative attitude is affecting the entire group.
No Follow-Through: A group member is irresponsible and doesn't perform assigned tasks.	1. Assign a mentor to help the group member. 2. Clarify that only those who do the work will be recognized for accomplishing the task. 3. Privately ask the irresponsible group member to do his or her share of the work. 4. If need be, confront the irresponsible group member as a group, explaining how the lack of follow-through is hurting the group.
Bully: A group member is unethically aggressive and verbally abusive and tries to take the credit for others' work.	1. Support those who are bullied. 2. Don't tolerate unethical behavior; describe the offensive behavior to the bully and explain its effect on the group. 3. As a group, confront the bully, explaining how the bullying behavior is hurting the group's emotional climate. 4. If need be, seek help from a person of authority outside the group (a supervisor or instructor); sometimes a bully responds only to a person with greater power.

Structuring Group and Team Problem Solving

10.2 List and describe the five steps of group problem solving (reflective thinking).

How many of us have uttered the plea, "Just tell me what to do"? When we do, we are usually looking for simple techniques or steps to help us achieve our goal. Several researchers have sought to identify the sequence that works best to help groups solve problems and achieve their goals. In fact, more than seventy methods or sequences of steps and techniques have been prescribed for structuring problem solving in groups and teams.[31] Despite all of these recommendations, however, researchers have concluded that there are no magic techniques that always enable a group to come up with the right solution to a problem. No single prescriptive method or series of steps works best in every situation. There is some good news, though: Research shows that *having some structured sequence of steps or questions works better than having no structure*.[32]

Another important conclusion reached by group researchers is that whatever structure a group uses must be balanced with interaction.

- **Structure** is the way a group or team discussion is organized to follow a prescribed agenda. Groups and teams need structure to keep them on task and on track.[33] Some group members have a strong preference for organized, structured conversation.[34] According to research, groups that engage in free-ranging discussion without

structure
The way a group or team discussion is organized, focusing on the group's agenda and the task that needs to be achieved.

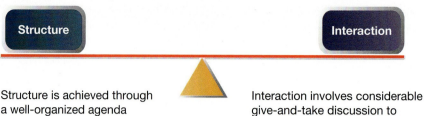

FIGURE 10.1 Groups Need a Balance of Structure and Interaction

Structure is achieved through a well-organized agenda and a clear discussion plan.

Interaction involves considerable give-and-take discussion to manage relationships and accomplish the task.

an agenda change topics about once a minute.[35] Besides having difficulty staying focused, a group without adequate structure or focus is more likely than a well-structured group to take excessive time to do its work, jump at the first solution recommended, find that one or more people dominate discussions, and have problems managing conflict.[36]

- **Interaction** among group members involves give-and-take discussion and responsiveness to the comments of others. In an interactive group, there are fewer long utterances, more people contribute, and more people take turns talking. People listen and thoughtfully respond to one another. In comparison, in a highly structured meeting there is more control over who talks, about what, and for how long; overly structured meetings include less interaction.

interaction
The give-and-take discussion within a group and the responsiveness of group members to the comments of others.

As Figure 10.1 suggests, the key is to find the right balance between structure and interaction. When there is too much interaction, the group experiences the chaos of unbridled talk; group and team members may bounce from topic to topic and need help focusing on one idea at a time. When there is too much structure, however, the group loses the freedom to listen and respond with sensitivity to what others are saying.

In the pages that follow, we present a series of steps that can help group members successfully navigate the problem-solving process. These five steps are inspired by educator and philosopher John Dewey, who in 1910 wrote a book called *How We Think*.[37] In essence, his book describes the scientific method that scientists still use to solve problems: defining and analyzing a problem, identifying solutions, picking a solution, and putting the solution into practice. He called this process **reflective thinking**. We present these steps here not as a one-size-fits-all prescription that you should always follow, but as a way of structuring the problem-solving process to manage uncertainty and ensure that the key functions we talked about earlier are accomplished during your discussion. These steps incorporate the ideas we previously presented when describing what effective group members do. In addition to describing each step of the reflective thinking process, we present several techniques to help you structure discussion.

reflective thinking
A problem-solving process based on the scientific method.

Step 1: Identify and Define the Problem

"What's your problem?" As we noted earlier, groups work best when they have identified a clear, elevating goal that unites their efforts. Whatever method or technique a group uses, it is essential that group members know precisely what problem they are trying to solve. To help your group reach a clear statement of the problem, consider asking the following questions:

- What is the specific problem that concerns us?
- What do we want more of or less of?[38]
- What terms, concepts, or ideas do we need to define so as to understand the problem?

It is also helpful to phrase the problem as a question and to clarify the problem.

Develop a Question To give your problem-solving task appropriate structure, most group experts recommend phrasing your problem in the form of a policy question that recommends some action (policy) to eliminate, reduce, or manage the problem. Policy questions typically begin with the words "What should be done about . . ." or "What could be done to improve . . . ."

Here are some examples:

- What should be done to lower the cost of tuition at our university?
- What could be done to decrease property taxes in our state?
- What should be done to make health care more affordable for all U.S. citizens?

Clarify the Problem One specific technique for clarifying a problem is to use the journalists' six questions method.[39] Most reporters are taught to include the answers to six questions—who, what, when, where, why, and how—when writing a news story. Answering each of these six questions about the problem the group has identified can help further define and limit the problem. For example, a group might ask *who* and *when* questions such as "Who is harmed by the problem?" and "When do the harmful effects of the problem occur?" The group's answers can also help it move to the next step in the process: analyzing the problem.

One way to help your group fully identify and define a problem is to use these six questions about the problem.
iQoncept, 2010/Used under license from Shutterstock

Step 2: Analyze the Problem

Many groups want to "cut to the chase" quickly and start spinning out solutions without taking the time to analyze a problem thoroughly. Resist this temptation. Analyzing a problem well is an important prerequisite to finding an effective solution. To analyze something is to break it down into smaller pieces. To analyze a problem is to consider its causes, effects, symptoms, history, and other information that will inform the group about how to best solve the problem. Essential questions that can help you analyze problems include the following:

- How long has the problem been in existence?
- How widespread is the problem?
- What are the causes of the problem?
- What are the effects of the problem?
- What are the symptoms of the problem?
- What methods already exist for managing the problem?
- What are the limitations of existing methods?
- What obstacles might keep the group from solving this problem?

Establish Criteria In addition to considering these questions, group members should develop **criteria**, which are standards for an acceptable solution to a problem. Identifying clear criteria can help you spot a good solution when you see one. Sample criteria for solutions include the following:

- The solution should be inexpensive.
- The solution should be implemented by a certain date.
- The solution should be agreed on by all group members.
- The solution should be agreed on by all individuals affected by the recommendations.

criteria
Standards for an acceptable solution.

Don't rely on your memory when you verbalize criteria. Write down on a highly visible dry-erase board, flipchart, or interactive whiteboard the list of criteria your group has identified. Include the list of criteria in the minutes or notes that summarize the meeting.

Analyze Problem Elements After collecting information and establishing criteria, your group may need to develop a systematic way of analyzing the information it's gathered. One technique that can help structure the analysis of your problem and also

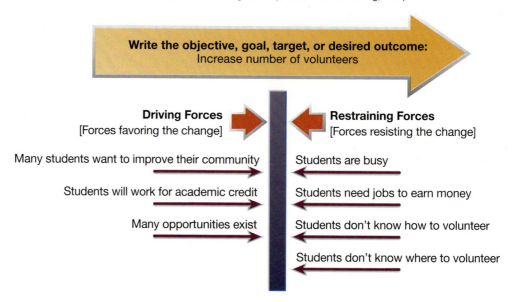

FIGURE 10.2 Force Field Analysis

This analysis was conducted by a group that wanted to increase the number of students who volunteer for community projects. The group's goal is written on the top arrow. Driving forces, shown on the left, are factors that increase the group's chance of achieving its goal. Restraining forces, listed on the right, are factors that reduce the group's ability to get more students to volunteer.

SOURCE: Adapted from Julius E. Eitington, *The Winning Trainer* (Houston: Gulf Publishing, 1989).

force field analysis technique
A method of analyzing a problem or issue by identifying forces that increase the likelihood that the desired goal will occur (driving forces) and forces that decrease the probability that the goal will occur (restraining forces).

help your team identify criteria is the **force field analysis technique** shown in Figure 10.2.[40] This technique works best when your group has identified a clear goal and needs to assess existing factors that would increase or decrease the probability of achieving that goal.

After identifying a goal, the group lists all the driving forces currently at work that would help achieve the goal. Then the group does just the opposite: It identifies the restraining forces that are keeping the group from achieving the goal. When the force field analysis is complete, the group's task in developing solutions is now clear: Increase the driving forces and decrease the restraining forces.

Step 3: Generate Creative Solutions

Now that you've identified a specific problem, analyzed its causes and history, and established clear criteria for solutions, you're ready to generate creative options to solve the problem. Keep in mind that sometimes it's a group's intuition rather than logical, structured strategies that result in more creative solutions to problems.[41] **Creativity** is the generation, application, combination, and extension of new ideas. Researchers have found that your entire group is more likely to be creative if individual group members are creative, are open to new ideas, have diverse backgrounds, and believe that they can be creative; it's important not to rely on others to be creative but to develop your own creative skill.[42] It's simply not true that only a few gifted and talented people are creative. Creative ideas can come from anyone. Your group is more likely to be creative if you do the following things:[43]

creativity
The generation, application, combination, and extension of new ideas.

- Make sure everyone in the group knows the precise nature of the problem.
- Review and summarize the analysis of the problem.
- Promote a climate of freedom; let people experiment and play with ideas.
- Don't prematurely judge and evaluate the ideas of others.
- Listen to minority points of view; you never know who may have the next great insight.
- Provide enough time for creativity to occur; don't rush the creative process.

Brainstorming is the classic technique for identifying possible solutions to a problem. This technique, in which group members try to generate as many ideas as possible within a set period of time *without evaluating them*, was developed by an advertising executive about sixty years ago to encourage a group to be creative.[44] You've probably used brainstorming before. Many groups, however, don't use the technique effectively.

brainstorming
A technique for identifying many possible solutions to a problem in which group members try to generate as many ideas as possible within a set period of time *without evaluating them*.

Problems with Traditional, Oral Brainstorming The key to making brainstorming work—to come up with as many creative ideas as possible—is to *separate the generation of ideas from the evaluation of ideas*. This means that group members should feel free to offer ideas without fear of criticism, snickering, or being made to feel foolish. Reality, however, may be quite different. When group members start suggesting ideas, there may be verbal or, more likely, nonverbal evaluation of those ideas. People may laugh at the more offbeat suggestions; or when someone announces a suggestion, others may frown, sneer, voice an editorial comment, or talk over the person and ignore the suggestion. Another subtle form of evaluation occurs when some group ideas are praised and some are not. Group members whose ideas are not praised may feel that others consider their ideas stupid. Clearly, when ideas are evaluated as soon as they're offered, brainstorming doesn't work well; members may become reluctant to share ideas. This is especially true of group members who are shy or uncomfortable talking in a group; however, these people may have great ideas worth sharing.

Better Brainstorming There are several strategies that can help groups improve on traditional, oral brainstorming. Consider the following suggestions.

Write down Your Ideas before Sharing Them with Others Consider having a period of **silent brainstorming** in which group members work individually before verbally sharing their ideas. Another name for silent brainstorming is the **nominal group technique**.[45] For a specified period of time, encourage group members to work individually and write down their ideas. During this time, they are a group in name only (hence the term *nominal*). After group members have brainstormed individually, they share their ideas with the group. When groups use silent brainstorming, it's usually best to go around the group one at a time to have members share what they have written down. For example, each member could be encouraged to present five to ten suggestions for solving the group's problem. Another option is to have group members privately brainstorm and then email their responses to the group leader or other members. Virtual groups can share ideas without meeting in person by using electronic brainstorming websites and apps. However, before any brainstorming begins, make sure group members have a clear understanding of the problem.[46]

silent brainstorming
A method of generating creative ideas; group members brainstorm individually and write down their ideas before meeting together to share them.

nominal group technique
Another name for silent brainstorming.

Piggyback off the Ideas of Others For groups that meet in person, members can brainstorm ideas silently for a few minutes and then move into smaller groups to share and piggyback ideas before the entire group comes back together. Another creative way to generate ideas is to have group members write each of their ideas or suggestions on sticky notes.[47] Once all of the ideas are on sticky notes, group members can stick them to the wall and then arrange them into categories. Seeing other group members' ideas may trigger additional creative ideas.

Evaluate All Ideas after They Are Shared In all variations of brainstorming, the goal is to separate generating or listing ideas from critiquing ideas. Evaluate the ideas *after* all the group members have finished sharing. When the two parts of brainstorming get mixed together, fewer ideas flow because of group members' fear of being criticized.

Provide Plenty of Time for Brainstorming One research team found that one way to make traditional, oral brainstorming more effective is to give groups more than just a few minutes to generate ideas.[48] Traditional brainstorming groups who generated ideas for more than ten minutes did just as well as groups using the nominal group technique

RECAP

Brainstorming Steps

1. Identify and define a problem that needs to be solved.
2. Discuss the history, causes, effects, symptoms, and background of the problem. Make sure the group establishes a set of criteria to clarify the issues and help evaluate solutions.
3. Tell the group to develop a creative mind-set:
   - Put aside judgments and evaluations.
   - Stress quantity of ideas.
   - Avoid criticizing anyone's ideas, including your own.
   - Try to come up with one or more wild ideas—stretch your imagination.
   - Provide enough time for creativity to occur; don't rush the process.
4. Start brainstorming. Give the group a time limit.
5. To reduce the possibility that people will evaluate ideas, consider using a period of silent brainstorming before having people verbalize their ideas.
6. Write all the ideas on a dry-erase board, flipchart, or interactive whiteboard. Piggyback off other people's ideas.
7. Keep reminding the group not to evaluate others' ideas when they are first expressed.
8. After all ideas have been presented, evaluate them based on the specific criteria established by the group.

(in which group members worked individually before sharing ideas collaboratively).[49] Research has confirmed that the nominal group technique has benefits because ideas are generated without others evaluating them. However, with adequate time, traditional brainstorming can also achieve positive results. When given enough time to do their work, traditional brainstorming groups also reported more cohesiveness than teams using the nominal group technique.[50]

As we've noted, the purpose of brainstorming is to think of as many ideas as possible. To generate a lot of options, encourage members to piggyback off each other's ideas. List all of the ideas where everybody can see them; referring to the list can fuel more ideas. Try to identify one or more zany or wild ideas—this triggers creativity and may lead to a less zany but workable idea.

Step 4: Select the Best Solution

After the group has generated a long list of ideas, the next step is to evaluate them to determine which ones best meet the criteria the group identified when they analyzed the problem. It's really important that group members have both a clear goal and specific criteria. Without them, group members will have difficulty recognizing a good solution when they see it.

It is usually easier for groups to expand alternatives (brainstorm) than to narrow alternatives. The methods that groups use to whittle a long list down to a manageable number for more serious debate include these five approaches:

1. *Decision by expert.* Let someone who has high credibility narrow the list.
2. *Rank.* Tell group members to rank their top five choices from 1 to 5.
3. *Rate.* Ask group members to evaluate each solution on a scale from 1 to 5; the solutions that are rated highest get the most serious discussion.
4. *Majority vote.* Group members vote for the ideas they like.
5. *Consensus.* Members seek a solution that everyone in the group or team can accept.

ETHICS & COMMUNICATION

What If Someone Can't Stop Judging?

Sarah likes to be in charge of group meetings. She has lots of good ideas, and other group members benefit from her leadership and wealth of suggestions. But during traditional brainstorming sessions, she can't stop criticizing other people's ideas. A couple of group members have asked Sarah not to evaluate others' ideas during brainstorming sessions because they have noticed how some members don't share as frequently because of her criticism, but she just can't seem to stop.

Sarah makes important contributions to the group and is a good leader except for this one flaw of continually evaluating what others say. What would you do if you were in this group with Sarah? Would you speak to Sarah, as other group members have done, to ask her to stop critiquing? Or would you say nothing? What are your ethical obligations to help the group perform as effectively as possible?

Some members have suggested asking Sarah to leave the group during brainstorming sessions, because her behavior hurts group creativity. On the basis of what you've read so far in this chapter, what other ideas might help Sarah avoid critiquing ideas as they are generated?

TABLE 10.2 Suggestions for Reaching Group and Team Consensus

Effective Group Members	Ineffective Group Members
Keep the Group Oriented toward Its Goal	
Remind the group what the goal is.	Go off on tangents and do not stay focused on the agenda.
Write facts and key ideas on a dry-erase board, flipchart, or interactive whiteboard.	Fail to summarize in writing or rely only on oral summaries to keep group members focused on the goal.
Talk about the discussion process, and ask questions that keep the group focused on the agenda.	Do little to help clarify group discussion.
Listen to the Ideas of Others	
Clarify misunderstandings.	Do not clarify misunderstandings or check to see whether others understand their message.
Emphasize areas of agreement.	Ignore areas of agreement.
Maintain eye contact when listening to someone and remain focused on the speaker without interrupting.	Avoid eye contact with the speaker, do not focus attention on the speaker, or interrupt the speaker.
Promote Honest Dialogue and Discussion	
Seek out differences of opinion.	Do not seek other opinions from group members.
Do not change their minds quickly to avoid conflict.	Quickly agree with other group members to avoid conflict.
Try to involve everyone in discussions.	Permit one person or just a few people to talk too much and dominate the conversation.

Develop Consensus Consensus occurs when there is enough agreement that all group members support a decision. Consensus doesn't mean that everyone agrees enthusiastically and completely with what the group has decided, but that no one will stand in the way of what the group has decided. The advantage of reaching a consensus decision is that all group members can verbalize support for the decision. But reaching consensus takes time.

The three primary strategies summarized in Table 10.2 can help groups reach consensus:[51]

1. Focus on the goal.[52]
2. Listen.
3. Promote honest discussion.

consensus
Agreement among all members of a group or team to support an idea, proposal, or solution.

Avoid Groupthink Be cautious if all group members agree too quickly or too consistently. You may be experiencing groupthink instead of consensus. **Groupthink** occurs when group members seem to agree but primarily just want to avoid conflict. On the surface, it seems as though group members have reached consensus, but it may be an illusion of agreement. Another way of describing groupthink is to call it *faulty consensus*; too little disagreement often reduces the quality of group decisions. Research has found that honest, substantive conflict can help groups and teams reach effective decisions.[53] If a group does not seriously examine the pros and cons of an idea, the quality of the decision it makes is likely to suffer.[54]

Failure to test ideas and the resulting groupthink can have serious consequences in the form of wrong, dangerous, or stupid decisions. The following list identifies a few well-known disasters or problems in which groupthink was a key factor:

groupthink
A faulty sense of agreement that occurs when members of a group fail to challenge an idea; a false consensus reached when conflict is minimized and group members do not express concerns or reservations about an idea or proposal.

- In 1986, American TV viewers, including thousands of schoolchildren, watched in horror as the *Challenger* space shuttle, carrying the first teacher in space, exploded on their screens. The tragedy resulted from both faulty engineering and groupthink: Some scientists knew that the shuttle might not fly in cold temperatures but, because of pressure to stay on schedule, decided not to stop the launch.[55]

"All those in favor say 'Aye.'"
"Aye." "Aye." "Aye." "Aye." "Aye."

- In 1999, several students were killed in a traditional pre–football game bonfire at Texas A&M University. Some people thought the bonfire construction unsafe before the accident occurred, but because of tradition, the bonfire continued to be built and tragedy was the result.[56]

- The commission that investigated the September 11, 2001, terrorist attacks concluded that the nation's lack of preparedness for the attacks was attributable in part to groupthink.[57] The commission found that evidence of a terrorist threat existed before the attacks, yet not enough action was taken to fully address the problem.

News headlines are not the only places to look for examples of groupthink. If you think about it, you'll find plenty of examples in groups and teams you've worked with.

Causes of Groupthink Groupthink is more likely to occur in your group under the following conditions:

- The group feels apathetic about its task.
- Group members don't expect to be successful.
- One group member has very high credibility—group members tend to believe what he or she says.
- One group member is very persuasive.
- Group members don't usually challenge ideas—it's expected that they will agree with one another.[58]

Be on the lookout for these symptoms in your groups and teams.

Of course, as the saying goes, "Hindsight is 20/20." After the fact, it can be easy to spot an example of groupthink. The hard part is to be aware of groupthink when it is occurring in your group. Knowing the causes and symptoms of groupthink can help you spot it and then put an end to it.

How to Avoid Groupthink The first thing to do is to be aware when groupthink is occurring. In addition to awareness, here are several additional strategies to avoid groupthink:[59]

- Don't agree with someone just because that person has high status; examine the evidence and others' ideas carefully, regardless of their position.
- Consider asking someone from outside the group to evaluate the group's decisions and decision-making process.
- Assign someone to be a devil's advocate—to look for disadvantages to a proposed idea.[60]
- Ask group members to break into smaller teams or pairs to consider both the pros and the cons of a proposed solution.

Step 5: Take Action

Once you have identified your solution or solutions, your group needs to consider the question, "Will it work?" You may want to do a pilot (practice) test or ask a small group of people what they think of your idea before you "go public" with it. Bouncing your proposed solution off an expert and checking to see whether your solution has been successful when others have adopted it can help you test its effectiveness.

If your group has to identify a solution *and* put it into action, your group will need to utilize a results-driven structure to make sure details don't get overlooked in getting the job done. Perhaps you know the people in the following story:

> This is a story about four people: Everybody, Somebody, Anybody, and Nobody. There was an important job to be done, and Everybody was asked to do it. Everybody was sure Somebody would do it. Anybody could have done it, but Nobody did it. Somebody got angry about that because it was Everybody's job. Everybody thought Anybody could do it, but Nobody realized that Everybody wouldn't do it. It ended up that Everybody blamed Somebody when actually Nobody asked Anybody.

Make a list of who should do what. At the next group meeting, follow up to see whether the assignments have been completed. Effective groups and teams develop an action plan and periodically review it to make sure Anybody asked Somebody.

RECAP
Reflective-Thinking Steps and Techniques

Steps	Techniques
1. Identify and define the problem.	• Phrase the problem as a policy question. • Use the journalists' six questions method (Who? What? When? Where? Why? How?) to help define the issues.
2. Analyze the problem.	• Use force field analysis to identify driving and restraining forces. • Develop criteria to clarify the issues and help evaluate solutions.
3. Generate creative solutions.	• Use brainstorming. • Use silent brainstorming (nominal group technique) or electronic brainstorming.
4. Select the best solution.	• Narrow alternatives by ranking, rating, majority vote, consensus, or relying on an expert decision. • Reach consensus by being goal oriented, by listening, and by promoting honest dialogue.
5. Take action.	• Develop a clear action plan. • Make a written list of who should do what.

Enhancing Group and Team Leadership

10.3 Compare and contrast the trait, functional, styles, situational, and transformational approaches to understanding leadership.

Leadership is the ability to influence others through communication to achieve a goal. Some people view a leader as someone who delegates and directs the group. Others see a leader as someone who is primarily responsible for ensuring that whatever task is assigned or designed by the group is completed. Actually, most groups have many leaders, not just one person who influences others. In fact, each group or team member undoubtedly influences what the group does or does not achieve. Regardless of who serves as leader, research suggests that the quality of group and team leadership has a significant effect on how satisfied team members are.[61] Members of an effectively led team feel greater satisfaction, are more productive, and are less likely to be absent than members of less effective groups.[62] The quality of team leadership influences virtually every aspect of what it feels like to be a team member. Researchers have analyzed the behavior of effective leaders and identified the following five prevailing approaches to leadership: trait, functional, styles, situational, and transformational.

Trait Approach

Are leaders born or made? The **trait approach to leadership** suggests that there are certain attributes or traits that make good leaders. According to this approach, if you are born with these traits or if you cultivate leadership skills, you will be a leader. Research has identified intelligence, confidence, social skills, general administrative skill, physical energy, and enthusiasm as some of the traits effective leaders possess.[63]

---

leadership
The ability to influence the behavior of others through communication to achieve a goal.

trait approach to leadership
A view of leadership that identifies specific qualities or characteristics of effective leaders.

▲ According to the trait approach to leadership, personal characteristics such as intelligence, confidence, social skills, physical energy, and enthusiasm make good leaders. Nelson Mandela, who served as president of South Africa and won the Nobel Peace Prize, possessed several traits of an effective leader. However, positive traits alone do not guarantee that someone will be a good leader.
Roger Bacon/REUTERS/Alamy Stock Photo

functional approach to leadership
A view of leadership that identifies the key task and process roles that need to be performed in a group.

task function
A leadership behavior that helps a group accomplish its job.

process function
A leadership behavior that helps maintain a positive group climate.

Researchers have also found that effective leaders develop persuasive arguments and are comfortable expressing their ideas to others.[64] Another research study found support for two of the Communication Principles for a Lifetime presented in this book: Effective leaders are self-aware and adapt to the people they lead and the context in which they lead.[65] Although many leaders do seem to have traits or special skills that can enhance their ability to influence others, just having these traits does not mean you will be an effective leader. Traits alone will not ensure effective leadership behavior. Leadership is more complicated than that.

Functional Approach

Rather than focusing on personality characteristics or other traits, the **functional approach to leadership** emphasizes essential leadership behaviors or functions that need to be performed to enhance the workings of a group. According to the functional approach, there are two broad leadership functions: (1) task functions and (2) process functions. These two functions should look familiar. They are similar to the types of group roles discussed in Chapter 9.

Task Leadership Functions **Task functions** include behaviors that help the group or team get the work done. Whether a leader is appointed or elected, one of his or her responsibilities is to ensure that the group completes the task it is tackling. The functional approach to leadership suggests that several people can share leadership functions. The following are some of the jobs that often need to be done:

- Helping set the group's agenda
- Recording what the group does
- Determining when meetings begin and end
- Preparing and distributing handouts
- Initiating or proposing new ideas
- Seeking and giving information
- Suggesting options
- Elaborating on the ideas of others
- Evaluating ideas

In most groups, these key functions are assumed by many if not most group members. A group member who rarely helps with any of these tasks often earns the uncoveted title of "slacker."

Process Leadership Functions **Process functions** are the second major type of function leaders assume in groups. Process leaders seek to maintain a friendly environment that promotes honest, frank discussion. Process leaders have "people skills." They listen sensitively to others and are observant of nonverbal cues. They focus on managing relationships by adapting to the needs of individual members. Another key process leadership task is to seek support from people and resources outside the team. An effective team leader keeps the team informed about how external influences affect the team's work goals.[66] Although a single person can perform all these functions, just as with task leadership, it is more than likely that several people will take on these process roles. Specific process roles include the following:

- Energizing the team by encouraging team members to keep at it
- Mediating conflict
- Compromising or helping others to compromise
- Gatekeeping: monitoring discussion to ensure that some members don't talk too much and others too little

In most groups or teams, these process roles are not formally assigned. Although some task functions may be explicitly assigned ("Daria, could you make copies of this report?"), process roles are assumed when needed; they emerge according to the needs of the group and the personality, skills, sensitivity, and past experiences of the members who are present. It is unlikely that you will start a meeting by saying, "Okay, Reya, you're in charge of settling the arguments between Ken and Hai. And Carl, you try to encourage Flor and Russell to talk more." Effective leaders look for opportunities to enhance the overall climate of the group. They try to catch people doing something right and then offer sincere praise and recognition.

Styles Approach

The **styles approach to leadership** suggests that leaders operate in one of three primary styles: (1) authoritarian, (2) democratic, or (3) laissez-faire. The methods used by leaders to influence group members usually fall into one of these broad categories, as outlined in Table 10.3.[67]

styles approach to leadership
A view of leadership that identifies three methods of interacting when leading others: authoritarian, democratic, and laissez-faire.

Authoritarian Leadership **Authoritarian leaders** influence others by giving orders and asserting control. Dictators and military officers assume this leadership style. But you don't have to be in the military or living in a dictatorship to experience an authoritarian leadership style. Perhaps you've felt like mumbling, "Who put *her* in charge?" during a group meeting. Or maybe you noticed that something needed to get done and you asked someone in the group to do what you thought was needed. As we discussed, groups need a certain amount of structure. The authoritarian leader assumes that he or she knows the type and amount of structure the group needs and proceeds to tell others what to do. Authoritarian leaders may be self-aware and may

authoritarian leader
One who leads by directing, controlling, telling, and ordering others.

TABLE 10.3 Leadership Styles

Authoritarian	Democratic	Laissez-Faire
The leader makes all policy decisions.	The leader discusses all policy decisions with group members. The group makes decisions by consensus.	Group members must initiate discussions about policy and procedures. The leader provides minimal direction during discussions about policy decisions.
The leader determines what will happen one step at a time; future steps are unclear or uncertain.	The group discusses what steps need to be taken. Group members work together to develop both short-term and long-term action steps.	The leader may supply information about what steps need to be taken, if asked. The leader does not volunteer information.
The leader tells people what to do.	The leader facilitates a collaborative approach to accomplishing the group's work.	The leader does not participate in creating work assignments.

use appropriate verbal and nonverbal messages, but they are not always known for listening and responding to others. They also may not be worried about adapting their messages to those whom they lead. They often speak and expect others to follow. Of the three primary leadership styles, the authoritarian leader is the least effective over a long period of time.[68] Yet when a group or team experiences increased stress, a decisive leader is perceived as more charismatic than other types of leaders.[69] Group members don't like an authoritarian leader all the time, but they may tolerate or even appreciate a bold, charismatic leader when there's a need for someone to make an important decision quickly.

Democratic Leadership The **democratic leader**, as you might guess from the name, consults with other group members before issuing edicts. This type of leader listens and adapts messages to others. Rather than bulldozing or shoving the group into an action its members may resent, the democratic leader seeks to participate in the process of influencing. Sometimes formal votes are taken in larger groups or assemblies; in smaller groups, the leader or leaders gauge the group's reaction through dialogue and nonverbal cues. The democratic leader leads by developing a consensus rather than telling people what to do or think.

democratic leader
One who leads by developing a consensus among group members; a leader who asks for input and then uses that input when leading and making decisions.

Laissez-Faire Leadership The **laissez-faire leader** takes a hands-off, laid-back approach to influencing. This type of leader shies away from actively influencing the group. He or she influences only when pushed to lead. Like the authoritarian leader, this type of leader often does not adapt to the needs of the group. A laissez-faire approach is easiest to spot when an elected or appointed leader simply won't lead. Laissez-faire leaders may adopt a hands-off approach because they fear making a mistake, or they just want to be liked and don't want to ruffle anyone's feathers. Sometimes, a laissez-faire approach may fit the group's needs. But as the slogan goes, "Not to decide is to decide." The laissez-faire leader influences the group by his or her silence or inactivity. The team may have a problem to unravel, but the laissez-faire leader leaves the task entirely to rest on the shoulders of the group members.

laissez-faire leader
One who fails to lead or who leads or exerts influence only when asked or directed by the group.

Which leadership style works best? As we discuss next, it depends on the situation. It also depends on the leader and the group members. One study found that a democratic, collaborative leadership style works best when the leader is perceived as credible and charismatic.[70] And as we'll see, a more directive, authoritarian style of leadership is generally more effective when group members doubt they can effectively accomplish the work and value direct assistance and guidance. Remember that leadership in groups and teams is usually shared by several people. Even when someone has been appointed or elected to be "the leader," leadership roles are often assumed by several group members.

Situational Approach

situational approach to leadership
A view of leadership as an interactive process in which a leader gauges how to lead based on such factors as the quality of the relationships among group members, the power of the leader, the nature of the task, and the maturity of the group.

The **situational approach to leadership** views leadership as an interactive process in which such factors as culture, time limitations, group member personalities, and the work the group needs to do determine a particular style of leadership. The situational leadership approach is based on Principle Five: appropriately adapt messages to others. An effective leader adapts his or her style to fit the needs of the group and the task at hand. Sometimes a group needs a strong, authoritarian leader to make decisions quickly so that it can achieve its goal. Although most groups prefer a democratic leadership style, during times of crisis a group needs a decisive leader who can help manage uncertainty and provide appropriate structure. An authoritarian style may be acceptable then.[71]

Groups with highly structured goals and a high level of stress may also operate best with a more authoritarian leadership style. For example, firefighters who are battling a

SOCIAL MEDIA & COMMUNICATION

Do We Still Need Face-to-Face Meetings?

The COVID-19 pandemic drove most meetings online with participants having to quickly learn how to use Zoom and Microsoft Teams.

The journal *Nature* carried out a poll of 900 readers about continuing with online meetings after the pandemic. The consensus was that meetings and presentations should continue to be online, at least until the end of the pandemic, with the principle reason being the ease of attendance. However, it was recognized that virtual meetings are no substitute for real-life networking with colleagues. Two major concerns were "screen-time fatigue" because participants had to be in a constant state of alert throughout the meeting, and issues related to time-zone differences and meeting schedules.[72]

Conference and meeting organizers were working on improvements to meetings well before the pandemic. In 2019, the Conference on Cognitive Computational Neuroscience in Berlin premiered a "mind-matching" session. Participants submitted three abstracts of their work and an algorithm was used to match them to six other participants, allowing them to have 15-minute online conversations. It was a first attempt at replicating face-to-face networking. Participants found it invaluable, with some being matched with those who were working on almost identical problems and carrying out similar research.[73]

According to research papers published by the Harvard Business Review, virtual meetings have three major advantages over face-to-face meetings: better polling, restructured off-site events, and improved brainstorming. Better polling means that software can be used to instantly total votes for and against as well as abstentions or "not sure" votes when a decision is being made. Restructured off-site events refer to annual "get-togethers" at a single site involving individuals from many locations that are working for a global business. Virtual meetings allow regional events to be launched, cutting down on costs and travel time, and these are then networked online to connect with similar regional events. The improved brainstorming means virtual break-out rooms to discuss situations and find solutions. Carefully appointed leaders are assigned to each room, and each virtual room has a good balance of participants. In an example cited in the research, a CEO had nine potential areas to grow the business.[74]

A blog post on the *British Medical Journal* suggested a compromise between virtual and real meetings and conferences. It put forward the notion that there might be fewer conferences in the future, but they would be better and more productive. They would be held for the right reasons, and not just because having conferences was the thing to do.[75]

However, according to the International Congress and Convention Association (ICCA), the appetite for live meetings has not really diminished as many organizations are not satisfied with virtual meetings.[76] Online meetings can make it difficult to pick up on posture, gestures, tones, eye contact, and other factors. Nonverbal messages are hard to spot during online meetings and some reports suggest that 90 percent of communication is nonverbal. Such meetings may continue to be an essential part of the future but it can be argued that it is only in the face-to-face meetings that full communication and understanding can be achieved.[77]

---

house fire with a family of five inside have a clearly structured goal: to save lives. In this situation, the group needs decisive authoritarian leadership. In contrast, if the group's task is to solve a problem or make a decision collaboratively, the group will likely benefit from a democratic leadership style. If a group's goal is primarily social or creative, a laissez-faire leader may be best. Compared to the firefighters, for example, a book club that is trying to select its next reading selection has less structured goals (there are many possible options) and a less stressful situation (there is no fire!). This less structured and less stressful task calls for a more participative democratic style of leadership or a hands-off, laissez-faire style of leadership. So according to the situational approach, the answer to the question "What's the best leadership style?" is "It depends."[78]

The readiness of the group also plays a major role in which leadership style would work best.[79] *Readiness* refers to a group member's ability to assume responsibility to accomplish a task; his or her overall knowledge, background, and experience; and his or her general level of motivation. Leadership experts Paul Hersey and Ken Blanchard suggest that a directive or more authoritative "telling" style of leadership seems to work best when groups have a low level of readiness. In comparison, a group with a high degree of readiness would likely function better with a more delegating style of leadership. An exceptionally ready or mature group may need minimal direction—more of a laissez-faire leadership style. Wise leaders also consider the cultural backgrounds of

DIVERSITY & COMMUNICATION

Deep and Surface Diversity: Which Differences Make a Difference?

People work in groups because "two heads are better than one." More people bring more—and more varied—approaches to solving a problem or illuminating an issue. But are all differences created equal?

Researchers have found that some differences among group members are more significant than others.[82] **Surface-level diversity** encompasses the human differences that are easily visible to us, such as differences in ethnicity, race, age, sex, gender, and other social and observable features. **Deep-level diversity** involves differences that aren't always visible on the surface, such as differences in attitudes, opinions, values, information, cognitive structure, culture, and other factors that take time to become evident in groups.[83] Groups that identify and discuss their differences make better decisions.[84] The next time you meet with a group, keep the following suggestions in mind:

- *Be cautious of making sweeping generalizations about people who are from a culture that appears to be similar to yours.*[85]
- *Take time to explore group members' deep-level differences in perspectives and approaches.*
- *Encourage people to share ideas and information via email or text messages.*
- *Group members benefit from different perspectives.*

---

surface-level diversity
Human differences that are easily visible to us, such as differences in ethnicity, race, age, sex, gender, and other social and observable features.

deep-level diversity
Human differences that aren't always visible on the surface, such as differences in attitudes, opinions, values, information, culture, and other factors that take time to become evident in groups.

transformational approach to leadership
A view of leadership that defines a leader as one who leads by shaping the vision of the group and by developing trust through high-quality interpersonal relationships with group members.

those whom they lead. Research supports the important role of culture in influencing the style of leadership that seems to be best suited to a team.[80] Group members from collective cultures seem to appreciate more participative styles of leadership.

Depending on the situation, a leadership style may emerge naturally from a group. For example, in one-time-only groups, members may allow a more directive leadership approach. However, if a group will be together for some time and the quality of group relations is important to the functioning of the group, a more participative, democratic leadership style may be in order.[81]

Transformational Leadership

One of the newer leadership approaches to emerge is called the **transformational approach to leadership**.[86] The transformational leader influences the group or organization by *transforming* the group—giving it a new vision, energizing or realigning the group culture, or giving the group a new structure. The leader leads by helping members see all the possibilities within the group. The transformational leader also develops a relationship with those whom he or she leads.[87]

Skills of Transformational Leaders Author Peter Senge suggests that there are three fundamental skills transformational leaders have in common: the ability to (1) build a shared vision, (2) challenge existing ways of thinking, and (3) be a systems thinker—help a group or team see that everything is connected to everything else.[88] Articulating a shared, or collective, vision is an important part of what a transformational leader does. An authoritarian leader would just tell the group, "Here's your vision; now get to work." The democratic leader would ask, "What vision do you want?" The laissez-faire leader would do nothing about a vision unless asked to do something. The situational leader would say, "Let me see what type of group I'm leading and listen to group members, and then I'll share a vision."

Another skill of transformational leaders is the ability to encourage the development of new ideas. Teams that emphasize the importance of learning and being creative do a better job of both accomplishing tasks and fostering positive, supportive interpersonal relationships.[89] More often viewed as the "guide on the side" than the "sage on the stage," transformational leaders prefer to think of themselves as coaches or mentors rather than directive leaders who dictate who does what.

Effects of Transformational Leaders Research suggests that effectively functioning transformational leaders can enhance team cohesiveness and improve perceptions of team performance.[90] They achieve these benefits by linking with other groups and teams from either inside or outside the organization, helping the group span boundaries and stay connected with issues and forces that influence the group.[91] Transformational leaders are more effective when leading face to face rather than virtually because they can draw upon their personal, relational communication skills to motivate and boost the confidence of group members.[92]

Can transformational leadership skills—or any leadership skills—be taught, the way you can teach someone to drive a car? Some researchers suggest that experience is the best teacher.[93] You can study how to communicate, listen, relate, and solve problems, but having an opportunity to practice these skills in real-life settings may be the best way to develop your leadership skills. Whether you learn leadership skills and principles from a book or from the "school of life," the role of a good leader is that of a servant, helping others accomplish a goal. This ancient description of a wise leader offers considerable insight into what makes a leader great:

> The wicked leader the people despise.
> The good leader the people revere.
> Of the great leader the people say,
> "We did it ourselves."
> —Lao Tsu

RECAP

Leadership Approaches

Approach to Leadership	Guiding Principle
Trait	Leaders possess certain traits or characteristics that contribute to leadership effectiveness.
Functional	Leaders influence others through two primary functions: • Task functions, which help accomplish the work • Process functions, which help establish a positive climate
Styles	Leadership is enacted in three primary styles: • Authoritarian leaders direct and control others. • Democratic leaders solicit input from others and seek to lead by involving others in decisions. • Laissez-faire leaders intentionally influence others only when asked or directed by others to lead.
Situational	Leadership is an interactive process in which a leader adapts his or her approach based on such factors as: • The quality of group member relationships • The nature of the task • Time limitations
Transformational	A leader influences others by: • Developing a shared vision • Encouraging the development of new ideas • Using listening and relationship-building skills to create a climate of trust

Enhancing Group and Team Meetings

10.4 Develop and use strategies to structure meetings appropriately, keep meetings on track, and promote appropriate dialogue and interaction.

Humor columnist Dave Barry said, "If you had to identify, in one word, the reason why the human race has not achieved, and never will achieve, its full potential, that word would be *meetings*."[94] Meetings are an inescapable fact of life for most people and will undoubtedly be inescapable for you as well.

Why does meeting participation inspire such a negative reaction—not just from Dave Barry, but from many people? Often, it's because meeting leaders and participants have not mastered the principles we've stressed as fundamental to communication success in any context. Meetings are more productive if participants are aware of their behaviors and the behaviors of others and if they believe they have the necessary skills to make meetings effective.[95] Using and interpreting verbal and nonverbal messages are also vital skills required for meeting effectiveness, as are listening and responding to messages with sensitivity. Because of the complexity and uncertainty that arise when people collaborate, being able to adapt message content and message structure is essential.[96] We conclude this chapter by providing some tips for managing one of the most likely collaborative contexts you'll encounter: meetings.

What specific problems occur most frequently in meetings? According to a survey of meeting participants, the most common meeting "sin" is getting off the subject.[97] The second-biggest problem is not having clear goals or a meeting agenda. Meeting goers also reported that often meetings were too long, people weren't prepared, nothing really happened, meetings started late, and there were no follow-up action plans.

Meetings need two essential things to be effective: *structure* and *interaction*.[98] Sound familiar? As we noted earlier in this chapter, groups also need a balance of these two things.

Manage Meeting Structure

The essential weapon to combat disorganized, rambling meetings is a clear, well-developed **agenda**, which is a list of the key issues, ideas, and information to be discussed, in the order of discussion. How do you develop a well-crafted agenda? Consider these three steps.

agenda
A written plan for achieving the goals of a group meeting; it typically includes items for discussion, action, and information.

Step One: Determine Your Meeting Goals   Every meeting seeks to accomplish something. (If you don't have something to accomplish, don't hold a meeting!) Most meetings have one or more of the following three goals: (1) giving information, (2) discussing information, and (3) taking action.

- *Giving information.* An information-giving meeting is like a briefing or a series of short speeches. If the only task is to share information, you may not really need a meeting at all; a written memo or an email message will suffice. However, if you want to emphasize the importance of the information by sharing it with others face-to-face, then giving information is an appropriate primary meeting goal.
- *Discussing information.* An information-discussion meeting is one in which there is considerable give and take. The key to this type of meeting is not to let it become a series of long-winded speeches. If you're not careful, discussions will digress from the topic. The meeting leader or meeting participants should be aware of the goals of the discussion so that comments remain relevant.
- *Taking action.* A meeting may involve making a decision, solving a problem, or implementing a decision or solution. If the purpose of the meeting is to take action, it's helpful if group members know before they arrive for the meeting that they will be asked to take some action.

Step Two: Identify What Needs to Be Discussed to Achieve the Goal   After you have determined your goal (or goals), you need to determine how to structure the meeting to achieve that goal. What topics need to be covered? What information do you need? What issues do you need to focus on? Brainstorm answers to these questions, but don't focus on organizing the items on your agenda yet; wait until you know what you need to discuss.

Step Three: Organize the Agenda   Once you have identified your meeting goals (giving information, discussing information, taking action) and assessed what you need to talk about, take time to arrange the items on your agenda in the most effective way. Table 10.4 identifies several meeting problems and possible solutions. In addition, here are several specific strategies for organizing effective meetings:[99]

- Organize the agenda around your meeting goals. If you're meeting to solve a problem, you could use the five problem-solving steps as an agenda-setting guide: (1) Identify and define the problem, (2) analyze the problem, (3) generate creative options, (4) select the best option, and (5) take action. A single meeting may focus on only one or two of those steps; don't feel that you have to cram all five problem-solving steps into every meeting.

TABLE 10.4 Solving Meeting Agenda Problems

Potential Meeting Agenda Problem	Suggested Meeting Agenda Strategy
Meeting participants tend to spend more time on the first or second agenda item than on later items.	Make sure the early agenda items are something the group needs to spend time on.
Meeting participants want to talk, even if the meeting leader wants them to just listen.	Take advantage of the desire to participate by inviting input and discussion early in the meeting rather than trying to squelch discussion or having to deal with interruptions from group members.
Meeting participants aren't prepared. They haven't done their "homework."	Allow a few minutes for silent reading. Let members get up to speed by reviewing information or quickly looking at key pieces of data.
Meeting participants won't stick to the agenda.	Continue to remind the group of the agenda and the overall goal of the meeting. Make sure to distribute a written agenda ahead of the meeting.
There is an agenda item that may produce conflict and disagreement.	Help the group develop a sense of success by putting one or more noncontroversial items on the agenda ahead of the item that may produce conflict. Build on the group's ability to reach agreement.

- Use the subheads "Information Items," "Discussion Items," and "Action Items" as you construct your agenda to signal to group members the goal of each item, as shown in the sample meeting agenda.
- Consider putting your most important agenda item first, because what is introduced first usually takes the most time.
- There may be times when you will want to discuss your most challenging issue in the middle of the meeting. This gives the group a chance to get oriented at the beginning of the meeting and ease out of the discussion at the end.[100]
- Consider making your first agenda item something that will immediately involve all meeting participants in active discussion. If you start with routine reports (a common practice), you establish a norm of passivity, and boredom is the usual result.
- If you are going to discuss a conflict-producing topic, you may want that agenda item to follow an issue on which you think the group will reach agreement. Groups may be more likely to reach agreement on a contentious issue if they have already reached agreement on another point.
- Start the meeting by asking participants whether they have any other agenda items to consider. That way, you aren't as likely to be surprised by people who want to add something after you've planned the meeting agenda.
- After you've prepared your agenda, estimate how long you think the group will take to discuss each agenda item. Most groups take more time than you would expect to talk about issues and ideas.

Refer to the sample meeting agenda provided. Notice that this meeting has clear goals and that many of the agenda items are phrased as questions. Questions give an agenda focus and help to manage discussion.

Sample Meeting Agenda

Meeting Goals:

1. Discuss new product proposal: evaluate the pros and cons.
2. Decide whether to implement the personnel policy and mentor program.
3. Receive updates from committees.

   I. Discussion Items

   A. How should we revise today's agenda?

   B. Personnel policy: What new issues or problems have you identified about the new personnel policy?

   C. New product team proposal (distributed earlier by email): What are the pros and cons of the proposal?

   II. Action Items

   A. Should we approve the new compensation policy (distributed by email)?

   B. Should we implement the new mentor program? If so, what should the program policies be?

   III. Information Items

   A. New employee orientation report

   B. Planning committee report

   C. Finance committee report

   D. Announcements

When your job is to lead the meeting, you have several specific tasks to perform, including the following:

1. Call the group together; find out when is the best time to meet (finding time is often a major problem for busy people).
2. Develop an agenda, using the steps already described.
3. Determine whether there is a **quorum**—the minimum number of people who must be present at a meeting to conduct business.
4. Call the meeting to order.
5. Keep notes (or delegate note-taking). Use a flipchart, dry-erase board, or an interactive whiteboard to make notes visible to members during the meeting. Such written meeting notes become the "group mind" and help everyone stay on track.
6. Decide when to take a vote.
7. Prepare meeting minutes or a final report, or delegate the task to another group member.

quorum
The minimum number of people who must be present at a meeting to conduct business.

Manage Meeting Interaction

Interaction, as you recall, is the back-and-forth dialogue and discussion in which participants engage during meetings. Without interaction, meetings would be like a monologue, a speech, or a seminar rather than a lively discussion. It's important for people in a meeting to be involved in the discussion and share information with one another.[102] Research has found that meetings that have more equal participation generally are more effective than meetings dominated by a few people.[103] But too much unfocused interaction can result in a disorganized, chaotic discussion. To keep a meeting on track, meeting leaders and participants need to practice their facilitation skills. The most important facilitation skills include being a gatekeeper, using metadiscussion, monitoring discussion time, and structuring discussion techniques to keep the meeting focused.

Use Gatekeeping Skills   A gatekeeper encourages less-talkative members to participate and tries to limit long-winded contributions by other group members. Gatekeepers

CRITICAL/CULTURAL PERSPECTIVES & COMMUNICATION

Who Controls the Agenda?

A good meeting always has a clear agenda—*always*. But who determines what's on the agenda? Wise leaders don't just dictate what will be on the agenda, but invite all members of the group to contribute questions and issues. There are times when the meeting leader is expected to set the agenda and determine the focus of the meeting, yet input from other group members should also be included. There is evidence that dominant leaders often aren't aware of their own position of power.[101] One way to assess who holds the most power and thereby controls the meeting is to consider these questions:

- Are others invited to contribute to the agenda prior to the meeting?
- Are there opportunities during the meeting to suggest modifications to the agenda?
- Who has the final say as to what is included on the agenda?

A good meeting should stick to the agenda. But a good meeting also invites participation to maximize interaction. Of course, there are exceptions. For example, meeting cultures at some corporations, or within the government or the military, may have different rules regarding who sets the agenda. Nonetheless, a meeting with too much structure—a prescribed, dictated agenda without input from others—can reduce the effectiveness of group and team deliberation.

need to be good listeners so they can help manage the flow of conversation. Gatekeepers make such comments as:

> "Ashley, we haven't heard your ideas yet. Won't you share your thoughts with us?"
>
> or
>
> "Mateo, thanks for sharing, but I'd like to hear what others have to say."

Polite, tactful invitations to talk or limit talk usually work. As we noted earlier in this chapter, you may need to speak privately with chronic oververbalizers to let them know that you would appreciate a more balanced discussion.

Use Metadiscussion **Metadiscussion** literally means "discussion about discussion."[104] It's a comment about the discussion process rather than about the topic under consideration. Metadiscussional statements include "I'm not following this conversation. What is our goal?" "Can someone summarize what we've accomplished so far?" and "Peggy, I'm not sure I understand how your observation relates to our meeting goal." These comments contain information and advice about the communication process rather than about the issues being discussed.

Metadiscussional phrases are helpful ways to keep the team or group focused on the task. Obviously, metadiscussional statements should not be phrased to personally attack others. Don't just blurt out "You're off task" or "Oh, let's not talk about that anymore." Instead, use tactful ways of letting other group members know you'd like to return to the issues at hand. Use "I" messages rather than "you" messages to bring the group back on track. An **"I" message** begins with the word *I*, such as "I am not sure where we are in our discussion" or "I am lost here." A **"you" message** is a way of phrasing a message that makes others feel defensive—for example, "You're not following the agenda" or "Your point doesn't make any sense." Another way to express these same ideas, but with less of a negative edge, is to use "I" messages such as "I'm not sure where we are on the agenda" or "I'm not sure I understand how your point relates to the issue we are discussing." The ability to use the metadiscussion technique is an exceptionally powerful skill because you can offer metadiscussional statements even if you are not the appointed leader.

Monitor Time Being sensitive to the time the group is spending on an issue is yet another skill that is necessary to manage meeting interaction. Think of your agenda as a map, helping you plan where you want to go. Think of the clock as your gas gauge, telling you the amount of fuel you have to get where you want to go. In a meeting, keeping one eye on the clock and one eye on the agenda is analogous to focusing on the map and the gas gauge on a car trip. If you are running low on fuel (time), you will need to either get more gas (budget more time) or recognize that you will not get where you want to go. Begin each meeting by asking how long members can meet. If you have two or three crucial agenda items and one-third of your group has to leave in an hour, you may need to reshuffle your agenda to make sure that you can achieve your goals.

Use Structure to Manage Interaction Another way to manage interaction is to use some of the prescriptive structures we talked about earlier. For example, silent brainstorming is a way to gain maximum participation from everyone. Yet another strategy is to ask people to come to the meeting with written responses to questions you posed in the agenda, which group members received in advance of the meeting. This signals that you want people to prepare for the meeting beforehand rather than doing their "homework" at the meeting.

An essential task of the meeting facilitator is to orchestrate meaningful interaction during the meeting so that all group or team members have the opportunity to share. Another structured method of inviting involvement is to have group members first write down their ideas individually and then share them with the group. Having

metadiscussion
Discussion about the discussion process; comments that help the group remain focused on the goals of the group or that point out how the group is doing its work.

"I" message
A message in which you state your perspective or point of view.

"you" message
A message that is likely to create defensiveness in others because it emphasizes how another person has created a problem rather than describing the problem from one's own perspective ("I" message).

RECAP

Strategies for Effective Meetings: Balance Structure and Interaction

How to Give a Meeting Structure

Prepare an effective agenda by

- Determining your meeting goals.
- Identifying what needs to be discussed to achieve the goals.
- Organizing the agenda to achieve the goals.

How to Ensure Managed Interaction

Keep discussion on track by

- Using effective gatekeeping skills.
- Using metadiscussion to help the group focus on the goals.
- Helping the group be sensitive to elapsed time and time remaining for deliberation.
- Using strategies to manage interaction (for example, writing before speaking or silent brainstorming).

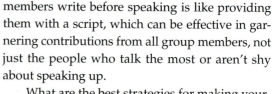

members write before speaking is like providing them with a script, which can be effective in garnering contributions from all group members, not just the people who talk the most or aren't shy about speaking up.

What are the best strategies for making yourself a valuable meeting leader or participant? The five Communication Principles for a Lifetime that we emphasize throughout the text will serve you well. In general, be aware of your own behavior and the behavior of others. Monitor your verbal and nonverbal messages to make sure that you are making comments relevant to the task at hand, but also be sensitive to the needs of the people in your group. You develop that sensitivity by listening to others and responding thoughtfully. Ineffective meeting participants make little effort to link their comments to what others are saying. They also don't adapt to the messages of others. Effective communicators adapt what they say and do to help achieve the goals of the group. There is evidence that putting these principles into practice will enhance group and team performance.[105]

Assessing Group and Team Problem-Solving Competencies[106]

Use the following evaluation form to assess the presence or absence of small group communication competencies in a group or team discussion. *Competencies* are specific behaviors that group and team members perform. The assessment form includes nine competencies organized into four general categories. Here's how to use the form:

1. Observe a group or team that is attempting to solve a problem. Write the names of the group members at the top of the form. (If the group includes more than five members, photocopy the form so that each group member can be evaluated.)

2. When using the form, first decide whether each group member has performed each competency. Circle NO if the group member was not observed performing the competency. Circle YES if you did observe the group member performing the competency (for example, defining the problem, analyzing the problem, or identifying criteria).

3. For each competency for which you circled YES, determine how effectively the competency was performed. Use a scale from 0 to 3:

   0 = The group member performed this competency but did so inappropriately or inadequately. For example, the person observed tried to define the problem but did so poorly.
   1 = Overall, the person's performance of this competency was adequate.
   2 = The person performed this competency twice.
   3 = The person performed this competency three or more times.

4. Total the score for each group member in each of the following four categories.

   Problem-oriented competencies consist of items 1 and 2. These are behaviors that help the group or team define and analyze the problem. If a group member performed these competencies, his or her point total for this category would range from 0 to 6. The more points the person scores, the better he or she performed this competency.

   Solution-oriented competencies include items 3, 4, and 5; the point total for this category ranges from 0 to 9. These competencies focus on how well the group or team member helped to develop and evaluate a solution to the problem.

   Discussion management competencies include items 6 and 7. These competencies help the group or team remain focused and manage interactions. The point total for this category ranges from 0 to 6.

   Relational competencies are behaviors that focus on dealing with conflict and developing a positive, supportive group climate. Items 8 and 9 reflect this competency; the point total for this category ranges from 0 to 6.

5. You can also assess the group's or team's overall ability to perform these competencies. The column marked "Group Assessment" can be used to record your overall impressions of how effectively the group or team behaved. Circle NO if no one in the group performed a particular competency. Circle YES if at least one person in the group or team performed this competency. Then evaluate how well the entire group performed this competency, using the scale already described.

Sometimes it is difficult to make so many judgments about group competencies by just viewing a group discussion once. Many people find that it's easier to make a video recording of the group discussion so that they can observe it more than once.

Competent Group Communicator

Problem-Solving Group Communication Competencies	Group Member A	Group Member B
COMPETENCIES		
Problem-Oriented Competencies		

1. Defined the problem the group attempted to solve	NO YES
	       0 1 2 3
		NO YES
		       0 1 2 3

2. Analyzed the problem the group attempted to solve. Used relevant information, data, or evidence; discussed the causes, obstacles, history, symptoms, or significance of the problem.	NO YES
	       0 1 2 3
		NO YES
		       0 1 2 3

Solution-Oriented Competencies		

3. Identified criteria for an appropriate solution to the problem	NO YES
	       0 1 2 3
		NO YES
		       0 1 2 3

4. Generated solutions or alternatives to the problem	NO YES
	       0 1 2 3
		NO YES
		       0 1 2 3

5. Evaluated solution(s): Identified positive or negative consequences of the proposed solutions	NO YES
	       0 1 2 3
		NO YES
		       0 1 2 3

Discussion Management Competencies		

6. Maintained task focus: Helped the group stay on, or return to, the task, issue, or topic the group was discussing	NO YES
	       0 1 2 3
		NO YES
		       0 1 2 3

7. Managed group interaction: Appropriately initiated and terminated discussion, contributed to the discussion, or invited others to contribute to the discussion. Didn't dominate or withdraw.	NO YES
	       0 1 2 3
		NO YES
		       0 1 2 3

Relational Competencies		

8. Managed conflict: Appropriately and constructively helped the group stay focused on issues rather than personalities when conflict occurred	NO YES
	       0 1 2 3
		NO YES
		       0 1 2 3

9. Maintained climate: Offered positive verbal comments or nonverbal expressions that helped maintain a positive group climate	NO YES
	       0 1 2 3
		NO YES
		       0 1 2 3

Scoring		

NO = Not observed

YES

0 = Overall inappropriate or inadequate performance of competency

1 = Overall adequate performance of competency

2 = Person performed this competency twice

3 = Person performed this competency three or more times

Group Member C		Group Member D		Group Member E		Group Assessment	
NO	YES 0 1 2 3	NO	YES 0 1 2 3	NO	YES 0 1 2 3	NO	YES 0 1 2 3
NO	YES 0 1 2 3	NO	YES 0 1 2 3	NO	YES 0 1 2 3	NO	YES 0 1 2 3
NO	YES 0 1 2 3	NO	YES 0 1 2 3	NO	YES 0 1 2 3	NO	YES 0 1 2 3
NO	YES 0 1 2 3	NO	YES 0 1 2 3	NO	YES 0 1 2 3	NO	YES 0 1 2 3
NO	YES 0 1 2 3	NO	YES 0 1 2 3	NO	YES 0 1 2 3	NO	YES 0 1 2 3
NO	YES 0 1 2 3	NO	YES 0 1 2 3	NO	YES 0 1 2 3	NO	YES 0 1 2 3
NO	YES 0 1 2 3	NO	YES 0 1 2 3	NO	YES 0 1 2 3	NO	YES 0 1 2 3
NO	YES 0 1 2 3	NO	YES 0 1 2 3	NO	YES 0 1 2 3	NO	YES 0 1 2 3
NO	YES 0 1 2 3	NO	YES 0 1 2 3	NO	YES 0 1 2 3	NO	YES 0 1 2 3

Problem-Oriented Competencies (0–6)

Solution-Oriented Competencies (0–9)

Discussion Management Competencies (0–6)

Relational Competencies (0–6)

STUDY GUIDE: PRINCIPLES FOR A LIFETIME

CHAPTER 10

What Effective Group and Team Members Do

10.1 Identify six functions that effective group members perform.

PRINCIPLE POINTS: Effective group members identify a clear, elevating goal; develop a results-driven structure; gather and share appropriate information; develop options; evaluate ideas; and are sensitive to group social and relationship concerns.

PRINCIPLE TERM:

results-driven structure

PRINCIPLE SKILLS:

1. After reviewing the list of disadvantages of working in groups, identify specific strategies you could use to avoid having these disadvantages occur in your group.
2. Which of the six functions of effective group members do you usually perform? Select a group function that you usually don't perform and then identify ways you could serve this function during your next group meeting.

Structuring Group and Team Problem Solving

10.2 List and describe the five steps of group problem solving (reflective thinking).

PRINCIPLE POINTS: Although there is no single series of steps that will ensure high performance, the following five steps can help groups organize the problem-solving process: (1) Identify and define the problem, (2) analyze the problem, (3) generate creative solutions, (4) select the best solution, and (5) take action.

PRINCIPLE TERMS:

structure	creativity
interaction	brainstorming
reflective thinking	silent brainstorming
criteria	nominal group technique
force field analysis technique	consensus
	groupthink

PRINCIPLE SKILLS:

1. Reflect on your last group or team meeting. Overall, would the group or team have benefited from having more structure (such as a clear agenda) or more interaction (such as participation from every group member)? What could you do to enhance either group structure or group interaction?
2. Assess which of the five problem-solving steps are the easiest for you and your group to perform. Which of the five steps are the most challenging for you and your group? Identify strategies for increasing your ability to implement one or more of the five problem-solving steps during your next group problem-solving discussion.

Enhancing Group and Team Leadership

10.3 Compare and contrast the trait, functional, styles, situational, and transformational approaches to understanding leadership.

PRINCIPLE POINTS: High-performing groups have competent group leaders. Researchers have devised several approaches to analyzing leadership. The trait approach to leadership seeks to identify certain characteristics or traits that all leaders possess. The functional approach to leadership suggests that leaders need to be concerned with both task functions and group process functions. A third approach to understanding leadership, the styles approach, identifies leaders as authoritarian, democratic, or laissez-faire. No one style seems to work best all the time. The situational leadership approach suggests that the best leadership style depends on a variety of factors, including the readiness of the group, group members' cultures, the urgency of the problem, and the type of issue the group is discussing. Finally, transformational leadership is an approach that encourages leaders to help shape the group's vision and goals.

PRINCIPLE TERMS:

leadership	democratic leader
trait approach to leadership	laissez-faire leader
functional approach to leadership	situational approach to leadership
task function	surface-level diversity
process function	deep-level diversity
styles approach to leadership	transformational approach to leadership
authoritarian leader	

PRINCIPLE SKILLS:

1. What are strategies group members could use to work more effectively if a group leader is using an authoritarian style of leadership and the group would prefer a more participative, democratic leadership style?

2. Reflect upon the last time you exerted some leadership influence in a group. What was your predominant leadership style? How effective was your leadership?

Enhancing Group and Team Meetings

10.4 Develop and use strategies to structure meetings appropriately, keep meetings on track, and promote appropriate dialogue and interaction.

PRINCIPLE POINTS: An effective meeting needs a balance of structure and interaction. Groups maintain appropriate structure if meeting planners develop and use an agenda to keep the discussion focused and on track. Meetings also need appropriate amounts of dialogue and discussion. Effective meeting participants monitor the amount of participation from other group or team members and serve as gatekeepers to ensure that ververbalizers don't monopolize the discussion and quiet members don't feel intimidated.

PRINCIPLE TERMS:

agenda "I" message
quorum "you" message
metadiscussion

PRINCIPLE SKILLS: Using the suggestions and examples presented in this chapter, draft a brief agenda for an upcoming meeting of a group you're in.

UNIT IV   PUBLIC SPEAKING

CHAPTER 11

DEVELOPING YOUR SPEECH

Freedom of speech is of no use to a man who has nothing to say. —FRANKLIN D. ROOSEVELT

SDI Productions/E+/Getty Images

CHAPTER OUTLINE

- Overviewing the Public Speaking Process
- Building Your Confidence
- Selecting and Narrowing Your Topic
- Identifying Your Purpose
- Developing Your Central Idea
- Generating Main Ideas
- Gathering Supporting Material
- Study Guide: *Principles for a Lifetime*

LEARNING OBJECTIVES

11.1 List and explain the components of the audience-centered public speaking model.

11.2 Apply specific strategies for becoming a more confident speaker.

11.3 Select and narrow a speech topic that is appropriate to the audience, the occasion, and yourself.

11.4 Write an audience-centered, specific-purpose statement for a speech.

11.5 Develop a central idea for a speech.

11.6 Generate main ideas from a central idea.

11.7 Describe five potential sources and seven types of supporting material for a speech, and use each type effectively.

A good friend of ours who lived in Hong Kong for several years once remarked that she found traveling back to the United States exhausting. Her reason? It was not so much the long plane trip or the thirteen-hour time difference, but, as she explained, "When I begin to hear airport public announcements in English instead of Cantonese, I suddenly feel compelled to pay attention to every word. All that listening wears me out!"

Few of us can take for granted that others will listen to us merely because we are speaking their native language. However, when we study the public speaking process and learn its component skills and principles, we increase the likelihood that others will listen to us out of genuine, compelling interest.

Far from being a rare talent possessed only by an inspired few, the skill of **public speaking** is a teachable, learnable process of developing, supporting, organizing, and orally presenting ideas. The skills you will develop as you learn and practice this process will be of practical use in the future. They will give you an edge in other college courses that require oral presentations. They may help you convince a current or future boss that you deserve a raise. They may even land you a job.

Let's begin our discussion with an overview of the public speaking process. Then we will offer suggestions for building your confidence as a public speaker before focusing specifically on the first five stages of the public speaking process—discovering and narrowing your topic, identifying your purpose, developing a central idea, generating main ideas, and gathering supporting material for your speech—all firmly grounded in the five communication principles.

public speaking
A teachable, learnable process of developing, supporting, organizing, and orally presenting ideas.

CRITICAL/CULTURAL PERSPECTIVES & COMMUNICATION

Using Public Advocacy to Address Positions of Power

Using public speaking skills to influence decision makers in legal, social, political, environmental, and/or cultural social structures is known as *public advocacy*. Public advocates promote change, educate the public, and form networks to effect change. In addition, public advocates provide a voice for those who need their own voices augmented to overcome barriers and address issues of power.

An example of a public advocacy group in the United States is the National Court Appointed Special Advocate (CASA)/Guardian ad Litem (GAL) Association for Children. Trained CASA and GAL volunteers advocate for children by working with legal and child welfare professionals, educators, and service providers to ensure that judges have all the information they need to make the most well-informed decisions for each child.[1]

FIGURE 11.1 An Audience-Centered Model of the Public Speaking Process

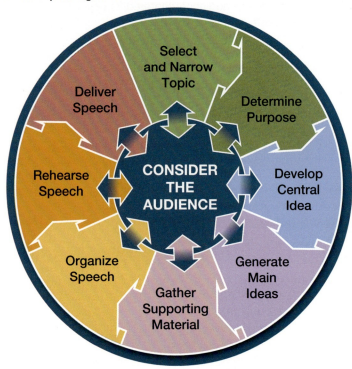

Overviewing the Public Speaking Process

11.1 List and explain the components of the audience-centered public speaking model.

You don't have to read an entire book on public speaking before you give your first speech. An overview of the public speaking process can help you with your early assignments even if you have to speak before you have a chance to read Chapters 11 through 15. Figure 11.1 illustrates the public speaking process. At the center of the model is "Consider the audience." Double arrows connect this center with every other stage, illustrating that at any point, you may revise your ideas or strategies as you learn more about your audience. Your audience influences every decision you make.

Audience-centered public speakers are inherently sensitive to the diversity of their audiences. While guarding against generalizations that might be offensive, they acknowledge that cultural, ethnic, and other traditions affect the way people process messages. They apply the fundamental principle of appropriately adapting their messages to others. How? They might choose to use pictures to help them communicate. They might select topics and use illustrations with universal themes such as family and friendship. They might adjust the formality of their delivery and even their clothing to whatever is expected by the majority of the audience members. The fundamental communication principle of adapting to the audience is central to the success of any speech.

Now view the model as a clock, with "Select and narrow topic" at 12 o'clock. From this stage, the process proceeds clockwise in the direction of the arrows, to "Deliver speech." Each stage is one of the tasks of the public speaker:

1. Select and narrow topic.
2. Determine purpose.
3. Develop central idea.
4. Generate main ideas.
5. Gather supporting material.
6. Organize speech.
7. Rehearse speech.
8. Deliver speech.

audience-centered public speaker
Someone who considers and adapts to the audience at every stage of the public speaking process.

DEVELOPING YOUR SPEECH STEP BY STEP

Considering Your Audience

A well-known Chinese proverb says that a journey of a thousand miles begins with a single step. Developing and delivering a speech may seem like a daunting journey. But if you take it one step at a time and keep your focus on your audience, you'll be rewarded with a well-crafted and well-delivered message.

To help you understand how the audience-centered speaking process unfolds, this Developing Your Speech Step by Step feature will provide a window through which you can see how one student prepared and delivered a speech. Dezerae Reyes, an undergraduate student at Texas State University, developed the persuasive speech entitled "The Health Risks of Soft Drinks" that is outlined in Chapter 12.[2] In the pages ahead, we'll walk through the process Dezerae used to develop her speech.

Even before selecting her speech topic, Dezerae thinks about her audience. Because her listeners will include her university classmates and instructor, she knows that she can discuss complex issues, using a fairly advanced vocabulary. Her challenge is to find a topic that will interest her fellow students as well as her instructor.

Building Your Confidence

11.2 Apply specific strategies for becoming a more confident speaker.

The previous overview of the stages of the public speaking process should help you understand how to prepare for your first speaking assignment, but if you still feel nervous at the prospect, you are definitely not alone.[3] One study found that more than 80 percent of us feel anxious when we speak to an audience.[4] Other surveys have discovered that the fear of public speaking is more common than the fear of death![5]

If you are taking a communication class online, you might think you will experience less **public speaking anxiety** than you would if you were speaking to a live audience. But recent research suggests that in fact slightly *more* students report feeling anxious about web-based speech delivery than the number who report anxiety about face-to-face delivery.[6]

What additional factors cause us to feel anxious about speaking in public? Figure 11.2 summarizes the results of studies that have explored the answers to this question.[7]

Fortunately, regardless of the reasons you may feel nervous about speaking in public, you can learn strategies to help you build your confidence. Figure 11.3 outlines these strategies, which are also explained in detail in the following paragraphs.

public speaking anxiety
Also known as stage fright or speaker anxiety; anxiety about speaking in public that is manifested in physiological symptoms such as rapid heartbeat, butterflies in the stomach, shaking knees and hands, quivering voice, and increased perspiration.

FIGURE 11.2 Some Reasons We May Feel Anxious about Speaking in Public

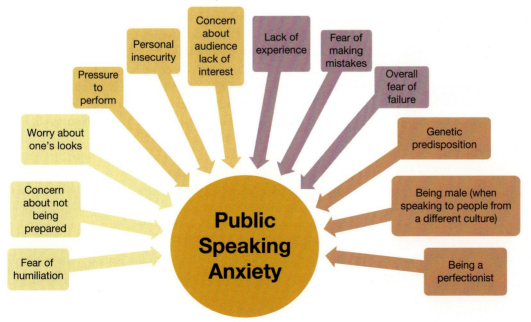

FIGURE 11.3 Building Your Confidence

- Understand public speaking anxiety.
- Know how to develop a speech.
- Be prepared.
- Give yourself a mental pep talk.
- Use deep-breathing techniques.

Building Your Confidence

- Focus on your audience.
- Focus on your message.
- Take advantage of opportunities to speak.
- Explore additional resources.

▲ Actor Samuel L. Jackson has admitted experiencing public speaking anxiety. We all need to take positive steps to control anxiety before a performance. Jim Smeal/BEI/Shutterstock

illusion of transparency
The mistaken belief that the physical manifestations of a speaker's nervousness are apparent to an audience.

Understand Public Speaking Anxiety

Regardless of why you may feel anxious, the physical symptoms of public speaking anxiety result from your brain signaling your body to help with a challenging task. Your body responds by increasing your breathing rate and blood flow and by pumping more adrenaline, which in turn results in the all-too-familiar symptoms of a rapid heartbeat, butterflies in the stomach, shaking knees and hands, quivering voice, and increased perspiration.[8]

Although these symptoms may annoy and worry you, the increased oxygen, blood flow, and adrenaline that cause you to feel uncomfortable can actually be helpful. Due to these biological changes, your brain thinks faster and more clearly, and you may speak with heightened enthusiasm. Overall, your state of increased physical readiness can help you speak better.[9]

Keep in mind, too, that most speakers *feel* more nervous than they *look*. Although the adage "Never let 'em see you sweat" suggests that our increased perspiration, along with our shaking hands and knocking knees, is likely to be visible to our audience, rarely is that true. Communication researchers call this mistaken belief the **illusion of transparency** and have found that simply informing speakers that their nervousness is not as apparent as they think can improve the quality of their speeches.[10]

Know How to Develop a Speech

Communication researchers have found that instruction in public speaking decreases students' perception of their own public speaking anxiety.[11] By reading the first part of this chapter, you have already taken this first step toward managing your anxiety: learning about the public speaking process. Just knowing what you need to do to develop an effective speech can boost your confidence in being able to do it.

Be Prepared

Being well prepared will decrease your public speaking anxiety. Communication researchers have found that one way for speakers to manage anxiety is to follow the recommended steps for preparing a speech, which include developing a logical and clear outline.[12] Being prepared also involves discovering an appropriate topic and researching that topic thoroughly. Perhaps most importantly, it includes rehearsing your speech. Research suggests that people who spend more time rehearsing experience less public speaking anxiety than those who rehearse less.[13]

When you rehearse your speech, imagine that you are giving it to the audience you will actually address. Stand up. Speak aloud rather than rehearsing silently. If you cannot rehearse in the room where you will deliver the speech, at least imagine that room. If you will be either recording your speech or delivering it live on Zoom or another video conferencing platform, practice it—and later deliver it—in a professional setting rather than a kitchen or bedroom.[14] Thorough preparation that includes realistic rehearsal will increase your confidence when it is time to deliver your speech.

Give Yourself a Mental Pep Talk

Researchers have suggested that "prespeaking exercises" may be the most effective antidotes for anxiety both before and during a speech.[15] Rather than allowing yourself to dwell on how nervous you are, give yourself a mental pep talk before getting up to speak: "I know I can give this speech. I have prepared and practiced, and I'm going to do a great job." A recent study found that speakers who recast their anxiety as excitement by stating, "I am excited" actually *felt* more excited and were perceived by their listeners as more confident than speakers who tried to tell themselves, "I am calm."[16]

Use Deep-Breathing Techniques

Two physical symptoms of nervousness are shallow breathing and rapid heart rate. To counter these symptoms, draw on the breathing techniques employed by practitioners of yoga.[17] Take a few slow, deep breaths before you get up to speak. As you slowly inhale and exhale, try to relax your entire body. These simple strategies will increase your oxygen intake and slow your heart rate, making you feel calmer and more in control.

Focus on Your Audience

Being audience centered is key to reducing public speaking anxiety. As you prepare your speech, consider the needs, goals, and interests of your audience. The more you know about your listeners and how they are likely to respond to your message, the more comfortable you will feel about delivering that message. As you rehearse your speech, visualize your audience members and imagine how they may respond; practice adapting your speech to the responses you imagine. And as you finally deliver your speech, look for positive, reinforcing feedback from audience members.[18] The more you concentrate on your audience, the less you attend to your own nervousness.

Focus on Your Message

Focusing on your message can be another anxiety-reducing strategy. Like focusing on your audience, it keeps you from thinking too much about how nervous you are. In the few minutes before you begin your speech, think about what you are going to say. Mentally review your main ideas. Silently practice your opening lines and your conclusion. Once you start speaking, maintain your focus on your message and your audience rather than on your fears.

habituation
The process of becoming more comfortable as you speak.

Take Advantage of Opportunities to Speak

As you gain public speaking experience, you will feel more in control of your nervousness. Communication researchers have found that most public speakers become progressively more comfortable as they speak, a phenomenon they call **habituation**.[19] Past successes build confidence. Your communication course will provide opportunities for frequent practice, which will increase your skill and confidence.[20]

Explore Additional Resources

For a few people, the above strategies may not be enough help. These people may still experience a level of public speaking anxiety that they consider debilitating. If you believe that you may be such a person, ask your communication instructor for additional resource

RECAP
Building Your Confidence

- Understand public speaking anxiety.
- Know how to develop a speech.
- Be prepared.
- Focus on your audience.
- Focus on your message.
- Give yourself a mental pep talk.
- Use deep-breathing techniques.
- Take advantage of opportunities to speak.
- Explore additional resources.

recommendations. For example, some college or university departments of communication have labs that teach students additional strategies to help manage counterproductive anxiety.

Selecting and Narrowing Your Topic

11.3 Select and narrow a speech topic that is appropriate to the audience, the occasion, and yourself.

Sometimes a speaker is invited or assigned to speak on a certain topic and doesn't have to think about selecting one. Other times, however, a speaker is given some guidelines—such as time limits and perhaps the general purpose for the speech—but otherwise is free to choose a topic. When that happens to you, as it almost certainly will in your communication class, your task may be made easier by exploring three questions: Who is the audience? What is the occasion? What are my interests and experiences?

Who Is the Audience?

As we have noted several times throughout this book, the principle of appropriately adapting messages to others is central to the communication process. In public speaking, that adaptation begins with topic selection. Who are the members of your audience? What interests and needs do they have in common? Why did they ask you to speak?

One professional speaker calls the answers to such questions "actionable intelligence"—information that you can use as you select your topic.[21] Your college classmates are likely to be interested in such topics as college loans and the job market. Older adults might be more interested in hearing a speaker address such topics as the cost of prescription drugs and investment tax credits. Thinking about your audience can often yield an appropriate topic.

What Is the Occasion?

You might also consider the occasion for which you are being asked to speak. A Veterans' Day address calls for such topics as patriotism and service to one's country. A university centennial address will focus on the successes in the institution's past and a vision for its future.

What Are My Interests and Experiences?

Self-awareness, another communication principle you already know, can also help you discover a topic. Exploring your own interests, attitudes, and experiences may suggest topics about which you know a great deal and feel passionate about, resulting in a speech you can deliver with energy and genuine enthusiasm. One international student selected as her topic "breaking cultural stereotyping."[22] Another student speaker's thinking about her own interests and experiences quickly produced the following list of possible topics:

- San Antonio, Texas: City of cultural diversity
- Ballet Folklórico
- Light pollution and dark skies
- What a forensic anthropologist does

Even after considering the audience, the occasion, and personal interests and experiences, you may still find yourself facing a speaking assignment for which you just cannot come up with a satisfactory topic. When that happens, you might try silent brainstorming, scanning web directories and web pages, or listening and reading for topic ideas.

Conducting Silent Brainstorming

Silent brainstorming, which was discussed in Chapter 10 as a technique used by small groups to generate creative ideas, is a useful strategy for coming up with possible topics for speeches. A silent brainstorming session of about three minutes yielded the sixteen potential topics shown in Figure 11.4.

Having generated a list of topics, you can now go back and eliminate the ones that don't have much promise or that you know you would never use. For example, you may not have any real interest in or reason for discussing SARS or MERS. However, perhaps your own experience as a COVID-19 survivor motivates you to talk about treatment with convalescent plasma. Keep the topics you like in your class notebook. You can reconsider them for future assignments.

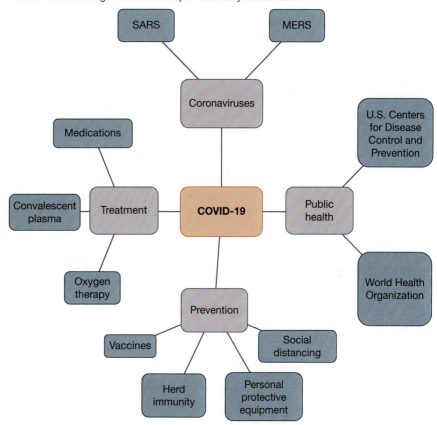

FIGURE 11.4 Brainstorming a Topic

Creating a cluster or concept map such as this one might help you visualize connections between ideas and generate more topic ideas as you brainstorm.

Scanning Web Directories and Web Pages

You know how addicting it can be to surf the web, following various categories and links out of interest and curiosity. What may seem an idle pastime can actually be a good way to discover potential speech topics. For example, a recent random search on Best of the Web (botw.org), starting with the general menu heading *Museums*, yielded the categories and possible topics illustrated in Figure 11.5.

An additional advantage of this strategy is that you now have both possible topics and potential sources for your speech.

Listening and Reading for Topic Ideas

It is not unusual to see on television or read in a news source something that triggers an idea for a speech. For example, the following list of topics was suggested by recent headlines:

- Conservative European politicians
- Likely Supreme Court nominees
- World Cup expansion
- Amazon Echo versus Google Home

You might also discover a topic in one of your courses. Perhaps you recently had an interesting discussion in your criminology class about minimum mandatory sentencing. It might make a good topic for a speech, and your criminology instructor would probably be happy to suggest additional resources.

FIGURE 11.5 Possible Topics from a Web Directory Search

DEVELOPING YOUR SPEECH STEP BY STEP

Selecting and Narrowing Your Topic

While surfing the web one afternoon, Dezerae comes across a list of "30 Health Reasons Not to Drink Soda or Diet Soda." As she scans the list, she is startled by the number and severity of health conditions with known links to soft drinks. She vows to cut down on her own consumption. As she ponders this idea, another thought goes through her mind: Maybe the health risks associated with soft drinks would make a good topic for her upcoming persuasive speech. She is personally interested and thinks her audience would be as well.

Even a subject that comes up in casual conversation with friends may make a good speech topic. Perhaps everyone in your dorm seems to be sniffling and coughing all at once. "It's sick-building syndrome," gasps one. Sick-building syndrome might be an interesting topic for a speech.

The point is to keep your eyes and ears open. You never know when you might see or hear a potential topic. When you do, write it down. Nothing is as frustrating as knowing that you had a good idea for a topic but now can't remember what it was.

Even if you discover potential topics through brainstorming, surfing the web, listening, or reading, you should still consider the communication principles of adapting to your audience and being aware of your own interests and experiences before making your final topic selection. You will also need to consider the time limits of the speaking assignment. Many good topics need to be narrowed down before they are appropriate for a given assignment. The key to narrowing your topic is sustaining your focus on your audience. One professional speaker advises,

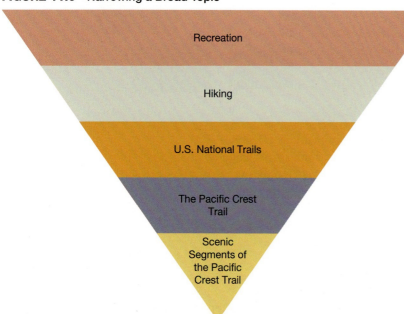

FIGURE 11.6 Narrowing a Broad Topic

> You have to research the group, look on their website, and talk to people in the group to assess what they need and want to know about a topic....[23]

With your audience's needs and expectations in mind, you might continue the process of narrowing your topic by constructing the kinds of categories created by web directories. Write your general topic at the top of a list, making each succeeding word or phrase more specific and narrow. Figure 11.6 illustrates how the broad topic *recreation* might be narrowed to a workable topic for a speech.

If you think your audience is unlikely to be interested in the Pacific Crest Trail, you can go

RECAP

Selecting and Narrowing Your Topic

- Consider the audience, the occasion, and your interests and experiences.
- Practice silent brainstorming.
- Scan web directories and web pages.
- Listen and read for topic ideas.
- Narrow your topic.

back a step and consider other U.S. national trails. For example, the Appalachian Trail may be more likely to interest your audience if they live on the East Coast of the United States.

Identifying Your Purpose

11.4 Write an audience-centered, specific-purpose statement for a speech.

Now that you have a topic in mind, you need to determine your purpose for your speech. A clear purpose can help you select main ideas, an organizational strategy, and supporting material. It can even influence how you deliver your speech. You should determine both your general purpose and your specific purpose for every speech you give.

General Purpose

Your **general purpose** is the broad reason for giving your speech: to inform, to persuade, or to entertain.

- *To inform*. When you inform, you teach. You define, describe, or explain a thing, person, place, concept, or process. Although you may use some humor in your speech or encourage your audience to seek out further information about your topic, your primary purpose for speaking is to give information.
- *To persuade*. If you are using information to try to change or reinforce your audience's ideas or convictions or to urge your audience to do something, your general purpose is persuasive. The insurance agent who tries to get you to buy life insurance, the candidate for state representative who asks for your vote, and the coordinator of Habitat for Humanity who urges your school organization to get involved in building homes all have persuasive general purposes. They may offer information, but they use it to convince you or to get you to do something. Their primary purpose is persuasive.
- *To entertain*. The speaker whose purpose is to entertain tries to get the members of his or her audience to smile, laugh, and generally enjoy themselves. For the audience members, learning something or being persuaded about something is secondary to having a good time. Most after-dinner speakers speak to entertain, as do most stand-up comedians and storytellers.

▲ The three main general purposes for public speaking are to inform, to persuade, and to entertain. Which appears to be this speaker's purpose?
Comstock/Stockbyte/Getty Images

general purpose
The broad reason for giving a speech: to inform, to persuade, or to entertain an audience.

ETHICS & COMMUNICATION

Is It Ethical to Buy a Speech?

An online "speech mill" advertises that for $13 per page, "highly qualified writers" will prepare a custom speech for you. The ad goes on to claim that the speeches are "original" and "from scratch," designed to "let you escape the whole preparation process."

Would it be ethical to use this or a similar website to prepare a speech for a class assignment? Why or why not? Are you comfortable with the site's "plagiarism-free guarantee"? Would it be ethical to buy a speech from such a site for a personal occasion, such as a great-aunt's funeral or your cousin's wedding? How do online speechwriters for hire compare, ethically, with professional speechwriters, who are regularly hired by executives and politicians?

TABLE 11.1 Examples of General and Specific Purposes

General Purposes	Specific Purposes
To inform	At the end of my speech, the audience will be able to list two benefits of learning to play a musical instrument as an adult.
To persuade	At the end of my speech, the audience will enroll in a music appreciation course.
To entertain	At the end of my speech, the audience will be laughing at my misadventures as an adult cello student.

In your speech class, the general purpose for each assignment will probably be set by your instructor. Because the general purpose influences the way you develop and organize your speech, as well as the way you deliver it, it is important to be aware of your general purpose throughout the process of developing and delivering your speech.

Specific Purpose

Knowing whether you want to inform, persuade, or entertain clarifies your general purpose for speaking. You also need to determine your specific purpose. A **specific purpose** is a concise statement indicating what you want your listeners to be able to do when you finish your speech. In other words, a specific purpose is an audience-centered behavioral goal for your speech. Table 11.1 shows examples of general and specific purposes.

A specific-purpose statement is intended not to become part of your speech, but to guide your own speech preparation. You can begin a specific-purpose statement for any speech with the words:

> At the end of my speech, the audience will . . .

Then you can specify a behavior. For example, if you are giving an informative speech on eating disorders, you might state,

> At the end of my speech, the audience will be able to explain the causes of anorexia.

If your topic is cell phone spyware and your general purpose is to persuade, you might say,

> At the end of my speech, the audience will be able to disable spyware on their cell phones.[24]

As in the examples above, the wording of your specific purpose will help you keep your audience foremost in your mind during the entire speech preparation process.

Every subsequent decision you make while preparing and delivering your speech should be guided by your specific purpose. As soon as you have formulated it, add it to the reminders on your smartphone or write it on a note card and keep it with you while you are working on your speech. Think of it as a compass pointing true north—toward your audience. Refer to it often.

specific purpose
A concise statement of what listeners should be able to do by the time the speaker finishes the speech.

RECAP

Identifying Your Purpose

General Purpose

- To inform — To define, describe, or explain a thing, person, place, concept, or process
- To persuade — To change or reinforce audience members' ideas or convictions, or to urge them to do something
- To entertain — To amuse an audience

Specific Purpose

- Specifies what you want audience members to be able to do by the end of your speech
- Guides you in developing your speech
- Uses the words "At the end of my speech, the audience will . . ."

DEVELOPING YOUR SPEECH STEP BY STEP

Identifying Your Purpose

Dezerae's assignment is to prepare and deliver a persuasive speech, so she knows that her general purpose is to persuade—to change or reinforce her audience's ideas, or to urge them to do something. She will talk about the health hazards associated with soft drinks and urge her listeners to cut down on their consumption.

Dezerae knows that her specific purpose should begin with the phrase "At the end of my speech, the audience will . . . ," so she jots down,

> At the end of my speech, the audience will know about the health hazards of soft drinks.

As Dezerae considers this draft specific purpose, she sees some problems with it. How can she determine what her audience "knows" at the end of her speech? And what, specifically, should her listeners do with the information she gives them? She edits her purpose statement to read,

> At the end of my speech, the audience will list the health hazards associated with soft drinks.

Although more specific, this version is more appropriate for an informative speech than for a persuasive one. Dezerae wants her audience to take action. Maybe a better purpose statement would be,

> At the end of my speech, the audience will consume fewer soft drinks.

Dezerae is pleased with this third version. It specifies what she wants her audience members to *do* by the end of her speech.

Developing Your Central Idea

11.5 Develop a central idea for a speech.

Your specific purpose indicates what you want your *audience* to know or do by the end of your speech, but your **central idea** makes a definitive point about your *topic*. It focuses on the content of the speech. Unlike the specific purpose, which guides your preparation but is *not* stated in your final speech, the central idea *is* stated.

central idea
A statement that makes a definitive point about your topic.

Sometimes, as in the following example, wording the central idea can be as simple as copying the part of the specific-purpose statement that specifies what the audience should be able to do.

TOPIC: World-language education

SPECIFIC PURPOSE: At the end of my speech, the audience will be able to explain two reasons world-language education should begin in the elementary grades.

CENTRAL IDEA: World-language education should begin in the elementary grades.

Figure 11.7 summarizes how the specific purpose and central idea differ.

Professional speech coach Judith Humphrey explains the importance of developing a central idea:

> Ask yourself before writing a speech . . . "What's my point?" Be able to state that message in a single clear sentence. Everything else you say will support that single argument.[25]

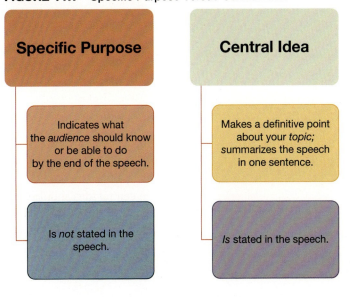

FIGURE 11.7 Specific Purpose Versus Central Idea

DEVELOPING YOUR SPEECH STEP BY STEP

Developing Your Central Idea

Dezerae knows from reading Chapter 11 of this text that her central idea should state a single audience-centered idea. She jots down,

> Why should people consume fewer soft drinks?

She thinks her first draft is not bad. It is certainly relevant to her purpose. Then she remembers that the central idea should be a *declarative* sentence, not a question. So she revises the question to read,

> People should consume fewer soft drinks.

This second draft meets all the criteria for a central idea: It is audience-centered, reflects a single idea, is a complete declarative sentence, and uses direct, specific language.

To be most useful to both speaker and listeners, the "single clear sentence" to which Humphrey refers should be an audience-centered idea, reflect a single idea, be a complete declarative sentence, and use direct, specific language.

An Audience-Centered Idea

If your specific purpose is focused on your audience, your central idea probably will be, too. It should reflect a topic in which the audience has a reason to be interested and should provide some knowledge that they do not already have or make some claim about the topic that they may not have previously considered. Consider the appropriateness of the central ideas in Figure 11.8 for an audience of students already attending college.

FIGURE 11.8 The central idea should be appropriate for the audience.

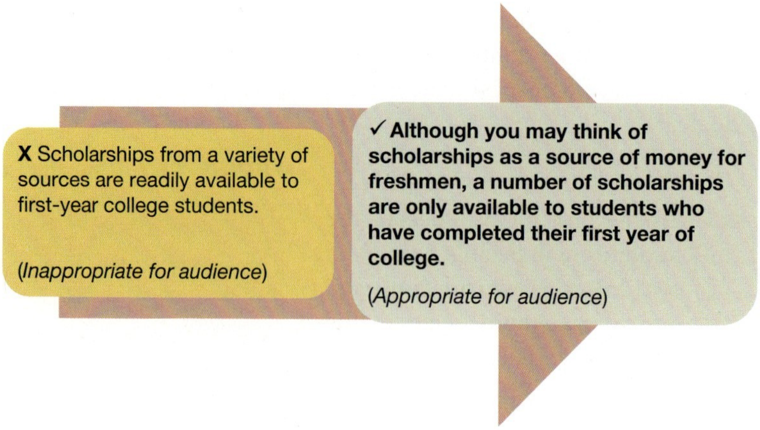

✗ Scholarships from a variety of sources are readily available to first-year college students.

(Inappropriate for audience)

✓ Although you may think of scholarships as a source of money for freshmen, a number of scholarships are only available to students who have completed their first year of college.

(Appropriate for audience)

A Single Idea

A central idea should be a single idea. Trying to cover more than one topic, even if the multiple topics are related, only muddles your speech and confuses the audience. The example in Figure 11.9 illustrates this guideline.

A Complete Declarative Sentence

Your central idea should be more than just the word or phrase that is your topic; it should also make a claim about your topic. In addition, avoid wording your central idea as a question. Questions may help you come up with a central idea, but because they don't make any kind of claim, questions themselves are not good central ideas. Figure 11.10 illustrates how a central idea should be a complete **declarative sentence**, not a topic and not a question.[26]

FIGURE 11.9 The central idea should be a single idea.

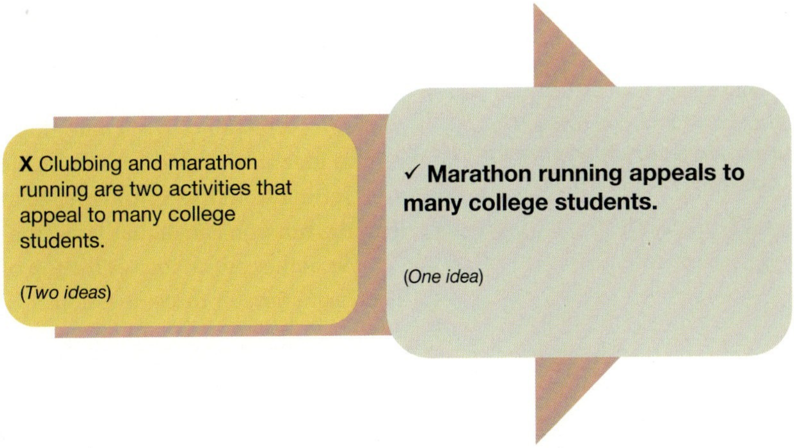

✗ Clubbing and marathon running are two activities that appeal to many college students.
(Two ideas)

✓ Marathon running appeals to many college students.
(One idea)

FIGURE 11.10 The central idea should be a complete declarative sentence.

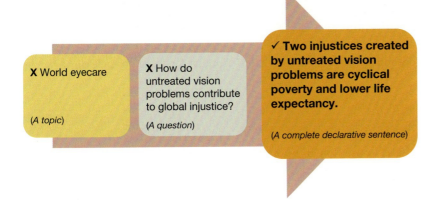

✗ World eyecare
(A topic)

✗ How do untreated vision problems contribute to global injustice?
(A question)

✓ Two injustices created by untreated vision problems are cyclical poverty and lower life expectancy.
(A complete declarative sentence)

declarative sentence
A complete sentence that makes a statement as opposed to asking a question.

Direct, Specific Language

As illustrated in Figure 11.11,[27] a good central idea uses direct, specific language rather than qualifiers and vague generalities.

FIGURE 11.11 The central idea should be worded in direct, specific language.

✗ It seems that desert fairy circles may not be what they appear to be.
(Qualified, vague language)

✓ Although long attributed to fairies, formations dotting the African Namib Desert mark the territory of termites.
(Direct, specific language)

RECAP

The Central Idea Should . . .
Be audience-centered.
Reflect a single topic.
Be a complete declarative sentence.
Use direct, specific language.

Generating Main Ideas

11.6 Generate main ideas from a central idea.

If the central idea of a speech is like the thesis statement of a paper, the **main ideas** of a speech correspond to the paragraph topics of a paper. They support or subdivide the central idea and provide more detailed points of focus for developing the speech.

Getting from the central idea to related but more specific main ideas can seem challenging, but you can actually use the central idea to generate main ideas. Here's how.

Write the central idea at the top of a sheet of paper or a word-processing document. Then ask yourself three questions:

1. Does the central idea have *logical divisions*?
2. Can I think of several *reasons* the central idea is true?
3. Can I support the central idea with a series of *steps* or a *chronological sequence*?

You should be able to answer yes to one of these questions and to write down the corresponding divisions, reasons, or steps. Let's apply this strategy to several examples.

main ideas
Subdivisions of the central idea of a speech that provide detailed points of focus for developing the speech.

Does the Central Idea Have *Logical Divisions*?

Suppose that your central idea is "Undocumented students face three obstacles to obtaining a college degree."[28] The phrase *three obstacles* is a flag that indicates that this central idea does indeed have logical divisions. You list the three obstacles:

1. Enrollment
2. Attendance
3. Graduation

You don't need to use Roman numerals or to worry particularly about the order in which you have listed the obstacles. Right now, you are simply trying to generate main ideas. They are not set in concrete, either. You may revise them—and your central idea—several times before you actually deliver the speech. For example, you may decide that you need to include "admission" as a fourth obstacle so you revise your central idea to read "four obstacles" and add "admission" to your list. If your central idea has logical divisions, you may organize those logical divisions topically, spatially, or according to cause–effect or problem–solution (these organizational strategies will be discussed in Chapter 12).

Can You Think of Several *Reasons* the Central Idea Is True?

If your central idea is "Refugee children in developing nations lack educational opportunities," you may not be able to find readily apparent logical divisions.[29] Simply describing the refugee populations of Afghanistan, Somalia, and Myanmar,[30] for example, would not necessarily support the argument that refugee children in developing nations lack educational opportunities. However, the second question—*Can I think of several reasons the central idea is true?*—is more productive. You can develop the central idea with *reasons* why refugee children lack educational opportunities:

1. Developing countries lack educational infrastructure.
2. The focus of international development and support is misguided.

Unlike the list of obstacles to obtaining a college degree, this list is written in brief complete sentences. You may or may not use full sentences in your own list. The purpose of your first list of main ideas is just to get the ideas in written form, whether using words, phrases, or sentences. You can and will revise them later. If your main ideas are reasons your central idea is true, you will probably organize them according to effect–cause.

> ## DEVELOPING YOUR SPEECH STEP BY STEP
>
> ### Generating Your Main Ideas
>
> With her central idea ("People should consume fewer soft drinks") in hand, Dezerae is ready to generate main ideas for her speech. She applies three questions:
>
> - Does the central idea have logical divisions?
> - Can I think of several reasons the central idea is true?
> - Can I support my central idea with a series of steps or a chronological sequence?
>
> Dezerae doesn't find logical divisions in her central idea. Nor can she support it with a series of steps or a chronological sequence. But she can certainly list reasons it is true. She begins her list:
>
> 1. Soft drinks are high in sugar.
> 2. High sugar consumption leads to obesity.
> 3. Obesity puts people at risk for a variety of lifestyle diseases such as heart disease and diabetes.
>
> Dezerae feels confident that she now has three main ideas that both support her central idea and fulfill her specific purpose. Because she also wants her audience to take action (decrease their consumption of soft drinks), she can make that action step her fourth point:
>
> 4. You should consume fewer soft drinks.
>
> Now Dezerae feels confident that she has four main ideas that both support her central idea and fulfill her specific purpose.

Can You Support the Central Idea with a Series of *Steps* or a *Chronological Sequence?*

"Free speech was alternately challenged and defended in the U.S. throughout the twentieth century." This central idea seemed like a pretty good idea when you drafted it, but now what do you do? It does not have any logical divisions. You cannot really come up with reasons it is true. You could, however, support this central idea with a chronological sequence or a history of free speech in the twentieth century. You jot down the following list:

1. 1919: The Supreme Court suggests that speech presenting a "clear and present danger" may be restricted.
2. 1940: Congress declares it illegal to urge the violent overthrow of the federal government.
3. 1964: The Berkeley Free Speech Movement arises from protest over the arrest of student activists.
4. 1989: The Supreme Court defines the burning of the U.S. flag as a speech act.
5. 1997: The Supreme Court defends free speech on the Internet by striking down the Communications Decency Act of 1996.

These five events, arranged in chronological order, could become the main ideas of your speech.

How many main ideas should you have? Your topic and time limit will help you decide. A short speech (three to five minutes) might have only two main ideas. A longer one (eight to ten minutes) might have four or five. If you have more potential main ideas than you can use, decide which main ideas are likely to be most interesting, relevant, and perhaps persuasive to your audience, or combine two or more closely related ideas.

Gathering Supporting Material

11.7 Describe five potential sources and seven types of supporting material for a speech, and use each type effectively.

supporting material
Verbal or visual material that clarifies, amplifies, and provides evidence to support the main ideas of a presentation.

By the time you have decided on your main ideas, you have a skeleton speech. Your next task is to flesh out that skeleton with **supporting material**, both verbal and visual. Verbal supporting material includes illustrations, explanations, descriptions, definitions, analogies, statistics, and opinions—material that will clarify, amplify, and provide evidence to support your main ideas and your thesis. Visual supporting material includes images, text, video, audio, objects, and people. The speaker who seeks out strong verbal and visual supporting material is adhering to the fundamental communication principles of using verbal and nonverbal messages effectively.

Sources of Supporting Material

Like a chef who needs to know where to buy high-quality fresh fruits and vegetables for gourmet recipes, you need to know where to turn for supporting material that will effectively develop your speech and achieve your specific purpose. We will discuss five potential sources of supporting material: personal knowledge and experience, the Internet, online databases, traditional library holdings, and interviews.

vertical search engine
A website that indexes information in a specialized area.

Boolean search
A web search that ties words together so that a search engine can hunt for the resulting phrase.

Personal Knowledge and Experience If you were self-aware as you selected your topic, you may have chosen a topic based on your passionate interest in rescuing feral cats or cooking. Or you may have chosen a topic with which you have had some personal experience, such as negotiating a favorable apartment lease. Although most well-researched speeches will include some objective material gathered from the Internet or from library resources, your listeners will respect your authority if they realize that you have firsthand knowledge of your topic.

▼ A smartphone lets you do Internet research anywhere, but there are also times when you may need to visit a library or interview someone to get information for your speech.
Damircudic/E+/Getty Images

The Internet Although easy to use and generally helpful, search engines such as Google or Bing can yield an overwhelming number of resources. The following relatively simple strategies can help you narrow thousands or even millions of hits to a more workable number:

- *Vertical search engines.* A **vertical search engine** is a specialized tool that may index, for example, only academic sources (Google Scholar) or job websites (Indeed).
- *Boolean searches.* A **Boolean search** allows you to enclose phrases in quotation marks or parentheses so that a search yields only those sites on which all words or the phrase appear in that exact order, and eliminates sites that contain the words at random. Boolean searches also let you exclude words or phrases from your search, or restrict the dates of documents to a specified time frame.
- *Criteria for evaluating web resources.* A third strategy for sorting through information you discover on the Internet has to do with the principles of appropriately interpreting verbal and nonverbal messages. Specifically, you can use a consistent standard to evaluate the sites you discover. The six criteria in Table 11.2 can serve as such a standard.[31]

Inevitably, one of the first hits in almost any Internet search is *Wikipedia*. Because it is continually updated, *Wikipedia* can provide valuable information about current events and cutting-edge technology. But users should keep in mind that because anyone, regardless of expertise, can add or edit a *Wikipedia* entry, the site's reliability and appropriateness for academic use are limited.

TABLE 11.2 Six Criteria for Evaluating Internet Resources

CRITERION	APPLYING THE CRITERION	DRAWING CONCLUSIONS
Accountability: Who is responsible for the site?	• The site's title and/or its URL may indicate the individual or organization responsible for its content. • See whether the site is signed. • Follow links or search for the author's name to determine his or her expertise and authority. • If the site is unsigned, search for a sponsoring organization. Follow links, search for the organization's name, or consider the domain to determine reputability.	• Check the *domain*, the last three letters of the site's URL. For example, *.gov* indicates a government entity; *.edu* indicates an educational institution. • If you cannot identify or verify an author or sponsor, be wary of the site.
Accuracy: Is the information correct?	• Consider whether the author or sponsor is a credible authority. • Assess the care with which the site has been written. • Consult other sources to fact check the information on the site.	• If the author or sponsor is a credible authority, the information is more likely to be accurate. • A site should be relatively free of writing errors. • You may be able to verify or refute the information by consulting another resource.
Objectivity: Is the site free of bias?	• Consider the interests, philosophical or political biases, and the source of financial support for the author or sponsor of the site. • Does the site include advertisements that might influence its content?	• The more objective the author and sponsor of the site are, the more credible their information may be.
Timeliness: Is the site current?	• Look at the bottom of the site for a statement indicating when the site was created and when it was last updated. • If you cannot find a date on the site, click on Page Info (for example, from the Tools menu at the top of the browser screen in Firefox) to find a "Last Modified" date. • Enter the title of the site in a search engine. The resulting information should include a date.	• In general, when you are concerned with factual data, the more recent it is, the better.
Usability: Do the layout and design of the site facilitate its use?	• Does the site load fairly quickly without crashing the browser or freezing the screen? • Is a fee required to gain access to any of the information on the site?	• Balance slow-loading websites and any fees against practical efficiency.
Diversity: Is the site inclusive?	• Do language and graphics reflect and respect differences in gender, ethnicity, race, and sexual preference? • Do interactive forums invite divergent perspectives? • Is the site friendly to people with disabilities (e.g., does it offer a large-print or video option)?	• A site should be free of bias, representative of diverse perspectives, and accessible by people with disabilities.

online database
A subscription-based electronic resource that may offer access to bibliographic information, abstracts, or full texts.

Online Databases **Online databases** provide access to bibliographic information, abstracts, and full texts for a variety of resources, including periodicals, newspapers, government documents, and even books. Like websites, online databases are accessed via a networked computer. Unlike websites, most databases are restricted to the patrons of libraries that subscribe to them. Your library may subscribe to several or all of the following popular full-text databases:

- *Academic Search Ultimate*. This popular database offers many full-text articles from 1887 to the present, covering a wide variety of subjects.
- *JSTOR*. This multisubject database provides full-text journal articles from the first volume to the present.
- *LexisNexis Academic*. Focusing on business, finance, industry, and law, this database provides many full-text articles from newspapers, magazines, journals, newsletters, and wire services. Dates of coverage vary.

Traditional Library Holdings Despite the proliferation of Internet and database resources in recent years, the more traditional holdings of libraries, both paper and electronic, remain rich sources of supporting material. Spend some time becoming familiar with your library's services and layout so that you know how and where to access books and reference materials.

- *Books*. The **stacks** are where libraries house their collections of books. They are organized by call numbers, which are included in electronic catalog entries. Many university libraries today house their stacks in off-campus archives. Schedule into your research plan the time it may take to retrieve a book from an archive.
- *Reference resources*. Print **reference resources**—which include encyclopedias, dictionaries, atlases, almanacs, and books of quotations—are indexed with a *ref* prefix on their call numbers to show that they are housed in the reference section of the library. Like periodicals, newspapers, and microfilm, print reference resources are usually available only for in-house research and cannot be checked out. If you plan to use the reference section, visit the library during daytime working hours. A full-time reference librarian is more likely to be on hand and available to help you at that time than in the evenings or on weekends.

stacks
Where libraries house their collections of books.

reference resources
Material housed in the reference section of a library, such as encyclopedias, dictionaries, atlases, almanacs, and books of quotations.

> **RECAP**
> **Sources of Supporting Material**
> 1. *Personal knowledge and experience*. Take advantage of your own expertise.
> 2. *The Internet*. Use vertical search engines, conduct Boolean searches, and apply evaluation criteria to choose the best information.
> 3. *Online databases*. For access to abstracts and full texts for a variety of resources, explore the databases to which your library subscribes.
> 4. *Traditional library holdings*. Get to know your reference librarian for help mining traditional library resources.
> 5. *Interviews*. When only an expert can provide the information you need, interview that person.

Interviews If you need detailed information that only an expert can provide, you may want to interview that person. For example, a member of the city council may be able to explain the reasons for the continuing controversy surrounding

SOCIAL MEDIA & COMMUNICATION

Why Do People Share Disinformation?
In 2020, the U.K. government produced two reports on sharing misinformation across social media. Whether it is done deliberately or unwittingly depends on the individual's motivation. Some content is shared by mistake (the sharers believe it to be true and are well-intentioned), but in many cases it is a deliberate and malicious act. The reports suggest there were deliberate sharers, accidental sharers, and a wider audience that is unable to tell whether information is true or false. Lower digital literacy implies individuals believe misinformation and act on them. Dealing with the "organic reach" of disinformation remains a considerable challenge for social media platforms.[32]

granting a liquor license to the new restaurant opening on the edge of campus. Appendix A offers guidelines and strategies for conducting an information-gathering interview.

Types of Supporting Material

If you have explored your own knowledge and insights and those of people you know, discovered material on the Internet, consulted databases, and examined a variety of library resources, you probably have a wealth of potential supporting material. Now you will need to decide what to use in your speech.

Keeping in mind your listeners' knowledge, interests, and expectations will help you determine where an illustration might stir their emotions, where an explanation might help them to understand a point, and where statistics might convince them of the significance of a problem. Let's discuss these and other types of supporting material and consider suggestions for using them effectively.

Illustrations An **illustration** offers an example of, or tells a story about, an idea, issue, or problem a speaker is discussing. Illustrations can be as brief as a word or phrase, or as long as a well-developed paragraph. Student speaker Jocelyn offered a poignant illustration of the needs of families of individuals with disabilities:

> As my brother Lucas nears the age of twenty, my family is starting to think about his future. He loves Christmas, making fun of my driving, and stealing my leftovers. Lucas is severely disabled, nonverbal, and needs help with all of his daily needs, including using the bathroom. In the next ten years, we will have to choose a group home to place my brother in for the rest of his life.[33]

Like Jocelyn's story, an illustration can come from your personal experience. You may also discover relevant illustrations in the course of your research. Or you may create a **hypothetical illustration**, prefaced by a word such as *imagine* to clarify to your audience that you are about to tell a story that has not actually occurred, but *might* happen.

Whatever the length or source of your illustration, remember this principle: Everybody likes to hear a story. An illustration almost always ensures audience interest. In addition, communication researchers have found that listeners are less likely to generate counterarguments to a persuasive message supported by examples and personal narratives than one not so supported.[34]

illustration
A story or anecdote that provides an example of an idea, issue, or problem the speaker is discussing.

hypothetical illustration
A plausible example or story that has not actually occurred.

▲ Everybody loves a good story. David Sedaris is famous for illustrations that capture his audience's attention. What principles can you use from this chapter to hold your listeners' attention?
Adm Golub/Modesto Bee/ZUMAPRESS.com/Alamy Stock Photo

DEVELOPING YOUR SPEECH STEP BY STEP

Gathering Supporting Material

With a draft of her specific purpose, central idea, and main ideas in hand, Dezerae begins to research the health hazards of soft drinks. The article that launched her topic mentions studies done by Harvard University.

She finds and electronically bookmarks fact sheets and other information from the Harvard studies. She also decides to do a Google search. She finds relevant and convincing data from the Centers for Disease Control and Prevention and the National Institutes of Health. Dezerae creates electronic bookmarks for these additional sources.

She then begins to read each resource more carefully and to take notes. As she does so, she puts quotation marks around any material she copies verbatim and makes sure that she has copied it accurately.

The following suggestions should help you use illustrations effectively in your speeches:

- Be sure that your illustrations are directly relevant to the idea or point they are supposed to support.
- Choose illustrations that are typical, not exceptions.
- Make your illustrations vivid and specific.
- Use illustrations with which your listeners can identify.
- Remember that the most effective illustrations are often personal ones.

Descriptions A **description** provides the details that allow an audience to see, hear, smell, touch, or taste whatever you are talking about. Descriptions can make people and scenes come alive for an audience. In her Nobel Prize acceptance speech, writer Doris Lessing described Africa as she remembered it:

> . . . the banks of the Zambesi, where it rolls between pale grassy banks, it being the dry season, dark-green and glossy, with all the birds of Africa around its banks . . . . elephants, giraffes, lions and the rest . . . the sky at night, still unpolluted, black and wonderful, full of restless stars.[35]

description
A word picture.

explanation
A statement that makes clear how something is done or why it exists in its present or past form.

definition
A statement of what something means.

classification
A type of definition that first places a term in the general class to which it belongs and then differentiates it from all other members of that class.

operational definition
A definition that shows how a term works or what it does.

analogy
A comparison between two ideas, things, or situations that demonstrates how something unfamiliar is similar to something the audience already understands.

Explanations An **explanation** of how something works or why a situation exists can help an audience understand conditions, events, or processes. Discussing why fewer American women than Canadian women are in the workforce, Mary Daly, president and chief executive officer of the Federal Reserve Bank of San Francisco, explained,

> . . . this difference can be attributed in part to Canada's generous parental leave policies and child-care subsidies, which allow women to remain attached to the labor market after childbirth.[36]

Although descriptions and explanations are part of most speeches, they lack the inherent interest factor that illustrations have. The following suggestions may help you keep audiences from yawning:

- Avoid too many descriptions and explanations.
- Keep your descriptions and explanations brief.
- Use specific and concrete language.

Definitions A **definition** has two justifiable uses in speeches. First, a speaker should be sure to define any and all specialized, technical, or little-known terms in his or her speech. Such definitions are usually achieved by **classification**, the kind of definition you would find in a dictionary. Alternatively, a speaker may define a term by showing how it works or how it is applied in a specific instance—what is known as an **operational definition**. In her 2020 commencement speech on social media, Oprah used first a definition by classification and then an operational definition:

> . . . "graduation" was a term used in alchemy to mean a tempering or refining. Every one of us is now being called to graduate, to step toward something, even though we don't know what.[37]

To use definitions effectively, consider the following suggestions:

- Use definitions only when necessary.
- Be certain that your definitions are understandable.
- Be sure that any definition you provide accurately reflects your use of the word or phrase throughout the speech.

Analogies An **analogy** demonstrates how unfamiliar ideas, things, and situations are similar to something the audience already understands. Speakers can use two types of

analogies in their speeches. The first is a **literal analogy**, or comparison of two similar things. In the spring of 2020, Michigan Governor Gretchen Whitmer used a literal analogy to compare her state's COVID-19 reopening policy to the policies of cities during the 1918 influenza pandemic:

> . . . re-engaging our state too soon or too fast will lead to a second wave of COVID-19 in Michigan. . . . During the flu pandemic of 1918, some cities lifted social distancing measures too fast, too soon, and created a second wave of pandemic.[38]

literal analogy
A comparison between two similar things.

The second type of analogy is a **figurative analogy**, a comparison of two seemingly dissimilar things that in fact share a significant common feature. In his speech on child slavery in the chocolate industry, student speaker Saeed used a chocolate-related figurative analogy to introduce his solution to the problem:

> I have a 2-step solution that's as simple as an M&M.[39]

figurative analogy
A comparison between two seemingly dissimilar things that share some common feature on which the comparison depends.

Two suggestions can help you use analogies more effectively in your speeches:

- Be certain that the two things you compare in a literal analogy are very similar.
- If you're using a figurative analogy, make sure the similarity between the two things being compared is apparent to the audience.

Statistics **Statistics**, or numerical data, can represent hundreds or thousands of illustrations, helping a speaker express the significance or magnitude of a situation. Statistics can also help a speaker express the relationship of a part to the whole. In her speech on opioid-related deaths in U.S. jails and prisons, student speaker Richkisha used both types of statistics to communicate the magnitude of the problem:

statistics
Numerical data that summarize examples.

> . . . there are about 456,000 individuals held in state, local, federal, youth, and military prisons combined for possession, trafficking, or other nonviolent drug offenses. That is one in five persons being held.[40]

Skilled speakers learn how to use statistics to their greatest advantage. For example, they try to make numbers more dramatic for their audiences. British Member of Parliament (MP) Rosie Duffield dramatized the rate of domestic violence by making a statistic personal:

> There are 650 MPs in this place—650 human beings. Statistically, it is highly likely that some of us here will have directly experienced an abusive relationship, and we are just as likely as anyone else to have grown up in a violent household.[41]

And student speaker Kaylee dramatized a statistic by *compacting* it—expressing it in units readily understandable to her audience:

> . . . in the ten minutes I stood up here in front of you today, someone out there was able to assemble [a] 3D printed gun.[42]

In addition to dramatizing statistics, you can use statistics more effectively if you apply the following suggestions:

- Round off large numbers.
- Use visual aids to present your statistics.
- Cite the sources of your statistics.

expert testimony
The opinion of someone who is an acknowledged expert in the field under discussion.

Opinions The opinions of others can add authority, drama, and style to a speech. A speaker can use three types of opinions: expert testimony, lay testimony, and literary quotations.

Expert testimony is often employed by speakers to make a point memorable. In his address to Virginia Commonwealth University, Michael Rao, president of Virginia Commonwealth University, drew on President Lyndon Johnson's avowal of the responsibility of the presidency:

lay testimony
The opinion of someone who experienced an event or situation firsthand.

literary quotation
A citation from a work of fiction or nonfiction, a poem, or another speech.

Just days into his presidency, Johnson pushed for civil rights legislation that got stalled in Congress. An adviser told him he was wasting his time, that the bill would be far too difficult to advance. But he was undeterred and said: "Well, what's the presidency for?"[43]

Someone who has experienced an event or situation firsthand can provide memorable **lay testimony**. With consent, student speaker Emily shared the lay testimony of Rose, a deaf survivor of domestic abuse:

> [Rose's] partner stole her social security checks each month and only gave her enough to survive. She desperately wanted to leave, but doing so meant living on the streets. And her abuser knew it.[44]

Finally, speakers may wish to include **literary quotations** in their speeches. Salem State College Professor Robert Brown quoted architect Buckminster Fuller to make a point about how the English language has become increasingly visual and kinesthetic:

> As the architectural visionary Buckminster Fuller was fond of saying, "I am a verb." In English, with every innovation that comes to market, we transform things into actions, and nouns into verbs, as when I say: "Let me friend you."[45]

Whether you use expert testimony, lay testimony, or literary quotations, consider the following suggestions for using opinions effectively in your speeches:

- Be certain that any authority you cite is actually an expert on the subject you are discussing.
- Identify your sources.
- Cite unbiased authorities.
- Cite representative opinions, or identify dissenting viewpoints as such.
- Quote or paraphrase your sources accurately and note the context in which the remarks were originally made.
- Use literary quotations sparingly.

As you select your illustrations, descriptions, explanations, definitions, analogies, statistics, and opinions, be guided not only by the suggestions provided in this chapter but also by the five Communication Principles for a Lifetime:

- **Be aware of your communication with yourself and others.** The best supporting material reflects self-awareness, taking advantage of your own knowledge and experience.

RECAP

Supporting Your Speech

Type of Supporting Material	Guidelines for Use
Illustrations	• Make illustrations directly relevant to the idea or point they support. • Choose illustrations that are typical. • Make illustrations vivid and specific. • Use illustrations with which your listeners can identify. • Remember that the most effective illustrations are often personal ones.
Descriptions and Explanations	• Avoid too many descriptions and explanations. • Keep descriptions and explanations brief. • Use specific and concrete language.
Definitions	• Use definitions only when necessary. • Be certain that definitions are understandable. • Be sure that a definition accurately reflects your use of the word or phrase.
Analogies	• Be certain that the two things you compare in a literal analogy are very similar. • Make apparent to the audience the similarity between the two things compared in a figurative analogy.
Statistics	• Round off large numbers. • Use visual aids. • Cite your sources.
Opinions	• Be certain that any authority you cite is actually an expert on the subject you are discussing. • Identify your sources. • Cite unbiased authorities. • Cite representative opinions, or identify dissenting viewpoints as such. • Quote or paraphrase accurately and in context. • Use literary quotations sparingly.

- **Effectively use and interpret verbal messages.** Effective verbal supporting material is appropriately worded, concrete, and vivid enough that your audience can visualize what you are talking about.
- **Effectively use and interpret nonverbal messages.** Use visual aids to present statistics.
- **Listen and respond thoughtfully to others.** If listeners find a speech boring, the speaker has probably not used the fundamental principles of communication as criteria for selecting supporting material.
- **Appropriately adapt messages to others.** Lin-Manuel Miranda, celebrated creator of the hit musical *Hamilton*, told recent graduates at the University of Pennsylvania that

> This act of choosing—the stories we tell versus the stories we leave out—will reverberate across the rest of your life. Don't believe me? Think about how you celebrated this senior week, and contrast that with the version you shared with the parents and grandparents sitting behind you.[46]

Miranda's "act of choosing" will help you select the verbal and visual supporting material that is most appropriately adapted to your audience.

Acknowledgment of Supporting Material

In the United States and most other Western cultures, using the words, sentence structures, or ideas of another person without crediting the source is a serious breach of ethics. Once you have supporting material in hand, you must decide whether and how to acknowledge the source.

Determining What Should Be Acknowledged Some information is so widely known that you may not need to acknowledge a source. For example, you need not cite a source if you say that former FBI official Mark Felt was identified as the long-anonymous Watergate informant "Deep Throat." This fact is general knowledge and is widely available in a variety of sources. If you decide to use any of the following, however, you must acknowledge the source:

- Direct quotations, even if they are only brief phrases
- Others' opinions, assertions, or ideas, even if you paraphrase them rather than quote them verbatim

DIVERSITY & COMMUNICATION

Global English

Learning to speak a foreign language such as English can be a major challenge for some people, particularly if the learner wants to be confident with the nuances and colloquialisms of the language.

Global English is a growing phenomenon that does away with many of the nuances and idiosyncrasies of standard English. It instead features different sentence structures and use of verbs. Global English uses shorter sentences, avoids the passive voice, metaphors, and figurative language, and it aims to be both logical and literal. It is developing and transforming through use, so there are very few established rules. Many see it as a means by which the language can be much clearer and more suitable for nonnative English speakers.[47]

The market for English language learning was worth an estimated $33.5 billion in 2018 and is expected to rise to $54.8 billion in 2024. Growing globalization is one of the key drivers. English is already spoken by 20 percent of the global population. In many countries English is seen as a basic necessity, particularly if an individual or organization wishes to operate in the international market. Global English therefore has an important part to play in delivering a workable version of the language. Digital learning has helped to accelerate the dissemination of Global English as a language learning option. This is being driven by nonnative English countries like China and other Asian countries where the demand to learn English has fast outpaced supply.[48] Delivering speeches and other communications in Global English may soon become the most effective way of communicating with global audiences.

- Statistics
- Any non-original visual materials, including graphs, tables, and pictures

plagiarism
The presentation of someone else's words or ideas without acknowledging the source.

oral citation
The oral presentation of such information about a source as the author, title, and publication date.

Understanding Plagiarism and its Consequences Presenting someone else's words or ideas without acknowledging the source constitutes **plagiarism**, a breach of academic honesty that can have dire consequences.

A few years ago, one of your authors heard a student's excellent speech on the importance of detecting cancer early. The only problem was that she heard the same speech again in the following class period! On finding the "speech"—actually a *Reader's Digest* article that was several years old—both students were certain that they had discovered a shortcut to an A. Instead, they failed the assignment, ruined their course grades, and lost their instructor's trust. The consequences of plagiarism in other arenas can be even more severe, including the loss of a job or the end of a promising career.

Acknowledging Sources in Oral Citations To acknowledge your source, you can integrate an **oral citation** into your speech. In her speech on pollution by the U.S. military, student speaker Fonda provided this oral citation:

> *The Guardian*, December 18, 2019, reported the U.S. is among the top seven countries with the most deaths caused by pollution—with almost 200,000 premature deaths in 2017.[49]

STUDY GUIDE: PRINCIPLES FOR A LIFETIME — CHAPTER 11

Overviewing the Public Speaking Process

11.1 List and explain the components of the audience-centered public speaking model.

PRINCIPLE POINTS: The stages of the public speaking process center on consideration of audience members, who influence every decision a speaker makes. A speaker's tasks include selecting and narrowing a topic, identifying a general and specific purpose, developing the central idea, generating main ideas, gathering supporting material, organizing the speech, and rehearsing and delivering the speech.

PRINCIPLE TERMS:
public speaking   audience-centered public speaker

PRINCIPLE SKILLS:

1. How is the behavior of a speaker who adapts to his or her audience different from that of a speaker who does *not* adapt to the audience?

2. Pat has been asked to attend Monday night's city council meeting to speak on behalf of neighbors who do not want the council to issue an alcohol use permit to a new restaurant in their neighborhood. What strategies could Pat use to adapt her speech to the members of the city council?

Building Your Confidence

11.2 Apply specific strategies for becoming a more confident speaker.

PRINCIPLE POINTS: Understanding public speaking anxiety, knowing how to develop a speech, being prepared, giving yourself mental pep talks, using deep-breathing techniques, and focusing on your audience and message can help you become a more confident speaker, as can taking advantage of opportunities to speak and exploring additional resources.

PRINCIPLE TERMS:
public speaking anxiety   habituation
illusion of transparency

PRINCIPLE SKILLS:

1. Xavier, one of your best friends from high school, went on to play football for your flagship state university. Now he has been invited back to address the annual football banquet at your old high school. Not having taken an oral communication course yet, Xavier is anxious about his upcoming speech. Based on what you have learned about becoming a more confident speaker, what advice would you give Xavier?

2. Complete the paper-pencil Personal Report of Public Speaking Anxiety (PRPSA) available at www.jamescmccroskey.com/measures/prpsa.htm to assess your level of communication apprehension. At the end of the communication course in which you are currently enrolled, complete the self-evaluation again to see whether this course has affected your level of communication apprehension.

Selecting and Narrowing Your Topic

11.3 Select and narrow a speech topic that is appropriate to the audience, the occasion, and yourself.

PRINCIPLE POINTS: As you begin to prepare your speech, you will first have to select and narrow your topic, keeping in mind the audience, the occasion, and your own interests and experiences. You may find helpful such strategies as silent brainstorming, scanning web directories and websites, and listening and reading for topic ideas.

PRINCIPLE SKILLS:

1. One speaker's self-awareness helped her generate a list of possible topics that began with "San Antonio, Texas: City of cultural diversity." Use your own interests and experiences to help generate a list of five to seven topics.

2. The chair of the Department of Communication Studies visits your required communication class to discuss what you can do with a degree in communication studies. Analyze her choice of topic according to the topic selection guidelines presented in this chapter.

Identifying Your Purpose

11.4 Write an audience-centered, specific-purpose statement for a speech.

PRINCIPLE POINTS: Once you have a topic, you need to identify both your general purpose and your specific purpose. General purposes include to inform, to persuade, and to entertain. Specific purposes are determined by the general purpose, the topic, and the audience.

PRINCIPLE TERMS:

general purpose   specific purpose

PRINCIPLE SKILLS:

1. Given the broad topic "ocean tides," write three specific-purpose statements: one for a speech to inform, one for a speech to persuade, and one for a speech to entertain.

2. Revise the following draft of a specific-purpose statement so that it better meets the criteria presented in this chapter: To explain why I use public transportation instead of my own car.

Developing Your Central Idea

11.5 Develop a central idea for a speech.

PRINCIPLE POINTS: Your central idea will focus on the content of your speech. It should be centered on your audience; reflect a single idea; be a complete declarative sentence; and use direct, specific language.

PRINCIPLE TERMS:

central idea   declarative sentence

PRINCIPLE SKILLS:

1. Following the guidelines in this chapter, write a central idea for a speech on the topic of buying car insurance.

2. Revise each of the following central ideas according to the criteria presented in this chapter:
   a. Bicycling and jewelry making are fun hobbies.
   b. How do you change your academic major?

Generating Main Ideas

11.6 Generate main ideas from a central idea.

PRINCIPLE POINTS: The main ideas of a speech support or subdivide the central idea. They are usually logical divisions of the central idea, reasons the central idea is true, or a series of steps or a chronological sequence that develops the central idea.

PRINCIPLE TERM:

main ideas

PRINCIPLE SKILLS:

1. Divide the central idea you wrote about buying car insurance into two or more main ideas, using the three questions recommended in this chapter.

2. Check the main ideas you drafted for the previous question against the following specific-purpose statement: "At the end of my speech, the audience will explain

three criteria for buying car insurance." If your main ideas do not contribute to this specific purpose, make appropriate revisions to either the specific purpose or the main ideas.

Gathering Supporting Material

11.7 Describe five potential sources and seven types of supporting material for a speech, and use each type effectively.

PRINCIPLE POINTS: You have at least five potential sources of supporting material: personal knowledge and experience, the Internet, online databases, traditional library holdings, and interviews. The types of supporting material available in these sources include illustrations, descriptions, explanations, definitions, analogies, statistics, and opinions. Simple guidelines can help you use each type of supporting material effectively and cite your sources correctly.

PRINCIPLE TERMS:

supporting material
vertical search engine
Boolean search
online database
stacks
reference resources
illustration
hypothetical illustration
description
explanation
definition
classification
operational definition
analogy
literal analogy
figurative analogy
statistics
expert testimony
lay testimony
literary quotation
plagiarism
oral citation

PRINCIPLE SKILLS:

1. Think back to a recent speech you have heard. Identify an illustration, statistic, or other piece of supporting material from this speech that you found highly memorable.

2. Use each of the five Communication Principles for a Lifetime to explain *why* the supporting material you identified in the previous question was memorable.

CHAPTER 12

ORGANIZING AND OUTLINING YOUR SPEECH

Don't agonize. Organize. —FLORYNCE R. KENNEDY

SFIO CRACHO/Shutterstock

CHAPTER OUTLINE

- Organizing Your Main Ideas
- Organizing Your Supporting Material
- Signposting: Organizing Your Speech for the Ears of Others
- Introducing and Concluding Your Speech
- Outlining Your Speech
- Study Guide: *Principles for a Lifetime*

LEARNING OBJECTIVES

12.1 List and explain five strategies for organizing the main ideas of a speech.

12.2 Explain how to organize supporting material.

12.3 Use verbal and nonverbal signposts to organize your speech for the ears of others.

12.4 Explain the functions of, and several strategies for, speech introductions and conclusions.

12.5 Develop a preparation outline and speaking notes for a speech.

One study found that college students report spending, on average, nearly half of their total speech preparation time outlining and revising their speeches.[1] This chapter will help you use that preparation time effectively.

Chapter 11 explained the first five stages of audience-centered speech preparation:

1. Select and narrow a topic.
2. Determine your purpose.
3. Develop your central idea.
4. Generate main ideas.
5. Gather supporting material.

Now it is time to put your speech together. You will need to consider first how best to organize your main ideas. Then you will organize your supporting material for maximum effect, and devise signposts to guide your audience through your speech. You will develop an effective introduction and conclusion. Finally, once you have made the necessary decisions about these component parts, you will be ready to outline the entire speech and prepare your speaking notes.

Organizing Your Main Ideas

12.1 List and explain five strategies for organizing the main ideas of a speech.

A logically organized speech includes an introduction, a body, and a conclusion. The body presents the most important content of the speech—the main ideas that you generated with the help of your central idea. At least five strategies can help you determine an effective order in which to present those main ideas.

Organizing Ideas Topically

If your main ideas are logical divisions of your central idea, you will probably arrange them according to **topical organization**. This strategy is used most frequently. There are four principles of topical organization that can help you arrange your main ideas effectively: personal preference, recency, primacy, and complexity.

topical organization
Organization determined by personal preference, recency, primacy, or complexity.

SOCIAL MEDIA & COMMUNICATION

Your Speech as a "Content Sandwich"

Developed by LinkedIn as a best practice for blogging, the "content sandwich" can also be a useful model for organizing a speech.[2] Here, adapted for speakers and their listeners, is how to make a content sandwich:

The top bun should draw the audience in. Main ideas and supporting material—lettuce, tomato, and cheese—should engage the audience. Signposts are the mustard and mayo that hold the fillings together. And the bottom bun is a call to action.

Personal preference is simply an arbitrary arrangement of main ideas that are fairly equal in importance. At other times, topical organization is less arbitrary. The principle of **recency** suggests that audiences remember best what they hear *last*. When following this principle, you move from your least to your most important idea, or from your weakest to your strongest one. In contrast, if you organize your main ideas according to **primacy**, you discuss your most important or strongest idea *first*. And if you apply the principle of **complexity**, you move from your simplest ideas to more complex ones. Figure 12.1 illustrates these four principles of topical organization.

personal preference
Arbitrary arrangement of ideas that are fairly equal in importance.

recency
Arrangement of ideas from least important to most important, or from weakest to strongest.

primacy
Arrangement of ideas from most important to least important, or from strongest to weakest.

complexity
Arrangement of ideas from simplest to most complex.

FIGURE 12.1 Topical Organization

The personal preference sample topic is from S. Njapa, "Changing the African Perception," *Winning Orations* 2019 (Mankato, MN: Interstate Oratorical Association, 2019): 72–74.

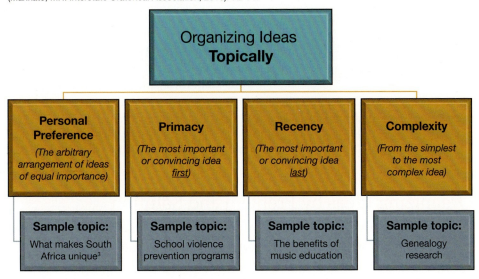

Organizing Ideas Chronologically

If you determine that you can best develop your central idea through a series of steps, you will probably organize those steps—your main ideas—chronologically. **Chronological organization** is based on time or sequential order according to when each step or event occurred or should occur. For example, you could explain a process, like how to strip and refinish furniture, by organizing the steps of that process from first to last. If you are providing a historical overview of an event, movement, or policy, you might begin with the end result and trace its history backward in time. Figure 12.2 illustrates the strategies of chronological organization.

chronological organization
Organization by time or sequence.

FIGURE 12.2 Chronological Organization

The historical sample topic is adapted from P. Steiger, "A Closer Look: Three Golden Ages of Journalism?" *Vital Speeches of the Day* 80.8 (2014): 111–114.

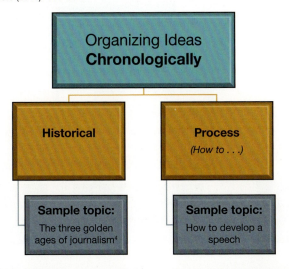

FIGURE 12.3 Spatial Organization

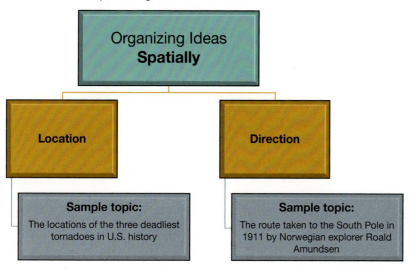

spatial organization
Organization according to location or direction.

cause and effect organization
Organization by discussing a situation and its effects, or a situation and its causes.

problem and solution organization
Organization by discussing first a problem and then various solutions.

Organizing Ideas Spatially

Spatial organization means arranging items according to their location or direction. Speeches that rely on description are especially good candidates for spatial organization. Figure 12.3 offers two topics that might be organized spatially.

Organizing Ideas to Show Cause and Effect

Cause and effect organization actually refers to two related patterns: identifying a situation and then discussing the resulting effects (cause–effect), and presenting a situation and then exploring its causes (effect–cause). If your main ideas are *logical divisions* of your central idea, you might organize them according to cause–effect. If your main ideas are *reasons* your central idea is true, you would probably want to organize them according to effect–cause. As the recency principle would suggest, a cause–effect pattern emphasizes effects; an effect–cause pattern emphasizes causes. Figure 12.4 illustrates two applications of cause and effect organization.

Organizing Ideas by Problem and Solution

If, instead of exploring causes or consequences of a problem or issue, you want either to explore how best to solve the problem or to advocate a particular solution, you will probably choose **problem and solution organization**. This strategy is appropriate for organizing logical divisions of a central idea in either an informative or persuasive speech. If your general purpose is to persuade, you will urge your audience to support or adopt one or more of the solutions you discuss. Figure 12.5 illustrates two applications of problem and solution organization.

How do you decide which organizational pattern to use when a topic lends itself to organization by either cause and effect, or problem and solution? Your specific purpose can

FIGURE 12.4 Cause and Effect Organization

The cause-effect sample topic is adapted from A. Zerull, "Resident Evil: How America's Teaching Hospitals Neglect the Care of Our Caregivers," *Winning Orations* 2016 (Mankato, MN: Interstate Oratorical Association, 2016): 161–166. The effect-cause sample topic is adapted from R. Walcott, "Dying from Withdrawal: Opioid-Related Deaths in U.S. Jails and Prisons," *Winning Orations* 2019 (Mankato, MN: Interstate Oratorical Association, 2019): 84–86.

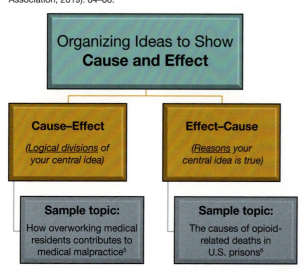

FIGURE 12.5 Problem and Solution Organization

The problem-solution sample topic is from F. Pham, "The U.S. Military's Invisible War," prepared for Individual Events/Persuasive Speaking competition, The University of Texas, Spring 2020.

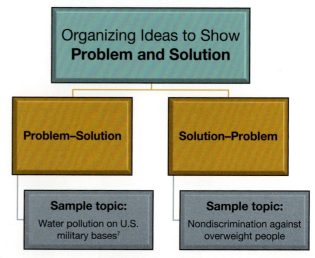

DIVERSITY & COMMUNICATION

Public Speaking—The Cultural Diversity Question

Internet apps and platforms have made it even more likely that if you make a public speech then it will be communicated around the world, and people from different cultures may listen to it. It should not be surprising that different cultures place radically different emphasis on communications and may also have differing expectations.

In many cultures simply being straightforward and to the point will seem to be overly forceful. Some cultures respond better to a more descriptive, narrative driven form of communication. They may favor a message in a story, to give it context and greater meaning.[8]

In some cultures, references to family, gender, clothing, and commentary on government actions and performances are often best avoided, unless comments are respectful and directly relevant to the main points of a speech. Some cultures may place a value on starting and finishing a speech at an agreed time, but others may focus on giving the speaker limitless opportunity to draw conclusions.

Humor is very culture based and you should never assume that humor will be understood, appreciated, or relevant to an audience. When preparing a speech, research what an audience might perceive as valuable and what may concern them.

You should try to show an understanding of an audience's native language, a simple greeting can help to establish a rapport, and could be seen as being courteous and interested in the audience.

Problems can arise when you are delivering to a diverse group of cultures at the same time. It is important to ensure that no one in the audience is marginalized or ignored. However, this does not mean drawing attention to and highlighting people's differences. It is better to consider the commonalities of the audience rather than the differences.[9]

---

help you make the decision. For example, if you want your audience to be able to explain how to end discrimination against overweight people, select the problem–solution organizational strategy. If you want your audience to be able to explain the harmful effects of discrimination against those who are overweight, use the cause and effect strategy. Let both your general and your specific purpose continue to guide your speech as you organize your main ideas.

Organizing Your Supporting Material

12.2 Explain how to organize supporting material.

After you have organized your main ideas, you are ready to organize the supporting material for each idea. Suppose you have two brief illustrations, a statistic, and an opinion in

RECAP

Organizing Your Main Ideas

Strategy	Description	Applicable to Main Ideas That Are . . .
Topical	Arbitrary arrangement of topics, or organization according to recency, primacy, or complexity	Logical divisions
Chronological	Organization by time or sequence	Steps or a chronological sequence
Spatial	Organization according to location or direction	Logical divisions
Cause and effect	Organization by discussing a situation and its causes (effect and cause) or a situation and its effects (cause and effect)	Reasons (effect and cause) Logical divisions (cause and effect)
Problem and solution	Organization by discussing a problem and then various solutions	Logical divisions

ETHICS & COMMUNICATION

The Ethics of Primacy and Recency

Nico knows that according to the principle of recency, he should discuss last what he wants his audience to remember best. In his speech on the risk of counterfeit prescription drugs, however, Nico thinks that it may be more ethical to reveal immediately to his audience how costly the problem is in terms of both dollars and human lives. Is it ethical for Nico to save that important statistic for last?

---

support of your first main idea. How can you organize these materials to communicate your verbal message most effectively?

The now-familiar strategies of chronology, primacy, recency, and complexity can help you organize your supporting material. For example, you might arrange a group of brief illustrations *chronologically*. At other times, you might apply the principle of *recency* and save your most convincing statistic for last. If you decide to present first the opinion with which you are certain your audience will agree, you apply the principle of *primacy*. Or you might arrange two explanations according to the principle of *complexity*, presenting the simplest one first and working up to the more complex one.

At other times, you may need to turn to an organizational strategy more specifically adapted to supporting material: specificity or soft-to-hard evidence.

- **Specificity.** Your supporting material may include specific illustrations and statistics, as well as more general explanations and opinions. The principle of **specificity** suggests that you offer first specific illustrations or statistics, followed by a general explanation or opinion, or—as student speaker Kate did in her speech on service animal training in shelters—first a general explanation or opinion, followed by more specific illustrations or statistics:

  > Animal shelters are overcrowded and unable to care for the millions of homeless pets in the United States. According to the ASPCA—the American Society for the Prevention of Cruelty to Animals—over 6.5 million animals enter U.S. animal shelters nationwide every year.[10]

- **Soft-to-Hard Evidence.** Another principle that can help you organize your supporting material is moving from "soft" to "hard" evidence. Illustrations, descriptions, explanations, definitions, analogies, and opinions are usually considered **soft evidence**, whereas statistics are **hard evidence**. In explaining to his student audience what motivated him to market an early blood-based screening test for cancer, GRAIL CEO Jeff Huber moved from a personal illustration (soft) to a statistic (hard):

  > [My wife] Laura's cancer is just one story out of millions. There are eight million cancer deaths, every year.[11]

specificity
Organization from specific information to a more general statement, or from a general statement to specific information.

soft evidence
Illustrations, descriptions, explanations, definitions, analogies, and opinions.

hard evidence
Statistics.

RECAP

Organizing Your Supporting Material

Strategy	Description
Chronology	Organization by time or sequence
Recency	Most important material last
Primacy	Most convincing material first
Complexity	From simple to more complex material
Specificity	From specific information to general overview or from general overview to specific information
Soft-to-Hard Evidence	From hypothetical illustrations and opinions to facts and statistics

Signposting: Organizing Your Speech for the Ears of Others

12.3 Use verbal and nonverbal signposts to organize your speech for the ears of others.

You now have a fairly complete, logically organized plan for your speech, but if you tried to deliver it at this point, your audience would probably become confused. What are your main ideas? How is one main idea related to the next? What supporting material develops which main idea? To adapt your logically organized message to your audience, you need to include **signposts**, organizational cues for the audience's ears. You do this by adding previews, transitions, and summaries that provide coherence as you move from one idea to the next throughout the speech.

Previews

A **preview** "tells them what you're going to tell them"; it is a statement of what is to come. Previews help audience members anticipate and remember the main ideas of your speech. They also help you move smoothly from the introduction to the body of your speech and from one main idea to the next.

Initial Preview The **initial preview** is usually presented in conjunction with the central idea. Consider student speaker Anastasia's speech on abuse of homeschooled students. After stating her central idea that the system allows severe abuse to go unnoticed, she previewed her three main ideas:

> Today, we'll look at the problem of severe abuse in homeschooling environments, the deregulation that led to it, and how we can ensure that [homeschooled] children . . . are protected in the future.[12]

Internal Preview In addition to providing an initial preview, a speaker may also offer, at various points throughout a speech, an **internal preview**. Internal previews introduce and outline ideas that will be developed as the speech progresses. Student speaker Carson provided an internal preview just before the second main idea of her speech on the U.S. Chamber of Commerce, the top-spending lobbyist in Washington:

> With coercion as its top priority, we are left to question how the [U.S. Chamber of Commerce] is allowed to continue manipulating the public. There are two causes: the legal status of the organization and public misconception.[13]

Hearing this preview, Carson's listeners knew she was going to explain two possible causes of the problem she had described and documented. Her internal preview generated anticipation, which increased the likelihood that her audience would hear and later remember these causes.

Verbal and Nonverbal Transitions

A **transition** is a verbal or nonverbal signpost that a speaker is moving from one idea to the next.

signpost
A verbal or nonverbal organizational signal.

preview
A statement of what is to come.

initial preview
First statement of the main ideas of a speech, usually presented with or near the central idea.

internal preview
A preview within the speech that introduces ideas still to come.

transition
A word, phrase, or nonverbal cue that indicates movement from one idea to the next or the relationship between ideas.

CRITICAL/CULTURAL PERSPECTIVES & COMMUNICATION

Structures for Effecting Change

Whether you are speaking to inform or to persuade (or some combination of both), you are seeking a response from your audience that will contribute to understanding and transforming issues of power. Essential to eliciting that response is organizing your message in a way that will help your listeners learn, remember, and act on it.

When former President Barack Obama used a Zoom town hall to address the 2020 protests following the death of George Floyd and other recent acts of police brutality, he asked, "What can we do?" and proceeded to outline and enumerate three specific steps. The clear organization of his solution left his audience without doubt as to how they could change the broken power structure that had led to Floyd's death.

Logical organization of your speech will enhance your own clarity of thought, as well as your success in leading your audience members to join you in effecting positive change.

verbal transition
A word or phrase that indicates the relationship between two ideas.

nonverbal transition
A facial expression, vocal cue, or physical movement that indicates that a speaker is moving from one idea to the next.

summary
A recap of what has been said.

internal summary
A recap within the speech of what has been said so far.

final summary
A recap of all the main ideas of a speech, usually occurring just before or during the conclusion.

Verbal Transition To use verbal messages effectively, include **verbal transitions**, words or phrases that show relationships between ideas in your speech. They include simple enumeration (*first, second, third*); synonyms or pronouns that refer to earlier key words or ideas (the word *they* at the beginning of this sentence refers to the phrase "verbal transitions" in the previous sentence); and words and phrases that show relationships between ideas (*in addition, not only . . . but also, in other words, in summary, therefore, however*). As you begin to rehearse your speech, you might need to experiment with various verbal transitions to achieve a flow that seems natural and logical to you. If none of the verbal alternatives seems quite right, consider a nonverbal transition.

Nonverbal Transition Sometimes used alone and sometimes used in combination with verbal transitions, an effective **nonverbal transition** might take the form of a facial expression, a pause, a change in vocal pitch or speaking rate, or movement. Most good speakers will use a combination of verbal and nonverbal transitions to signpost their progression from one idea to the next throughout their speeches.

Summaries

A **summary** "tells them what you've told them"; it provides an opportunity for the audience to grasp a speaker's most important ideas. Most speakers use two types of summaries: internal summaries and a final summary.

Internal Summary After you have discussed two or three main ideas, you might want to provide an **internal summary** to ensure that the audience keeps these ideas firmly in mind before you move on to another main idea. You can combine an internal summary with an internal preview. In her speech comparing the Brothers Grimm and Disney versions of *Cinderella*, student speaker Grace combined an internal summary and preview in this way:

> So now that we've talked a little bit about the differences in the characters between the two versions and the differences in the royal ball scene, I'd like to discuss the way that Disney omitted some violence from their version of *Cinderella* compared to the Brothers Grimm version.[14]

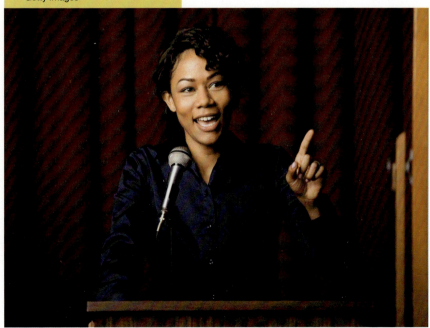

▼ Simply telling listeners you are making your first (or second or third) point can help them understand the organization of your speech.
Hill Street Studios/DigitalVision/Getty Images

Final Summary In your conclusion, you may want to provide your audience with a final opportunity to hear and remember your main ideas. Whereas your initial preview gave your audience members their first exposure to your main ideas, your **final summary** will give them their last exposure to those ideas. Near the end of Rockefeller Foundation President Rajiv Shah's speech on universal health care, he provided this final summary of his three main ideas:

> If you remember nothing else tonight, please remember these three women—a frontline health worker, a mother—actually a grandmother—and a baby girl. . . . Because they also make clear what we value: A health worker's desire to serve her community. A mother's love. A child's future.[15]

Signposting with previews, transitions, and summaries applies the fundamental principles of using both verbal and nonverbal messages effectively and of adapting your message to others. It increases the likelihood that your audience will grasp your main ideas and the logic of your organizational strategy.

Introducing and Concluding Your Speech

12.4 Explain the functions of, and several strategies for, speech introductions and conclusions.

At this point, you have developed and organized the ideas and content of the body of your speech, but you might not have thought about how you are going to begin and end the speech. That's okay. Even though you will deliver your introduction first, you usually plan it last. This is because you need to know what you're introducing—especially your central idea and main ideas. Once you do, it is time to plan how you will introduce and conclude your speech. Although your introduction and conclusion make up a relatively small percentage of the total speech, they provide your audience with first and final impressions of you and your speech. They are important considerations in adapting your message to others.

Introductions

Your **introduction** should convince your audience to listen to you. More specifically, it must perform six functions: getting the audience's attention, introducing the topic, giving the audience a reason to listen, establishing your credibility, stating your central idea, and previewing your main ideas. Let's briefly consider each of these functions.

Get the Audience's Attention   If an introduction does not capture the attention of audience members, the rest of the speech may be wasted on them. You have to use verbal messages effectively to wake up your listeners and make them want to hear more.

There are several good ways to gain an audience's attention. One commonly used and quite effective way is to open with an illustration or personal anecdote. When National Football League (NFL) quarterback Peyton Manning announced his retirement from the Denver Broncos, he opened his speech with this anecdote:

> In my very first NFL game, I completed my first pass to Hall of Fame running back Marshall Faulk. I threw a touchdown in that same game to Marvin Harrison, who would be inducted into the Hall of Fame. . . .[16]

Other strategies for gaining an audience's attention are to ask a rhetorical question, relate a startling fact or statistic, or quote an expert or a literary text. Student speaker Robert opened his speech with two rhetorical questions:

> Let's talk about the birds, and the bees. But what if the bees . . . didn't exist? What if the act of the birds and the bees helped fix that problem?[17]

Still other speakers might capture their audience's attention by referring to the occasion, historical or recent events, or something said by a preceding speaker. Speaking to the United Nations in 2019, Indian Prime Minister Narendra Modi began by acknowledging the historical context:

> . . . this year, the entire world is celebrating the 150th birth anniversary of Mahatma Gandhi. His message of truth and non-violence is very relevant for us even today, for peace, development, and progress in the world.[18]

introduction
The opening lines of a speech, which must catch the audience's attention, introduce the topic, give the audience a reason to listen, establish the speaker's credibility, state the central idea, and preview the main ideas.

▼ In the introduction to his retirement speech, NFL quarterback Peyton Manning used an anecdote about his first professional football game to capture his audience's attention.
David Zalubowski/ASSOCIATED PRESS

Although not all of these strategies will work for all speeches, at least one of them should be an option for any speech you make. With a little practice, you may be able to choose from several good possibilities for a single speech.

Introduce the Topic   Within the first few seconds of listening to you, your audience should have a pretty good idea of what your topic is.

Give the Audience a Reason to Listen   Not only do you have to get your audience's attention and introduce your topic, but you also have to motivate your listeners to continue to listen. Show your listeners how your topic affects them and those they care about. Student speaker Rebecca combined a hypothetical illustration, rhetorical question, and startling statistic to engage her audience in her speech on mental illness in adolescents:

> Imagine you're sitting in your favorite class, and you're looking around at the people around you. What do you notice? Probably what they're wearing. Who they're talking to. What they're doing. What you can't see is that, for every five of those students, one of them has some sort of a mental illness.[19]

By the end of your introduction, your audience should be thinking, "This concerns *me*!"

Establish Your Credibility   A credible speaker is one whom the audience judges to be believable, competent, and trustworthy. Be aware of the background and experiences you have had that are related to your topic. You can increase your credibility by telling your audience about your expertise. For example, comedian Sacha Baron Cohen offered his credentials in his speech accepting the Anti-Defamation League's International Leadership Award:

> I've been passionate about challenging bigotry and intolerance throughout my life. As a teenager in the U.K., I marched against the fascist National Front and to abolish apartheid. As an undergraduate, I traveled around America and wrote my thesis about the civil rights movement, with the help of the archives of the ADL. And as a comedian, I've tried to use my characters to get people to let down their guard and reveal what they actually believe, including their own prejudice.[20]

State Your Central Idea   You should usually state your central idea at or near the end of your introduction, as in the following example from student speaker Emma's speech on the problem of public bathrooms that are inaccessible to people with disabilities:

> Inaccessible restrooms deny disabled people access to restaurants, to school, to work, to public life.[21]

Preview Your Main Ideas   Previewing your main ideas allows your listeners to anticipate and begin to listen for those main ideas. You can provide your initial preview immediately after stating your central idea.

▲ Looking the audience in the eye with a friendly smile as you deliver your well-prepared introduction can help establish your credibility.
GlobalStock/E+/Getty Images

▼ Comedian Sacha Baron Cohen established his credibility by sharing his background and experiences when giving a speech in acceptance of the Anti-Defamation League's International Leadership Award.
© 2020 Anti-Defamation League. All rights reserved

Here is the initial preview of main ideas for student speaker Kaylee's speech on 3-D printed guns:

> So in order to understand the complexity of . . . 3-D printed guns, first, we will unload the problems that are associated with these 3-D guns; second, we will target the causes behind these issues; before finally scoping out some potential solutions . . . .[22]

Conclusions

Your introduction creates a critically important first impression, and your **conclusion** leaves an equally important final impression. Long after you finish speaking, your audience will hear the echo of your compelling final words. An effective conclusion serves four functions: to summarize the speech, to reemphasize the central idea in a memorable way, to motivate the audience to respond, and to provide closure. Let's consider each of these functions.

conclusion
The closing lines of a speech, which leave a final impression.

Summarize the Speech The conclusion offers a speaker a last chance to repeat his or her main ideas. Most speakers summarize their main ideas between the body of the speech and its conclusion or in the first part of the conclusion. Here is how student speaker Caleb summarized his main ideas in his conclusion:

> After analyzing why the [second American civil] war would start, what it could look like, and its implications, it's evident we might be closer to civil conflict than we think.[23]

Reemphasize the Central Idea in a Memorable Way The conclusions of a number of famous speeches contain many of the lines we remember best:

> . . . and that government of the people, by the people, for the people, shall not perish from the earth. *(Abraham Lincoln)*[24]

> Old soldiers never die; they just fade away. *(General Douglas MacArthur)*[25]

> . . . we will be with our friends again; we will be with our families again; we will meet again. *(Queen Elizabeth II)*[26]

Note, too, the brevity of these memorable lines. As Aaron Beverly, a competitor in the Toastmasters World Championship of Public Speaking, remarked with irony,

> Leave a lasting memory using as few words as possible and strive with every fiber in your being to avoid being the type of person who rambles on and on with no end in sight, more likely than not causing listeners to sit and think to themselves, "Oh my goodness can somebody please make this stop."[27]

Use your final verbal message effectively. Word your thoughts so that your audience cannot help but remember them.

Motivate the Audience to Respond Think back to your specific purpose. What do you want your audience to be able to do by the end of your speech? If your purpose is to inform, you may want your audience to think about your topic or seek more information about it. If your purpose is to persuade, you may want your audience to take some sort of action, such as write a letter, make a phone call, or volunteer for a cause. Your conclusion is where you can motivate your audience to respond. Student speaker Manny concluded his speech on body brokering with a specific opportunity for action:

> On this pamphlet I have provided a QR code that includes the contact information for your state representatives. Please contact them and encourage them to advocate for H.R. 1835 [regulation of body brokering].[28]

Provide Closure Have you ever listened to a speech and felt surprised or uncertain when it ended? If so, you were listening to a speaker who did not achieve the last purpose of an effective conclusion: providing **closure**, or a sense that the speech is finished.

closure
The sense that a speech is finished.

▲ Effective speakers often use nonverbal signposts as they transition to their conclusions.
PG Arphexad / Alamy Stock Photo

You can provide closure by referring to your introduction and finishing a story, answering a rhetorical question, or reminding your audience of where you started. In the introduction of her speech on the opioid epidemic, student speaker Abbie told her audience about Matthew LaGreca:

> After a football-related injury, Matthew was prescribed 100 pills of Oxycodone, an opioid created, marketed, and sold by Purdue Pharma. Due to his prescription, Matthew became addicted to opioids and died of an overdose....[29]

Then, in her conclusion, Abbie returned to Matthew's story:

> Sadly, it's too late for Matthew LaGreca, his family, and hundreds of thousands like him....

You can also achieve closure by using verbal and nonverbal signposts. For example, you might use such verbal transitions as *finally* or *in conclusion* as you move into your conclusion. You might also pause before you begin the conclusion, slow your speaking rate as you deliver your final sentence, or signal by falling vocal inflection that you are making your final statement. Experiment with these strategies until you are certain that your speech "sounds finished."

RECAP
The Purposes of Introductions and Conclusions

Your introduction should...
- Get your audience's attention.
- Introduce your topic.
- Give your audience a reason to listen.
- Establish your credibility.
- State your central idea.
- Preview your main ideas.

Your conclusion should...
- Summarize your speech.
- Reemphasize your central idea in a memorable way.
- Motivate your audience to respond.
- Provide closure.

Outlining Your Speech

12.5 Develop a preparation outline and speaking notes for a speech.

With your introduction and conclusion planned, you are almost ready to begin rehearsing your speech. By this point, you should have your preparation outline nearly complete. A **preparation outline** is a fairly detailed outline of your central idea, main ideas, and supporting material. It may also include your specific purpose, introduction, and conclusion. A second outline, which you will prepare shortly, will become the speaking notes from which you will eventually deliver your speech.

Preparation Outline

A detailed preparation outline can help you ensure that your main ideas are clearly related to your central idea and are logically and adequately supported. When you create a preparation outline, you are applying the first fundamental principle of communication: becoming increasingly aware of your communication. In addition

preparation outline
A detailed outline of a speech that includes the central idea, main ideas, and supporting material, and may also include the specific purpose, introduction, and conclusion.

to helping you judge the unity and coherence of your speech, the preparation outline also serves as an early rehearsal outline and is usually handed in as part of a class requirement.

Instructors who require you to turn in a preparation outline will probably have their own specific requirements. For example, some instructors ask for the introduction and conclusion as part of the outline, whereas others want only an outline of the body of the speech. Some instructors ask that you incorporate signposts into the outline or write your specific purpose at the top of the outline. Be certain that you carefully listen to and follow your instructor's specific requirements regarding which elements to include.

Almost certainly, your instructor will require that you use **standard outline format**. Using standard outline format can help you become more aware of the exact relationships among the various main ideas, subpoints, and supporting material in your speech. Even if you haven't had much experience with formal outlines, the following guidelines can help you produce a correct outline.

standard outline format
Conventional use of numbered and lettered headings and subheadings to indicate the relationships among parts of a speech.

Use Standard Numbering Outlines are numbered with Roman and Arabic numerals and uppercase and lowercase letters followed by periods, as follows:

    I. First main idea
        A. First subdivision of I
        B. Second subdivision of I
            1. First subdivision of B
            2. Second subdivision of B
                (a) First subdivision of 2
                (b) Second subdivision of 2
   II. Second main idea

You will probably not need to subdivide beyond the level of lowercase letters in most speech outlines.

Use at Least Two Subdivisions, If Any, for Each Point You cannot divide anything into fewer than two parts. On an outline, every I should be followed by a II, every A should be followed by a B, and so on. If you have only one subdivision, fold it into the level above it.

Line Up Your Outline Correctly Main ideas, indicated by Roman numerals, are written closest to the left margin. The *periods* following these Roman numerals need to line up so that the first letters of the first words also line up:

    I. First main idea
   II. Second main idea
  III. Third main idea

Letters or numbers of subdivisions begin directly underneath the first letter of the first *word* of the point above:

    I. First main idea
        A. First subdivision of I
        B. Second subdivision of I

If a main idea or subdivision takes up more than one line, the second line begins under the first letter of the first word of the preceding line:

    I. First main idea
        A. If a rather lengthy subdivision runs more than one line, then the second line
           should begin under the first letter of the first word in the preceding line
        B. Second subdivision

Within Each Level, Make the Headings Grammatically Parallel Regardless of whether you write your preparation outline in complete sentences or in phrases, be consistent within each level. In other words, if I is a complete sentence, II should also be a complete sentence. If A is an infinitive phrase (one that begins with *to* plus a verb, such as "to guarantee greater security"), B should also be an infinitive phrase.

In this chapter, we have included a sample preparation outline for the speech by Dezerae Reyes in the Developing Your Speech Step by Step feature.[30] As you review this outline, please keep in mind that your instructor may have additional or alternative requirements for what your preparation outline should include or how it should be formatted.

Sample Preparation Outline

Purpose
At the end of my speech, the audience will consume fewer soft drinks.

Writing her purpose statement at the top of the outline will help Dezerae keep it in mind, but always follow your instructor's specific requirements for how to format your preparation outline.

Introduction
Imagine that your doctor calls you, and she says, "Hey, I know you're stressed, but I have a solution for you. I'm going to prescribe a daily pill that will give you all the energy you need to go through your day, and it's also really affordable for students, and it tastes pretty good, too. But it has side effects: It's mildly addictive, it will burn your mouth, and you'll start to feel sick and sluggish after a while—but it will get the job done." Most of us would not consider that situation. But we have, because that "pill" I just described is soda. And I used to feel those experiences myself. I used to be a daily—even hourly—soda drinker. But I've made the decision to stop drinking soda, and the change has been significant.

Dezerae catches her listeners' attention by combining a hypothetical illustration and personal anecdote. Other strategies for effectively getting your audience's attention were discussed earlier in the chapter.

Central Idea
So today I'm going to tell you just how bad drinking soda is, in the hopes that you can also transition from soda to healthier drinks.

Preview
First, I'm going to tell you about the biggest problem associated with soda; second, how that problem can cause weight gain and obesity; and finally, how it can cause disease.

Dezerae writes out and labels her central idea and the initial preview that follows. Again, follow your instructor's requirements.

Body
I. Let's discuss the biggest problem with drinking soda: It is high in sugar.
   A. I know we know that soda contains sugar, but I don't think we know the significance of just how much. With one 20-ounce soda, we are consuming more than our daily sugar intake recommendation.
   B. In 2014, the World Health Organization suggested that sugars should make up only about 5 percent of daily calorie intake (6 teaspoons or 25 grams).
   C. So if we convert that: 3 teaspoons = 1 tablespoon, 6 teaspoons = 2 tablespoons.
   D. On the other hand, I have a 20-ounce Coca-Cola, which has 65 grams of sugar. The amount of sugar in this soda: 4 grams = 1 teaspoon, 65 grams divided by 4 = 16.25 teaspoons, 16.25 teaspoons = almost 5 ½ tablespoons.

The first main idea of the speech is indicated by the Roman numeral I. This main idea has four subpoints, indicated by A, B, C, and D.

As Dezerae calculates the measurements orally, she uses presentation aids to help her audience visualize the amounts.

Sample Preparation Outline (continued)

The World Health Organization says that the average American consumes 19.25 teaspoons of sugar every day, which is far higher than the 6 we're supposed to consume.

Signpost: Now that you know about the problem of high sugar consumption, how does that lead to obesity?

    II. Consuming such a vast amount of excess calories from foods and drinks high in free sugars contributes to unhealthy weight gain, which can lead to obesity.

        A. According to the Obesity Society, added sugar consumption has increased by 30 percent over the last three decades.

        B. According to the U.S. Department of Health and Human Services, 68.8 percent of adults age 20 or older are overweight or obese. And drinks like soda are partially to blame because they add so much sugar to our already sugary diets.

> Dezerae provides written citations of her orally cited sources in the references section at the end of her outline. Make sure you follow your instructor's requirements for including and formatting source citations in your outline.

Signpost: So high soda consumption can cause obesity, which in turn can lead to disease.

    III. Being overweight and/or obese can put you at risk for a variety of lifestyle diseases, such as heart disease and diabetes.

        A. According to the American Heart Association, drinking sugar-sweetened beverages every day is associated with an increase in a particular type of body fat that may affect a person's risk for developing heart disease and even diabetes.

        B. It's important that we know this fact because heart disease, which is a lifestyle disease, is the number one killer in the U.S. for both men and women, according to the Centers for Disease Control and Prevention. And this is a big reason I stopped drinking soda. Several years ago, I witnessed one of my own family members have a heart attack and eventually pass away from heart disease. I decided to reduce my risk while I still could.

> Dezerae continues to use signposts to organize her speech for the ears of her listeners—in this case, transitioning from her second main idea (II) to her third (III).

Signpost: Now you know how excess sugar consumption from drinking soda can damage your health.

Conclusion

In order to decrease these health risks, drink less soda and drink healthier alternatives instead. So if you're craving soda, whether that be today, next week, or next month, try drinking a sparkling flavored water. There's no sugar, but it's still carbonated, and it's flavored. Even better, drink a glass of water, tea, or even coffee for a week, and you'll start to feel a difference in your body. If you want to take the first step today, I'll be passing out sparkling flavored water at the end of class. I hope this sparkling water is the first step of many steps to a healthier, happier life.

> In her conclusion, Dezerae brings closure to her speech with an action step that reflects the specific purpose of her speech. By telling her audience that she will have healthier drinks available at the end of class, she both reemphasizes her central idea in a memorable way and motivates her audience to respond.

(continued)

Sample Preparation Outline (continued)

References

30 health reasons not to drink soda or diet soda. (n.d.). Retrieved from http://hccua.org/health/healthandwellness.cfm?id=311

Beverages. (2014). Retrieved from www.sugarstacks.com/beverages.htm

Gunnars, K. (n.d.). *Daily intake of sugar - how much sugar should you eat per day?* Retrieved from https://authoritynutrition.com/how-much-sugar-per-day/

Healthy diet. (September 2015). Retrieved from World Health Organization site: www.who.int/mediacentre/factsheets/fs394/en/

How sweet is it? (2012). Retrieved from Harvard University site: https://cdn1.sph.harvard.edu/wp-content/uploads/sites/30/2012/10/how-sweet-is-it-color.pdf

Leading causes of death. (2016). Retrieved from Centers for Disease Control and Prevention site: www.cdc.gov/nchs/fastats/leading-causes-of-death.htm

Overweight and obesity statistics. (2012). Retrieved from National Institute of Diabetes and Digestive and Kidney Diseases site: www.niddk.nih.gov/health-information/health-statistics/Pages/overweight-obesity-statistics.aspx

Soft drinks and disease. (2016). Retrieved from Harvard University T. H. Chan School of Public Health site: www.hsph.harvard.edu/nutritionsource/healthy-drinks/soft-drinks-and-disease

Sugary drinks and the obesity epidemic. (2012). Retrieved from Harvard University T. H. Chan School of Public Health site: https://cdn1.sph.harvard.edu/wp-content/uploads/sites/30/2012/10/sugary-drinks-and-obesity-fact-sheet-june-2012-the-nutrition-source.pdf

U.S. adult consumption of added sugars increased by more than 30% over three decades. (2014). Retrieved from Obesity Society site: www.obesity.org/news/press-releases/us-adult

Following her instructor's requirements, Dezerae includes a list of her references in her preparation outline, formatted in APA style.

Speaking Notes

As you rehearse your speech, you will need to look at your preparation outline less and less. You should now have both the structure and the content of your speech quite well in mind. At this point, you are ready to develop a shorter outline to serve as your speaking notes.

Speaking notes should provide all the information you will need to make your speech as you have planned, but should not be so detailed that you will be tempted to read rather than speak to your audience. Here are a few suggestions for developing speaking notes.

Use Note Cards, a Smartphone, or a Tablet Your speaking notes should be small enough to hold in one hand, quiet to handle, and readily legible.

Note cards are generally preferable to sheets of paper because they do not rustle when you handle them, and they are small enough to hold in one hand. Prepare your note cards according to logical blocks of material, using one note card for your introduction, one or two for the body of your speech, and one for your conclusion. Number

RECAP

Two Types of Speech Outlines

Type	Purpose
Preparation Outline	Allows speaker to examine speech for completeness, unity, coherence, and overall effectiveness. May serve as first rehearsal outline.
Speaking Notes	Include supporting material, signposts, and delivery cues.

your note cards in case they get out of order while you are speaking. If you choose instead to put your speaking notes on an electronic device, you should be able to scroll through your outline as you progress through the speech. Regardless of whether you use note cards or an electronic device, be sure your font is large enough to read easily.

Use Standard Outline Format Standard outline format will help you find your exact place when you glance down at your speaking notes. You will know, for example, that your second main idea is indicated by "II."

Include Your Introduction and Conclusion in Abbreviated Form Even if your instructor does not require you to include your introduction and conclusion on your preparation outline, include shortened versions of them in your speaking notes. You might even feel more comfortable delivering the speech if you have your first and last sentences written out in front of you.

Include Your Central Idea, But Not Your Purpose Statement Be sure to include your central idea in your speaking notes. Do not include your purpose statement because you will not actually say it during your speech.

Include Supporting Material and Signposts Write out in full any statistics and direct quotations and their sources. Write down your key signposts—your initial preview, for example—to help you transition smoothly from one idea to the next.

Include Delivery Cues Writing such cues as "Louder," "Pause," or "Walk two steps left" will remind you to communicate the nonverbal messages you have planned. Use a different color font or ink so that you don't confuse your delivery cues with your verbal content.

Figure 12.6 illustrates speaking notes for Dezerae's speech on the health risks of soft drinks.

FIGURE 12.6 Sample Speaking Notes

Preview
1. Today I'm going to discuss [hold up one finger] first the biggest problem with drinking soda;
2. [hold up two fingers] second, how that problem can cause obesity and disease;
3. [hold up three fingers] finally, how you can consume fewer sodas.

Body
I. High in sugar.
  A. 20 ounce soda = > daily sugar recommendation
  B. World Health Organization:
   • Healthy diet = < 10% energy intake from sugars
   • (12 teaspoons = 4 tablespoons, based on 2,000 daily calorie diet)

STUDY GUIDE: PRINCIPLES FOR A LIFETIME
CHAPTER 12

Organizing Your Main Ideas

12.1 List and explain five strategies for organizing the main ideas of a speech.

PRINCIPLE **POINTS:** Once you have found supporting material, you are ready to organize your ideas and information. Depending on your topic, purpose, and audience, you can organize the main ideas of your speech chronologically, topically, spatially, by cause and effect, or by problem and solution.

PRINCIPLE **TERMS:**

topical organization
personal preference
recency
primacy
complexity
chronological organization

spatial organization
cause and effect organization
problem and solution organization

PRINCIPLE **SKILLS:**

1. For each of the five strategies of organization discussed, suggest a topic that might be organized according to that strategy.

2. Take notes as you listen to a speech, either live or online. Then organize your notes into an outline that you think reflects both the speaker's organization and the intended relationship among ideas and supporting material.

Organizing Your Supporting Material

12.2 Explain how to organize supporting material.

PRINCIPLE **POINTS:** You can often organize supporting material according to one of the same strategies used to organize main ideas: chronology, recency, primacy, or complexity. You can also organize supporting material by specificity or from soft-to-hard evidence.

PRINCIPLE **TERMS:**

specificity   hard evidence
soft evidence

PRINCIPLE **SKILLS:**

1. Select one of the speeches in Appendix B. Identify the supporting material for one main idea in this speech. What principle did the speaker use to organize his or her supporting material?
2. Reread the Ethics & Communication feature box in this chapter. Based on how you responded to the question posed there, discuss whether either primacy or recency may be a more ethical choice than the other.

Signposting: Organizing Your Speech for the Ears of Others

12.3 Use verbal and nonverbal signposts to organize your speech for the ears of others.

PRINCIPLE **POINTS:** With your speech organized, you will want to add signposts—previews, transitions, and summaries—to make your organization clearly apparent to your audience.

PRINCIPLE **TERMS:**

signpost   verbal transition
preview   nonverbal transition
initial preview   summary
internal preview   internal summary
transition   final summary

PRINCIPLE **SKILLS:**

1. In a recent speech, class lecture, or Technology, Entertainment, Design (TED) talk you have viewed online, identify one or more signposts.
2. For one of the speeches in Appendix B, find at least one example of each of the following:
   a. A verbal transition
   b. An internal preview
   c. An internal summary

Introducing and Concluding Your Speech

12.4 Explain the functions of, and several strategies for, speech introductions and conclusions.

PRINCIPLE **POINTS:** A carefully planned introduction will capture your audience's attention, introduce your topic, give the audience a reason to listen, establish your credibility, state your central idea, and preview your main ideas. An equally carefully planned conclusion will summarize your speech, reemphasize the central idea in a memorable way, motivate your audience to respond, and provide closure.

PRINCIPLE **TERMS:**

introduction   closure
conclusion

PRINCIPLE **SKILLS:**

1. Draft an introduction for a speech on one of the following topics:
   a. Strategies for surviving a tsunami
   b. Private-school vouchers
   c. Mars up close
   d. Celebrities and the press

   In addition to introducing the topic and previewing your main ideas, be sure to plan strategies for getting the attention of audience members and giving them a reason to listen. Also devise a way to establish your own credibility as a speaker on that topic.
2. Give an example of a memorable speech introduction you've heard. Explain how that introduction effectively caught your attention and gave you a reason to listen.

Outlining Your Speech

12.5 Develop a preparation outline and speaking notes for a speech.

PRINCIPLE **POINTS:** A final step before beginning to rehearse your speech is to prepare a detailed preparation outline and speaking notes. Your preparation outline should follow the guidelines provided by your instructor.

PRINCIPLE **TERMS:**

preparation outline   standard outline format

PRINCIPLE **SKILLS:**

1. What alternative method of formatting might work for speakers who do not wish to use a standard outline for their speaking notes?
2. Why do you think it is important not to read your speaking notes?

CHAPTER 13

DELIVERING YOUR SPEECH

O the orator's joys! To inflate the chest, to roll the thunder of the voice out from the ribs and throat, to make the people rage, weep, hate, desire. —WALT WHITMAN

Lightpoet/123RF

CHAPTER OUTLINE

- Methods of Delivery
- Effective Verbal Delivery
- Effective Nonverbal Delivery
- Effective Presentation Aids
- Some Final Tips for Rehearsing and Delivering Your Speech
- Criteria for Evaluating Speeches
- Study Guide: *Principles for a Lifetime*

LEARNING OBJECTIVES

13.1 List and describe the four methods of delivery, and provide suggestions for effectively using each one.

13.2 List and explain three criteria for effective verbal delivery.

13.3 Identify and illustrate characteristics of effective nonverbal delivery.

13.4 Discuss how to prepare and use presentation aids effectively.

13.5 Make the most of your rehearsal time, and deliver your speech effectively.

13.6 Understand and apply criteria for evaluating speeches.

Which is more important, the content of a speech or the way it is delivered? Speakers and speech teachers have argued about the answer to this question for thousands of years, and the debate continues.

One researcher concluded that delivery is almost twice as important as content when students give self-introduction speeches and three times as important when students give persuasive speeches.[1] Other scholars have found that delivery provides important information about a speaker's feelings and emotions and will in turn affect listeners' emotional responses to the speaker.[2] Most speech teachers today agree that both content and delivery contribute to the effectiveness of a speech. As a modern speechwriter and communication coach has observed,

> In the real world—the world where you and I do business—content and delivery are always related.[3]

In this chapter, we will discuss how you can apply the five Communication Principles for a Lifetime to your verbal and nonverbal delivery of speeches. We will also discuss how to determine what presentation aids might be effective for your audience, and we will offer guidelines for both preparing and using various presentation aids. In addition, we will offer tips for making the most of your rehearsal time and delivering your final speech as effectively as possible. Finally, we will talk briefly about evaluating both your own speeches and those you hear.

Methods of Delivery

13.1 List and describe the four methods of delivery, and provide suggestions for effectively using each one.

Different audiences expect and prefer different delivery styles. For example, if you are using a microphone to speak to an audience of 1,000 people, your listeners may expect a relatively formal delivery style. On the other hand, your communication class would probably find it odd if you delivered a formal oration to your twenty-five classmates.

People from different cultures also have different expectations of what is considered effective speech delivery. Listeners from Japan and China, for example, prefer subdued gestures to a more flamboyant delivery. British listeners expect a speaker to stay behind a lectern and use relatively few gestures.

Another factor in delivery style is whether your speech is face-to-face or mediated. For example, when delivering a mediated speech, either recorded or in real time, you should tone down your gestures and facial expressions, as a camera lens only inches away tends to amplify movement.

Speakers should consider and adapt to their audience's expectations, their topic, and the speaking situation as they select from four basic methods of delivery: manuscript speaking, memorized speaking, impromptu speaking, and extemporaneous speaking.

Manuscript Speaking

Perhaps you remember the first speech you ever had to give, maybe as long ago as elementary school. Chances are that you wrote out your message and read it to your audience. Unfortunately, **manuscript speaking** is rarely done well enough to be interesting. Most speakers who rely on a manuscript read it either in a monotone or with a pattern of vocal inflection that makes the speech "sound read." They are so afraid of losing their place that they keep their eyes glued to the manuscript and seldom look at the audience. These challenges are significant enough that most speakers should avoid reading from a manuscript most of the time. However, you might need to deliver a manuscript speech if you ever have to speak on a sensitive, critical, or controversial issue. One experienced speaker points out that manuscript speaking "should not be dismissed as only a crutch for new and timid speakers" but is in fact a "skill essential to politicians and top business executives."[4] For example, because an awkward statement made by the U.S. Secretary of State could cause an international crisis, his or her remarks on critical issues are usually carefully scripted. If you ever have to deliver a manuscript speech, consider the suggestions in Figure 13.1.

FIGURE 13.1 Tips for Effective Manuscript Speaking

- Type your manuscript in short, easy-to-scan phrases on the upper two-thirds of the paper so you won't have to look too far down the page.
- Practice with your manuscript before you deliver your speech.
- Unobtrusively use your index finger to keep your place in the text.

→ EFFECTIVE MANUSCRIPT SPEAKING

Memorized Speaking

After that first speech you read in elementary school, you probably became a savvier speaker. Perhaps the next time you had to give a speech, you wrote it out and memorized it. You thought that no one would be able to tell. What you didn't know then, but probably do now, is that most **memorized speaking** sounds stiff and recited. In addition, you run the risk of forgetting parts of your speech and having to search awkwardly for words in front of your audience. By memorizing your speech, you also forfeit the ability to adapt to your audience while you are speaking.

On occasion, speaking from memory is justifiable. If you must deliver a short speech within a narrow time limit, memorizing and rehearsing it will allow you to time it more accurately. The three guidelines in Figure 13.2 can help you use nonverbal messages effectively when you deliver a speech from memory.

manuscript speaking
Reading a presentation from a written text.

memorized speaking
Delivering a speech word for word from memory without using notes.

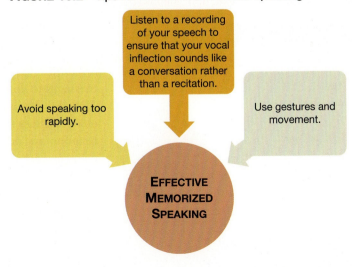

FIGURE 13.2 Tips for Effective Memorized Speaking

- Avoid speaking too rapidly.
- Listen to a recording of your speech to ensure that your vocal inflection sounds like a conversation rather than a recitation.
- Use gestures and movement.

→ EFFECTIVE MEMORIZED SPEAKING

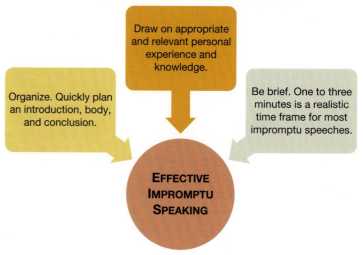

FIGURE 13.3 Tips for Effective Impromptu Speaking

Impromptu Speaking

During President Bill Clinton's 1993 health care speech before a joint session of Congress, the teleprompter scrolled the wrong text for nine minutes. Drawing on his years of experience, the president kept speaking. As political advisor and commentator Paul Begala marveled, "Nine minutes the guy went without a note, and no one could tell."[5]

Although you may plan your speeches, there are times—as illustrated by Clinton's experience—when the best plans go awry. A more likely possibility is that you will be asked to answer a question or respond to an argument without advance warning or time to prepare. At such times, you will have to call on your skills in **impromptu speaking**, or speaking "off the cuff."

Having a solid grasp of the topic on which you are asked to speak can help you in such instances. The three additional guidelines in Figure 13.3 can also help you avoid fumbling for words or rambling.

impromptu speaking
Delivering a presentation without advance preparation.

Extemporaneous Speaking

extemporaneous speaking
Delivering a well-developed, well-organized, carefully rehearsed speech without having memorized the exact wording.

We have saved for last the method of speaking most appropriate for most circumstances, preferred by most audiences, and most often taught in public speaking classes: **extemporaneous speaking**. The extemporaneous speech is a well-developed and well-organized message delivered in an interesting and vivid manner. It reflects your understanding of how to use both verbal and nonverbal messages effectively and your ability to adapt these messages to your audience. Although we offer numerous guidelines for extemporaneous speaking in this text, consider the three tips in Figure 13.4 before you rehearse and deliver your speech.

RECAP

Methods of Delivery

Manuscript	Reading a speech from a written text
Memorized	Giving a speech word for word from memory without using notes
Impromptu	Delivering a speech without advance preparation
Extemporaneous	Speaking from a written or memorized outline without having memorized the exact wording of the speech

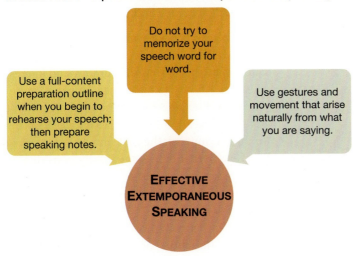

FIGURE 13.4 Tips for Effective Extemporaneous Speaking

Effective Verbal Delivery

13.2 List and explain three criteria for effective verbal delivery.

In an examination of some 125 years' worth of student speeches prepared for intercollegiate competition, researchers Leah White and Lucas Messer found remarkable consistency in students' use of stylized language. White and Messer explain, "Style and delivery are often tightly connected. Speeches rich in language strategies lend themselves to engaging deliveries."[6] Although you will not write out most speeches word for word, you will want to plan and rehearse words, phrases, and sentences that clearly, accurately, and memorably communicate your ideas. Let's examine some guidelines for effectively using and understanding words and word structures in a speech.

Using Words Clearly

Clarity is essential to making meaning. Clear words are specific and concrete, simple, and vivid. Building on our discussion in Chapter 3 of the power of verbal messages, we will examine each of these characteristics in turn.

Specific, Concrete Words A **specific word** refers to an individual member of a general class—for example, *ammonite* as opposed to the more general term *fossil*, or *sodium* as opposed to *chemical*. Specific words are often **concrete words**, appealing to one of the five senses and communicating an image clearly, as Figure 13.5 demonstrates.

In each case, the second word is more specific and concrete than the first and better communicates the image the speaker intends. For maximum clarity in your speeches, use more specific, concrete words than general, abstract ones.

Simple Words **Simple words** are generally an asset to a speaker. An audience will immediately understand them. In his classic essay "Politics and the English Language," George Orwell includes this prescription for simplicity:

> Never use a long word where a short one will do. . . . Never use a foreign phrase, a scientific word, or a jargon word if you can think of an everyday English equivalent.[7]

specific word
A word that refers to an individual member of a general class.

concrete word
A word that appeals to one of the five senses and communicates an image clearly.

simple word
A word known to most people who speak the same language.

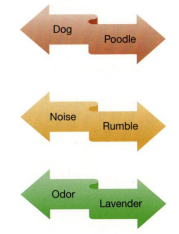

FIGURE 13.5 Which word in each of the following pairs creates a more specific, concrete mental image?

▲ This word cloud visualizes the frequency with which teenage Swedish environmental activist Greta Thunberg used various words in her speech at the 2019 United Nations Climate Action Summit. Many of the words in larger font, which are those Thunberg used most, are simple words that communicate clearly. How can you use simple, specific words to drive home your messages? *Source*: Generated from Greta Thunberg's speech delivered on September 23, 2019, in New York. Susan J. Beebe/Pearson Education

vivid word
A colorful word.

thesaurus
A list of synonyms.

correct word
A word that means what the speaker intends and is grammatically correct in the phrase or sentence in which it appears.

unbiased word
A word that does not stereotype, discriminate against, or insult any gender, ethnic, cultural, or religious group.

Selected thoughtfully, simple words can communicate with both accuracy and power.

Vivid Words **Vivid words** add color and interest to your language. Like concrete words, they help you communicate mental images more accurately and interestingly. Most speakers who try to make their language more vivid think first of adding adjectives to nouns—for example, *distressed oak table* instead of *table*, or *scruffy tabby cat* instead of *cat*. In these examples, the first phrase is certainly more vivid. However, what is less frequently considered and potentially more powerful is substituting vivid verbs for "blah" verbs—for example, *sprout* instead of *grow*, and *devour* instead of *eat*.

When searching for a vivid word, you might want to consult a **thesaurus**, or collection of synonyms. But do not assume that the most obscure or unusual synonym you find will necessarily be the most vivid. Sometimes a simple word can evoke a vivid image for your audience.

Using Words Accurately

In addition to using words clearly, using words accurately is essential to ensuring understanding. The most accurate words are correct and unbiased.

Correct Words Perhaps most obviously, you should use **correct words** when you speak. Grammatical and usage errors communicate a lack of preparation and can lower your credibility with your audience. Be aware of errors that you make habitually. If you are uncertain about how to use a word, look it up in a dictionary or ask someone who knows. If you are stumped by whether to say, "Neither the people nor the president *knows* how to solve the problem" or "Neither the people nor the president *know* how to solve the problem," seek assistance from a credible online site such as the Purdue OWL. (By the way, the first sentence is the correct one.)

Unbiased Words **Unbiased words** do not disparage, either intentionally or unintentionally, any gender or racial, cultural, or religious group, nor do they offend any audience member who may belong to one of these groups.

Although speakers can fairly easily avoid overtly offensive language, they must be especially mindful to avoid language that more subtly stereotypes or discriminates as it could offend others and embarrass themselves.[9] As the former National Transportation

CRITICAL/CULTURAL PERSPECTIVES & COMMUNICATION

Words Constitute Meaning

Even the most carefully chosen words do not objectively transfer meaning from speaker to listener. Instead, words are *constitutive*; they create or constitute meaning for both speaker and listener. A speaker's words may stir her own emotions, even as she voices them. These same words may contribute to listeners' judgments about the speaker's credibility, to listeners' collective identity as a community, to the agency or power that listeners feel, and to the way listeners respond to the speaker's message as a whole. Words do not *transfer* meaning, they *constitute* meaning.

Safety Board Chair Deborah Hersman told attendees at the International Women in Aviation Conference,

> I don't want to hear anybody say "I saw a woman mechanic!"
> Or "I saw an all-woman flight crew!"
> Or "I saw a woman engineer!"
> Or "I saw a woman CEO!"
> Or "I saw a woman in space exploration!"
> Not because there are none of us there, but because there are so many of us there![10]

When possible, adapt to your audience by choosing unbiased gender-neutral language.

> **RE**CAP
> ### Using Words Well
> Use specific, concrete words to communicate clearly and specifically.
> Use simple words to be understood readily.
> Use vivid words to add color and interest to your language.
> Use correct words to enhance your credibility.
> Use unbiased words to avoid offending people of any gender or from any ethnic, cultural, or religious group.

Crafting Memorable Word Structures

We have discussed the importance of using words that are clear and accurate. Now we will turn our attention to crafting memorable word structures that create the figurative language, drama, and cadences needed to provide what one marketing communication specialist calls "ear appeal."[11]

Figurative Language One way to make your message memorable is to use **figurative language**, including **metaphors** (implied comparisons), **similes** (overt comparisons using *like* or *as*), and **personification** (the attribution of human qualities to nonhuman things or ideas). Such language is memorable because it is used in a way that is a little different from its ordinary, expected usage. Figure 13.6 provides examples of each type of figurative language.

Drama Another way to make the word structures in your speech more memorable is to use language to create **drama** by phrasing something in an unexpected way. Three specific devices that can help you achieve verbal drama are omission, inversion, and suspension:

- *Omission.* When you strip a phrase or sentence of nonessential words that the audience expects or with which they are so familiar that they will mentally fill them in,

figurative language
Language that deviates from its ordinary, expected usage to make a description or comparison unique, vivid, and memorable.

metaphor
An implied comparison between two things.

simile
An overt comparison between two things that uses the word *like* or *as*.

personification
The attribution of human qualities to inanimate things or ideas.

drama
A characteristic of a speech created when something is phrased in a way that differs from what the audience expects.

FIGURE 13.6 Figurative Language[12]

Metaphor: . . . there is a green light on the other side of this red light that we're in right now (Actor Matthew McConaughey).

Simile: stars that shone like diamonds on black velvet (Girl Scout Interim CEO Sylvia Acevedo).

Personification: The hard times and vicissitudes of life will ultimately visit everyone (Filmmaker Ken Burns).

omission
Leaving out a word or phrase the audience expects to hear.

inversion
Reversing the normal word order of a phrase or sentence.

suspension
Withholding a key word or phrase until the end of a sentence.

cadence
The rhythm of language.

parallelism
Using the same grammatical structure for two or more clauses or sentences.

antithesis
Using a two-part parallel structure in which the second part contrasts in meaning with the first.

repetition
Emphasizing a key word or phrase by using it more than once.

alliteration
The repetition of a consonant sound (usually the first consonant) several times in a phrase, clause, or sentence.

you are using **omission**. Journalist Bill Moyers described modifications of a major American newspaper with the succinct phrase "More money, less news."[13]

- *Inversion.* **Inversion**—reversing the normal order of words in a phrase or sentence—can also create drama in a speech. In his 2017 presidential inaugural address, Donald Trump inverted the usual subject–verb sentence pattern to verb–subject to make this declaration emphatic and memorable: "Now arrives the hour of action."[14]

- *Suspension.* A third way to create drama through sentence structures is to employ verbal **suspension**, saving an important word or group of words for the end of a sentence rather than placing it at the beginning. Speaking in his eulogy for Kobe Bryant, Michael Jordan used suspension to focus on Bryant's strong desire to compete:

> No matter where he saw me, it was a challenge.[15]

Cadence   A final way to create memorable word structures is to use **cadence**, or language rhythm, in your speech. A speaker does so not by speaking in a singsong pattern, but by using such stylistic devices as parallelism, antithesis, repetition, and alliteration:

- *Parallelism.* **Parallelism** occurs when two or more clauses or sentences have the same grammatical pattern. Governor Andrew Cuomo used parallelism to address the citizens of New York during the coronavirus pandemic in the spring of 2020:

> This is going to be a long day and it's going to be a hard day, and it's going to be an ugly day, and it's going to be a sad day.[16]

The parallel noun phrases, *long day, hard day, ugly day,* and *sad day* emphasized the somber nature of the struggle to come.

- *Antithesis.* Similar to parallelism, except that the two structures contrast in meaning, **antithesis** is often marked by the conjunctions "not only. . . but (also)." In a speech marking the fiftieth anniversary of John F. Kennedy's "Moon Shot" speech, President Joe Biden noted that Kennedy's character was

> a reflection not only of his generation, but of America's character.[17]

- *Repetition.* **Repetition** of an important word or phrase can add emphasis to a key idea and memorability to your message. At the close of a commencement address, GRAIL CEO Jeff Huber repeated his denial of the cliché *Things happen for a reason*:

> Things don't "happen for a reason." But you can find purpose and meaning in things that do happen.
>
> Things don't happen for a reason. But how you respond can reveal your true character.
>
> Things don't happen for a reason. But they do often happen because nobody has yet found a better way.[18]

- *Alliteration.* A final strategy for creating cadence is to use **alliteration**, the repetition of an initial consonant sound several times in a phrase, clause, or sentence. Student

RECAP

Crafting Memorable Word Structures

To make your message memorable, use . . .

Figurative Language

Metaphor	Making an implied comparison
Simile	Making a comparison using *like* or *as*
Personification	Attributing human qualities to nonhuman things or ideas

Drama

Omission	Leaving nonessential words out of a phrase or sentence
Inversion	Reversing the normal order of words in a phrase or sentence
Suspension	Withholding the key ideas in a phrase or sentence until the end

Cadence

Parallelism	Using two or more clauses or sentences with the same grammatical structure
Antithesis	Using a two-part parallel structure in which the second part contrasts in meaning with the first
Repetition	Using a key word or phrase more than once
Alliteration	Repeating a consonant sound

SOCIAL MEDIA & COMMUNICATION

Coded Language on Social Media

Originally a genre of music and dance from the mid-twentieth century, the term *boogaloo* later became a gaming community meme for describing any unwanted sequel after the release of the film *Breakin' 2: Electric Boogaloo*. Today the meme has morphed again, into coded language for pending civil war, used on social networking sites by militant fringe movements to deter the detection efforts of the sites' anti-violence policies.[8]

The rapidly changing meaning of this term illustrates the challenge of identifying and avoiding offensive or discriminatory language. If you have any questions about the meaning of a word you are using in a speech, or a word that you hear someone else use, research that word so that you can be aware of any colloquial or slang meaning or connotation.

speaker Saeed used alliteration to help his audience remember two steps for solving the problem of child slavery in the chocolate industry:

> Munch and mobilize.[19]

Repeating the *m* sound added cadence—and memorability—to Saeed's two steps.

Effective Nonverbal Delivery

13.3 Identify and illustrate characteristics of effective nonverbal delivery.

At this point, you understand how important it is to deliver your speech effectively and what delivery style most audiences today prefer. You are familiar with the four methods of delivery and know how to maximize the use of each one. You also have some ideas about how to use effective and memorable language. Still, you may wonder, "What do I do with my hands?" "Is it all right to move around while I speak?" "How can I make my voice sound interesting?" To help answer these and similar questions, and to help you use nonverbal messages more effectively, we will examine five major categories of nonverbal delivery: eye contact, physical delivery, facial expression, vocal delivery, and personal appearance. This discussion further develops the fundamental principle of using and interpreting nonverbal messages that we introduced in Chapter 4.

Eye Contact

Of all the nonverbal delivery variables discussed in this chapter, the most important one in a public speaking situation for North Americans is **eye contact**. Eye contact with your audience members lets them know that you are interested in and ready to talk to them. It also permits you to determine whether they are responding to you. In addition, most listeners will think that you are more capable and trustworthy if you look them in the eye than if you avoid eye contact. Some studies document a relationship between eye contact and speaker credibility, as well as between eye contact and listener learning in both face-to-face and mediated environments.[20]

eye contact
Looking at audience members directly in their eyes during a presentation.

How much eye contact do you need? One study found that speakers with less than 50 percent eye contact are considered unfriendly, uninformed, inexperienced, and even dishonest by their listeners.[21] On the other hand, is there such a thing as too much eye contact? For North American audiences, the answer is probably not. Be aware, though, that not all people from all cultures prefer as much eye contact as North Americans do. Many Asian cultures, for example, generally prefer less.

If you are recording your speeches for an online class, you will need to establish eye contact with the device you're using to record your speech, which can be challenging. Although doing so may seem easier than looking at a live audience, more than two-thirds of respondents in one study felt that it was actually more difficult.[22]

DIVERSITY & COMMUNICATION

The Academic Quarter

When speaking at a Polish university a few years ago, one of your authors expected to begin promptly at 11:00 a.m., as announced in the program and on posters. By 11:10, it was clear that the speech would not begin on time, and your author began to despair of having any audience at all.

In Poland, it turns out, both students and professors expect to adhere to the "academic quarter." In other words, most lectures begin at least fifteen minutes (a quarter of an hour) after the announced starting time.

If your author had asked a Polish professor about the audience's expectations, he would have known about this custom in advance. One way to avoid such misunderstandings is to talk with people you know who are familiar with the cultural expectations. Another way is to observe other speakers presenting to similar audiences. Ask specific questions, including the following:

1. Where does the audience expect me to stand while speaking?
2. Do listeners expect direct eye contact?
3. When will the audience expect me to start and stop my talk?
4. Will listeners find movement and gestures distracting or welcome?
5. Do listeners expect presentation aids?

Keep cultural differences in mind as you rehearse and deliver speeches to diverse audiences.

---

physical delivery
A person's gestures, movement, and posture, which influence how a message is interpreted.

gestures
Movements of the hands and arms to communicate ideas.

▼ This speaker's gesture acknowledging his fellow graduates is simple, natural, and definite. Focusing on your audience and your message during rehearsals can help you to gesture effectively when you deliver your speech to an audience.
Comstock/Stockbyte/Getty Images

The following suggestions can help you use eye contact more effectively when giving a speech:

- Establish eye contact with your audience before you say anything. Eye contact sends listeners a message to tune in as you start your talk.
- Maintain eye contact with your audience as you deliver your opening sentence without looking at your notes.
- Try to establish eye contact with people throughout your audience, not just with the front row or only one or two people. Briefly look into the eyes of an individual, and then transfer your eye contact to someone else.
- Do not look over your listeners' heads. They will notice if you do so and may even turn around to try to find out what you are looking at.
- If you are giving a mediated speech with no audience present, look into the camera lens. If you can see your audience on a shared screen, look at the audience members rather than only at the lens.

Physical Delivery

Gestures, movement, and posture are the three key elements of **physical delivery**. A good speaker knows how to use effective gestures, make meaningful movements, and maintain appropriate posture while speaking to an audience.

Gestures The hand and arm movements you use while speaking are called **gestures**. Nearly all people from all cultures use some gestures when they speak. In fact, research suggests that gesturing is instinctive and that it is intrinsic to speaking and thinking.[23] Yet even if you gesture easily and appropriately in the course of everyday conversation, you may feel awkward about what to do with your hands when you are in front of an audience. To minimize this challenge, consider the following guidelines:

- Focus on the message you want to communicate. As in ordinary conversation, your hands should help emphasize or reinforce your verbal message. Your gestures should coincide with what you are saying.
- Again, as in conversation, let your gestures flow with your message. They should appear natural, not tense or rigid.
- Be definite. If you want to gesture, go ahead and gesture. Avoid making minor hand movements that will be masked by the lectern or that may appear to your audience as accidental brief jerks.
- Vary your gestures. Try not to use the same hand or one all-purpose gesture all the time. Think of the different gestures you can use, depending on whether you want to enumerate, point, describe, or emphasize ideas.
- Don't overdo your gestures. You want your audience to focus not on your gestures, but on your message.
- Make your gestures appropriate to your audience and the situation. When speaking to a large audience in a relatively formal face-to-face setting, use bolder, more sweeping, and more dramatic gestures than you would use when speaking to a small audience in an informal or online setting. Also consider the culture-based expectations of your audience. Americans in general tend to use more gestures than speakers from other cultures. If you are speaking to a culturally diverse audience, you may want to tone down your gestures.

Movement Another element of physical delivery is **movement**. You may wonder, "Should I walk around during my speech, or should I stay in one place?" "Should I stay behind the lectern, or could I stand beside or in front of it?" "Can I move around among the audience?" The following criteria may help you answer these questions:

movement
A purposeful change of location during a presentation.

- Like gestures, any movement should be purposeful. It should be consistent with the verbal content of your message; otherwise, it will appear to be aimless wandering. You might signal the beginning of a new idea or major point in your speech with movement, or you might move to signal a transition from a serious idea to a more humorous one. The bottom line is that your movement should make sense to your listeners.
- If a physical barrier such as a lectern, a row of chairs, or an overhead projector makes you feel cut off from your listeners, move closer to the audience. Studies suggest that physical proximity enhances learning.[24]
- Adapt to the cultural expectations of your audience. British listeners, for example, have commented to us that American lecturers tend to stand too close to an audience when speaking. If you think moving closer to your audience will make them uncomfortable, stay in one carefully chosen spot to deliver your speech.

Posture **Posture** is the third element of physical delivery to consider when delivering a speech. One study suggests that your posture may reflect on your credibility as a speaker.[25] Certainly, slouching lazily across a lectern does not communicate enthusiasm for or interest in your audience or your topic. On the other hand, you should adapt your posture to your topic, your audience, and the level of formality of the speaking occasion. For example, during a very informal speech, it may be perfectly appropriate, as well as comfortable and natural, to lean against the edge of a desk.

posture
A speaker's stance.

Few speech teachers or texts advocate specific speaking postures. Instead, you should observe some commonsense guidelines about posture:

- Avoid slouching, shifting from one foot to the other, or drooping your head.
- Unless you are unable to stand, avoid sitting when delivering a face-to-face speech. An exception might be perching on or leaning against the edge of a desk or stool (which would still elevate you slightly above your audience) during a very informal speech.

Like your gestures and movement, your posture should not call attention to itself. Rather, it should reflect your interest in and attention to your audience and your message.

Facial Expression

facial expression
An arrangement of the facial muscles to communicate thoughts, emotions, and attitudes.

Your **facial expression** plays a key role in expressing your thoughts, emotions, and attitudes.[26] Your audience sees your face before they hear what you are going to say, giving you the opportunity to set the tone for your message even before you begin to speak. Social psychologist Paul Ekman has found that facial expressions of primary emotions are virtually universal, so even a culturally diverse audience should be able to read many of your facial expressions clearly.[27]

Throughout your speech, your facial expression, like your body language and eye contact, should be appropriate to your message. Relate somber news wearing a serious expression. Tell a humorous story with a smile. To communicate interest in your listeners, keep your expression alert and friendly. To ensure that you are maximizing the use of this important nonverbal delivery cue, rehearse your speech in front of a mirror; better yet, record and analyze videos of yourself rehearsing your speech. Consider as objectively as possible whether your face is reflecting the emotional tone of your ideas.

Vocal Delivery

vocal delivery
Nonverbal voice cues, including volume, pitch, rate, and articulation.

We have already discussed the importance of selecting words and phrases that will most effectively communicate your ideas and information. We referred to this element of delivery as verbal delivery. **Vocal delivery**, on the other hand, involves nonverbal vocal cues—not the words you say, but the way you say them. Effective vocal delivery requires you to speak so that your audience can understand you and will remain interested in what you are saying. Nonverbal vocal elements include volume, pitch, rate, and articulation.

volume
The softness or loudness of a speaker's voice.

Volume Volume is the softness or loudness of your voice. It is the most fundamental determinant of audience understanding. If you do not speak loudly enough, even the most brilliant presentation will be ineffective, because the audience simply will not hear you. In addition, volume can signal important ideas in your speech; for example, you can deliver a key idea either more loudly or more softly than you have been speaking. To help you appropriately adapt the volume of your voice to your audience's needs, consider these guidelines:

- Speak loudly enough so that the audience members farthest from you can hear you without straining. Doing so will ensure that everyone else in the room can hear you, too. If you are delivering a mediated speech, conduct a microphone test before the speaking event or class begins.
- Vary the volume of your voice in a purposeful way. Indicate important ideas by turning your volume up or down.
- For face-to-face speeches, be aware of whether you need a microphone to amplify your volume. If you do, and one is available, use it.

You will probably use the microphone built into your computer or earbuds for a mediated speech. To amplify volume for face-to-face speeches, there are three kinds of microphones, only one of which demands much technique:

1. *Lavaliere or Wireless Hand-Held.* Both lavaliere and wireless hand-held microphones allow a speaker to move freely while speaking. Often worn on the front of a shirt or a jacket lapel by news reporters and interviewees, a lavaliere microphone requires no particular care other than not thumping it or accidentally knocking it off.

2. *Boom.* A boom microphone is used by filmmakers. It hangs over the heads of the speakers and is controlled remotely, so the speakers need not be particularly concerned with it.
3. *Stationary.* A stationary microphone may attach to a lectern, sit on a desk, or stand on the floor. Generally, today's stationary microphones are multidirectional. Even so, you will have to keep your mouth at about the same distance from the microphone at all times to avoid distracting fluctuations in the volume of sound. You can turn your head from side to side and use gestures, but you will have to limit other movements.

Under ideal circumstances, you will be able to practice with your microphone. If you have the chance, figure out where to stand for the best sound quality and to determine how sensitive the microphone is to extraneous noise. Practice will accustom you to any voice distortion or echo that might occur so that these sound qualities do not surprise you during your presentation.

Pitch Whereas volume is the loudness or softness of your voice, **pitch** refers to how high or low your voice is. To some extent, pitch is determined by physiology. The faster the folds in your vocal cords vibrate, the higher the habitual pitch of your voice. In general, female vocal folds vibrate much faster than do those of males. You can, however, raise or lower your habitual pitch within a certain range.

Variation in pitch, called **inflection**, is a key factor in communicating the meaning of your words. You know that a startled "Oh!" in response to something someone has told you communicates something quite different from a lower-pitched, questioning "Oh?" Your vocal inflection indicates your emotional response to what you have heard.

Vocal inflection also helps to keep an audience interested in your message. If you speak in a monotone, without changing your pitch, the audience will probably become bored quickly. To help you monitor and practice your pitch and inflection as you prepare to speak, record and play back your speech at least once as you rehearse. Listen carefully to your pitch and inflection. If you think that you are speaking in too much of a monotone, practice again with exaggerated variations in pitch. Eventually, you will find a happy medium.

Rate Another vocal variable is **rate**, or speed. How fast do you talk? Most speakers average between 120 and 180 words per minute. Good speakers vary their rate to add interest to their delivery and to emphasize key ideas. To determine whether your speaking rate is appropriate and purposeful, become conscious of it. Record your presentation during rehearsal and listen critically to your speech speed. If you are speaking too slowly, make a conscious effort to speed up. If you are speaking too quickly, insert a strategic **pause** before presenting a key idea, after sharing an important point, and after asking a question.[28]

pitch
How high or low a speaker's voice is.

inflection
Variation in vocal pitch.

rate
How fast or slowly a speaker speaks.

pause
A few seconds of silence during a speech, used both to slow a fast pace and to signal a key idea.

DEVELOPING YOUR SPEECH STEP BY STEP

Rehearsing Your Speech

Dezerae begins to rehearse her speech. From the beginning, she stands and speaks aloud, practicing gestures and movement that seem appropriate to her message.

At first, Dezerae rehearses from her preparation outline (see Chapter 12). These early rehearsals go quite well, but the speech runs a little short. Dezerae knows that she tends to speak fairly rapidly, so she decides to plan more pauses throughout the speech—some to allow her listeners to think about an important point she has just made, and others to provide nonverbal transitions. When she prepares her speaking notes, Dezerae writes the delivery cue "Pause" in several strategic places.

articulation
The production of clear and distinct speech sounds.

dialect
A consistent style of pronunciation and articulation that is common to an ethnic group or geographic region.

appearance
A speaker's dress and grooming.

Articulation   Articulation is the enunciation of sounds. As a speaker, you want to articulate distinctly to ensure that your audience can determine what words you are using. Sometimes we fall into the habit of mumbling or slurring—saying *wanna* instead of *want to*, or *chesterdrawers* instead of *chest of drawers*. Some nonstandard articulation may be part of a speaker's **dialect**, a speech style common to an ethnic group or a geographic region. One dialect with which most of us are familiar is the dialect of the southern United States, characterized by a distinctive drawl.

Although most native speakers of English can understand different English dialects, studies have shown that North American listeners assign more favorable ratings to, and can recall more information presented by, speakers with dialects similar to their own.[29] If your dialect is significantly different from that of your listeners, or you suspect that it could be potentially distracting, you may want to work to improve your articulation or standardize your dialect. To do so, be aware of words or phrases that you have a tendency to drawl, slur, or chop. Once you have identified them, practice saying them distinctly and correctly.

Appearance

What would you wear to deliver a speech to your class? To address your city council? The fact that you would probably wear something different for each of these occasions suggests that you are already aware of the importance of a speaker's **appearance**. There is considerable evidence that your personal appearance affects how your audience will respond to you and your message. If you violate your audience's expectations, you will be less successful in achieving your purpose. The following guidelines may make selecting a wardrobe a bit easier when you are next called on to speak:

- Never wear anything potentially distracting, such as a T-shirt with writing on it. You want your audience to listen to you, not read your shirt.
- Consider that appropriate clothing can be a presentation aid. For example, if you are a nurse or an emergency technician, wear your uniform when you speak about your profession. (We will discuss presentation aids in more detail shortly.)
- Take cues from your audience. If you know that they will be dressed in business attire, dress similarly. If anything, you want to be a bit more dressed up than the members of your audience.
- When in doubt about what to wear, select something conservative.
- Dress for a mediated speech as you would for a face-to-face speech.

RECAP
Characteristics of Effective Nonverbal Delivery

- Eye contact should be established before you say anything and should be sustained as much as possible throughout your speech.
- Gestures should be relaxed, definite, varied, and appropriate to your audience and the speaking situation.
- Movement should be purposeful and adapted to the audience's cultural expectations.
- Posture should feel natural and should be appropriate to your topic, your audience, and the occasion.
- Facial expression should be alert, friendly, and appropriate to your message.
- Volume should be loud enough that you can be easily heard and should be purposefully varied.
- Pitch should be varied so that the inflection in your voice helps sustain your audience's interest.
- Rate should be neither too fast nor too slow and can be varied to add interest and emphasize key ideas.
- Articulation should be clear and distinct.
- Appearance should conform to what the audience expects.

Effective Presentation Aids

13.4 Discuss how to prepare and use presentation aids effectively.

We have already discussed two elements of delivery: verbal delivery and nonverbal delivery. A third element used with increasing frequency in this era of sophisticated computer presentation software is the **presentation aid**. The term *presentation aid* refers to anything your audience can listen to or look at to help them understand your ideas. Images, text, video, audio, objects, models, and people are some of the types of presentation aids frequently used by speakers.

As long as they *aid* the speaker, rather than *replace* the speaker or the speech, presentation aids can be invaluable. They help you gain and maintain your audience's attention.[30] They communicate the organization of your ideas. They illustrate sequences of events or procedures. They help your audience understand and remember your message. In addition, chances are that for at least one assignment in your communication class, you will be required to use a presentation aid. Because presentation aids are valuable supplements to your speeches and because students of communication are so often required to use them, let's discuss first the types of available presentation aids. Then we will discuss guidelines for using computer-generated presentation aids and, finally, provide some general suggestions for using presentation aids effectively.

presentation aid
Any tangible item used to help communicate ideas to an audience.

Types of Presentation Aids

If you are required to use a presentation aid for an assignment or you think that a presentation aid might enhance your message, you have a number of options from which to select. You could use drawings, photographs, maps, graphs, charts, text, video, audio, objects, models, or people.

Images The most commonly used presentation aids are two-dimensional images: drawings, photographs, maps, graphs, and charts.

- **Drawings.** You can use simple drawings to help illustrate or explain ideas that you are talking about. For example, you could sketch the tunnels of a fire ant mound to show your audience why it is so difficult to eradicate an entire ant colony. You could sketch the plants and animals that are crucial to the life cycle of the Florida Everglades. If you are not a confident illustrator, you could ask a friend to help you prepare a drawing, or you could use computer software to generate a simple image. Your drawings do not have to be original artwork. Just be sure to credit your source if you use someone else's sketch. A good way to display your drawing to your audience is to scan it and then put it into a computer-generated slide. Keep your drawings large and simple. Line drawings are often more effective than more detailed ones.
- **Photographs.** If you are giving a speech on urban forestry, you might want to show your audience high-quality photographs of trees that are appropriate for urban sites in your area. In this case, photographs would show color and detail that would be nearly impossible to achieve with drawings.

    The biggest challenge to using photographs as presentation aids is size; most printed photos are simply too small to be seen clearly from a distance. If you want to display photos, bring the digital image files up on your smartphone or computer screen, and use a projection system to enlarge them for your audience.
- **Maps.** Like photographs, most maps are too small to be useful as presentation aids; to be effective, they must be enlarged in some way. You can accomplish this by scanning and transferring your map to a computer-generated slide. Be sure to highlight the areas or routes you are going to talk about in your speech.
- **Charts.** Charts can summarize and organize a great deal of information in a small space. Consider using a chart any time you need to present information that could be organized under several headings or in several columns. The chart in Figure 13.7 displays the number of COVID-19 cases in the United States by age group on July 7, 2020.[31] You can prepare charts quite easily by using the table feature in your

FIGURE 13.7 Chart

COVID-19 Cases in the U.S., by Age Groups, July 7, 2020 (Rounded to Nearest Thousands)	
< 18	140,000
18–49	846,000
50–64	939,000
65–74	211,000
75–84	130,000
85+	125,000

word-processing program. Again, be sure your chart is large enough to be seen easily. Make it visually simple and do not put too much information in one chart.
- **Graphs.** Graphs are effective ways to present statistical relationships to your audience and help make data more concrete. You are probably already familiar with the three basic types of graphs:

1. *Bar graph.* A **bar graph** consists of bars of various lengths that represent percentages or numbers. It is useful for making comparisons.
2. *Pie graph.* A round **pie graph** shows how data are divided proportionately.
3. *Line graph.* A **line graph** can show both trends over a period of time and relationships among variables.

We recommend that you use raw data and a computer program like Microsoft Word or Excel to generate graphs. Your graphs should be simple and uncluttered. Figure 13.8 illustrates the three basic types of graphs.[32] These examples were created using Microsoft Excel.

bar graph
A graph consisting of bars of various lengths that represent numbers or percentages.

pie graph
A circular graph that shows how a set of data is divided proportionately.

line graph
A graph that shows trends over a period of time and relationships among variables.

FIGURE 13.8 Three Types of Graphs: (A) Bar Graph, (B) Pie Graph, and (C) Line Graph

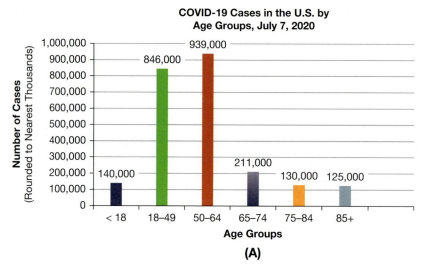

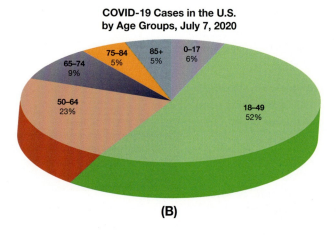

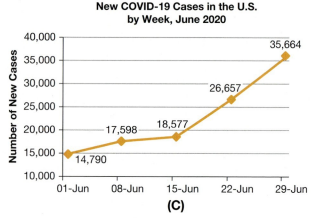

Text In addition to—or instead of—using images, many speakers use a word, phrase, or bulleted outline as a presentation aid. Although some speakers still occasionally display text on chalkboards, dry-erase boards, flipcharts, or posters, most speakers today use slides created with PowerPoint or similar presentation software. Although presentation software helps you adapt your message to audiences who increasingly expect sophisticated visual aids, do not use it simply to project your speaking notes. Rather than letting your slides *become* your presentation, use them to *supplement* it. Figure 13.9 offers suggestions for effectively using text as a presentation aid.

FIGURE 13.9 Effectively Using Text as a Presentation Aid

Using Text Effectively

Make certain the text conveys significant information.

Don't use too much text. Some experts suggest no more than seven lines of text on any single slide.

Make informed and mindful decisions about fonts, color, and layout. A light background with darker-colored words in a simple 28-point or larger font usually works well.

Audio and Video Audio, such as music or excerpts from speeches or interviews, can be used as a presentation aid. Similarly, you could show clips from a movie, an excerpt from a training film, or a brief original video. Make sure any recordings stored on flash drives, smartphones, or tablets, or streamed from the Internet, offer good picture and sound quality and permit freeze-frame viewing. Most video devices allow you to replay a scene several times if you want your audience to listen or watch for different specific elements.

If you plan to use an audio or video presentation aid, consider the suggestions provided in Figure 13.10.

FIGURE 13.10 Effectively Using Video and Audio Presentation Aids

Using Video and Audio Effectively

Use only brief clips and excerpts. Audio and video should always supplement, rather than supplant, your speech.

Have the equipment set up and ready to go in the room where you are speaking.

Be certain the volume is amplified enough that your audience can hear it without straining.

Be certain your audience can see your video. If you have an audience of 25 to 30 people, you can use a 25-inch screen for video. For larger audiences, you will need to use several television monitors or projection technology.

ETHICS & COMMUNICATION

Profanity in an Audio Presentation Aid

Matt wants to talk to his college classmates about the use of profanity in rap music. He plans to play audio clips of several profane song lyrics to illustrate his point. Should Matt play these songs, even though doing so might offend several members of his audience? Why or why not?

Objects and Models The first type of presentation aid you ever used—perhaps as long ago as preschool "show and tell"—was probably an object. You took to school your favorite teddy bear or the new remote-control car you got for your birthday. Remember how the kids crowded around to see what you had brought?

Because listeners of all ages like tangible, real things, using objects as presentation aids can still help you engage your audience. In his speech on the lead danger from water pipes, student speaker Nick held up two water bottles as he said,

> I have two water bottles here. The brown water is from Flint, Michigan, and the clear water is from my apartment in the nearby city of Detroit. Which bottle contains a dangerous level of lead? The answer? Both do.[33]

He had his audience's full attention. Figure 13.11 includes guidelines for effectively using objects and models as presentation aids.

If it is not possible to bring an object to class, you may be able to substitute a model. For example, you cannot bring a 1956 Ford Thunderbird into a classroom, but you may be able to construct and bring a model. You probably could not acquire a dog's heart to bring to class, but you might be able to find a model to use for your explanation of how heartworms damage that vital organ. If you use a model as a presentation aid, be sure it is large enough to be seen by all members of your audience.

People You might not think of people as potential presentation aids, but they can be. George W. Bush used ordinary people as visual aids for some of his most important presidential speeches, "asking them to stand and then telling stories of their sacrifices or heroism . . . a way of coming down from the stage, as it were, and mingling with the crowd."[34] In other instances, people can model costumes, play an instrument, or demonstrate a dance. If you are going to ask someone to assist you by acting as a presentation aid for a speech, consider the guidelines provided in Figure 13.12.

Additional Guidelines for Preparing and Using Presentation Aids

In addition to the specific guidelines provided for various types of presentation aids, the following general guidelines can help you prepare and use all types of presentation aids more effectively.

FIGURE 13.11 Effectively Using Objects and Models as Presentation Aids

Using Objects and Models Effectively

- **Make certain the object or model is neither too large nor too small.** If it is too large, it may be unwieldy; if it is too small, your audience won't be able to see it.
- **Don't use dangerous or illegal objects as presentation aids.** They may make your audience members uneasy or actually put them at risk.

FIGURE 13.12 Effectively Using People as Presentation Aids

Using People Effectively

- **Rehearse with the person who will be helping you.**
- **Don't have the person stand beside you, doing nothing.** Wait and introduce the person to your audience when needed.
- **Don't let your presentation aid steal the show.** Make his or her role specific and fairly brief. As the speaker, you should remain the "person of the hour."

Select the Right Presentation Aids As is evident from the above discussion, you have a number of options for presentation aids. If you are trying to decide which to use, consider these suggestions:

1. Be constantly aware of your specific purpose. Be certain that your presentation aid contributes to it.
2. Adapt to your listeners. Let their interests, experiences, and knowledge guide your selection of presentation aids. For example, an audience of accountants would readily understand arbitrage charts that might be incomprehensible to a more general audience. If you will be speaking to a large audience, be certain that everyone will be able to see or hear your presentation aid.
3. Consider your own skill and experience. Use equipment with which you have had experience, or allow yourself ample time to practice.
4. Take into account the room in which you will speak. If it has large windows and no shades, for example, do not plan to use a visual presentation aid that will require a darkened room. If you plan to use PowerPoint slides, be sure that both hardware and software are available and in good working order.

> ## RECAP
> **Types of Presentation Aids**
>
> - Keep *drawings* simple and large.
> - Be sure that *photographs* are large enough to be seen easily.
> - Highlight on a *map* the geographic areas you will discuss.
> - Limit the amount of information you put on any single *chart*.
> - Keep *graphs* simple and uncluttered.
> - Use only brief *video and audio clips*, make sure they can be easily seen or heard, and have equipment ready to go before you speak.
> - Use *objects* and *models* that you can handle easily and that are safe and legal.
> - Rehearse with *people* who will serve as presentation aids, and don't let them steal the show.

Use Presentation Aids Thoughtfully One speechwriter and presentation coach warns against this bleak but all-too-common scenario:

> The presenter says, "And now, I'd like to talk about quality." And lo and behold . . . the word *quality* flashes on a screen. Now, folks, does this slide offer any new information? Does it clarify a complex point? Does it strengthen the bond between presenter and audience? You know the answer: a resounding "no."[35]

Be sure that the aids you use help you communicate your message.

Rehearse with Your Presentation Aids The day of your speech should not be the first time you deliver your presentation while holding up your model, advancing your PowerPoint slides, or cueing up your video clip. Practice setting up and using your presentation aids until you feel at ease with them. If you will be delivering a mediated speech, practice using the feature of your video conferencing software that allows you to share your screen, or to switch back and forth between the two screens. Consider during rehearsal what you would do at various stages of the speech if you had to carry on without a particular presentation aid. For example, what if a software application crashes, the Wi-Fi stops working, your equipment fails to show up, or the electricity goes off? Have contingency plans.

Maintain Eye Contact with Your Audience, Not with Your Presentation Aids You can glance at your presentation aids during your speech, but do not talk to them. Keep looking at your audience.

Explain Your Presentation Aids Always talk about and explain your presentation aids. Do not assume that the audience will understand their relevance and how to interpret them.

Time the Display of Your Presentation Aids to Coincide with Your Discussion of Them Don't put a presentation aid in front of your audience until you are ready to use it. Likewise, remove or cover your presentation aid after you finish with it. Keeping presentation aids in front of an audience before or after you use them will only serve to distract from your message.

▲ Before delivering a mediated speech, practice using the feature of your video conferencing software that allows you to share your screen.
Kayoko Hayashi/E+/Getty Images

Do Not Pass Objects, Pictures, or Other Small Items among Audience Members Passing things around distracts audience members. Either people are focused on whatever they are looking at, or they are counting the number of people who will handle the object before it reaches them. If the item is too small for everyone to see it when you hold it up, it is not a good presentation aid.

Use Handouts Effectively Handing out papers during your speech can distract your audience. If possible, wait to distribute handouts until after you have spoken. If your audience needs to refer to the material while you are speaking about it, go ahead and pass out the handouts; then, at various points in your speech, tell audience members where in the handout they should focus.

Use Small Children and Animals with Caution Small children and even the best-trained animals are unpredictable. In a strange environment, in front of an audience, they may not behave in their usual way. The risk of having a child or animal detract from your message may be too great to justify using either as a presentation aid.

Some Final Tips for Rehearsing and Delivering Your Speech

13.5 Make the most of your rehearsal time, and deliver your speech effectively.

Throughout this chapter, we have described and offered suggestions for effective verbal and nonverbal delivery and use of presentation aids. In addition to those tips, the following suggestions will help you make the most of your rehearsal time and ultimately deliver your speech successfully:

- *Finish your preparation outline several days before you must deliver the speech.* Begin to rehearse from the preparation outline. Revise the speech as necessary, and then prepare your speaking notes. Continue to rehearse and modify your speaking notes as necessary.

- *Practice, practice, practice.* Rehearse aloud as often as possible. Only by rehearsing will you gain confidence in both the content of the speech and your delivery of it. As the author of the bestselling book *Quiet: The Power of Introverts in a World That Can't Stop Talking* points out,

  > If you went to a job interview without fixing your tie or applying your lipstick in front of the mirror, you would hope that there's no scarlet lip gloss smeared across your teeth, but how could you know for sure? Better to take the guesswork out of it.[36]

- *Use good delivery skills while rehearsing.* Rehearse your speech standing up. Pay attention to your gestures, posture, eye contact, facial expression, and vocal delivery, as well as the verbal message. Rehearse with your presentation aids.

- *If possible, practice your speech in front of someone.* Researchers in one study found that students who practice their speeches before an audience score higher on evaluations than those who practice without an audience.[37]
- *Use audio or video technology to record your speech, but try not to be overly critical when you listen to or watch yourself, as many of us tend to be.* Notice whether you use too many filler sounds or words, such as "uh," "er," "okay," "you know," and "like." Realize, however, that you're developing a delivery style unique to you, so don't try to change too much.
- *Prepare the room and equipment.* You may want to rearrange the furniture or any equipment. If you are using technology, check to see that it is working properly, and set up your presentation aids carefully.
- *Re-create the speaking situation in your final rehearsals.* Try to rehearse in a room similar to the one where you will deliver the speech. Use the speaking notes you will use the day you deliver the speech. Give the presentation without stopping. The more realistic the rehearsal, the more confidence you will gain.
- *Get plenty of rest the night before you speak.* Being well rested is more valuable than squeezing in a frantic, last-minute rehearsal.
- *Arrive early.* If you do not know for certain the location of the room in which you will make your presentation, give yourself plenty of time to find it. Set up and check your presentation aids.
- *Review and apply the suggestions offered in Chapter 11 for becoming a more confident speaker.* As the moment for delivering your speech nears, remind yourself of the effort you have spent preparing it. Visualize yourself delivering the speech effectively. Silently practice your opening lines. Think about your audience. Breathe deeply. Relax.
- *If something unforeseen (a ringing cell phone, for example) briefly interrupts your speech, remain composed as you pause briefly and then pick up where you left off.* If the incident is

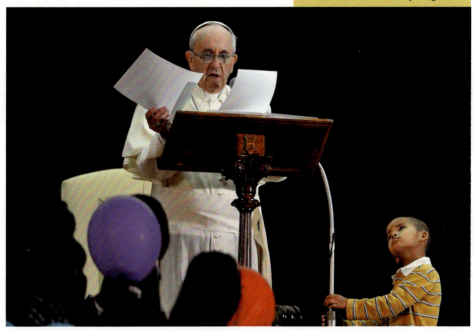

▼ When a small boy insisted on participating in one of Pope Francis's early speeches, the Pope seemed delighted rather than distracted. How can you prepare to deliver your speech with similar composure?
TIZIANA FABI/AFP/Getty Images

DEVELOPING YOUR SPEECH STEP BY STEP

Delivering Your Speech

The long-awaited day of Dezerae's speech has arrived at last. She got a full night's sleep last night and ate a light breakfast before setting out for class.

As she waits to speak, Dezerae visualizes herself delivering her speech calmly and confidently. When her name is called, she rises, walks to the front of the room, and establishes eye contact with her audience before she begins to speak. Dezerae focuses on adapting her message to her listeners. She looks at individual members of her audience, uses purposeful and well-timed gestures, and speaks loudly and clearly.

Even before she hears her classmates' applause, Dezerae knows that her speech has gone well.

amusing, you can laugh along with your audience. When the presidential seal fell off Barack Obama's lectern and crashed to the stage during a speech, he quipped, "That's all right, all of you know who I am."[38]

- *After you have delivered your speech, seek feedback from members of your audience.* Use the information you gain to improve your next presentation.

Criteria for Evaluating Speeches

13.6 Understand and apply criteria for evaluating speeches.

What makes a speech successful? Our purpose here is not to take you through the centuries of dialogue and debate about this issue, but rather to offer practical ways to evaluate your own speeches as well as those of others.

Your instructor will probably use a rubric or evaluation form that lists precise criteria. Underlying any list of what a successful speaker should do, however, are two fundamental goals: A successful speech should be *effective*, and it should be *ethical*.

- *Effective.* To be effective, a speech should be understandable to listeners and should achieve the speaker's intended purpose.[39]
- *Ethical.* A good speaker is an ethical speaker—one who tells the truth, cites sources for nonoriginal words and ideas, and is sensitive and responsive to listeners. Even if a message can be understood clearly and achieves the speaker's purpose, if the speaker has used unethical means to achieve that purpose, the speech is not successful.

STUDY GUIDE: PRINCIPLES FOR A LIFETIME — CHAPTER 13

Methods of Delivery

13.1 List and describe the four methods of delivery, and provide suggestions for effectively using each one.

PRINCIPLE POINTS: As you consider how you will deliver your presentation speech, you will select from four methods of delivery: manuscript speaking, memorized speaking, impromptu speaking, and extemporaneous speaking. Extemporaneous speaking is the style taught today in most presentational public speaking classes and preferred by most audiences.

PRINCIPLE TERMS:

manuscript speaking	impromptu speaking
memorized speaking	extemporaneous speaking

PRINCIPLE SKILLS: Answering an instructor's question or presenting a summary of a small group discussion to the larger class may call for impromptu speaking skills. Based on your observations and experiences in such situations, what tips can you add to those provided in Figure 13.3?

Effective Verbal Delivery

13.2 List and explain three criteria for effective verbal delivery.

PRINCIPLE POINTS: Once you know what method of delivery you will use, you should think about and rehearse words, phrases, and sentences that will best communicate your intended message and give it a distinct and memorable style. The most effective language is clear, accurate, and memorable.

PRINCIPLE TERMS:

specific word	personification
concrete word	drama
simple word	omission
vivid word	inversion
thesaurus	suspension
correct word	cadence
unbiased word	parallelism
figurative language	antithesis
metaphor	repetition
simile	alliteration

PRINCIPLE SKILLS: A friend asks you for advice on making the word choice in her speech as effective as possible. Offer her at least three suggestions based on the criteria in this chapter for using words effectively.

Effective Nonverbal Delivery

13.3 Identify and illustrate characteristics of effective nonverbal delivery.

PRINCIPLE POINTS: Nonverbal variables are critical to effective delivery. Physical delivery includes a speaker's gestures, movement, and posture. Eye contact is perhaps the most important delivery variable, determining to a large extent your credibility with your audience. Facial expression plays a key role in expressing your thoughts, emotions, and attitudes. Vocal delivery includes such elements as volume, pitch, rate, and articulation. Finally, your personal appearance can affect how your audience responds to you and your message.

PRINCIPLE TERMS:

eye contact	pitch
physical delivery	inflection
gestures	rate
movement	pause
posture	articulation
facial expression	dialect
vocal delivery	appearance
volume	

PRINCIPLE SKILLS:

1. Which of the characteristics of nonverbal delivery described so far—eye contact, gesturing, movement, posture, or facial expression—are you confident you can use effectively? Which are most challenging for you? Which of the tips in this chapter do you plan to use to help you overcome your challenges?
2. For a speech you have viewed either live or online, consider the speaker's nonverbal delivery. Did he or she make appropriate eye contact with the audience? Did the speaker use appropriate volume and vocal variation? Did he or she use gestures effectively? Explain your responses.

Effective Presentation Aids

13.4 Discuss how to prepare and use presentation aids effectively.

PRINCIPLE POINTS: Presentation aids include images, text, video, audio, objects, models, and people. All presentation aids should be easy to see and simple. Also be sure to select the right presentation aids, use presentations aids thoughtfully, rehearse with your presentation aids, explain your presentation aids, time the use of your presentation aids, refrain from passing things around or using handouts indiscriminately, and remember that small children and animals are unpredictable presentation aids.

PRINCIPLE TERMS:

presentation aid	pie graph
bar graph	line graph

PRINCIPLE SKILLS: What is the least effective use of presentation aids you've witnessed? Based on this chapter, what advice would you give to that speaker to help improve his or her use of presentation aids?

Some Final Tips for Rehearsing and Delivering Your Speech

13.5 Make the most of your rehearsal time, and deliver your speech effectively.

PRINCIPLE POINTS: Final suggestions for rehearsing your speech include allowing ample time, rehearsing it aloud while standing up, practicing your speech in front of someone, recording and listening to or watching your speech, and re-creating the actual speaking situation in your final rehearsals. Make sure you get plenty of rest the night before you speak, arrive early, and apply the suggestions offered in Chapter 11 for becoming a more confident speaker.

PRINCIPLE SKILLS:

1. How can you determine when you have rehearsed long enough that you can extemporaneously deliver your speech, but not so long that you have memorized it?
2. Record your speech while you rehearse. When reviewing the recording, objectively and critically observe your gestures, posture, eye contact, facial expression, and vocal delivery, as well as your verbal message. Make necessary adjustments.

Criteria for Evaluating Speeches

13.6 Understand and apply criteria for evaluating speeches.

PRINCIPLE POINTS: Underlying any list of what a successful speaker should do are two fundamental goals: A successful presentation should be effective, and it should be ethical.

PRINCIPLE SKILLS:

1. What kinds of comments from classmates evaluating your speeches would you find most helpful? What types of remarks would be *least* useful? Explain your answers.
2. Is it ethical to make only positive comments and no suggestions for improvement when evaluating a classmate's speech? Explain your answer.

CHAPTER 14

SPEAKING TO INFORM

To me to be a storyteller is really to . . . be able to absorb life and take in life and be able to interpret it in a way that anybody in this room could say, 'Man, that's my story, I can relate to that.' And it's just finding the humanity in the stories and the creativity in the stories. —COMMON

Larry French/Stringer/Getty Images

CHAPTER OUTLINE

- Types of Informative Speeches
- Strategies for Organizing Your Informative Speech
- Strategies for Making Your Informative Speech Clear
- Strategies for Making Your Informative Speech Interesting
- Strategies for Making Your Informative Speech Memorable
- Study Guide: *Principles for a Lifetime*

LEARNING OBJECTIVES

14.1 Describe five types of informative speeches.

14.2 Identify and use appropriate strategies for organizing informative speeches.

14.3 Identify and use strategies for making informative speeches clear.

14.4 Identify and use strategies for making informative speeches interesting.

14.5 Identify and use strategies for making informative speeches memorable.

One survey of both speech teachers and students who had taken a communication course found that the single most important skill taught in a public speaking class is how to give an informative speech.[1] Given the importance in our lives of sending and receiving information, this finding is not surprising.

Important as it may be, informing or teaching others can also be a challenge because of one simple fact: *Presenting information does not mean that communication has occurred.* One of the cofounders of Common Craft, a company known for explaining complex ideas and processes in short, easy-to-understand videos, says that

> Creating a great explanation involves stepping out of your own shoes and into the audience's. It is a process built on empathy, on being able to understand and share the feelings of another.[2]

In other words, a speaker must be audience-centered to communicate information successfully.

In this chapter, we will examine different types of informative tasks and identify specific strategies to help you organize your messages and make them clear, interesting, and memorable. Throughout our discussion, we will continue to apply the five Communication Principles for a Lifetime.

Types of Informative Speeches

14.1 Describe five types of informative speeches.

The purpose of a message to **inform** is to share information with others to enhance their knowledge or understanding of the objects, procedures, people, events, or ideas you discuss. Identifying which of the five types of informative speeches you are giving can help you select and narrow your topic, organize your message, and choose appropriate supporting material.

inform
To share information with others to enhance their knowledge or understanding of the information, concepts, and ideas you present.

Speeches about Objects

A speech about an object might be about anything tangible—anything you can see or touch. You may or may not show the actual object to your audience while you are talking about it. Objects that could form the basis of an interesting speech include the following:

- Items from your own collection (guitars, vintage vinyl, baseball cards)
- Brunelleschi's Dome
- Celtic harps
- Isle of Skye
- The Franklin Delano Roosevelt Memorial in Washington, D.C.

Speeches about Procedures

A speech about a procedure discusses how something works (for example, how blood travels through the human circulatory system) or describes a process that produces a particular outcome (such as how grapes become wine). At the close of such a presentation, your audience should be able to describe, understand, or perform the procedure you have described. Here are some examples of procedures that could be topics of effective informative speeches:

How to access and use a Virtual Private Network (VPN)

How state laws are made

How to refinish furniture

How to select a cell phone provider

How to garden organically

How to select and purchase stocks

Notice that all these examples start with the word *how*. A speech about a procedure usually focuses on how a process is completed or how something can be accomplished. Speeches about procedures are often presented in workshops or other training situations in which people learn skills.

One good way to teach people a skill is to follow the acronym T-E-A-C-H, as shown in Figure 14.1.[3]

Many speeches about procedures include visual aids. Whether you are teaching people how to install a Wi-Fi router or how to give a speech, showing them how to do something—the *Example* step of the T-E-A-C-H acronym—is almost always more effective than just telling them how to do it.

Speeches about People

Most of us enjoy hearing about the lives of real people, whether famous or unknown, living or dead, who have some special quality. Examples of subjects for such speeches include the following:

Joan of Arc

Mother Teresa

FIGURE 14.1 Remember TEACH to teach.

The letters in the acronym TEACH stand for Tell-Example-Apply-Coach-Help and summarize an effective process you can use to teach people new skills.

T • TELL: Describe what you want your listeners to know.

E • EXAMPLE: Show listeners an example of how to perform the skill.

A • APPLY: Give listeners an opportunity to apply the knowledge by performing the skill.

C • COACH: Provide positive coaching to encourage listeners.

H • HELP: Help listeners learn by correcting mistakes.

ETHICS & COMMUNICATION

Confidential or Potentially Dangerous Information

Mike, a computer engineering major, understands how a computer hacker recently accessed confidential personal information files on faculty members at his university. The procedure is actually simple enough that even people without sophisticated technical ability could understand and replicate it. Mike thinks that the procedure might be a good topic for an interesting informative speech. Meanwhile, Mike's classmate Paul, a chemistry major, considers whether to give an informative speech on how to create homemade explosives. If you are privy to confidential or potentially dangerous information, is it ethical to share it with others in an informative speech?

Mahatma Gandhi

Harry Truman

Banksy

Your seventh-grade social studies teacher

The key to making an effective biographical speech is to be selective. Don't try to cover every detail of your subject's life. Relate the key elements in the person's career, personality, or other significant life features so that you build to a particular point, rather than just recite facts about the individual. One speaker gave a memorable speech about his friend:

> To enter Charlie's home was to enter a world of order and efficiency. His den reflected his many years as an Air Force officer; it was orderly and neat. He always knew exactly where everything was. When he finished reading the morning paper, he folded it so neatly by his favorite chair that you would hardly know that it had been read. Yet for all of his efficiency, you knew the minute you walked into his home that he cared for others, that he cared for you. His jokes, his stories, his skill in listening to others drew people to him. He never met a stranger. He looked for opportunities to help others.

Notice how the details capture Charlie's personality and charm. Speeches about people should give your listeners the feeling that the person is a unique, authentic individual.

A specific type of speech about a person is an introduction of another speaker and his or her topic. There are two cardinal rules for introducing another speaker: Be brief and be accurate. Remember that the audience has come to hear the main speaker, not you. And be certain that you know how to pronounce the speaker's name.

▼ You may have seen a recording of the CBS news bulletin on the assassination of John F. Kennedy. Legendary newscaster Walter Cronkite's ability to describe the event while reflecting the incredible emotion of the moment has made that broadcast a classic. Just as Cronkite was able to do, your purpose as an informative speaker describing an event is to make that event come alive for your listeners.
CBS Photo Archive/Getty Images

Speeches about Events

Did you experience firsthand any of the following events?

Hurricane Harvey

The California Camp Fire of 2018

The EF-4 Nashville tornado of 2020

The coronavirus pandemic

Or perhaps you witnessed the inauguration of a president, or the winning game of the World Series. A major event, whether it is one you have experienced firsthand or one you have researched, can form the basis of a fascinating informative speech. Your goal as a speaker is to describe the event in concrete, tangible terms, bringing the experience to life for your audience.

Speeches about Ideas

By nature, speeches about ideas are more abstract than other types of speeches. The following principles, concepts, and theories might make good topics for idea speeches:

Principles of time management

Freedom of speech

Evolution

Theories of communication

Buddhism

Animal rights

As you look at this list, you may think that these topics seem boring, but as British writer G. K. Chesterton once said, "There is no such thing on earth as an uninteresting subject; the only thing that can exist is an uninterested person."[4] The selection and use of illustrations, examples, and anecdotes to make an otherwise abstract idea seem both interesting and relevant to your listeners are keys to gaining and maintaining interest in your speech about an idea.

Strategies for Organizing Your Informative Speech

14.2 **Identify and use appropriate strategies for organizing informative speeches.**

As with any presentation, your audience will better understand your informative speech if you organize your ideas logically.[5] Regardless of the length or complexity of your message, you must follow a logical pattern to be understood. The topic of your informative speech may lend itself to a particular organizational pattern.

Organizing Speeches about Objects

Speeches about objects may be organized topically; a topical pattern is structured around logical divisions of the object you're describing. Here is a sample topical outline for a speech about an object—a nuclear power plant:

    I. The reactor core
        A. The nuclear fuel in the core
        B. The placement of the fuel in the core

    II. The reactor vessel
        A. The walls of a reactor vessel
        B. The function of the coolant in the reactor vessel

    III. The reactor control rods
        A. The description of the control rods
        B. The function of the control rods

Speeches about objects may also be organized chronologically. A speaker might, for example, focus on the history and development of nuclear power plants. Or, depending on the speaker's specific purpose, the speech could be organized spatially, describing the physical layout of a nuclear power plant.

Organizing Speeches about Procedures

Speeches about procedures are usually organized chronologically, according to the steps involved in the process. One speaker chose a chronological organization for her explanation of how to develop a new training curriculum in teamwork skills:

I. Conduct a needs assessment of your department.
   A. Identify the method of assessing department needs.
   B. Implement the needs assessment.

II. Identify the topics that should be presented in the training.
   A. Specify topics that all members of the department need.
   B. Specify topics that only some members of the department need.

III. Write training objectives.
   A. Write objectives that are measurable.
   B. Write objectives that are specific.
   C. Write objectives that are attainable.

IV. Develop lesson plans for the training.
   A. Identify the training methods you will use.
   B. Identify the materials you will need.

Notice that the speaker grouped the tasks into four steps. Audience members will remember these four general steps of the curriculum development process much more easily than if each individual task had been listed as a separate step.

▼ Chefs who teach classes in person or on television, such as Bobby Flay, often arrange their speeches chronologically, to show the procedure of following a recipe from start to finish. What procedures could you describe to an audience?
Vespasian/Alamy Stock Photo

Organizing Speeches about People

One way to talk about a person's life is in chronological order: birth, school, career, family, professional achievements, death. However, if you are interested in presenting a specific theme, such as "Winston Churchill, master of English prose," you may decide instead to organize Churchill's life experiences topically:

I. Journalist
II. Author
III. Orator

Organizing Speeches about Events

Although a speech about an event might describe the complex issues or causes behind it and be organized topically, most speeches about events follow a chronological arrangement. Perhaps you lived in Midland,

Michigan, where the dam breaches on May 21, 2020, caused unprecedented flooding. Organizing your speech chronologically, you might proceed like this:

I. Seven inches of rainfall over 48 hours
II. Alert of imminent dam failure
III. Evacuation of 10,000 people
IV. Edenville Dam break and catastrophic flooding

Although these main points are chronological, specific subpoints may be organized topically. However you choose to organize your speech about an event, remember that your goal should be to ensure that your audience is enthralled by your vivid description.

Organizing Speeches about Ideas

Most speeches about ideas are organized topically (by logical subdivisions of the central idea) or according to complexity (from simple ideas to more complex ones). The following example illustrates how one speaker used a topical organization for his informative speech about the three major branches of philosophical study:

I. Metaphysics
   A. The study of ontology
   B. The study of cosmology

II. Epistemology
   A. Knowledge derived from thinking
   B. Knowledge derived from experiencing

III. Logic
   A. Types of reasoning
   B. Types of proof

Table 14.1 summarizes typical organizational patterns used for major categories of informational speech topics.

TABLE 14.1 Organizing Informative Speeches

Speech Type	Description	Typical Organizational Patterns	Sample Topics
OBJECTS	Present information about tangible things	Topical Spatial Chronological	The Rosetta Stone Electronic tablets International Space Station

PROCEDURES	Review how something works, or describe a process	Chronological
		Topical
		Complexity
			How to . . .
			  clone a dog
			  trap lobsters

PEOPLE	Describe either a famous person or a personal acquaintance	Chronological Topical	Rosa Parks Your grandmother
EVENTS	Describe something that has happened, is happening, or will happen	Chronological Topical Complexity Spatial	Chinese New Year Juneteenth
IDEAS	Present abstract information or information about principles, concepts, theories, or issues	Topical Complexity	Communism Microeconomic theory Tao Te Ching

Strategies for Making Your Informative Speech Clear

14.3 Identify and use strategies for making informative speeches clear.

Think of the best teacher you ever had. He or she probably possessed a special talent for making information clear, interesting, and memorable. Some speakers, like some teachers, are better than others at presenting information clearly.

A message is clear when the listener understands it in the way the speaker intended. As described in the Diversity & Communication feature, translating your speech into the audience's language is a basic step toward helping listeners understand.

How else do you make your messages clear to others?[6] You can help your audience make sense of your message by expressing your ideas simply, presenting information at a reasonable pace, and relating new information to what the audience already knows.

Simplify Ideas

Your job as a public speaker is to communicate with your audience, not to see how many complex words and ideas you can cram into your speech. The simpler your ideas and phrases, the greater the chance that your audience will understand and remember them.

DIVERSITY & COMMUNICATION

Using an Interpreter

It is quite possible that you may at some time be asked to speak to an audience of people who do not understand English or who cannot hear. In such a situation, you will need an interpreter to translate your message so that your audience can understand you. When using an interpreter, consider the following tips:

1. *Edit your message to fit within the time limit.* A speech that may take you thirty minutes to deliver without an interpreter will take at least an hour to present with an interpreter.
2. *Slow your speaking rate a bit.* Pause after every two or three sentences to give the interpreter time to translate your message.
3. *Don't say anything that you don't want your audience to hear.* Don't assume that your audience doesn't understand you just because you're using an interpreter.
4. *Give your interpreter a written copy of any facts, figures, or other detailed data.*
5. *Use humor with caution.* Humor often doesn't translate well. Even a very skilled interpreter may have difficulty communicating the intended meaning of your humor.
6. *Avoid slang, jargon, or terms that will be unfamiliar to your listeners or the interpreter.*
7. *When possible, talk with your interpreter before you deliver your speech.* Tell him or her the general points you will present. Give the interpreter an outline or, if you are using a manuscript, a transcript of your speech.

Vernault Quentin/NurPhoto/Getty Images

Let's say that you decide to talk about state-of-the-art wireless earbuds. Given the lack of headphone jacks on some current smartphone models, that's a fine topic, but don't try to make your audience as sophisticated as you are about wireless earbuds in a five-minute speech. Discuss only major features and name one or two leaders in the field. Don't load your speech with complex details. Edit ruthlessly.

Pace Your Information Flow

If you present too much new information too quickly, you may overwhelm your listeners, and their ability to understand may falter. Arrange your supporting material so that you present an even flow of information rather than bunching up many significant details around one point. Remember that signposts offer your listeners both a break from listening to new information and help in processing that information. Preview your main ideas in your introduction, and use frequent internal summaries.[7]

Relate New Information to Old

Most of us learn by building on what we already know. As a speaker, you can apply this learning principle to help make your informative speech clear. Professional speaker and trainer John Zimmer explains,

> It is always helpful to anchor your (new) ideas to something with which the audience is familiar. That is why metaphors and analogies are so powerful.[8]

For example, tell bewildered new students how their first year of college will be similar to high school and how it will be different. Or describe to young 4-H members how raising cattle is similar to taking care of any animal; they all need food, water, and shelter. By building on the familiar, you can help your listeners understand how information or a new concept relates to their experience.

> **RECAP**
>
> **Strategies for Making an Informative Speech Clear**
>
> Simplify ideas.
>
> Pace the information flow.
>
> Relate new information to old.

Strategies for Making Your Informative Speech Interesting

14.4 Identify and use strategies for making informative speeches interesting.

He had them. No one moved. They hung on every word.

How can you create such interest when *you* speak? Here are several strategies to keep your audiences yearning for more.

Relate to Your Listeners' Interests

Your listeners may be interested in your topic for a variety of reasons. It may affect them directly, it may add to their knowledge, it may satisfy their curiosity, or it may entertain them. These reasons are not mutually exclusive. For example, if you were speaking at your local public library on how integration affected black businesses in your town, your audience of community members would be interested because your talk would affect them directly, add to their knowledge, and satisfy their curiosity.[9]

Another way to make your message interesting is to think about why you yourself are interested in the topic. Once you are aware of how your own interests and background relate to your topic, you can often find ways to establish common bonds with your audience.

Use Attention-Getting Supporting Material

Consider the following tips for selecting supporting material to best capture and sustain your listeners' attention:

- Research suggests that you can increase audience interest if you first provide a simple overview with an analogy, model, picture, or vivid description.[10]
- As you discuss the object, process, person, event, or idea, keep in mind the *who, what, when, where,* and *why* questions outlined in Figure 14.2.

Establish a Motive for Your Audience to Listen to You

> There will be a test covering my lecture tomorrow. It will count as 50 percent of your semester grade.

Such statements may not make a teacher popular, but they will certainly motivate the class to listen. Lacking a teacher's power to assign grades, you will need to find more creative ways to get your audience to listen to you. We suggest you use the following strategies of questioning, engaging, and relating:

- *Question:* One way to arouse the interest of your listeners is to ask them a question, such as one of the following:

  "How many of you are interested in saving tuition dollars this year?"

  "Who would like to save money on their income taxes?"

  "How many of you would like to learn an effective way of preparing your next speech?"

FIGURE 14.2 Attention-Getting Supporting Material: Who, What, When, Where, and Why?

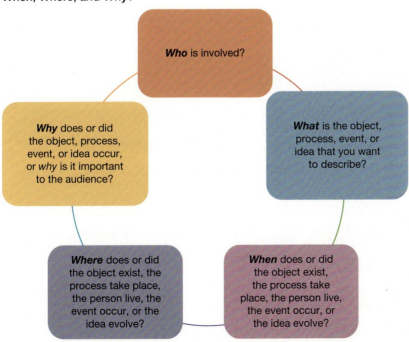

These questions could stimulate your listeners' interest and motivate them to give you their attention.

- *Engage:* Capture your listeners' interest by beginning your speech with an anecdote, a startling statistic, or some other attention-getting strategy. Sustain your listeners' interest by telling stories that are relevant to both your audience and your topic. Researchers have found that speakers who tell stories effectively hold their listeners' attention and help them remember the message.[11] Online, as well as face-to-face, the most memorable presentations are those that tell a story.[12]

- *Relate:* Tell your listeners explicitly how the information in your speech will be of value to them.

Use Word Pictures

word picture
A vivid description that invites listeners to draw on their senses.

A **word picture** is a vivid description that helps your listeners form a mental image by appealing to one or more of their senses of sight, sound, smell, touch, and taste. Such powerful images can gain and hold an audience's attention. Use as many of your senses as possible to construct effective word pictures, as illustrated in Figure 14.3.

In addition to providing sensory images, you can enhance a word picture by describing the emotion a listener might feel if he or she were to experience the situation you relate. Use specific adjectives rather than general terms such as *happy* or *sad*. Enumerating some of the qualities of animals that help to calm people, student speaker Kate described "a dog's soft ears" and "the quiet rumble of a cat's purr."[13]

Create Interesting Presentation Aids

Each day, audiences are exposed to a barrage of messages conveyed through such highly visual electronic media as streaming video. They have grown to depend on more than words alone to help them remember ideas and information. Research suggests that presentation aids can help you get and maintain audience members' attention, as well as increase their retention of the information in your speech.[14] For example, if you need

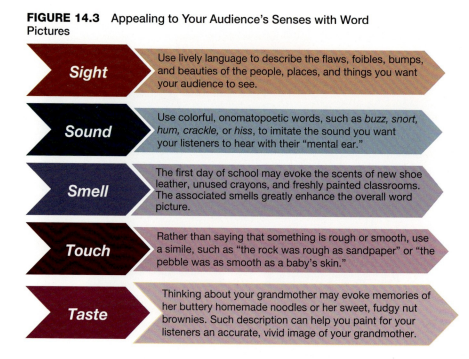

FIGURE 14.3 Appealing to Your Audience's Senses with Word Pictures

Sight	Use lively language to describe the flaws, foibles, bumps, and beauties of the people, places, and things you want your audience to see.
Sound	Use colorful, onomatopoetic words, such as *buzz*, *snort*, *hum*, *crackle*, or *hiss*, to imitate the sound you want your listeners to hear with their "mental ear."
Smell	The first day of school may evoke the scents of new shoe leather, unused crayons, and freshly painted classrooms. The associated smells greatly enhance the overall word picture.
Touch	Rather than saying that something is rough or smooth, use a simile, such as "the rock was rough as sandpaper" or "the pebble was as smooth as a baby's skin."
Taste	Thinking about your grandmother may evoke memories of her buttery homemade noodles or her sweet, fudgy nut brownies. Such description can help you paint for your listeners an accurate, vivid image of your grandmother.

SOCIAL MEDIA & COMMUNICATION

Informative Speaking via Zoom for a Baseball Season Cut Short

When their Spring 2020 season was canceled because of the coronavirus pandemic, The University of Texas Longhorns men's baseball team turned to Zoom to hear information from some of the most significant names in professional baseball.[15]

Angels manager Joe Maddon talked to the players about establishing a team identity and the various stages of a ballplayer's career. Dodgers executive Andrew Friedman talked to the team about preparation and scouting prospects. Listening to these informative talks kept the players engaged and underscored the messages they received from their own coaches.

to summarize data, a well-crafted line graph can quickly and memorably reinforce the words and numbers you cite.

Use Humor

"Humor is the spice of speeches," says comedian Michael Klepper. "Too little and your message may be bland or lifeless, too much and it can burn the mouth."[16] The challenge is to use just the right kind of humor in the right amounts. The following suggestions can help you use humor wisely:[17]

- *Be certain your humor is appropriate to your listeners.* Because your audience "gives attempts at humor their success or failure," you should avoid topics or language that might offend your listeners and create so much emotional noise for them that they cannot focus on your message.[18]

- *Use humor to make a point.* Don't tell a joke just for the sake of getting a laugh. Make sure that your story or punch line relates to your message. Here's an example of how one presenter used a brief joke to make a point about the value of teamwork:

    > I read recently about a veterinarian and a taxidermist who decided to share a shop in a small town in Ohio. The sign in the front window read: "Either way, you get your dog back."
    >
    > There is an important lesson there. We need to work together to solve our problems. People from marketing need to work with operations people. Designers need to work with engineers.

▼ Judicious use of humor will help keep your audience's attention and can help them remember and understand your points. Before using humor, be sure to evaluate carefully whether the joke or story you want to use is appropriate for the occasion and the audience, and whether you have the ability to tell it well.
Digital Vision/Photodisc/Getty Images

Then, when we find a problem that one part of the organization can't solve, someone else may suggest a solution. It doesn't matter who comes up with the solution. The important thing is to "get your dog back."[19]

- *Poke fun at yourself.* Audiences love it when you tell a funny or embarrassing story about yourself. In addition, if the joke's on you, you don't have to worry about whether you will offend someone else.[20]
- *Use humorous quotations.* You don't have to be a comedy writer to be funny. Quote humorous proverbs, poetry, or sayings from others. Remember, however, that what may be funny to you may not be funny to your audience. Try out your quotes and jokes on others before you present them from behind the lectern. And don't try to pass off a quotation from someone else as one of your own; always give credit for the quotations you use.
- *Use cartoons.* A cartoon may be an effective way to make a point. Make sure that your cartoon is large enough to be seen by everyone in the audience. As with any humor, though, don't overdo your use of cartoons.

> **RECAP**
>
> **Strategies for Making an Informative Speech Interesting**
>
> Relate to your listeners' interests.
>
> Use attention-catching supporting material.
>
> Establish a motive for your audience to listen to you.
>
> Use word pictures.
>
> Create interesting presentation aids.
>
> Use humor.

Strategies for Making Your Informative Speech Memorable

14.5 Identify and use strategies for making informative speeches memorable.

If you have made your message clear and interesting, you're well on your way to ensuring that your audience members will remember what you say. Presenting a well-organized message will also help your listeners remember what you say. In this section, we'll discuss several additional strategies for making your speech memorable.

Build in Redundancy

Seldom do writers need to repeat themselves. If readers don't quite understand a passage, they can go back and read it again. However, most speech teachers advise their students to structure their speeches as follows:

1. *Tell them what you're going to tell them.* In the introduction of your speech, provide a broad overview of the purpose of your message. Identify the major points you will present.
2. *Tell them.* In the body of your speech, develop each of the main points mentioned during your introduction.
3. *Tell them what you've told them.* Finally, in your conclusion, summarize the key ideas discussed in the body of your speech.

Use Adult Learning Principles

People remember what is important to them, so it is not surprising that one key to making your message memorable is to adapt it to your listeners. If your audience comprises adult listeners, make sure you deliver your message in the way that adults learn best. **Adult learning principles** suggest that adults prefer the following:[21]

- Relevant information that they can use immediately
- Active involvement in the learning process
- Connections between the new information and their life experiences

adult learning principles
Preferences of adult learners for what and how they learn.

Most people with office jobs have in-boxes (or "in-piles") on their desks, where they place work that needs to get done. Similarly, adult learners tend to have "mental in-boxes"; as audience members, they have mental agendas of what they want or need to gain from listening to a speech. Remember these characteristics of adult learners, as well as the importance of adapting your message to others. If you tailor your information to address *their* agenda, you will make your message memorable and also have more success in informing your audience.

Reinforce Key Ideas Verbally

Suppose you have four suggestions for helping your listeners chair a meeting, and your last suggestion is the most important one. How can you make sure that your audience knows that? Just tell them. You can reinforce an idea by using a phrase such as "This is the most important point" or "Be sure to remember this next point; it's the most crucial one." Be careful, however, not to overuse this technique. If you claim that every other point is a key point, soon your audience will not believe you.

Reinforce Key Ideas Nonverbally

You can also signal the importance of a point with nonverbal emphasis. Gestures can accent or emphasize key phrases, just as italics do in written communication. A well-placed pause can emphasize and reinforce a point. Pausing just before or after you make an important point will focus attention on your thought. Raising or lowering your voice can also reinforce a key idea.

Movement can also help to emphasize major ideas. Moving from behind the lectern to tell a personal anecdote can signal that something special and more intimate is about to be shared. Remember that your movement and gestures should be meaningful and natural, rather than seeming arbitrary or forced. Your need to emphasize an idea can provide the motivation to make a meaningful movement.

The sample informative speech about a person (Elvis Presley) that appears at the end of this chapter is organized chronologically. In this speech, student speaker Angelitta Armijo applies a number of strategies for making an informative speech clear, interesting, and memorable:

- *Clear.* Angelitta makes her speech clear by providing signposts at strategic points to give her audience opportunities to process new information.
- *Interesting.* Angelitta took an important step in making her speech interesting when she initially selected her topic. By speaking on a subject in which she is

CRITICAL/CULTURAL PERSPECTIVES & COMMUNICATION

What Makes Fake News Fake

Just because someone proclaims a news story is fake does not make it fake. Those who seek power and influence, as well as those who have power, often use the claim of "fake news" as an easy way to discredit information or a conclusion heard or read in the media. To determine whether a news story really is biased or untrue, consider these suggestions:

- Read the entire story, not just the headline.
- Check the date to determine whether the story is "old news" and, therefore, no longer accurate.
- Look for credible evidence to support a claim or conclusion. Are the quotations verifiable? Are there enough examples to prove the point? Are the examples typical? Is the evidence recent?
- Consider the source. Assess whether the media outlet is known to be biased. Even if you don't consider the source biased, do others consider it biased?

> **RECAP**
>
> **Strategies for Making an Informative Speech Memorable**
> Build in redundancy.
> Use adult learning principles.
> Reinforce key ideas verbally.
> Reinforce key ideas nonverbally.

personally interested and to which her listeners can relate, Angelitta captures and sustains their attention.

- *Memorable.* Finally, Angelitta makes her speech memorable by relating key information to her listeners and using main ideas to focus that information, by dramatizing statistics, and by closing with a line that her listeners will relate to Elvis.

Sample Informative Speech

Elvis

Angelitta Armijo[22]
Texas State University

Can you imagine being a singer with 150 different albums and singles that have been certified gold, platinum, or multiplatinum? Neither can I. But according to Elvis.com, that's the reality for Elvis Presley.

Angelitta introduces her speech with a rhetorical question.

Although Elvis is no longer with us, his influence on the rock industry remains prevalent today. After all, he paved the way for groups such as the Beatles and Led Zeppelin. I personally have been an Elvis fan for as long as I can remember. I grew up on him, and I own many of his albums on CD, cassette, and vinyl. I also own every movie that he's ever starred in, including some of his TV specials, which I'll talk about later.

Angelitta establishes a motive for her audience to listen to her by sharing her personal interest in Elvis.

Elvis Presley was an American kid who grew up on the wrong side of the tracks and later became the King of Rock 'N' Roll. To better understand Elvis, you need to know about his early days of life before he was famous, his early career, and his shift in career focus, which was prevalent until the end of his life.

Angelitta previews the three main ideas of her presentation, organized chronologically.

Let's begin with Elvis's humble beginnings. Elvis was born into a poor family, but he kept his eyes on his dreams and his love of music. Elvis Aaron Presley was born January 8, 1935, in Tupelo, Mississippi, to Gladys and Vernon Presley. Actually, Elvis was born as a twin, but his brother, Jesse Garon, died at birth, leaving Elvis to be raised as an only child, according to the A&E Network. Also, according to the A&E Network, Elvis was very dedicated to his family and especially to his mother, whom he loved very much. His family encouraged him to be active in church, and it was in church that he discovered his love of singing and music. When he was ten years old, he received his first guitar, and throughout his childhood and young adult life, he was involved in many talent shows.

Angelitta provides her audience with details about Elvis's early life, having selected those that influenced his music career.

According to Elvis.com, the family moved to Memphis in 1948 to seek financial and job security. Soon after graduating high school in 1953 in Memphis, Elvis became a truck driver. It was during his truck driving years that Elvis recorded a few songs at Sun Records for his mother for her birthday. It was at Sun Records where his career began, because Sam Phillips asked him to record more songs, in hopes of finding a star.

Sample Informative Speech (continued)

So now that you know about Elvis's beginnings, we can discuss his rise to fame and early successes. Elvis's career began at Sun Records and grew as his fans wanted to see him on stage, on TV, and on the silver screen. According to *Rolling Stone*, one of the recordings requested by Sam Phillips, "That's Alright Momma," became Elvis's first single in 1954. This single, and many of Elvis's other singles, showed the influence of blues music, which he discovered in Memphis. By 1955, Elvis was signed to RCA, a premier record label. In 1956, his first album was released, titled *Elvis Presley*. According to Elvis.com, this record was #1 on the Billboard Pop Charts for 10 weeks and was also Elvis's first gold album, selling over a million copies.

Throughout the rest of the '50s, Elvis appeared on many variety shows such as the *Ed Sullivan Show* and starred in his first movie, *Love Me Tender*. In 1960, after two years in the army, Elvis taped a special *Welcome Home Elvis* edition of Frank Sinatra's TV show. He received $125,000 for appearing on the show—which, according to Elvis.com, was a record sum of money for an appearance at that time. According to IMDb, Elvis released 27 films throughout the '60s. This was obviously his career focus at that time. He also put out many soundtracks for these movies; some of them include *GI Blues*, *Blue Hawaii*, and *Viva Las Vegas*.

After covering Elvis's early life and career, we can now discuss his career change. The obvious shift from movies to music came with Elvis's 1968 *Comeback Tour Special*, initially entitled *Elvis*. Elvis used the 1968 *Comeback Special* to be taken more seriously, and he ended the special on a personal note, by closing with the song *If I Can Dream*. This song was in response to the tragedies that had occurred in the 1960s, such as the assassination of JFK, Martin Luther King Jr., and Bobby Kennedy, all men whom Elvis respected. This was a sign he was ready to be taken more seriously. His movies changed as well; he finished up his acting career with a few movies that were less cheesy and had more serious plots.

In 1973, Elvis made history. His *Aloha from Hawaii Special* was broadcast via satellite to 40 countries and viewed by 1 to 1.5 billion people, according to Elvis.com. Also, according to Elvis.com, 51 percent of Americans viewed the *Aloha from Hawaii Special*. That means it was seen in more American households than the walk on the moon was! Elvis continued to sell out shows and venues such as Madison Square Garden and Las Vegas until his career ended in 1977 with his death.

You can see that Elvis's life is something for the history books. He came from humble beginnings and catapulted himself into a thriving career to become the King of Rock 'N' Roll. Now you know about his life before fame, his early fame and rise to stardom, and a career shift that he focused on. Now—as Elvis would say—"Thank you, thank you very much."

Angelitta provides a signpost to summarize her first main idea and preview her second one.

Angelitta knows that the key to making an effective biographical speech is to be selective. To support her second main idea, she has selected the key events of Elvis's meteoric rise to fame.

Angelitta provides another signpost to summarize her second main idea and preview her third one.

Again, Angelitta is selective in relating details about Elvis's later career, focusing on those that emphasize the increasingly serious nature of his work.

Having provided data about the viewership of Elvis's 1973 Aloha from Hawaii Special, Angelitta makes these numbers more dramatic for her listeners by comparing them with the numbers of American households who watched the first moon walk.

After summarizing her main ideas, Angelitta provides closure to her speech with Elvis's signature sign-off.

STUDY GUIDE: PRINCIPLES FOR A LIFETIME — CHAPTER 14

Types of Informative Speeches

14.1 Describe five types of informative speeches.

PRINCIPLE **POINTS:** There are five basic types of informative speeches. A speech about an object is about anything tangible, whereas a speech about a procedure discusses how something works or describes a process that produces a particular outcome. Speeches about people can be about either the famous or the little known. Speeches about events describe major occurrences or personal experiences and speeches about ideas are often abstract and generally discuss principles, concepts, or theories.

PRINCIPLE **TERM:**
inform

PRINCIPLE **SKILLS:** Which type of informative speech have you heard most often? Which type do you think you are most likely to give?

Strategies for Organizing Your Informative Speech

14.2 Identify and use appropriate strategies for organizing informative speeches.

PRINCIPLE **POINTS:** Strategies for organizing your informative speech will vary according to the type of informative speech and your specific purpose. A speech about an object may be organized topically, chronologically, or spatially. A speech about a procedure will usually be organized chronologically. Speeches about either people or events are also usually organized chronologically but can be organized topically. A speech about an idea will probably be organized topically.

PRINCIPLE **SKILLS:**

1. How could you organize a speech about a brain-imaging project in which you have been involved?
2. Use the following checklist to assess the *organization* of an informative speech you have developed for your communication class:

   _____ Introduction that states the central idea

   _____ Body organized in a logical way

   _____ Conclusion that restates the central idea and provides closure

Strategies for Making Your Informative Speech Clear

14.3 Identify and use strategies for making informative speeches clear.

PRINCIPLE **POINTS:** To make your message clear, use simple rather than complex ideas and phrases, pace the flow of your information, and relate new information to old ideas.

PRINCIPLE **SKILLS:** Use the following checklist to assess the *clarity* of an informative speech you have developed for your communication class:

_____ Clear, one-sentence declarative central idea

_____ Main ideas relate to the central idea as logical divisions, reasons, or chronological steps

_____ Preview of main ideas in the speech's introduction

_____ Main ideas developed in the body of the speech

_____ Summary of the main ideas in the speech's conclusion

Strategies for Making Your Informative Speech Interesting

14.4 Identify and use strategies for making informative speeches interesting.

PRINCIPLE **POINTS:** To increase interest in your speech, relate information to your listeners' interests, find and use attention-getting supporting material, establish a motive for your audience to listen to you, use vivid word pictures, create intriguing and clear presentation aids, and use humor appropriately.

PRINCIPLE **TERM:**
word picture

PRINCIPLE **SKILLS:**

1. Think about something you have seen or experienced recently. Draft a word picture that describes the image or experience.
2. Before giving a speech to your class in which you share a humorous or interesting story that includes information about a friend, should you ask that friend's permission? Explain your answer.

Strategies for Making Your Informative Speech Memorable

14.5 Identify and use strategies for making informative speeches memorable.

PRINCIPLE POINTS: To make messages memorable, build in some redundancy (tell your audience what you're going to tell them, tell them, and then tell them what you've told them), apply principles of adult learning, and reinforce key ideas both verbally and nonverbally.

PRINCIPLE TERM:

adult learning principles

PRINCIPLE SKILLS:

1. What strategies does your communication teacher use in class to make information memorable?

2. Use the following checklist to help ensure that an informative speech you have developed for your communication class is *memorable*:

    _____ Adapted to the needs, interests, and background of the audience

    _____ Evident connection between new information and listeners' life experiences

    _____ Redundancy and reinforcement of key ideas

    _____ Nonverbal reinforcement of key ideas

CHAPTER 15

SPEAKING TO PERSUADE

Give me the right word and the right accent and I will move the world. —JOSEPH CONRAD

Junial Enterprises/Shutterstock

CHAPTER OUTLINE

- Understanding Persuasion
- Developing Your Audience-Centered Persuasive Speech
- Supporting Your Persuasive Message with Credibility, Logic, and Emotion
- Organizing Your Persuasive Message
- Adapting Ideas to People and People to Ideas
- Study Guide: *Principles for a Lifetime*

LEARNING OBJECTIVES

15.1 Define persuasion and describe five ways listeners may be motivated.

15.2 Explain how to select and narrow a persuasive topic, identify a persuasive purpose, and develop and support a persuasive proposition.

15.3 Use credibility, logical reasoning, and emotional appeals to make your persuasive speech more effective.

15.4 Organize your persuasive message.

15.5 Provide specific suggestions for adapting to receptive audiences, neutral audiences, and unreceptive audiences.

You don't have to be an attorney, an advertiser, or a politician to use the highly valued skill of persuasion. Whether you're asking your roommate to help you clean the kitchen, seeking an extension on your term paper from your professor, or trying to convince your city council to support a library expansion, you too need the power to persuade.

In 333 BCE, Aristotle was among the first to write a comprehensive guide to persuasion. His work, *Rhetoric*, was used by other Greek and Roman writers who sought to summarize principles and strategies of persuasion. The chapter you are reading draws on some of that classic advice and updates it with contemporary research. We first define persuasion, noting how it is both similar to and different from informing others. We then explore how persuasion works by explaining how to motivate an audience. We also offer strategies for developing a persuasive speech; present ideas to help you organize your persuasive message; provide methods to help you move an audience with your credibility, logic, reasoning, and emotional appeals; and help you adapt your message not only to receptive audiences but also to those who are neutral or unreceptive.

Understanding Persuasion

15.1 Define persuasion and describe five ways listeners may be motivated.

As we have already noted, since the time of Aristotle, people have been trying to understand and explain what persuasion is and how it works. In this section, we will examine some of the most fundamental ideas about persuasion.

Persuasion Defined

Persuasion is the process of attempting to change or reinforce attitudes, beliefs, values, or behavior. When we persuade, we are urging someone to modify or maintain the way he or she thinks, feels, or behaves.

Using force to achieve your goal is **coercion**, not persuasion. Weapons, threats, and other unethical strategies may momentarily achieve what you want, but such means are certainly not appropriate or ethical. Efforts to persuade should be grounded in giving people options, rather than forcing them to respond in a certain way.

The Psychology of Persuasion

How does persuasion work? What makes you dial the phone to have a piping hot pepperoni pizza delivered to your door after you watch a television commercial for pizza? What motivates people to do things that they wouldn't do unless they were persuaded to do so? Let's look at five explanations of why people respond to efforts to persuade.

persuasion
The process of attempting to change or reinforce a listener's attitudes, beliefs, values, or behavior.

coercion
The use of force to get another person to think or behave as you wish; coercion is unethical because it takes away free choice.

ETHICS & COMMUNICATION

More Than Just A Customer Loyalty Card
Jameel, a supermarket owner in the Middle East, wants to launch a new customer loyalty card. It will offer money off deals, low pricing on food essentials, a guarantee that card holders will always be offered low stock items first and access to members only events and activities. How could he persuade his managers, in a staff meeting that the loyalty card is a valuable marketing tool?

cognitive dissonance
A sense of mental discomfort that occurs when new information conflicts with a person's current attitudes, beliefs, values, or behavior.

Cognitive Dissonance When you are presented with information that is inconsistent with your current attitudes, beliefs, values, or behavior, you experience a kind of mental discomfort called **cognitive dissonance**. For example, if you frequently drive when you are drowsy and then learn that driving when drowsy is a major contributor to traffic accidents, this theory predicts that you will experience cognitive dissonance. The incompatibility between your customary behavior and your new knowledge will make you feel uncomfortable. Your discomfort may prompt you to change your thoughts, likes or dislikes, feelings, or behavior so that you can restore your comfort level or sense of balance. In this case, you may decide to stop driving when drowsy.

Skilled persuasive speakers know that creating dissonance and then offering their listeners a way to restore balance is an effective persuasive strategy. For example, student speaker Malena wants to persuade her listeners of the need for cancer treatments that do not damage the heart while destroying the cancer:

> We are so focused on killing the cancer that we forget to think about the human the cancer is affecting.[1]

Malena is deliberately creating dissonance. She knows that her audience members value their health and the health of family members who might undergo treatment for cancer. Her next task is to restore her listeners' sense of balance. She assures them that solutions already exist, in the forms of more holistic, individualized cancer treatments and the use of remote ischemic conditioning (RIC) to protect the heart during chemotherapy. The need to resolve dissonance provides one explanation of why people may respond to a speaker's attempts to persuade.

Needs Need is one of the best motivators. A shopper who just broke the heel off a shoe is much more likely to buy new shoes than someone who is just browsing. When you are a speaker, the better you understand what your listeners need, the better you can adapt to them. And the more you can adapt, the greater the chance that you can persuade them to change an attitude, belief, or value or get them to take some action.

The classic theory that outlines our basic needs was developed by Abraham Maslow.[2] If you've taken a psychology course, you have undoubtedly encountered this theory, which has important applications for persuasion. Maslow suggested that a **hierarchy of needs**, illustrated in Figure 15.1, motivates the behavior of all people:

hierarchy of needs
Abraham Maslow's classic theory that humans have five levels of needs and that lower-level needs must be met before people can be concerned about higher-level needs.

- *Physiological needs.* At the bottom of the hierarchy are basic physiological needs (such as food, water, and air), which have to be satisfied before we can attend to any other concern.
- *Safety needs.* Once our physiological needs have been met, we think next about safety needs. We need to feel safe and be able to protect those we love.
- *Social needs.* If we are comfortable and secure, we attend next to social needs, including the need to be loved and the need to belong to a group.
- *Self-esteem needs.* The next level of need is for self-esteem, or our judgment of self-worth.
- *Self-actualization needs.* Finally, if the first four levels of need have been satisfied, we may attend to the need for self-actualization, or achieving our highest potential.

Understanding and applying the hierarchy of needs helps you adapt to your audience. One practical application is to do everything in your power to ensure that your audience's physiological needs are met. For example, if your listeners are sweating and fanning themselves, they are unlikely to be very interested in whether Bigfoot exists or whether the city should reopen River Park. If you can turn on the air conditioning or fans, you will stand a greater chance of persuading your audience than if you continue your speech in that stifling atmosphere.

FIGURE 15.1 Maslow's Hierarchy of Needs
SOURCE: Maslow, Abraham (1954). *Motivation and Personality.* New York: HarperCollins.

Another way you can apply the hierarchy of needs is by appealing to an audience's basic need for safety. For example, Mike knows that most of his audience members have young friends or family members who routinely ride school buses. As he begins to talk about the problem of safety hazards on school buses, he appeals to the audience's need to protect those they love.

Fear Appeals One of the oldest ways to convince people to change their minds or their behavior is by scaring them into compliance. Fear works. The appeal to fear often takes the form of a verbal message—an "if–then" statement. *If* you do (or don't do) X, *then* something awful will happen to you:

- If you don't get a flu shot, then you will probably catch the flu.
- If you text and drive, then you are more likely to die in an automobile accident.
- If you smoke cigarettes, then you are at greater risk for lung cancer.

These statements are all examples of fear appeals. A variety of research studies support the principles outlined in Figure 15.2 for using fear as a motivator.[3]

The effectiveness of fear appeals is based on both cognitive dissonance and Maslow's hierarchy of needs. The fear aroused creates dissonance. Taking action reduces the fear and can meet a need, such as living a long life, being safe from harm, having good friends, or achieving a fulfilling career.

Of course, you have an ethical responsibility not to overstate your case or fabricate evidence when using a fear appeal. The persuader always has an ethical responsibility to be truthful when trying to arouse fear in the listener.

Positive Motivation A political candidate's Facebook page declares: "Vote for me! You'll have lower taxes and higher wages, and your children will be better educated." Does this politician's promise sound familiar? It sounds like what most politicians offer: better days ahead if you'll vote for that candidate. Politicians, salespeople, and most other successful persuaders know that one way to change or reinforce your attitudes, beliefs, values, or behavior is to use positive motivation.

Positive motivational appeals are verbal messages promising that good things will happen if the speaker's advice is followed. The key to using positive motivation is to know what your listeners value. Most Americans value a comfortable, prosperous life; stimulating, exciting activity; a sense of accomplishment; world, community, and personal peace; and overall happiness and contentment. In a persuasive speech, you can motivate your listeners to respond to your message by describing what advantages they will experience if they follow your advice.

The Elaboration Likelihood Model (ELM) One of the newest frameworks for understanding persuasion is called the **elaboration likelihood model (ELM)**.[4] ELM theory, which focuses on how audience members interpret persuasive messages, includes a

elaboration likelihood model (ELM)
A contemporary theory that people can be persuaded both directly and indirectly.

FIGURE 15.2 Using Fear to Motivate Listeners

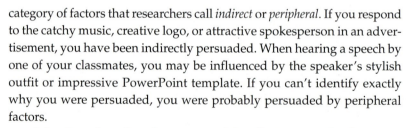

Make the threat applicable to listeners' loved ones.	"If your parents don't have a smoke alarm in their house, they are ten times more likely to die in a house fire."
Make the threat credible.	"Doctors agree that lack of sleep poses a threat to students' health and academic performance."
Make the threat imminent.	"An overly fatty diet coupled with lack of exercise is the primary cause of heart disease in the United States. Eat less fat and get more exercise, or you may die prematurely."
Make the threat strong.	"After the Category 5 hurricane comes ashore, most of the coastal area will remain uninhabitable for weeks if not months."

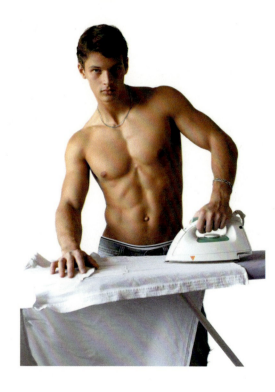

▼ According to the elaboration likelihood model, we are often persuaded by indirect factors that are not central to the product or message. What indirect factors do the advertisers of this product hope will persuade shoppers to buy it?
Vladimir Wrangel/Shutterstock

category of factors that researchers call *indirect* or *peripheral*. If you respond to the catchy music, creative logo, or attractive spokesperson in an advertisement, you have been indirectly persuaded. When hearing a speech by one of your classmates, you may be influenced by the speaker's stylish outfit or impressive PowerPoint template. If you can't identify exactly why you were persuaded, you were probably persuaded by peripheral factors.

Advertisers have long been aware of the effectiveness of indirect persuasion. One researcher points out,

> In current advertising practice, it is rare to find magazine ads that lead off with a direct verbal claim such as "[Brand X] gets clothes clean." Instead of straightforward claims that a brand possesses some attribute or delivers some benefit, one encounters pictures of . . . measuring cups full of blue sky.[5]

Like consumers, voters can also be persuaded indirectly—by a political party preference, or by a candidate's favorability or image.[6]

Because ELM theory is a more audience-centered model than other persuasive theories, it can be especially valuable in helping you understand how you have been indirectly persuaded. And as a speaker, you should be aware of any peripheral factors that could be adapted to influence your listeners, such as your delivery, appearance, and general impression of preparedness.

Developing Your Audience-Centered Persuasive Speech

15.2 Explain how to select and narrow a persuasive topic, identify a persuasive purpose, and develop and support a persuasive proposition.

Now that you have an understanding of what persuasion is and is not, you're probably wondering how best to develop a persuasive message. The audience-centered model of public speaking, which we introduced in Chapter 11, can help you design and deliver a persuasive speech, just as it can an informative one. As Figure 15.3 illustrates, you should prepare for a persuasive speech in the same way that you would for any speech: by considering the needs, interests, and background of your audience. Ethically adapting to listeners is important in any communication situation, but it is especially important when persuading others.

Narrowing Your Topic

As with any speech, after you've thought about your audience, the next step is to select and narrow your topic. The best persuasive topic is one about which you feel strongly. If your listeners sense that you are committed to, and excited about, your topic, chances are that they will be interested and involved as well.

The principle of appropriately adapting messages to others can help guide your choice of a persuasive topic. Know the local, state, national, and international issues that interest and affect your listeners:

- Should the city build a new power plant?
- Should convicted child molesters be permitted to live in any neighborhood they like?
- Should the United States drop economic sanctions against Iran?

These and other significant controversial issues make excellent persuasive speech topics. Avoid frivolous topics, such as "why you should make your own potholders," when so many important issues challenge the world and your listeners.

Remain informed about important issues of the day. Facebook posts and tweets can provide ideas for persuasive speeches. Other potential sources include talk radio, daily newspapers, and online news sites. After you have chosen a topic for your persuasive message, staying up to date on current events can help you narrow your topic and find interesting and appropriate supporting material for your speech.

FIGURE 15.3 Audience-Centered Model of the Public Speaking Process

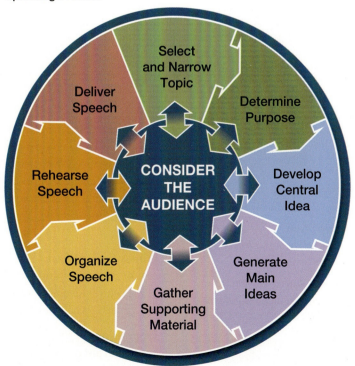

Identifying Your Purpose

Attitudes, beliefs, and values, identified in Chapter 2 as components of a person's self-concept, are also integral to understanding how to persuade others. When your general purpose is to persuade, your specific purpose should target your listeners' attitudes, beliefs, or values, or their behavior.

FIGURE 15.4 Targeting Attitudes, Beliefs, and Values in Specific Purpose Statements

Attitudes—our likes and dislikes—are much more likely to change than are our beliefs or values. Our sense of what is right and wrong—our values—are least likely to change.

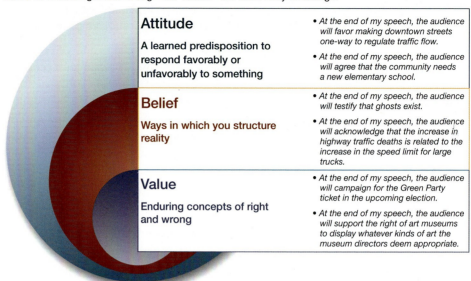

Figure 15.4 defines attitudes, beliefs, and values; provides examples of specific purpose statements that target each one; and illustrates that attitudes lie fairly close to the surface of our convictions, with values the most deeply ingrained in the center of the model.

Be aware of whether your specific purpose targets an attitude, a belief, a value, or a behavior, and be realistic in assessing what you will need to do in your speech to effect change. Recall, too, from our definition of *persuasion* that you can try to *reinforce* attitudes, beliefs, values, and behavior that audience members already hold, or you can try to *change* their attitudes, beliefs, values, or behavior. Reinforcing what listeners already know or think is relatively easy; it's more of a challenge to change their minds.

Developing Your Central Idea as a Persuasive Proposition

After clarifying their specific purpose, most persuasive speakers find it useful to cast their central idea as a **proposition**, a statement with which they want their audience to agree. A well-worded proposition is a verbal message that can help you fine-tune your persuasive objective and develop strategies for convincing your audience that your proposition is true. There are three categories of propositions: propositions of fact, propositions of value, and propositions of policy. Let's examine each type in more detail.

Propositions of Fact A **proposition of fact** is a claim that something is or is not the case or that something did or did not happen. A speaker who uses a proposition of fact as the central idea of a persuasive speech focuses on changing or reinforcing the listeners' beliefs—what they think is true.

Propositions of Value As the word *value* suggests, a **proposition of value** calls for the listener to judge the worth or importance of something. A simple example is "Tattoos are beautiful." Other value propositions compare two ideas, things, or actions and suggest that one is better than the other.

proposition
A claim with which you want your audience to agree.

proposition of fact
A claim that something is or is not the case or that something did or did not happen.

proposition of value
A claim that calls for the listener to judge the worth or importance of something.

Propositions of Policy The third type of proposition, the proposition of policy, advocates a specific action, such as changing a regulation, procedure, or behavior. **Propositions of policy** include the word *should*.

Figure 15.5 provides an example of each of the three types of persuasive propositions.

With your specific purpose and central idea in hand, you are ready to move to the next stages in the public speaking process. In most cases, you can draw your main ideas from several reasons *why* the persuasive proposition is true. Then you will be ready to begin selecting supporting material.

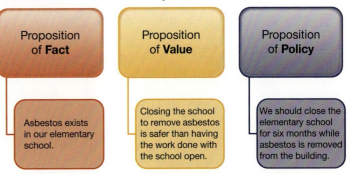

FIGURE 15.5 Persuasive Propositions

proposition of policy
A claim advocating a specific action to change a regulation, procedure, or behavior.

Supporting Your Persuasive Message with Credibility, Logic, and Emotion

15.3 Use credibility, logical reasoning, and emotional appeals to make your persuasive speech more effective.

Aristotle defined **rhetoric** as the process of "discovering the available means of persuasion."[7] What exactly are those "available means"? They are the various strategies you can use to support your persuasive proposition. Aristotle suggested three: (1) **ethos**, emphasizing the credibility or ethical character of a speaker; (2) **logos**, using logical arguments; and (3) **pathos**, using emotional appeals to move an audience.

Ethos: Establishing Your Credibility

If you were going to buy a new computer, to whom would you turn for advice? Perhaps you would consult your brother, who is a computer geek, or your roommate, who is a computer science major? Alternatively, you could seek advice from *Consumer Reports*, a monthly publication providing reviews and ratings of various consumer products. In other words, you would turn to a source that you consider credible.

For centuries, teachers and researchers have sought to understand the factors that audiences consider in deciding whether a speaker is credible. Aristotle thought that a public speaker should be ethical, possess good character, display common sense, and be concerned for the well-being of his audience. Quintilian, a Roman teacher of public speaking, advised that a speaker should be "a good man speaking well." These ancient speculations about the elements that enhance a speaker's credibility are reflected in our modern understanding of **credibility**. When you give a speech, your credibility depends upon the audience's perception of your competence, trustworthiness, and dynamism. Your listeners, not you, determine whether you have credibility.

Competence One clear factor in credibility is **competence**. A speaker should be informed, skilled, or knowledgeable about the subject he or she is discussing. You will be more persuasive if you can convince your listeners that you know something about your topic. How can you do that?

You can use verbal messages effectively by talking about your relevant personal experience with the topic. If you have taken and enjoyed a cruise, for instance, you can tell your audience about the highlights of your trip. You can also cite evidence to support your ideas. Even if you have not taken a cruise yourself, you can be prepared with information about what a good value a cruise is—how much it costs and what is included—in comparison to how much the same trip would cost if one were to travel by air and stay and eat in hotels.

rhetoric
The process of discovering the available means of persuasion.

ethos
The credibility or ethical character of a speaker.

logos
Logical arguments.

pathos
Emotional appeals.

credibility
An audience's perception of a speaker's competence, trustworthiness, and dynamism.

competence
An aspect of a speaker's credibility that reflects whether the speaker is perceived as informed, skilled, and knowledgeable.

▲ Audiences often perceive a dynamic, charismatic speaker, such as this one, as credible. What steps can you take to be more dynamic in your delivery, or to assure your audience of your competence or trustworthiness?
Wavebreak Media Ltd/123RF

Trustworthiness A second factor in credibility is **trustworthiness**. While delivering a speech, you need to convey honesty and sincerity to your audience. You cannot simply say, "Trust me." You have to earn the audience's trust by demonstrating that you are interested in and experienced with your topic. Again, speaking from personal experience makes you appear to be a more trustworthy speaker. Conversely, having something to gain by persuading your listeners may make you suspect in their eyes, which is why salespeople and politicians often lack credibility; if you do what they say, they will clearly benefit by earning sales commissions or being elected to public office.

Dynamism A third factor in credibility is a speaker's **dynamism**, or energy. Dynamism is often projected through delivery. If we apply the communication principle of using and understanding nonverbal messages effectively, a speaker who maintains eye contact, has enthusiastic vocal inflection, and moves and gestures purposefully is likely to be seen as dynamic. **Charisma** is a form of dynamism. A charismatic speaker possesses charm, talent, magnetism, and other qualities that make the person attractive and energetic. Many people considered President Franklin Roosevelt and Pope John Paul II charismatic speakers.

Stages of Credibility You have opportunities before, during, and after your speech to enhance your credibility. **Initial credibility** is the impression your listeners have of you before you even begin to speak. They grant you initial credibility on the basis of such factors as your appearance and your credentials. **Derived credibility** is the perception your listeners form as you deliver your speech. And **terminal credibility** is the perception your listeners have when you finish your speech. Figure 15.6 provides specific suggestions for enhancing your credibility at each of these three stages.

trustworthiness
An aspect of a speaker's credibility that reflects whether the speaker is perceived as believable and honest.

dynamism
An aspect of a speaker's credibility that reflects whether the speaker is perceived as energetic.

charisma
Talent, charm, and attractiveness.

initial credibility
The impression of a speaker's credibility that listeners have before the speaker begins to speak.

derived credibility
The impression of a speaker's credibility based on what the speaker says and does during the speech.

terminal credibility
The final impression listeners have of a speaker's credibility, after the speech has been concluded.

FIGURE 15.6 Enhancing Your Credibility

To enhance **initial credibility** (before you speak)	To enhance **derived credibility** (as you speak)	To enhance **terminal credibility** (after you speak)
• Dress appropriately. • Prepare a summary of your qualifications for the person who introduces you.	• Establish common ground with listeners. • Support your arguments with evidence. • Organize your message well.	• Prepare a strong conclusion. • Deliver your conclusion well. • Maintain eye contact after your closing sentence.

Logos: Using Evidence and Reasoning

In addition to being considered a credible speaker, you will gain influence with your audience if you can effectively use logically structured arguments supported with evidence. As we noted earlier, Aristotle called logical arguments *logos*, which, translated from Greek, means "the word." Using words effectively to communicate your arguments is vital to persuading thoughtful and informed listeners.[8]

The goal is to provide logical proof for your arguments. **Proof** consists of both evidence and reasoning. **Evidence** is another word for the illustrations, definitions, statistics, and opinions that are your supporting material. **Reasoning** is the process of drawing conclusions from your evidence. There are three major ways to draw logical conclusions: inductively, deductively, and causally.

Inductive Reasoning Reasoning that arrives at a general conclusion from specific instances or examples is known as **inductive reasoning**. You reason inductively when you claim that a conclusion is probably true because of specific evidence.

Reasoning by analogy is a special type of inductive reasoning. An analogy demonstrates how an unfamiliar idea, thing, or situation is similar to something the audience already understands. If you develop an original analogy, rather than quote one you find in a printed source, you are reasoning inductively. Here's an example of reasoning by analogy: Mandatory rear seatbelt laws that were enacted in Missouri saved lives; therefore, Kansas should also develop mandatory rear seatbelt laws. The key to arguing by analogy is to claim that the two things you are comparing (such as driving habits in Missouri and Kansas) are similar, so your argument is sound. Here's another example: England has a relaxed policy toward violence being shown on television and has experienced no major rise in violent crimes; therefore, the United States should relax its policy on showing violence on TV.

Deductive Reasoning Reasoning from a general statement or principle to reach a specific conclusion is called **deductive reasoning**. Deductive reasoning can be structured as a **syllogism**, a three-part argument that consists of a major premise, a minor premise, and a conclusion. For example, if you were attempting to convince your audience to vote for an upcoming school bond issue, your syllogism might look like the following:

> MAJOR PREMISE: Keeping schools in good repair extends the number of years that school buildings can be used.
> MINOR PREMISE: The proposed school bond issue provides money for school repairs.
> CONCLUSION: The proposed school bond issue will extend the number of years that we can use our current school buildings.

Contemporary logicians note that when you reason deductively, the certainty of your conclusion rests primarily on the validity of the major premise and secondarily on the truth of the minor premise. If you can prove that keeping schools in good repair extends the useful life of school buildings, and if it is true that the proposed bond issue provides money for school repairs, your conclusion will be certain.

Causal Reasoning You use **causal reasoning** when you relate two or more events in such a way as to conclude that one or more of the events probably caused the others. For example, you might argue that public inoculation programs during the twentieth century eradicated smallpox.

As we noted in Chapter 12 when we discussed cause and effect as an organizational strategy, there are two ways to structure a causal argument. One is by reasoning from cause to effect—that is, predicting a result from a known fact. For example, you

---

proof
Evidence plus reasoning.

evidence
The material used to support a point or premise.

reasoning
The process of drawing a conclusion from evidence.

inductive reasoning
Using specific instances or examples to reach a probable general conclusion.

reasoning by analogy
A special kind of inductive reasoning that draws a comparison between two ideas, things, or situations that share some essential common feature.

deductive reasoning
Moving from a general statement or principle to reach a certain specific conclusion.

syllogism
A three-part argument, including a major premise, a minor premise, and a conclusion.

causal reasoning
Relating two or more events in such a way as to conclude that one or more of the events caused the others.

DIVERSITY & COMMUNICATION

"Elementary Reasoning, My Dear Watson"[9]

Although we frequently use the word *diversity* to refer to readily discernible differences in sex, gender, race, culture, and age, diversity can also involve differences in perspective or point of view. As the following narrative shows, people may draw different conclusions from the same evidence.

Sherlock Holmes and Dr. Watson went on a camping trip. After a good meal and a bottle of wine, they lay down for the night and went to sleep. Some hours later, Holmes awoke and nudged his faithful friend.

"Watson, look up at the sky and tell me what you see."

Watson replied, "I see millions and millions of stars."

"What does that tell you?" inquired Holmes.

Watson pondered for a minute. "Astronomically, it tells me that there are millions of galaxies and potentially billions of planets. Astrologically, I observe that Saturn is in Leo. Horologically, I deduce that the time is approximately a quarter past three. Theologically, I can see that God is all powerful and that we are small and insignificant. Meteorologically, I suspect that we will have a beautiful day tomorrow. What does it tell you?"

Holmes was silent for a moment and then spoke. "Watson, you idiot! Someone has stolen our tent!"

---

logical fallacy
Attempting to persuade without adequate evidence or with arguments that are irrelevant or inappropriate.

causal fallacy
Making a faulty cause and effect connection between two things or events.

know that it has rained more than an inch over the last few days, so you predict that the aquifer level will rise. The inch of rain is the cause, and the rising aquifer is the effect. The other way to structure a causal argument is by reasoning from a known effect to the cause. National Transportation Safety Board accident investigators reason from effect to cause when they reconstruct airplane wreckage to determine the cause of an air disaster.

The key to developing any causal argument is to be certain that a causal relationship actually exists between the two factors you are investigating. A few summers ago, a young science student took part in a bird population project involving counting chimney swifts in a given area just before sunset. He counted the most chimney swifts on the Fourth of July. It would not have been valid, however, to argue that fireworks (or parades or hot dogs or anything else connected with the Fourth of July) caused an increase in the number of chimney swifts seen in the area. The Fourth of July holiday and the bird count were not related by cause and effect.

Logical Fallacies Unfortunately, not all people who try to persuade you will use sound evidence and reasoning. Some will try to develop arguments in ways that are irrelevant or inappropriate. Such reasoning is called a **logical fallacy**. To be a better-informed consumer, as well as a more ethical persuasive speaker, be aware of the following eight common logical fallacies:

- Making a faulty cause and effect connection is a **causal fallacy**, or, to use its Latin term, *post hoc, ergo propter hoc* ("after this; therefore, because of this").

RECAP

Inductive, Deductive, and Causal Reasoning

Type of Reasoning	Reasoning begins with . . .	Reasoning ends with . . .	Conclusion is . . .	Example
Inductive	specific examples	a general conclusion	probable or not probable	Dell, HP, and Acer computers are all reliable. Therefore, PCs are reliable.
Deductive	a general statement	a specific conclusion	certain or not certain	All professors at this college have advanced degrees. Tom Bryson is a professor at this college. Therefore, Tom Bryson has an advanced degree.
Causal	something known	a speculation about causes or effects of what is known	likely or not likely	The number of people with undergraduate degrees has risen steadily since 1960. This increasing number has caused a glut in the job market of people with degrees.

- A **bandwagon fallacy** gets its name from the colloquial expression "jumping on the bandwagon," thinking or doing something just because everybody else is.
- An **either–or fallacy** artificially limits choices or solutions to only two.
- A person who reaches a conclusion without adequate supporting evidence is making a **hasty generalization**.
- A **personal attack** focuses on an individual associated with an idea, rather than the idea itself.
- Someone who argues against an issue by bringing up irrelevant facts or arguments is using a **red herring**, a fallacy that takes its name from the old trick of distracting dogs who are following a scent by dragging a smoked herring across a trail.
- Using a spokesperson who lacks appropriate authority or credentials is an **appeal to misplaced authority**.
- And finally, if a reason has nothing to do with the conclusion, the fallacy is a **non sequitur** (Latin for "it does not follow").

Figure 15.7 further defines and provides examples of each of these eight common logical fallacies.

Persuasive speakers who provide logical proof (evidence and reasoning) for their arguments and who avoid logical fallacies heighten their chances for success with their audience. But good speakers also know that evidence and reasoning are not their only tools. Emotion is another powerful strategy for moving an audience to support a persuasive proposition.

FIGURE 15.7 Logical Fallacies

Causal Fallacy	Bandwagon Fallacy	Either–or Fallacy	Hasty Generalizatiion
Making a faulty cause-and-effect connection between two things or events.	Suggesting that because everyone believes something or does something, it must be valid, accurate, or effective.	Oversimplifying an issue as offering only two choices.	Reaching a conclusion without adequate supporting evidence.
Example: A scientist counted more chimney swifts on the Fourth of July, because of the fireworks.	**Example:** Everybody knows that taxes are too high.	**Example:** Either we support the bond issue, or we end up busing our students to another school district.	**Example:** The math test was too hard because one person failed it.

Personal Attack	Red Herring	Appeal to Misplaced Authority	Non Sequitur
Attacking irrelevant personal characteristics of someone connected with an idea, rather than addressing the idea itself.	Using irrelevant facts or information to distract someone from the issue under discussion.	Using someone without the appropriate credentials or expertise to endorse an idea or product.	Presenting an idea or conclusion that does not logically follow the previous idea (Latin for "it does not follow").
Example: The new federal health care plan is a bad idea because it was proposed by that crazy senator.	**Example:** A congressional representative, indicted for misuse of federal funds, devotes a press conference to talking about a colleague's sexual indiscretions.	**Example:** A professional baseball player endorses breakfast cereal.	**Example:** Students should give blood because it is nearly time for final exams.

bandwagon fallacy
Suggesting that because everyone believes something or does something, it must be valid, accurate, or effective.

either–or fallacy
Oversimplifying an issue as offering only two choices.

hasty generalization
Reaching a conclusion without adequate supporting evidence.

personal attack
Attacking irrelevant personal characteristics of someone connected with an idea, rather than addressing the idea itself.

red herring
Using irrelevant facts or information to distract someone from the issue under discussion.

appeal to misplaced authority
Using someone without the appropriate credentials or expertise to endorse an idea or product.

non sequitur
Presenting an idea or conclusion that does not logically follow the previous idea or conclusion; Latin for "it does not follow."

Pathos: Using Emotion

People often make decisions based not on logic but on emotion. Advertisers know all about it; just think of soft-drink commercials. There is little rational reason for people to spend any part of their food budget on soft drinks that are "empty calories." So soft-drink advertisers turn instead to emotional appeals, striving to connect feelings of pleasure with their product. Smiling people, upbeat music, and good times are usually part of the formula for selling soft drinks.

One way to make an emotional appeal is with emotion-arousing verbal messages. Words such as *mother, flag, freedom*, and *slavery* trigger emotional responses in listeners. Patriotic slogans, such as "Remember the Alamo" and "Give me liberty, or give me death," are examples of phrases that have successfully aroused emotions in listeners.

Another way to appeal to emotions is to use concrete illustrations and descriptions. Although illustrations and descriptions are themselves types of evidence or supporting material, their effect is often emotional, as in the following example:

> Before he reached the age of 16, Tyler threatened to bomb his school, attempted to stab both of his siblings, and was suspected of having strangled a cat with his bare hands. Tyler was finally placed in the hands of our juvenile justice system....[10]

Effective use of nonverbal messages can also appeal to audience members' emotions. As a speaker, you can use visual aids, such as pictures, slides, or video, to evoke both positive and negative emotions. For example, a photograph of a dirty, ragged child alone in a big city can evoke sadness and pain. A video clip of an airplane crash can arouse fear and horror. A picture of a smiling baby makes most of us smile, too.

When you use emotional appeals, you have an obligation to be ethical and forthright. Making false claims, misusing evidence or images, or relying exclusively on emotion without any evidence or reasoning violates standards of ethical public speaking.

RECAP

Tips for Using Emotion to Persuade

- Use emotion-arousing words.
- Use concrete illustrations and descriptions to appeal to people's emotions.
- Use visual aids to evoke both positive and negative emotions.
- Be ethical and forthright. Avoid making false claims, misusing evidence or images, or relying exclusively on emotion without any evidence or reasoning.

Organizing Your Persuasive Message

15.4 Organize your persuasive message.

An audience-centered persuasive speaker adapts the organization of the speech to the audience's needs, attitudes, beliefs, behaviors, and background. Most persuasive speeches are organized according to one of four strategies: problem–solution, cause and effect, refutation, or the motivated sequence. The first two strategies were also discussed in Chapter 12; the last is a special variation of the problem–solution format.

Problem–Solution

When you use a problem–solution organization for your persuasive message, apply the principle of appropriately adapting messages to others. If you are speaking to an apathetic audience or one that is not aware that a problem exists, emphasize the problem portion of the message. If your audience is already aware of the problem, emphasize the solution or solutions. In either case, your challenge will be to provide ample evidence that your perception of the problem is accurate and reasonable. You'll also need to convince your listeners that the solution or solutions you advocate are the most appropriate ones to solve the problem.

Notice how student speaker Nicholas organizes his speech "The Death of Reading" in a problem–solution pattern:[11]

I. PROBLEM: Reading is a dying activity.
   A. Each year more than 500 courts hear arguments to ban books.
   B. Since 1990, more than 2,000 libraries across America have closed.
   C. Leisure reading has decreased more than 50 percent since 1975.
II. SOLUTIONS:
   A. Teach children that reading as an activity has worth and beauty.
   B. Teach children that books in and of themselves only express ideas and should not be banned.
   C. Support programs such as "One City, One Book" that encourage community involvement and literary discussion.
   D. Give books as gifts.
   E. Allow others to see you read.

The sample persuasive speech about private ambulance companies at the end of this chapter is an example of a message organized by first stating the problem and then presenting some specific solutions.

Cause and Effect

If two or more situations are causally related, a cause and effect strategy can work well for a persuasive speech. Here is an example of a persuasive outline organized from cause to effect:[12]

I. CAUSE: The foster care system is in crisis.
   A. Since 1987, there has been a 90 percent increase in the number of children placed in foster care nationally.
   B. During that same time, there has been a 3 percent decrease in the number of licensed foster homes.
II. EFFECT: Children in foster care are at risk.
   A. Children in the foster care system are five times more likely to die as a result of abuse than children in the general population.
   B. Eighty percent of federal prisoners spent time in our nation's foster care system as children.

▼ This speaker uses a graph to persuade his audience that a new marketing plan has affected profits. How would relating cause and effect help you to persuade your audience?
Thinkstock Images/Getty Images

An effect may have more than one cause. For example, standardized test scores may be low in your state both because of low per-pupil expenditures and because of a lack of parental involvement in the schools. To argue that only one of the two factors causes the low test scores would probably be inaccurate.

It is also possible for two situations to coexist but not be causally related. Suppose that standardized test scores are indeed low in your state and that your state has a lottery. Both situations exist, but one does not cause the other.

Refutation

refutation
Organization according to objections your listeners may have to your ideas and arguments.

Refutation is an organizational strategy in which you identify likely objections to your proposition and then refute those objections with arguments and evidence. This third way to organize your persuasive speech is especially useful when you are facing an unreceptive audience—one that does not agree with your point of view or your specific proposition.

You will be most likely to organize your persuasive message by refutation if you know your listeners' chief objections to your proposition. In fact, if you do not acknowledge such objections, the audience will probably think about them during your speech anyway. Credible facts and statistics will generally be more effective in supporting your points of refutation than will emotional arguments.

One speaker organized a persuasive speech on organ donation by providing the following refutations for four common misconceptions about the process:[13]

I. Anyone who decides to become a donor can reconsider that decision at any time.
II. Doctors will do everything to save the life of an organ donor that they would do for a non-donor.
III. No one who views the body of an organ donor will be able to tell that organs have been removed.
IV. Families of organ donors do not pay for any procedure related to the organ donation.

The Motivated Sequence

motivated sequence
Alan H. Monroe's five-step plan for organizing a persuasive message: attention, need, satisfaction, visualization, and action.

The **motivated sequence**, devised by Alan Monroe, is a five-step organizational plan that integrates the problem–solution method with principles that have been confirmed by research and practical experience.[14] The five steps are attention, need, satisfaction, visualization, and action.

SOCIAL MEDIA & COMMUNICATION

Influencers and Social Media Houses

Los Angeles is home to dozens of social media influencer "collab" houses. These houses, which are often rented by brands or management companies, are where Gen Z influencers live and work together on content they post primarily to TikTok, but also to YouTube, Instagram, and Twitter. These collaborations allow influencers (and the brands they represent) to increase their reach through cross-promotion. Most young social media influencers believe that to succeed, they need to live in one of these L.A. houses, where, as one explained,

. . . if you talk to four people, one is probably going to have over 100,000 followers on Instagram.[15]

YouTube collab houses, such as the Vlog Squad and the Clout House, have existed for some time. But with more than two billion downloads in March of 2020, TikTok became the focus of influencers' attention. The number of TikTok influencer collab houses has increased along with TikTok users, with the Girls in the Valley, Drip Crib, and Kids Next Door houses attracting influencers and their vast audiences.

Attention Your first task in applying the motivated sequence is to get your listeners' attention. (This is also the first stage in appropriately adapting your message to others.) You already know attention-getting strategies for introductions: rhetorical questions, illustrations, startling facts or statistics, quotations, humorous stories, and references to historical or recent events. The attention step is, in essence, your application of one of these strategies.

Samin begins his persuasive speech about landmines with this attention-catching illustration:

> In Angola, little Tusnia became yet another one of the town's orphans. She was out in the field playing with her friends when she stumbled onto the ground and screamed. Her mother went running to see what happened, stepped in the wrong place, and was mutilated instantly. Parts from her body were found as far as 30 meters from the explosion site.[16]

Need After getting your audience's attention, establish why your topic, problem, or issue should concern your listeners. Tell your audience about the problem. Adapt your message to them by convincing them that the problem affects them directly. Argue that there is a need for change. During the need step (which corresponds to the problem step in a problem–solution strategy), you should develop logical arguments backed by evidence. At this point, you can create dissonance or use a credible fear appeal to motivate listeners to respond to your solution. Samin outlines his need step as follows:

> Citizens of countries with landmines face two major problems: risk of death or serious injury, and disruption of daily routines.

Satisfaction After you explain and document a need or problem, identify your plan (or solution) and explain how it will satisfy the need. You need not go into painstaking detail. Present enough information for your listeners to gain a general understanding of how the problem may be solved. Samin recommends two solutions in his satisfaction step:

visualization
A word picture of the future.

positive visualization
A word picture of how much better things will be if a solution is implemented.

negative visualization
A word picture of how much worse things will be if a solution is not implemented; a fear appeal.

> One possible solution is to spread awareness. Luckily, this process has already been started by the United Nations Children's Fund or UNICEF. . . . And a second solution is to teach successful de-mining technology to indigenous populations.

Visualization Now you need to give your audience a sense of what it would be like if your solution were adopted or, conversely, not adopted. **Visualization**—a word picture of the future—applies the fundamental principle of using and understanding verbal messages effectively. An appropriate presentation aid can also help your audience visualize the implications of your persuasive message. With a **positive visualization** approach, you paint a rosy picture of how wonderful the future will be if your satisfaction step is implemented. With a **negative visualization** approach, you paint a bleak picture of how terrible the future will be if nothing changes; you use a fear appeal to motivate your listeners to do what you suggest to avoid further problems. You might also combine the two approaches: The problem will be solved if your solution is adopted, but things will get increasingly worse if it is not. An ethical speaker makes sure that a positive or negative visualization message is accurate and not overstated. Samin offers a positive visualization to communicate what can happen if his second solution is implemented:

> Perhaps in the future Tusnia can use this technology to start de-mining Angola so that the horrific atrocity that she faced will not happen to anyone else.

Action The final step of the motivated sequence requires you to adapt your solution to your audience. Offer your listeners some specific action they can take to solve the problem you have discussed. Identify exactly what you want them to do. Give them

FIGURE 15.8 The Motivated Sequence

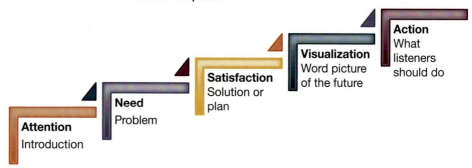

simple, clear, and easy-to-follow steps. At the end of your speech, provide a website to go to for more information, an address to which they can write a letter of support, or a petition to sign. Samin suggests a specific action step his listeners can take to solve the problem of landmines:

> First, sign the People's Treaty to Support the Convention on Cluster Munitions, which is a de-mining effort. Second, help the International Campaign to Ban Landmines by donating money to their cause.

Figure 15.8 illustrates the steps in the motivated sequence. You can adapt this strategy to both your topic and the needs of your audience. For example, if you are speaking to a knowledgeable, receptive audience, you do not need to spend a great deal of time on the need step. Your listeners already know that the need is serious. However, they may feel helpless to do anything about it. In this case, you would want to emphasize the satisfaction and action steps.

On the other hand, if you are speaking to neutral or apathetic audience members, you will need to spend time getting their attention and proving that a problem exists, is significant, and affects them personally. In this case, you will emphasize the attention, need, and visualization steps.

The organizational strategies for persuasive speeches are summarized in Table 15.1. Is there one best way to organize a persuasive message? The answer is no. The organizational strategy you select depends on your audience, message, and desired

TABLE 15.1 Organizational Patterns for Persuasive Speeches

Organizational Pattern	Definition	Example
Problem–Solution	Organization by discussing a problem and then its various solutions	I. Tooth decay threatens children's dental health. II. Inexpensive, easy-to-apply sealants make teeth resistant to decay.
Cause and Effect	Organization by discussing a situation and its causes, or a situation and its effects	I. Most HMOs refuse to pay for treatment they deem "experimental." II. Patients die who might have been saved by "experimental" treatment.
Refutation	Organization according to objections your listeners may have to your ideas and arguments	I. Although you may think that college football players get too much financial aid, they work hard for it, spending twenty to thirty hours a week in training and on the field. II. Although you may think that college football players don't spend much time on academics, they have two hours of enforced study every weeknight.
Motivated Sequence	Alan H. Monroe's five-step plan for organizing a persuasive message: attention, need, satisfaction, visualization, and action	I. Attention: "An apple a day keeps the doctor busy." What has happened to the old adage about keeping the doctor away? Why has it changed? II. Need: Pesticides are poisoning our fresh fruits and vegetables. III. Satisfaction: Growers must seek environmentally friendly alternatives to pesticides. IV. Visualization: Remember the apple poisoned by Snow White's wicked stepmother? You may be feeding such apples to your own children. V. Action: Buy organically grown fruits and vegetables.

objective. Just remember that your chosen strategy can have a major effect on your listeners' response to your message.

Adapting Ideas to People and People to Ideas

15.5 Provide specific suggestions for adapting to receptive audiences, neutral audiences, and unreceptive audiences.

Scholar Donald C. Bryant's definition of rhetoric emphasizes the principle of appropriately adapting a message to an audience, which he calls the *process of adjusting ideas to people and people to ideas*.[17] With this thought, we've now come full circle in the process of developing a persuasive message. As we have emphasized throughout our discussion of public speaking, analyzing your audience members and adapting to them is at the heart of the speech-making process; it's one of the fundamental Communication Principles for a Lifetime. In a persuasive speech, adapting begins with identifying your specific purpose and understanding whether you are trying to change or reinforce attitudes, beliefs, values, or behavior. It continues when you select an organizational strategy.

For example, if your audience members are unreceptive toward your ideas, you might organize your speech by refutation and address their objections directly. In addition, research studies and experienced speakers can offer other useful suggestions to help you adapt to your audience. Let's look at some specific strategies for persuading receptive, neutral, and unreceptive audiences.

The Receptive Audience

It is usually a pleasure to address an audience that already supports you and your message. In these situations, you can explore your ideas in depth and can be fairly certain of a successful appeal to action. The following suggestions can help you engage receptive audience members:

- *Identify with your audience.* Emphasize your similarities and common interests. A good place to do so is often in the introduction of your speech.
- *State your speaking objective overtly.* Tell your audience members exactly what you want them to do, and ask them for an immediate show of support. If your listeners are already receptive, you do not have to worry that being overt will antagonize them. Rather, it will give you more time to rouse them to passionate commitment and action.
- *Use emotional appeals.* If your listeners already support your position, you can spend less time providing detailed evidence and instead focus on using strong emotional appeals to move them to action.

CRITICAL/CULTURAL PERSPECTIVES & COMMUNICATION

Persuasion as Dialogue: The Power of Listening and Responding

The success of a persuasive speech is usually measured in terms of the speaker's skill in developing, supporting, organizing, and delivering an effective persuasive message. But studying persuasion is a means to becoming not only a better advocate to persuade others, but also a more knowledgeable and critical listener. The listener is at least equally accountable for the outcome of the persuasive event. Listeners have an ethical responsibility to listen critically, be sensitive to and tolerant of differences, and communicate expectations and feedback to the speaker—including, when appropriate, to challenge the speaker's message. To be both effective and ethical, persuasion must be a dialogue, with both speaker and listener sharing responsibility for the outcome. Speakers have power to influence and evoke change only if listeners grant them that power.

▲ Most audiences will start out fairly neutral toward your persuasive goal. To persuade such an audience, you can establish common ground between their needs and your goals and appeal to their interests.
Wavebreak Media Ltd/123RF

The Neutral Audience

Many audiences will fall somewhere between being wildly enthusiastic and being hostile and will simply be neutral. The listeners' neutrality may take the form of indifference: They know about the topic or issue, but they do not see how it affects them, or they cannot make up their minds about it. Alternatively, their neutrality may take the form of ignorance: They just do not know much about the topic. Regardless of whether they are indifferent or ignorant, your challenge is to get them interested in your message. Otherwise, they may escape by sleeping through your speech or engaging in such self-distracting activities as texting or checking social media. The following suggestions can help you engage your neutral audience members:

- *Hook your neutral audience with an especially engaging introduction or attention step.* Anna hooked her student audience with the following introduction to her persuasive speech about mortgage discrimination:

    > With a degree from Northwestern and a successful career in computer tech, Rachelle Farouk expected no trouble buying her first place. But when she applied for a mortgage loan, she was denied.[18]

- *Appeal to common ground.* Another strategy for persuading neutral audiences is to refer to universal beliefs or common concerns. For example, protecting the environment and having access to good health care might be common concerns.

- *Appeal to your listeners' interests.* Show how the topic affects not only them but also people they care about. For example, parents will be interested in issues and policies that affect their children.

- *Limit your persuasive purpose.* Be realistic about what you can accomplish. People who are neutral at the beginning of your speech are unlikely to change their opinion in just a few minutes. Persuasion is unlikely to occur all at once or after only one presentation of arguments and issues.

The Unreceptive Audience

As a speaker, you will find that one of your biggest challenges is to persuade audience members who are unreceptive toward you or your message. If they are unreceptive toward you personally, you need to find ways to enhance your credibility and persuade them to listen to you. If they are unreceptive toward your point of view, the following strategies may help:

- *Focus on universal beliefs and concerns.* Do not immediately announce your persuasive purpose. Explicitly telling unreceptive listeners that you plan to change their minds can make them defensive. Instead, refer to areas of agreement, as you would with a neutral audience. Rather than saying, "Wear a face mask to protect others from the coronavirus" you might say, "I share your concern for your neighbors."

- *Following the principle of primacy, advance your strongest arguments first.* If you save your best argument for last (the recency principle), your audience may already have stopped listening.
- *Acknowledge the opposing points of view that audience members may hold.* Summarize the reasons they may oppose your point of view; then cite evidence and use arguments to refute the opposition and support your conclusion. In speaking to students seeking to hold down tuition costs, a dean might say, "I am aware that many of you struggle to pay for your education. You work nights, take out loans, and live frugally." Then the dean could go on to identify how the university could provide additional financial assistance to students.
- *Be especially aware of, and effectively use, nonverbal messages.* One study suggests that unreceptive audiences may more negatively evaluate speakers who do not gesture than they do those who use gestures.[19]

RECAP
Adapting Ideas to People and People to Ideas

Persuading the Receptive Audience	Persuading the Neutral Audience	Persuading the Unreceptive Audience
• Identify with your audience.	• Gain and maintain your audience's attention.	• Do not tell listeners that you are going to try to convince them to support your position.
• Emphasize common interests.	• Refer to beliefs and concerns that are important to listeners.	• Present your strongest arguments first.
• Provide a clear objective; tell your listeners what you want them to do.	• Show how the topic affects people your listeners care about.	• Acknowledge opposing points of view.
• Appropriately use emotional appeals.	• Be realistic about what you can accomplish.	• Use appropriate gestures.

In the following persuasive speech on private ambulance companies, Blake Bergeron argues a proposition of policy. He supports his speech by being a knowledgeable, well-prepared speaker; using evidence and reasoning; and making emotional appeals. He organizes his persuasive speech according to cause and effect, and problem–solution patterns.

Sample Persuasive Speech

Private Ambulances

Blake Bergeron[20]
The University of Texas

When 81-year-old Tennessee resident Donna Maher woke up with chest pain and shortness of breath, she knew what to do: dial 911. After she was told paramedics would leave as quickly as they could, *Jacobin Magazine* on January 5, 2017, describes surveillance footage showing Rural/Metro employee Cortney Bryson receiving the dispatch and lighting a cigarette. In those moments, Donna slips into a coma and ten days later, passes away.

Blake captures his listeners' attention with an illustration.

(continued)

Sample Persuasive Speech (continued)

This second-rate response from a first responder is horrifying, but to be expected. Rural/Metro is a private company with no loyalty to the county or its residents. The June 25, 2016, *New York Times* laments that one in four of the ambulances we pay taxes for is owned and operated by private corporations with little oversight. Danielle Ivory, one of the authors of that *New York Times* article, reveals in a February 13, 2017, interview that the financial crisis left municipalities cash-strapped and unable to provide basic ambulance services. But where cities saw disaster, corporate giants like Rural/Metro, Transcare, and American Medical Response saw opportunity and stepped in, bringing with them a complete disregard for our safety. *The Week* on July 6, 2016, warns that, from the ambulance workers who slept through an emergency call, to the company who sent a $761 collections notice to an infant, private ambulances are in a state of emergency. With more than 50 million calls going to private ambulances this year, it's clear: We need greater protections from the dangers of private ambulances. So, let's first look at why residents are left helpless, next understand this corporate takeover's effects, and finally learn how we can fight back—because when you dial 911, big business shouldn't answer.

In 2010, Lifestar Response employee Jim Ralston approached CEO Danny Platt about rampant medical fraud occurring in the company. His response: It's fine; "we['re] profitable." Lifestar's [schemes] persist for two reasons: unsystematic oversight and consumer deception.

First, corporations exploit a lack of standardization within emergency services. The August 3, 2016, *Democracy Now* elaborates that since privatization really started after the financial crisis, regulations haven't caught up—a problem exacerbated by the fact that there is no national standard for what emergency services have to report, or what even constitutes a late arrival time. Companies take advantage of this lack of oversight and coerce municipalities to keep regulations as lax as possible. *Alternet* on August 5, 2016, warns that the municipality loses all forms of agency. Like Edgewater, Colorado—this municipality is supposed to charge Rural/Metro for response times over seven minutes, but with no reporting requirements, enforcement is impossible. Without standard metrics, we don't know if companies actually do their jobs.

Second, we're unprotected because private ambulances keep us in the dark. The February 2017 *Journal of Emergency Medical Services* reveals that 72 percent of U.S. ambulance use is not medically needed, something companies do not want us to know. Private ambulances capitalize on our simplistic view of emergency response, urging us to call them as soon as things get rough. But to make things worse, we think this necessity is paid for by taxes. It's not. The *Bradenton Herald* on January 8, 2017, reveals that the average ambulance costs us approximately $1,000. But when residents think costs are covered, why would companies tell us about subscription services, or when ambulances are not needed? By keeping us blind, they've created the perfect storm, feeding on an illusion they know they can exploit.

For fourteen years, New York's Chez Valenta was forced by his company to participate in the practice of "ER Shopping," where one paramedic is a lookout while the other steals whatever he or she can from the emergency room. Chez's former employer embodies two effects of this corporate takeover: poor quality of service and increased risk of bankruptcy.

Blake moves from his opening illustration to facts and statistics that make it clear to his audience that "This issue concerns you."

Blake states his central idea in a single concise declarative statement. He then previews his main ideas in an organizational pattern that moves from cause to effect and then to solution.

Blake poses a rhetorical question to his listeners to help sustain their attention.

Sample Persuasive Speech (continued)

First, private ambulances bring about deadly consequences. *EMS1* on January 15, 2017, asserts a company is at "level zero" when no fully staffed or stocked ambulances are available. Because private ambulances are motivated to keep profits high and costs low, they experience as much as 400 percent more level zeros. *EMS1* on July 29, 2016, narrates that in 2015, Pamela and her husband Larry were riding their motorcycle together when they ran into a tree. Pamela, who was mildly injured, frantically dialed 911, who dispatched the ambulance provider, Opportunity EMS. They were at level zero, sent a crew without proper equipment, and caused Pamela to watch her husband die right in front of her. It's normally hard to point fingers for a patient's death, but for Pamela it couldn't be clearer. They left her a widow.

At this point in the speech, another specific illustration increases the likelihood that audience members will think, "This could happen to me."

Second, privatization dramatically increases the risk of bankruptcy. The July 2, 2016, *Des Moines Register* cautions that privatization is risky because businesses go bankrupt far more often than municipalities do. And when emergency services go bankrupt, as five have in the past year, we're left stranded. The February 14, 2017, *Wall Street Journal* calls out Transcare. In February 2016, some 1,700 people woke up jobless, approximately 5,000 emergency calls went unanswered, and dozens of city officials scrambled to figure out what to do when 911 dispatchers across ten cities heard one message: "out of service." Their last line of defense fell out from under them. It's familiar. Lax regulations and prioritization of profits left us wrecked in 2008; nearly a decade later and those same symptoms turn us into prey in our most vulnerable moments.

Jay Robbins was one of Transcare's employees. As a first responder who was at Ground Zero on 9/11, he cries, "Transcare betrayed us." Look, we can't abolish private ambulances because some municipalities have no other option, but we can change how these corporations operate, in two ways: by establishing enforcement standards and by increasing preparedness.

Blake offers an internal preview of the solution section of his speech.

First, corporations exploit a lack of standardization. So I've worked with Lisa Horton from Aurora, Colorado, to create a standard based on Aurora's contract with Falck Ambulance. Under these guidelines, ambulances would be required to reveal all response times and pay strict penalties for times over seven minutes and the number of instances of level zero. We can take these standards to our local governments and demand revamped regulations. Write down your name, email, and address, and I'll mail the guidelines to your city or county's government. Private ambulances are in all 50 states, meaning that your city may not be private, but some city in your state is; it's up to us to keep residents safe. Municipalities are pretty slow, y'all. So, we've got to get the ball rolling now. Starting this movement on the local level is the only way to ensure our interests get met.

Blake suggests a specific action step for his first solution.

Second, since private ambulances stay silent, let's shed some light on how to properly handle emergencies. First, since ambulances have $45 a year subscriptions, call yours and find out. Next, I've got simple questions to determine whether you actually need an ambulance. If you just need transportation to the ER, call a taxi, rideshare, friend, whatever. If you broke your arm, but there's no blood, a rideshare would definitely be cheaper and probably be faster. Fort Worth, Texas, launched a campaign with that message and in just one year, cut down on over 10,000 rides. To help spread the word, I've created a toolkit. It's got a pamphlet, magnet, flyer—literally everything you need to remind yourself and others. We've been told since we were young that if there's an emergency, dial 911, but now it's time we ensure companies enter this industry not to provide a quick buck, but to provide a pivotal public service.

Blake provides tools to help his listeners enact a second solution.

(continued)

Sample Persuasive Speech (continued)

When *New York Times* reporter Danielle Ivory visited Transcare's bankruptcy auction, she found herself in awe. She describes seeing "expired medical supplies," broken heart monitors, and former employees brought to tears wondering what to do now. Today, we've examined the causes, effects, and solutions so we can all better protect ourselves from private ambulances. While a Tennessee county may have lost one of their very own, hopefully we can ensure that this story doesn't have to tell itself again.

Blake provides closure by referring in his final sentence to his opening illustration.

CHAPTER 15
STUDY GUIDE: PRINCIPLES FOR A LIFETIME

Understanding Persuasion

15.1 Define persuasion and describe five ways listeners may be motivated.

PRINCIPLE POINTS: Persuasion is the process of attempting to change or reinforce attitudes, beliefs, values, or behaviors. Cognitive dissonance is a sense of mental discomfort that arises when new information conflicts with a person's current attitudes, beliefs, values, or behavior. Maslow's classic hierarchy of needs attempts to explain why people may be motivated to respond to persuasive appeals. Both fear appeals and positive motivational appeals can prompt listeners to respond to a persuasive message. The elaboration likelihood model (ELM) explains how listeners may be motivated by such peripheral factors as the speaker's appearance.

PRINCIPLE TERMS:

persuasion
coercion
cognitive dissonance
hierarchy of needs
elaboration likelihood model (ELM)

PRINCIPLE SKILLS:

1. Describe a time when you experienced cognitive dissonance, whether as a result of persuasive communication or not, and explain how you resolved the feeling.
2. Using the definition of *persuasion* provided in this chapter, explain what makes the end-of-chapter speech "Private Ambulances" a persuasive speech.

Developing Your Audience-Centered Persuasive Speech

15.2 Explain how to select and narrow a persuasive topic, identify a persuasive purpose, and develop and support a persuasive proposition.

PRINCIPLE POINTS: Your specific persuasive purpose targets your audience's attitudes, beliefs, values, or behavior. Attitudes are learned predispositions to respond favorably or unfavorably toward something. A belief is one's sense of what is true or false. Values are enduring conceptions of right or wrong, or good or bad. Of the three, attitudes are most susceptible to change, and values are least likely to change. After clarifying your specific purpose, you can word your central idea as a proposition of fact, value, or policy.

PRINCIPLE TERMS:

proposition
proposition of fact
proposition of value
proposition of policy

PRINCIPLE SKILLS:

1. Brainstorm three topics that would make a good persuasive speech for an audience of your communication classmates. Explain whether these topics target your audience members' attitudes, beliefs, values, or behavior.
2. State an attitude, a belief, and a value that you hold related to the topic of transportation. Use your attitude, belief, and value to develop a proposition of fact,

a proposition of value, and a proposition of policy that could each be a central idea for a persuasive speech.

3. Use the following checklist to assess your choice of topic and purpose for a persuasive speech you are developing for your communication class:

    _____ Topic focused on an important issue

    _____ Topic narrowed to fit time limits

    _____ Persuasive general purpose—to change or reinforce listeners' attitudes, beliefs, values, or behavior

    _____ Audience-centered specific purpose

    _____ General and specific purposes achieved

    _____ Central idea is a clear, declarative one-sentence summary of the speech

    _____ Central idea is a proposition of fact, value, or policy

Supporting Your Persuasive Message with Credibility, Logic, and Emotion

15.3 **Use credibility, logical reasoning, and emotional appeals to make your persuasive speech more effective.**

PRINCIPLE POINTS: Support for your persuasive proposition can include credibility, logic, and emotion. Credibility is your audience's perception of your competence, trustworthiness, and dynamism. Enhancing your initial credibility before you speak, your derived credibility during your speech, and your terminal credibility after your speech will help you improve your overall credibility as a speaker. Reasoning, the process of drawing a conclusion from evidence, is integral to your persuasive process. The three primary types of reasoning are inductive, deductive, and causal. You can also reason by analogy. Be a more effective and ethical persuader by avoiding such reasoning fallacies as the causal fallacy, bandwagon fallacy, either–or fallacy, hasty generalization, personal attack, red herring, appeal to misplaced authority, and non sequitur. In addition to persuading others because of who you are (ethos) or how well you reason (logos), you can move an audience to respond by using emotional appeals (pathos).

PRINCIPLE TERMS:

rhetoric
ethos
logos
pathos
credibility
competence
trustworthiness
dynamism
charisma
initial credibility
derived credibility
terminal credibility
proof
evidence
reasoning
inductive reasoning
reasoning by analogy
deductive reasoning
syllogism
causal reasoning
logical fallacy
causal fallacy
bandwagon fallacy
either–or fallacy
hasty generalization
personal attack
red herring
appeal to misplaced authority
non sequitur

PRINCIPLE SKILLS:

1. Imagine you are giving a speech to your classmates near the end of the term. What specific strategies can you use to enhance your credibility with this audience?

2. Use the following checklist to assess the credibility, logical reasoning, and emotional appeals in a persuasive speech you are developing for your communication class:

    _____ Ethos evident in speaker's appearance, credentials, preparation, and delivery

    _____ Logos evident in logically reasoned arguments supported by evidence

    _____ Pathos evident in emotion-arousing words and phrases, concrete illustrations and descriptions, and evocative presentation aids

Organizing Your Persuasive Message

15.4 **Organize your persuasive message.**

PRINCIPLE POINTS: Ways to organize your persuasive message include problem–solution, cause and effect, refutation, and the motivated sequence. The motivated sequence includes five steps: attention, need, satisfaction, visualization, and action.

PRINCIPLE TERMS:

refutation
motivated sequence
visualization
positive visualization
negative visualization

PRINCIPLE SKILLS:

1. You want your listeners to support a local ordinance that will restrict noise after 10:00 p.m. in your community. Using the motivated sequence, identify a way to catch their attention, establish a need, identify a solution, visualize the benefits of this proposal, and present a specific action step they could take to help the ordinance pass.

2. Use the following checklist to assess the organization of a persuasive speech you are developing for your communication class:

   _____ Introduction caught attention, established motive for audience to listen, stated central idea, and previewed main ideas

   _____ Body organized in a logical way—for example, according to problem–solution, cause and effect, refutation, or the motivated sequence

   _____ Conclusion restated central idea, summarized main ideas, and provided closure

   _____ Positive and negative emotions and visualization evoked by presentation aids, if any

Adapting Ideas to People and People to Ideas

15.5 Provide specific suggestions for adapting to receptive audiences, neutral audiences, and unreceptive audiences.

***PRINCIPLE* POINTS:** Be prepared to adapt your persuasive messages to receptive, neutral, and unreceptive audiences. If your listeners are receptive, identify with them, be overt in stating your speaking objective, and use emotional appeals. If they are neutral, hook them with your introduction, refer to universal beliefs and common concerns, show them how the topic affects them and those they care about, and be realistic about what you can accomplish. If your listeners are unreceptive, focus on areas of agreement, present your strongest arguments first, acknowledge opposing points of view, and use appropriate gestures.

***PRINCIPLE* SKILLS:**

1. You want to persuade members of your communication class to buy snacks from the campus World Environment Club, whose members donate profits to save South American rainforests. Most of your classmates do not even know or care much about rainforests half a world away and some have stereotyped the Environment Club as a bunch of out-of-touch hippies. What persuasive speaking strategies would be helpful in achieving your goal?

2. For a speech you are preparing for your communication class, consider whether your classmates are a receptive, neutral, or unreceptive audience. What specific strategies offered in this chapter will help you adapt to your audience?

APPENDIX

INTERVIEWING

APPENDIX OUTLINE

- Interview Types
- Interview Phases
- How to Be Interviewed for a Job
- How to Be Interviewed in an Information-Gathering Interview
- Interviewer Responsibilities
- Study Guide: *Principles for a Lifetime*

APPENDIX OBJECTIVES

A.1 Define what an interview is and identify five different kinds of interviews.

A.2 Describe the three phases of a well-structured interview.

A.3 Identify and describe how to be interviewed for a job, including how to develop a well-worded resume.

A.4 Identify and describe how to be interviewed in an information-gathering interview.

A.5 Explain how to conduct an interview.

Not that long ago you would pick up a newspaper and scour the "want ads" for a job. Once you found a vacancy that fit your skills and talents, you would dutifully type up your resume and cover letter, and mail your application to the address listed in the ad. Then you would wait. Eventually, someone would read your application, decide if you were a possible candidate, and give you a call, or you would receive a polite, "thanks, but no thanks," letter in the mail.

Today it's more likely you'll learn about a job vacancy online, or if you have a profile on LinkedIn, Indeed, or another popular job search site, *you* may be the one first notified of a vacancy if your credentials match an employer's needs. If you apply for a job online, your resume will probably be scanned for keywords by a computer software program to determine if you are a good fit for the position. Only after someone reviews the computer triage results, may you then be invited for an interview. Your first interview may be via Zoom or Skype.

Although the job search process has certainly evolved during the past quarter century, what has not changed is the importance of making a good impression in an interview, whether via video or in person.[1] Your resume does not get you the job, *you get the job based on your ability to communicate during an interview*.[2]

In this introduction to interviewing, we'll discuss communication strategies that can enhance your job interview skills, whether interviewing in person or via Zoom, Skype, FaceTime, or another video messaging application. We'll also offer tips about how to participate in an information-gathering interview. We'll conclude the appendix by identifying strategies that can help you polish your talents if you are the person interviewing others.

Interview Types

A.1 Define what an interview is and identify five different kinds of interviews.

An **interview** is a form of oral interaction structured to achieve a goal; it often involves just two people who take turns speaking and listening, but it can include more than two people. An effective interview is not a random conversation; rather, the person conducting the interview has carefully framed the objectives of the interview and developed a structured plan for achieving those objectives. The person being interviewed should also prepare by considering the kinds of questions he or she may be asked and being ready to give appropriate responses.

The planned or structured nature of the interview sets it apart from other communication situations, yet interviews sometimes include elements of interpersonal, group, and presentational communication. Interviews embody interpersonal communication in that there are two or more people participating in the interview who must establish a relationship. If the goal of the interview is to find a solution to a vexing problem, the interview may resemble elements of a group discussion in which a problem is defined and analyzed and solutions are generated, evaluated, and then implemented. Preparing for a job interview is like a public speaking situation; you focus on your audience (the interviewer), keep your purpose in mind as you research the company you're interviewing with, organize your ideas, and even rehearse your responses to questions you think you may be asked.

When people think of the term *interview*, what most commonly comes to mind is a job interview. Yet interviews can also be a means of gathering information, sharing job performance feedback, solving problems, and persuading others. Even though we are focusing primarily on employment and information-gathering interviews, the strategies we present can help you with *any* interview situation.

interview
A form of oral interaction structured to achieve a goal; it involves two or more people who take turns speaking and listening.

Information-Gathering Interview

Just as the name suggests, **information-gathering interviews** are designed to seek information from the person being interviewed. *Public-opinion polls* are one type of information-gathering interview. When you leave an organization, you may be asked to participate in an *exit interview*, an interview designed to assess why you are leaving the company. A reporter for an online publication, magazine, newspaper, radio, or TV station interviews people to gather information for a story.

The people who are most skilled at conducting information-gathering interviews do their homework before the interview. They come prepared with specific questions and have already conducted background research. In addition to preparing questions, a skilled information-gathering interviewer listens and develops questions that stem from the information that is shared during the interview.

information-gathering interview
An interview, such as an opinion poll, designed to seek information from another person.

Appraisal Interview

An **appraisal interview**, sometimes called a *performance review*, occurs when a supervisor or employer shares information with you about your job performance. Such an interview enables you to see how others perceive your effectiveness and helps you determine whether you are likely to get a promotion or a layoff. During an appraisal interview, you can typically express your observations about the organization and your goals for the future. Usually, a supervisor prepares a written report summarizing your strengths and weaknesses and then meets with you to review it.

When you are receiving feedback from a supervisor, the best approach is to listen and gather as much information about the supervisor's perceptions as possible. In an evaluation situation, especially if the feedback is negative, it is easy to become defensive. Instead, you should try to manage your emotions and use the information to your benefit. If you disagree with your supervisor's evaluation, consider using the conflict management skills we discussed in Chapter 8. In addition, provide specific examples to support your position. Just saying that you don't like the review is likely to do more harm than good.

appraisal interview
An interview during which a supervisor or employer shares information with an employee about his or her job performance.

Problem-Solving Interview

A **problem-solving interview** is designed to resolve a problem that affects one or both parties involved in the interview. A disciplinary interview to consider corrective action toward an employee or a student is one type of problem-solving interview. Grievance interviews are also problem-solving interviews; one person brings a grievance or complaint against another person, and solutions are sought to resolve the problem or conflict.

The strategies presented in Chapter 10 for structuring a problem-solving group discussion can also help you organize a problem-solving interview. Before trying to solve or manage a problem, first define the issues; then analyze the causes, history, and symptoms of the problem. Rather than focusing on only one solution, brainstorm several possible solutions, and then evaluate the pros and the cons of the potential solutions before settling on a single one.

problem-solving interview
An interview, such as a grievance or disciplinary interview, that is designed to solve a problem.

Persuasion Interview

During a **persuasion interview**, one person seeks to change or reinforce the attitudes, beliefs, values, or behavior of one or more other people. The sales interview is a classic example of an interview in which the goal is to persuade. A political campaign interview is another example of a persuasion interview.

persuasion interview
An interview that attempts to change or reinforce attitudes, beliefs, values, or behavior, such as a sales interview.

job interview
A focused, structured conversation that is used to assess a person's credentials and skills for employment.

Our discussion in Chapter 15 of the principles and strategies of persuading others can help you prepare for a persuasion interview. The advantage of trying to persuade someone during an interview rather than in a speech is the size of the audience; during a persuasive interview, you may have an audience of one. It is especially important to analyze and adapt to your listener when seeking to persuade.

Job Interview

A **job interview** is a focused, structured conversation that is used to assess a person's credentials and skills for employment. The job interview may involve elements of each of the types of interviews we've already discussed. Information is both gathered and shared, and a job interview will certainly solve a problem if you're the one looking for a job and you are hired. Elements of persuasion are also involved in a job interview. If you are seeking a job, you're trying to persuade the interviewer to hire you; if you are the interviewer and you're interviewing an exceptionally talented person, your job is to persuade the interviewee to join your organization.

Regardless of the purpose or format of the interview, the five Communication Principles for a Lifetime that we've used to organize our discussion of interpersonal, group and team, and presentational communication situations will serve you well when you participate in an interview. Whether you are the interviewer or the interviewee, it is important to be aware of how you are coming across to others. Using and interpreting verbal and nonverbal messages are critical to having a successful interview. In our definition of an interview, we noted that all individuals involved both talk and listen. Adapting to others is also essential. Effective interview participants listen, respond, and speak extemporaneously rather than delivering overly scripted, planned messages.

Interview Phases

A.2 Describe the three phases of a well-structured interview.

Just as a speech or term paper has a beginning, a middle, and an end, so does a well-structured interview.[3] No matter what type, most interviews have three phases:

1. *The opening.* The interviewer puts the interviewee at ease and presents an overview of the interview agenda.
2. *The body.* During the longest part of an interview, the interviewer asks questions, and the interviewee listens and responds. The interviewee may also ask questions.
3. *The conclusion.* The interviewer summarizes what will happen next and usually gives the interviewee an opportunity to ask any final questions.

It is the responsibility of the interviewer, the person leading the interview, to develop a structure for the interview. But it's also helpful for the interviewee to understand the overall structure in advance to know what to expect both before and during the interview. So whether you're the interviewer or the interviewee, understanding the interview structure we discuss in this appendix should be of value to you.

The Opening

The opening of any interview is crucial because it creates a climate for positive and open communication. When interviewing someone, you should strive to establish rapport and to clarify the goals of the interview.

To establish rapport, start the conversation with something that will put the interviewee at ease. The discussion could be about something as simple as the weather, recent events both of you attended, or other light topics. Make direct eye contact, smile appropriately, and offer a firm handshake to establish a warm atmosphere.

Besides making the interviewee comfortable, the interviewer should clarify the goals of the interview by explicitly stating the general purpose for the meeting. After the opening conversation, it may be helpful for the interviewer to provide a general overview of the nature and purpose of the interview and an estimate of how long it will last. Clarifying a meeting's purpose helps both parties get their bearings and check their understanding. A good interviewer makes sure that everyone is on the same wavelength before the actual questioning begins.

Both the interviewer and the interviewee should arrive a few minutes early for the interview. The interviewee should be prepared, however, to wait patiently if necessary. If you are the interviewer and have decided to use a recording device, set it up. You may keep it out of sight once the interviewee has seen it, but *never* try to hide the fact that you are recording the interview—such a ploy is unethical and in some states, illegal. If you are going to take written notes, get out your paper and pen. Now you are ready to begin asking your prepared questions.

The Body: Asking Questions

Once the interviewee has been put at ease during the opening of the interview, the bulk of the interview will consist of the interviewer asking the interviewee questions. Even though both parties listen and speak, the interviewer has the primary responsibility for questioning. If the interviewer has done a good job of identifying and clarifying his or her objectives and gathering information, the key questions to be asked are usually fairly obvious.

Question Types Interview questions fall into one of four categories: open, closed, probing, or hypothetical.[4] A typical interview usually includes some of each type.

Open Questions **Open questions** are broad and unstructured questions that allow interviewees considerable freedom to determine the amount and kind of information they will provide. Because they encourage the interviewee to share information almost without restriction, open questions are useful in determining opinions, values, and perspective. Such questions as "What are your long- and short-term career goals?" "Why are you seeking employment here?" and "How do you feel about gun control?" prompt personal and wide-ranging responses.

open question
A question that is broad and unstructured and that allows the respondent considerable freedom to determine the amount and kind of information to provide.

Closed Questions **Closed questions** limit the range of possible responses. They may ask for a simple yes or no—"Do you enjoy working in teams?"—or they may allow interviewees to select responses from a number of specific alternatives: "How often do you go to the movies? (1) Less than once a month, (2) Once a month, (3) Twice a month, (4) Once a week." Closed questions enable the interviewer to gather specific information by restricting interviewees' freedom to express personal views or elaborate on responses. Closed questions are most often used when an interviewer is trying to obtain a maximum amount of information in a short period of time.

closed question
A question that limits the range of possible responses and requires a simple, direct, and brief answer.

Probing Questions **Probing questions** encourage interviewees to clarify or elaborate on partial or superficial responses. Through the use of these questions, interviewers attempt to clarify or direct responses. Such questions as "Could you elaborate on your coursework in the area of communication?" "Do you mean to say that you already own three vacuum cleaners?" and "Will you tell me more about your relationship with your supervisor?" call for further information in a particular area. Often spontaneous, probing questions follow up on the key questions that interviewers have prepared in advance.

probing question
A question that encourages the interviewee to clarify or elaborate on partial or superficial responses and that usually takes the discussion in a desired direction.

Hypothetical Questions Interviewers use **hypothetical questions** when they describe a set of conditions and ask interviewees what they would do if they were in that situation. Such questions are generally used either to gauge reactions to emotion-arousing or value-laden circumstances or to reveal an interviewee's likely response to a real

hypothetical question
A question used to gauge an interviewee's reaction to an emotion-arousing or value-laden situation or to reveal an interviewee's likely reactions to a real situation.

RECAP
Types of Interview Questions

	Uses	Example
Open Question	Prompts wide-ranging responses. Answers reveal interviewee's opinions, values, and perspectives.	Tell me about your previous job duties. How would you describe your son's problems in school?
Closed Question	Requests simple yes or no response or forces interviewee to select a response from limited options.	Have you been skiing in the past month? Which one of the following drinks would you buy? Coke Pepsi 7-Up
Probing Question	Encourages clarification of, or elaboration on, previous responses. Leads response in a specific direction.	Can you tell me more about the pain in your side? We've talked about your mother. Can you describe how you felt about your father's long absences from home when you were a child?
Hypothetical Question	Gauges reactions to emotional or value-laden situations. Elicits response to a real or imaginary situation.	How would you support your opponent if she were elected chair of the board? What would you do if your secretary lost an important file?

situation. A police officer might ask an eyewitness to a murder, "What if I told you that the man you identified as the murderer in the line-up was the mayor?" During an exit interview, a personnel manager might ask, "If we promoted you to chief sanitary engineer and paid you $4 an hour more, would you consider staying with Bob's Landfill and Landscaping?"

Questioning Sequences Open, closed, probing, and hypothetical questions may be used in any combination, as long as their sequence is thoughtfully planned. Depending on the purpose, these questions may be arranged into three basic sequences: funnel, inverted funnel, and tunnel.

The Funnel Sequence As Figure A.1 shows, the **funnel sequence** begins with broad, open questions and proceeds to more closed questions. The advantage of this format is that it allows an interviewee to express views and feelings without restriction, at least early in an interview. For example, it may be more useful to begin a grievance interview with the question "How would you describe your relationship with your supervisor?" than with "What makes you think that your supervisor treats you like an idiot?" The first question allows the free expression of feelings, whereas the second clearly reflects an interviewer's bias, immediately forcing the discussion in a negative direction. The following series of questions provides an example of a funnel sequence that might be used for an information-gathering interview:

1. Why do you find communication interesting?
2. What area of communication are you primarily interested in?
3. How long have you studied interpersonal communication?
4. Why do you think interpersonal attraction theory is useful?
5. What would you do to test interpersonal attraction theory?

Notice that the questions start by asking for general information and then focus on more specific ideas.

The Inverted Funnel Sequence The opposite of the funnel sequence is the **inverted funnel sequence**, as shown in Figure A.2, which begins with closed questions and proceeds to more open questions. An interview designed to gather information about a worker's grievance might be based on the inverted funnel and might include the following series of questions:

1. Do you believe that your supervisor wants to fire you?
2. What makes you think that you'll be fired soon?
3. What do you think has caused this problem between you and your supervisor?
4. How has this problem affected your work?
5. How would you describe the general working climate in your department?

funnel sequence
A questioning sequence that begins with broad, open questions and proceeds toward more closed questions.

FIGURE A.1 The Funnel Sequence

Getting at pieces of specific information through the use of direct questioning

inverted funnel sequence
A questioning sequence that begins with closed questions and proceeds to more open questions, intended to encourage an interviewee to respond easily early in the interview.

The relatively closed questions that begin the inverted funnel sequence are intended to encourage an interviewee to respond easily, because they require only brief answers (yes or no, short lists, and the like). As the sequence progresses, the questions become more open and thus require more elaborate answers and greater disclosure.

The inverted funnel sequence is appropriate when an interviewer wants to direct the interview along specific lines and encourage an interviewee to respond with short, easily composed answers. An interviewer can follow up with more general questions to solicit increasingly broad information—the "big picture."

The Tunnel Sequence Finally, the **tunnel sequence** consists of a series of related open or closed questions or a combination of the two; the sequence is intended to gather a wide range of information. This sequence does not include probing questions; it goes into less depth than the other two sequences. An interviewer may use the tunnel sequence to gather information about attitudes and opinions without regard for the reasons behind an interviewee's answers or the intensity of their feelings. The following is a typical tunnel sequence for an information-gathering interview:

1. What are the three major issues in the presidential campaign this year?
2. Which candidate would you vote for if the election were held today?
3. Who will you vote for in the race for U.S. senator?
4. Are you a registered voter in this state?
5. What do you think of the proposition to set up a nuclear waste dump in this state?

The tunnel sequence is most appropriate when an interviewer wants some general information on a variety of topics in a relatively short period of time.

Although these sequences have been discussed as if they were independent and easily distinguishable, a good questioning strategy will probably combine one or more of these question sequences. The key to effective interviewing is to prepare a set of questions that will get the amount and kinds of information you need. An interviewer should remain flexible enough to add, subtract, and revise questions as a discussion proceeds. Such an approach ensures that the objectives of the interview will be accomplished.

As you conduct the interview, use the questions you have prepared as a general guide but not a rigid schedule. If the person you are interviewing mentions an interesting angle you did not think of, don't be afraid to pursue the point. Listen carefully to the person's answers, and ask for clarification of any ideas you don't understand.

FIGURE A.2 The Inverted Funnel Sequence

Building the "big picture" with repeated questioning, integrating previous responses

tunnel sequence
A way of structuring interview questions so that parallel open or closed questions (or a combination of open and closed questions) are asked to gather a large amount of information in a short amount of time; no probing questions are asked.

The Conclusion

Opinion polls, marketing surveys, and sales pitches often end rather abruptly with a "Thank you for taking the time to help me." Many other kinds of interviews require follow-up meetings or some form of future contact. For this reason, and for reasons of common courtesy, the conclusion of an interview is very important. Conclusions can summarize the interview and establish a basis for a continued relationship as well as bringing the meeting to a close.

Summarizing A primary function of the conclusion is to summarize the proceedings. All parties should be aware of and agree on what happened during the meeting. To ensure understanding and agreement, an interviewer summarizes the highlights of the discussion, asking for and offering clarification if necessary.

Continuing the Relationship Another function of the conclusion is to encourage a continued, friendly relationship. The positive communication climate developed during the interview should be carried into its conclusion. The interviewer may need to establish interpersonal harmony if he or she asked questions that resulted in conflict or made the interviewee uncomfortable. Comments such as "I'm glad we had a chance to talk about this problem" or "Thank you for sharing and listening" enable both parties to feel like they have had a positive and productive encounter.

Clarifying Expectations An interviewer can tell the interviewee when to expect further contact or action, if appropriate. A job applicant wants to know when to expect a phone call about a follow-up interview or a job offer. An expert, interviewed by a journalist, wants to know how his or her comments will be used and when the story is likely to be published.

Ending the Meeting At the end of virtually any interview, good manners require both the interviewer and the interviewee to say, "Thank you." Because an interview requires mutual effort, both parties deserve recognition. One final suggestion: Do not prolong the interview beyond the time limits of your appointment.

RECAP
Organizing an Interview

Phase	Goals
Opening	Put the interviewee at ease.
	Review the purpose.
	Establish rapport.
	Provide a general overview.
Body	Use questions appropriate to the interview type and objective:
	• Use open questions to elicit wide-ranging responses.
	• Use closed questions to get specific responses.
	• Use probing questions to seek clarification or elaboration.
	• Use hypothetical questions to gauge a reaction to an imaginary situation.
	Design questioning sequences appropriate to the interview purpose:
	• Use the funnel sequence to elicit general comments first and specific information later.
	• Use the inverted funnel sequence to elicit specific information first and more general comments later.
	• Use the tunnel sequence to gather a lot of information without probing too deeply.
Conclusion	Summarize the proceedings.
	Encourage friendly relations.
	Arrange further contact(s).
	Exchange thank-yous.

How to Be Interviewed for a Job

A.3 Identify and describe how to be interviewed for a job, including how to develop a well-worded resume.

Perhaps you've heard this often-quoted observation, "80 percent of success is showing up."[5] We suggest that you do more than just show up for a job interview, however. Like giving an effective speech, having a successful job interview involves thoughtful preparation and careful planning. According to *CareerBuilder*, a popular website for job hunters, it takes an average of seventeen interviews to get one job offer.[6] To increase your odds of getting hired after an interview, we present research-based suggestions and strategies that can help you make your first impression your best impression when looking for employment.

Be Aware of Your Skills and Abilities

The first communication principle we introduced in this book is to be aware of your communication. Before you interview for a job, it is important to be aware not only of your communication as you interact with others, but also of your unique skills, talents, and abilities. Many people select a career because they think they might like to *be* a lawyer, doctor, or teacher. But rather than thinking about what you want to be, we suggest considering what you like to *do*. Ask yourself these questions:

What do I like to do in my free time?

What are my best skills and talents?

What education and training do I have?

What experiences or previous jobs have I had?

In addition to answering these questions, write down responses to complete this statement: "I can . . . ." For example, you might respond, "I can cook, write, and relate well to others." List as many answers as possible. Here's another statement to complete: "I have . . . ." You might answer, "I have traveled, worked on a farm, and sold smoothies at the mall." Responding to the "I can" and "I have" statements will help you develop an awareness of your skills and experiences that will help you respond readily when you are asked about them during an interview. Reflecting on your interests can help you decide which career will best suit your talents; you will also be able to develop a resume that reflects your best abilities.

Prepare Your Resume

We imagine that you won't be as unwise as the job applicant who put on his resume that his availability for work was limited because Friday, Saturday, and Sunday were "drinking time." Nonetheless, you can still benefit from reading tips, strategies, and suggestions for preparing your resume.

A **resume** is a written, concise, well-organized description of your qualifications for a job. A resume is essentially your professional story. And like a story, it has a main character (you), a story background (your credentials), and a plot (your professional work history). How long should a resume be? Many employers don't expect a resume to be longer than two printed pages; some will look only at a one-page resume. (Resumes of experienced career professionals may be longer than two pages, however.) Today most resumes are posted and distributed online via such sites as LinkedIn, Glassdoor, Indeed, or Monster.com.

resume
A written, concise, well-organized description of a person's qualifications for a job.

Throughout our discussion of presentational speaking we emphasized the importance of analyzing and adapting to your audience. The same principle of being audience-centered holds true when preparing your resume. The specific decisions you make about what to include on a resume should be based on your understanding of the people who will review it. The best resumes are ethically adapted to showcase how your skills and experiences can meet the needs of prospective employers.

One of the best ways to understand what qualifications potential employers seek is to network with those who may have a job for you.[7] **Networking** is the process of communicating with others, sharing information, developing new career contacts, and learning about the needs of prospective employers. You can network using your own contacts or you can reach out to family, friends, and colleagues for their contacts.

networking
The process of communicating with others to share information, develop career contacts, and learn the needs of prospective employers.

Although your resume is important in helping you land a job, its key function is to help you get an interview. How you perform in the interview will determine whether you get the job. Employers rarely hire someone only on the basis of a resume. Most employers spend less than a minute—and some only a few seconds—looking at each resume. In fact, many resumes are never even read by a human being—they are first reviewed by a computer software program to confirm your compatibility for the position. Therefore, your resume should be clear and easy to read and should focus on the essential information an employer seeks.

Elements of a Resume Most employers will be looking for standard information on your resume. (Study the sample resume that appears in this appendix.[8]) Most resumes include the following information:

- *Personal information.* Employers will look for your name, address, phone numbers, email address, and website address (if you have one). Provide phone numbers where you can be reached during both the day and the evening.
- *Career objective.* Many employers will want to see your career objective. Make it brief, clear, and focused. Customize your career objective for each different position you seek. Communicate truthfully about how your goals mesh with the goals and needs of the employer.
- *Education.* Include your major, your degree, your graduation date, and the institution you attended.
- *Experience.* Describe your relevant work experience, listing your most recent job first. Include the names of employers, dates when you worked, and a very brief description of your duties.
- *Honors and special accomplishments.* List any awards, honors, offices held, or other leadership responsibilities.
- *Optional information.* If you have volunteer experience, have traveled, or have computer skills or other pertinent experience, be sure to include it if it is relevant to your objective and the job.
- *References.* List the names, phone numbers, and email addresses of people who can speak positively about your skills and abilities. Or you may indicate that your references are available on request.

Formatting Your Resume Virtually all resumes are sent electronically today, so it's important to use techniques to make sure your resume is accurately transmitted and, once it gets to an employer, stands out in the e-crowd. Career-search expert Katherine Hansen has several useful tips for submitting your resume online:[9]

- *Use their words.* Many resumes are first "read" by a computer software program that scans it for keywords that are mentioned in the job posting or are used frequently in your career field. To avoid having your resume screened out or never even reaching a human being, make liberal use of appropriate keywords as well as specific action verbs. As you write your resume, remember the importance of staying truthful.
- *Keep it simple.* Text formatting, such as boldfaced text, larger fonts in headings, or lines to divide sections, helps people find key information in your resume more quickly. However, that same formatting can create problems when you submit your resume electronically. Many larger employers have online applications that require you to paste your resume into a blank form, for example. In other cases, you may be able to submit your resume as an email attachment or upload it to an online application. By saving your resume as a PDF, you can preserve any formatting.

- *Be (a little) creative.* You can use bullets, asterisks (*), lower-case letter o's (o), and carets (>) to format lists of accomplishments in a plain-text resume. It's also possible to create lines or boxes using text characters such as equal signs (======), plus signs (++++++), and tildes (~~~~~~~~), but don't overdo it.
- *Prepare to be published.* Prepare your resume with formatting that looks good to the human eye as well as the electronic eye. Numerous print and online resume guides can provide formatting tips. No matter what format you choose, one task is essential: Before submitting your resume to employers, carefully review a printed copy to spot and correct any errors that could cause you to be rejected.
- *Publish yourself.* In some career fields, employers expect you to establish your own website or social media profile where you provide your resume in HTML format, along with a portfolio of work samples. Although the HTML format permits you to use more graphics, remember that unless you are a graphic designer, the purpose of any graphics should be to help tell your story simply and effectively, not to dazzle the reader with your design talent.
- *Adapt.* Rather than preparing only one resume and sending it to every job posting, follow our Communication Principle Five and customize your story for each audience. Appropriately adapt not only the content of your resume but also the format to ensure that it meets each prospective employer's requirements.[10]

When developing your resume, be sure to use specific action verbs to describe your experience. Also use these action words during interviews. Rather than using a general verb such as "I *worked* on a project," use more descriptive action words that clarify the role you assumed. Consider using some of the following words when listing or describing your activities or accomplishments:

accelerated	evaluated	promoted
accepted	expanded	proposed
accomplished	expedited	provided
achieved	facilitated	recommended
adapted	found	reduced
administered	generated	researched
analyzed	guided	resulted in
approved	improved	reviewed
built	increased	revised
completed	initiated	selected
conceived	instructed	solved
conducted	interpreted	stimulated
controlled	maintained	structured
coordinated	managed	supervised
created	mastered	tested
delegated	motivated	trained
demonstrated	negotiated	translated
designed	operated	traveled
developed	organized	updated
directed	originated	utilized
effected	participated	won
eliminated	planned	

Sample Resume

MARIA SANCHEZ
3124 West Sixth Street
San Marcos, TX 78666
(512) 555-0102
(512) 555-0010
mariasanchez@emailprovider.com

PROFESSIONAL OBJECTIVE: Seeking a position in human resources as a training specialist.

EDUCATION:

Bachelor of Arts Degree
Major: Communication Studies
Minor: English
Texas State University
Graduation Date: May 20XX

PROFESSIONAL EXPERIENCE:

20XX–Present, Intern, GSD&M, Austin, Texas

- Assisted in creating a leadership training program
- Designed flyers and display ads using desktop publishing software
- Made cold calls to prospective clients

20XX–August 20XX, Intern, Target Market, Houston, Texas

- Developed a sales training seminar
- Coordinated initial plan for writing copy for Crest Inc.'s advertising campaign

20XX–20XX, Supervisor, S&B Associates, San Marcos, Texas

- Supervised three employees editing training materials

20XX–20XX, Advertising Sales and Reporter, *University Star*, San Marcos, Texas

- Sold ads for university paper and worked as social events reporter

OTHER EXPERIENCE:

20XX–20XX, Summer job at Target, San Marcos, Texas
20XX–20XX, Summer job at YMCA, Austin, Texas

SKILLS: Team Leadership, Photography, Computer Proficiency, Research and Analysis, Public Speaking, Customer Service

ACCOMPLISHMENTS & HONORS: Paid for majority of my college education while maintaining a 3.5 grade point average, Presidential Scholarship, Vice President of Texas State University Communication Club, Editor/Historian of MortarBoard, John Marshall High School Vice President of Junior Class, Yearbook Coordinator

PROFESSIONAL ORGANIZATIONS: Lambda Pi Eta, American Society for Training and Development, Communication Club, National Communication Association

INTERESTS: Photography, Tennis, Softball, Theater

REFERENCES: Available at your request

Identify the Needs of Your Potential Employer

After you have analyzed your skills and abilities and have prepared a well-crafted resume, try to anticipate the needs and goals of your potential employer. A good interviewee adapts his or her message to the interviewer.[11]

How do you find information that will help you adapt your message to fit an organization's needs? In a word: research. Gather as much information as you can about not only the person who will interview you but also the needs and goals of the organization or company where you want to work. As a starting point, search for information about the organization online. Virtually every organization these days has a web presence. But do more than just look at the organization's home page; click on the various links to learn more about what the organization does.

Look and Communicate Your Best

The opportunity to assess your appearance and the way in which you express yourself nonverbally is one of the most important reasons an interviewer wants to meet with you face-to-face.

Dress for Success As we discussed in Chapter 4, don't forget about the power of nonverbal messages in making a good impression. Dressing for success is crucial. Regardless of the type or level of the job for which you are applying, most experts suggest that you dress conservatively and give special attention to your grooming. For many professional positions, men may be expected to wear a coat and tie or a suit and well-polished shoes, while women may be expected to wear a dress, suit, or other coordinated attire. However, more casual dress is increasingly becoming the norm. There are many jobs, of course, for which wearing a business suit to the interview would be overkill, but if you're not certain what to wear, it's better to err on the side of dressing up rather than dressing down.

Communicate Your Best What determines whether you are hired for the job? In short, it's the way you communicate. By the time you get to an interview, your interviewer has already determined that you have at least the minimum qualifications for the job. Your ability to apply the Communication Principles for a Lifetime that we've reiterated throughout this text is key to making a good impression on your interviewer. In Chapter 1, when we discussed why it's important to learn about communication, we noted that the top three key factors that employers look for in a job applicant focus on your communication skills.[12] Your ability to listen, respond, and relate to your interviewer is one of the best predictors of whether you will be hired for a job. Other areas that an interviewer may try to assess during an interview are the following:

- *Self-expression.* Are you clear or are you vague when you respond to questions? Do you make effective eye contact? Do you talk too much or too little?
- *Maturity.* Are you likely to make good judgments and effective decisions?
- *Personality.* What's your overall style of relating to people? Are you outgoing, shy, quiet, overbearing, enthusiastic, warm, friendly?
- *Experience.* Can you do the job? Do you have a track record that suggests you can effectively do what needs to be done?
- *Enthusiasm.* Do you seem interested in this job and the organization? Do you seem to be genuine and authentic, or is your enthusiasm phony?
- *Goals.* Where are you heading in life? Are your short- and long-term goals compatible with the needs of the organization?

If you are being interviewed via Zoom, Skype, FaceTime, or some other video conferencing technology, keep in mind that gestures and facial expressions may seem amplified when viewed by others on a screen. Consider minimizing your gestures and expressions (as most newscasters do) when communicating via video. Practice your video interview ahead of time by recording yourself with your smartphone or another digital device. By watching the recording, you can gain insight into how an interviewer might view you on screen.

Marketing experts know the importance of developing a brand name (such as Coke, Kleenex, or Starbucks) to make a product memorable and distinctive. A **personal brand** works the same way. Your personal brand is the impression you leave when the interview has concluded. As career counselor Delores Dean notes, "The goal in branding is to leave behind an impression of you that will be remembered. You must stand out above the rest and be the best."[13] How do you develop yourself as a memorable brand? During the interview, if you project a positive attitude when you speak, you can leave a lasting, positive impression. A memorable, appropriate, and well-told brief story in response to a question can also help you be remembered. The goal of the interview is not only to *make* a positive impression, but also to *leave* a positive impression that will be remembered when the interviewer sifts through his or her notes and memories of multiple interviews. Because your social media presence is often used by employers to identify information about you, it should also reflect the positive impression you want to leave behind.

personal brand
The clear impression an interviewee leaves when the interview has concluded.

Polish Your Online Appearance

Journalist Andy Simmons noted, "Every American has, at some point, appeared naked, drunk, unconscious, rude, crude or felonious online. Okay, maybe not everyone, but surf the Net and that's the impression you'll get."[14] Simmons's point is that it's important to make sure your online impression is as presentable as your live-and-in-person appearance. If you have a Facebook, Instagram, or other social media account, make sure that it contains no embarrassing photos or quotes that might damage your reputation. Keep in mind that employers are searching online to see whether applicants are as credible as their resumes or personal impressions suggest.[15] According to *CareerBuilder*, when employers used the Internet to check the facts on people's resumes, here's what they found:

- 31 percent had lied about their qualifications.
- 24 percent had some link to criminal behavior.
- 19 percent had made negative comments about a past employer.
- 19 percent had bragged about drinking or using illegal drugs.
- 15 percent had shared confidential information about their former employers.
- 11 percent had posted unflattering or sexually explicit photos.
- 8 percent had used an obscene or unprofessional online screen name.

According to Monster.com, the most common lies on resumes have to do with education, employment dates, job titles, and technical skills.[16] Although you may think no one will check or know if you fudge information on your resume, it's easy for employers to double-check its accuracy. Career counselor Liz Ryan cautioned, "People think that they can make up and embellish details about companies that have been sold or gone out of business. But LinkedIn, Facebook and our wide-ranging networks will put a quick stop to most efforts to change history in our favor."[17]

So always be truthful, and monitor your online presence. Don't assume that no one will find out about something you have fabricated on your resume or a "friend" of yours has posted about you online. Increasingly, employers are using social networks such as Facebook and Twitter to see whether your cyberpersonality is consistent with the well-scrubbed, polished appearance you presented in your interview and on your resume. We provide specific tips and suggestions for putting your best online image forward in the Social Media & Communication box.

SOCIAL MEDIA & COMMUNICATION

Putting Your Best Facebook Image Forward

Perhaps you should think twice before posting that photo from last night's wild party to your Facebook page or retweeting that slightly offensive joke. According to one source, 70 percent of all employers routinely review social media sites such as Facebook and Twitter to gain a broader picture of job candidates and their skills.[18] Another source suggests that more than 90 percent of employers use social media sites for recruiting purposes.[19] So if you're looking for a job, make sure your social media accounts put your best image forward. Among the top reasons employers did not hire someone after conducting research online include finding inappropriate content posted, evidence of excessive drinking or drug use, negative comments about previous employers, or lies about qualifications.[20] Here are several tips for making sure your social media profiles don't become an obstacle to your employment.[21]

Privacy. Review the privacy settings on your social media accounts to make sure you are in control of the information you want others to see.

Photos. Remove any unflattering images that might highlight your party skills but not your work skills. Consider updating your profile photo to project the professional image you wish to promote.

Monitor What You and Others Post About You. Review what you and others have posted, including comments on blogs and other social media outlets, to ensure that your posts don't detract from your credibility as a potential employee. Consider what you have posted from the perspective of someone who may hire you.

Review Your Friends List and Those Whom You Have Tagged. Even if you have carefully scrubbed *your* profile information and adjusted *your* privacy settings, a prospective employer may glean unflattering information about you from your friends' pages or through those you have tagged.

Google Yourself. One of the first things many prospective employers do is search for your name using Google. We recommend that you preemptively Google yourself to find out what a prospective employer may see and read about you. By signing up for a Google Alert, you'll find out when your name pops up on the Internet. Consider how you might need to modify your online presence to relay a more positive image. Of course, there may be some information you cannot change. But some Internet content you can alter, such as the images and information you share on your own social media accounts.

Monitor Your Online Name. Avoid what you and your friends may think are cute or funny screen names, such as Imlazyandbored or hottotrot. It's unlikely a prospective employer will be amused and, therefore, it's less likely you'll be hired.

One final tip: Make sure your voicemail greeting is professional and appropriate. Using a fake accent, giving yourself a "cute" nickname, attempting humor that may offend, or referencing inappropriate racial, ethnic, cultural, or sexual orientation stereotypes will not enhance your credibility or employability.

Listen, Respond, and Ask Appropriate Questions

Because an interview is a structured, planned discussion, it is important to demonstrate effective listening and responding skills. Stay focused on what your interviewer is asking you. Remember to stop, look, and listen for both the details and the major points of the questions.

When you respond to questions, you should project genuine enthusiasm and competence. Don't put on an act: Be yourself while being professional. Be friendly and pleasant without being overly effusive or giddy. Communication researcher Mary Minto found that how you respond to an interviewer's questions could be even more important than what you say.[22] Your tone of voice, use of pauses and gestures, and posture are vital in expressing your personality and overall mood. Talking rapidly and nonstop without periodically pausing, for example, communicates that you are not sensitive to others.

Practicing your interview skills can be beneficial. Research confirms that interview skills can be improved with training.[23] One of the best ways to prepare for an interview

TABLE A.1 Typical Questions Asked during Job Interviews

I. Education

1. Why did you select your major?
2. Why did you select your college/university?
3. If you were starting college again, what would you do differently? Why?
4. What subjects were most and least interesting to you? What ones were the most useful? Why?
5. Other than the courses you studied, what is the most important thing you learned from your college experience?
6. How did you finance your college education?

II. Experience

7. What do you see as your strengths as an employee?
8. You say one of your strengths is ___. Give me some indication, perhaps an example, that illustrates this strength.
9. What special skills would you bring to this position?
10. Describe your last few work experiences. Why did you leave each one?
11. What were the best and worst aspects of your last job?
12. What were some of your achievements and disappointments in your last job?
13. Do you see yourself as a leader/manager of people? Why?
14. What kinds of work situations would you like to avoid? Why?
15. What frustrations have you encountered in your work experience? How have you handled these frustrations?
16. What do you look for in a boss?
17. Most employees and bosses have some disagreements. What are some things that you and your current or previous boss have disagreed about?

III. Position and Company

18. Why did you select this company?
19. Why did you decide to apply for this particular position?
20. How do you see yourself being qualified for this position?
21. Are you willing to relocate?

IV. Self-Evaluation

22. Tell me a little bit about yourself. Describe yourself.
23. What do you see as your personal strengths? Talents? How do you know that you possess these? Give examples of each.
24. What do you see as your weak points? Areas for improvement? Things you have difficulty doing? What have you done to deal with these weak areas?
25. Describe a specific work problem you had. Explain what you did to solve this problem.
26. What do you consider to be your greatest work achievement? Why?

V. Goals

27. Where do you see yourself professionally in five years? In ten years? How did you establish these goals? What will you need to do to achieve these goals?
28. What are your salary expectations for this position? Starting salary? Salary in five years?

is to anticipate an interviewer's questions. Table A.1 lists typical questions that may be asked during an interview.[24] We don't recommend that you memorize "canned" or overly rehearsed answers, but it may be helpful to think about possible responses to these questions. Also be prepared to answer questions about your unique experiences, such as military service, vocational training, or membership on sports teams. Keep in mind that when an interviewer asks "Can you tell me a little about yourself?" he or she is likely not only listening for the content of your answer, but assessing your social skills.

Make sure you get a good night's sleep before the interview and eat sensibly (don't skip breakfast; don't stuff yourself at lunch) so that you can stay alert. Long interviews can be physically demanding.

Consider the interview an opportunity to ask questions as well as to answer them; toward the end of an interview, most interviewers will give you an opportunity to ask whatever questions you'd like. Asking questions about an organization is a way to display enthusiasm for the job as well as a means of assessing whether you really want to join the organization. You will want to know the following:

- Will there be any job training for this position?
- What are the opportunities for advancement?
- What is the atmosphere like in the workplace? (If it is an in-person interview, you will be able to observe the workplace.)
- What hours do people work?
- Is there flexibility in scheduling the work day?
- When do you anticipate making a decision about this position?

When it's your opportunity to ask questions, the very first question you ask should *not* be "How much does this job pay?" Usually, the interviewer will discuss salary and benefits with you during the interview. If it is a preliminary interview and there is a chance that you will be called back for another interview, you may want to defer questions about salary and benefits until you know that the organization is seriously considering you for the position.

During the interview, maintain eye contact and speak assertively. The goal in an interview is to project a positive attitude to the interviewer. As motivational speaker Zig Ziglar once noted, "Your attitude, not your aptitude, will determine your altitude."

Follow Up after the Interview

After the interview, it is wise to write a brief letter (yes, a written note) or email to thank the interviewer and to provide any additional information that may have been requested. You may also want to send a thank-you message to others in the organization, such as a secretary or administrative assistant, for helping to arrange the interview. If the interviewer asked for references, make sure to let your reference providers know as soon as possible that they may be contacted. If you are asking your references to send or respond to an online request for a letter of recommendation, expedite the process by providing an addressed, stamped envelope or the appropriate email address and a copy of your resume so that they can personalize their letter with specific information.

Is it appropriate to call the person who interviewed you to ask when a decision will be made about hiring someone? Some employers abide by the philosophy "Don't call or email us, we'll call or email you," but many others would interpret your contact as a sign of your interest in the position and a testament to your ability to follow through. You may want to take the direct approach and simply ask the interviewer toward the end of the interview, "Would it be all right if I emailed you in a few days to find out if you have made a decision or if you need additional information?" If the interviewer tells you that a decision will be made by a certain date and then that date passes by, it is probably okay to ask whether the job has been offered to someone else and to express your continued interest in the position if it hasn't been filled.

How to Be Interviewed in an Information-Gathering Interview

A.4 Identify and describe how to be interviewed in an information-gathering interview.

The bulk of the responsibility for an effective information-gathering interview falls on the person who is doing the interviewing. If you are the interviewer in an information-gathering interview, review the suggestions we discussed earlier in this appendix for structuring the interview. Most information-gathering interviews follow this general structure.

If you are the person being interviewed, however, your primary responsibilities are to be prepared, to listen carefully, and to respond appropriately to questions.

In addition, a good interviewee knows what to expect in an information-gathering interview. You should prepare responses to anticipated questions, pay close attention to requests for specific information, and answer questions directly and accurately.

Prepare for the Interview

In most cases, an interviewee has some advance knowledge of the purpose and objective of an interview, especially if someone is seeking specific information or advice. You can therefore anticipate probable topics of discussion. If you are uncertain what the interview is about, it is appropriate to ask the person who will interview you how best to prepare for the questions he or she plans to ask. Yes, sometimes a broadcast news reporter will pop up on the street, thrust a microphone in someone's face, and ask a pointed question. In most cases, however, NBC news anchor Lester Holt (or his equivalent) is not going to ambush you.

Depending on the nature of the interview, you might want to brush up on the facts you may be asked about. Jot down a few notes to remind you of names, dates, and places. In some cases, you may want to do some background reading on the topic of the interview.

Finally, think about not only what you will say in the interview but also how you will respond nonverbally. Be on time. Maintain an attitude of interest with eye contact, attentive body positions, alert facial expressions, and an appropriately firm handshake.

Listen Effectively

Interviewing situations require you to listen to determine the amount and depth of information desired. If your responses are to be appropriate and useful, you must know what is being requested. If questions are unclear, ask for clarification or elaboration. By doing so, you can respond more fully and relevantly.

Successful interviewees practice empathy. Interviewers are people, and interviewing situations are interpersonal encounters. An effective interviewee considers situations from the interviewer's point of view, listens "between the lines" to what someone says to focus on underlying emotions, and watches for nonverbal cues. When interviewees listen to all facets of the communication, they can better adapt to the situation.

Respond Appropriately

Just as questioning is the primary responsibility of an interviewer, responding is the primary responsibility of an interviewee. Keep answers direct, honest, and appropriate in depth and relevance. For example, in response to the question "How would you describe the quality of your relationship with your family?" don't give a fifteen-minute speech about your problems with your ex-spouse, keeping the children in clothes, and finding dependable home care for your aging parents. To make sure that you give the best possible answer, listen carefully when a question is posed and, if necessary, take a few moments to think before you answer. A response that is well thought out, straightforward, and relevant will be much more appreciated than one that is hasty, evasive, and unrelated to the question.

Using language and vocabulary that are appropriate to the situation is also important. The use of too much slang or technical terminology in an attempt to impress an interviewer can easily backfire by distracting the interviewer or distorting communication. Direct and simple language promotes understanding.

Finally, be flexible and adapt to the needs of the interviewing situation. Some interviewers will ask questions to throw you off guard. If that happens to you, take a moment to think before you respond. Try to discover the reason for the question and respond to the best of your ability. Listen carefully for the content *and* intent of questions so that you provide the information requested, especially when the interviewer changes topics. Flexibility and adaptability depend on good listening, empathy, accurate reading and interpretation of nonverbal communication, and practice. Just remember: "Engage brain before opening mouth."

Interviewer Responsibilities

A.5 Explain how to conduct an interview.

So far, we've emphasized how to behave when you are the person being interviewed. As you assume leadership positions in your profession and community, you will undoubtedly be called on to interview others. In addition to knowing how to structure the opening, body, and conclusion of an interview, which we discussed earlier, there are several other characteristics of effective interviewers, whether you are seeking to hire an employee or simply gathering information.

Adapt to an Interviewee's Behavior

Skilled interviewers observe, evaluate, and adapt to the communication behavior of their interviewees. Because no two interviews—and no two interviewees—are exactly alike, interviewers adapt their communication behavior accordingly. A flexible communication style is a necessity. Interviewers should have predetermined plans, but they should not be thrown off balance if an interviewee suddenly turns the tables and asks, "How much money do *you* make for *your* job?"

Adaptability also includes the use of appropriate language and vocabulary. You should consciously choose language and vocabulary that your interviewees will understand. Little is gained by using technical, ambiguous, or vague terms. Words should be straightforward, simple, and specific but not so simple that interviewees feel "talked down" to. Empathy is important in determining the most appropriate language and vocabulary to use.

Deal Wisely with Sensitive Content

When planning questions for an interview, consider possible sensitive topics that should be avoided. A question in a grievance interview such as "Why were you fired from your last job?" will provoke a defensive reaction.

Good judgment and careful word choice play crucial roles in interviews. One ill-chosen question can destroy the positive and open communication developed in an opening. Effective interviewers avoid potentially troublesome topics and attempt to put interviewees at ease. They discuss sensitive issues *if and only if* they are related to the purpose of the interview. When a sensitive subject must be discussed, experienced interviewers choose their words carefully; for example, the question "Why were you fired?" might be rephrased as "How would you describe your relationship with your previous supervisor?"

Listen Effectively

The admonition to listen effectively has appeared frequently in this appendix. Effective listening is at the heart of any interview. No matter how well interviewers have prepared, the time will have been wasted if they are poor listeners. They need strong listening skills to make sure they are receiving the amount and kind of information they need. They must be able to identify partial or irrelevant responses.

Highly developed listening skills also increase the ability to accurately perceive and interpret unintentional messages and beliefs, attitudes, and values. Interviewers learn a great deal from nonverbal as well as verbal communication.

Record Information

The information accumulated from an interview is useless if it is not recorded completely and accurately. A partial or inaccurate report can lead to poor decisions and mistaken actions. Take appropriate, legible, written notes. If you plan to record audio or video, ask the interviewee in advance for permission to do so.

CRITICAL/CULTURAL PERSPECTIVES & COMMUNICATION

Becoming an Unbiased Person of Conscience
Interviewers sometimes let their unconscious biases and prejudices influence hiring decisions unfairly and illegally. A person's race, ethnicity, sex, gender, sexual orientation, and pregnancy are among the many factors that have been documented as unfairly, yet sometimes unconsciously, influencing a hiring decision.[25] The first step to making unbiased, ethical, and legal hiring decisions is to become conscious of your own bias and prejudices. How do you do that? Review decisions that you have made in the past. Honestly examine whether you have made a decision about hiring someone, or even becoming friends with someone, because of such factors as a person's race, ethnicity, or sexual orientation. Be aware of your cultural context. Each of us has a set of beliefs, attitudes, and values based on a lifetime of experiences that influence how we receive, interpret, and evaluate incoming stimuli. If the most qualified person is to be hired, an interviewer must be aware of his or her own biased processes in order to make accurate and objective decisions. After mindfully working to become conscious of your biases and prejudices, apply clear, unbiased criteria to ensure that the best candidate is selected for the position. Moving from biased and prejudicial unconscious incompetence to conscious competence will take effort, but that effort can fulfill the Declaration of Independence's promise: All people are created equal.

Ask Appropriate Questions

The success of most interviews will be determined by the quality of the questions asked. Think of questions as "mental can openers" designed to reveal how the other person thinks and behaves. Earlier, we discussed question types (open, closed, probing, and hypothetical) and question sequences (funnel, inverted funnel, and tunnel). Some of your questions should be planned. Other questions may evolve from the discussion. The best questions during an interview emerge from simply listening to what the other person is saying and then probing or following up on information and verbalized ideas.

If you are interviewing a job applicant, be aware that there are certain questions that you should *not* ask. These questions are inappropriate because they ask for information that either laws or court interpretations of laws suggest could lead to illegal discrimination. Here's a list of topics you should not bring up during an employment interview when you're asking the questions:[26]

arrest records	insurance claims
less-than-honorable discharges	judgments
gender and marital status	citizenship or national origin
maiden name	mother's maiden name
number of children	place of birth
ages of children	disabilities
number of preschool children	handicap
spouse's name	illnesses or accidents
spouse's education	hospitalizations
spouse's income	current or prior medication/treatment
form of birth control	workers' compensation claims
family plans	weight
child care arrangements	religion
car accidents	church affiliation
lawsuits	social organizations
legal complaints	loans
ownership of home	wage assignments or garnishments
rental status	bankruptcy
length of residence	credit cards
date of high school graduation	form of transportation
age	ownership of car
sexual orientation	

STUDY GUIDE: PRINCIPLES FOR A LIFETIME

APPENDIX A

Interview Types

A.1 Define what an interview is and identify five different kinds of interviews.

PRINCIPLE **POINTS:** An interview is a form of oral interaction that is structured to achieve a goal and that involves two or more people who take turns speaking and listening. We have identified five types of interview situations: the information-gathering interview, the appraisal interview, the problem-solving interview, the persuasion interview, and the job interview.

PRINCIPLE **TERMS:**

interview
information-gathering interview
appraisal interview
problem-solving interview
persuasion interview
job interview

PRINCIPLE **SKILLS:**

1. It may seem as though the supervisor does most of the preparation for an appraisal interview, but what should an employee do to prepare for one?
2. Reflect on the last time you were interviewed. What kind of interview was it? How would you evaluate your overall interview skills? What interview skills (if any) do you think you need to improve?

Interview Phases

A.2 Describe the three phases of a well-structured interview.

PRINCIPLE **POINTS:** All interviews have an opening, in which the interviewee is put at ease; a body, during which questions are asked and answered; and a conclusion, which brings the interview to a comfortable close.

PRINCIPLE **TERMS:**

open question
closed question
probing question
hypothetical question
funnel sequence
inverted funnel sequence
tunnel sequence

PRINCIPLE **SKILLS:**

1. Imagine that you're an employer who is interviewing candidates for a social media manager position at your organization. Write a series of interview questions that follow either the funnel sequence or the inverted funnel sequence.
2. Review the list of key terms for this section and identify the question types in which you are most skilled in asking and answering. Also, identify the types of questions in which you may need to enhance your skill in either asking or answering.

How to Be Interviewed for a Job

A.3 Identify and describe how to be interviewed for a job, including how to develop a well-worded resume.

PRINCIPLE **POINTS:** When you are seeking employment, start by becoming aware of your skills and abilities; then use your personal inventory to develop a well-written resume. Focus on the needs of your prospective employer: Research the organization where you seek a job. During the interview, listen carefully to the questions asked by the interviewer and respond appropriately. After the interview, it may be appropriate to send a thank-you note to the interviewer.

PRINCIPLE **TERMS:**

resume
networking
personal brand

PRINCIPLE **SKILLS:**

1. Before submitting your resume to a prospective employer, use the following checklist to ensure that it meets the criteria of an effective resume.

   _____ My name, mailing address, email address, and all contact numbers are accurate.

   _____ My career objective matches the advertised need of the employer.

   _____ My employment dates are accurate.

   _____ I've described the projects I've completed and skills I possess using action verbs and appropriate keywords.

   _____ My resume is clearly formatted.

   _____ There are no spelling errors.

   _____ There are no grammar or punctuation errors.

2. Conduct a social media audit of all the information available about you online. What needs to be changed, edited, or modified to improve your online image?

How to Be Interviewed in an Information-Gathering Interview

A.4 Identify and describe how to be interviewed in an information-gathering interview.

PRINCIPLE **POINTS:** When you are preparing to be interviewed for an information-gathering interview, you have three primary tasks. First, prepare for the interview by reviewing information you think that the interviewer will ask you about. Second, listen closely to the questions you are being asked. Finally, respond appropriately by keeping answers direct and honest. Don't ramble. Observe the interviewer's nonverbal responses to determine whether you are answering the questions appropriately.

PRINCIPLE **SKILLS:**

1. A visit to your doctor or dentist for a regular checkup is, in part, an interview in which the practitioner gathers information from you. How can you prepare for the typical questions you'll be asked at your next checkup?
2. Watch an information-gathering interview on *60 Minutes* or *Today*, or another news or news magazine program. Identify the types of questions that the interviewer asks (open, closed, probing, or hypothetical). On the basis of the information presented in this appendix, evaluate the effectiveness of both the interviewer and the interviewee.

Interviewer Responsibilities

A.5 Explain how to conduct an interview.

PRINCIPLE **POINTS:** The key to any interview is the quality of the questions asked. As the interviewer, you are responsible for asking clear, appropriate, and answerable questions. Although it's useful to have a list of questions, be prepared to adapt to the interviewee's behavior. Listening well is the hallmark of an effective interviewer. Develop a strategy to record the information you gather from the interview. When you interview others, don't let your own biases and prejudices interfere with your job of listening and responding to the interviewee. Don't ask illegal questions during a job interview, and handle sensitive questions with tact and diplomacy.

PRINCIPLE **SKILLS:**

1. As an interviewer, what are some ways you could adapt a planned list of questions to specific interviewees?
2. Imagine that you are an employer interviewing a job applicant. The applicant's answers to your first few questions have not impressed you, and you are growing fairly certain that this is not the right person for the job. How should you proceed in the interview?

APPENDIX B

SAMPLE SPEECHES FOR DISCUSSION AND EVALUATION

Informative Speech

Recuperandos

by Manuel Reyes[1]

Renato Da Silva Junior harbors ambitions of becoming a lawyer. There is just one obstacle: According to the *Guardian* on April 2, 2018, he is one-quarter of the way through serving a twenty-year jail sentence for murder. Da Silva, an inmate at the Brazilian Association for the Protection and Assistance of the Convicted, or APAC, believes his dreams are bigger than his mistakes, and APAC not only agrees, but is helping him reach his goal. Valdeci Ferreira, director of the Brazilian Fraternity of Assistance to the Convicted, explained in a September 2018 interview that "the APAC (prisons) in Brazil practice an alternative methodology of incarceration and rehabilitation, humanizing the punishment and preparing offenders to re-enter society." At an APAC facility, there are no guards or weapons. The individuals who live in these facilities are not referred to as inmates or prisoners. They are referred to as *recuperandos*: "people in the process of rehabilitation." They wear their regular clothes, prepare their own food, are in charge of facility security, and are even given the keys to their cells. Brutality, violence, and severe overcrowding make Brazil one of the worst penal systems in the world. Previous attempts to reform the country's incarceration policies have failed, until now. Today, we will first examine the presence of APAC in Brazil. Next, we will explore how APAC functions for both the incarcerated and the incarcerator. Finally, we will discuss the implications this system could have on society. If more countries adopted APAC, it could significantly alter how society addresses incarceration and reform. Recuperandos from APAC facilities have a mere 5 percent recidivism rate, because as Valdeci Ferreira explained, "APAC shows human beings who made a mistake that someone believes in them again."

Prison scholar Ruth Gilmore Wilson explained in *OpenGlobalRights* from November 29, 2018, that proper prison reform requires us to "create awareness of the inhumanity of the prison system, find as many alternatives to incarceration as possible, and tie human rights and development to the reformation of prisons." These have been the guiding tenets behind the rising presence of APAC in Brazil. There are two important aspects of APAC's development: first, its history; and second, the current state of APAC throughout the country. First, journalist Fino Menezes in March 2019 reports that the reoffending rate of Brazilian prisoners is extremely high at around 70 percent. To address the crippling system, lawyer Dr. Mario Ottoboni created APAC in 1972. According to Dan Van Ness, lawyer and restorative justice advocate in 2018, APAC began as a response to the prison system's overcrowding.

This system provides prisoners an opportunity for growth and advancement, while also addressing the failed state prison system. While the implementation of APAC was promising in the 1970s, this system remains largely unused. According to *La Civiltà Cattolica* on December 13, 2018, many politicians and judges are skeptical of APAC because they believe prison should be a place for punishment, not a rehabilitation center. Dr. Walter Mswaka, writing for Huddersfield University in May 2018, said that the Brazilian justice system has always favored a heavy-handed approach to crime, and these open systems are perceived as too soft a punishment for "criminals." As a result of this mentality, most APAC prisons were suspended throughout the country. But due to public support, they are now being reinstated.

Now that we've examined the history and current state of APAC, we can explore what makes this system so unique. Tatiane Correia de Lima, a 26-year-old mother of two, told the previously cited *Guardian*, "Other prisons take away your womanhood. We weren't allowed proper mirrors. When I saw my reflection here, at first I didn't know who I was." APAC is helping her and many others find themselves with unique selection process expectations and unique functions, which we will explore by first discussing the selection process and expectations, and second, exploring how APAC functions.

First the selection process. *CSIS Prosper* on December 14, 2018, explains that all APAC recuperandos are hand selected from individuals who have expressed interest in serving their sentence in APAC. APAC does not take into account the severity of the conviction before choosing to accept or reject the individuals. Due to this highly selective process, all members have specific jobs, including security for the facility. According to the European Commission's International Cooperation and Development website, updated June 9, 2019, the members take classes, learn trades, work a job, and are taught how to reenter society a changed individual. Second, we'll learn how APAC does this by discussing its functions. Tanya Erzen explained on March 24, 2017, that when the idea for APAC was conceived, a judge granted APAC's founder, Dr. Ottoboni, complete authority over how it would be run. He believed, "It was imperative to restore in the prisoner the sense of human dignity and divine affiliation so that he can turn himself to goodness." And to do so, Dr. Ottoboni dictated that religion be foundational to the development and daily functioning of all aspects of APAC facilities and administration. A strict schedule of faith-based training, education, and service is required for all recuperandos. Another unique advantage is that this system is cheaper, too, by 550 U.S. dollars per prisoner.

According to public health advocate Loren Walker, writing about her own experience visiting an APAC facility, last accessed Sept. 7, 2019, APAC functions in a way that makes people feel worthy, respected, and able to restore their lives. While this sounds like an excellent model for reform, it does have interesting implications that must be examined. First, the power of politics. According to SBS Dateline, October 19, 2018, Judge Ernani Neves notes, "Brazil faces a very big problem in the prisons related to the lack of government funds. We have a crisis of investment and our correctional centers don't have the same capacity to rehabilitate people like other countries." APAC's results prove its value in a prison system that is struggling to house and rehabilitate inmates, but, like any other unconventional model, until properly funded and politically supported, its impact will remain minimal.

Despite these challenges, we cannot ignore how APAC's approach restores humanity to the prison system, bringing us to our second implication. As explained by the World Economic Forum on August 24, 2018, the APAC system gives people a second chance and treats the convicted with dignity. It allows them to feel human and gives them opportunities to change by providing education and training. When people feel respected and are left with their dignity, they are more likely to invest in personal change. And respect and dignity are foundational to every aspect of APAC facilities. Sanitation, lodging accommodations, and food are all held to much higher standards. All APAC facilities impose a limit of 200 recuperandos to prevent overcrowding.

The residents are treated as people who deserve another chance and are given the opportunity to change. However, because this model is firmly rooted in a faith-based approach to rehabilitation and training, it magnifies the complicated questions that surround prison reform regarding the intersection of politics, religion, funding, and privatization. Despite these issues, APAC does open the door to approaching prison reform from a more empathetic and dignified place. According to the European Commission, last accessed August 15, 2019, Jelletly, an APAC recuperando, had been arrested for stealing, drug trafficking, and drug abuse six times as a young adult. If held in a traditional prison system, Jelletly would likely continue to cycle in and out of crime and incarceration. But at APEC, he was able to receive an education, job training, and an opportunity to escape the cycle of crime and transform his life.

Today, we have seen how APAC could help not only improve the lives of its members, but also restore humanity in the prison industrial complex by looking at the history, operations, and implications of this revolutionary model. While there are some challenges that impact the APAC system, many of the challenges facing individuals like Renato, Tatiane, and Jelletly have been removed, allowing them the opportunity to pursue their dreams and have a life after their sentence, showing that a little respect, trust, and love can truly change one's life.

Persuasive Speech
Queers of the Court
by Caleb Newton[2]

At three different points in this creative and unique speech, Caleb selects an audience member at random to choose between two options. He then addresses whichever option is selected. Therefore, the speech has the potential to change each time he delivers it. According to Caleb, the point behind the structure is that queer defendants in the justice system are forced to make quick choices that will have huge impacts on their lives.

Before the jury even reached their decision, they knew: Charles Rhines was guilty. After Rhines was charged with the murder of a young man, the June 11, 2018, *Marshall Project* explains that, for the first time in almost fifty years, a South Dakota jury handed down a death sentence. Their reasoning? Jury members decided that since Rhines was gay, he would have enjoyed life in prison too much. But it's not just juries doing the discriminating. The *University of Miami Law Review* in 2017 laments that 79 percent of queer defendants still report hearing belittling comments from court employees, attorneys, and even judges. And it's only getting worse. The 2018 *University of Richmond Law Review* warns that a third of President Donald Trump's federally appointed judges are setting anti-queer criminal precedents. So it makes sense that the Williams Institute, last accessed April 9, 2020, explains that, compared to their straight counterparts, queer defendants are three times more likely to end up behind bars. For queer women, trans folks, and queer people of color, the idea of a fair trial is a pipedream. The Texas Criminal Justice Coalition in 2018 estimates that more than 300,000 queer people are funneled through the U.S. criminal justice system each year—a system that assumes you're innocent until proven queer. Listen, we can't overhaul the entire system in ten minutes, but we can teach queer people how to navigate a hostile court. So, let's follow every step of the process: first, pretrial; next, in the courtroom; and finally, during sentencing. Each step is directly followed by solutions. We don't have statistics on the prevalence of queerphobia in the courtroom, but what we do have is queer people's stories and the choices they made. So I'll be calling on individual audience members to make the same choices at each step of the process. If making these choices feels difficult or uncomfortable, imagine how queer defendants in this position feel. This isn't a "choose your own adventure." This isn't an adventure at all. You're on trial. Choose wisely.

After being kicked out by your queerphobic family, you're nothing more than a statistic. And after living on the street for months, like thousands of queer homeless, you turn to sex for survival. Inevitably, you get caught and are charged with prostitution. Now begins the pretrial period, during which you make key decisions about your case. The DA presents you with a choice: Do you hire an attorney or accept a plea deal?

[This is the first point in the speech at which Caleb selects an audience member at random to choose between these two options, here designated Option 1 and Option 2. He addresses whichever of the options is selected.]

[Option 1: Hire an attorney.] Sixteen-year-old Destiny made the same decision as you. While that would normally work, let's examine how her legal defense failed, and then how to help. The 2017 *Boston College Law Review* details how in court, Destiny's public attorney hid her transgender identity, which got her placed in a men's prison. After Destiny was sexually assaulted, her attorney still refused to help her move to the correct facility. And it was completely legal. Law Professor Sarah Valentine's 2011 article, "When Your Attorney is Your Enemy," explains why: Attorneys can legally substitute their clients' wishes for what they think is best, even if the motivation is queerphobic. Our laws give attorneys the benefit of the doubt, but that power can easily be abused by bigoted lawyers.

[Option 2: Accept the plea deal.] Robert Suttle made the same decision as you. While that would normally work, let's examine first how a plea deal disenfranchised Robert, and then how to help. The 2016 Movement Advancement Project explains how, too poor to hire an attorney, Robert thought a plea deal negotiated by his public defender was his only option. But when he went to sign his statement of guilt, his attorney wasn't there. The Project further explains the terrifying reason: Prosecutors hide clauses in plea deals to make queer defendants waive their right to legal representation, leaving half of queers with no representation at all. Plea deals already disenfranchise marginalized communities; prosecutors have just found their next target, sending a clear message: Waive your rights; we're going to take them anyway.

So what can we do? Whatever choice you made, you should know the solutions for both, so I've made an online guidebook. Follow the QR code. The guide tells queer folks never to waive their right to representation in trade for a plea deal. Once we get representation, we have to call out queerphobic attorneys. That's why I've included the ethical guidelines for attorneys and where to report them, should they step out of line. Also, since you might not have the money to hire a gaggle of gay lawyers, I have listed on my website queer-friendly law firms that provide low-cost to pro-bono defense. The courts may turn a blind eye to our discrimination, but we can't unsee it.

In the end, you decide not to accept the DA's ridiculous terms. After weeks in a concrete cage, you're ecstatic when your new lawyer comes to visit. With your trial coming up, you are given a choice: Do you choose to take the stand and defend yourself, or let witnesses be called to do it for you? *[Caleb again selects an audience member at random to choose between two options, here numbered Option 3 and Option 4. He addresses whichever of the options is selected.]*

[Option 3: Take the stand and defend yourself.] Earl Ford thought the same thing as you. Sometimes that could work, but let's see how your own words can be turned against you, and then how to protect you. The 2018 Williams Institute reports that after Ford took the stand, prosecutors berated him about his sexuality. Court documents recount that although Ford's lawyer objected, the judge overruled that objection. The *Cardozo Law Review*, last accessed March 21, 2020, explains why, under evidentiary rules, the prosecution can use cross examination to turn someone's sexuality into a piece of evidence. During closing statements, prosecutors said, "I'm not bisexual bashing . . . But . . . that's [basically] what he is charged with." How can you speak out when your voice is the very weapon they'll use against you?

[Option 4: Let witnesses be called to do it for you.] Bernina Mata thought the same thing as you. Sometimes that could work, but let's see how witness testimony was

weaponized against her and how to prevent it. The 2017 *University of Miami Law Review* explains that after Bernina killed her attacker in self-defense, prosecutors argued, "murder is a natural response for a lesbian." To prove it, they called forward ten witnesses and made each read from her collection of queer literature, which is perfectly legal. The *Washington Journal of Law and Policy* argues, "it is ethically defensible to . . . exploit . . . racism, sexism, [or] homophobia" to win a case. The second you walk into the courtroom, the most dangerous weapon that could be used against you, is who you are.

So: solutions. In my guidebook are resources to challenge prosecutorial misconduct. To protect someone's identity and avoid outing someone on the stand, I've included motions to make the court use gender-neutral language. Additionally, changing legislation is often futile, since lawmakers are the ones rolling back protections. So let's attack the roots of this issue. Every year, attorneys are required to take continuing education requirements. On my website is the contact for every state's bar association. Call them to expand continuing legal education credits! I'm currently in the process of making my state accountable. The people who represent countless queer lives should know the conditions for our survival.

Finally, the dreaded day arrives. The guards drag you from your cell and to the courthouse in tight handcuffs. So now it's up to you: Do you place your fate in the hands of a jury of your peers or a single judge? *[For the third and final time, Caleb selects an audience member at random to choose between two options, here numbered Option 5 and Option 6. He addresses whichever of the options is selected.]*

[Option 5: Jury.] You and Christian Delp have that in common. That's ordinarily the right choice, but let's understand how his jury discriminated against him and how to prevent it. The 2018 *Williams Institute* reports that during Christian's trial, a juror was recorded saying, "[When I] heard Christian . . . I [knew he was] a homosexual and from that point accepted [the prosecutor's arguments] as gospel." You'd think Delp's appeal would be easy. But the June 6, 2018, *Marshall Project* reminds us that last year the Supreme Court rejected a similar appeal, finding no jury discrimination—which is damning, considering that a 2018 publication by the UCLA Law School reveals that one out of eight jurors admitted they could "not be fair to a queer defendant." Clearly, if you can't be straight, you can't be innocent, either.

[Option 6: Single judge.] You and Kaushal Niroula have that in common. That's ordinarily the right choice, but let's understand how a judge discriminated against Kaushal and how to end it. The *Los Angeles Times* on April 12, 2018, explains that when he received a motion, Judge David Downing refused to open the envelope. After being caught on record saying, "[L]ord knows where his tongue has been," Downing added, "[It's my court.] I can say what I want." The most frightening part: He's right. The Administrative Office of the U.S. Courts in their 2017 report found that of the 1,270 complaints against judges, only twelve were adjudicated. That's less than 2 percent. From bail to sentencing, one queerphobic person can serve as the judge, jury, and executioner.

Luckily, there are some precautions we can take. We can't prevent queerphobic conversations. But to try to prevent queerphobic jury decisions, on my website are *voir dire* questions for your lawyer to ask during jury selection. A judge understanding our problems isn't enough, so I've also included scholarship opportunities for queer students going to law school. There's no feasible way to reteach a whole court system, so let's start from the bottom up and create a new generation of lawyers and eventually judges queering the courtroom.

At this point, you might be wondering whether, if you had made different choices, would there have been different outcomes? Charles Rhines has been asking this question every night for the past twenty-five years. But Rhines and other queer individuals like him are more than attention-getting devices for this speech. So take one of these cards. Each features a different defendant who needs help. Fight for them, using my suggestions on the back. For countless queer defendants, ending up in our broken justice system was never a decision they made. And now the decision is ours: What do you choose?

Endnotes

Chapter 1

1. R. Emanuel, J. Adams, K. Baker, E. K. Daufin, C. Ellington, E. Fitts, J. Himsel, L. Holladay, and D. Okeowo, "How College Students Spend Their Time Communicating," *International Journal of Listening* 22 (2008): 12–28; E. T. Klemmer and F. W. Snyder, "Measurement of Time Spent Communicating," *Journal of Communication* 20 (1972): 142; B. Krivokapic-Skoko, R. Duncan, and K. Tilbrook, "The Use of the Time Diary Method to Explore Academic Time Management: Insights from an Australian University," *Proceedings of the European Conference on Research Methods for Business & Management Studies* (2012): 199–206.
2. For information about how an introductory course in communication is beneficial to students, see K. Nordin and M. A. Broeckelman-Post, "Can I Get Better? Exploring Mindset Theory in the Introductory Communication Course," *Communication Education* 68 (2019): 44–60.
3. We thank our friend Tom Burkholder, University of Nevada, Las Vegas, for this idea.
4. J. C. Humes, *The Sir Winston Method: The Five Secrets of Speaking the Language of Leadership* (New York: William Morrow, 1991).
5. V. Marchant, "Listen Up!" *Time* (June 28, 1999): 72.
6. A. Vangelisti and J. A. Daly, "Correlates of Speaking Skills in the United States: A National Assessment," *Communication Education* 38 (1989): 132–143.
7. M. Cronin, ed., "The Need for Required Oral Communication Education in the Undergraduate General Education Curriculum," unpublished paper, 1993, available from the National Communication Association, Washington, DC.
8. J. Ayres and T. S. Hopf, "The Long-Term Effect of Visualization in the Classroom: A Brief Research Report," *Communication Education* 39 (1990): 75–78.
9. See J. C. McCroskey and M. Beatty, "The Communibiological Perspective: Implications for Communication in Instruction," *Communication Education* 49 (2000): 1; also see J. C. McCroskey, J. A. Daly, M. M. Martin, and M. J. Beatty, eds., *Communication and Personality: Trait Perspectives* (Cresskill, NJ: Hampton Press, 1998).
10. J. H. McConnell, *Are You Communicating? You Can't Manage without It* (New York: McGraw-Hill, 1995).
11. M. Schwantes, "Warren Buffett Says You Will Be Worth 50 Percent More if You Improve This 1 Human Skill," *Inc.* (January 18, 2018) https://www.inc.com/marcel-schwantes/warren-buffett-says-this-is-1-simple-habit-that-separates-successful-people-from-everyone-else.html, (accessed May 15, 2020).
12. Schwantes, "Warren Buffett Says."
13. Value Investors Portal, "Warren Buffet on Communication Skills," *YouTube*, December 6, 2010, www.youtube.com/watch?v=tpgcEYpLzP0 (accessed May 14, 2013).
14. Hart Research Associates, "Falling Short? College Learning and Career Success," *Association of American Colleges and Universities*, January 20, 2015, www.aacu.org (accessed February 12, 2017); Hart Research Associates, "Employer Priorities for Most Important College Learning Outcomes," *Association of American Colleges and Universities*, January 20, 2015, www.aacu.org (accessed February 12, 2017); "Staffing in Special Markets," *Society for Human Resources Management*, September 3, 2016, www.shrm.org (accessed February 12, 2017). Also see J. L. Winsor, D. Curtis, and R. D. Stephens, "National Preferences in Business and Communication Education: A Survey Update," *Journal of the Association of Communication Administration* 3 (1997): 170–179. For a summary of the values and virtues of studying communication, see S. P. Morreale and J. C. Pearson, "Why Communication Education Is Important: The Centrality of the Discipline in the 21st Century," *Communication Education* 57.2 (2008): 224–240; also see S. P. Morreale, D. W. Worley, and B. Hugenberg, "The Basic Communication Course at Two- and Four-Year U.S. Colleges and Universities: Study VIII—The 40th Anniversary," *Communication Education* 59.4 (2010): 405–430; Hart Research Associates "Raising the Bar: Employers' Views on College Learning in the Wake of the Economic Downturn," Washington, DC, Association of American Colleges and Universities (January 10, 2010); D. Sellnow, "Integrated Composition and Communication: Addressing the Needs of the 21st Century," paper presented at the annual meeting of the Rhetoric Society of America, Minneapolis, Minnesota (May 2010); T. A. Coffelt, D. Grauman, and F. L. M. Smith, "Employers' Perspectives on Workplace Communication Skills: The Meaning of Communication Skills," *Business and Professional Communication Quarterly* 82 (2019): 418–439.
15. Career Services, "What Skills and Attributes Employers Seek When Hiring Students," *University of Wisconsin–River Falls*, www.uwrf.edu/ccslskills/htm (accessed June 7, 2007); C. Luckenbaugh and K. Gray, "Employers Describe Perfect Job Candidate," *Association of Colleges and Employers Survey*, www.naceweb.org/press/display.asp?year=2003&prid=169 (accessed June 4, 2007); R. S. Hansen and K. Handson, "What Do Employers Really Want? Top Skills and Values Employers Seek from Job Seekers," *Quintessential Careers*, www.quintcareers.com/job_skills_values.html (accessed June 4, 2007). For evidence that communication skills can be developed, see R. F. Brown, C. L. Bylund, J. A. Gueguen, C. Diamond, J. Eddington, and D. Kissane, "Developing Patient-Centered Communication Skills Training for Oncologists: Describing the Content and Efficacy of Training," *Communication Education* 59.3 (2010): 235–248; G. Sulcas and J. English, "A Case for Focus on Professional Communication Skills at Senior Undergraduate Level in Engineering and the Built Environment," *Southern African Linguistics & Applied Language Studies* 28.3 (2010): 219–226; J. Keyton, J. M. Caputo, E. A. Ford, R. Fu, S. A. Leibowitz, T. Lio, and C. Wu, "Investigating Verbal Workplace Communication Behaviors," *International Journal of Business Communication* 50 (2013): 152–169; J. T. Goodwin, J. Goh, S. Verkoeyen, and K. Lithgow, "Can Students Be Taught to Articulate Employability Skills?" *Education + Training* 61 (2019): 445–460; J. A. Rios, G. Ling, R. Pugh, D. Becker, and A. Bacall, "Identifying Critical 21st-Century Skills for Workplace Success: A Content Analysis of Job Advertisements," *Educational Researcher* 49 (2020): 80–89.
16. For a discussion of the prominence of LinkedIn in the job market, see S. Rivera, "You Heard it Here First: LinkedIn is the New (and Improved) Facebook," *Study Breaks* (November 2016): 34.
17. P. Gillooly, "Why You Need Social Media," *New York Times*, Business (December 4, 2016): 8.
18. *Pathway to Careers in Communication* (Washington D.C., National Communication Association, 2020) https://www.natcom.org/academic-professional-resources/why-study-communication (accessed May 15, 2020).
19. M. M. Robles, "Executive Perceptions of the Top 10 Soft Skills Needed in Today's Workplace," *Business Communication Quarterly* 75.4 (2012): 453–465.

20. K. E. Davis and M. Todd, "Assessing Friendship: Prototypes, Paradigm Cases, and Relationship Description," in *Understanding Personal Relationships*, edited by S. W. Duck and D. Perlman (London: Sage, 1985); B. Wellman, "From Social Support to Social Network," in *Social Support: Theory, Research and Applications*, edited by I. G. Sarason and B. R. Sarason (Dordrecht, Netherlands: Nijhoff, 1985); R. Hopper, M. L. Knapp, and L. Scott, "Couples' Personal Idioms: Exploring Intimate Talk," *Journal of Communication* 31 (1981): 23–33.
21. M. Argyle and M. Hendershot, *The Anatomy of Relationships* (London: Penguin Books, 1985): 14.
22. D. Goleman, "Emotional Intelligence: Issues in Paradigm Building," in *The Emotionally Intelligent Workplace*, edited by C. Chemiss and D. Goleman (San Francisco: Jossey-Bass, 2001): 13; also see R. Wang, H. Chen, Y. Liu, and Y. Yao, "Neighborhood Social Reciprocity and Mental Health Among Older Adults in China: The Mediating Effects of Physical Activity, Social Interaction, and Volunteering," *BMC Public Health* 19 (2019) https://doi.org/10.1186/s12889-019-7385-x (accessed May 19, 2020).
23. V. Satir, *People Making* (Palo Alto, CA: Science and Behavior Books, 1972): 1.
24. The former Surgeon General of the United States has summarized literature documenting the importance of human interaction; see V. H. Murthy, *Together: The Healing Power of Human Connection in a Sometimes Lonely World* (New York: Harper Wave, 2020).
25. L. C. Hawkley and J. T. Cacioppo, "Loneliness Matters: A Theoretical and Empirical Review of Consequences and Mechanisms," *Annals of Behavioral Medicine* 40 (2010): 218–227; J. Holt-Lunstad, T. B. Smith, M. Baker, T. Harris, and D. Stephenson, "Loneliness and Social Isolation as Risk Factors for Mortality," *Perspectives on Psychological Science* 10 (2015): 227–237. Also see Murthy, *Together*, 13.
26. M. Argyle, *The Psychology of Happiness* (London: Routledge, 2001).
27. J. Lynch, *The Broken Heart: The Medical Consequences of Loneliness* (New York: Basic Books, 1977).
28. D. P. Phillips, "Deathday and Birthday: An Unexpected Connection," in *Statistics: A Guide to the Unknown*, edited by J. M. Tanur (San Francisco: Holden-Day, 1972); also see F. Korbin and G. Hendershot, "Do Family Ties Reduce Mortality? Evidence from the United States 1968," *Journal of Marriage and the Family* 39 (1977): 737–746; K. Heller and K. S. Rook, "Distinguishing the Theoretical Functions of Social Ties: Implications of Support Interventions," in *Handbook of Personal Relationships* 2e, edited by S. W. Duck, K. Dindia, W. Ickes, R. Milardo, R. S. L. Mills, and B. R. Sarason (Chichester, UK: Wiley, 1997); B. R. Samson, L. G. Sarason, and R. A. R. Gurung, "Close Personal Relationships and Health Outcomes: A Key to the Role of Social Support," in *Handbook of Personal Relationships* 2e, edited by S. W. Duck, K. Dindia, W. Ickes, R. Milardo, R. S. L. Mills, and B. R. Sarason (Chichester, UK: Wiley, 1997); S. Duck, *Relating to Others* (Buckingham, UK: Open University Press, 1999): 1.
29. Hawkley and Cacioppo, "Loneliness Matters."; also see W. von Hipple, *The Social Leap: The New Evolutionary Science of Who We Are, Where We Come From, and What Makes Us Happy* (New York: Harper Wave, 2018).
30. Pamela Paul, "Does Facebook Make Someone Social Offline?" *New York Times* (January 30, 2011): Style 8; also see S. Craig Watkins and H. Erin Lee, "Got Facebook? Investigating What's Social about Social Media," University of Texas at Austin, www.theyoungandthedigital.com/wp-content/uploads/2010/11/watkins_lee_facebookstudy-nov-18.pdf (accessed January 31, 2011).
31. F. E. X. Dance and C. Larson, *Speech Communication: Concepts and Behavior* (New York: Holt, Rinehart and Winston, 1972).
32. Dance and Larson, *Speech Communication*.
33. J. T. Masterson, S. A. Beebe, and N. H. Watson, *Invitation to Effective Speech Communication* (Glenview, IL: Scott, Foresman, 1989).
34. M. Gladwell, *Blink: The Power of Thinking without Thinking* (New York: Little, Brown, 2005).
35. L. Barker, R. Edwards, C. Gaines, K. Gladney, and F. Holley, "An Investigation of Proportional Time Spent in Various Communication Activities of College Students," *Journal of Applied Communication Research* 8 (1981): 101–109.
36. D. Barnlund, *Interpersonal Communication: Survey and Studies* (Boston: Houghton Mifflin, 1968).
37. See, for instance, C. R. Berger and J. J. Bradac, *Language and Social Knowledge: Uncertainty in Interpersonal Relations* (London: Arnold, 1982).
38. O. Wiio, *Wiio's Laws—and Some Others* (Espoo, Finland: Welin-Goos, 1978).
39. T. Watzlawick, J. B. Bavelas, and D. Jackson, *The Pragmatics of Human Communication* (New York: W. W. Norton, 1967).
40. D. Thompson and R. Filik, "Sarcasm in Written Communication: Emoticons Are Efficient Markers of Intention" *Journal of Computer-Mediated Communication* 21 (2016): 105–120.
41. S. B. Shimanoff, *Communication Rules: Theory and Research* (Beverly Hills, CA: Sage, 1980).
42. H. Lasswell, "The Structure and Function of Communication in Society," in *The Communication of Ideas*, edited by L. Bryson (New York: Institute for Religious and Social Studies, 1948): 37.
43. For an excellent summary of critical/cultural approaches to communication, see K. Ono, "Critical/Cultural Approaches to Communication," *21st Century Communication: A Reference Handbook* edited by W. Eadie (Los Angeles: Sage, 2009): 74–81.
44. Also see D. L. Fassett and J. T. Warren, *Critical Communication Pedagogy* (Thousand Oaks, CA: Sage, 2007); M. Foucault, *The Foucault Reader* (P. Rabinow, Trans.) (New York: Pantheon Books, 1984); M. Foucault, *Discipline and Punish* (New York: Antheon, 1977); b. hooks, *Feminist Theory: From Margin to Center* (Boston: South End Press, 1984); Bourdieu, *Distinction* (London: Routledge, 1984); D. K. Mumby, *Communication and Power in Organizations: Discourse, Ideology and Domination* (Norwood, NJ: Ablex, 1988); K. Ashcraft and D. Mumby, *A Revoking Gender: A Feminist Communicology of Organization* (Thousand Oaks, CA: Sage, 2004); D. S. Dougherty, *The Reluctant Farmer: An Exploration of Work, Social Class & the Production of Food* (Leics, United Kingdom: Troubador Publishing Ltd., 2015).
45. C. S. Lewis, *The Magician's Nephew* (London: The Bodley Head, 1955): 123.
46. For a brief discussion of standpoint theory, see S. A. Beebe, S. J. Beebe, and M. V. Redmond, *Interpersonal Communication: Relating to Others* (Boston: Pearson, 2020): 70; also see M. Stoetzler and N. Yuval-Davis, "Standpoint Theory, Situated Knowledge and the Situated Imagination," *Feminist Theory* 3 (2002): 315–333.
47. See V. E. Cronen, W. B. Pearce, and L. M. Harris, "The Coordinated Management of Meaning: A Theory of Communication," in *Human Communication Theory: Comparative Essays*, edited by F. E. X. Dance (New York: Harper & Row, 1982): 61–89.
48. This section is based on Masterson, Beebe, and Watson, *Invitation to Effective Speech Communication*. We are especially indebted to J. T. Masterson for this discussion.
49. M. Orzeata, "Ways of Obtaining Communication Efficiency," *International Journal of Communication Research* 8 (2018): 185–190.
50. See R. P. Wolff, *About Philosophy* (Upper Saddle River, NJ: Prentice Hall, 2000): 308–335.
51. C. S. Lewis, *The Abolition of Man* (New York: Macmillan, 1947); also see A. M. Nicholi Jr., *The Question of God: C. S. Lewis and Sigmund Freud Debate God, Love, Sex, and the Meaning of Life* (New York: Free Press, 2002).
52. C. Christians and M. Traber, *Communication Ethics and Universal Values* (Beverly Hills, CA: Sage, 1997); also see S. Bok, *Common Values* (Columbia: University of Missouri Press, 2002).
53. Christians and Traber, *Communication Ethics and Universal Values*.
54. For additional discussion of the ethical values taught in the world's religions, see H. Smith, *The World's Religions* (San Francisco: HarperSanFrancisco, 1991).
55. Adapted from W. Ham, *Man's Living Religions* (Independence, MO: Herald Publishing House, 1966): 39–40.

56. "NCA Credo for Communication Ethics," *National Communication Association*, 1999, www.natcom.org/conferences/Ethicslethicsconfcred099.htm (accessed June 27, 2001).
57. M. Iqbal, "Tinder Revenue and Usage Statistics," *Business of Apps* (April 2020) https://www.businessofapps.com/data/tinder-statistics/ (accessed May 21, 2020).
58. M. Iqbal, "Tinder Revenue and Usage Statistics."
59. Pew Research Center, "The Virtues and Downsides of Online Dating," *Survey of U.S. Adults Conducted October 16-28, 2019* reported by M. Iqbal, "Tinder Revenue and Usage Statistics."
60. Pew Research Center, "The Virtues and Downsides of Online Dating."
61. E. Darics, "The Blurring Boundaries Between Synchronicity and Asynchronicity: New Communicative Situations in Work-Related Instant Messaging" *International Journal of Business Communication* 51:4 (2014): 337–358.
62. Broadband Search, *Average Time Spent Daily on Social Media (Latest 2020 Data)* https://www.broadbandsearch.net/blog/average-daily-time-on-social-media (accessed May 21, 2020).
63. N. S. Baron, *Always On: Language in an Online and Mobile World* (New York: Oxford University Press, 2008); also see D. Crystal, *txtng: The gr8 db8* (Oxford, UK: Oxford University Press, 2008); S. Turkle, *Alone Together: Why We Expect More from Technology and Less from Each Other* (New York: Basic Books, 2011); M. A. Dourin, "College Students' Text Messaging, Use of Textese, and Literacy Skills," *Journal of Assisted Learning* 27.1 (2011): 67.
64. M. Seo, J. Kim, and P. David, "Always Connected or Always Distracted? ADHD Symptoms and Social Assurance Explain Problematic Use of Mobile Phone and Multicommunicating," *Journal of Computer-Mediated Communication* 20 (2015): 667–681.
65. A. Sedghi, "Facebook: 10 Years of Social Networking, in Numbers," *The Guardian*, February 4, 2014, www.theguardian.com/news/datablog/2014/feb/04/facebook-in-numbers-statistics (accessed March 28, 2014).
66. R. S. Tokunaga, "A Meta-Analysis of the Relationships Between Psychosocial Problems and Internet Habits: Synthesizing Internet Addiction, Problematic Internet Use, and Deficient Self-Regulation Research," *Communication Monographs* 84 (2017): 423–446.
67. S. Kemp, "Digital 2020: July Global Statshot," DataReportal, July 21, 2020, https://datareportal.com/reports/digital-2020-july-global-statshot (accessed May 4, 2021); and Statista 2021 "Most Popular Social Networks Worldwide as of January 2021, Ranked by Number of Active Users," We are Social; Various sources (company data); Hootsuite; DataReportal; https://www.statista.com/statistics/272014/global-social-networks-ranked-by-number-of-users (accessed May 4, 2021).
68. T. Bern, "Social Media Trends Report: Key Insights From Q4 2020," Socialbakers data, January 19, 2021, https://www.socialbakers.com/blog/social-media-trends-report-q4-2020 (accessed May 4, 2021).
69. Ofcom, Children and Parents: Media Use and Attitudes Report 2019, February 4, 2020, https://www.ofcom.org.uk/__data/assets/pdf_file/0023/190616/children-media-use-attitudes-2019-report.pdf (accessed May 4, 2021).
70. TikTok website, https://www.tiktok.com/ (accessed May 4, 2021).
71. Influencer Marketing Hub, The State of Social Media – Benchmark Report 2021, February 15, 2021, https://influencermarketinghub.com/social-media-benchmark-report-2021/ (accessed May 4, 2021).
72. App Annie website, https://www.appannie.com/en/ (accessed May 4, 2021).
73. Insider Intelligence, eMarketer, https://www.emarketer.com/ (accessed May 4, 2021).
74. M. Iqbaal, "Facebook Revenue and Usage Statistics (2021)," BuisnessofApps, April 6, 2021, https://www.businessofapps.com/data/facebook-statistics/ (accessed May 4, 2021).
75. C. Newberry, "47 Facebook Stats That Matter to Marketers in 2021," HootSuite, January 11, 2021, https://blog.hootsuite.com/facebook-statistics/#general (accessed May 4, 2021).
76. Social Media Perth, Facts & Figures // Facebook Statistics for 2021, November 3, 2020, https://www.smperth.com/resources/facebook/facebook-statistics/ (accessed May 4, 2021).
77. J. Chen, "20 Facebook Stats to Guide Your 2021 Facebook Strategy," sproutsocial, February 17, 2021, https://sproutsocial.com/insights/facebook-stats-for-marketers/ (accessed May 4, 2021).
78. Watkins and Lee, "Got Facebook?"
79. B. Jin and J. F. Pena, "Mobile Communication in Romantic Relationships: Mobile Phone Use, Relational Uncertainty, Love, Commitment, and Attachment Styles," *Communication Reports* 23.1 (2010): 39–51.
80. K. Sehl, "27 Top Facebook Demographics That Matter to Social Media Marketers."
81. For an excellent discussion of the power of dialogue to enrich the quality of communication, see D. Yankelovich, *The Magic of Dialogue: Transforming Conflict into Cooperation* (New York: Simon & Schuster, 1999).
82. We appreciate and acknowledge our friend and colleague M. Redmond for his contributions to our understanding of interpersonal communication. For more information, see S. A. Beebe, S. J. Beebe, and M. V. Redmond, *Interpersonal Communication: Relating to Others* 9e (Hoboken, NJ: Pearson, 2020).
83. S. A. Beebe and J. T. Masterson, *Communicating in Small Groups: Principles and Practices* 12e (Boston: Pearson, 2020).
84. Poole and Ahmed, "Group Decision Support Systems," in *21st Century Communication*; also see M. C. Poole, "Collaboration, Integration, and Transformation: Directions for Research on Communication and Information Technologies," *Journal of Computer-Mediated Communication* 14 (2009): 753–763.
85. See D. Ofri, "The Conversation Placebo," *New York Times* Sunday Review (January 22, 2017): 2.
86. For an excellent review of intrapersonal communication theory and research, see D. Voate, *Intrapersonal Communication: Different Voices, Different Minds* (Hillsdale, NJ: Lawrence Erlbaum, 1994).
87. D. Quinn, *My Ishmael* (New York: Bantam Books, 1996).
88. B. Plester and C. Wood, "Exploring Relationships between Traditional and New Media Literacies: British Preteen Texters at School," *Journal of Computer-Mediated Communication* 14 (2009): 1108–1129.
89. R. Fulghum, *All I Really Need to Know I Learned in Kindergarten* (New York: Ballantine Books, 1988).
90. Barker et al., "An Investigation of Proportional Time Spent in Various Communication Activities of College Students."
91. S. A. Beebe, **"Structure-Interaction Theory: Conceptual, Contextual and Strategic Influences on Human Communication,"** *Russian Journal of Linguistics Vestnik Rudn: Special Issue: Intercultural Communication Theory and Practice* 19 (2015): 7–24.

Chapter 2

1. A. Perrin and M. Anderson, "Share of U.S. Adults Using Social Media, Including Facebook, Is Mostly Unchanged Since 2018," April 10, 2019, https://www.pewresearch.org/fact-tank/2019/04/10 (accessed June 16, 2020).
2. S. R. Covey, *The Seven Habits of Highly Effective People*, Anniversary Edition (New York: Simon & Schuster, 2013): 74.
3. D. W. Johnson, *Reaching Out: Interpersonal Effectiveness and Self-Actualization* 11e (Boston: Pearson, 2012): 51.
4. E. Young, "Who Do You Think You Are?" *New Scientist* 229 (2016): 30.
5. S. E. Wood, E. Green Wood, and D. Boyd, *Mastering the World of Psychology* 6e (Boston: Pearson, 2017): 115.
6. N. R. Branscombe and R. A. Baron, *Social Psychology* 14e (Boston: Pearson, 2016).
7. C. Scaffidi Abbate, S. Boca, and G. H. E. Gendolla, "Self-Awareness, Perspective-Taking, and Egocentrism," *Self & Identity*

15 (2016): 371–380; S. M. McNaughton, "Developing Pre-Requisites for Empathy: Increasing Awareness of Self, the Body, and the Perspectives of Others," *Teaching in Higher Education* 21 (2016): 501–515; Young, "Who Do You Think You Are?"; A. Sutton, "Measuring the Effects of Self-Awareness: Construction of the Self-Awareness Outcomes Questionnaire," *Europe's Journal of Psychology* 12 (2016): 645–658.

8. K. Horney, *Neurosis and Human Growth* (New York: W. W. Norton, 1991): 17.

9. A. Elliott, *Concepts of the Self* 3e (Cambridge, UK: Polity Press, 2013); K. J. Gergen, *The Saturated Self: Dilemmas of Identity in Contemporary Life* (New York: Basic Books, 2000); B. Goss, *Processing Communication: Information Processing in Intrapersonal Communication* (Belmont, CA: Wadsworth, 1982): 72.

10. S. Harter and W. M. Bukowski, *The Construction of the Self* 2e (New York: Guilford, 2015); D. O. Oyserman, K. E. Elmore, and G. S. Smith, "Self, Self-Concept, and Identity," in *Handbook of Self and Identity* 2e, edited by M. R. Leary and J. Price Tangney (New York: Guilford, 2013): 69–104.

11. W. James, *Principles of Psychology* (New York: Henry Holt, 1890). For a discussion and critique of James's approach to the self, see C. Lemert, "A History of Identity: The Riddle at the Heart of the Mystery of Life," in *Routledge Handbook of Identity Studies* 2e, edited by A. Elliott (Abingdon, UK: Routledge, 2020): 18–45.

12. V. Rubinsky, A. M. Hosek, and N. Hudak, "'It's Better to Be Depressed Skinny Than Happy Fat': College Women's Memorable Body Messages and Their Impact on Body Image, Self-Esteem, and Rape Myth Acceptance," *Health Communication* 34.13 (2019): 1555–1563; H. El Jurdi and S. Smith, "Mirror, Mirror: National Identity and the Pursuit of Beauty," *Journal of Consumer Marketing* 35.1 (2018): 40–50; M. Ura and K. S. J. Preston, "The Influence of Thin-Ideal Internalization on Women's Body Image, Self-Esteem, and Appearance Avoidance: Covariance Structure Analysis," *American Communication Journal* 17 (2015): 15–26.

13. W. Pan and J. Pena, "Looking Down on Others to Feel Good about the Self: The Exposure Effects of Online Model Pictures on Men's Self-Esteem," *Health Communication* 35.6 (2020): 731–738; M. Cordes, S. Vocks, R. Dtising, A. Bauer, and M. Waldorf, "Male Body Image and Visual Attention Towards Oneself and Other Men," *Psychology of Men & Masculinity* 17 (2016): 243–254; L. DeFeciani, "Eating Disorders and Body Image Concerns among Male Athletes," *Clinical Social Work Journal* 44 (2016): 114–123; M-E. Brierley, K. R. Brooks, J. Mond, R. J. Stevenson, and I. D. Stephen, "The Body and the Beautiful: Health, Attractiveness, and Body Composition in Men's and Women's Bodies," *PLoS One* 11 (2016): 1–16; Z. Sylvia, T. K. King, and B. J. Morse, "Virtual Ideals: The Effect of Video Game Play on Male Body Image," *Computers in Human Behavior* 37 (2014): 183–188; L. A. Ricciardelli and M. P. McCabe, "Body Image Development in Adolescent Boys," in *Body Image: A Handbook of Science, Practice, and Prevention* 2e, edited by T. F. Cash and L. Smolak (New York: Guilford, 2013): 85–92.

14. H. Ball and R. Elsner, "Tattoos Increase Self-Esteem Among College Students," *College Student Journal* 53.3 (2019): 293–300.

15. K. Hou, "Zhuzh Up Your Zoom Meetings," *New York* (March 30-April 12, 2020): 70.

16. K. P. McIntyre, B. A. Mattingly, and G. W. Lewandowski, "When 'We' Changes 'Me,'" *Journal of Social & Personal Relationships* 32 (2015): 857.

17. P. Lau, T. Anctil, G. T. Ee, J. L. S. Jaafar, and T. G. Kin, "Self-Concept, Attitudes Toward Career Counseling, and Work Readiness of Malaysian Vocational Students," *The Career Development Quarterly*, Volume 68, Issue 1 (2020): 18–31.

18. Z. Ishak, S. Jamaluddin, and F.P Chew, "Factors Influencing Students' Self-Concept among Malaysian Students," *World Academy of Science, Engineering and Technology* 66 (2010), https://core.ac.uk/download/pdf/162013615.pdf

19. G. Khor, L. Cobiac, G. Skrzypiec, "Gender Differences in Eating Behavior and Social Self Concept among Malaysian University Students," *Malaysian Journal of Nutrition*, 8.1 (Mar 2002): 75–98.

20. C. H. Cooley, *Human Nature and the Social Order* (New York: Scribner's, 1912).

21. G. H. Mead, *Mind, Self, and Society* (Chicago: University of Chicago Press, 1934); A. Aron and N. Nardone, "Self and Close Relationships," in *Handbook of Self and Identity*, 520–541.

22. E. Taniguchi and R. M. Dailey, "Parental Confirmation and Emerging Adult Children's Body Image: Self-Concept and Social Competence as Mediators," *Communication Research* 47.3 (2020): 373–401; R. M. Dailey, "Testing Components of Confirmation: How Acceptance and Challenge from Mothers, Fathers, and Siblings Are Related to Adolescent Self-Concept," *Communication Monographs* 77 (2010): 592–617.

23. J. N. Martin and T. K. Nakayama, *Experiencing Intercultural Communication* 6e (New York: McGraw-Hill, 2017).

24. T. C. DeMarco and A-K. Newheiser, "Attachment to Groups: Relationships with Group Esteem, Self-Esteem, and Investment in Ingroups," *European Journal of Social Psychology* 49 (2019): 63–75; M. A. Hogg, "Social Identity and the Psychology of Groups," in *Handbook of Self and Identity*, 502–519.

25. D. K. Ivy, *GenderSpeak: Communicating in a Gendered World* 6e (Dubuque, IA: Kendall Hunt, 2017); M. Forman-Brunnell and J. D. Whitney (eds.), *Dolls Studies: The Many Meanings of Girls' Toys and Play* (London: Peter Lang, 2015); D. Ehrensaft, *Gender Born, Gender Made: Raising Healthy Gender-Nonconforming Children* (New York: The Experiment, 2011); J. E. O. Blakemore and R. E. Centers, "Characteristics of Boys' and Girls' Toys," *Sex Roles* 53 (2005): 619–634.

26. J. E. Stake, "Gender Differences and Similarities in Self-Concept within Everyday Life Contexts," *Psychology of Women Quarterly* 16 (1992): 349–363.

27. S. Lamb, L. M. Brown, and M. Tappan, *Packaging Boyhood: Saving Our Sons from Superheroes, Slackers, and Other Media Stereotypes* (New York: St. Martin's, 2009); S. Lamb and L. M. Brown, *Packaging Girlhood: Rescuing Our Daughters from Marketers' Schemes* (New York: St. Martin's, 2006).

28. D. Chaffee, "Reflexive Identities," in *Routledge Handbook of Identity Studies* 2e, 118–129; Elliott, *Concepts of the Self*; A. Elliott and P. du Gay, *Identity in Question* (Thousand Oaks, CA: Sage, 2009); J. Jorgenson, "Reflexivity in Feminist Research Practice: Hearing the Unsaid," *Women & Language* 34 (2011): 115–118; C. E. Medved and L. H. Turner, "Qualitative Research: Practicing Reflexivity," *Women & Language* 34 (2011): 109–112.

29. M. McKay and P. Fanning, *Self-Esteem: A Proven Program of Cognitive Techniques for Assessing, Improving, and Maintaining Your Self-Esteem* 4e (Oakland, CA: New Harbinger Publications, 2016).

30. G. Steinem, *Revolution from Within: A Book of Self-Esteem* (Boston: Little, Brown, 1993): 26.

31. M. Tajmirriyahi and W. Ickes, "Self-Concept Clarity as a Predictor of Self-Disclosure in Romantic Relationships," *Journal of Social and Personal Relationships* 37.6 (2020): 1873–1891; J. D. Campbell, P. D. Trapnell, S. J. Heine, I. M. Katz, L. F. Lavallee, and D. R. Lehman, "Self-Concept Clarity: Measurement, Personality Correlates, and Cultural Boundaries," *Journal of Personality and Social Psychology* 70 (1996): 141–156.

32. For more information on self-concept clarity, see A. E. Wong, R. R. Vallacher, and A. Nowak, "Intrinsic Dynamics of State Self-Esteem: The Role of Self-Concept Clarity," *Personality & Individual Differences* 100 (2016): 167–172; C. Fullwood, B. M. James, and C-H. Chen-Wilson, "Self-Concept Clarity and Online Self-Presentation in Adolescents," *CyberPsychology, Behavior & Social Networking* 19 (2016): 716–720; R. E. Fite, M. I. H. Lindeman, A. P. Rogers, E. Voyles, and A. M. Durik, "Knowing Oneself and Long-Term Goal Pursuit: Relations among Self-Concept Clarity, Conscientiousness, and Grit," *Personality & Individual Differences* 108 (2017): 191–194.

33. T. Altmann and M. Roth, "The Self-Esteem Stability Scale (SESS) for Cross-Sectional Direct Assessment of Self-Esteem Stability," *Frontiers in Psychology* 9 (2018): doi: 10.3389/fpsyg.2018.00091; N. Schubert and A. Bowker, "Examining the Impostor Phenomenon in Relation to Self-Esteem Level and Self-Esteem Instability,"

Current Psychology 38.3 (2019): doi.10.1007/s12144-017-9650-4; L. Rill, E. Baiocchi, M. Hopper, K. Denker, and L. N. Olson, "Exploration of the Relationship Between Self-Esteem, Commitment, and Verbal Aggressiveness in Romantic Dating Relationships," *Communication Reports* 22 (2009): 102–113; T. DeHart and B. W. Pelham, "Fluctuations in State Implicit Self-Esteem in Response to Daily Negative Events," *Journal of Experimental Social Psychology* 43 (2007): 157–165.

34. A. J. Holmstrom, J. C. Russell, and D. D. Clare, "Assessing the Role of Job-Search Self-Efficacy in the Relationship between Esteem Support and Job-Search Behavior among Two Populations of Job Seekers," *Communication Studies* 66 (2015): 277–300; A. J. Holmstrom, J. C. Russell, and D. D. Clare, "Esteem Support Messages Received during the Job Search: A Test of the CETESM," *Communication Monographs* 80 (2013): 220–242.

35. Ivy, *GenderSpeak*.

36. W. Bleidorn, J. J. A. Denissen, J. E. Gebauer, R. C. Arslan, P. J. Rentfrow, J. Potter, and S. D. Gosling, "Age and Gender Differences in Self-Esteem—A Cross-Cultural Window," *Journal of Personality & Social Psychology* 111 (2016): 396–410; C. Mason, K. Mason, and A. Mathews, "Aspiring to Lead: An Investigation into the Interactions between Self-Esteem, Patriarchal Attitudes, Gender, and Christian Leadership," *Journal of Psychology & Theology* 44 (2016): 244–256; B. M. Hill, S. M. Ogletree, and K. M. McCrary, "Body Modifications in College Students: Considering Gender, Self-Esteem, Body Appreciation, and Reasons for Tattoos," *College Student Journal* 50 (2016): 246–52; S. Sprecher, J. E. Brooks, and W. Avogo, "Self-Esteem among Young Adults: Differences and Similarities Based on Gender, Age, and Cohort (1990–2012)," *Sex Roles* 69 (2013): 264–275; G. D. Webster, L. A. Kirkpatrick, J. B. Neziek, C. V. Smith, and E. L. Paddock, "Different Slopes for Different Folks: Self-Esteem Instability and Gender as Moderators of the Relationship between Self-Esteem and Attitudinal Aggression," *Self and Identity* 6 (2007): 74–94.

37. K. Kay and C. Shipman, *The Confidence Code: The Science and Art of Self-Assurance—What Women Should Know* (New York: Harper Business, 2014); S. Sandberg, *Lean In: Women, Work, and the Will to Lead* (New York: Alfred A. Knopf, 2013); M. Brzezinski, *Knowing Your Value: Women, Money, and Getting What You're Worth* (New York: Weinstein Books, 2011).

38. K. T. Luong, S. Knobloch-Westerwick, and S. Niewiesk, "Superstars within Reach: The Role of Perceived Attainability and Role Congruity in Media Role Models on Women's Social Comparisons," *Communication Monographs* 87.1 (2020): 4–24; E. Pila, A. Stamiris, A. Castonguay, and C. M. Sabiston, "Body-Related Envy: A Social Comparison Perspective in Sport and Exercise," *Journal of Sport & Exercise* 36 (2014): 93–106; V. Hoorens and C. Van Damme, "What Do People Infer from Social Comparisons? Bridges between Social Comparison and Person Perception," *Social & Personality Psychology Compass* 6 (2012): 607–618; B. Butzer and N. A. Kuiper, "Relationships between the Frequency of Social Comparisons and Self-Concept Clarity, Intolerance of Uncertainty, Anxiety, and Depression," *Personality and Individual Differences* 41 (2006): 167–176; L. Festinger, "A Theory of Social Comparison Processes," *Human Relations* 2 (1954): 117–140.

39. Perrin and Anderson, "Share of U.S. Adults Using Social Media, Including Facebook, Is Mostly Unchanged Since 2018."

40. B. K. Johnson and S. Knobloch-Westerwick, "When Misery Avoids Company: Selective Social Comparisons to Photographic Online Profiles," *Human Communication Research* 43 (2017): 54–75; J. Liu, C. Li, N. Carcioppolo, and M. North, "Do Our Facebook Friends Make Us Feel Worse? A Study of Social Comparison and Emotion," *Human Communication Research* 42 (2016): 619–640; J. Fox and M. A. Vendemia, "Selective Self-Presentation and Social Comparison through Photographs on Social Networking Sites," *CyberPsychology, Behavior & Social Networking* 19 (2016): 593–600; C-C. Yang, "Instagram Use, Loneliness, and Social Comparison Orientation: Interact and Browse on Social Media, But Don't Compare," *CyberPsychology, Behavior & Social Networking* 19 (2016): 703–708; H. Appel, J. Crusius, and A. L. Gerlach, "Social Comparison, Envy, and Depression on Facebook: A Study Looking at the Effects of High Comparison Standards on Depressed Individuals," *Journal of Social & Clinical Psychology* 34 (2015): 277–289; K. Wilcox and A. T. Stephen, "Are Close Friends the Enemy? Online Social Networks, Self-Esteem, and Self-Control," *Journal of Consumer Research* Supplement (2014): S63–S76; N. Haferkamp and N. C. Kramer, "Social Comparison 2.0: Examining the Effects of Online Profiles on Social-Networking Sites," *CyberPsychology, Behavior, & Social Networking* 14 (2011): 309–314.

41. P. Sheldon and A. Wiegand, "'Am I as Pretty and Smart as She Is?' Competition for Attention and Social Comparison on Instagram," *Carolinas Communication Annual* 35 (2019): 63–75; F. Reer, T. Y. Wai, and T. Quandt, "Psychosocial Well-Being and Social Media Engagement: The Mediating Roles of Social Comparison Orientation and Fear of Missing Out," *New Media & Society* 21.7 (2019): 1486–1515; L. M. Amaro and N. T. Joseph, "Social Comparison and Emotion across Social Networking Sites for Mothers," *Communication Reports* 32.2 (2019): 82–97.

42. M. Raggatt, C. J. C. Wright, E. Carrotte, R. Jenkinson, K. Mulgrew, I. Prichard, and M. S. C. Lim, "'I Aspire to Look and Feel Healthy Like the Posts Convey': Engagement with Fitness Inspiration on Social Media and Perceptions of Its Influence on Health and Wellbeing," *BMC Public Health* 18 (2018): doi.org/10.1186/s12889-018-5930-7.

43. K. Toffoletti and J. Thorpe, "Bodies, Gender, and Digital Affect in Fitspiration Media," *Feminist Media Studies* (2020): doi.org/10.1080/14680777.2020.1713841; B. T. Bell, N. Deighton-Smith, and M. Hurst, "'When You Think of Exercising, You Don't Really Want to Think of Puking, Tears, and Pain': Young Adolescents' Understanding of Fitness and #Fitspiration," *Journal of Health Psychology* (2019): 1–15: doi: 10.1177/1359105319869798.

44. I. Prichard, E. Kavanagh, K. E. Mulgrew, M. S. C. Lim, and M. Tiggeman, "The Effect of Instagram #Fitspiration Images on Young Women's Mood, Body Image, and Exercise Behavior," *Body Image* 33 (2020): 1–6; B. Davies, M. Turner, and J. Udell, "Add a Comment . . . How Fitspiration and Body Positive Captions Attached to Social Media Image Influence the Mood and Body Esteem of Young Female Instagram Users," *Body Image* 33 (2020): 101–105.

45. K. E. Lommerud, D. R. Straume, and S. Vagstad, "Mommy Tracks and Public Policy: On Self-Fulfilling Prophecies and Gender Gaps in Hiring and Promotion," *Journal of Economic Behavior & Organization* 116 (2016): 540–554; S. Wurm, L. M. Warner, J. P. Ziegelmann, J. K. Wolff, and B. Schuz, "How Do Negative Self-Perceptions of Aging Become a Self-Fulfilling Prophecy?" *Psychology & Aging* 28 (2013): 1088–1097.

46. A. Eryilmaz and H. Atak, "Investigation of Starting Romantic Intimacy in Emerging Adulthood in Terms of Self-Esteem, Gender, and Gender Roles," *Educational Sciences: Theory & Practice* 11 (2011): 595–600; S. Zhang and L. Stafford, "Perceived Face Threat of Honest but Hurtful Evaluative Messages in Romantic Relationships," *Western Journal of Communication* 72 (2008): 19–39; M. H. Kernis, C. E. Lakey, and W. L. Heppner, "Secure Versus Fragile High Self-Esteem as a Predictor of Verbal Defensiveness: Converging Findings across Three Different Markers," *Journal of Personality* 76 (2008): 477–512.

47. Goss, *Processing Communication*, 72.

48. J. Roessler, "Thinking, Inner Speech, and Self-Awareness," *Review of Philosophy and Psychology* 7 (2016): 541–557; E. J. Oliver, D. Marklan, and J. Hardy, "Interpretation of Self-Talk and Post-Lecture Affective States of Higher Education Students: A Self-Determination Theory Perspective," *British Journal of Educational Psychology* 80 (2010): 307–323; J. Hardy, R. Roberts, and L. Hardy, "Awareness and Motivation to Change Negative Self-Talk," *Sport Psychologist* 23 (2009): 435–450; L. C. Lederman, "The Impact of Gender on the Self and Self-Talk," in *Women and Men Communicating: Challenges and Changes* 2e, edited by L. P. Arliss and D. J. Borisoff (Prospect Heights, IL: Waveland, 2001), 78–89;

J. R. Johnson, "The Role of Inner Speech in Human Communication," *Communication Education* 33 (1984): 211–222; J. Ayres, "The Power of Positive Thinking," *Communication Education* 37 (1988): 289–296.

49. A. T. Latinjak, M. Torregrosa, and J. Renom, "Combining Self Talk and Performance Feedback: Their Effectiveness with Adult Tennis Players," *Sport Psychologist* 25 (2011): 18–31; N. Zourbanos et al., "The Social Side of Self-Talk: Relationships between Perceptions of Support Received from the Coach and Athletes' Self-Talk," *Psychology of Sport & Exercise* 12 (2011): 407–414; A. V. Tovares, "Managing the Voices: Athlete Self-Talk as a Dialogic Process," *Journal of Language & Social Psychology* 29 (2010): 261–277.

50. McKay and Fanning, *Self-Esteem*.

51. B. R. Schlenkere, S. A. Wowra, R. M. Johnson, and M. L. Miller, "The Impact of Imagined Audiences on Self-Appraisals," *Personal Relationships* 15 (2008): 247–260; see J. Ayres and T. S. Hopf, "The Long-Term Effect of Visualization in the Classroom: A Brief Research Report," *Communication Education* 39 (1990): 75–78; J. Ayres and T. S. Hopf, "Visualization: Is It More Than Extra-Attention?" *Communication Education* 38 (1989): 1–5.

52. B. M. Al-Sobaihi and A. Helsdingen "Facebook Interaction Effects on Self Esteem and Narcissistic Behavior," *International Journal of Psychosocial Rehabilitation*, 24.1 (2020): 294–304.

53. Juliet Dinkha, "The Online Looking Glass: The Study of Self Esteem and Narcissism on Social Media," *Psychology and Behavioral Science International Journal*, 7.1 (2017).

54. N. Stanger, N. Alnaghaimshi, and E. Pearson, "How do Saudi youth engage with social media?" *First Monday*, 22.5 (2017) https://firstmonday.org/article/view/7102/6101.

55. Y. Al-Saggaf, S. Utz, and R. Lin, "Venting Negative Emotions on Twitter and the Number of Followers and Followees," *International Journal of Sociotechnology and Knowledge Development (IJSKD)*, 8.1, (2016): 44–55.

56. P. Pan, M. Alharethi, and M. Bhandari, "Using Instagram as Online Shopping Channel: Key Predictors of Consumers' Purchase Involvement on Instagram in Saudi Arabia," *The Journal of Social Media in Society*, 8.2 (2019): 63–83.

57. K. Wilcox and A. T. Stephen, "Are Close Friends the Enemy? Online Social Networks, Self-esteem, and Self-control," *Journal of Consumer Research*, 40.1 (2013): 90–103.

58. J. Ayres, T. S. Hopf, and D. M. Ayres, "An Examination of Whether Imaging Ability Enhances the Effectiveness of an Intervention Designed to Reduce Speech Anxiety," *Communication Education* 43 (1994): 252–258.

59. D. S. Doblhofer, A. Hauser, A. Kuonath, K. Haas, M. Agthe, and D. Frey, "Make the Best Out of the Bad: Coping with Value Incongruence through Displaying Facades of Conformity, Positive Reframing, and Self-Disclosure," *European Journal of Work and Organizational Psychology* 28.5 (2019): 572–593; C. Samios, "Couple Adjustment to a Stressful Life Event: A Dyadic Investigation of the Roles of Positive Reframing and Perceived Benefits," *Anxiety, Stress & Coping: An International Journal* 31.2 (2018): 188–205.

60. A concept related to bravado and confidence is *communication bravado*, introduced by K. Quintanilla and J. Mallard, "Understanding the Role of Communication Bravado: An Important Issue for Trainers/Educators," *Texas Speech Communication Journal* 33 (2008): 44–49.

61. K. Cortes, J. V. Wood, and J. Prince, "Repairing One's Mood for the Benefit of Others: Agreeableness Helps Motivate Low Self-Esteem People to Feel Better," *Journal of Social and Personal Relationships* 36.11-12 (2019): 3835–3854.

62. T. F. Waddell, "When Inspiration Comes with Baggage: How Prior Moral Transgressions Affect Feelings of Elevation and Disgust," *Communication Research Reports* 36.4 (2019): 277–286; B. N. Frisby, R. J. Sidelinger, and M. Booth-Butterfield, "No Harm, No Foul: A Social Exchange Perspective on Individual and Relational Outcomes Associated with Relational Baggage," *Western Journal of Communication* 79 (2015): 555–572; R. J. Sidelinger and M. Booth-Butterfield, "Starting Off on the Wrong Foot: An Analysis of Mate Value, Commitment, and Partner 'Baggage' in Romantic Relationships," *Human Communication* 12 (2009): 403–419.

63. P. R. Hinton, *The Perception of People: Integrating Cognition and Culture* 2e (New York: Routledge, 2015).

64. E. B. Goldstein and J. R. Brockmole, *Sensation and Perception* 10e (Belmont, CA: Cengage Learning/Wadsworth, 2016); A. S. Rancer, F. F. Jordan-Jackson, and D. A. Infante, "Observers' Perceptions of an Interpersonal Dispute as a Function of Mode of Presentation," *Communication Reports* 16 (2003): 35–48; D. A. Kenny, *Interpersonal Perception: The Foundation of Social Relationships* 2e (New York: Guilford, 2020).

65. A. J. Lee, M. J. Sidari, S. C. Murphy, J. M. Sherlock, and B. P. Zietsch, "Sex Differences in Misperceptions of Sexual Interest Can Be Explained by Sociosexual Orientation and Men Projecting Their Own Interest onto Women," *Psychological Science* 31.2 (2020): 184–192; M. Merleau-Ponty, *Phenomenology of Perception* (New York: Routledge, 2013); Z. Wang, M. Huifang, J. Yexin, and L. Fan, "Smile Big or Not? Effects of Smile Intensity on Perceptions of Warmth and Competence," *Journal of Consumer Research* 43 (2017): 7887–7805; L. Vingilis-Jaremko, D. Maurer, G. Rhodes, and L. Jeffery, "The Influence of Averageness on Adults' Perceptions of Attractiveness: The Effect of Early Visual Deprivation," *Perception* 45 (2016): 1399–1411.

66. A. Carrier, B. Dompnier, and V. Yzerbyt, "Of Nice and Mean: The Personal Relevance of Others' Competence Drives Perceptions of Warmth," *Personality and Social Psychology Bulletin* 45.11 (2019): 1549–1562; U. Lyngs, E. Cohen, W. T. Hattori, M. Newson, and D. T. Levin, "Hearing in Color: How Expectations Distort Perception of Skin Tone," *Journal of Experimental Psychology: Human Perception and Performance* 42 (2016): 2068–2076; B. Fink, P. J. Matts, S. Roder, R. Johnson, and M. Burquest, "Differences in Visual Perception of Age and Attractiveness of Female Facial and Body Skin," *International Journal of Cosmetic Science* 33 (2011): 126–131; S. F. O'Neil and M. A. Webster, "Adaptation and the Perception of Facial Age," *Visual Cognition* 19 (2011): 534–550.

67. C. M. Steele, *Whistling Vivaldi: How Stereotypes Affect Us and What We Can Do* (New York: W. W. Norton, 2011); L. C. Aguilar, *Ouch! That Stereotype Hurts . . . Communicating Respectfully in a Diverse World* (Bedford, TX: Walk the Talk Company, 2006); D. J. Schneider, A. H. Hastorf, and P. C. Ellsworth, *Person Perception* 2e (Reading, MA: Addison-Wesley, 1979).

68. S. Wright, J. E. Haskett, and J. Anderson, "When Your Students Are Hungry and Homeless: The Crucial Role of Faculty," *Communication Education* 69.2 (2020): 260–267; A. Varma, "When Empathy Is Not Enough," *Journalism Practice* 13.1 (2019): 105–121; E. Leake, "'Should You Encounter': The Social Conditions of Empathy," *Poroi: An Interdisciplinary Journal of Rhetorical Analysis & Invention* 14.1 (2018): 1–26; M. Ziegele, C. Koehler, and M. Weber, "Socially Destructive? Effects of Negative and Hateful User Comments on Readers' Donation Behavior toward Refugees and Homeless Persons," *Journal of Broadcasting & Electronic Media* 62.4 (2018): 636–653; R. Asgary, B. Sckell, A. Alcabes, R. Naderi, P. Adongo, and G. Ogedegbe, "Perceptions, Attitudes, and Experience Regarding mHealth among Homeless Persons in New York City Shelters," *Journal of Health Communication* 20 (2015): 1473–1480.

69. D. T. Kenrick, S. L. Neuberg, and R. B. Cialdini, *Social Psychology: Goals in Interaction* 6e (Boston: Pearson, 2014), 360.

70. A. H. Eagly, C. Nater, D. I. Miller, M. Kaufmann, and S. Sczesny, "Gender Stereotypes Have Changed: A Cross-Temporal Meta-Analysis of U.S. Public Opinion Polls from 1946 to 2018," *American Psychologist* 75.3 (2020): 301–315; A. M. Castano, Y. Fontanil, and A. L. Garcia-Izquierdo, "'Why Can't I Become a Manager?' A Systematic Review of Gender Stereotypes and Organizational Discrimination," *International Journal of Environment Research and Public Health* 16 (2019): doi.10.3390/ijerph16101813; M. Marquet,

A. L. Chasteen, J. E. Plaks, and L. Balasubramaniam, "Understanding the Mechanisms Underlying the Effects of Negative Age Stereotypes and Perceived Age Discrimination on Older Adults' Well-Being," *Aging & Mental Health* 23.12 (2019): 1666–1673.

71. J. A. van Breen, R. Spears, T. Kuppens, and S. de Lemus, "Subliminal Gender Stereotypes: Who Can Resist?" *Personality and Social Psychology Bulletin* 44.12 (2018): 1648–1663; C. N. Macrae, G. V. Bodenhausen, A. B. Milne, and J. Jetten, "Out of Mind but Back in Sight: Stereotypes on the Rebound," *Journal of Personality and Social Psychology* 67 (1994): 808–817.

72. R. Lagos, E. Canessa, and S. E. Chaigneau, "Modeling Stereotypes and Negative Self-Stereotypes as a Function of Interactions Among Groups with Power Asymmetries," *Journal for the Theory of Social Behavior* 49 (2019): 312–333.

73. This chapter benefited from the fine scholarship and work of M. V. Redmond, coauthor of *Interpersonal Communication: Relating to Others* 9e (Hoboken, NJ: Pearson, 2020).

Chapter 3

1. English Language Smart Words, "Text Message—SMS—E-Mail—Chat," https://www.smart-words.org (accessed June 9, 2020); N. Kemp, "Textese: Language in the Online World," in *Oxford Handbook of Cyberpsychology*, edited by A. Attrill-Smith, C. Fullwood, M. Keep, and D. Kuss (Oxford, UK: Oxford University Press, 2019), 151–172; A. Hussain and I. Lukmana, "An Exploratory Study to the Characteristics of Terxtisms in Text Messaging," *3rd Asian Education Symposium* (2018): 469–472; A. Grace, N. Kemp, F. H. Martin, and R. Parrila, "Undergraduates' Attitudes to Text Messaging Language Use and Intrusions of Textisms into Formal Writing," *New Media & Society* 17 (2015): 792–809; D. Wray, "An Exploration of the Views of Teachers Concerning the Effects of Texting on Children's Literacy Development," *Journal of Information Technology Education* 14 (2015): 271–282; D. K. Ivy and S. T. Wahl, *Nonverbal Communication for a Lifetime* 3e (Dubuque, IA: Kendall Hunt, 2019).

2. R. E. Tamargo Guzzardo, J. R. Kroff Valdés, and P. E. Dussias, "Examining the Relationship between Comprehension and Production Processes in Code-Switched Language," *Journal of Memory & Language* 89 (2016): 138–161; A. N. Amicucci, "How They Really Talk," *Journal of Adolescent & Adult Literacy* 57 (2014): 483–491; K. H. Turner, "Flipping the Switch: Code-Switching from Text Speak to Standard English," *English Journal* 98 (2009): 60–65.

3. National Association of Colleges and Employers, Job Outlook Survey 2020, "Key Attributes Employers Want to See on Students' Résumés," January 13, 2020, https://www.naceweb.org (accessed June 9, 2020).

4. J. A. Rios, G. Ling, R. Pugh, D. Becker, and A. Bacall, "Identifying Critical 21st-Century Skills for Workplace Success: A Content Analysis of Job Advertisements," *Educational Researcher* 49.2 (2020): 80–89.

5. B. L. Whorf, "Science and Linguistics," in *Language, Thought, and Reality*, edited by J. B. Carroll (Cambridge: Massachusetts Institute of Technology Press, 1956).

6. R. F. Verderber and K. S. Verderber, "Elements of Language," in *Making Connections: Readings in Relational Communication* 5e, edited by K. M. Galvin (New York: Oxford University Press, 2011), 51–60.

7. *Oxford Desk Dictionary and Thesaurus, American Edition* (New York: Oxford University Press, 2007).

8. Y. Neuman, Y. Cohen, and D. Assaf, "How Do We Understand the Meaning of Connotations? A Cognitive Computational Model," *Semiotica* 2015 (2015): 1–16; B. Lawton, "What's in a Name? Denotation, Connotation, and 'A Boy Named Sue'," *Communication Teacher* 25.3 (2011): 136–138.

9. P. Ferre, M. Guasch, T. Garcia-Chico, and R. Sanchez-Casas, "Are There Qualitative Differences in the Representation of Abstract and Concrete Words? Within-Language and Cross-Language Evidence from the Semantic Priming Paradigm," *Quarterly Journal of Experimental Psychology* 68 (2015): 2402–2418; S. T. Kousta, G. Vigliocco, D. P. Vinson, M. Andrews, and E. Del Campo, "The Representation of Abstract Words: Why Emotion Matters," *Journal of Experimental Psychology* 140 (2011): 14–34.

10. E. R. Fyle, N. M. McNeil, and B. Rittle-Johnson, "Easy as ABCABC: Abstract Language Facilitates Performance on a Concrete Patterning Task," *Child Development* 86 (2015): 927–935; L. M. Bauer, E. L. Olheiser, and J. Altarriba, "Word Type Effects in False Recall: Concrete, Abstract, and Emotion Word Critical Lures," *American Journal of Psychology* 122 (2009): 469–481; A. Parker and N. Dagnall, "Concreteness Effects Revisited: The Influence of Dynamic Visual Noise on Memory for Concrete and Abstract Words," *Memory* 17 (2008): 397–410.

11. A. G. Smith, ed., *Communication and Culture* (New York: Holt, Rinehart and Winston, 1966).

12. "Milestones," *Ms.* (Fall 2017), p. 7.

13. "A Gender-Neutral Honorific, Mx: Words We're Watching," https://www.merriam-webster.com (accessed June 9, 2020).

14. D. K. Ivy, *GenderSpeak: Communicating in a Gendered World* 6e (Dubuque, IA: Kendall Hunt, 2017).

15. K. Berry, "LGBT Bullying in School: A Troubling Relational Story," *Communication Education* 67.4 (2018): 502–513; J. Close Conoley, "Sticks and Stones Can Break My Bones and Words Can Really Hurt Me," *School Psychology Review* 37 (2008): 217–220.

16. P. Anurit, W. Pornpatcharapong, S. Chongpakdeepong, K. Sataman, P. Dinh, T. Yu, and E. Naing, "Influences of Social Media on the Use of Thai Language," *International Journal of Academic Research in Business and Social Sciences*, 1 (2011): 109–122.

17. S. Phrakru, N. Polyiam, and I. Kraisin, "Effect on Social Media: Its Impacts on Thai Education," Academic MCU Buriram Journal, 5.1 (2020): 248–261, https://so06.tci-thaijo.org/index.php/ambj/article/view/240919.

18. T. Phanitprachaya, "Meet the Thai Language Teacher Stirring up Social Media," *Top Tables Bangkok*, January 13, 2015, https://toptables.asia-city.com/city-living/news/almost-famous; and P. Theeraphong, "Time Out Bangkok Meets Jakkrit Yompayorm," *Time Out*, September 22, 2016.

19. Y. Osward, *Every Word Has Power: Switch on Your Language and Turn on Your Life* (New York: Atria Books/Simon & Schuster, 2008); P. Denton, *The Power of Our Words: Teacher Language That Helps Children Learn* (Turners Falls, MA: Northwest Foundation for Children, 2007).

20. "Mansplaining," *Merriam-Webster Dictionary*, https://www.merriam-webster.com (accessed June 10, 2020); B. Conner, K. McCauliff, C. Shue, and G. H. Stamp, "Explaining Mansplaining," *Women & Language* 41.2 (2018): 143–167.

21. C. M. Frisby, "Sticks 'n' Stones May Break My Bones, but Words They Hurt Like Hell: Derogatory Words in Popular Songs," *Media Report to Women* 38 (2010): 12–18; H. A. Schroth, J. Bain-Chekal, and D. F. Caldwell, "Sticks and Stones May Break Bones and Words Can Hurt Me: Words and Phrases That Trigger Emotions in Negotiations and Their Effects," *International Journal of Conflict Management* 16 (2005): 102–127; A. Palayiwa, P. Sheeran, and A. Thompson, "'Words Will Never Hurt Me!': Implementation Intentions Regulate Attention to Stigmatizing Comments About Appearance," *Journal of Social and Clinical Psychology* 29 (2010): 575–598; A. Ellis, *A New Guide to Rational Living* (North Hollywood, CA: Wilshire Books, 1977).

22. "Introducing 78 More Feelings: Some Scientists Believe We Have Infinite Emotions, So Long as We Can Name Them—and So We Did," *New York* (February 3-16, 2020), 28–39.

23. J. L. Dibble, N. M. Punyanunt-Carter, A. Morris, and R. Hair, "A New Look for the 'Little Black Book': Prospective Sex Partners, Back Burner Relationships, and Modern Communication Technology," in *Contemporary Studies of Sexuality & Communication: Theoretical & Applied Perspectives*, edited by J. Manning and C. M. Noland (Dubuque, IA: Kendall Hunt, 2016), 189–202.

24. A. M. Croom, "Slurs, Stereotypes, and In-Equality: A Critical Review of 'How Epithets and Stereotypes Are Racially Unequal'," *Language Sciences* 52 (2015): 139–154; D. Archer, "Slurs, Insults, (Backhanded) Compliments, and Other Strategic Facework Moves," *Language Sciences* 52 (2015): 82–97; C. J. O'Dea, S. S. Miller, E. B. Andres, M. H. Ray, D. F. Till, and D. A. Saucier, "Out of Bounds: Factors Affecting the Perceived Offensiveness of Racial Slurs," *Language Sciences* 52 (2015): 155–164; J. Rahman, "Missing the Target: Group Practices That Launch and Deflect Slurs," *Language Sciences* 52 (2015): 70–81; M. Harris, "Flying Solo: Negotiating the Matrix of Racism and Sexism in Higher Education," *Women & Language* 35 (2012): 103–107; J. Hartigan, *What Can You Say? America's National Conversation on Race* (Stanford, CA: Stanford University Press, 2010).
25. About #BlackLivesMatter, https://blacklivesmatter.com (accessed June 10, 2020).
26. Ice-T, "Party Lines," *New York* (July 25-August 7, 2016), 90.
27. T. Lan and L. Jingxia, "On the Gender Discrimination in English," *Advances in Language and Literary Studies* (2019), http:dx.doi.org/10.7575/aiac.alls.v.10n.3p.155; A. H. Bailey and M. LaFrance, "Who Counts as Human? Antecedents to Androcentric Behavior," *Sex Roles* 76 (2017): 682–693; S. Sczesny, M. Formanowicz, and F. Moser, "Can Gender-Fair Language Reduce Gender Stereotyping and Discrimination?" *Frontiers in Psychology* 7 (2016): 1–11; S. Koeser, E. A. Kuhn, and S. Sczesny, "Just Reading? How Gender-Fair Language Triggers Readers' Use of Gender-Fair Forms," *Journal of Language & Social Psychology* 34 (2015): 343–357; K. M. Douglas and R. M. Sutton, "'A Giant Leap for Mankind,' But What about Women? The Role of System-Justifying Ideologies in Predicting Attitudes toward Sexist Language," *Journal of Language & Social Psychology* 33 (2014): 667–680; A. Taylor, M. J. Hardman, and C. Wright, *Making the Invisible Visible: Gender in Language* (Bloomington, IN: IUniverse LLC, 2013).
28. A. Lindqvist, E. A. Renstrom, and M. G. Senden, "Reducing a Male Bias in Language? Establishing the Efficiency of Three Different Gender-Fair Language Strategies," *Sex Roles* 81 (2019): 109–117; M. Budziszewska, K. Hansen, and M. Bilewicz, "Backlash over Gender-Fair Language: The Impact of Feminine Job Titles on Men's and Women's Perception of Women," *Journal of Language & Social Psychology* 33 (2014): 681–691; C. Kramarae, "Muted Group Theory and Communication: Asking Dangerous Questions," *Women & Language* 28 (2005): 55–61; S. Ardener, "Muted Groups: The Genesis of an Idea and Its Praxis," *Women & Language* 28 (2005): 50–54; J. K. Swim, R. Mallett, and C. Stangor, "Understanding Subtle Sexism: Detection and Use of Sexist Language," *Sex Roles* 51 (2004): 117–128; J. Briere and C. Lanktree, "Sex-Role Related Effects of Sex Bias in Language," *Sex Roles* 9 (1983): 625–632; L. Brooks, "Sexist Language in Occupational Information: Does It Make a Difference?" *Journal of Vocational Behavior* 23 (1983): 227–232.
29. S. Killerman, *The Social Justice Advocate's Handbook: A Guide to Gender* 2e (Austin, TX: Impetus Books, 2017); B. D. Earp, "The Extinction of Masculine Generics," *Journal for Communication & Culture* 2 (2012): 4–19; J. Flanigan, "The Use and Evolution of Gender Neutral Language in an Intentional Community," *Women & Language* 36 (2013): 27–41.
30. Earp, "The Extinction of Masculine Generics"; Killerman, *The Social Justice Advocate's Handbook* 2e; P. Gygax, U. Gabriel, O. Sarrasin, J. Oakhill, and A. Garnham, "Some Grammatical Rules Are More Difficult Than Others: The Case of the Generic Interpretation of the Masculine," *European Journal of Psychology of Education* 24 (2009): 235–246; M. A. Clason, "Feminism, Generic 'He,' and the *TNIV* Bible Translation Debate," *Critical Discourse Studies* 3 (2006): 23–35; J. L. Stinger and R. Hopper, "Generic *He* in Conversation?" *Quarterly Journal of Speech* 84 (1998): 209–221; J. Gastil, "Generic Pronouns and Sexist Language: The Oxymoronic Character of Masculine Generics," *Sex Roles* 23 (1990): 629–641; D. K. Ivy, L. Bullis-Moore, K. Norvell, P. Backlund, and M. Javidi, "The Lawyer, the Babysitter, and the Student: Inclusive Language Usage and Instruction," *Women & Language* 18 (1994): 13–21; W. Martyna, "What Does 'He' Mean? Use of the Generic Masculine," *Journal of Communication* 28 (1978): 131–138.
31. H. J. MacArthur, J. L. Cundiff, and M. R. Mehl, "Estimating the Prevalence of Gender-Biased Language in Undergraduates' Everyday Speech," *Sex Roles* 82 (2020): 81–93.
32. "Bias-Free Language Guidelines," *Publication Manual of the American Psychological Association: The Official Guide to APA Style* 7e (Washington, DC: American Psychological Association, 2020) 131–149.
33. L. Madson and R. M. Hessling, "Does Alternating between Masculine and Feminine Pronouns Eliminate Perceived Gender Bias in a Text?" *Sex Roles* 41 (1999): 559–576; D. Kennedy, "Review Essay: She or He in Textbooks," *Women & Language* 15 (1992): 46–49.
34. L. Madson and J. Shoda, "Alternating between Masculine and Feminine Pronouns: Does Essay Topic Affect Readers' Perceptions?" *Sex Roles* 54 (2006): 275–285; T. Strahan, "'They' in Australian English: Non-Gender-Specific or Specifically Non-Gendered?" *Australian Journal of Linguistics* 28 (2008): 17–29.
35. A. Hess, "Multiple Choice," *New York Times Magazine* (April 3, 2016): 13–15; Killerman, *Social Justice Advocate's Handbook*.
36. J. M. Ryan, "Communicating Trans Identity: Toward an Understanding of the Selection and Significance of Gender Identity-Based Terminology," *Journal of Language & Sexuality* 8.2 (2019): 221–241; R. Kaveney, "Why Trans Is In, But Tranny Is Out," www.theguardian.com (accessed February 24, 2017); P. E. Wagner, A. Kunkel, and B. L. Compton, "(Trans)lating Identity: Exploring Discursive Strategies for Navigating the Tensions of Identity Gaps," *Communication Quarterly* 64.3 (2016): 251–272; M. Heinz, *Entering Transmasculinity: The Inevitability of Discourse* (Bristol, UK: Intellect, 2016).
37. Ivy, *GenderSpeak*.
38. R. B. B. Abdullah, "Gender Bias in Malay Language," *International Journal of Social Science and Humanity*, 6.6 (June 2016): 456–461.
39. T. K. Seong and A. P. M. B. Seksis, *Pelita Bahasa*, 8.6 (1996): 2-4, Kuala Lumpur: DBP; and R. Hamdan, "Gender Perspective in Malay Proverbs," *The Middle-East Journal of Scientific Research*, 22.1 (2014): 99–106.
40. Y. J. Ng, L. V. Y. Chiew, S. T. Chong, Y. L. Lee, T. Ahmad, and Mohd Ariff, "An Analysis on Gender-based Language and Illustrations in Malaysian Secondary Schools' English Language and Literature Textbooks," *International Journal of Humanities and Social Science*, 3.18 (2013): 155–127.
41. H. Ansary and E. Babaii "Subliminal Sexism in Current ESL/EFL Textbooks," *Asian-EFL Journal*, 5.1 (2003).
42. Ivy, *GenderSpeak*.
43. F. Fasoli, P. Hegarty, and A. Carnaghi, "Sounding Gay, Speaking as a 'Fag': Auditory Gaydar and the Perception of Reclaimed Homophobic Language," *Journal of Language and Social Psychology* 38.5-6 (2019): 798–808; M. Fischer, "It's Judith Butler's World," *New York* (July 13–26, 2016): 38–44; D. S. Strasser and K. Hobson, "'You Had Sex, Right?': Theorizing Desire, Identity, Reciprocity, and Sex in Queer Friendships," in *Contemporary Studies of Sexuality & Communication*, 169–187; J. Sanders, "The Questioning Continuum: Seeking Sexuality as a Lifelong Process," *Bitch* (Spring 2016): 71–73.
44. S. Criniti and E. R. Green, "Understanding Transgender Identities and Experiences," in *Contemporary Studies of Sexuality & Communication*, 125–142; L. G. Spencer, IV, "Introduction: Centering Transgender Studies and Gender Identity in Communication Scholarship," in *Transgender Communication Studies: Histories, Trends, and Trajectories*, edited by L. G. Spencer, IV, and J. C. Capuzza (Lanham, MD: Lexington, 2015); A. Silman, "Laverne Cox Talks Battling Transphobia on 'Orange Is the New Black'," www.salon.com (accessed June 26, 2015).

45. S. Tanno, "France Could Ban 'confusing' Gender Neutral Words That 'endanger the Language' under Law Proposed by 60 MPs," *The Daily Mail*, February 25, 2021, https://www.dailymail.co.uk.
46. B. Dodman, "'Françaises, Français': Could the French Language be Less Sexist?" https://www.france24.com/en/culture/20210225-fran%C3%A7aises-fran%C3%A7ais-why-the-french-language-need-not-be-so-sexist, February 25, 20121.
47. "Guide Pour Une Communication Publique Sans Stéréotype de Sexe (Guide for Public Communication without Gender Stereotypes)," République Française, November 2015, https://www.haut-conseil-egalite.gouv.fr/IMG/pdf/hcefh__guide_pratique_com_sans_stereo-_vf_2015_11_05.pdf.
48. P.C. Jandau, "What is Inclusive Writing and Why is it a Problem?" *Sud Ouest*, October 13, 2017, https://www.sudouest.fr/2017/10/12/qu-est-ce-que-l-ecriture-inclusive-et-pourquoi-pose-t-elle-probleme-3856018-4699.php?nic.
49. "Belgian Law to be Updated with Gender-Neutral Language," *The Brussels Times*, April 17, 2021. https://www.brusselstimes.com/news/belgium-all-news/163756/french-dutch-civil-code-belgian-law-to-be-updated-with-gender-neutral-language/.
50. P. Williams, "In Landmark Case, Supreme Court Rules LGBTQ Workers Are Protected from Job Discrimination," June 15, 2020, https://www.nbcnews.com (accessed June 16, 2020).
51. P. C. McCabe, E. A. Dragowski, and F. Rubinson, "What Is Homophobic Bias Anyway? Defining and Recognizing Microaggressions and Harassment of LGBTQ Youth," *Journal of School Violence* 12 (2013): 7–26; M. Kantor, *Homophobia: The State of Sexual Bigotry Today* 2e (Santa Barbara, CA: Praeger, 2009); G. Griffin, "Understanding Heterosexism: The Subtle Continuum of Homophobia," *Women & Language* 21 (1998): 33–39.
52. C. Flores-Sandoval and E. A. Kinsella, "Overcoming Ageism: Critical Reflexivity for Gerontology Practice," *Educational Gerontology* 46.4 (2020): 223–234; C. Berridge and N. Hooyman, "The Consequences of Ageist Language Are Upon Us," *Journal of Gerontological Social Work* (2020), https://doi.org/10.1080/01634372.2020.1764688; J. F. Nussbaum (ed.), *Communication across the Lifespan* (International Communication Association Conference Theme Book Series, vol. 3; New York: Peter Lang, 2016); A. Applewhite, *This Chair Rocks: A Manifesto Against Ageism* (Networked Books, 2016).
53. N. Isenberg, *White Trash: The 400-Year Untold History of Class in America* (New York: Viking, 2016); B. Jensen, *Reading Classes: On Culture and Classism in America* (Ithaca, NY: ILR Press, 2012); R. K. S. Macaulay, *Talk That Counts: Age, Gender, and Social Class Differences in Discourse* (New York: Oxford University Press, 2005); M. Argyle, *The Psychology of Social Class* (New York: Routledge, 1993).
54. J. S. Seiter, J. Larsen, and J. Skinner, "'Handicapped' or 'Handicapable'? The Effects of Language about Persons with Disabilities on Perceptions of Source Credibility and Persuasiveness," *Communication Reports* 11 (1998): 21–31.
55. R. McRuer, *Crip Times: Disability, Globalization, and Resistance* (New York: New York University Press, 2018); J. St. Pierre, "Cripping Communication: Speech, Disability, and Exclusion in Liberal Humanist and Posthumanist Discourse," *Communication Theory* 25 (2015): 330–348; A. Kafer, *Feminist, Queer, Crip* (Bloomington: Indiana University Press, 2013), 14.
56. J. R. Gibb, "Defensive Communication," *Journal of Communication* 11 (1961): 141–148. For other research on communication climate, see G. L. Bradley and A. C. Campbell, "Managing Difficult Workplace Conversations: Goals, Strategies, and Outcomes," *International Journal of Business Communication* 53 (2016): 443–464; G. L. Forward, K. Czech, and C. M. Lee, "Assessing Gibb's Supportive and Defensive Communication Climate: An Examination of Measurement and Construct Validity," *Communication Research Reports* 28 (2011): 1–15; J. M. Reagle, "'Be Nice': Wikipedia Norms for Supportive Communication," *New Review of Hypermedia & Multimedia* 16 (2010): 161–180.
57. J. H. Kim and J. Kim, "The Dynamics of Polarization and Compromise in Conflict Situations: The Interaction between Cultural Traits and Majority-Minority Influence," *Communication Monographs* 84 (2017): 128–141.
58. L. H. Turner, "Message from the President," *Spectra* (November, 2011), www.natcom.org (accessed February 25, 2017).
59. B. Clark, "50 Trigger Words and Phrases for Powerful Multimedia Content," *copyblogger*, April 20, 2009, www.copyblogger.com/trigger-words; E. T. Booth, "Assign This: Trigger Words," *Spectra* (Washington, DC: National Communication Association, June/July 2007).
60. M. R. Andreychik, "I Like That You Feel My Pain, but I Love That You Feel My Joy: Empathy for a Partner's Negative versus Positive Emotions Independently Affect Relationship Quality," *Journal of Social & Personal Relationships* 36.3 (2019): 834–854; M. Huo, J. L. Fuentecilla, K. S. Birditt, and K. L. Fingerman, "Older Adults' Empathy and Daily Support Exchanges," *Journal of Social & Personal Relationships* 36.11-12 (2019): 3814–3834; S. M. Jones, G. D. Bodie, and S. D. Hughes, "The Impact of Mindfulness on Empathy, Active Listening, and Perceived Provisions of Emotional Support," *Communication Research* 46.6 (2019): 838–865; S. M. McNaughton, "Developing Pre-Requisites for Empathy: Increasing Awareness of Self, the Body, and the Perspectives of Others," *Teaching in Higher Education* 21 (2016): 501–515; R. Krznaric, *Empathy: Why It Matters and How to Get It* (New York: Perigee Books, 2014); K. McLaren, *The Art of Empathy: A Complete Guide to Life's Most Essential Skill* (Louisville, CO: Sounds True Publishers, 2013); M. V. Redmond, "The Functions of Empathy (Decentering) in Human Relations," *Human Relations* 42 (1993): 593–606.
61. C. Streit, G. Carlo, and S. E. Killoren, "Family Support, Respect, and Empathy as Correlates of U.S. Latino/Latina College Students' Prosocial Behaviors toward Different Recipients," *Journal of Social & Personal Relationships* 27.5 (2020): 1513–1533; A. K. Meinecke and S. Kauffeld, "Engaging the Hearts and Minds of Followers: Leader Empathy and Language Style Matching during Appraisal Interviews," *Journal of Business & Psychology* 34.4 (2019): 485–501; D. B. Whiteside and L. J. Barclay, "The Face of Fairness: Self-Awareness as a Means to Promote Fairness Among Managers with Low Empathy," *Journal of Business Ethics* 137 (2016): 721–730; F. Barone, P. S. Hutchings, H. J. Kimmel, H. L. Traub, J. T. Cooper, and C. M. Marshall, "Increasing Empathic Accuracy through Practice and Feedback in a Clinical Interviewing Course," *Journal of Social and Clinical Psychology* 24 (2005): 156–171.
62. T. Challies, "The Art and Science of the Humblebrag," Challies.com, October 22, 2013, www.challies.com (accessed June 19, 2014); *The Rachel Maddow Show*, MSNBC, June 23, 2012, Television.

Chapter 4

1. M. Kaneko and J. Mesch, "Eye Gaze in Creative Sign Language," *Sign Language Studies* 13 (2013): 372–400; M. Fox, *Talking Hands: What Sign Language Reveals About the Mind* (New York: Simon & Schuster, 2008); R. B. Grossman and J. Kegl, "Moving Faces: Categorization of Dynamic Facial Expressions in American Sign Language by Deaf and Hearing Participants," *Journal of Nonverbal Behavior* 31 (2007): 23–38.
2. D. Keltner, D. Sauter, J. Tracy, and A. Cowen, "Emotional Expression: Advances in Basic Emotion Theory," *Journal of Nonverbal Behavior* 43 (2019): 133–160; L. J. Youngvorst and A. C. High, "'Anyone Free to Chat?' Using Technological Features to Elicit Quality Support Online," *Communication Monographs* 85.2 (2018): 203–223; H. Toscano, T. W. Schubert, and S. R. Giessner, "Eye Gaze and Head Posture Jointly Influence Judgments of Dominance, Physical Strength, and Anger," *Journal of Nonverbal Behavior* 42.3 (2018): 285–309; S. L. Aloia and D. H. Solomon, "Emotions Associated with Verbal Aggression Expression and Suppression," *Western Journal of Communication* 80 (2016): 3–20; C. Civile and S. Obhi, "Power Eliminates the Influence of Body Posture on Facial Emotion Recognition," *Journal of Nonverbal*

Behavior 40 (2016): 283–299; U. Hess, C. Blaison, and K. Kafetsios, "Judging Facial Emotion Expressions in Context: The Influence of Culture and Self-Construal Orientation," *Journal of Nonverbal Behavior* 40 (2016): 55–64.

3. A. Mehrabian, *Nonverbal Communication* (Chicago: Aldine-Atherton, 1972).
4. R. L. Birdwhistell, *Kinesics and Context* (Philadelphia: University of Pennsylvania Press, 1970).
5. J. A. Hall, M. A. Ruben, and Swatantra, "First Impressions of Physicians According to Their Physical and Social Group Characteristics," *Journal of Nonverbal Behavior* 44 (2020): 279–299; T. Kinley, J. Strubel, and A. Amlani, "Impression Formation of Male and Female Millennial Students Wearing Eye Glasses or Hearing Aids," *Journal of Nonverbal Behavior* 43 (2019): 357–379; A. Todorov, *Face Value: The Irresistible Influence of First Impressions* (Princeton: Princeton University Press, 2017); D. Re and N. Rule, "Making a (False) Impression: The Role of Business Experience in First Impressions of CEO Leadership Ability," *Journal of Nonverbal Behavior* 40 (2016): 235–245.
6. R. Petrican, A. Todorov, and C. Grady, "Personality at Face Value: Facial Appearance Predicts Self and Other Personality Judgments among Strangers and Spouses," *Journal of Nonverbal Behavior* 38 (2014): 259–277.
7. A. Gunia, "'I Don't Think We Should Ever Shake Hands Again.' Dr. Fauci Says Coronavirus Should Change Some Behaviors for Good," April 9, 2020. https://time.com (accessed June 6, 2020).
8. W. E. Chaplin, J. B. Phillips, J. D. Brown, N. R. Clanton, and J. L. Stein, "Handshaking, Gender, Personality, and First Impressions," *Journal of Personality and Social Psychology* 79 (2000): 110–117.
9. Y. Katsumi, S. Dolcos, S. Kim, K. Sung, and F. Dolcos, "When Nonverbal Greetings 'Make It or Break It': The Role of Ethnicity and Gender in the Effect of Handshakes on Social Appraisals," *Journal of Nonverbal Behavior* 41 (2017): 345–365; R. Ryan, *60 Seconds and You're Hired* Rev. Ed. (New York: Penguin, 2016); G. L. Stewart, S. L. Dustin, M. R. Barrick, and T. C. Darnold, "Exploring the Handshake in Employment Interviews," *Journal of Applied Psychology* 93 (2008): 1139–1146.
10. D. K. Ivy and S. T. Wahl, *Nonverbal Communication for a Lifetime* 3e (Dubuque, IA: Kendall Hunt, 2019); K. Fujiwara, M. Kimura, and I. Daibo, "Rhythmic Features of Movement Synchrony for Bonding Individuals in Dyadic Interaction," *Journal of Nonverbal Behavior* 44 (2020): 173–193; N. E. Dunbar, H. Giles, Q. Bernhold, A. Adams, M. Giles, N. Zamanzadeh, K. Gangi, S. Coveleski, and K. Fujiwara, "Strategic Synchrony and Rhythmic Similarity in Lies about Ingroup Affiliation," *Journal of Nonverbal Behavior* 44 (2020): 153–172; K. Yokotani, G. Takagi, and K. Wakashima, "Nonverbal Synchrony of Facial Movements and Expressions Predict Therapeutic Alliance during a Structured Psychotherapeutic Interview," *Journal of Nonverbal Behavior* 44 (2020): 85–116; J. Hale, J. A. Ward, F. Buccheri, D. Oliver, and A. F. de C. Hamilton, "Are You on My Wavelength? Interpersonal Coordination in Dyadic Conversations," *Journal of Nonverbal Behavior* 44 (2020): 63–83; T. Lischetzke, M. Cugialy, T. Apt, M. Eid, and M. Niedeggen, "Are Those Who Tend to Mimic Facial Expressions Especially Vulnerable to Emotional Contagion?" *Journal of Nonverbal Behavior* 44 (2020): 133–152.
11. S. Farley, "Introduction to the Special Issue on Nonconscious Mimicry: History, Applications, and Theoretical and Methodological Innovations," *Journal of Nonverbal Behavior* 44 (2020): 1–4; K. A. Duffy, P. A. Green, and T. L. Chartrand, "Mimicry and Modeling of Health(-Risk) Behaviors: How Others Impact Our Health(-Risk) Behaviors Without Our Awareness," *Journal of Nonverbal Behavior* 44 (2020): 5–40; Q. S. Bernhold and H. Giles, "Vocal Accommodation and Mimicry," *Journal of Nonverbal Behavior* 44 (2020): 41–62; A. L. Skinner, A. Osnaya, B. Patel, and S. P. Perry, "Mimicking Others' Nonverbal Signals Is Associated with Increased Attitude Contagion," *Journal of Nonverbal Behavior* 44 (2020): 117–131; A. J. Arnold and P. Winkielman, "The Mimicry Among Us: Intra- and Inter-Personal Mechanisms of Spontaneous Mimicry," *Journal of Nonverbal Behavior* 44 (2020): 195–212; L. Lakin, V. W. Jefferis, C. M. Cheng, and T. L. Chartrand, "The Chameleon Effect as Social Glue: Evidence for the Evolutionary Significance of Nonconscious Mimicry," *Journal of Nonverbal Behavior* 27 (2003): 145–161.
12. M. Argyle, *Bodily Communication* (New York: Methuen, 1988).
13. J. N. Martin and T. K. Nakayama, *Experiencing Intercultural Communication* 6e (New York: McGraw-Hill, 2018); D. Matsumoto and H. S. Hwang, "Cultural Influences on Nonverbal Behavior," in *Nonverbal Communication: Science and Applications*, edited by D. Matsumoto, M. G. Frank, and H. S. Hwang (Thousand Oaks, CA: Sage, 2018); U. Hess, C. Blaison, and K. Kafetsios, "Judging Facial Emotion Expressions in Context: The Influence of Culture and Self-Construal Orientation," *Journal of Nonverbal Behavior* 50 (2016): 55–64; P. A. Andersen, "Tactile Traditions: Cultural Differences and Similarities in Haptic Communication," in *The Handbook of Touch: Neuroscience, Behavioral, and Health Perspectives*, edited by M. J. Hertenstein and S. J. Weiss (New York: Springer, 2011), 351–371; D. Matsumoto, A. Olide, J. Schug, B. Willingham, and M. Callan, "Cross-Cultural Judgments of Spontaneous Facial Expressions of Emotion," *Journal of Nonverbal Behavior* 33 (2009): 213–238;. E. Axtell, *Gestures: Do's and Taboos of Body Language around the World* (New York: Wiley, 1998).
14. D. Matsumoto and H. Hwang, "Cultural Similarities and Differences in Emblematic Gestures," *Journal of Nonverbal Behavior* 37 (2013): 1–27; E. Vennekens-Kelly, *Subtle Differences, Big Faux Pas: Test Your Cultural Competence* (Scottsdale, AZ: Summertime, 2012); L. A. Samovar, R. E. Porter, E. R. McDaniel, and C. S. Roy, "Approaches to Intercultural Communication," in *Intercultural Communication: A Reader* 14e, edited by L. A. Samovar, R. E. Porter, E. R. McDaniel, and C. S. Roy (Belmont, CA: Wadsworth, 2014), 1–4.
15. K. Steinmetz, "Standing Too Close. Not Covering Coughs. If Someone Is Violating Social Distancing Rules, What Do You Do?" April 13, 2020. https://time.com (accessed June 4, 2020).
16. See J. K. Burgoon and S. B. Jones, "Toward a Theory of Personal Space Expectations and Their Violations," *Human Communication Research* 2 (1976): 131–146. For discussions and applications of expectancy violations theory, see C. N. Wright and M. E. Roloff, "You Should Just Know Why I'm Upset: Expectancy Violation Theory and the Influence of Mind Reading Expectations (MRE) on Responses to Relational Problems," *Communication Research Reports* 32 (2015): 10–19; A. Miller-Ott and L. Kelly, "The Presence of Cell Phones in Romantic Partner Face-to-Face Interactions: An Expectancy Violation Theory Approach," *Southern Communication Journal* 80 (2015): 253–270; W. Walther-Martin, "Media-Generated Expectancy Violations: A Study of Political Humor, Race, and Source Perceptions," *Western Journal of Communication* 79 (2015): 492–507; B. W. Chiles and M. E. Roloff, "Apologies, Expectations, and Violations: An Analysis of Confirmed and Disconfirmed Expectations for Responses to Apologies," *Communication Reports* 27 (2014): 65–77; E. L. Cohen, "Expectancy Violations in Relationships with Friends and Media Figures," *Communication Research Reports* 27 (2010): 97–111.
17. A. Tilton Ratcliff, "(Un)safe Refuge: The Built-In Ableism in Queer Spaces," *Bitch* (Spring 2020): 36–41; M. N. Enzinna, "Reconsidering Nonverbal Communication Among Children with Mental and Physical Disabilities," *Journal of the Communication, Speech, and Theatre Association of North Dakota* 29 (2016/2017): 56–70; I. Marini, X. Wang, C. Etzbach, and A. Del Castillo, "Ethnic, Gender, and Contact Differences in Intimacy Attitudes toward Wheelchair Users," *Rehabilitation Counseling Bulletin* 56 (2013): 135–145; D. W. Worley, "Communication and Students with Disabilities on College Campuses," in *Handbook of Communication and People with Disabilities: Research and Application*, edited by D. O. Braithwaite and T. L. Thompson (New York: Routledge, 2000), 125–140.
18. J. Fast, *Body Language* (New York: M. Evans, 1970).

19. J. Clement, "Second Screen Usage—Statistics and Facts," January 29, 2019. https://www.statisa.com (accessed June 4, 2020).
20. P. Ekman and W. V. Friesen, "The Repertoire of Nonverbal Behavior: Categories, Origins, Usage, and Coding," *Semiotica* 1 (1969): 49–98.
21. American Society for Aesthetic Plastic Surgery, "Cosmetic Surgery National Data Bank Statistics, 2019," https://www.surgery.org/sites/default/files/Aesthetic-Society_Stats2019Book_FINAL.pdf (accessed June 4, 2020).
22. A. Arroyo, T. J. Burke, and V. J. Young, "The Role of Close Others in Promoting Weight Management and Body Image Outcomes: An Application of Confirmation, Self-Determination, Social Control, and Social Support," *Journal of Social & Personal Relationships* 37 (2020): 1030–1050; M. Meltzer, "Big Feels," *New York* (March 2-15, 2020): 39–40; A. Yazdanparast and N. Spears, "The New Me or the Me I'm Proud of?" *European Journal of Marketing* 52 (2018): 279–301; M. Cordes, S. Vocks, R. Dtising, A. Bauer, and M. Waldorf, "Male Body Image and Visual Attention Towards Oneself and Other Men," *Psychology of Men & Masculinity* 17 (2016): 243–254; L. DeFeciani, "Eating Disorders and Body Image Concerns among Male Athletes," *Clinical Social Work Journal* 44 (2016): 114–123; M-E. Brierley, K. R. Brooks, J. Mond, R. J. Stevenson, and I. D. Stephen, "The Body and the Beautiful: Health, Attractiveness, and Body Composition in Men's and Women's Bodies," *PloS One* 11 (2016): 1–16; M. Ura and K. S. J. Preston, "The Influence of Thin-Ideal Internalization on Women's Body Image, Self-Esteem, and Appearance Avoidance: Covariance Structure Analysis," *American Communication Journal* 17 (2015): 15–26.
23. S. Han, Y. Li, S. Liu, Q. Xu, Q. Tan, and L. Zhang, "Beauty is in the Eye of the Beholder: The Halo Effect and Generalization Effect in the Facial Attractiveness Evaluation," *Acta Psychologica Sinica* 50.4 (2018): 363–376; J. Gibson and J. Gore, "Is He a Hero or a Weirdo? How Norm Violations Influence the Halo Effect," *Gender Issues* 33 (2016): 299–310; W. J. Lammers, S. Davis, O. Davidson, and K. Hogue, "Impact of Positive, Negative, and No Personality Descriptors on the Attractiveness Halo Effect," *Psi Chi Journal of Psychological Research* 21 (2016): 29–34.
24. A. L. Jones, J. J. Tree, and R. Ward, "Personality in Faces: Implicit Associations between Appearance and Personality," *European Journal of Social Psychology* 49 (2019): 658–669; B. Verhulst, M. Lodge, and H. Lavine, "The Attractiveness Halo: Why Some Candidates Are Perceived More Favorably Than Others," *Journal of Nonverbal Behavior* 34 (2010): 111–117; L. P. Naumann, S. Vazire, P. J. Rentfrow, and S. D. Gosling, "Personality Judgments Based on Physical Appearance," *Personality & Social Psychology Bulletin* 35 (2009): 1661–1671.
25. J. J. Guyer, P. Brinol, R. E. Petty, and J. Horcajo, "Nonverbal Behavior of Persuasive Sources: A Multiple Process Analysis," *Journal of Nonverbal Behavior* 43 (2019): 203–231; J. Trekels and S. Eggermont, "Beauty is Good: The Appearance Culture, the Internalization of Appearance Ideals, and Dysfunctional Appearance Beliefs Among Tweens," *Human Communication Research* 43 (2017): 173–192.
26. M. Parry, "Researchers Find Ratemyprofessors.com Useful, If Not Chili-Pepper Hot," *The Chronicle of Higher Education* (December 2, 2011): A4; R. Wilson, "Being Hot Leaves Some Professors Cold," *The Chronicle of Higher Education* (August 13, 2010): A1, A9; K. Soper, "RateMyProfessor'sAppearance.com," *The Chronicle of Higher Education* (September 17, 2010): B24; T. A. Moriarty, "They Love Me, They Love Me Not," *The Chronicle of Higher Education* (April 24, 2009): A27; R. Toor, "Can't We Be Smart and Look Good, Too?" *The Chronicle Review* (April 3, 2009): B4–B5; C. Edwards, A. Edwards, Q. Qing, and S. T. Wahl, "The Influence of Computer-Mediated Word-of-Mouth Communication on Student Perceptions of Instructors and Attitudes toward Learning Course Content," *Communication Education* 56 (2007): 255–277; T. H. Feeley, "Evidence of Halo Effects in Student Evaluations of Communication Instruction," *Communication Education* 51 (2002): 225–236.
27. D. Kuster, E. G. Krumhuber, and U. Hess, "You Are What You Wear: Unless You Moved—Effects of Attire and Posture on Person Perception." *Journal of Nonverbal Behavior* 43 (2019): 23–38; R. A. R. Gurung, E. Punke, M. Brickner, and V. Badalamenti, "Power and Provocativeness: The Effects of Subtle Changes in Clothing on Perceptions of Working Women," *The Journal of Social Psychology* 158 (2018): 252–255; D. J. Gurney, N. Howlett, K. Pine, M. Tracey, and R. Moggridge, "Dressing Up Posture: The Interactive Effects of Posture and Clothing on Competency Judgments," *British Journal of Psychology* 108 (2017): 436–451.
28. T. C. Ford, "Sunday Best: The Beauty and Timelessness of Black Adornment Rituals," *Bitch* (Fall 2019): 24–30; C. A. Zestcott, M. G. Bean, and J. Stone, "Evidence of Negative Implicit Attitudes toward Individuals with a Tattoo Near the Face," *Group Processes & Intergroup Relations* 20 (2017): 186–201; L. Dunden and A. Francis, "Inking and Thinking: Honor Students and Tattoos," *College Student Journal* 50 (2016): 219–223; B. M. Hill, S. M. Ogletree, and K. M. McCrary, "Body Modifications in College Students: Considering Gender, Self-Esteem, Body Appreciation, and Reasons for Tattoos," *College Student Journal* 50 (2016): 246–252.
29. A. H. Bailey, R. Lambert, and M. LaFrance, "Implicit Reactions to Women in High Power Body Postures: Less Wonderful But Still Weaker," *Journal of Nonverbal Behavior* 44 (2020): 329–350.
30. Z. M. Flack, M. Naylor, and D. A. Leavens, "Pointing to Visible and Invisible Targets," *Journal of Nonverbal Behavior* 42 (2018): 221–236; N. Dargue and N. Sweller, "Not All Gestures Are Created Equal: The Effects of Typical and Atypical Iconic Gestures on Narrative Comprehension," *Journal of Nonverbal Behavior* 42 (2018): 327–345; D. B. Givens, "Reading Palm-Up Signs: Neurosemiotic Overview of a Common Hand Gesture," *Semiotica* 210 (2016): 235–250; B. S. Hasler, O. Salomon, P. Tuchman, A. Lev-Tov, and D. Friedman, "Real-Time Gesture Translation in Intercultural Communication," *Artificial Intelligence & Society* 32 (2017): 25–35.
31. B. Blaskovits and C. Bennell, "Are We Revealing Hidden Aspects of Our Personality When We Walk?" *Journal of Nonverbal Behavior* 43 (2019): 329-356; S. Halovic and C. Kroos, "Not All Is Noticed: Kinematic Cues of Emotion-Specific Gait," *Human Movement Science* 57 (2018): 478–488.
32. I. Prichard, E. Kavanagh, K. E. Mulgrew, M. S. C. Lim, and M. Tiggeman, "The Effect of Instagram #Fitspiration Images on Young Women's Mood, Body Image, and Exercise Behavior," *Body Image* 33 (2020): 1–6; B. Davies, M. Turner, and J. Udell, "Add a Comment....How Fitspiration and Body Positive Captions Attached to Social Media Image Influence the Mood and Body Esteem of Young Female Instagram Users," *Body Image* 33 (2020): 101–105; B. T. Bell, N. Deighton-Smith, and M. Hurst, "'When You Think of Exercising, You Don't Really Want to Think of Puking, Tears, and Pain': Young Adolescents' Understanding of Fitness and #fitspiration," *Journal of Health Psychology* (2019): 1–15. doi: 10.1177/1359105319869798; M. Raggatt, C. J. C. Wright, E. Carrotte, R. Jenkinson, K. Mulgrew, I. Prichard, and M. S. C. Lim, "'I Aspire to Look and Feel Healthy Like the Posts Convey': Engagement with Fitness Inspiration on Social Media and Perceptions of Its Influence on Health and Wellbeing," *BMC Public Health* 18 (2018): doi.org/10.1186/s12889-018-5930-7.
33. A. Arroyo and S. R. Brunner, "Negative Body Talk as an Outcome of Friends' Fitness Posts on Social Networking Sites: Body Surveillance and Social Comparison as Potential Moderators," *Journal of Applied Communication Research* 44 (2016): 216–235.
34. E. M. Lamberg and L. M. Muratori, "Cell Phones Change the Way We Walk," *Gait & Posture* 35 (2012): 688–690.
35. K. Heaney, "Can You Tell If Someone Is Smiling by Their Eyes?" April 13, 2020. www.thecut.com (accessed June 5, 2020); J. Thomas, "Spotting a Duchenne Smile: How to Identify a Genuine Smile," March 28, 2020. www.betterhelp.com (accessed June 5, 2020).
36. K. M. Quintanilla and S. T. Wahl, *Business and Professional Communication: Keys for Workplace Excellence* 4e (Thousand Oaks, CA: Sage, 2019); A. Pico, A. Gracanin, M. Gadea, A. Boeren, M. Alino,

and A. Vingerhoets, "How Visible Tears Affect Observers' Judgements and Behavioral Intentions: Sincerity, Remorse, and Punishment," *Journal of Nonverbal Behavior* 44 (2020): 215–232; Toscano et al., "Eye Gaze and Head Posture Jointly Influence Judgments of Dominance, Physical Strength, and Anger"; R. Lawson, "I Just Love the Attention: Implicit Preference for Direct Eye Contact," *Visual Cognition* 23 (2015): 450–488; D. Tang and B. Schmeichel, "Look Me in the Eye: Manipulated Eye Gaze Affects Dominance Mindsets," *Journal of Nonverbal Behavior* 39 (2015): 181–194; S. A. Beebe, "Eye Contact: A Nonverbal Determinant of Speaker Credibility," *Speech Teacher* 23 (1974): 21–25.

37. M. L. Knapp, J. A. Hall, and T. G. Horgan, *Nonverbal Communication in Human Interaction* 8e (Belmont, CA: Wadsworth/Cengage Learning, 2013).

38. S. C. Koch, C. G. Baehne, L. Kruse, F. Zimmermann, and J. Zumbach, "Visual Dominance and Visual Egalitarianism: Individual and Group-Level Influences of Sex and Status in Group Interactions," *Journal of Nonverbal Behavior* 34 (2010): 137–153; J. A. Hall, "Women's and Men's Nonverbal Communication: Similarities, Differences, Stereotypes, and Origins," in *The SAGE Handbook of Nonverbal Communication*, edited by V. Manusov and M. L. Patterson (Thousand Oaks, CA: Sage, 2006).

39. P. Ekman and W. Friesen, *Unmasking the Face* (Englewood Cliffs, NJ: Prentice Hall, 1975); R. L. Birdwhistell, "The Language of the Body: The Natural Environment of Words," in *Human Communication: Theoretical Explorations*, edited by A. Silverstein (New York: Wiley, 1974), 203–220.

40. C. Darwin, *Expression of Emotions in Man and Animals* (London, UK: Appleton; reprinted University of Chicago Press, 1965).

41. Keltner et al., "Emotional Expression"; A. Widmann, E. Schroger, and N. Wetzel, "Emotion Lies in the Eye of the Listener: Emotional Arousal to Novel Sounds Is Reflected in the Sympathetic Contribution to the Pupil Dilation Response and the P3," *Biological Psychology* 133 (2018): 10–17; V. L. Kinner, L. Kuchinke, A. M. Dierolf, C. J. Merz, T. Otto, and O. T. Wolf, "What Our Eyes Tell Us about Feelings: Tracking Pupillary Responses during Emotion Regulation Processes," *Psychophysiology* 54 (2017): 508–518; R. G. Lea, P. Qualter, S. K. Davis, J-C. Perez-Gonzalez, and M. Bangee, "Trait Emotional Intelligence and Attentional Bias for Positive Emotion: An Eye Tracking Study," *Personality and Individual Differences* 128 (2018): 88–93; A. Campbell, J. E. Murray, L. Atkinson, and T. Ruffman, "Face Age and Eye Gaze Influence Older Adults' Emotion Recognition," *The Journals of Gerontology: Series B: Psychological Sciences and Social Sciences* 72.4 (2017): 633–636; Z. Wang, M. Huifang, J. Yexin, and L. Fan, "Smile Big or Not? Effects of Smile Intensity on Perceptions of Warmth and Competence," *Journal of Consumer Research* 43 (2017): 787–805; U. Hess, K. Kafetsios, H. Mauersberger, C. Blaison, and C. L. Kessler, "Signal and Noise in the Perception of Facial Emotion Expressions: From Labs to Life," *Personality and Social Psychology Bulletin* 42 (2016): 1092–1110.

42. Z. H. Gong and E. P. Bucy, "When Style Obscures Substance: Visual Attention to Display Appropriateness in the 2012 Presidential Debates," *Communication Monographs* 83 (2016): 349–372; C. M. Hurley and M. G. Frank, "Executing Facial Control During Deception Situations," *Journal of Nonverbal Behavior* 35 (2011): 119–131; M. Mendolia, "Explicit Use of Categorical and Dimensional Strategies to Decode Facial Expressions of Emotion," *Journal of Nonverbal Behavior* 31 (2007): 57–75; A. P. Atkinson, J. Tipples, D. M. Burt, and A. W. Young, "Asymmetric Interference Between Sex and Emotion in Face Perception," *Perception and Psychophysics* 67 (2005): 1199–1213.

43. P. Collett, "The Seven Faces of Donald Trump—a Psychologist's View," *The Guardian*, January 15, 2017. www.theguardian.com (accessed March 11, 2017).

44. Ekman and Friesen, *Unmasking the Face*.

45. D. Shichuran, T. Yong, and A. M. Martinez, "Compound Facial Expressions of Emotion," *Proceedings of the National Academy of Sciences* 111 (2014): 1454–1462.

46. P. M. Cole, "Children's Spontaneous Control of Facial Expression," *Child Development* 57 (1986): 1309–1321.

47. Y. L. A. Kwok, J. Gralton, and M-L. McLaws, "Face Touching: A Frequent Habit That Has Implications for Hand Hygiene," *American Journal of Infection Control* 43 (2015): 112–114; C. Stieg, "Why You Can't Stop Touching Your Face, According to Science and Psychology," *CNBC Make It Health and Wellness*, March 20, 2020. https://www.cnbc.com/2020/03/20/why-you-touch-your-face-so-much-and-how-to-stop (accessed May 14, 2020).

48. B. K. Jakubiak and B. C. Feeney, "Hand-in-Hand Combat: Affectionate Touch Promotes Relational Well-Being and Buffers Stress during Conflict," *Personality and Social Psychology Bulletin* 45.3 (2019): 431–446; M. A. Fabello, "Touch Too Much," *Bitch* (Winter 2019): 31–33; C. J. Cascio, D. Moore, and F. McGlone, "Social Touch and Human Development," *Developmental Cognitive Neuroscience* 35 (2018): 5–11; B. K. Jakubiak and B. C. Feeney, "Affectionate Touch to Promote Relational, Psychological, and Physical Well-Being in Adulthood: A Theoretical Research Model and Review of the Research," *Personality and Social Psychology Review* 21.3 (2017): 228–252; K. Floyd, *The Loneliness Cure: Six Strategies for Finding Real Connections in Your Life* (Fort Collins, CO: Adams Media, 2016).

49. K. Floyd and C. Hesse, "Affection Deprivation Is Conceptually and Empirically Distinct from Loneliness," *Western Journal of Communication* 81.4 (2017): 446–465; C. Hesse and A. C. Mikkelson, "Affection Deprivation in Romantic Relationships," *Communication Quarterly* 65 (2017): 20–38; K. Floyd, "Affection Deprivation Is Associated with Physical Pain and Poor Sleep Quality," *Communication Studies* 67 (2016): 379–398.

50. Ivy and Wahl, *Nonverbal Communication for a Lifetime*.

51. D. H. Mansson, F. Marko, K. Bachrata, Z. Daniskova, J. Gajdosikova Zeleiova, V. Janis, and A. S. Sharov, "Young Adults' Trait Affection Given and Received as Functions of Hofstede's Dimensions of Cultures and National Origin," *Journal of Intercultural Communication Research* 45 (2016): 404–418; Andersen, "Tactile Traditions."

52. Matsumoto and Hwang, "Cultural Influences on Nonverbal Behavior"; R. DiBiase and J. Gunnoe, "Gender and Culture Differences in Touching Behavior," *Journal of Social Psychology* 144 (2004): 49–62; E. T. Hall, *The Hidden Dimension* (Garden City, NY: Anchor, 1990); E. T. Hall, *Beyond Culture* (New York: Doubleday, 1981); M. S. Remland, T. S. Jones, and H. Brinkman, "Interpersonal Distance, Body Orientation and Touch: Effect of Culture, Gender, and Age," *Journal of Social Psychology* 135 (1995): 281–295.

53. M. H. Burleson, N. A. Roberts, D. W. Coon, and J. A. Soto, "Perceived Cultural Acceptability and Comfort with Affectionate Touch: Differences between Mexican Americans and European Americans," *Journal of Social and Personal Relationships* 36.3 (2019): 1000–1022.

54. N. S. Eckland, T. M. Leyro, W. Berry Mendes, and R. J. Thompson, "The Role of Physiology and Voice in Emotion Perception During Social Stress," *Journal of Nonverbal Behavior* 43 (2019): 493–511; P. Sorokowski, D. Puts, J. Johnson, O. Zolkiewicz, A. Oleszkiewicz, A. Sorokowska, M. Kowal, B. Borkowska, and K. Pisanski, "Voice of Authority: Professionals Lower Their Vocal Frequencies When Giving Expert Advice," *Journal of Nonverbal Behavior* 43 (2019): 257–269; A. DeWaele, A-S. Claeys, V. Cauberghe, and G. Fannes, "Spokespersons' Nonverbal Behavior in Times of Crisis: The Relative Importance of Visual and Vocal Cues," *Journal of Nonverbal Behavior* 42 (2018): 441–460; M. Morningstar, M. A. Dirks, and S. Huang, "Vocal Cues Underlying Youth and Adult Portrayals of Socio-Emotional Expressions," *Journal of Nonverbal Behavior* 41 (2017): 1–29; V. Hughes, S. Wood, and P. Foulkes, "Strength of Forensic Voice Comparison Evidence from the Acoustics of Filled Pauses," *International Journal of Speech, Language & the Law* 23 (2016): 99–132; M. G. Frank, A. Maroulis, and D. J. Griffin, "The Voice," in *Nonverbal Communication: Science and Application*, edited by D. Matsumoto, M. G. Frank, and H. S. Hwang (Thousand Oaks, CA: Sage, 2013), 53–74; M. Imhof, "Listening to Voices and Judging People," *International*

Journal of Listening 24 (2010): 19–33; A. Karpf, *The Human Voice: How This Extraordinary Instrument Reveals Essential Clues about Who We Are* (New York: Bloomsbury, 2006).

55. Y. Tian, T. Maruyama, and J. Ginzburg, "Self Addressed Questions and Filled Pauses: A Cross-Linguistic Investigation," *Journal of Psycholinguistic Research* 46 (2017): 905–922; A. M. Goberman, S. Hughes, and T. Haydock, "Acoustic Characteristics of Public Speaking: Anxiety and Practice Effects," *Speech Communication* 53 (2011): 867–876; F. Roberts, A. L. Francis, and M. Morgan, "The Interaction of Inter-Turn Silence with Prosodic Cues in Listener Perceptions of 'Trouble' in Conversation," *Speech Communication* 48 (2006): 1079–1093; T. DeGroot and S. J. Motowidlo, "Why Visual and Vocal Interview Cues Can Affect Interviewers' Judgments and Predict Job Performance," *Journal of Applied Psychology* 84 (1999): 986–993; N. Christenfeld, "Does It Hurt to Say Um?" *Journal of Nonverbal Behavior* 19 (1995): 171–186.

56. M. Zuckerman and V. Sinicropi, "When Physical and Vocal Attractiveness Differ: Effects on Favorability of Interpersonal Impressions," *Journal of Nonverbal Behavior* 35 (2011): 75–86.

57. L. Zimman, "Transgender Voices: Insights on Identity, Embodiment, and the Gender of the Voice," *Language and Linguistics Compass* (2018): https://doi.org/10.1111/lnc3.12284.

58. A. Ziegler, T. Henke, J. Wiedrick, and L. B. Helou, "Effectiveness of Testosterone Therapy for Masculinizing Voice in Transgender Patients: A Meta-Analytic Review," *International Journal of Transgenderism* 19 (2018): 25–45; A. B. Hancock, K. D. Childs, and M. S. Irwig, "Trans Male Voice in the First Year of Testosterone Therapy: Make No Assumptions," *Journal of Speech, Language, and Hearing Research* 60 (2017): 2472–2482; M. Mills, G. Stoneham, and I. Georgiadou, "Expanding the Evidence: Developments and Innovations in Clinical Practice, Training and Competency within Voice and Communication Therapy for Trans and Gender Diverse People," *International Journal of Transgenderism* 18 (2017): 328–342; J. Meister, H. Kuhn, W. Shehata-Dieler, R. Hagen, and N. Kleinsasser, "Perceptual Analysis of the Male-to-Female Transgender Voice after Glottoplasty," *Laryngoscope* 127 (2017): 875–881; A. B. Hancock and G. Haskin, "Speech-Language Pathologists' Knowledge and Attitudes Regarding Lesbian, Gay, Bisexual, Transgender, and Queer (LGBTQ) Populations," *American Journal of Speech-Language Pathology* 24 (2015): 206–221; J. Sawyer, J. L. Perry, and A. Dobbins-Scaramelli, "A Survey of the Awareness of Speech Services Among Transgender and Transsexual Individuals and Speech-Language Pathologists," *International Journal of Transgenderism* 15 (2014): 146–163; L. Garabedian and A. Hancock, "Transgender Voice and Communication Treatment: A Retrospective Chart Review of 25 Cases," *International Journal of Language and Communication Disorders* 48 (2013): 54–65.

59. K. Strassler, "What We Lose When We Go from the Classroom to Zoom," May 4, 2020. https://nytimes.com/2020/05/04/sunday-review (accessed May 11, 2020); M. Tillman, "Best Zoom Backgrounds: Fun Virtual Backgrounds for Zoom Meetings," May 4, 2020. https://www.pocket-lint.com (accessed June 8, 2020); T. Maddox, "Photos: The 54 Coolest Virtual Backgrounds to Use in Zoom Meetings," April 15, 2020. https://222.techrepublic.com (accessed June 8, 2020).

60. E-M. Sohn and K-W. Lee, "The Effect of Chefs' Nonverbal Communication in Open Kitchens on Service Quality," *Journal of Foodservice Business Research* 21.5 (2018): 483–492; K. Erlandson, "Stay Out of My Space," *Journal of College & University Student Housing* 387 (2012): 46–61; M. Costa, "Territorial Behavior in Public Settings," *Environment & Behavior* 44 (2012): 713–721; T. Bringslimark, T. Hartig, and G. Grindal Patil, "Adaptation to Windowlessness: Do Office Workers Compensate for a Lack of Visual Access to the Outdoors?" *Environment & Behavior* 43 (2011): 469–487.

61. A. Soriano, M. W. Kozusznik, J. M. Peiro, and C. Mateo, "The Role of Employees' Work Patterns and Office Type Fit (and Misfit) in the Relationships between Employee Well-Being and Performance," *Environment & Behavior* 52.2 (2020): 111–138; T. Sugiyama, N. T. Hadgraft, G. N. Healy, N. Owen, and D. W. Dunstan, "Perceived Availability of Office Shared Spaces and Workplace Sitting: Moderation by Organizational Norms and Behavioral Autonomy," *Environment & Behavior* 51.7 (2019): 856–878; C. Bodin Danielsson and T. Theorell, "Office Employees' Perception of Workspace Contribution: A Gender and Office Design Perspective," *Environment & Behavior* 51.9-10 (2019): 995–1026; J. Kim and R. DeDear, "Workspace Satisfaction: The Privacy-Communication Trade-Off in Open-Plan Offices," *Journal of Environmental Psychology* (2013): 18–26; I. Vilnai-Yavetz, A. Rafaeli, and C. Schneider-Yaacov, "Instrumentality, Aesthetics, and Symbolism of Office Design," *Environment & Behavior* 37 (2005): 533–551; J. Sandberg, "Want to Know Someone's Job Status? Look at Desk Location," *Corpus Christi Caller Times* (March 2, 2003): D4.

62. H. Gang, L. Feng, S. Cheng, and S. Xiaochen, "Effect of Workplace Environment Cleanliness on Judgement of Counterproductive Work Behavior," *Social Behavior & Personality: An International Journal* 45 (2017): 599–604; S. Hadavi, "Direct and Indirect Effects of the Physical Aspects of the Environment on Mental Well-Being," *Environment & Behavior* 49 (2017): 1071–1104; C. C. Andrade, M. L. Lima, A. S. Devlin, and B. Hernandez, "Is It the Place or the People? Disentangling the Effects of Hospitals' Physical and Social Environments on Well-Being," *Environment & Behavior* 48 (2016): 299–323.

63. L. Scannel, M. Hodgson, J. G. M. Villarreal, and R. Gifford, "The Role of Acoustics in the Perceived Suitability of, and Well-Being in, Informal Learning Spaces," *Environment & Behavior* 48 (2026): 769–795; A. Joseph, Y.-S. Choi, and X. Quan, "Impact of Physical Environment of Residential Health, Care, and Support Facilities (RHCSF) on Staff and Residents: A Systematic Review of Literature," *Environment & Behavior* 48 (2016): 1203–1241; A. Fenko and C. Loock, "The Influence of Ambient Scent and Music on Patients' Anxiety in a Waiting Room of a Plastic Surgeon," *Health Environments Research & Design Journal* 7 (2014): 33–59.

64. P. Dev and L. Haynes, "Teacher Perspectives on Suitable Learning Environments for Students with Disabilities: What Have We Learned from Inclusive, Resource, and Self-Contained Classrooms?" *International Journal of Interdisciplinary Social Sciences: Annual Review* 9 (2015): 53–64; A. S. Sief, A. Pruski, and A. Bennia, "A New Approach for Handling Element Accessibility Problems Faced by Persons with a Wheelchair," *Journal of Automation, Mobile Robotics & Intelligent Systems* 10 (2016): 27–39; P. Monaghan, "Design for Disability Will Become the Norm," *The Chronicle Review* (February 12, 2010): B6–B7; T. R. Vandenbark, "Tending a Wild Garden: Library Web Design for Persons with Disabilities," *Information Technology & Libraries* 29 (2010): 23–29; D. K. White et al., "Are Features of the Neighborhood Environment Associated with Disability in Older Adults?" *Disabilities & Retention* 32 (2010): 639–645.

65. For more information on design for people with disabilities, see M. Andersen, "Ramped Up: Navigating Through Ableist Architecture," *Bitch* (Summer 2018): 20–21; R. Adams, "Bring Down the Barriers—Seen and Unseen," *The Chronicle of Higher Education* (November 11, 2011): A80; G. Pullin, *Design Meets Disability* (Cambridge, MA: MIT Press, 2011).

66. Matsumoto and Hwang, "Cultural Influences on Nonverbal Behavior"; M. Pearce and R. Woodford-Smith, "The (Dis)location of Time and Space: Trans-Cultural Collaborations in Tokyo," *Journal of Media Practice* 13 (2012): 197–213.

67. Hall, *The Hidden Dimension*; H. Overhill, "Apple Pie Proxemics: Edward T. Hall in the Kitchen Work Triangle," *Design Issues* 30 (2014): 67–82.

68. Farley, "Nonverbal Reactions to an Attractive Stranger"; S. Li and Y. Li, "How Far Is Far Enough? A Measure of Information Privacy in Terms of Interpersonal Distance," *Environment & Behavior* 39 (2007): 317–331; D. Matsumoto, "Culture and Nonverbal Behavior," in *The SAGE Handbook of Nonverbal Communication*, edited by V. Manusov and M. L. Patterson (Thousand Oaks, CA: Sage, 2006), 219–235; C. M. J. Beaulieu, "Intercultural Study of Personal Space: A Case Study," *Journal of Applied Social Psychology* 34 (2004): 794–805.

69. A. Schneeweis, "Power, Gender, and Ethnic Spaces," *Journal of Communication Inquiry* 40 (2016): 88–105; S. Canagarajah, "Agency and Power in Intercultural Communication: Negotiating English in Translocal Spaces," *Language & Intercultural Communication* 13 (2013): 202–224; T. T. Prabhu, "Proxemics: Some Challenges and Strategies in Nonverbal Communication," *IUP Journal of Soft Skills* 4 (2010): 7–14; L. Van Doorn, "Perception of Time and Space of (Formerly) Homeless People," *Journal of Human Behavior in the Social Environment* 20 (2010): 218–238; D. R. Carney, J. A. Hall, and L. Smith LeBeau, "Beliefs about the Nonverbal Expression of Social Power," *Journal of Nonverbal Behavior* 29 (2005): 105–123.

70. D. K. Ivy, *GenderSpeak: Communicating in a Gendered World* 6e (Dubuque, IA: Kendall Hunt); V. Santilli and A. N. Miller, "The Effects of Gender and Power Distance on Nonverbal Immediacy in Symmetrical and Asymmetrical Power Conditions: A Cross-Cultural Study of Classrooms and Friendships," *Journal of International and Intercultural Communication* 4 (2011): 3–22; M. Costa, "Interpersonal Distances in Group Walking," *Journal of Nonverbal Behavior* 34 (2010): 15–26; J. A. Hall, "Women's and Men's Nonverbal Communication: Similarities, Differences, Stereotypes, and Origins," in *The SAGE Handbook of Nonverbal Communication*, 201–218.

71. C. Roveri Marin, R. C. Gasparino, and A. C. Puggina, "The Perception of Territory and Personal Space Invasion Among Hospitalized Patients," *PloS One* 13.6 (2018): e0198989; L. Lewis, H. Patel, M. D'Cruz, and S. Cobb, "What Makes a Space Invader? Passenger Perceptions of Personal Space Invasion in Aircraft Travel," *Ergonomics* 60.11 (2017): 1461–1470; G. Brown and S. L. Robinson, "Reactions to Territorial Infringement," *Organization Science* 22 (2011): 210–224; S. M. Lyman and M. B. Scott, "Territoriality: A Neglected Sociological Dimension," in *The Nonverbal Communication Reader: Classic and Contemporary Reading* 2e, edited by L. K. Guerro, J. DeVito, and M. L. Hecht (Prospect Heights, IL: Waveland, 1999), 175–183.

72. M. L. Miller Henningsen, K. S. Valde, M. J. Entzminger, D. T. Dick, and L. B. Wilcher, "Student Disclosures about Academic Information: Student Privacy Rules and Boundaries," *Communication Reports* 32.1 (2019): 29–42; L. Baruh, E. Secinti, and Z. Cemalcilar, "Online Privacy Concerns and Privacy Management: A Meta-Analytical Review," *Journal of Communication* 67 (2017): 26–53; M. H. Millham and D. Atkin, "Managing the Virtual Boundaries: Online Social Networks, Disclosure, and Privacy Behaviors," *New Media & Society* 20 (2018): 50–67; C. Baraniuk, "Ghosts in the Machine," *New Scientist* 227 (2015): 38–41; Ivy and Wahl, *Nonverbal Communication for a Lifetime*; Knapp, Hall, and Horgan, *Nonverbal Communication in Human Interaction*.

73. Mehrabian, *Nonverbal Communication*.

74. For applications of Mehrabian's immediacy principle, see A. Bainbridge Frymier, Z. W. Goldman, and C. J. Claus, "Why Nonverbal Immediacy Matters: A Motivation Explanation," *Communication Quarterly* 67.5 (2019): 526–539; E. Meiners, "Instructor Verbal and Nonverbal Immediacy as Goal-Driven and Intuitive Processes," *Florida Communication Journal* 46.2 (2018): 33–49; L. Zhu and D. Anagondahalli, "Predicting Student Satisfaction: The Role of Academic Entitlement and Nonverbal Immediacy," *Communication Reports* 31.1 (2018): 41–52; M. D. Dixson, M. R. Greenwell, C. Rogers-Stacy, R. Weister, and S. Lauer, "Nonverbal Immediacy Behaviors and Online Student Engagement: Bringing Past Instructional Research into the Present Virtual Classroom," *Communication Education* 66 (2017): 37–53.

75. Argyle, *Bodily Communication*.

76. P. A. Andersen, *Nonverbal Communication: Forms and Functions* 2e (Long Grove, IL: Waveland, 2008): 168.

77. Lakens and Stel, "If They Move in Sync, They Must Feel in Sync"; Wilt, Funkhouser, and Revelle, "The Dynamic Relationships of Affective Synchrony to Perceptions of Situations"; K. McGinty, D. Knox, and M. E. Zusman, "Nonverbal and Verbal Communication in 'Involved' and 'Casual' Relationships among College Students," *College Student Journal* 37 (2003): 68–71; B. Le Poire, A. Duggan, C. Shepard, and J. Burgoon, "Relational Messages Associated with Nonverbal Involvement, Pleasantness, and Expressiveness in Romantic Couples," *Communication Research Reports* 19 (2002): 195–206.

78. Toscano et al., "Eye Gaze and Head Posture Jointly Influence Judgments of Dominance, Physical Strength, and Anger"; J. K. Burgoon and N. E. Dunbar, "Nonverbal Expressions of Dominance and Power in Human Relationships," in *The SAGE Handbook of Nonverbal Communication*, 279–297; D. R. Carney and L. Smith LeBeau, "Beliefs about the Nonverbal Expression of Social Power," *Journal of Nonverbal Behavior* 29 (2005): 105–123.

79. M. L. Knapp, W. Earnest, D. J. Griffin, and M. S. McGlone, *Lying and Deception in Human Interaction* 3e (Dubuque, IA: Kendall Hunt, 2020); J. Masip and N. Sanchez, "How People *Really* Suspect Lies: A Re-examination of Novotny et al.'s (2018) Data," *Journal of Nonverbal Behavior* 43 (2019): 481–492; E. P. Lloyd, K. M. Summers, K. Hugenberg, and A. R. McConnell, "Revisiting Perceiver and Target Gender Effects in Deception Detection," *Journal of Nonverbal Behavior* 42 (2018): 427–440; A. Vrij, "Nonverbal Communication and Deception," in *The SAGE Handbook of Nonverbal Communication*, 341–359.

80. Ivy and Wahl, *Nonverbal Communication for a Lifetime*; S. Mann, A. Vrij, S. Leal, P. A. Granhag, L. Warmelink, and D. Forrester, "Windows to the Soul? Deliberate Eye Contact as a Cue to Deceit," *Journal of Nonverbal Behavior* 36 (2013): 205–215; F. M. Marchak, "Detecting False Intent Using Eye Blink Measures," *Frontiers in Psychology* 4 (2013): doi:10.3389/fpsyg.2013.00736.

81. M. Boltz, R. Dyer, and A. Miller, "Are You Lying to Me? Temporal Cues for Deception," *Journal of Language and Social Psychology* 29 (2010): 458–466; L. Anolli and R. Ciceri, "The Voice of Deception: Vocal Strategies of Naive and Able Liars," *Journal of Nonverbal Behavior* 21 (1997): 259–284.

82. T. Mapala, L. Warmelink, & S. A. Linkenauger, "Jumping the Gun: Faster Response Latencies to Deceptive Questions in a Realistic Scenario," *Psychonomic Bulletin & Review* 24 (2017): 1350–1358.

83. Tian et al., "Self Addressed Questions and Filled Pauses"; V. Hughes, S. Wood, and P. Foulkes, "Strength of Forensic Voice Comparison Evidence from the Acoustics of Filled Pauses," *International Journal of Speech, Language and the Law* 23 (2016): 99–132.

84. J. K. Burgoon, R. Schuetzler, and D. W. Wilson, "Kinesic Patterning in Deceptive and Truthful Interactions," *Journal of Nonverbal Behavior* 39 (2015): 1–25.

85. J. Tierney, "At Airports, a Misplaced Faith in Body Language," *New York Times*, March 23, 2014. www.nytimes.com/2014 (accessed April 1, 2014); C. F. Bond, Jr., and B. M. DePaulo, "Accuracy of Deception Judgments," *Review of Personality and Social Psychology* 10 (2006): 214–234.

Chapter 5

1. A. K. Przybylski and N. Weinstein, "Can You Connect with Me Now? How the Presence of Mobile Communication Technology Influences Face-to-Face Conversation Quality," *Journal of Social and Personal Relationships* 30.3 (2012): 237–246. R. J. Allred and J. P. Crowley, "The 'Mere Presence' Hypothesis: Investigating the Nonverbal Effects of Cell-Phone Presence on Conversation Satisfaction," *Communication Studies* 68.1 (2017): 1–21.

2. G. Bodie, M. E. Pence, M. Rold, M. D. Chapman, J. Lejune, and L. Anzalone, "Listening Competence in Initial Interactions II: Applying Trait Centrality to Discover the Relative Placement of Listening Competence Among Implicit Competency Theories," *Communication Studies* 66.5 (2015): 528–548.

3. For additional support for the importance of listening in interpersonal relationships, see L. Sparks, S. S. Travis, and S. R. Thompson, "Listening for the Communication Signals of Humor, Narratives, and Self-Disclosure in the Family Caregiver Interview," *Health & Social Work* 30.4 (2005): 340–343; S. Wright, "The Beauty of Silence: Deep Listening Is a Key Nursing Skill That Can Be Learned with Practice," *Nursing Standard* 20.50

(2006): 18–20; M. R. Jalongo, "Listening in Early Childhood: An Interdisciplinary Review of the Literature," *International Journal of Listening* 24.1 (2010): 1–18.

4. R. Emanuel, J. Adams, K. Baker, E. K. Daufin, C. Ellington, F. Fits, J. Himsel, L. Holladay, and D. Okeowo, "How College Students Spend Their Time Communicating," *International Journal of Listening* 22 (2008): 13–28; also see L. Barker et al., "An Investigation of Proportional Time Spent in Various Communication Activities for College Students," *Journal of Applied Communication Research* 8 (1981): 101–109; also see K. Dindia and B. L. Kennedy, "Communication in Everyday Life: A Descriptive Study Using Mobile Electronic Data Collection," paper presented at the annual meeting of the National Communication Association, Chicago (November 2004); L. A. Janusik and A. D. Wolvin, "24 Hours in a Day: A Listening Update to the Time Studies," *The International Journal of Listening* 23 (2009): 104–120; L. Cooper and T. Buchanan, "Listening Competency on Campus: A Psychometric Analysis of Student Learning," *The International Journal of Listening* 24 (2010): 141–163.

5. For an excellent review of listening research, see M. L. Beall, J. Gill-Rosier, J. Tate, and A. Matten, "State of the Context: Listening in Education," *International Journal of Listening* 22 (2008): 123–132; also see A. D. Wolvin, "Listening Engagement: Intersecting Theoretical Perspectives," in *Listening and Human Communication in the 21st Century*, edited by A. D. Wolvin (Oxford, UK: Wiley-Blackwell, 2010): 7–30; also see Janusik and Wolvin, "24 Hours in a Day."

6. For a review of the literature documenting what researchers have found about approximate time spent communicating over the years dating back to 1926 see Janusik and Wolvin, "24 Hours in a Day."

7. One study found that only 5 percent of colleges and universities offered a course in listening. See K. G. Wacker and K. Hawkins, "Curricula Comparison for Classes in Listening," *International Journal of Listening* 9 (1995): 14–28.

8. J. Hackenbracht and K. Gasper, "I'm All Ears: The Need to Belong Motivates Listening to Emotional Disclosure," *Journal of Experimental Social Psychology* 49 (2013): 915–921; G. S. Bodie, C. C. Gearhart, J. P. Denham, and A. J. Vickery, "The Temporal Stability and Situational Contingency of Active-Empathic Listening," *Western Journal of Communication* 77.2 (2013): 113–138.

9. For a provocative discussion of the role of empathy and compassion in our interactions with others, see P. Bloom, *Against Empathy: The Case for Rational Compassion* (New York: ECCO/HarperCollins, 2016).

10. K. L. Geiman and J. O. Greene, "Listening and Experiences of Interpersonal Transcendence," *Communication Studies* 70 (2019): 114–128.

11. K. Wright, "Similarity, Network Convergence, and Availability of Emotional Support as Predictors of Strong-Tie/Weak-Tie Support Network Preference on Facebook," *Southern Communication Journal* 77.5 (2012): 389–402; M. Scott and S. Sale, "Consumers Use Smartphones for 195 Minutes Per Day, But Spend Only 25% of That Time on Communications," *Analysys Mason* (May 2014), www.analysysmason.com/About-Us/News/Insight/consumers-smartphone-usag

12. C. Jacobs and D. Coghlan, "Sound of Silence: On Listening in Organizational Learning," *Human Relations* 58.1 (2005):115–138.

13. P. Skaldeman, "Converging or Diverging Views of Self and Other: Judgment of Relationship Quality in Married and Divorced Couples," *Journal of Divorce & Remarriage* 44 (2006): 145–160.

14. K. Savitsky, B. Keysar, N. Epley, T. Carter, and A. Swanson, "The Closeness-Communication Bias: Increasing Egocentrism Among Friends Versus Strangers," *Journal of Experimental Social Psychology* 47 (2011): 269–273.

15. Andre Maurois, *Memoris 1885-1967* (London: Bodley Head, 1970): 218.

16. For a review of the role of listening in business contexts, see J. Flynn, T. R. Valikoski, and J. Grau, "Listening in the Business Context: Reviewing the State of Research," *International Journal of Listening* 22 (2008): 141–151.

17. For a review of literature documenting the importance of listening in the health professions, see D. L. Roter and J. A. Hall, *Doctors Talking with Patients/Patients Talking with Doctors: Improving Communication in Medical Visits* (Westport, CT: Praeger, 2006); J. Davis, C. R. Thompson, A. Foley, C. D. Bond, and J. DeWitt, "An Examination of Listening Concepts in the Healthcare Context: Differences Among Nurses, Physicians, and Administrators," *International Journal of Listening* 22 (2008): 152–167.

18. K. Kristensson, I. J. Jonsdottir, and S. K. Snorrason, "Employees' Perceptions of Supervisors' Listening Skills and Their Work-Related Quality of Life," *Communication Reports* 32 (2019): 137–147.

19. S. K. Maben and C. C. Gearhart, "Organizational Social Media Accounts: Moving Toward Listening Competency," *International Journal of Listening* 32 (2019): 101–114.

20. T. Brown, M. Yu, and J. Etherington, "Are Listening and Interpersonal Communication Skills Predictive of Professionalism in Undergraduate Occupational Therapy Students?" *Health Professions Education* 30 (2020): 1–14; J. Brownell, "Perceptions of Effective Listeners: A Management Study," *Journal of Business Communication* 27 (1990): 401–415; D. A. Romig, *Side by Side Leadership* (Austin, TX: Bard, 2001).

21. "Robert Caro on the Fall of New York and Glenn Close on Complicated Characters," New Yorker Radio Hour, WNYC (May 4, 2018), as reported by K. Murphy, *You're Not Listening: What You're Missing and Why It Matters* (New York: Celadon, 2019): 124.

22. K. W. Hawkins and B. P. Fullion, "Perceived Communication Skill Needs for Work Groups," *Communication Research Reports* 16 (1999): 167–174.

23. J. Burnside-Lawry, "Listening and Participatory Communication: A Model to Assess Organizational Listening Competency," *The International Journal of Listening* 26 (2012): 102–121; C. Jacobs and D. Coghlan, "Sound of Silence."

24. K. R. Meyer and S. K. Hunt, "The Lost Art of Lecturing: Cultivating Student Listening and Notetaking," *Communication Education* 66 (2017): 239–241.

25. R. Bommelje, J. M. Houston, and R. Smither, "Personality Characteristics of Effective Listeners: A Five Factor Perspective," *International Journal of Listening* 17 (2003): 32–46.

26. M. S. Conaway, "Listening: Learning Tool and Retention Agent," in *Improving Reading and Study Skills*, edited by A. S. Algier and K. W. Algier (San Francisco: Jossey-Bass, 1996), 51–63.

27. Y. Liu, E. A. Piazza, E. Simony, P. A. Sherwokis, B. Onaral, U. Hasson, and H. Ayaz, "Measuring Speaker-Listener Neural Coupling with Functional Near Infrared Spectroscopy," *Scientific Reports* 7 (2017): https://www.nature.com/articles/srep43293?ncid=txtlnkusaolp00000618 (accessed April 21, 2020); also see V. Aryadoust, L. Y. Ng, S. Foo, and G. Esposito, "A Neurocognitive Investigation of Test Methods and Gender Effects in Listening Assessment," *Computer Assisted Language Learning* (2020): https://doi.org/10.1080/09588221.20201744667 (accessed May 8, 2020).

28. For a review of how listening is discussed in public speaking textbooks, see W. C. Adams and E. S. Cox, "The Teaching of Listening as an Integral Part of an Oral Activity: An Examination of Public-Speaking Texts," *International Journal of Listening* 24.2 (2010): 89–105.

29. Adapted from the International Listening Association's definition of *listening*, which may be found on its website, www.listen.org; for a theoretical explanation of the attending listening process, see L. A. Janusik, "Building Listening Theory: The Validation of the Conversational Listening Span," *Communication Studies* 5.2 (June 2007): 139–156; see also G. D. Bodie, K. St. Cyr, M. Pence, M. Rold, and J. Honeycutt, "Listening Competence in Initial Interactions I: Distinguishing between What Listening Is and What Listeners Do," *The International Journal of Listening* 26 (2012): 1–28; also see D. L. Worthington and G. D. Bodie (eds.)

The Sourcebook of Listening Research: Methodology and Measures (Hoboken, NJ: John Wiley & Sons, 2018).

30. S. C. Bentley, "Listening in the 21st Century," *International Journal of Listening* 14 (2000): 129–142; also see A. D. Wolvin and C. G. Coakley, "Listening Education in the 21st Century," *International Journal of Listening* 14 (2001): 143–152. For an excellent literature review of definitions and perspectives on defining listening, see S. Bentley, "Benchmarking Listening Behaviors: Is Effective Listening What the Speaker Says It Is?" *International Journal of Listening* 11.1 (2008): 51–68.

31. A. McSpadden, "You Now Have a Shorter Attention Span Than a Goldfish," *Time*, May 14, 2015. https://time.com/3858309/attention-spans-goldfish/ (accessed May 30, 2020).

32. D. Mount and A. Mattila, "Last Chance to Listen: Listening Behaviors and Their Effect on Call Center Satisfaction," *Journal of Hospitality & Tourism Research* 26.2 (2002): 124–137.

33. A. Mulanx and W. G. Powers, "Listening Fidelity Development and Relationship to Receiver Apprehension and Locus of Control," *International Journal of Listening* 17 (2003): 69–78.

34. W. L. Randall, S. M. Prior, and M. Skarborn, "How Listeners Shape What Tellers Tell: Patterns of Interaction in Lifestory Interviews and Their Impact on Reminiscence by Elderly Interviewees," *Journal of Aging Studies* 20.4 (2006): 381–396.

35. K. W. Watson, L. L. Barker, and J. B. Weaver, *The Listener Style Inventory* (New Orleans: Spectra, 1995); D. Worthington, G. D. Bodie, and C. Gearhart, "The Listening Styles Profile Revised (LSP-R): A Scale Revision and Validation," paper presented at the annual meeting of the Eastern Communication Association, Arlington, VA (April 2011); G. D. Bodie and D. L. Worthington, "Revisiting the Listening Styles Profile (LSP-16): A Confirmatory Factor Analytic Approach to Scale Validation and Reliability Estimation," *International Journal of Listening* 24.2 (2010): 69–88; G. D. Bodie, C. C. Gearhart, and D. L. Worthington, "The Listening Styles Profile-Revised (LSP-R): A Scale Revision and Evidence for Validity," *Communication Quarterly* 61.1 (2014): 72–90; G. D. Bodie, J. P. Denham, and C. C. Gearhart, "Listening as a Goal-Directed Activity," *Western Journal of Communication* 78.5 (2014): 668–684; also see D. L. Worthington and G. D. Bodie (eds.) *The Sourcebook of Listening Research.*

36. Bodie, Denham, and Gearhart, "Listening as a Goal-Directed Activity"; G. D. Bodie, C. C. Gearhart, J. P. Denham, and A. J. Vickery, "The Temporal Stability and Situational Contingency of Active-Empathetic Listening," *Western Journal of Communication* 77:2 (2013): 113–138.

37. D. L. Worthington, "Exploring the Relationship between Listening Style Preference and Personality," *International Journal of Listening* 17 (2003): 68–87; D. L. Worthington, "Exploring Juror's Listening Processes: The Effect of Listening Style Preference on Juror Decision Making," *International Journal of Listening* 17 (2003): 20–37.

38. Worthington, "Exploring Juror's Listening Processes"; L. R. Salazar, "The Influence of Business Students' Listening Styles on Their Compassion and Self-Compassion," *Business and Professional Communication Quarterly* 80 (2017): 426–442; M. J. Diaz-Valentin, M. Garriod-Abejar, R. M. Fuentes-Chancon, M. D. Serrano-Parra, M. E. Larranaga-Rubia, and S. Yubero-Jimenez, "Influencia del Estilo de Escucha Sobre la Capacidad Empática en Estudiantes de Enfermería," *Metas Enferm* 22 (2019): 21–26.

39. Worthington, "Exploring Juror's Listening Processes."

40. Worthington, "Exploring Juror's Listening Processes."

41. J. B. Weaver III and M. Kirtley, "Listening Styles and Empathy," *Southern Communication Journal* 2 (1995): 131–141.

42. Bodie, Denham, and Gearhart, "Listening as a Goal-Directed Activity."

43. K. Thompson, P. Leintz, B. Nevers, and S. Witkowski, "The Integrative Listening Model: An Approach to Teaching and Learning Listening," *The Journal of General Education* 53 (2004): 225–246; also see F. Ferrari-Bridgers, R. Vogel, and B. Lynch, "Fostering and Assessing Critical Listening Skills in the Speech Course," *International Journal of Listening* 32 (2017): 19–32.

44. S. L. Sargent and J. B. Weaver, "Correlates between Communication Apprehension and Listening Style Preferences," *Communication Research Reports* 14 (1997): 74–78.

45. M. K. Johnston, J. B. Weaver, K. W. Watson, and L. L. Barker, "Listening Styles: Biological or Psychological Differences?" *International Journal of Listening* 14 (2000): 14–31.

46. See C. Kiewitz, J. B. Weaver III, B. Brosius, and G. Weimann, "Cultural Differences in Listening Style Preferences: A Comparison of Young Adults in Germany, Israel, and the United States," *International Journal of Public Opinion Research* 9 (1997): 233–248; N. Dragon and J. C. Sherblom, "The Influence of Cultural Individualism and Collectivism on U.S. and Post Soviet Listening Styles," *Human Communication* 11 (2008): 177–192.

47. L. L. Barker and K. W. Watson, *Listen Up* (New York: St. Martin's Press, 2000); also see M. Imhof, "Who Are We as We Listen? Individual Listening Profiles in Varying Contexts," *International Journal of Listening* 18 (2004): 36–45. Although Barker and Watson use different labels for listening styles than the current discussion, their results are applicable.

48. Imhof, "Who Are We as We Listen?"

49. Bodie, Denham, and Gearhart, "Listening as a Goal-Directed Activity."

50. G. Itzchakov, D. R. Castro, and A. N. Kluger, "If You Want People to Listen to You, Tell a Story," *The International Journal of Listening* 30 (2016): 120–133.

51. W. Winter, A. J. Ferreira, and N. Bowers, "Decision-Making in Married and Unrelated Couples," *Family Process* 12 (1973): 83–94.

52. R. Montgomery, *Listening Made Easy* (New York: Amacom, 1981); also see O. Hargie, C. Sanders, and D. Dickson, *Social Skills in Interpersonal Communication* (London, UK: Routledge, 1994); *The Handbook of Communication Skills,* edited by O. Hargie (London, UK: Routledge, 1997).

53. R. G. Owens, "Handling Strong Emotions," in *The Handbook of Communication Skills*, edited by O. Hargie (London: Croom Helm/New York University Press, 1986).

54. J. L. Gonzalez-Balado (ed.), *Mother Teresa: In My Own Words* (New York: Gramercy Books, 1997).

55. K. Murphy, *You're Not Listening: What You're Missing and Why It Matters* (New York: Celadon, 2019): 22.

56. R. G. Nichols, "Factors in Listening Comprehension," *Speech Monographs* 15 (1948): 154–163; G. M. Goldhaber and C. H. Weaver, "Listener Comprehension of Compressed Speech When the Difficulty, Rate of Presentation, and Sex of the Listener Are Varied," *Speech Monographs* 35 (1968): 20–25.

57. M. Fitch-Hauser, D. A. Barker, and A. Hughes, "Receiver Apprehension and Listening Comprehension: A Linear or Curvilinear Relationship?" *Southern Communication Journal* 56 (1988): 62–71; P. E. King and R. R. Behnke, "Patterns of State Anxiety in Listening Performance," *Southern Communication Journal* 70.1 (2004): 72–81.

58. Fitch-Hauser et al., "Receiver Apprehension and Listening Comprehension."

59. C. R. Sawyer, K. Gayle, A. Topa, and W. Powers, "Listening Fidelity Among Native and Nonnative English-Speaking Undergraduates as a Function of Listening Apprehension and Gender," *Communication Research Reports* 31 (2014): 62–71.

60. Fitch-Hauser et al., "Receiver Apprehension and Listening Comprehension."

61. For a review of the literature on gender, listening, and communication, see D. K. Ivy, *GenderSpeak: Communicating in a Gendered World* 6e (Dubuque, IA: Kendall Hunt, 2020); also see C. Leaper, "Young Adults' Conversational Strategies during Negotiation and Self-Disclosure in Same-Gender and Mixed-Gender Friendships," *Sex Roles* 81 (2019): 561–575.

62. B. R. Burleson, L. K. Hanasono, G. D. Bodie, A. J. Holmstrom, J. D. McCullough, J. J. Rack, and J. Gill Rosier, "Are Gender Differences in Responses to Supportive Communication a Matter of Ability, Motivation, or Both? Reading Patterns of Situation

Effects Through the Lens of a Dual-Process Theory," *Communication Quarterly* 59 (2011): 37–60.
63. Sargent and Weaver, "Correlates between Communication Apprehension and Listening Style Preferences."
64. J. Silverman, "Attentional Styles and the Study of Sex Differences," in *Attention: Contemporary Theory and Analysis*, edited by D. I. Mostofsky (New York: Appleton-Century-Crofts, 1970): 61–79.
65. K. Watson, L. Barker, and J. Weaver, "The Listening Styles Profile (LPP16): Development and Validation of an Instrument to Assess Four Listening Styles," *Journal of International Listening Association* (1995), research cited on *20/20*, ABC television network, September 1998.
66. J. O. Yum, "The Impact of Confucianism on Interpersonal Relationships and Communication Patterns in East Asia," *Communication Monographs* 55 (1988): 374–388.
67. T. S. Lebra, *Japanese Patterns of Behavior* (Honolulu: University Press of Hawaii, 1976).
68. For a discussion of the type of listening training that enhances listening skill of non-native speaking individuals see S. Roussel, R. Gruson, and J. P. Galan, "What Types of Training Improve Learners' Performances in Second Language Listening Comprehension?" *The International Journal of Listening* 33 (2019): 39–52.
69. Imhof, "Who Are We as We Listen?"
70. Bodie et al., "Listening Competence in Initial Interactions I."
71. Bodie et al., "Listening Competence in Initial Interactions I."
72. A. Carruthers, "Listening, Hearing and Changing," *Business Communication* 5 (2004): 3; for a discussion of strategies and perspectives for managing internal listening barriers see L. Lipari, *Listening, Thinking, Being: Toward an Ethics of Attunement* (University Park, PA: The Pennsylvania State University Press, 2010).
73. For excellent recommendations about how to enhance mindfulness skill see J. Kabat-Zinn, *Meditation Is Not What You Think: Mindfulness and Why It Is so Important* (New York: Hachette, 2018); J. Kabat-Zinn, *Falling Awake: How to Practice Mindfulness in Everyday Life* (New York: Hachette, 2018).
74. There is evidence that we sometimes use cognitive strategies about which we are not always aware to help us when listening. For more information, see L. Janusik and S. A. Keaton, "Toward Developing a Cross-Cultural Metacognition Instrument for Listening in First Language (L^1) Contexts: The (Janusik–Keaton) Metacognitive Listening Instrument," *Journal of Intercultural Communication Research* 44:4 (2015): 288–306.
75. K. K. Halone and L. L. Pecchioni, "Relational Listening: A Grounded Theoretical Model," *Communication Reports* 14 (2001): 59–71.
76. Kabat-Zinn, *Meditation Is Not What You Think*; Kabat-Zinn, *Falling Awake*.
77. M. V. Redmond, "The Functions of Empathy (Decentering) in Human Relations," *Human Relations* 42 (1993): 593–606.
78. A. Mehrabian, *Nonverbal Communication* (Chicago: Aldine Atherton, 1970); A. Mehrabian, *Silent Messages* (Belmont, CA: Wadsworth, 1981); also see D. Lapakko, "Three Cheers for Language: A Closer Examination of a Widely Cited Study of Nonverbal Communication," *Communication Education* 46 (1997): 63–67.
79. M. Imhof, "Listening to Voices and Judging People," *International Journal of Listening* 24.1 (2010): 19–33.
80. H. J. Ferguson and R. Breheny, "Listeners' Eyes Reveal Spontaneous Sensitivity to Others' Perspectives," *Journal of Experimental Social Psychology* 48 (2012): 257–263.
81. M. Argyle and M. Cook, *Gaze and Mutual Gaze* (Cambridge, UK: Cambridge University Press, 1976).
82. Hargie et al., *Social Skills in Interpersonal Communication*; Hargie, *The Handbook of Communication Skills*.
83. For an excellent review of listening skills and research supporting listening skill development, see J. Brownell, "The Skills of Listening-Centered Communication," in *Listening and Human Communication in the 21st Century*, edited by A. D. Wolvin (Oxford, UK: Wiley-Blackwell, 2010): 141–157.
84. Gearhart, Denham, and Bodie, "Listening as a Goal-Directed Activity."
85. A. D. Wolvin and S. D. Cohen, "An Inventory of Listening Competency Dimensions," *The International Journal of Listening* 26 (2012): 64–66.
86. F. Ferrari-Bridgers, R. Vogel and B. Lynch, "Fostering and Assessing Critical Listening Skills in the Speech Course," *International Journal of Listening* 32 (2017): 19–32; F. Ferrari-Bridgers, K. Stroumbakis, M. Drini, B. Lynch, and R. Vogel, "Assessing Critical-Analytical Listening Skills in Math and Engineering Students: An Exploratory Inquiry of How Analytical Listening Skills Can Positively Impact Learning," *International Journal of Listening* 31 (2017): 121–141.
87. For a review of literature about measuring empathy, see G. D. Bodie, "The Active Empathic Listening Scale."
88. See R. G. Nichols and L. A. Stevens, "Listening to People," *Harvard Business Review* 35 (September–October 1957): 85–92.
89. W. T. Mickelson and S. A. Welch, "A Listening Competence Comparison of Working Professionals," *International Journal of Listening* 27.2 (2013): 85–99.
90. D. Perkova, "Beyond Silence: A Cross-Cultural Comparison between Finnish 'Quietude' and Japanese 'Tranquility,'" *Eastern Academic Journal* 4 (2015); 1–14; also see research summary in K. Murphy, *You're Not Listening*.
91. K. McComb and F. M. Jablin, "Verbal Correlates of Interviewer Empathic Listening and Employment Interview Outcomes," *Communication Monographs* 51 (1984): 353–371.
92. A. Clark, "Communication Confidence and Listening Competence: An Investigation of the Relationships of Willingness to Communicate, Communication Apprehension, and Receiver Apprehension to Comprehension of Content and Emotional Meaning in Spoken Messages," *Communication Education* 38 (1989): 237–248.
93. J. T. Kaplan, S. I. Gimbel, and S. Harris, "Neural Correlates of Maintaining One's Political Beliefs in the Face of Counterevidence," *Scientific Reports* 6 (2016), https://doi.org/10.1038/step39589; also see K. Murphy, *You're Not Listening*, 47–48.
94. Halone and Pecchioni, "Relational Listening"; J. Vickery, S. A. Keaton, and G. D. Bodie, "Intrapersonal Communication and Listening Goals: An Examination of Attributes and Functions of Imagined Interactions and Active-Empathic Listening Behaviors," *Western Communication Journal* 80.1 (2015): 20–38.
95. Pearce et al., "Assessment of the Listening Styles Inventory."
96. Pearce et al., "Assessment of the Listening Styles Inventory."
97. G. D. Bodie, "The Nature of Supportive Listening II: The Role of Verbal Person Centeredness and Nonverbal Immediacy," *Western Journal of Communication* 76 (2012): 250–269.
98. S. K. Maben and C. C. Gearhart, "Organizational Social Media Accounts: Moving Toward Listening Competency," *International Journal of Listening* 32 (2019): 101–114; see also Bodie et al., "Listening Competence in Initial Interactions I."
99. Bodie et al., "Listening Competence in Initial Interactions I."
100. A. L. B. Eggenberger, "Active Listening Skills as Predictors of Success in Community College Students," *Community College Journal of Research and Practice* 10 (2019): 1–10.
101. E. A. Doohan, "Listening Behaviors of Married Couples: An Exploration of Nonverbal Presentation to a Relational Insider," *International Journal of Listening* 21 (2007): 24–41.
102. W. R. Miller, K. E. Hedrick, and D. R. Orlofsky, "The Helpful Responses Questionnaire: A Procedure for Measuring Therapeutic Empathy," *Journal of Clinical Psychology* 47 (1991): 444–448; A. Paukert, B. Stagner, and K. Hope, "The Assessment of Active Listening Skills in Helpline Volunteers," *Stress, Trauma, and Crisis* 7 (2004): 61–76; D. H. Levitt, "Active Listening and Counselor Self-Efficacy: Emphasis on One Micro-Skill in Beginning

Counselor Training," *Clinical Supervisor* 20 (2001): 101–115; V. B. Van Hasselt, M. T. Baker, S. J. Romano, K. M. Schlessinger, M. Zuker, R. Dragone, and A. L. Perera, "Crisis (Hostage) Negotiation Training: A Preliminary Evaluation of Program Efficacy," *Criminal Justice and Behavior* 33 (2006): 56–69; H. Weger Jr., G. R. Castle, and M. C. Emmett, "Active Listening in Peer Interviews: The Influence on Perceptions of Listening Skill," *International Journal of Listening* 24 (2010): 34–49.

103. G. Bodie, A. J. Vickery, and K. Cannava, "Supportive Communication and the Adequate Paraphrase," *Communication Research Reports* 33 (2016): 166–172.

104. Weger et al., "Active Listening in Peer Interviews"; also see M. R. Wood, "What Makes for Successful Speaker-Listener Technique? Two Case Studies," *Family Journal* 18.1 (2010): 50–54.

105. Vickery et al., "Intrapersonal Communication and Listening Goals."

106. K. Crawford, "Following You: Disciplines of Listening in Social Media," *Journal of Media & Cultural Studies* 23 (2009): 525–535; also see S. Keaton and D. L. Worthington, "Listening in Mediated Context: Introduction to a Special Issue," *International Journal of Listening* 32 (2018): 65–68.

107. For a classic discussion of empathy and interpretive listening, see J. Stewart, "Interpretive Listening: An Alternative to Empathy," *Communication Education* 32 (1983): 379–391; Bommelje et al., "Personality Characteristics of Effective Listeners"; J. Håkansson and H. Montgomery, "Empathy as an Interpersonal Phenomenon," *Journal of Social & Personal Relationships* 20 (2003): 267–284.

108. H. J. M. Nouwen, "Listening as Spiritual Hospitality," in *Bread for the Journey* (New York: HarperCollins, 1997).

109. H. Weger, "Instructor Active Empathic Listening and Classroom Incivility," *International Journal of Listening* 32 (2018): 49–64.

110. C. R. Rogers, "Empathic: An Unappreciated Way of Being," in *A Way of Being* (Boston: Houghton Mifflin, 1980): 137–163.

111. J. C. McCroskey and M. J. Beatty, "The Communibiological Perspective: Implications for Communication in Instruction," *Communication Education* 49 (2000): 1–6; M. J. Beatty and J. C. McCroskey, "Theory, Scientific Evidence and the Communibiological Paradigm: Reflections on Misguided Criticism," *Communication Education* 49 (2001): 36–44.

112. M. E. Pence and A. J. Vickery, "The Roles of Personality and Trait Emotion Intelligence in the Active-Empathic Listening Process: Evidence from Correlational and Regression Analyses," *The International Journal of Listening* 26 (2012): 159–174.

113. D. F. Barone, P. S. Hutchings, H. J. Kimmel, H. L. Traub, J. T. Cooper, and C. M. Marshall, "Increasing Empathic Accuracy through Practice and Feedback in a Clinical Interviewing Course," *Journal of Social and Clinical Psychology* 24 (2005): 156–171; B. Umaadevi and S. P. Sasi Rekha, "The Impact of Listening Strategies on Improving Learners' Listening Skill," *Language in India* 19 (2019): www.languageinindia.com (accessed April 15, 2020).

114. Weaver and Kirtley, "Listening Styles and Empathy."

115. D. Goleman, *Emotional Intelligence* (New York: Bantam Books, 1994).

116. A. de Saint-Exupéry, as quoted in Goleman, *Emotional Intelligence*.

117. P. Toller, "Learning to Listen, Learning to Hear: A Training Approach," *Time to Listen to Children: Personal and Professional Communication*, edited by C. Birgit (Florence, KY: Taylor, Frances/Routledge, 1999): 48–61; T. Drollinger, L. B. Comer, and P. T. Warrington, "Development and Validation of the Active Empathetic Listening Scale," *Psychology & Marketing* 23.2 (2006): 161–180; S. L. Do and D. L. Schallert, "Emotions and Classroom Talk: Toward a Model of the Role of Affect in Students' Experiences of Classroom Discussions," *Journal of Educational Psychology* 96.4 (2004): 619–634.

118. For an excellent review of emotional intelligence research, see D. Grewal and P. Salovey, "Feeling Smart: The Science of Emotional Intelligence," *American Scientist* 93 (2005): 330–339. Also see J. Keaton and L. Kelly, "Emotional Intelligence as a Mediator of Family Communication Patterns and Reticence," *Communication Reports* 21.2 (2008): 104–116; R. Pishghadam, "Emotional and Verbal Intelligences in Language Learning," *Iranian Journal of Language Studies* 3.1 (2009): 43–64.

119. Goleman, *Emotional Intelligence*; Grewal and Salovey, "Feeling Smart."

120. Goleman, *Emotional Intelligence*.

121. G. Bodie, A. J. Vickery, K. Cannava, and S. M. Jones, "The Role of 'Active Listening' in Informal Helping Conversations: Impact on Perceptions of Listener Helpfulness, Sensitivity, and Discloser Emotional Improvement," *Western Journal of Communication* 79.2 (2015): 151–173; G. Bodie, A. J. Vickery, and K. Cannava, "Supportive Communication and the Adequate Paraphrase."

122. Hargie et al., *Social Skills in Interpersonal Communication*; R. Boulton, *People Skills* (New York: 1981). We also acknowledge others who have presented excellent applications of listening and responding skills in interpersonal and group contexts: D. A. Romig and L. J. Romig, *Structured Teamwork* (D Guide) (Austin, TX: Performance Resources, 1990); S. Deep and L. Sussman, *Smart Moves* (Reading, MA: Addison-Wesley, 1990); P. R. Scholtes, *The Team Handbook* (Madison, WI: Joiner Associates, 1988); Hargie, *The Handbook of Communication Skills*.

123. See P. Ellis and J. Abbot, "Active Listening, Part Two: Showing Empathy," *Journal of Kidney Care* 3 (2018): 193–195; E. G. Zugaro and C. G. Zugaro, "The Listening Leader: How to Drive Performance by Using Communicative Leadership," *British Journal of Occupational Therapy* (2020): 1–12.

124. G. D. Bodie, S. A. Keaton, and S. M. Jones, "Individual Listening Values Moderate the Impact of Verbal Person Centeredness on Helper Evaluations: A Test of the Dual-Process Theory of Supportive Message Outcomes," *International Journal of Listening* 32 (2018): 127–139.

125. Bodie et al., "Individual Listening Values Moderate the Impact of Verbal Person Centeredness on Helper Evaluations"; W. Strom, "Do Moral Communicators Make Better Listeners? Personality, Virtue and Receiver Apprehension as Predictors of Active Empathic-Listening," *International Journal of Listening* 18 (2020): 51–60.

126. S. M. Jones, "Supportive Listening," *The International Journal of Listening* 25 (2011): 85–103.

127. Our discussion of appropriate and inappropriate social support responses is taken from B. D. Burleson, "Emotional Support Skill," in *Handbook of Communication and Social Interaction Skills*, edited by O. Greene and B. R. Burleson (Mahwah, NJ: Lawrence Erlbaum, 2003): 566–568. See also Bodie et al., "The Nature of Supportive Listening, I"; J.A. Harvey, V. Manusov, and E. A. Sanders, "Improving Cancer Caregivers' Emotion Regulation and Supportive Message Characteristics: Results of a Randomized Controlled Expressive Writing Intervention," *Communication Monographs* 86 (2019): 1–22.

128. M. April and P. Schrodt, "Person-Centered Messages, Attributions of Responsibility, and the Willingness to Forgive Parental Infidelity," *Communication Studies* 70 (2019): 79–98; Harvey et al., "Improving Cancer Caregivers' Emotion Regulation and Supportive Message Characteristics."

129. L. B. Comer and T. Drollinger, "Active Empathic Listening and Selling Success: A Conceptual Framework," *Journal of Personal Selling & Sales Management* 19 (1999): 15–29; S. B. Castleberry, C. D. Shepherd, and R. Ridnour, "Effective Interpersonal Listening in the Personal Selling Environment: Conceptualization, Measurement, and Nomological Validity," *Journal of Marketing Theory and Practice* 7 (1999): 30–38.

130. F. C. B. Hansen, H. Resnick, and J. Galea, "Better Listening: Paraphrasing and Perception Checking: A Study of the Effectiveness of a Multimedia Skills Training Program," *Journal of Technology in Human Services* 20 (2002): 317–331; D. Ifert Johnson and K. Long, "Evaluating the Effectiveness of Listening Instruction in Introductory Communication Courses," paper presented at the

annual meeting of the International Communication Association (May 2008).
131. A. M. Nicotera, J. Steele, A. Catalani, and N. Simpson, "Conceptualization and Test of an Aggression Competence Model," *Communication Research Reports* 29 (2012): 12–25.
132. R. Lemieux and M. R. Tighe, "Attachment Styles and the Evaluation of Comforting Responses: A Receiver Perspective," *Communication Research Reports* 21 (2004): 144–153; also see W. Samter, "How Gender and Cognitive Complexity Influence the Provision of Emotional Support: A Study of Indirect Effects," *Communication Reports* 15 (2002): 5–16.

Chapter 6

1. Research documents several culture-based differences in communication, including approaches to leadership, deception, and conflict management styles. See N. Ensari and S. E. Murphy, "Cross-Cultural Variations in Leadership Perceptions and Attribution of Charisma to the Leader," *Organizational Behavior and Human Decision Processes* 92 (2003): 52–66; M. K. Lapinski and T. R. Levine, "Culture and Information Manipulation Theory: The Effects of Self-Construal and Locus of Benefit on Information Manipulation," *Communication Studies* 5 (2000): 55–73; D. Cai and E. L. Fink, "Conflict Style Differences between Individualists and Collectivists," *Communication Monographs* 69 (2002): 67–87; M. S. Kim and A. S. Ebesu Hubbard, "Intercultural Communication in the Global Village: How to Understand 'The Other'," *Journal of Intercultural Communication Research* 36.3 (2007): 223–235.
2. For a discussion of the role of self-awareness as a strategy for enhancing intercultural competence, see R. C. Weigl, "Intercultural Competence through Cultural Self-Study: A Strategy for Adult Learners," *International Journal of Intercultural Relations* 33 (2009): 346–360.
3. For a review of research identifying the importance of adapting to cultural differences, see Y. Hu and W. Fan, "An Exploratory Study on Intercultural Communication Research Contents and Methods: A Survey Based on the International and Domestic Journal Papers Published from 2001 to 2005," *International Journal of Intercultural Relations* 35 (2011): 554–566.
4. D. K. Ivy, *GenderSpeak: Communicating in a Gendered World* 6e (Dubuque, IA: Kendall Hunt Publishers, 2017).
5. J. Gray, *Men Are from Mars, Women Are from Venus* (New York: HarperCollins, 1992).
6. D. K. Ivy, *GenderSpeak*; D. J. Canary and T. R. Emmers Sommer, *Sex and Gender Differences in Personal Relationships* (New York: Guilford, 1997).
7. D. Tannen, *You Just Don't Understand* (New York: William Morrow, 1990).
8. Ivy, *GenderSpeak*.
9. S. D. Farley, A. M. Ashcraft, M. F. Stasson, and R. L. Nusbaum, "Nonverbal Reactions to Conversational Interruption: A Test of Complementarity Theory and the Status/Gender Parallel," *Journal of Nonverbal Behavior* 34.4 (2010): 193–206.
10. A. C. Selbe, *Are You from Another Planet or What?* Workshop presented at the Joint Service Family Readiness Matters Conference, Phoenix, AZ (July 1999).
11. R. Garfield, *Breaking the Male Code: Unlocking the Power of Friendship* (New York: Gotham Books, 2015); R. B. Rubin, E. M. Perse, and C. A. Barbato, "Conceptualization and Measurement of Interpersonal Communication Motives," *Human Communication Research* 14 (1988): 602–628; D. Tannen, *That's Not What I Meant!* (London: Dent, 1986).
12. "A Survey of LGBT Americans: Attitudes, Experiences and Values in Changing Times," *Pew Research Social & Demographic Trends*, June 13, 2013, www.pewsocialtrends.org/2013/06/13/a-survey-of-lgbt-americans (accessed March 18, 2014); T. Mottet, "The Role of Sexual Orientation in Predicting Outcome: Value and Anticipated Communication Behaviors," *Communication Quarterly* 43 (2000): 223–239; for an excellent review of literature summarizing attitudes toward gay men and lesbians, see J. Soliz, E. Ribarsky, M. M. Harrigan, and S. Tye-Williams, "Perceptions of Communication with Gay and Lesbian Family Members: Predictors of Relational Satisfaction and Implications for Outgroup Attitudes," *Communication Quarterly* 58.1 (2010): 77–95.
13. L. Abrahms, "This Map Shows Which Countries Still Haven't Legalized Same-Sex Marriage," *Culture Trip* (January, 2019) https://theculturetrip.com/europe/articles/this-map-shows-which-countries-still-havent-legalized-same-sex-marriage/ (accessed June 4, 2020); "73 Countries Where Homosexuality is Illegal" (December, 2019) https://76crimes.com/76-countries-where-homosexuality-is-illegal/; R. Perper, Business Insider, "The 29 Countries Around the World Where Same-Sex Marriage Is Legal" (May, 2020) https://www.businessinsider.com/where-is-same-sex-marriage-legal-world-2017-11 (accessed June 4, 2020).
14. R. Barnes, "Supreme Court Says Gay, Transgender Workers Are Protected by Federal Law Forbidding Discrimination on the Basis of Sex," *The Washington Post* (June 15, 2020) https://www.washingtonpost.com/politics/courts_law/supreme-court-says-gay-transgender-workers-are-protected-by-federal-law-forbidding-discrimination-on-the-basis-of-sex/2020/06/15/2211d5a4-655b-11ea-acca-80c22bbee96f_story.html (accessed July 5, 2020).
15. "A Survey of LGBT Americans: Attitudes, Experiences and Values in Changing Times," *Pew Research Social & Demographic Trends*, June 13, 2013, www.pewsocialtrends.org/2013/06/13/a-survey-of-lgbt-americans (accessed March 18, 2014).
16. G. M. Herek, "Heterosexuals' Attitudes Toward Lesbian and Gay Men: Correlates and Gender Differences," *Journal of Sex Research* 25 (1988): 451–477.
17. Herek, "Heterosexuals' Attitudes Toward Lesbian and Gay Men"; M. S. Weinberg and C. J. Williams, *Male Homosexuals: Their Problems and Adaptations* (New York: Free Press, 1974); Mottet, "The Role of Sexual Orientation in Predicting Outcome."
18. "A Survey of LGBT Americans."
19. J. Soliz, et al., "Perceptions of Communication with Gay and Lesbian Family Members."
20. "Removing Bias in Language; Sexuality," *American Psychological Association*, www.apastyle.org/sexuality.html (accessed March, 2006); J. W. Peters, "The Decline and Fall of the 'H' Word," *New York Times*, Sunday Styles (March 23, 2014): 10.
21. A. Williams and P. Garrett, "Communication Evaluations across the Life Span: From Adolescent Storm and Stress to Elder Aches and 'Pains'," *Journal of Language and Social Psychology* 21 (June 2002): 101–126; also see D. Cai, H. Giles, and K. Noels, "Elderly Perceptions of Communication with Older and Younger Adults in China: Implications for Mental Health," *Journal of Applied Communication Research* 26 (1998): 32–51.
22. J. Montepare, E. Koff, D. Zaitchik, and M. Albert, "The Use of Body Movements and Gestures as Cues to Emotions in Younger and Older Adults," *Journal of Nonverbal Behavior* 23 (1999): 133–152.
23. J. Harwood, E. B. Ryan, H. Giles, and S. Tysoski, "Evaluations of Patronizing Speech and Three Response Styles in a Non-Service-Providing Context," *Journal of Applied Communication Research* 25 (1997): 170–195.
24. T. C. Segrin, "Age Moderates the Relationship between Social Support and Psychosocial Problems," paper presented at the annual meeting of the International Communication Association, San Diego, CA (May 2003).
25. N. Howe and W. Strauss, *Millennials Rising: The Next Great Generation* (New York: Vintage Books, 2000); N. Howe and W. Strauss, *The Fourth Turning: An American Prophecy* (New York: Broadway Books, 1997).
26. K. Meyers and K. Sadaghiani, "Millennials in the Workplace: A Communication Perspective on Millennials' Organizational Relationships and Performance," *Journal of Business & Psychology* 25.2 (2010): 225–238.
27. "Millennials in Adulthood: Detached from Institutions, Networked with Friends," *Pew Research Social & Demographic*

Trends, March 7, 2014, www.pewsocialtrends.org/2014/03/07/millennials-in-adulthood (accessed March 20, 2014).
28. Howe and Strauss, *Millennials Rising*.
29. Living Facts, "Generation Z" https://www.livingfacts.org/en/articles/2020/generation-z?utm_campaign=adwords_sustained&utm_source=adwords&utm_medium=paid&utm_content=genz&utm_term=ad2&gclid=Cj0KCQjwuJz3BRDTARIsAMg-HxUrReNr1xa8mrwtBdfBcx3yT0LQGT0KfbaHsVk-9BtZSVdErPZpVe4aAoBZEALw_wcB (accessed June 15, 2020).
30. Living Facts, "Generation Z" https://www.livingfacts.org/en/articles/2020/generation-z?utm_campaign=adwords_sustained&utm_source=adwords&utm_medium=paid&utm_content=genz&utm_term=ad2&gclid=Cj0KCQjwuJz3BRDTARIsAMg-HxUrReNr1xa8mrwtBdfBcx3yT0LQGT0KfbaHsVk-9BtZSVdErPZpVe4aAoBZEALw_wcB (accessed June 15, 2020).
31. Our discussion of generational differences and communication is also based on J. Smith, "The Millennials Are Coming," workshop presented at Texas State University, San Marcos, TX (2006).
32. Howe and Strauss, *Millennials Rising*; H. Karp, C. Fuller, and D. Sirias, *Bridging the Boomer-Xer Gap: Creating Authentic Teams for High Performance at Work* (Palo Alto, CA: Davies-Black, 2002).
33. R. Lewontin, "The Apportionment of Human Diversity," *Evolutionary Biology* 6 (1973): 381–397.
34. D. Matsumoto and L. Juang, *Culture and Psychology* (Belmont, CA: Wadsworth/Thomson, 2004), 16; also see H. A. Yee, H. H. Fairchild, F. Weizmann, and E. G. Wyatt, "Addressing Psychology's Problems with Race," *American Psychologist* 48 (1994): 1132–1140.
35. Allen, *Differences Matter*.
36. Allen, *Differences Matter*.
37. Argyle, *The Psychology of Social Class* (London: Routledge, 1994), 62.
38. Allen, *Differences Matter*, 113.
39. Argyle, *Social Class*, 62.
40. See K. W. Crenshaw, "Mapping the Margins: Intersectionality, Identity Politics, and Violence Against Women of Color," *Stanford Law Review* 43 (1991): 1241–1299; K. W. Crenshaw, "Demarginalizing the Intersection of Race and Sex: A Black Feminist Critique of Antidiscrimination Doctrine, Feminist Theory, and Antiracist Politics," *University of Chicago Legal Forum* 1 (1989): 139–167; L. Alcoff, "Cultural Feminism versus Post-Structuralism: The Identity Crisis in Feminist Theory Signs," 13 (1988): 405–436; A. Kezar and J. Lester, "Breaking the Barriers of Essentialism in Leadership Research: Positionality as a Promising Approach," *Feminist Formations* 22 (2010): 163–185; A. G. Stamou, "Studying the Interactional Construction of Identities in Critical Discourse Studies: A Proposed Analytical Framework," *Discourse & Society* 29 (2018): 568–589; P. R. Jensen, J. Cruz, E. K. Eger, J. N. Hanchey, A. N. Gist-Mackey, K. Ruiz-Mesa, and A. Villamil, "Pushing Beyond Positionalities and through 'Failures' in Qualitative Organizational Communication: Experiences and Lessons on Identities in Ethnographic Praxis," *Management Communication Quarterly* 34 (2020): 121–151; L. Cooks, "Pedagogy, Performance, and Positionality: Teaching about Whiteness in Interracial Communication," *Communication Education* 52 (2003): 245–257; H. Masri, "Communication Studies' Hollow Intersectionality Rhetoric," *Communication Education* 42 (2019): 417–421.
41. G. A. Yep, "Toward Thick(er) Intersectionalities: Theorizing, Researching, and Activating the Complexities of Communication and Identities," *Globalizing Intercultural Communication: A Reader*, edited by K. Sorrells and S. Sekimoto (Los Angeles, CA: Sage, 2015): 86.
42. See A. E. Hoover, T. Hack, A. L. Garcia, W. Goodfriend, and M. M. Habashi, "Powerless Men and Agentic Women: Gender Bias in Hiring Decisions," *Sex Roles: A Journal of Research* 80 (2019): 667–680.
43. S. Roberts, *Who We Are Now: The Changing Face of America in the Twenty-First Century* (New York: Henry Holt, 2004).
44. See T. Friedman, *The World Is Flat: A Brief History of the Twenty-First Century* (New York: Farrar, Straus and Giroux, 2005).
45. Adapted from *Information Please Almanac* (Boston: Houghton Mifflin, 1990) and *World Almanac and Book of Facts* (New York: World Almanac, 1991), as cited by M. W. Lustig and J. Koester, *Intercultural Competence: Interpersonal Communication across Cultures* (Boston: Allyn & Bacon, 2009), 11.
46. For a discussion of globalization and change see T. Friedman, *Thank You for Being Late: An Optimist's Guide to Thriving in the Age of Accelerations* (New York: Farrar, Straus, and Girous, 2016).
47. A. G. Smith, ed., *Communication and Culture* (New York: Holt, Rinehart and Winston, 1966).
48. E. T. Hall, *Beyond Culture* (Garden City, NY: Doubleday, 1976).
49. "Current Population Estimates, Malaysia, 2020," Department of Statistics Malaysia Official Website, July 15, 2020, https://www.dosm.gov.my/.
50. Population and housing census of Malaysia 2000: General report of the population and housing census. Putrajaya: Department of Statistics, Malaysia (2005).
51. M. A. Khalid and L. Yang, "Income Inequality Among Different Ethnic Groups: The Case of Malaysia," The London School of Economics, September 11, 2019, https://blogs.lse.ac.uk/businessreview/2019/09/11/income-inequality-among-different-ethnic-groups-the-case-of-malaysia/.
52. M. Ravallion, "Ethnic Inequality and Poverty in Malaysia," The Society for the Study of Economic Inequality (ECINEQ), July 2019, http://www.ecineq.org/ecineq_paris19/papers_EcineqPSE/paper_406.pdf.
53. S. Z. Abidin, "Do We Really Understand Cultural Diversity?" *New Straits Times*, July 27, 2015, https://www.nst.com.my/news/2015/09/do-we-really-understand-cultural-diversity.
54. R. Ibrahim, J. Tan, T. A. Hamid, and A. Ashari, "Cultural, Demographic, Socio-economic Background and Care Relations in Malaysia," *The Intimate and the Public in Asian and Global Perspectives*, 8 (2018): 41–98.
55. "Malaysia yet to Harness the Power of Diversity & Inclusion," HR Asia, December 21, 2018, https://hrasiamedia.com/top-news/malaysia-yet-to-harness-the-power-of-diversity-inclusion/; and G. Lim, "Malaysian Companies on Par with Asia Counterparts in Workplace Diversity," https://www.michaelpage.com.my.
56. "No Place For LGBT Malaysians?: The ASEAN Post, January 25, 2021, https://theaseanpost.com/article/no-place-lgbt-malaysians.
57. " Number of Students Enrolled in Public Higher Education Institutions in Malaysia from 2012 to 2019, by Gender," Statista.com, January 7, 2021.
58. F. Tjiptono, G. Khan, E. S. Yeong, and V. Kunchamboo, "Generation Z in Malaysia: The Four 'E' Generation," *The New Generation Z in Asia Dynamics, Differences, Digitalization*, Emerald Publishing Limited (2020): 147-161.
59. B. S. Ram, "Survey: Malaysians Find Ageism a Barrier to Work Opportunities," *New Straits Times*, February 12, 2020.
60. For example, see A. V. Matveeve and P. E. Nelson, "Cross Cultural Competence and Multicultural Team Performance: Perceptions of American and Russian Managers," *International Journal of Cross-Cultural Management* 4 (2004): 253–270.
61. G. Hofstede, *Culture's Consequences: International Differences in Work Related Values* (Beverly Hills, CA: Sage, 1980); G. Hofstede and G. J. Hofstede, *Cultures and Organizations: Software of the Mind* 3e (New York: McGraw-Hill, 2010).
62. H. J. Ladegaard, "Global Culture—Myth or Reality? Perceptions of 'National Cultures' in Global Corporation," *Journal of Intercultural Communication Research* 36.2 (2007): 139–163; also see T. R. Levine, H. S. Park, and R. K Kim, "Some Conceptual and Theoretical Challenges for Cross-Cultural Communication Research in the 21st Century," *Journal of Intercultural Communication Research* 36.3 (2007): 205–221.
63. E. R. Pedersen, C. Neighbors, M. E. Larimer, and C. M. Lee, "Measuring Sojourner Adjustment Among American Students Studying Abroad," *International Journal of Intercultural Relations* 35 (2011): 881–889; G/Gap. "The Effects of Intercultural Training upon the Organizational Performance of Multinational

Corporations in China," *International Journal of Business Anthropology* 1 (2009): 97–116.

64. For an excellent overview of issues in teaching intercultural communication, see Levine et al., "Some Conceptual and Theoretical Challenges for Cross-Cultural Communication Research in the 21st Century."

65. C. Ward, S. Bochner, and A. Furnham, *The Psychology of Culture Shock* (Hove, UK: Routledge, 2001).

66. T. L. Sandel, "'Oh, I'm Here!': Social Media's Impact on the Cross-cultural Adaptation of Students Studying Abroad," *Journal of Intercultural Communication Research* 45.1 (2014): 1–29.

67. C. H. Dodd, *Dynamics of Intercultural Communication* (New York: McGraw-Hill, 1998).

68. Hall, *Beyond Culture*.

69. L. A. Samovar, R. E. Porter, and L. A. Stefani, *Communication between Cultures* (Belmont, CA: Wadsworth, 1998).

70. Hofstede, *Culture's Consequences*; Hofstede and Hofstede, *Cultures and Organizations* 3e.

71. G. Hofstede, "Dimensionalizing Cultures: The Hofstede Model in Context," *Online Readings in Psychology and Culture* 2 (2011): 1–25; also see D. H. Mansson, F. Marko, K. Bachrata, Z. Daniskova, J. Gajdosikova Zeleiova, V. Janis, and A. S. Sharov, "Young Adults' Trait Affection Given and Received as Functions of Hofstede's Dimensions of Cultures and National Origin," *Journal of Intercultural Communication Research* 45.5 (2016): 404–418.

72. S. Ting-Toomey, "Applying Dimensional Values in Understanding Intercultural Communication," *Communication Monographs* 77.2 (2010): 169–180.

73. P. Coy, "The Future of Work," *Business Week* (August 20 and 27, 2007): 43.

74. See J. B. Walther, "Interpersonal Effects in Computer-Mediated Interaction: A Relational Perspective," *Communication Research* 19 (1992): 52–90; J. B. Walther, "Relational Aspects of Computer-Mediated Communication: Experimental and Longitudinal Observations," *Organizational Science* 6 (1995): 186–203; J. B. Walther, J. F. Anderson, and D. Park, "Interpersonal Effects in Computer-Mediated Interaction: A Meta-Analysis of Social and Anti-Social Communication," *Communication Research* 21 (1994): 460–487.

75. M. E. Heilman, S. Caleo, and M. L. Halim, "Just the Thought of It!: Effects of Anticipating Computer-Mediated Communication on Gender Stereotyping," *Journal of Experimental Social Psychology* 46.4 (2010): 672–675; M. Hansen, S. Fabriz, and S. Stehle, "Cultural Cues in Students' Computer-Mediated Communication: Influences on E-mail Style, Perception of the Sender, and Willingness to Help" *Journal of Computer-Mediated Communication* 20 (2015): 278–294.

76. Y. Mao and C. L. Hade "Relating Intercultural Communication Sensitivity to Conflict Management Styles, Technology Use, and Organizational Communication Satisfaction in Multinational Organizations in China," *Journal of Intercultural Communication Research* 44.2 (2015): 132–150.

77. C. U. Grosse, "Managing Communication within Virtual Intercultural Teams," *Business Communication Quarterly* 65 (2002): 22–38.

78. E. Glikson and M. Erez, "The Emergence of a Communication Climate in Global Virtual Teams," *Journal of World Business* (2019): https://www.sciencedirect.com/science/article/abs/pii/S1090951617308787 (accessed May 27, 2020).

79. J. Mittelmeir, B. Rienties, D. Tempelaar, and D. Whitelock, "Overcoming Cross-Cultural Group Work Tensions: Mixed Student Perspectives on the Role of Social Relationships," *Higher Education* 75 (2018): 149–166.

80. For research about the effect of individualistic and collectivistic cultural values on communication and conflict management, see R. Kaushal and C. T. Kwantes, "The Role of Culture and Personality in Choice of Conflict Management Strategy," *International Journal of Intercultural Relations* 30 (2006): 579–603.

81. A. S. Waterman's *The Psychology of Individualism* (Santa Barbara, CA: Praeger, 1984), 4–5.

82. W. B. Gudykunst, *Bridging Differences: Effective Intergroup Communication* (Newbury Park, CA: Sage, 1998).

83. H. C. Triandis, "The Many Dimensions of Culture," *Academy of Management Executive* 18 (2004): 88–93.

84. I. Kim, B. Feng, B. Wang, and J. Jang, "Examining Cultural and Gender Similarities and Differences in College Students' Value of Communication Skills in Romantic Relationships," *Chinese Journal of Communication* 11 (2018): 437–454.

85. M. Voronov and J. A. Singer, "The Myth of Individualism-Collectivism: A Critical Review," *Journal of Social Psychology* 142 (2002): 461–480.

86. For an excellent review of Hofstede's work, see J. W. Bing, "Hofstede's Consequences: The Impact of His Work on Consulting and Business Practices," *Academy of Management Executive* 18 (2004): 80–87.

87. Hofstede, *Culture's Consequence*; Hofstede and Hofstede, *Cultures and Organizations* 3e.

88. G. Hofstede, "Cultural Dimensions in Management and Planning," *Asia Pacific Journal of Management* (January 1984): 81–98; Hofstede and Hofstede, *Cultures and Organizations* 3e.

89. For a discussion of a nation's long- and short-term time orientation, see Hofstede and Hofstede, *Cultures and Organizations* 3e, 210–238.

90. Hofstede and Hofstede, *Cultures and Organizations* 3e.

91. *The Declaration of Independence*. http://www.ushistory.org/declaration/document/ (accessed January 23, 2017).

92. Hofstede, "Dimensionalizing Cultures."

93. Hofstede, "Dimensionalizing Cultures."

94. Hofstede, "Dimensionalizing Cultures."

95. J. W. Neuliep, "Assessing the Reliability and Validity of the Generalized Ethnocentrism Scale," *Journal of Intercultural Communication Research* 31 (2002): 201–215. For additional research on the role of ethnocentrism in communication, see Y. Lin, A. Rancer, and A. Sunhee Lim, "Ethnocentrism and Intercultural Willingness to Communicate: A Cross-Cultural Comparison Between Korean and American College Students," *Journal of Intercultural Communication Research* 32 (2003): 117–128.

96. See Ensari and Murphy, "Cross-Cultural Variations in Leadership Perceptions and Attribution of Charisma to the Leader"; Lapinski and Levine, "Culture and Information Manipulation Theory"; Cai and Fink, "Conflict Style Differences between Individualists and Collectivists."

97. C. Kluckhohn and S. Murray, 1953, as quoted by J. S. Caputo, H. C. Hazel, and C. McMahon, *Interpersonal Communication* (Boston: Allyn & Bacon, 1994), 304.

98. Y. Kashima, E. S. Kashima, U. Kim, and M. Gelfand, "Describing the Social World: How Is a Person, a Group, and a Relationship Described in the East and in the West?" *Journal of Experimental Social Psychology* 42 (2006): 388–396.

99. D. E. Brown, "Human Universals and Their Implications," in *Being Humans: Anthropological Universality and Particularity in Transdisciplinary Perspectives*, edited by N. Roughley (New York: Walter de Gruyter, 2000, 156–174). For an applied discussion of these universals, see S. Pinker, *The Blank Slate: The Modern Denial of Human Nature* (London: Penguin Books, 2002).

100. D. W. Kale, "Ethics in Intercultural Communication," in *Intercultural Communication: A Reader* 6e, edited by L. A. Samovar and R. E. Porter (Belmont, CA: Wadsworth, 1991).

101. L. A. Samovar and R. E. Porter, *Communication between Cultures* (Stamford, CT: Wadsworth and Thomson Learning, 2001), 29.

102. C. S. Lewis, *The Abolition of Man* (New York: Macmillan, 1944).

103. M. Hansen, S. Fabriz, and S. Stehle, "Cultural Cues in Students' Computer-Mediated Communication: Influences on E-mail Style, Perception of the Sender, and Willingness to Help," *Journal of Computer-Mediated Communication*, 20 (2015): 278–294; N. Zaidman and A. Malach-Pines, "Stereotypes in Bicultural Global Teams," *International Journal of Intercultural Relations* 40 (2014): 99–112.

104. S. Kamekar, M. B. Kolsawalla, and T. Mazareth, "Occupational Prestige as a Function of Occupant's Gender," *Journal of Applied Social Psychology* 19 (1988): 681–688.

105. R. Barnes, "Supreme Court Says Gay, Transgender Workers Are Protected by Federal Law Forbidding Discrimination on the Basis of Sex," *The Washington Post* (June 15, 2020) https://www.washingtonpost.com/politics/courts_law/supreme-court-says-gay-transgender-workers-are-protected-by-federal-law-forbidding-discrimination-on-the-basis-of-sex/2020/06/15/2211d5a4-655b-11ea-acca-80c22bbee96f_story.html (accessed June 15, 2020).
106. E. Roosevelt, as cited by Lustig and Koester, *Intercultural Competence*.
107. S. Ting-Toomey, "Intercultural Conflict Training: Theory-Practice Approaches and Research Challenges," *Journal of Intercultural Communication Research* 36.3 (2007): 255–271.
108. J. G. DeJaeghere and Y. Cao, "Developing U. S. Teachers' Intercultural Competence: Does Professional Development Matter?" *International Journal of Intercultural Relations* 33 (2009): 437–447; F. Miller, A. Denk, E. Lubaway, C. Salzer, A. Kozina, T. V. Perse, M. Rasmusson, I. Jugovic, B. L. Nielse, M. Rozman, A. Ojstersek, and S. Jurko, "Assessing Social, Emotional, and Intercultural Competencies of Students and School Staff: A Systematic Literature Review," *Educational Research Review* 29 (2020): 1–24.
109. See M. R. Hammer, M. J. Bennett, and R. Wiseman, "Measuring Intercultural Sensitivity: The Intercultural Development Inventory," *International Journal of Intercultural Relations* 27 (2003): 421–443; also see J. Emontospool and K. R. Hansen, "Bridging the Determinist-Interpretivist Divide in Intercultural Competence Research," *European Journal of International Management* 14 (2020): 251–272.
110. P. Holmes and G. O'Neill, "Developing and Evaluating Intercultural Competence: Ethnographies of Intercultural Encounters," *International Journal of Intercultural Relations* 36 (2012): 707–718.
111. For additional research about the validity of measuring intercultural adaptation, see J. F. Greenholtz, "Does Intercultural Sensitivity Cross Cultures? Validity Issues in Porting Instruments across Languages and Cultures," *International Journal of Intercultural Relations* 29 (2005): 73–89.
112. L. Holubnycha, I. I. Kostikova, O. Leiba, S. Lobzova, and R. Chornovol-Tkachenka, "Developing Students' Intercultural Competence at the Tertiary Level," *Revista Romanezsca pentru Educatie Multidimensionala* 11 (2019): 245–262.
113. B. W. Haas, "Enhancing the Intercultural Competence of College Students: A Consideration of Applied Teaching Techniques," *International Journal of Multicultural Education* 21 (2019): 81–96; M. M. Idris, "Assessing Intercultural Competence (IC) of State Junior High School English Teachers in Yogyakarta," *Indonesian Journal of Applied Linguistics* 9 (2020): 628–636.
114. W. B. Gudykunst and Y. Kim, *Communicating with Strangers* (New York: Random House, 1984); Gudykunst, *Bridging Differences*.
115. A. N. Miller and J. A. Samp, "Planning Intercultural Interaction: Extending Anxiety Uncertainty Management Theory," *Communication Research Reports* 24.2 (2007): 87–95.
116. B. J. Lough, "International Volunteers' Perceptions of Intercultural Competence," *International Journal of Intercultural Relations* 35 (2011): 452–464.
117. Holubnycha et al., "Developing Students' Intercultural Competence."
118. R. Peng, C. Zhu, and W. Wu, "Visualizing the Knowledge Domain of Intercultural Competence Research: A Bibliometric Analysis," *International Journal of Intercultural Relations* 74 (2020): 58–68.
119. R. Vollhardt, "Enhanced External and Culturally Sensitive Attributions after Extended Intercultural Contact," *British Journal of Social Psychology* 49.2 (2010): 363–383.
120. Miller and Samp, "Planning Intercultural Interaction."
121. Taking initiative when interacting with others from another culture can enhance intercultural competence. See E. S. Yakunina, I. K. Weigold, A. Weigold, S. Hercegovac, and N. Elsayed, "The Multicultural Personality: Does It Predict International Students' Openness to Diversity and Adjustment?" *International Journal of Intercultural Relations* 36 (2010): 533–540.
122. For a classic discussion of egocentrism and ethnocentrism, see T. W. Adorno, E. Frenkel-Brunswik, D. J. Levinson, and R. N. Sanford, *The Authoritarian Personality* (New York: Harper & Brothers, 1950).
123. Neuliep, "Assessing the Reliability and Validity of the Generalized Ethnocentrism Scale"; Lin et al., "Ethnocentrism and Intercultural Willingness to Communicate."
124. G. Goncalves, C. Sousa, L. A. Arasaratnam-Smith, N. Rodrigues, and R. Carvalheiro, "Intercultural Communication Competence Scale: Invariance and Construct Validation in Portugal," *Journal of Intercultural Communication Research* (2020): doi: 10.1080/17475759.2020.1746687.
125. M. V. Redmond, "The Functions of Empathy (Decentering) in Human Relations," *Human Relations* 42 (1993): 593–606; also see M. V. Redmond, "A Multidimensional Theory and Measure of Social Decentering," *Journal of Research in Personality* 1 (1995): 35–88; for an excellent discussion of the role of emotions in establishing empathy, see D. Goleman, *Emotional Intelligence* (New York: Bantam, 1995).
126. See B. J. Broome, "Building Shared Meaning: Implications of a Relational Approach to Empathy for Teaching Intercultural Communication," *Communication Education* 40 (1991): 235–249. Much of this discussion is based on the treatment of social decentering and empathy in S. A. Beebe, S. J. Beebe, and M. V. Redmond, *Interpersonal Communication: Relating to Others* 9e (Hoboken, NJ: Pearson, 2020).
127. F. Walter, M. S. Cole, and R. H. Humphrey, "Emotional Intelligence: *Sine Qua Non* of Leadership or Folderol?" *Academy of Management Perspectives* (2011): 45–59; Y. C. Lin, A. S. Y. Chen, and Y. C. Song, "Does Your Intelligence Help to Survive in a Foreign Jungle? The Effects of Cultural Intelligence and Emotional Intelligence on Cross-Cultural Adjustment," *International Journal of Intercultural Relations* 36 (2012): 541–552.
128. For an excellent discussion of empathy as it relates to intercultural communication, see D. W. Augsburger, *Pastoral Counseling across Cultures* (Philadelphia: Westminster Press, 1986), 28–30.
129. H. J. M. Nouwen, *Bread for the Journey* (New York: HarperCollins, 1997).
130. C. Gallois, T. Ogay, and H. Giles, "Communication Accommodation Theory: A Look Back and a Look Ahead," in W. B. Gudykunst (ed.), *Theorizing about Intercultural Communication*, (Thousand Oaks, CA: Sage, 2005): 121–148; also see Hansen et al., "Cultural Cues."
131. J. R. C. Kuntz, J. R. Kuntz, D. Elenkov, and A. Nabirukhina, "Characterizing Ethical Cases: A Cross-Cultural Investigation of Individual Differences, Organizational Climate, and Leadership on Ethical Decision-Making," *Journal of Business Ethics* (2013): 317–331.
132. R. H. Farrell (ed.), *Off the Record: The Private Papers of Harry S. Truman* (New York: Harper & Row, 1980), 310.
133. S. M. Fowler, "Training across Cultures: What Intercultural Trainers Bring to Diversity Training," *International Journal of Intercultural Relations* 30 (2006): 401–411.
134. See, for example, A. Molinsky, "Cross-Cultural Code-Switching: The Psychological Challenges of Adapting Behavior in Foreign Cultural Interactions," *Academy of Management Review* (2007): 622–640.
135. L. J. Carrell, "Diversity in the Communication Curriculum: Impact on Student Empathy," *Communication Education* 46 (1997): 234–244.
136. Ting-Toomey, "Intercultural Conflict Training"; D. F. Barone, P. S. Hutchings, H. J. Kimmel, H. L. Traub, J. T. Cooper, and C. M. Marshall, "Increasing Empathic Accuracy through Practice and Feedback in a Clinical Interviewing Course," *Journal of Social and Clinical Psychology* 24 (2005): 156–171; J. Hamilton and

R. Woodward-Kron, "Developing Cultural Awareness and Intercultural Communication through Multimedia: A Case Study from Medicine and Health Sciences," *System* 38.4 (2010): 560–568.

Chapter 7

1. M. Anderson, E. A. Vogels, and E. Turner, "The Virtues and Downsides of Online Dating," Pew Research Center, February 6, 2020. https://www.pewresearch.org (accessed May 15, 2020); S. R. Sumter and L. Vandenbosch, "Dating Gone Mobile: Demographic and Personality-Based Correlates of Using Smartphone-Based Dating Applications Among Emerging Adults," *New Media & Society* 21.3 (2019): 655–673; C. Seymour, "Facebook, Undergraduates, and Ruined Relationships: An Exploratory Study," *College Student Journal* 53.4 (2019): 405–416; J. S. Wrench and N. M. Punyanunt-Carter, "From the Front Porch to Swiping Right: The Impact of Technology on Modern Dating," in *The Impact of Social Media in Modern Romantic Relationships*, edited by N. M. Punyanunt-Carter and J. S. Wrench (Lanham, MD: Lexington, 2017): 1–12.

2. K. M. Galvin and C. A. Wilkinson, "The Communication Process: Impersonal and Interpersonal," in *Making Connections: Readings in Relational Communication* 5e, edited by K. M. Galvin (New York: Oxford University Press, 2011), 5–12.

3. E. Berscheid, "Interpersonal Attraction," in *The Handbook of Social Psychology*, edited by G. Lindzey and E. Aronson (New York: Random House, 1985), 413–484, as reported in J. A. Simpson and B. A. Harris, "Interpersonal Attraction," in *Perspectives on Close Relationships*, edited by A. L. Weber and J. H. Harvey (Boston: Allyn & Bacon, 1994), 45–66; W. G. Graziano and J. W. Bruce, "Attraction and the Initiation of Relationships: A Review of the Empirical Literature," in *Handbook of Relationship Initiation*, edited by S. Sprecher, A. Wenzel, and J. Harvey (New York: Psychology Press, 2008), 269–295; S. Sprecher and D. Felmlee, "Insider Perspectives on Attraction," in *Handbook of Relationship Initiation*, 297–313.

4. E. A Croes, M. L. Antheunis, A. Schouten, and E. J. Krahmer, "Social Attraction in Video-Mediated Communication: The Role of Nonverbal Affiliative Behavior," *Journal of Social and Personal Relationships* 36.4 (2019): 1210–1232; T. R. Wagner, "When Off-Line Seeks Information Online: The Effect of Modality Switching and Time on Attributional Confidence and Social Attraction," *Communication Research Reports* 35.4 (2018): 346–355.

5. D. K. Ivy and S. T. Wahl, *Nonverbal Communication for a Lifetime* 3e (Dubuque, IA: Kendall Hunt, 2019); L. K. Guerrero and K. Floyd, *Nonverbal Communication in Close Relationships* (Mahwah, NJ: Erlbaum, 2006); J. H. Harvey and A. L. Weber, *Odyssey of the Heart: Close Relationships in the 21st Century* 2e (Mahwah, NJ: Erlbaum, 2002).

6. M. Boler, "Hypes, Hopes, and Actualities: New Digital Cartesianism and Bodies in Cyberspace," in *The New Media and Cybercultures Anthology*, edited by P. K. Nayar (Malden, MA: Wiley-Blackwell, 2010), 185–208; D. Currier, "Assembling Bodies in Cyberspace: Technologies, Bodies, and Sexual Difference," in *The New Media and Cybercultures Anthology*, 254–267; J. A. McCown, D. Fisher, R. Page, and M. Homant, "Internet Relationships: People Who Meet People," *Cyberpsychology & Behavior* 4 (2001): 593–596; A. Cooper and L. Sportolari, "Romance in Cyberspace: Understanding Online Attraction," *Journal of Sex Education and Therapy* 22 (1997): 7–14; K. Y. A. McKenna, A. S. Green, and M. E. J. Gleason, "Relationship Formation on the Internet: What's the Big Attraction?" *Journal of Social Issues* 58 (2002): 9–31.

7. A. Cooper, I. P. McLoughlin, and K. M. Campbell, "Sexuality in Cyberspace: Update for the 21st Century," *Cyberpsychology & Behavior* 32 (2000): 521–536.

8. W. Wolfe Herd, "Welcome to the Hive," *Bumble* (April, 2019), 1; A. S. Breslow, R. Sandil, M. E. Brewster, M. C. Parent, A. Chan, A. Yucel, N. Bensmiller, and E. Glaeser, "Adonis on the Apps: Online Objectification, Self-Esteem, and Sexual Minority Men," *Psychology of Men & Masculinities* 21.1 (2020): 25–35; B. Miller, "A Picture Is Worth 1000 Messages: Investigating Face and Body Photos on Mobile Dating Apps for Men Who Have Sex with Men," *Journal of Homosexuality* (2019): doi.org/10.1080/00918369.2019.1610630; C. D. Wotipka and A. C. High, "An Idealized Self or the Real Me? Predicting Attraction to Online Dating Profiles Using Selective Self-Presentation and Warranting," *Communication Monographs* 83 (2016): 281–302; C. L. Toma and J. T. Hancock, "Looks and Lies: The Role of Physical Attractiveness in Online Dating Self-Presentation and Deception," *Communication Research* 37 (2010): 335–351; C. L. Toma and J. D. D'Angelo, "Connecting Profile-to-Profile: How People Self-Present and Form Impressions of Others through Online Dating Profiles," in *The Impact of Social Media in Modern Romantic Relationships*, 147–161; J. E. Brooks and H. A. Neville, "Interracial Attraction among College Men," *Journal of Social & Personal Relationships* 34 (2017): 166–183; K. A. Gibson, A. E. Thompson, and L. F. O'Sullivan, "Love Thy Neighbour: Personality Traits, Relationship Quality, and Attraction to Others as Predictors of Infidelity among Young Adults," *Canadian Journal of Human Sexuality*, 25 (2016): 186–198.

9. S. Niehus, A. Reifman, D. A. Weiser, N. M. Punyanunt-Carter, J. Flora, V. S. Arias, and C. R. Oldham, "Guilty Pleasure? Communicating Sexually Explicit Content on Dating Apps and Disillusionment with App Usage," *Human Communication Research* 46.1 (2020): 55–85; T. Van der Zanden, A. P. Schouten, M. B. J. Mos, and E. J. Krahmer, "Impression Formation on Online Dating Sites: Effects of Language Errors in Profile Texts on Perceptions of Profile Owners' Attractiveness," *Journal of Social and Personal Relationships* 37.3 (2020): 758–778; L. E. Lefebvre, "Swiping Me Off My Feet," *Journal of Social and Personal Relationships* 35.9 (2018): 1205–1229; M. Rosenfeld, "Are Tinder and Dating Apps Changing Dating and Mating in the USA?" in *Families and Technology*, edited by J. Van Hook, S. M. McHale, and V. King (Cham, Switzerland: Springer Nature Switzerland AG, Vol. 9, 2018), 103–117; Wrench and Punyanunt-Carter, "From the Front Porch to Swiping Right"; V. Santiago Arias, N. M. Punyanunt-Carter, and J. S. Wrench, "Future Directions for Swiping Right: The Impact of Technology on Modern Dating," in *The Impact of Social Media in Modern Romantic Relationships*, 261–272.

10. L. K. Guerrero, P. A. Andersen, and W. A. Afifi, *Close Encounters: Communicating in Relationships* 5e (Los Angeles: Sage, 2017), 54.

11. S. W. Duck, *Personal Relationships and Personal Constructs: A Study of Friendship Formation* (New York: Wiley, 1973).

12. F. O. Poulsen, T. B. Holman, D. M. Busby, and J. S. Carroll, "Physical Attraction, Attachment Style, and Dating Development," *Journal of Social and Personal Relationships* 30 (2013): 301–319; S. A. Takeuchi, "On the Matching Phenomenon in Courtship: A Probability Matching Theory of Mate Selection," *Marriage and Family Review* 40 (2006): 25–51; G. B. Forbes, L. E. Adams-Curtis, B. Rade, and P. Jaberg, "Body Dissatisfaction in Women and Men: The Role of Gender-Typing and Self-Esteem," *Sex Roles* 44 (2001): 461–484; D. Bar-Tal and L. Saxe, "Perceptions of Similarity and Dissimilarity of Attractive Couples and Individuals," *Journal of Personality and Social Psychology* 33 (1976): 772–781.

13. International Labor Organization, "Women in Business and Management, The business Case for Change," 2019.

14. International Finance Corporation, "Board gender diversity in ASEAN," 2019.

15. https://www.russellreynolds.com/en/Insights/thought-leadership

16. D. M. Amodio and C. J. Showers, "'Similarity Breeds Liking' Revisited: The Moderating Role of Commitment," *Journal of Social and Personal Relationships* 22 (2005): 817–836.

17. Z. Cemalcilar, L. Baruh, M. Kezer, R. Gizem Kamiloglu, and B. Higedli, "Role of Personality Traits in First Impressions: An Investigation of Actual and Perceived Personality Similarity Effects on Interpersonal Attraction across Communication

Modalities," *Journal of Research in Personality* 76 (2018): 139–149; R. Singh, Y. Y. Tay, and K. Sankaran, "Causal Role of Trust in Interpersonal Attraction from Attitude Similarity," *Journal of Social and Personal Relationships* 34.5 (2017): 717–731; R. Goei and R. Tamborini, "Disclosiveness, Similarity, Attraction and the Comfort of Strangers," *Kentucky Journal of Communication* 36.1 (2017): 52–66; Y. Cheng and D. Gruhn, "Perceived Similarity in Emotional Reaction Profiles between the Self and a Close Other as a Predictor of Emotional Well-Being," *Journal of Social & Personal Relationships* 33 (2016): 711–732; Y. Ng, C. Kulik, and P. Bordia, "The Moderating Role of Intergroup Contact in Race Composition, Perceived Similarity, and Applicant Attraction Relationships," *Journal of Business & Psychology* 31 (2016): 415–431; S. Sprecher, "Effects of Actual (Manipulated) and Perceived Similarity on Liking in Get-Acquainted Interactions: The Role of Communication," *Communication Monographs* 81 (2014): 4–27.

18. S. Peters and H. Salzsieder, "What Makes You Swipe Right?: Gender Similarity in Interpersonal Attraction in a Simulated Online Dating Context," *Psi Chi Journal of Psychological Research* 23.4 (2018): 320–329; P. M. Sias, H. Pedersen, E. B. Gallagher, and I. Kopaneva, "Workplace Friendship in the Electronically Connected Organization," *Human Communication Research* 38 (2012): 253–279; A. C. High and D. H. Solomon, "Locating Computer-Mediated Social Support within Online Communication Environments," in *Computer-Mediated Communication in Personal Relationships*, edited by K. B. Wright and L. M. Webb (New York: Peter Lang, 2010), 119–136.

19. M. J. McClure, E. Auger, and J. E. Lydon, "What They Say, How They Say It, or How They Look Saying It: Which Channels of Communication Link Attachment Anxiety and Problematic First Impressions?" *Journal of Social and Personal Relationships* 37.4 (2020): 1216–1224; O. Romaniuk, "The First Impression Matters: The Art of Male Romantic Communication in American Media Dating Culture," *Discourse & Interaction* 13.1 (2020): 67–91.

20. Fehr, "Friendship Formation"; Ivy and Wahl, *Nonverbal Communication for a Lifetime* 3e.

21. K. Koban and S. Kruger, "Out of Sight (Not Yet) Out of Mind: The Impact of Tie Strength on Direct Interaction and Social Surveillance Among Geographically Close and Long-Distance Facebook Friends," *Communication Research Reports* 35.1 (2018): 74–84; A. J. Johnson, E. Bostwick, and M. Bassick, "Long-Distance Versus Geographically Close Romantic Relationships: The Effects of Social Media on the Development and Maintenance of These Relationships," in *The Impact of Social Media in Modern Romantic Relationships*, 113–129; I. A. Cionea, S. V. Wilson Mumpower, and M. A. Bassick, "Serial Argument Goals, Tactics, and Outcomes in Long-Distance and Geographically Close Romantic Relationships," *Southern Communication Journal* 84.1 (2019): 1–16; C. J. Billedo, P. Kerkhof, and C. Finkenauer, "The Use of Social Networking Sites for Relationship Maintenance in Long-Distance and Geographically Close Romantic Relationships," *Cyberpsychology, Behavior and Social Networking* 18 (2015): 152–157; J. L. Borelli, H. F. Rasmussen, M. L. Burkhart, and D. A. Sbarra, "Relational Savoring in Long-Distance Romantic Relationships," *Journal of Social & Personal Relationships* 32 (2015): 1083–1108.

22. C. L. Jiang and J. T. Hancock, "Absence Makes the Communication Grow Fonder: Geographic Separation, Interpersonal Media, and Intimacy in Dating Relationships," *Journal of Communication* 63 (2013): 556–577; K. C. Maguire, D. Heinemann-LaFave, and E. Sahlstein, "'To Be Connected, Yet Not at All': Relational Presence, Absence, and Maintenance in the Context of a Wartime Deployment," *Western Journal of Communication* 77 (2013): 249–271; K. C. Maguire and T. A. Kinney, "When Distance Is Problematic: Communication, Coping, and Relational Satisfaction in Female College Students' Long-Distance Dating Relationships," *Journal of Applied Communication Research* 38 (2010): 27–46; L. Stafford, "Geographic Distance and Communication During Courtship," *Communication Research* 37 (2010): 275–297.

23. M. Prensky, "Digital Natives, Digital Immigrants," *On the Horizon* 9 (2001); *Digital Native*, accessed July 6, 2011, www.digitalnative.org/wiki.

24. L. Sharabi and J. P. Caughlin, "Usage Patterns of Social Media across Stages of Romantic Relationships," in *The Impact of Social Media in Modern Romantic Relationships*, 15–29; N. S. Rodriguez and J. Huemmer, "Male Same-Sex Dating in the Digital Age," in *The Impact of Social Media in Modern Romantic Relationships*, 81–89; P. B. Brandtzaeg, "Social Networking Sites: Their Users and Social Implications—A Longitudinal Study," *Journal of Computer-Mediated Communication* 17 (2012): 467–488; D. Ballard-Reisch, B. Rozzell, L. Heldman, and D. Kamerer, "Microchannels and CMC: Short Paths to Developing, Maintaining, and Dissolving Relationships," in *Computer Mediated Communication in Personal Relationships*, 56–78; K. Shonbeck, "Communicating in a Connected World," in *Making Connections* 5e, 393–400.

25. N. Lozza, C. Spoerri, U. Ehlert, M. Kesselring, P. Hubmann, W. Tschacher, and R. La Marca, "Nonverbal Synchrony and Complementarity in Unacquainted Same-Sex Dyads: A Comparison in a Competitive Context," *Journal of Nonverbal Behavior* 42.2 (2018): 179–197; M. Karampela, A. Tregear, J. Ansell, and S. Dunnett, "When Opposites Attract? Exploring the Existence of Complementarity in Self-Brand Congruence Processes," *Psychology & Marketing* 35.8 (2018): 573–585; P. M. Markey and C. N. Markey, "Romantic Ideals, Romantic Obtainment, and Relationship Experiences: The Complementarity of Interpersonal Traits among Romantic Partners," *Journal of Social and Personal Relationships* 24 (2007): 517–533; Guerrero et al., *Close Encounters*.

26. R. Watson, M. Daffern, and S. Thomas, "The Impact of Interpersonal Style and Interpersonal Complementarity on the Therapeutic Alliance between Therapists and Offenders in Sex Offender Treatment," *Sexual Abuse: Journal of Research and Treatment* 29 (2017): 107–127.

27. J. A. Hall, M. A. Ruben, and Swatantra, "First Impressions of Physicians According to Their Physical and Social Group Characteristics," *Journal of Nonverbal Behavior* 44 (2020): 279–299; T. Kinley, J. Strubel, and A. Amlani, "Impression Formation of Male and Female Millennial Students Wearing Eye Glasses or Hearing Aids," *Journal of Nonverbal Behavior* 43 (2019): 357–379; A. Todorov, *Face Value: The Irresistible Influence of First Impressions* (Princeton: Princeton University Press, 2017); D. Re and N. Rule, "Making a (False) Impression: The Role of Business Experience in First Impressions of CEO Leadership Ability," *Journal of Nonverbal Behavior* 40 (2016): 235–245; R. Petrican, A. Todorov, and C. Grady, "Personality at Face Value: Facial Appearance Predicts Self and Other Personality Judgments among Strangers and Spouses," *Journal of Nonverbal Behavior* 38 (2014): 259–277; H. Fisher, "The First Three Minutes," *O: The Oprah Winfrey Magazine* (November 2009): 140.

28. A. Mehrabian, *Nonverbal Communication* (Chicago: Aldine-Atherton, 1972).

29. L. Zhu and D. Anagondahalli, "Predicting Student Satisfaction: The Role of Academic Entitlement and Nonverbal Immediacy," *Communication Reports* 31.1 (2018): 41–25; C. E. Hill and S. Gupta, "The Use of Immediacy in Supervisory Relationships," in *Developing the Therapeutic Relationship: Integrating Case Studies, Research, and Practice*, edited by O. Tishby and H. Wiseman (Washington, DC: American Psychological Association, 2018), 289–314; S. Kelly, C. Rice, B. Wyatt, J. Ducking, and Z. Denton, "Teacher Immediacy and Decreased Student Quantitative Reasoning Anxiety: The Mediating Effect of Perception," *Communication Education* 64 (2015): 171–186; M. Jia, C. Jiuqing, and C. L. Hale, "Workplace Emotion and Communication: Supervisor Nonverbal Immediacy, Employees' Emotion Experience, and Their Communication Motives," *Management Communication Quarterly* 31 (2017): 69–87; G. Bodie, K. E. Cannava, A. J. Vickery, and S. M. Jones, "Patterns of Nonverbal Adaptation in Supportive Interactions," *Communication Studies* 67 (2016): 3–19; A. M. Ledbetter and A. T. Keating,

"Maintaining Facebook Friendships: Everyday Talk as a Mediator of Threats to Closeness," *Western Journal of Communication* 79 (2015): 197–217; R. Ranganath, D. Jurafsky, and D. A. McFarland, "Detecting Friendly, Flirtatious, Awkward, and Assertive Speech in Speed-Dates," *Computer Speech & Language* 27 (2013): 89–115; J. Deyo, P. Walt, and L. Davis, "Rapidly Recognizing Relationships: Observing Speed Dating in the South," *Qualitative Research Reports in Communication* 12 (2011): 71–78; M. L. Houser, S. M. Horan, and L. A. Furler, "Dating in the Fast Lane: How Communication Predicts Speed-Dating Success," *Journal of Social and Personal Relationships* 25 (2008): 749–768; P. W. Eastwick and E. J. Finkel, "Speed-Dating: A Powerful and Flexible Paradigm for Studying Romantic Relationship Initiation," in *Handbook of Relationship Initiation*, 297–313.

30. A. Bainbridge Frymier, A. W. Goldman, and C. J. Claus, "Why Nonverbal Immediacy Matters: A Motivation Explanation," *Communication Quarterly* 67.5 (2019): 526–539; P. Collett, *The Book of Tells* (London: Bantam, 2004); J. A. Daly, E. Hogg, D. Sacks, M. Smith, and L. Zimring, "Sex and Relationship Affect Social Self-Grooming," in *The Nonverbal Communication Reader: Classic and Contemporary Readings* 2e, edited by L. K. Guerrero, J. DeVito, and M. L. Hecht (Prospect Heights, IL: Waveland, 1999), 56–61.

31. J. A. Wade, "(I Think) You Are Pretty: A Behavior Analytic Conceptualization of Flirtation," *Perspectives on Behavior Science* 41.2 (2018): 615–636; J. White, H. Lorenz, C. Perilloux, and A. Lee, "Creative Casanovas: Mating Strategy Predicts Using—But Not Preferring—Atypical Flirting Tactics," *Evolutionary Psychological Science* 4.4 (2018): 443–455; S. A. Speer, "Flirting: A Designedly Ambiguous Action?" *Research in Language & Social Interaction* 50 (2017): 128–150; J. A. Hall, "Interpreting Social-Sexual Communication: Relational Framing Theory and Social-Sexual Communication, Attraction, and Intent," *Human Communication Research* 42 (2016): 138–164; J. A. Hall and C. Xing, "The Verbal and Nonverbal Correlates of the Five Flirting Styles," *Journal of Nonverbal Behavior* 39 (2015): 41–68; J. Hall, C. Xing, and S. Brooks, "Accurately Detecting Flirting: Error Management Theory, the Traditional Sexual Script, and Flirting Base Rate," *Communication Research* 42 (2015): 939–958; Guerrero et al., *Close Encounters*.

32. E. M. Ross and J. A. Hall, "The Traditional Sexual Script and Humor in Courtship," *Humor: International Journal of Humor Research* 33.2 (2020): 197–218.

33. K. Kaspar and J. Krull, "Incidental Haptic Stimulation in the Context of Flirt Behavior," *Journal of Nonverbal Behavior* 37 (2013): 165–173; J. A. Hall, S. Carter, M. J. Cody, and J. M. Albright, "Individual Differences in the Communication of Romantic Interest: Development of the Flirting Styles Inventory," *Communication Quarterly* 58 (2010): 365–393.

34. Anderson et al., "The Virtues and Downsides of Online Dating."

35. N. M. Punyanunt-Carter and T. R. Wagner, "Interpersonal Communication Motives for Flirting Face to Face and through Texting," *Cyberpsychology, Behavior, and Social Networking* 21.4 (2018): 229–233; E. L. Cohen, N. D. Bowman, and K. Borchert, "Private Flirts, Public Friends: Understanding Romantic Jealous Responses to an Ambiguous Social Networking Site Message as a Function of Message Access Exclusivity," *Computers in Human Behavior* 35 (2014): 533–541; C. Fleuriet, M. Cole, and L. K. Guerrero, "Exploring Facebook: Attachment Style and Nonverbal Message Characteristics as Predictors of Anticipated Emotional Reactions to Facebook Postings," *Journal of Nonverbal Behavior* 38 (2014): 429–450.

36. M. T. Whitty, "Cyber-Flirting: An Examination of Men's and Women's Flirting Behaviour Both Offline and on the Internet," *Behaviour Change* 21 (2004): 115–126. For more information on flirting and conveying attraction, see D. D. Henningsen, M. L. M. Henningsen, E. McWorthy, C. McWorthy, and L. McWorthy, "Exploring the Effects of Sex and Mode of Presentation in Perceptions of Dating Goals in Video-Dating," *Journal of Communication* 61 (2011): 641–658; D. D. Henningsen, F. Kartch, N. Orr, and A. Brown, "The Perceptions of Verbal and Nonverbal Flirting Cues in Cross-Sex Interactions," *Human Communication* 12 (2009): 371–381; J. M. Albright, "How Do I Love Thee and Thee and Thee: Self-Presentation, Deception, and Multiple Relationships Online," in *Online M@tchmaking*, edited by M. T. Whitty, A. Baker, and J. A. Inman (New York: Palgrave Macmillan, 2007), 81–93; D. D. Henningsen, M. Braz, and E. Davies, "Why Do We Flirt?" *Journal of Business Communication* 45 (2008): 483–502; M. T. Whitty and A. N. Carr, "Cyberspace as Potential Space: Considering the Web as a Playground to Cyber-Flirt," *Human Relations* 56 (2003): 869–891.

37. "Netflix and chill," Wikipedia, accessed March 11, 2017, from https://en.wikipedia.org.

38. P. Seargeant, *The Emoji Revolution* (Cambridge, UK: Cambridge University Press, 2019); A. Gregory, "Flirtmoji," *Bitch* (Fall 2016): 14; J. King-Slutzky, "An Emoji Guide for the Text Message Clueless," accessed March 11, 2017, from www.nerve.com; https://flirtmoji.com.

39. L. L. Sharabi and T. A. Dykstra-DeVette, "From First Email to First Date: Strategies for Initiating Relationships in Online Dating," *Journal of Social and Personal Relationships* 36.11-12 (2019): 3389–3407; L. Stafford and J. D. Hillyer, "Information and Communication Technologies in Personal Relationships," *Review of Communication* 12 (2012): 290–213; M. Lipinski-Harten and R. W. Tafarodi, "A Comparison of Conversational Quality in Online and Face-to-Face First Encounters," *Journal of Language and Social Psychology* 31 (2012): 331–341; J. P. Caughlin and L. L. Sharabi, "A Communicative Interdependence Perspective of Close Relationships: The Connections between Mediated and Unmediated Interactions Matter," *Journal of Communication* 63 (2013): 873–893.

40. Lefebvre, "Swiping Me Off My Feet"; S. Sprecher and S. Metts, "Logging on, Hooking up: The Changing Nature of Romantic Relationship Initiation and Romantic Relating," in *Human Bonding: The Science of Affectional Ties*, edited by C. Hazan and M. I. Campa (New York: Guilford, 2013), 197–225; A. L. Vangelisti, "Interpersonal Processes in Romantic Relationships," in *The SAGE Handbook of Interpersonal Communication* 4e, edited by M. L. Knapp and J. A. Daly (Thousand Oaks, CA: Sage, 2011), 597–632; J. B. Walther, "Theories of Computer-Mediated Communication and Interpersonal Relations," in *The SAGE Handbook of Interpersonal Communication*, 443–480.

41. G. E. Birnbaum, M. Mizrahi, and H. T. Reis, "Fueled by Desire: Sexual Activation Facilitates the Enactment of Relationship-Initiating Behaviors," *Journal of Social and Personal Relationships* 36.10 (2019): 3057–3074; D. Haunani Solomon and M. E. Roloff, "Relationship Initiation and Growth," in *The Cambridge Handbook of Personal Relationships* 3e, edited by A. L. Vangelisti and D. Perlman (Cambridge, UK: Cambridge University Press, 2018): 79–89; McClure et al., "What They Say, How They Say It, or How They Look Saying It"; Romaniuk, "The First Impression Matters"; D. A. Stinson, J. J. Cameron, and K. J. Robinson, "The Good, the Bad, and the Risky," *Journal of Social & Personal Relationships* 32 (2015): 1109–1136; L. K. Odom, E. Sahlstein Parcell, B. M. A. Baker, and V. Cronin-Fisher, "Communication and Female Date Initiation: Differences in Perceptions Based on Assertiveness of Initiator," *Iowa Journal of Communication* 47 (2015): 177–196; D. Pillet-Shore, "Doing Introductions: The Work Involved in Meeting Someone New," *Communication Monographs* 78 (2011): 73–95.

42. S. Turkle, *Reclaiming Conversation: The Power of Talk in a Digital Age* (New York: Penguin, 2016).

43. M. Sunnafrank and A. Ramirez, "At First Sight: Persistent Relational Effects of Get-Acquainted Conversations," *Journal of Social and Personal Relationships* 21 (2004): 361–379.

44. C. R. Berger and R. J. Calabrese, "Some Explorations in Initial Interaction and Beyond: Toward a Developmental Theory of Interpersonal Communication," *Human Communication Research* 1 (1975): 99–112; C. R. Berger and J. J. Bradac, *Language and Social Knowledge: Uncertainty in Interpersonal Relations* (Baltimore: Edward Arnold, 1982); W. Peng and Q. Huang, "An Examination of Surprise and Emotions in the Processing of Anecdotal Evidence," *Health Communication* 35.6 (2020): 766–777;

M. C. Stewart, "Uncertainty Reduction and Technologically Mediated Communication: Implications to Marital Communication During Wartime Deployment," *Ohio Communication Journal* 56 (2018): 136–148; A. Barrett, "Information-Seeking from Organizational Communication Sources During Healthcare Technology Change," *Communication Quarterly* 66.1 (2018): 58–78.

45. For more research on relational uncertainty, a topic related to uncertainty reduction theory, we refer you to the work of Leanne Knobloch and others; see L. K. Knobloch, E. D. Basinger, B. Abendschein, E. C. Wehrman, J. K. Monk, and K. G. McAninch, "Communication in Online Forums about the Experience and Management of Relational Uncertainty in Military Life," *Journal of Family Communication* 18.1 (2018): 13–31; L. K. Knobloch, A. T. Ebata, P. C. McGlaughlin, and J. A. Theiss, "Generalized Anxiety and Relational Uncertainty as Predictors of Topic Avoidance During Reintegration Following Military Deployment," *Communication Monographs* 80 (2013): 452–477; L. K. Knobloch and J. A. Theiss, "Relational Uncertainty and Relationship Talk within Courtship: A Longitudinal Actor-Partner Interdependence Model," *Communication Monographs* 78 (2011): 3–26; L. K. Knobloch, "Relational Uncertainty and Interpersonal Communication," in *New Directions in Interpersonal Communication Research*, 69–93; J. B. Stein, P. A. Mongeau, and N. I. Truscelli, "Identifying and Measuring Network-Based Relational Uncertainty: Looking Outside of the Dyadic Bubble," *Journal of Social and Personal Relationships* 37.2 (2020): 491–515; A. L. Delaney and L. L. Sharabi, "Relational Uncertainty and Interference from a Partner as Predictors of Demand/Withdraw in Couples with Depressive Symptoms," *Western Journal of Communication* 84.1 (2020): 58–78; D. Haunani Solomon and K. St. Cyr Brisini, "Relational Uncertainty and Interdependence Processes in Marriage: A Test of Relational Turbulence Theory," *Journal of Social and Personal Relationships* 36.8 (2019): 2416–2436; M. G. Blight, E. K. Ruppel, and K. Jagiello, "'Using Facebook Lets Me Know What He Is Doing': Relational Uncertainty, Breakups, and Renewals in On-Again/Off-Again Relationships," *Southern Communication Journal* 84.5 (2019): 328–339.

46. L. L. Sharabi and J. P. Caughlin, "Deception in Online Dating: Significance and Implications for the First Offline Date," *New Media & Society* 21.1 (2019): 229–247; D. M. Markowitz and J. T. Hancock, "Deception in Mobile Dating Conversations," *Journal of Communication* 68.3 (2018): 547–569; N. B. Ellison, J. T. Hancock, and C. L. Toma, "Profile as Promise: A Framework for Conceptualizing Veracity in Online Dating Self-Presentations," *New Media & Society* 14 (2012): 45–62; R. E. Guadagno, B. M. Okdie, and S. A. Kruse, "Dating Deception: Gender, Online Dating, and Exaggerated Self-Presentation," *Computers in Human Behavior* 28 (2012): 642–647; J. A. Hall, N. Park, S. Hayeon, and J. C. Michael, "Strategic Misrepresentation in Online Dating: The Effects of Gender, Self-Monitoring, and Personality Traits," *Journal of Social & Personal Relationships* 27 (2010): 117–135; J. T. Hancock and C. L. Toma, "Putting Your Best Face Forward: The Accuracy of Online Dating Photographs," *Journal of Communication* 59 (2009): 367–386; C. L. Toma and J. T. Hancock, "A New Twist on Love's Labor: Self-Presentation in Online Dating Profiles," in *Computer-Mediated Communication in Personal Relationships*, 41–55.

47. C. L. Kleinke, F. B. Meeker, and R. A. Staneski, "Preference for Opening Lines: Comparing Ratings by Men and Women," *Sex Roles* 15 (1986): 585–600; E. Weber, *How to Pick Up Girls!* (New York: Bantam Books, 1970).

48. C. Senko and V. Fyffe, "An Evolutionary Perspective on Effective vs. Ineffective Pick-Up Lines," *Journal of Social Psychology* 150 (2010): 648–667.

49. J. P. Anderson and C. Zou, "Exclusion of Sexual Minority Couples from Research," *Health Science Journal* 9.6 (2015): 1–9; K. Blair, "The State of LGBTQ-Inclusive Research Methods in Relationship Science and How We Can Do Better," *Relations Research News* 13 (2019): 7–12; E. S. Spengler, E. N. DeVore, P. M. Spengler, and N. A. Lee, "What Does 'Couple' Mean in Couple Therapy Outcomes Research? A Systematic Review of the Implicit and Explicit, Inclusion and Exclusion of Gender and Sexual Minority Individuals and Identities," *Journal of Marital and Family Therapy* 46.2 (2020): 240–255; D. Umberson, M. B. Thomeer, R. A. Kroger, A. C. Lodge, and M. Xu, "Challenges and Opportunities for Research on Same-Sex Relationships," *Journal of Marriage and Family* 77.1 (2015): 96–111.

50. M. L. Fisher, S. Coughlin, and J. T. Wade, "Can I Have Your Number? Men's Perceived Effectiveness of Pick-Up Lines Used by Women," *Personality and Individual Differences* 153 (2020): doi.org/10.1016/j.paid.2019.109664.

51. K. Stapleton, "Questioning," in *The Handbook of Communication Skills* 4e, edited by O. Hargie (Abingdon, UK: Routledge, 2019), 135–162.

52. Sharabi and Caughlin, "Usage Patterns of Social Media across Stages of Romantic Relationships."

53. S. Casale and V. Banchi, "Narcissism and Problematic Social Media Use: A Systematic Literature Review," *Addictive Behaviors Reports* 11 (2020): ArtID: 100252; J. Brailovskaia, H.-W. Bierhoff, E. Rohmann, F. Raeder, and J. Margraf, "The Relationship Between Narcissism, Intensity of Facebook Use, Facebook Flow and Facebook Addiction," *Addictive Behaviors Reports* 11 (2020): ArtID: 100265; W. Hart, J. Adams, K. A. Burton, and G. K. Tortoriello, "Narcissism and Self-Presentation: Profiling Grandiose and Vulnerable Narcissists' Self-Presentation Tactic Use," *Personality & Individual Differences* 104 (2017): 48–57; D. Wang, "A Study of the Relationship between Narcissism, Extraversion, Drive for Entertainment, and Narcissistic Behavior on Social Networking Sites," *Computers in Human Behavior* 66 (2017): 138–148.

54. A. L. Vangelisti, M. L. Knapp, and J. A. Daly, "Conversational Narcissism," *Communication Monographs* 57 (1990): 251–274; J. M. Twenge, S. Konrath, J. D. Foster, W. K. Campbell, and B. J. Bushman, "Egos Inflating over Time: A Cross-Temporal Meta-Analysis of the Narcissistic Personality Inventory," *Journal of Personality* 76 (2008): 875–901; J. M. Twenge, *Generation Me: Why Today's Young Americans Are More Confident, Assertive, Entitled—and More Miserable Than Ever Before* Revised/Updated (New York: Free Press, 2014); J. M. Twenge, *iGen: Why Today's Super-Connected Kids Are Growing Up Less Rebellious, More Tolerant, Less Happy—and Completely Unprepared for Adulthood—and What That Means for the Rest of Us* (New York: Atria Books, 2018); J. M. Twenge, "The Narcissism Epidemic: Narcissism Is on the Rise among Individuals and in American Culture," August 12, 2013, accessed June 15, 2014, www.psychtoday.com; F. Rhodewalt, "Contemporary Perspectives on Narcissism and the Narcissistic Personality Type," in *Handbook of Self and Identity* 2e, edited by M. R. Leary and J. Price Tangney (New York: Guilford, 2013), 571–586.

55. J. Lamkin, J. A. Lavner, and A. Shaffer, "Narcissism and Observed Communication in Couples," *Personality & Individual Differences* 105 (2017): 224–228; W. T. Behary and D. J. Siegel, *Disarming the Narcissist: Surviving and Thriving with the Self-Absorbed* (Oakland, CA: New Harbinger Publications, 2013); C. Malkin, *Rethinking Narcissism: The Secret to Recognizing and Coping with Narcissists* (New York: Harper, 2016)

56. K. Koc-Michalska, A. Schiffrin, A. Lopez, S. Boulianne, and B. Bimber, "From Online Political Posting to Mansplaining: The Gender Gap and Social Media in Political Discourse," *Social Science Computer Review* (2019): doi.org/10.1177/0894439319870259; J. Bridges, "Gendering Metapragmatics in Online Discourse: 'Mansplaining Man Gonna Mansplain. . . ,'" *Discourse, Context & Media* 20 (2017): 94–102.

57. J. Holmes, "Complimenting—A Positive Politeness Strategy," in *Language and Gender: A Reader* 2e, edited by J. Coates and P. Pichler (Malden, MA: Blackwell, 2011), 71–88.

58. J. C. Mirivel, *The Art of Positive Communication: Theory and Practice* (New York: Peter Lang, 2014); M. Strobel, *The Compliment Quotient: Boost Your Spirits, Spark Your Relationships, and Uplift the World* (New York: Wise Roads Press, 2011); C. Matheson, *The Art of the Compliment: Using Kind Words with Grace and Style* (New

York: Skyhorse Publishing, 2009); D. C. Marigold, J. G. Holmes, and M. Ross, "More Than Words: Compliments from Romantic Partners Foster Security in Low Self-Esteem Individuals," *Journal of Personality and Social Psychology* 92 (2007): 232–248; E. M. Doohan and V. Manusov, "The Communication of Compliments in Romantic Relationships: An Investigation of Relational Satisfaction and Sex Differences and Similarities in Compliment Behavior," *Western Journal of Communication* 68 (2004): 170–194; C. Parisi and P. Wogan, "Compliment Topics and Gender," *Women & Language* 29 (2006): 21–28.

59. R. Kahalon, N. Schnabel, and J. C. Becker, "'Don't Bother Your Pretty Little Head': Appearance Compliments Lead to Improved Mood but Impaired Cognitive Performance," *Psychology of Women Quarterly* 42.2 (2018): 136–150.

60. M. W. Placencia, A. Lower, and H. Powell, "Complimenting Behaviour on Facebook: Responding to Compliments in American English," *Pragmatics & Society* 7.3 (2016): 339–365; M. Beck, "Why It's Harder to Receive Than to Give," *O: The Oprah Winfrey Magazine* (September 2006): 81–83.

61. "The Health Benefits of Strong Relationships," *Harvard Women's Health Watch* 18 (December 2010): 1.

62. B. G. Ogolsky and J. K. Monk, "Maintaining the Literature on Relationship Maintenance," in *Relationship Maintenance: Theory, Process, and Context*, edited by B. G. Ogolsky and J. K. Monk (Cambridge, UK: Cambridge University Press, 2019), 1–14; B. G. Ogolsky and J. K. Monk, "Maintaining Relationships," in *The Cambridge Handbook of Personal Relationships* 3e, 523–537; L. Stafford, "Communication and Relationship Maintenance," in *Relationship Maintenance*, 109–133; M. Dainton and S. A. Myers, *Communication and Relationship Maintenance* (San Diego, CA: Cognella Academic Publishing, 2019); P. A. Mongeau, L. J. van Raalte, L. Bednarchik, and M. Generous, "Investigating and Extending Variation Among Friends with Benefits Relationships: Relationship Maintenance and Social Support," *Southern Communication Journal* 84.5 (2019): 275–286; A. Ledbetter, "Relational Maintenance Behavior and Shared TV Viewing as Mediators of the Association between Romanticism and Romantic Relationship Quality," *Communication Studies* 68 (2017): 95–114; C. Fowler and J. Gasiorek, "Depressive Symptoms, Excessive Reassurance Seeking, and Relationship Maintenance," *Journal of Social & Personal Relationships* 34 (2017): 91–113.

63. Harvey and Weber, *Odyssey of the Heart*, 105–106.

64. B. L. Lane and C. W. Piercy, "Making Sense of Becoming Facebook Official: Implications for Identity and Time," in *The Impact of Social Media in Modern Romantic Relationships*, 31–45.

65. S. Morgan, "Cybercrime To Cost The World $10.5 Trillion Annually By 2025," *Cybercrime Magazine*, November 13, 2020.

66. J. Myhre, "Privacy on Social Media Guards Against Identity Theft," *Business News Daily*, January 11, 2021.

67. J. Faden and G. Gorton, "The Doorknob Phenomenon in Clinical Practice," *American Family Physician* (2018), 52–53; D. Gitlin, "Doorknob Moments," *Psychotherapy Networker* 42 (2019): 17–19; M. N. Wittink, P. Walsh, W. Yilmaz, M. Mendoza, R. L. Street Jr., B. P. Chapman, and P. Duberstein, "Patient Priorities and the Doorknob Phenomenon in Primary Care: Can Technology Improve Disclosure of Patient Stressors?" *Patient Education and Counseling* 101 (2018): 214–220.

68. S. Jourard, *The Transparent Self* (Princeton, NJ: Van Nostrand, 1971).

69. D. W. Johnson, *Reaching Out: Interpersonal Effectiveness and Self-Actualization* 11e (Boston: Pearson, 2012), 48–49.

70. M. Tajmirriyahi and W. Ickes, "Self-Concept Clarity as a Predictor of Self-Disclosure in Romantic Relationships," *Journal of Social and Personal Relationships* 37.6 (2020): 1873–1891.

71. Y. E. Willems, C. Finkenauer, and P. Kerkof, "The Role of Disclosure in Relationships," *Current Opinion in Psychology* 31 (2020): 33–37; R. M. Horne and M. D. Johnson, "Gender Role Attitudes, Relationship Efficacy, and Self-Disclosure in Intimate Relationships," *The Journal of Social Psychology* 158.1 (2018): 37–50; A. M. Dotterer and E. Day, "Parental Knowledge Discrepancies: Examining the Roles of Warmth and Self-Disclosure," *Journal of Youth and Adolescence* 48 (2019): 459–468; E. K. Ruppel, C. Gross, A. Stoll, B. S. Peck, M. Allen, and S.-Y. Kim, "Reflecting on Connecting: Meta-Analysis of Differences between Computer-Mediated and Face-to-Face Self-Disclosure," *Journal of Computer-Mediated Communication* 22 (2017): 18–34; S. A. Rains, S. R. Brunner, and K. Oman, "Self-Disclosure and New Communication Technologies," *Journal of Social and Personal Relationships* 33 (2016): 42–61.

72. K. Shonbeck, "Thoughts on CMC by an E-mailer, IMer, Blog Reader, and Facebooker," in *Making Connections: Readings in Relational Communication* 4e, edited by K. M. Galvin and P. Cooper (Los Angeles: Roxbury, 2006), 372–378.

73. V. J. Derlega, B. Winstead, A. Mathews, and A. L. Braitman, "Why Does Someone Reveal Highly Personal Information? Attributions for and against Self-Disclosure in Close Relationships," *Communication Research Reports* 25 (2008): 115–130.

74. M. Luo and J. T. Hancock, "Self-Disclosure and Social Media: Motivations, Mechanisms and Psychological Well-Being," *Current Opinion in Psychology* 31 (2020): 110–115; R. Zhang and J. S. Fu, "Privacy Management and Self-Disclosure on Social Network Sites: The Moderating Effects of Stress and Gender," *Journal of Computer-Mediated Communication* 25.3 (2020): 236–251; M. Tsay-Vogel, J. Shanahan, and N. Signorielli, "Social Media Cultivating Perceptions of Privacy: A 5-Year Analysis of Privacy Attitudes and Self-Disclosure Behaviors Among Facebook Users," *New Media & Society* 20.1 (2018): 141–161; Z. Liu, X. Wang, Q. Min, and W. Li, "The Effect of Role Conflict on Self-Disclosure in Social Network Sites: An Integrated Perspective of Boundary Regulation and Dual Process Model," *Information Systems* 29 (2019): 279–316; W. Xie and C. Kang, "See You, See Me: Teenagers' Self-Disclosure and Regret of Posting on Social Network Sites," *Computers in Human Behavior* 52 (2015): 398–407; J. E. Wendorf and F. Yang, "Benefits of a Negative Post: Effects of Computer-Mediated Venting on Relationship Maintenance," *Computers in Human Behavior* 52 (2015): 271–277.

75. Sandra Petronio's body of work on communication privacy management (CPM theory) is our major source of information on this topic; see S. Petronio and J. T. Child, "Conceptualization and Operationalization: Utility of Communication Privacy Management Theory," *Current Opinion in Psychology* 31 (2020): 76–82; S. Petronio, "Privacy from a Communication Science Perspective," in *The Handbook of Privacy Studies: An Interdisciplinary Introduction*, edited by B. van der Sloot and A. de Groot (Amsterdam, The Netherlands: Amsterdam University Press, 2018), 387–408; S. Petronio, *Boundaries of Privacy: Dialectics of Disclosure* (Albany: SUNY Press, 2002); S. Petronio, "Brief Status Report on Communication Privacy Management Theory," *Journal of Family Communication* 13 (2013): 6–14; J. T. Child and S. Petronio, "Unpacking the Paradoxes of Privacy in CMC Relationships: The Challenges of Blogging and Relational Communication on the Internet," in *Computer-Mediated Communication in Personal Relationships*, 21–40. For extensions of Petronio's work, see A. M. Ledbetter, "Parent-Child Privacy Boundary Conflict Patterns during the First Year of College: Mediating Family Communication Patterns, Predicting Psychosocial Distress," *Human Communication Research* 45.3 (2019): 255–285; J. Kratzer, "Communication Privacy Management in Senior Citizen Romantic Relationships," *Iowa Journal of Communication* 50.1 (2018): 26–51; K. C. C. Yang, A. Pulido, and Y. Kang, "Exploring the Relationship between Privacy Concerns and Social Media Use Among College Students: A Communication Privacy Management Perspective," *Intercultural Communication Studies* 25 (2016): 46–62; S.-A. A. Jin, "Peeling Back the Multiple Layers of Twitter's Private Disclosure Onion: The Roles of Virtual Identity Discrepancy and Personality Traits in Communication Privacy Management on Twitter," *New Media & Society* 15 (2013): 813–833.

76. L. G. Spencer, IV, "Coming Out, Bringing Out: God's Love, Transgender Identity, and Difference," in *Transgender Communication Studies*, edited by L. G. Spencer, IV, and J. C. Capuzza

(New York: Lexington, 2016), 187–198; K. M. Norwood and P. J. Lannutti, "Families' Experiences with Transgender Identity and Transition: A Family Stress Perspective," in *Transgender Communication Studies*, 51–68; K. B. Carnelley, E. G. Hepper, C. Hicks, and W. Turner, "Perceived Parental Reactions to Coming Out, Attachment, and Romantic Relationship Views," *Attachment and Human Development* 13 (2011): 217–236; M. Vaughan and C. Waehler, "Coming Out Growth: Conceptualizing and Measuring Stress-Related Growth Associated with Coming Out to Others as a Sexual Minority," *Journal of Adult Development* 17 (2010): 94–109; L. Heatherington and J. A. Lavner, "Coming to Terms with Coming Out: Review and Recommendations for Family Systems-Focused Research," *Journal of Family Psychology* 22 (2008): 329–343; M. L. Rasmussen, "The Problem of Coming Out," *Theory into Practice* 43 (2004): 144–151.

77. I. Altman and D. Taylor, *Social Penetration: The Development of Relationships* (New York: Holt, Rinehart and Winston, 1973).

78. J. Luft, *Group Process: An Introduction to Group Dynamics* (Palo Alto, CA: Mayfield, 1970).

79. P. D. Bolls, "Understanding Emotion from a Superordinate Dimensional Perspective: A Productive Way Forward for Communication Processes and Effects Studies," *Communication Monographs* 77 (2010): 146–152.

80. A. Wagner, S. Marusek, and W. Yu, "Sarcasm, the Smiling Poop, and E-Discourse Aggressiveness: Getting Far Too Emotional with Emojis," *Social Semiotics* 30.3 (2020): 305–311; L. Fosslien and M. West Duffy, *No Hard Feelings: The Secret Power of Embracing Emotions at Work* (New York: Portfolio/Penguin, 2019); D. Keltner, J. Tracy, D. A. Sauter, D. C. Cordaro, and G. McNeil, "Expression of Emotions," in *Handbook of Emotions*, edited by L. Feldman Barrett, M. Lewis, and J. M. Haviland-Jones (New York: Guilford, 2016); S. Metts and S. Planalp, "Emotional Experience and Expression: Current Trends and Future Directions in Interpersonal Relationship Research," in *The SAGE Handbook of Interpersonal Communication*, 283–316; E. L. MacGeorge, B. Feng, and B. R. Burleson, "Supportive Communication," in *The SAGE Handbook of Interpersonal Communication*, 317–354.

81. U. Hess, C. Blaison, and K. Kafetsios, "Judging Facial Emotion Expressions in Context: The Influence of Culture and Self-Construal Orientation," *Journal of Nonverbal Behavior* 40 (2016): 55–64; Y. Xiaoqian, T. J. Andrews, and A. W. Young, "Cultural Similarities and Differences in Perceiving and Recognizing Facial Expressions of Basic Emotions," *Journal of Experimental Psychology: Human Perception & Performance* 42 (2016): 423–440.

82. L. A. Samovar, R. E. Porter, E. R. McDaniel, and C. Sexton Roy, *Communication Between Cultures* 9e (Boston: Cengage Learning, 2017); P. A. Andersen, "In Different Dimensions: Nonverbal Communication and Culture," in *Intercultural Communication: A Reader* 14e, edited by L. A. Samovar, R. E. Porter, E. R. McDaniel, and C. Sexton Roy (Belmont, CA: Wadsworth/Cengage Learning, 2014), 229–241.

83. J. Bennett, "How Emotions Play Out behind the Masks," *New York Times* (June 11, 2020): D3.

84. S. F. Waterloo, S. E. Baumgartner, J. Peter, and P. M. Valkenburg, "Norms of Online Expressions of Emotion: Comparing Facebook, Twitter, Instagram, and WhatsApp," *New Media & Society* 20.5 (2018): 1813–1831; U. Hess, R. B. Adams Jr., K. Grammer, and R. E. Kleck, "Face Gender and Emotion Expression: Are Angry Women More Like Men?" *Journal of Vision* 9 (2009): 1–8; A. Campbell and S. Muncer, "Intent to Harm or Injure? Gender and the Expression of Anger," *Aggressive Behavior* 34 (2008): 282–293; T. B. Kashdan, A. Mishra, W. E. Breen, and J. J. Froh, "Gender Differences in Gratitude: Examining Appraisals, Narratives, the Willingness to Express Emotions, and Changes in Psychological Needs," *Journal of Personality* 77 (2009): 1–40.

85. M. S. Kimmel, *Manhood in America: A Cultural History* (Oxford, UK: Oxford University Press, 2017); M. S. Kimmel, *Angry White Men: American Masculinity at the End of an Era* (New York: Nation Books, 2015); M. S. Kimmel, *Guyland: The Perilous World Where Boys Become Men* (New York: Harper Paperbacks, 2009).

86. Jourard, *The Transparent Self*.

87. B. B. Burleson, "Introduction to the Special Issue: Psychological Mediators of Sex Differences in Emotional Support," *Communication Reports* 15 (2002), 1–4; W. Pollack, *Real Boys: Rescuing Our Sons from the Myths of Boyhood* (New York: Owl Books, 1999); O. Silverstein and B. Rashbaum, *The Courage to Raise Good Men* (New York: Penguin, 1995).

88. C. Hesse and E. A. Rauscher, "Privacy Tendencies and Revealing/Concealing: The Moderating Role of Emotional Competence," *Communication Quarterly* 61 (2013): 91–112.

89. A. Arroyo, T. J. Burke, V. J. Young, "The Role of Close Others in Promoting Weight Management and Body Image Outcomes: An Application of Confirmation, Self-Determination, Social Control, and Social Support," *Journal of Social and Personal Relationships* 37.3 (2020): 1030–1050; K. Carr, "Rumination and Perceived Risk in Seeking Social Support as Mediators of the Stressful Impact of Adversity and Posttraumatic Growth," *Western Journal of Communication* 83.4 (2019): 463–482; R. M. McLaren and A. C. High, "The Effect of Under- and Over-Benefited Support Gaps on Hurt Feelings, Esteem, and Relationships," *Communication Research* 46.6 (2019): 785–810; S. A. Rains, C. Akers, C. A. Pavlich, E. Tsetsi, and M. Appelbaum, "Examining the Quality of Social Support Messages Produced Face-to-Face and in Computer-Mediated Communication: The Effects of Hyperpersonal Communication," *Communication Monographs* 86.3 (2019): 271–291; E. L. MacGeorge, L. M. Guntzviller, K. S. Brisini, L. C. Bailey, S. K. Salmon, K. Severen, S. E. Branch, H. M. Lillie, C. K. Lindley, R. G. Pastor, and R. D. Cummings, "The Influence of Emotional Support Quality on Advice Evaluation and Outcomes," *Communication Quarterly* 65 (2017): 80–96.

90. S. A. Rains, E. Tsetsi, C. Akers, C. A. Pavlich, and M. Appelbaum, "Factors Influencing the Quality of Social Support Messages Produced Online: The Role of Responsibility for Distress and Others' Support Attempts," *Communication Research* 46.6 (2019): 866–886; S. Li, B. Feng, and V. S. Wingate, "Give Thanks for a Little and You Will Find a Lot: The Role of a Support Seeker's Reply in Online Support Provision," *Communication Monographs* 86.2 (2019): 251–270; J. Owlett, "Communicating Grief and Loss Online: Evaluating Person-Centered Support Messages," *Communication Teacher* 32.4 (2018): 203–208; L. J. Youngvorst and A. C. High, "'Anyone Free to Chat?' Using Technological Features to Elicit Quality Support Online," *Communication Monographs* 85.2 (2018): 203–223.

91. J. G. Myrick, A. E. Holton, I. Himelboim, and B. Love, "#Stupidcancer: Exploring a Typology of Social Support and the Role of Emotional Expression in a Social Media Community," *Health Communication* 31 (2016): 596–605.

Chapter 8

1. L. Denworth, *Friendship: The Evolution, Biology, and Extraordinary Power of Life's Fundamental Bond* (New York: W. W. Norton, 2020); N. L. Galambos and L. A. Kotylak, "Transformations in Parent-Child Relationships from Adolescence to Adulthood," in *Relationship Pathways: From Adolescence to Young Adulthood*, edited by B. P. Laursen and W. A. Collins (Thousand Oaks, CA: Sage, 2011), 23–42; W. K. Rawlins, *The Compass of Friendship: Narratives, Identities, and Dialogues* (Los Angeles: Sage, 2009); M. Monsour, *Women and Men as Friends: Relationships across the Life Span in the 21st Century* (Mahwah, NJ: Lawrence Erlbaum, 2002); M. Paul, *The Friendship Crisis: Finding, Making, and Keeping Friends When You're Not a Kid Anymore* (New York: Rodale Books, 2005).

2. A. Steinhoff and M. Keller, "Pathways for Childhood Sociomoral Sensitivity in Friendship, Insecurity, and Peer Rejection to Adult Friendship Quality," *Society for Research in Child Development* (2020): doi.org/10.1111/cdev.13381; S. R. Asher and M. S. Weeks, "Friendships in Childhood," in *The Cambridge Handbook of Personal Relationships* 2e, edited by A. L. Vangelisti and D. Perlman (Cambridge, UK: Cambridge University Press, 2018), 119–134; N. Way, *Deep Secrets: Boys' Friendships and the Crisis of Connection* (Cambridge, MA: Harvard University Press, 2013).

3. S. D. Madsen and W. A. Collins, "Personal Relationships in Adolescence and Early Adulthood," in *The Cambridge Handbook of Personal Relationships*, 135–147; C. A. Hafen, B. Laursen, and D. DeLay, "Transformations in Friend Relationships across the Transition into Adolescence," in *Relationship Pathways*, 69–90.
4. J. Yager, *Friendshifts: The Power of Friendship and How It Shapes Our Lives* (Stamford, CT: Hannacroix Creek Books, 2013); C. M. Chow, H. Roelse, D. Buhrmeister, and M. K. Underwood, "Transformations in Friend Relationships across the Transition into Adulthood," in *Relationship Pathways*, 91–112; W. Rawlins, "Being There for Friends," in *Making Connections: Readings in Relational Communication* 4e, edited by K. M. Galvin and P. Cooper (Los Angeles: Roxbury, 2006), 329–332.
5. H. Reeder, "'He's Like a Brother': The Social Construction of Satisfying Cross-Sex Friendship Roles," *Sexuality & Culture* 21 (2017): 142–162; S. Nelson, *Frientimacy: How to Deepen Friendships for Lifelong Health and Happiness* (Berkeley, CA: Seal Press, 2016); B. McEwan and L. K. Guerrero, "Freshmen Engagement through Communication: Predicting Friendship Formation Strategies and Perceived Availability of Network Resources from Communication Skills," *Communication Studies* 61 (2010): 445–463; B. Fehr, "Friendship Formation," in *Handbook of Relationship Initiation*, edited by S. Sprecher, A. Wenzel, and J. Harvey (New York: Psychology Press, 2008), 29–54; G. Foster, "Making Friends: A Nonexperimental Analysis of Social Pair Formation," *Human Relations* 58 (2005): 1443–1465; A. J. Johnson, E. Wittenberg, M. M. Villagran, M. Mazur, and P. Villagran, "Relational Progression as a Dialectic: Examining Turning Points in Communication among Friends," *Communication Monographs* 70 (2003): 230–249.
6. J. M. McCabe, *Connecting in College: How Friendship Networks Matter for Academic and Social Success* (Chicago: University of Chicago Press, 2016).
7. R. Blieszner and A. M. Ogletree, "Close Relationships in Middle and Late Adulthood," in *The Cambridge Handbook of Personal Relationships*, 148–160; R. I. M. Dunbar, "The Anatomy of Friendship," *Trends in Cognitive Sciences* 22.1 (2018): 32–51; J. Harwood, *Understanding Communication and Aging* 2e (San Diego, CA: Cognella Academic Publishing, 2017); L. Gee, *Friends: Why Men and Women Are from the Same Planet* (New York: Bloomsbury, 2004); Monsour, *Women and Men as Friends*.
8. L. H. Turner and R. West, "The Challenge of Defining 'Family,'" in *The SAGE Handbook of Family Communication* 4e, edited by L. H. Turner and R. West (Thousand Oaks, CA: Sage, 2014), 10–25; E. A. Suter, L. A. Baxter, L. M. Seurer, and L. J. Thomas, "Discursive Constructions of the Meaning of 'Family' in Online Narratives of Foster Adoptive Parents," *Communication Monographs* 81 (2014): 59–78; V. Satir, "The Rules You Live By," in *Making Connections* 4e, 168–174; R. S. Miller, *Intimate Relationships* 6e (New York: McGraw-Hill, 2011).
9. *Miami Herald* (July 9, 1982): 12A.
10. "Stepfamily Statistics," *The Stepfamily Foundation*, www.stepfamily.org (accessed July 13, 2020); P. Schrodt, "Coparental Communication with Nonresidential Parents as a Predictor of Children's Feelings of Being Caught in Stepfamilies," *Communication Reports* 29 (2016): 63–74; M. L. Thorsen and V. King, "My Mother's Husband," *Journal of Social & Personal Relationships* 33 (2016): 835–851; K. Floyd and M. T. Morman, *Widening the Family Circle* 2e (Thousand Oaks, CA: Sage, 2013).
11. E. A. Suter, "Communication in Lesbian and Gay Families," in *The SAGE Handbook of Family Communication*, 235–247; J. Dixon and D. S. Dougherty, "A Language Convergence/Meaning Divergence Analysis Exploring How LGBTQ and Single Employees Manage Traditional Family Expectations in the Workplace," *Journal of Applied Communication Research* 42 (2014): 1–19; J. Koenig Kellas and E. A. Suter, "Accounting for Lesbian-Headed Families: Lesbian Mothers' Responses to Discursive Challenges," *Communication Monographs* 79 (2012): 475–498.
12. H. Prime, M. Wade, and D. T. Browne, "Risk and Resilience in Family Well-Being during the COVID-19 Pandemic," *American Psychologist* (2020), doi.org/10.1037/amp0000660.
13. "2021 Global Marketing Trends: Find Your Focus," Deloitte Development LLC, January 2021, https://www2.deloitte.com/content/dam/insights/us/articles/6963_global-marketing-trends/DI_2021-Global-Marketing-Trends_US.pdf.
14. J. Bowles, "How Zoom Defied Its Critics and Became the Go-to Video Conferencing App for Surviving the Pandemic," https://diginomica.com, January 18, 2021.
15. F. Richter, "Video Chat Apps Rise to Prominence Amid Pandemic," https://www.statista.com/, March 27, 2020.
16. "Software Bugs Don't Shelter in Place: What app usage and error data reveal during COVID-19," 2020, https://www.bugsnag.com/covid-19-app-usage-error-data-report.
17. "UK's Internet Use Surges to Record Levels," June 24, 2020, https://www.ofcom.org.uk/about-ofcom/latest/media/media-releases/2020/uk-internet-use-surges.
18. "Video Chat for Customer Service Sees 70% Growth in Europe," January 20, 2021, https://webhelp.com/news/video-chat-for-customer-service-sees-70-growth-in-europe/.
19. J. T. Goodwin, J. Goh, S. Verkoeyen, and K. Lithgow, "Can Students Be Taught to Articulate Employability Skills?" *Education + Training* 61 (2019): 445–460; J. A. Rios, G. Ling, R. Pugh, D. Becker, and A. Bacall, "Identifying Critical 21st-Century Skills for Workplace Success: A Content Analysis of Job Advertisements," *Educational Researcher* 49 (2020): 80–89.
20. P. M. Sias, H. Pedersen, E. B. Gallagher, and I. Kopaneva, "Workplace Friendship in the Electronically Connected Organization," *Human Communication Research* 38 (2012): 253–279.
21. V. Satir, *The New Peoplemaking* (Mountain View, CA: Science & Behavior Books, 1988), 4.
22. D. M. Keating, J. C. Russell, J. Cornacchione, and S. W. Smith, "Family Communication Patterns and Difficult Family Conversations," *Journal of Applied Communication Research* 41 (2013): 160–180; J. P. Caughlin, A. F. Koerner, P. Schrodt, and M. A. Fitzpatrick, "Interpersonal Communication in Family Relationships," in *The SAGE Handbook of Interpersonal Communication* 4e, edited by M. L. Knapp and J. A. Daly (Thousand Oaks, CA: Sage, 2011), 679–714.
23. P. Schrodt, P. L. Witt, and A. S. Messersmith, "A Meta-Analytical Review of Family Communication Patterns and Their Associations with Information Processing, Behavioral, and Psychosocial Outcomes," *Communication Monographs* 75 (2008): 248–269.
24. L. K. Knobloch, A. T. Ebata, P. C. McGlaughlin, and J. A. Theiss, "Generalized Anxiety and Relational Uncertainty as Predictors of Topic Avoidance during Reintegration Following Military Deployment," *Communication Monographs* 80 (2013): 452–477; L. K. Knobloch and S. R. Wilson, "Communication in Military Families across the Deployment Cycle," *The SAGE Handbook of Family Communication*, 370–385.
25. K. K. Myers, D. R. Seibold, and H. S. Park, "Interpersonal Communication in the Workplace," in *The SAGE Handbook of Interpersonal Communication*, 527–562; R. B. Adler, M. Maresh-Fuehrer, J. M. Elmhorst, and K. Lucas, *Communication at Work* 12e (New York: McGraw-Hill, 2018); D. O'Hair, G. W. Friedrich, and L. A. Dixon, *Strategic Communication in Business and the Professions* 8e (Boston: Pearson, 2015).
26. M. L. Knapp and A. Vangelisti, "Relationship Stages: A Communication Perspective," in *Making Connections*, 132–139; M. L. Knapp, A. L. Vangelisti, and J. P. Caughlin, *Interpersonal Communication and Human Relationships* 7e (Boston: Pearson, 2014); K. N. Dunleavy and M. Booth-Butterfield, "Idiomatic Communication in the Stages of Coming Together and Falling Apart," *Communication Quarterly* 57 (2009): 416–432; P. A. Mongeau and M. L. Miller Henningsen, "Stage Theories of Relationship Development: Charting the Course of Interpersonal Communication," in *Engaging Theories in Interpersonal Communication: Multiple Perspectives* 2e, edited by D. O. Braithwaite and P. Schrodt (Los Angeles: Sage, 2015), 391–402; L. K. Guerrero, P. A. Andersen, and W. A. Afifi, *Close Encounters: Communication in Relationships* 6e (Thousand Oaks, CA: Sage, 2021).

27. J. M. Honeycutt, "Dominance as Defined through Asymmetry in Predictability: An Exploration of the Relational Stage Model," *American Communication Journal* 21.1 (2019): 1–12; S. M. Horan, R. L. Cown, and E. G. Carberry, "Spillover Effects: Communication Involved with Dissolved Workplace Romances," *Communication Studies* 70.5 (2019): 564–581; G. D. Shipman, D. Vo, A. Brown, and N. Brody, "Humor Functions throughout Platonic Relationships: Knapp's Staircase Model," *Northwest Journal of Communication* 46.1 (2018): 33–48; L. Sharabi and J. P. Caughlin, "Usage Patterns of Social Media across Stages of Romantic Relationships," in *The Impact of Social Media in Modern Romantic Relationships*, edited by N. M. Punyanunt-Carter and J. S. Wrench (Lanham, MD: Lexington, 2017),15–29; J. Fox and C. Anderegg, "Romantic Relationship Stages and Social Networking Sites: Uncertainty Reduction Strategies and Perceived Relational Norms on Facebook," *Cyberpsychology, Behavior and Social Networking* 17 (2014): 685–691; J. Fox, K. M. Warber, and D. C. Makstaller, "The Role of Facebook in Romantic Relationship Development: An Exploration of Knapp's Relational Stage Model," *Journal of Social & Personal Relationships* 30 (2013): 771–794.

28. M. E. King and A. G. La Valley, "Partner Influence, Emotion, and Relational Outcomes: A Test of Relational Turbulence Theory in Early Dating Relationships," *Southern Communication Journal* 84.5 (2019): 287–300; L. K. Knobloch, "The Relational Turbulence Model: Communicating during Times of Transition," in *Engaging Theories in Interpersonal Communication*, 377–385; D. Hauani Solomon, K. M. Weber, and K. R. Steuber, "Turbulence in Relational Transitions," in *New Directions in Interpersonal Communication Research*, edited by S. W. Smith and S. R. Wilson (Los Angeles: Sage, 2010), 115–134; R. M. Dailey, A. D. Hampel, and J. B. Roberts, "Relational Maintenance in On-Again/Off-Again Relationships: An Assessment of How Relational Maintenance, Uncertainty, and Commitment Vary by Relationship Type and Status," *Communication Monographs* 77 (2010): 75–101; R. M. Dailey, K. Rossetto, R. A. Pfiester, and C. A. Surra, "A Qualitative Analysis of On-Again/Off-Again Romantic Relationships: 'It's Up and Down, All Around'," *Journal of Social & Personal Relationships* 26 (2009): 443–466; R. M. Dailey, R. A. Pfiester, B. Jin, G. Beck, and G. Clark, "On-Again/Off-Again Dating Relationships: How Are They Different from Other Dating Relationships?" *Personal Relationships* 16 (2009): 23–47.

29. Knapp and Vangelisti, "Relationship Stages"; Knapp et al., *Interpersonal Communication and Human Relationships*.

30. B. L. Lane and C. W. Piercy, "Making Sense of Becoming Facebook Official: Implications for Identity and Time," in *The Impact of Social Media in Modern Romantic Relationships*, 31–45.

31. S. W. Duck, "A Topography of Relationship Disengagement and Dissolution," in *Personal Relationships 4: Dissolving Relationships*, edited by S. W. Duck (New York: Academic Press, 1982); Guerrero et al., *Close Encounters*.

32. B. Laursen and C. A. Hafen, "Future Directions in the Study of Close Relationships: Conflict Is Bad (Except When It's Not)," *Social Development* 19 (2010): 858–872.

33. C. Harasymchuk and B. Fehr, "A Prototype Analysis of Relational Boredom," *Journal of Social and Personal Relationships* 30 (2012): 627–646.

34. Duck, "A Topography of Relationship Disengagement and Dissolution."

35. V. Lukacs and A. Quan-Haase, "Romantic Breakups on Facebook: New Scales for Studying Post-Breakup Behaviors, Digital Distress, and Surveillance," *Information, Communication & Society* 18 (2015): 492–508.

36. D. M. Frost, J. D. Rubin, and N. Darcangelo, "Making Meaning of Significant Events in Past Relationships," *Journal of Social and Personal Relationships* 33 (2016): 938–960.

37. N. Brody, L. E. LeFebvre, and K. G. Blackburn, "Holding On and Letting Go: Memory, Nostalgia, and Effects of Virtual Possession Management Practices on Post-Breakup Adjustment," *Journal of Social and Personal Relationships* 37.7 (2020): 2229–2249; M. Owenz and B. J. Fowers, "Perceived Post-Traumatic Growth May Not Reflect Actual Positive Change: A Short-Term Prospective Study of Relationship Dissolution," *Journal of Social and Personal Relationships* 36.10 (2019): 3098–3116; O. L. Haimson, N. Andalibi, M. De Choudhury, and G. R. Hayes, "Relationship Breakup Disclosures and Media Ideologies on Facebook," *New Media & Society* 20.5 (2018) 1931–1952; L. E. LeFebvre, K. G. Blackburn, and N. Brody, "Navigating Romantic Relationships on Facebook: Extending the Relationship Dissolution Model to Social Networking Environments," *Journal of Social & Personal Relationships* 32 (2015): 78–98; K. G. Blackburn, N. Brody, and L. E. LeFebvre, "The I's, We's, and She/He's of Breakups: Public and Private Pronoun Usage in Relationship Dissolution Accounts," *Journal of Language & Social Psychology* 33 (2014): 202–213; L. A. Lee and D. A. Sbarra, "The Predictors and Consequences of Relationship Dissolution: Breaking Down Silos," in *Human Bonding: The Science of Affectional Ties*, edited by C. Hazan and M. I. Campa (New York: Guilford, 2013), 308–342.

38. L. E. LeFebvre, M. Allen, R. D. Rasner, S. Garstad, A. Wilms, and C. Parrish, "Ghosting in Emerging Adults' Romantic Relationships: The Digital Dissolution Disappearance Strategy," *Imagination, Cognition, and Personality: Consciousness in Theory, Research, and Clinical Practice* 39.2 (2019): 125–150; R. B. Koessler, T. Kohut, and L. Campbell, "When Your Boo Becomes a Ghost: The Association between Breakup Strategy and Breakup Role in Experiences of Relationship Dissolution," *Collabra: Psychology* 5.1 (2019): 1–18; L. E. LeFebvre, "Phantom Lovers: Ghosting as a Relationship Dissolution Strategy in the Technological Age," in *The Impact of Social Media in Modern Romantic Relationships*, 219–235.

39. M. J. Rosenfeld, "Who Wants the Breakup? Gender and Breakups in Heterosexual Couples," in *Social Networks and the Life Course: Integrating the Decelopment of Human Lives and Social Relational Networks*, edited by D. F. Alwin, D. Felmlee, and D. Kreager (New York: Springer, 2018), 221–243.

40. T. Levine and S. L. Fitzpatrick, "You Know Why; The Question Is How? Relationships between Reasons and Methods in Romantic Breakups," paper presented at the meeting of the International Communication Association (May 2005), New York City, New York.

41. Knapp et al., *Interpersonal Communication and Human Relationships*; M. L. Knapp and A. L. Vangelisti, "Relational Decline," in *Making Connections* 4e, 269–273; W. R. Cupach, "Dialectical Process in the Disengagement of Interpersonal Relationships," in *Making Connections* 4e, 274–280; M. Pelaez, T. Field, M. Diego, O. Deeds, and J. Delgado, "Insecurity, Control, and Disinterest Behaviors Are Related to Breakup Distress in University Students," *College Student Journal* 45 (2010): 333–340; D. Davis, P. R. Shaver, and M. L. Vernon, "Physical, Emotional, and Behavioral Reactions to Breaking Up: The Roles of Gender, Age, Emotional Involvement, and Attachment Style," *Personality and Social Psychology Bulletin* 29 (2003): 871–884.

42. L. Locker Jr., W. D. McIntosh, A. A. Hackney, J. H. Wilson, and K. E. Wiegand, "The Breakup of Romantic Relationships: Situational Predictors of Perception of Recovery," *North American Journal of Psychology* 12 (2010): 565–578; D. Cullingson, *Breaking Up Blues: A Guide to Survival* (New York: Routledge, 2008); S. P. Banks, D. M. Altendorf, J. O. Greene, and M. Cody, "An Examination of Relationship Disengagement: Perceptions, Breakup Strategies, and Outcomes," *Western Journal of Speech Communication* 51 (1987): 19–41.

43. K. Matthews, "The Dear John Talk and Other Dreaded Conversations: Eight Ways to Make Them Easier, Kinder, Gentler," *O: The Oprah Winfrey Magazine* (August 2007): 144, 146.

44. D. K. Ivy, *GenderSpeak: Communicating in a Gendered World* 6e (Dubuque, IA: Kendall Hunt, 2017).

45. K. Tan, C. R. Agnew, L. E. VanderDrift, and S. M. Harvey, "Committed to Us: Predicting Relationship Closeness Following Nonmarital Romantic Relationship Breakup," *Journal of Social & Personal Relationships* 32 (2015): 456–471; M. O'Connor, "Winning the Breakup: A Generation Defines Itself by Post-Relationship Peacocking," *New York* (December 1–14, 2014), 28–32.

46. I. S. Abbasi and N. G. Alghamdi, "When Flirting Turns into Infidelity: The Facebook Dilemma," *The American Journal of Family Therapy* 45.1 (2017): 1–14; B. Kring, "Cyber Infidelity: The New Seduction," *Journal of Sex & Marital Therapy* 42 (2016): 751–753; A. Ferron, Y. Lussier, and S. Sabourin, "Spousal Problems Arising from Internet Usage: Cyber Infidelity and Sexting," *Integrating Science & Practice* 3 (2013): 27–31; V. S. Millner, "Internet Infidelity: A Case of Intimacy with Detachment," *Family Journal* 16 (2008): 78–82; B. H. Henline, L. K. Lamke, and M. D. Howard, "Exploring Perceptions of Online Infidelity," *Personal Relationships* 14 (2007): 113–128; K. M. Hertlein and F. P. Piercy, "Internet Infidelity: A Critical Review of the Literature," *Family Journal* 14 (2006): 366–371.
47. M. Rabbitt, "Is Infidelity Obsolete?" *Women's Health* (July/August 2010): 144.
48. E. A. Utley, *He Cheated, She Cheated, We Cheated: Women Speak about Infidelity* (Jefferson, NC: McFarland, 2019); A. M. Neal and E. P. Lemay, "The Wandering Eye Perceives More Threats: Projection of Attraction to Alternative Partners Predicts Anger and Negative Behavior in Romantic Relationships," *Journal of Social and Personal Relationships* 36.2 (2019): 450–468; D. M. Buss, "Sexual and Emotional Infidelity: Evolved Gender Differences in Jealousy Prove Robust and Replicable," *Perspectives on Psychological Science* 13.2 (2018): 155–160; K. A. V. Gibson, A. E. Thompson, and L. F. O'Sullivan, "Love Thy Neighbour: Personality Traits, Relationship Quality, and Attraction to Others as Predictors of Infidelity Among Young Adults," *The Canadian Journal of Human Sexuality* 25.3 (2016): 186–198; S. J. Watkins and S. D. Boon, "Expectations Regarding Partner Fidelity in Dating Relationships," *Journal of Social & Personal Relationships* 33 (2016): 237–256; E. A. Utley, "Rethinking the Other Woman: Exploring Power in Intimate Heterosexual Triangular Relationships," *Women's Studies in Communication* 39 (2016): 177–192.
49. B. Easterling, S. Kahn, D. Knox, and S. S. Hall, "Deception in Undergraduate Romantic Relationships: Who's Lying and Cheating?" *College Student Journal* 53.5 (2019): 277–284; I. Tsapelas, H. E. Fisher, and A. Aron, "Infidelity: When, Where, Why," in *The Dark Side of Close Relationships II*, edited by W. R. Cupach and B. H. Spitzberg (New York: Routledge, 2011), 175–196.
50. M. L. Hans, B. D. Selvidge, K. A. Tinker, and L. M. Webb, "Online Performances of Gender: Blogs, Gender-Bending, and Cybersex as Relational Examples," in *Computer-Mediated Communication in Personal Relationships*, edited by K. B. Wright and L. M. Webb (New York: Peter Lang, 2010), 302–323.
51. A. Vossler and N. P. Moller, "Internet Affairs: Partners' Perceptions and Experiences of Internet Infidelity," *Journal of Sex & Marital Therapy* 46.1 (2020): 67–77; K. Y. A. McKenna, A. S. Green, and P. K. Smith, "Demarginalizing the Sexual Self," *Journal of Sex Research* 38 (2001): 302–316; A. Cooper, I. P. McLoughlin, and K. M. Campbell, "Sexuality in Cyberspace: Update for the 21st Century," *Cyberpsychology & Behavior* 3 (2000): 521–536.
52. M. Washburn-Busk, A. Vennum, P. McAllister, and P. Busk, "Navigating 'Breakup Remorse': Implications for Disrupting the On-Again/Off-Again Cycles in Young Adult Dating Relationships," *Journal of Marital and Family Therapy* (2020), doi: 10.1111/jmft.12425; R. M. Dailey, K. R. Rossetto, A. A. McCracken, B. Jin, and E. W. Green, "Negotiating Breakups and Renewals in On-Again/Off-Again Dating Relationships: Traversing the Transitions," *Communication Quarterly* 60 (2012): 165–189; R. M. Dailey, B. Jin, A. Pfiester, and G. Beck, "On-Again/Off-Again Dating Relationships: What Keeps Partners Coming Back?" *Journal of Social Psychology* 151 (2011): 417–440; R. M. Dailey, A. V. Middleton, and E. W. Green, "Perceived Relational Stability in On-Again/Off-Again Relationships," *Journal of Social & Personal Relationships* 28 (2011): 1–25.
53. R. M. Dailey, L. Zhong, R. Pett, D. Scott, and C. Krawietz, "Investigating Relationship Dispositions as Explanations for On-Again/Off-Again Relationships," *Journal of Social and Personal Relationships* 37.1 (2020): 201–211; M. G. Blight, E. K. Ruppel, and K. Jagiello, "'Using Facebook Lets Me Know What He Is Doing': Relational Uncertainty, Breakups, and Renewals in On-Again/Off-Again Relationships," *Southern Communication Journal* 84.5 (2019): 328–339; R. M. Dailey, L. E. LeFebvre, B. Crook, and N. Brody, "Relational Uncertainty and Communication in On-Again/Off-Again Romantic Relationships: Assessing Changes and Patterns across Recalled Turning Points," *Western Journal of Communication* 80 (2016): 239–263; R. M. Dailey, A. A. McCracken, B. Jin, K. R. Rossetto, and E. W. Green, "Negotiating Breakups and Renewals: Types of On-Again/Off-Again Dating Relationships," *Western Journal of Communication* 77 (2013): 382–410; S. A. Robbins and A. F. Merrill, "Understanding Posttransgressional Relationship Closeness: The Roles of Perceived Severity, Rumination, and Communication Competence," *Communication Research Reports* 31 (2014): 23–32.
54. M. Coleman, L. Ganong, and S. N. Mitchell, "Divorce and Postdivorce Relationships," in *The Cambridge Handbook of Personal Relationships*, 106–116; N. Brody, L. E. LeFebvre, and K. G. Blackburn, "Post-Dissolution Surveillance on Social Networking Sites," in *The Impact of Social Media in Modern Romantic Relationships*, 237–257; P. J. Lannutti and K. A. Cameron, "Beyond the Breakup: Heterosexual and Homosexual Post-Dissolutional Relationships," *Communication Quarterly* 50 (2002): 153–170.
55. K. Koenig Kellas and S. Sato, "'The Worst Part Is, We Don't Even Talk Anymore': Post-Dissolutional Communication in Break Up Stories," in *Making Connections: Readings in Relational Communication* 5e, edited by K. M. Galvin (New York: Oxford University Press, 2011), 297–309; A. N. Lambert and P. C. Hughes, "The Influence of Goodwill, Secure Attachment, and Positively Toned Disengagement Strategy on Reports of Communication Satisfaction in Nonmarital Post-Dissolution Relationships," *Communication Research Reports* 27 (2010): 171–183; J. Koenig Kellas, D. Bean, C. Cunningham, and K. Y. Cheng, "The Ex-Files: Trajectories, Turning Points, and Adjustment in the Development of Post-Dissolutional Relationships," *Journal of Social & Personal Relationships* 25 (2008): 23–50.
56. L. A. Baxter, *Voicing Relationships: A Dialogic Perspective* (Thousand Oaks, CA: Sage, 2011); L. A. Baxter and D. O. Braithwaite, "Relational Dialectics Theory, Applied," in *New Directions in Interpersonal Communication Research*, 48–66; L. A. Baxter and K. M. Norwood, "Relational Dialectics Theory: Navigating Meaning for Competing Discourses," in *Engaging Theories in Interpersonal Communication*, 279–292; L. A. Baxter and B. M. Montgomery, *Relating: Dialogues and Dialectics* (New York: Guilford, 1996); L. A. Baxter and B. M. Montgomery, "Rethinking Communication in Personal Relationships from a Dialectical Perspective," in *Communication and Personal Relationships*, edited by K. Dindia and S. Duck (New York: Wiley, 2000), 31–53.
57. For more research on relational dialectics, see D. Haunani Solomon and M. E. Roloff, "Relationship Initiation and Growth," in *The Cambridge Handbook of Personal Relationships*, 79–89; B. Baker, "'We're Just Family, You Know?' Exploring the Discourses of Family in Gay Parents' Relational Talk," *Journal of Family Communication* 19.3 (2019): 213–227; V. Cronin-Fisher and E. Sahlstein Parcell, "Making Sense of Dissatisfaction During the Transition to Motherhood through Relational Dialectics Theory," *Journal of Family Communication* 19.2 (2019): 157–170; S. L. Faulkner and P. D. Ruby, "Feminist Identity in Romantic Relationships: A Relational Dialectics Analysis of E-Mail Discourse as Collaborative Found Poetry," *Women's Studies in Communication* 38 (2015): 206–226; J. Fox, J. L. Osborn, and K. W. Warber, "Relational Dialectics and Social Networking Sites: The Role of Facebook in Romantic Relationship Escalation, Maintenance, Conflict, and Dissolution," *Computers in Human Behavior* 35 (2014): 527–534.
58. J. L. Semlak and J. C. Pearson, "Big Macs/Peanut Butter and Jelly: An Exploration of Dialectical Contradictions Experienced by the Sandwich Generation," *Communication Research Reports* 28 (2011): 296–307; E. Sahlstein and T. Dun, "'I Wanted Time to Myself and He Wanted to Be Together All The Time': Constructing Breakups as Managing Autonomy-Connection," *Qualitative Research Reports in Communication* 9 (2008): 37–45.

59. L. Kelly and A. E. Miller-Ott, "Perceived Miscommunication in Friends' and Romantic Partners' Texted Conversations," *Southern Communication Journal* 83.4 (2018): 267–280; D. Halpern and J. E. Katz, "Texting's Consequences for Romantic Relationships: A Cross-Lagged Analysis Highlights Its Risks," *Computers in Human Behavior* 71 (2017): 386–394; B. McEwan and D. Horn, "ILY & Can U Pick up Some Milk: Effects of Relational Maintenance via Text Messaging on Relational Satisfaction and Closeness in Dating Partners," *Southern Communication Journal* 81 (2016): 168–181; A. Miller-Ott and L. Kelly, "The Presence of Cell Phones in Romantic Partner Face-to-Face Interactions: An Expectancy Violation Theory Approach," *Southern Communication Journal* 80 (2015): 253–270; R. L. Duran, L. Kelly, and T. Rotaru, "Mobile Phones in Romantic Relationships and the Dialectic of Autonomy Versus Connection," *Communication Quarterly* 59 (2011): 19–36; J. A. Hall and N. K. Baym, "Calling and Texting (Too Much): Mobile Maintenance Expectations, (Over) Dependence, Entrapment, and Friendship Satisfaction," *New Media & Society* 14 (2011): 316–331.

60. M. R. Leary and J. Acosta, "Acceptance, Rejection, and the Quest for Relational Value," in *The Cambridge Handbook of Personal Relationships*, 378–390; C. Prentice, "Relational Dialectics Among In-Laws," *Journal of Family Communication* 9 (2009): 67–89.

61. J. Vitak and N. B. Ellison, "Personal Relationships and Technology in the Digital Age," in *The Cambridge Handbook of Personal Relationships*, 481–493; P. W. Toller and D. O. Braithwaite, "Grieving Together and Apart: Bereaved Parents' Contradictions of Marital Interaction," *Journal of Applied Communication Research* 37 (2009): 257–277; A. F. Herrmann, "How Did We Get This Far Apart? Disengagement, Relational Dialectics, and Narrative Control," *Qualitative Inquiry* 13 (2007): 989–1007.

62. S. W. Whitton, N. James-Kangal, G. K. Rhoades, and H. J. Markman, "Understanding Couple Conflict" in *The Cambridge Handbook of Personal Relationships*, 297–310; W. A. Donohue and D. A. Cai, "Interpersonal Conflict: An Overview," in *Managing Interpersonal Conflict: Advances through Meta-Analysis*, edited by N. A. Burrell, M. Allen, B. M. Gayle, and R. W. Preiss (New York: Routledge, 2014), 22–41; S. Ting-Toomey and J. G. Oetzel, "Introduction to Interpersonal/International Conflict," in *The SAGE Handbook of Conflict Communication: Integrating Theory, Research, and Practice* 2e, edited by J. G. Oetzel and S. Ting-Toomey (Thousand Oaks, CA: Sage, 2013), 99–104.

63. J. Fox and J. Frampton, "Social Media Stressors in Romantic Relationships," *The Impact of Social Media on Modern Romantic Relationships*, 181–195; S. M. Horan, T. D. Guinn, and S. Banghart, "Understanding Relationships among the Dark Triad Personality Profile and Romantic Partners' Conflict Communication," *Communication Quarterly* 63 (2015): 156–170; D. Aldeis and T. D. Afifi, "Putative Secrets and Conflict in Romantic Relationships Over Time," *Communication Monographs* 82 (2015): 224–251; N. A. Burrell and J. D. Shields, "An Overview of Interpersonal Conflict Management Issues in Personal, Intimate, and Social Contexts," *Managing Interpersonal Conflict*, 251–254; C. Segrin, A. Hanzal, and T. J. Domschke, "Accuracy and Bias in Newlywed Couples' Perceptions of Conflict Styles and the Association with Marital Satisfaction," *Communication Monographs* 76 (2009): 207–233; R. Domingue and D. Mollen, "Attachment and Conflict Communication in Adult Romantic Relationships," *Journal of Social and Personal Relationships* 26 (2009): 678–696.

64. D. C. Jack and A. Ali, *Silencing the Self across Cultures: Depression and Gender in the Social World* (New York: Oxford University Press, 2010); M. Schuessler Harper, *Keeping Quiet: Self-Silencing and Its Association with Relational and Individual Functioning Among Adolescent Romantic Couples,* unpublished doctoral dissertation, University of Tennessee, Knoxville, 2004; "Unhealthy for Women Not to Speak Up during Marital Spats," *Harvard Women's Health Watch* (January 2008): 6–7; T. Parker-Pope, "Marital Spats, Taken to Heart," *New York Times*, October 7, 2007, nytimes.com.

65. L. S. Aloia and T. Worley, "The Role of Family Verbal Aggression and Taking Conflict Personally in Romantic Relationship Complaint Avoidance," *Communication Studies* 70.2 (2019): 190–207; L. S. Aloia, "Verbal Aggression in Romantic Relationships: The Influence of Family History, Destructive Beliefs about Conflict, and Conflict Goals," *Communication Quarterly* 66.3 (2018): 308–324.

66. L. S. Aloia and D. Haunani Solomon, "Cognitive and Physiological Systems Linked to Childhood Exposure to Family Verbal Aggression and Reactions to Conflict in Adulthood," *Communicating Interpersonal Conflict in Close Relationships: Contexts, Challenges, and Opportunities,* edited by J. A. Samp (New York: Routledge, 2016), 11–27; O. Hargie, *Skilled Interpersonal Communication: Research, Theory, and Practice* 6e (London: Routledge, 2017).

67. A. S. Rancer and T. A. Avtgis, *Argumentative and Aggressive Communication: Theory, Research, and Application* 2e (Thousand Oaks, CA: Sage, 2014). For more research on verbal aggression, see R. R. Roper, A. J. Johnson, and E. N. Bostwick, "A Target's Perspective: Verbal Aggressiveness, Coping Strategies, and Relational Harm," *Communication Research Reports* 34 (2017): 21–28; L. S. Aloia and D. Haunani Solomon, "Sex Differences in the Perceived Appropriateness of Receiving Verbal Aggression," *Communication Research Reports* 34 (2017): 1–10; N. S. Hoskins, A. Woszidlo, and A. Kunkel, "Words Can Hurt the Ones You Love: Interpersonal Trust as It Relates to Listening Anxiety and Verbal Aggression," *Iowa Journal of Communication* 48 (2016): 96–112; L. S. Aloia and D. Haunani Solomon, "Emotions Associated with Verbal Aggression Expression and Suppression," *Western Journal of Communication* 80 (2016): 3–20.

68. N. E. Dunbar, B. L. Lane, and G. Abra, "Power in Close Relationships: A Dyadic Power Theory Perspective," *Communicating Interpersonal Conflict in Close Relationships*, 75–92; P. T. Coleman, "Power and Conflict," *The Handbook of Conflict Resolution* 3e, edited by M. Deutsch, P. T. Coleman, and E. C. Marcus (New York: Jossey-Bass, 2014), 137–167.

69. C. R. Berger, "Social Power and Interpersonal Communication," in *Explorations in Interpersonal Communication,* edited by G. R. Miller (Newbury Park, CA: Sage, 1976).

70. "Country Comparison," Hofstede Insights, https://www.hofstede-insights.com/country-comparison/saudi-arabia,the-usa/; Saudi Arabia Culture Profile: Country Values, https://sites.google.com/site/moensaudiarabiamgt755/country-values; M. A. Cassell, R. J. Blake, and W. Virginia, "Analysis Of Hofstede's 5-D Model: The Implications Of Conducting Business In Saudi Arabia," *International Journal of Management & Information Systems*, 16.2 (2012).

71. A. J. Merolla and J. J. Harman, "Relationship-Specific Hope and Constructive Conflict Management in Adult Romantic Relationships: Testing an Accommodation Framework," *Communication Research* 45.3 (2018): 339–364; M. Deutsch, "Cooperation, Competition, and Conflict," in *The Handbook of Conflict Resolution: Theory and Practice* 3–28.

72. Deutsch, "Cooperation, Competition, and Conflict."

73. W. W. Wilmot and J. L. Hocker, *Interpersonal Conflict* 10e (New York: McGraw-Hill, 2017).

74. G. R. Miller and M. Steinberg, *Between People: A New Analysis of Interpersonal Communication* (Chicago: Science Research Associates, 1975).

75. T. Suwinyattichaiporn and M. A. Generous, "'Who's Doing the Phubbing?': Exploring Individual Factors That Predict Phubbing Behaviors during Interpersonal Interactions," *Ohio Communication Journal* (2019): 105–114; M. M. P. Vanden Abeele and M. Postma-Nilsenova, "More Than Just a Gaze: An Experimental Vignette Study Examining How Phone-Gazing and Newspaper-Gazing and Phubbing-While-Speaking and Phubbing-While-Listening Compare in Their Effect on Affiliation," *Communication Research Reports* 35.4 (2018): 303–313; V. Chotitayasunondh and K. M. Douglas, "The Effects of 'Phubbing' on Social Interaction," *Journal of Applied Social Psychology* 48.6 (2018): 304–316; J. A. Roberts and M. E. David, "My Life Has Become a Major Distraction from My Cellphone: Partner Phubbing and Relationship

76. I. A. Cionea, S. V. Wilson Mumpower, M. A. Bassick, "Serial Argument Goals, Tactics, and Outcomes in Long-Distance and Geographically Close Romantic Relationships," *Southern Communication Journal* 84.1 (2019): 1–16; I. A. Cionea, A. J. Johnson, and E. N. Bostwick, "Argument Interdependence: Connections to Serial Argument Goals and Tactics in Romantic Relationships," *Journal of Social and Personal Relationships* 36.7 (2019): 1975–1995; T. R. Worley and J. Samp, "Goal Variability and Perceived Resolvability in Serial Argumentation," *Communication Research* 45.3 (2018): 422–442; S. Morrison and P. Schrodt, "The Perceived Threat and Resolvability of Serial Arguments as Correlates of Relational Uncertainty in Romantic Relationships," *Communication Studies* 68.1 (2017): 56–71.

Satisfaction Among Romantic Partners," *Computers in Human Behavior* 54 (2016): 134–141.

77. P. T. Coleman, "Intractable Conflict," *The Handbook of Conflict Resolution*, 708–744; C. Waite Miller, "Irresolvable Interpersonal Conflicts: Students' Perceptions of Common Topics, Possible Reasons for Persistence, and Communication Patterns," *Making Connections*, 240–247.

78. Y. Mao and C. L. Hale, "Relating Intercultural Communication Sensitivity to Conflict Management Styles, Technology Use, and Organizational Communication Satisfaction in Multinational Organizations in China," *Journal of Intercultural Communication Research* 44 (2015): 132–150; S. Ting-Toomey, "Managing Intercultural Conflicts Effectively," in *Intercultural Communication: A Reader* 14e, edited by L. A. Samovar, R. E. Porter, E. R. McDaniel, and C. Sexton Roy (Belmont, CA: Wadsworth/Cengage Learning, 2014), 355–367; S. Ting-Toomey and L. C. Chung, *Understanding Intercultural Communication* 2e (New York: Oxford University Press, 2011); S. Ting-Toomey and J. G. Oetzel, "Culture-Based Situational Conflict Model: An Update and Expansion," *The SAGE Handbook of Conflict Communication*, 763–790; M. D. Hazen and R. Shi, "Harmony, Conflict, and the Process of Argument in Chinese Societies," in *Intercultural Communication: A Reader* 13e, edited by L. A. Samovar and R. E. Porter (Belmont, CA: Wadsworth/Cengage Learning, 2011), 445–456; S. E. Quasha and F. Tsukada, "International Marriages in Japan: Cultural Conflict and Harmony," *Intercultural Communication* 13e, 126–143; D. Tjosvold, K. Leung, and D. W. Johnson, "Cooperative and Competitive Conflict in China," *The Handbook of Conflict Resolution*, 654–678.

79. S. McCorkle and M. J. Reese, *Personal Conflict Management: Theory and Practice* 2e (New York: Routledge, 2018); G. D. Paul and L. L. Putnam, "Moral Foundations of Forgiving in the Workplace," *Western Journal of Communication* 81 (2017): 43–63; P. Hopeck and T. R. Harrison, "Reframing, Refocusing, Referring, Reconciling, and Reflecting: Exploring Conflict Resolution Strategies in End-of-Life Situations," *Health Communication* 32 (2017): 240–246; A. L. Mello and L. A. Delise, "Cognitive Diversity to Team Outcomes: The Roles of Cohesion and Conflict Management," *Small Group Research* 46 (2015): 204–226.

80. D. Hample and A. S. Richards, "Personalizing Conflict in Different Interpersonal Relationship Types," *Western Journal of Communication* 83.2 (2019): 190–209; V. S. Helgeson and K. Mascatelli, "Gender and Relationships," in *The Cambridge Handbook of Personal Relationships*, 186–198; Whitton et al., "Understanding Couple Conflict"; T. A. Spencer, A. Lambertsen, D. S. Hubler, and B. K. Burr, "Assessing the Mediating Effect of Relationship Dynamics between Perceptions of Problematic Media Use and Relationship Satisfaction," *Contemporary Family Therapy* 39.2 (2017): 80–86; P. Schrodt, P. L. Witt, and J. R. Shimkowski, "A Meta-Analytical Review of the Demand/Withdraw Pattern of Interaction and Its Associations with Individual, Relational, and Communicative Outcomes," *Communication Monographs* 81 (2014): 28–58; Satir, *The New Peoplemaking*; Wilmot and Hocker, *Interpersonal Conflict*.

81. L. L. Putnam and C. E. Wilson, "Communicative Strategies in Organizational Conflicts: Reliability and Validity of a Measurement Scale," in *Communication Yearbook* 6, edited by M. Burgoon (Beverly Hills, CA: Sage, 1982).

82. T. Curran, "Intergenerational Transmissions of Mother-Child Loneliness: A Modern Mediation Model of Familial Social Support and Conflict Avoidance," *Health Communication* 34.10 (2019): 1166–1172; Aloia and Worley, "The Role of Family Verbal Aggression and Taking Conflict Personally in Romantic Relationship Complaint Avoidance"; C. Gunsoy, S. E. Cross, A. K. Uskul, G. Adams, and B. Gercek-Swing, "Avoid or Fight Back? Cultural Differences in Responses to Conflict and the Role of Collectivism, Honor, and Enemy Perception," *Journal of Cross-Cultural Psychology* 46 (2015): 1081–1102; C-C. Cheng and C. Tardy, "A Cross-Cultural Study of Silence in Marital Conflict," *Media Report Overseas* 6 (2010): 95–105.

83. M. A. Gross, L. K. Guerrero, and J. K. Alberts, "Perceptions of Conflict Strategies and Communication Competence in Task-Oriented Dyads," *Journal of Applied Communication Research* 32 (2004): 249–270.

84. R. Fisher, W. Ury, and B. Patton, *Getting to Yes: Negotiating Agreement without Giving In* Revised Edition (New York: Penguin Books, 2011).

85. This information is based on several excellent discussions of conflict management skills. We acknowledge R. C. Arnett, L. McManus, and A. McKendree, *Conflict between Persons: The Origins of Leadership* (Dubuque, IA: Kendall Hunt, 2014); W. R. Cupach, D. J. Canary, and B. H. Spitzberg, *Competence in Interpersonal Conflict* 2e (Long Grove, IL: Waveland, 2009); Wilmot and Hocker, *Interpersonal Conflict*; O. Hargie, *Skilled Interpersonal Communication*; O. Hargie, *The Handbook of Communication Skills* 3e (London: Routledge, 2006); O. Hargie, C. Saunders, and D. Dickson, *Social Skills in Interpersonal Communication* 3e (London: Routledge, 1994); Fisher et al., *Getting to Yes*.

86. S. Planalp, J. Fitness, and B. A. Fehr, "The Roles of Emotion in Relationships," in *The Cambridge Handbook of Personal Relationships*, 256–267; E. Liu and M. E. Roloff, "To Avoid or Not to Avoid: When Emotions Overflow," *Communication Research Reports* 32 (2015): 332–339.

87. B. M. Gayle and R. W. Preiss, "Language Intensity Plus: A Methodological Approach to Validate Emotions in Conflicts," *Communication Reports* 12 (1999): 43–50; Wilmot and Hocker, *Interpersonal Conflict*.

88. A. S. Ebesu Hubbard, B. Hendrickson, K. S. Fehrenbach, and J. Sur, "Effects of Timing and Sincerity of Apology on Satisfaction and Changes in Negative Feelings During Conflicts," *Western Journal of Communication* 77 (2013): 305–322; Z. Qin and M. Andreychik, "Relational Closeness in Conflict: Effects on Interpersonal Goals, Emotion, and Conflict Styles," *Journal of International Communication* 19 (2013): 107–116; L. K. Guerrero, "Emotion and Communication in Conflict Interaction," *The SAGE Handbook of Conflict Communication*, 105–131; E. G. Lindner, "Emotion and Conflict: Why It Is Impossible to Understand How Emotions Affect Conflict and How Conflict Affects Emotions," *The Handbook of Conflict Resolution*, 268–293; C. R. Knee, C. Lonsbary, A. Canevello, and H. Patrick, "Self-Determination and Conflict in Romantic Relationships," *Journal of Personality and Social Psychology* 89 (2005): 997–1009.

89. A. Ellis, *A New Guide to Rational Living* (North Hollywood, CA: Wilshire Books, 1977).

90. J. Roessler, "Thinking, Inner Speech, and Self-Awareness," *Review of Philosophy and Psychology* 7 (2016): 541–557.

91. Fisher et al., *Getting to Yes*.

92. K. Leo, F. R. Leifker, D. H. Baucom, and B R. W. Baucom, "Conflict Management and Problem Solving as Relationship Maintenance," in *Relationship Maintenance: Theory, Process, and Context*, edited by B. G. Ogolsky and J. K. Monk (Cambridge, UK: Cambridge University Press, 2019), 194–214.

Chapter 9

1. M. L. King, Jr. "A Christmas Sermon on Peace (1967)," *A Testament of Hope: The Essential Writings and Speeches of Martin Luther*

King, edited by J. M. Washington (New York: HarperCollins, 1991): 253.
2. For a comprehensive review of group process research, see G. Randsley de Moura, T. Leader, J. Pelletier, and D. Abrams, "Prospects for Group Processes and Intergroup Relations Research: A Review of 70 Years' Progress," *Group Processes & Intergroup Relations* 11 (2008): 575–596; also see S. Sloman and P. Fernback, *The Knowledge Illusion: Why We Never Think Alone* (New York: Riverhead Books, 2017).
3. M. S. Weber and H. Kim, "Virtuality, Technology Use, and Engagement within Organizations," *Journal of Applied Communication Research* 43.4 (2015): 358–407; V. Penarroja, V. Orengo, and A. Zornoza, "Reducing Perceived Social Loafing in Virtual Teams: The Effect of Team Feedback with Guided Reflexivity," *Journal of Applied Social Psychology* 47 (2017): 424–435; H. C. Xie, "The Role of Computer Mediated Communication Competence on Unique Information Pooling and Decision Quality in Virtual Teams," Unpublished M.A. Thesis, Michigan State University, Department of Psychology (2015).
4. R. K. Mosvick and R. B. Nelson, *We've Got to Start Meeting Like This[!]* (Glenview, IL: Scott, Foresman, 1987). Also see B. Lam, "The Wasted Workday," *The Atlantic*, December 4, 2014, accessed April 15, 2017, www.theatlantic.com/business/archive/2014/12/the-wasted-workday/383380/.
5. Mosvick and Nelson, *We've Got to Start Meeting Like This[!]*; also see S. Duckweiler, "How Much Time Do We Spend in Meetings?: The Ugly Truth About Meetings," *The Muse*, accessed April 15, 2017, www.themuse.com/advice/how-much-time-do-we-spend-in-meetings-hint-its-scary.
6. D. C. Strubler and K. M. York, "An Exploratory Study of the Team Characteristics Model Using Organizational Teams," *Small Group Research* 38 (2007): 670–695.
7. K. Halvorsen, "Team Decision Making in the Workplace: A Systematic Review of Discourse Analytic Studies," *Journal of Applied Linguistics and Professional Practice* 3 (2013): 273–296.
8. K. W. Hawkins and B. P. Fillion, "Perceived Communication Skill Needs for Work Groups," *Communication Research Reports* 16 (1999): 167–174; also see S. Burkhalter, J. Gastil, and T. Kelshaw, "A Conceptual Definition and Theoretical Model of Public Deliberation in Small Face-to-Face Groups," *Communication Theory* 12 (2002): 398–422.
9. S. A. Beebe and J. T. Masterson, *Communicating in Small Groups: Principles and Practices* 12e (Hoboken, NJ: Pearson, 2020).
10. J. S. Mueller, "Why Individuals in Larger Teams Perform Worse," *Organizational Behavior and Human Decision Processes* 117 (2012): 111–124.
11. C. Lee, J. L. Farh, and Z. J. Chen, "Promoting Group Poetency in Project Teams: The Importance of Group Identification," *Journal of Organizational Behavior* 32 (2011): 1147–1162.
12. For a discussion of the importance of arguments in helping a group achieve its goals, see M. B. Fornoff and D. D. Henningsen, "Testing the Linear Discrepancy Model in Perceptions of Group Decision-Making," *Western Journal of Communication* 81.4 (2017): 507–521.
13. J. Kotlarsky, B. V. D. Hooff, and L. Houtman, "Are We on the Same Page? Knowledge Boundaries and Transactive Memory System Development in Cross-Functional Teams," *Communication Research* 42.3 (2015): 319–344.
14. B. Bell and S. W. J. Kozlowski, "A Typology of Virtual Teams: Implications for Effective Leadership," *Group & Organizational Management* 27 (2002): 14–49; A. Thatcher, "Small Group Decision-Making in Face-to-Face and Computer-Mediated Environments: The Role of Personality," *Behavior & Information Technology* 22 (2003): 203–218; D. R. Lemus, D. R. Seibold, A. J. Flanagin, and M. J. Metzger, "Argument and Decision Making in Computer Mediated Groups," *Journal of Communication* 54 (2004): 302–320; E. V. Hobman, P. Bordia, B. Irmer, and A. Chang, "The Expression of Conflict in Computer-Mediated and Face-to-Face Groups," *Small Group Research* 33 (2002): 439–464; R. Benbunan-Fich, S. R. Hiltz, and M. Turoff, "A Comparative Content Analysis of Face-to-Face vs. Asynchronous Group Decision Making," *Decision Support Systems* 34 (2002): 457–469; D. S. Staples and J. Webster, "Exploring Traditional and Virtual Team Members' 'Best Practices': A Social Cognitive Theory Perspective," *Small Group Research* 38 (2007): 60–97; S. Z. Schiller and M. Mandviwalla, "Virtual Team Research: An Analysis of Theory Use and a Framework for Theory Appropriation," *Small Group Research* 38 (2007): 12–59; J. T. Polzer, C. B. Crisp, S. L. Jarvenpaa, and J. W. Kim, "Extending the Faultline Model to Geographically Dispersed Teams: How Colocated Subgroups Can Impair Group Functioning," *Academy of Management Journal* 4 (2006): 679–692; also see C. Garon and K. Wegryn, *Managing Without Walls: Maximize Success with Virtual, Global and Cross-Cultural Teams* (Lewisville, TX: MC Press, 2006); T. Brake, *Where in the World Is My Team? Making Success of Your Virtual Global Workplace* (San Francisco: Jossey-Bass, 2008); D. Derosa and R. Lepsinger, *Virtual Team Success: A Practical Guide for Working and Leading from a Distance* (San Francisco: Jossey-Bass, 2010).
15. J. M. Wilson, S. G. Straus, and B. McEvily, "All in Due Time: The Development of Trust in Computer-Mediated and Face-to-Face Teams," *Organizational Behavior and Human Decision Processes* 99 (2006): 16–33; also see C. A. Nystrom and V. Asproth, "Virtual Teams—Support for Technical Communication?" *Journal of Organisational Transformation & Social Change* 10 (2013): 64–80; M. del C. Triana, B. L. Kirkman, and M. F. Wagstaff, "Does the Order of Face-to-Face and Computer-Mediated Communication Matter in Diverse Project Teams? An Investigation of Communication Order Effects on Minority Inclusion and Participation," *Journal of Business Psychology* 27 (2013): 57–70.
16. Wilson et al., "All in Due Time."
17. N. N. Bazarova and Y. C. Yuan, "Expertise Recognition and Influence in Intercultural Groups: Differences between Face-to-Face and Computer-Mediated Communication," *Journal of Computer-Mediated Communication* 18 (2013): 437–453.
18. C. E. Timmerman and C. R. Scott, "Virtually Working: Communicative and Structural Predictors of Media Use and Key Outcomes in Virtual Work Teams," *Communication Monographs* 73 (2006): 108–136.
19. M. Washington, E. Okoro, and P. Cardon, "Perceptions of Civility for Mobile Phone Use in Formal and Informal Meetings," *Business and Professional Communication* 77 (2013): 52–64.
20. Washington et al., "Perceptions of Civility for Mobile Phone Use."
21. Washington et al., "Perceptions of Civility for Mobile Phone Use."
22. N. Katz and G. Koenig, "Sports Teams as a Model for Workplace Teams: Lessons and Liabilities," *Academy of Management Executive* 15 (2001): 56–67; L. G. Snyder, "Teaching Teams about Teamwork: Preparation, Practice, and Performance Review," *Business Communication Quarterly* (2009): 74–79.
23. Our discussion of teams and teamwork is from Beebe and Masterson, *Communicating in Small Groups*; for an excellent review of teamwork theoretical models, see V. Rousseau, C. Aube, and A. Savoie, "Teamwork Behaviors: A Review and an Integration of Frameworks," *Small Group Research* 27 (2006): 540–570.
24. T. D. Fletcher and D. A. Major, "The Effects of Communication Modality on Performance and Self-Ratings of Teamwork Components," *Journal of Computer-Mediated Communication* 11 (2006): 557–576.
25. A. G. Sheard and A. P. Kakabadse, "From Loose Groups to Effective Teams: The Nine Key Factors of the Team Landscape," *Journal of Management Development* 21 (2002): 133–151; also see R. A. Meyers and D. R. Seibold, "Making Foundational Assumptions Transparent: Framing the Discussion About Group Communication and Influence," *Human Communication Research* 35 (2009): 286–295.
26. See F. C. Broadbeck and T. Breitermeyer, "Effects of Individual versus Mixed Individual and Group Experience in Rule

Induction on Group Member Learning and Group Performance," *Journal of Experimental Social Psychology* 36 (2002): 621–648.
27. S. B. Shimanoff, *Communication Rules: Theory and Research* (Beverly Hills, CA: Sage, 1980).
28. M. Hoegl, "Goal Setting and Team Performance in Innovative Projects: On the Moderating Role of Teamwork Quality," *Small Group Research* 34 (2003): 3–19; A. W. Woolley, M. E. Gerbasi, C. F. Chabris, S. M. Kosslyn, and J. R. Hackman, "Bringing in the Experts: How Team Composition and Collaborative Planning Jointly Shape Analytic Effectiveness," *Small Group Research* 39 (2008): 352–371; H. Van Mierlo and A. Kleingeld, "Goals, Strategies, and Group Performance: Some Limits of Goal Setting in Groups," *Small Group Research* 41 (2010): 524–555; H. V. Mierlo and E. A. J. Van Hooft, "A Group-Level Conceptualization of the 2 X 2 Achievement Goal Framework: Antecedents and Motivational Outcomes," *Group & Organization Management* 40 (2015): 776–808; M. P. Healey, T. Vuori, and G. Hodgkinson, "When Teams Agree While Disagreeing: Reflection and Refection in Shared Cognition," *Academy of Management Review* 40 (2015): 399–422; L. Alexander and D. V. Knippernberg, "Teams in Pursuit of Radical Innovation: A Goal Orientation Perspective," *Academy of Management Review* 39 (2014): 423–438.
29. R. Rico, M. Sanchez-Manzanares, F. Gil, and C. Gibson, "Team Impact Coordination Processes: A Team Knowledge-Based Approach," *Academy of Management Review* 33 (2008): 163–184; M. Schaeffner, H. Huettermann, D. Gebert, S. Boerner, E. Kearney, and L. Song, "Swim or Sink Together: Collective Team Member Alignment for Separating Task and Relationship Conflicts," *Group and Organization Management* 40 (2015): 467–499; N. Lehmann-Willenbrock, M. M. Chiu, Z. Lei, and S. Kauffeld, "Understanding Positivity within Dynamic Team Interactions: A Statistical Discourse Analysis," *Group & Organizational Management* 42 (2017): 39–78.
30. Beebe and Masterson, *Communicating in Small Groups*.
31. J. E. Mathieu, S. I. Tannenbaum, M. R. Kukenberger, J. S. Donsbach, and G. M. Alliger, "Team Role Experience and Orientation: A Measure and Tests of Construct Validity," *Group & Organization Management* 40 (2015): 6–34.
32. M. Priesemuth, A. Arnuad, and M. Schminke, "Bad Behavior in Groups: The Impact of Overall Justice Climate and Functional Dependence on Counterproductive Work Behavior in Work Units," *Group & Organization Management* 38 (2013): 230–257.
33. C. Savelsbergh, J. M. P. Gevers, B. I. J. M. van der Heijden, and R. F. Poell, "Team Role Stress: Relationships with Team Learning and Performance in Project Teams," *Group & Organization Management* 37 (2012): 67–100.
34. K. D. Benne and P. Sheats, "Functional Roles of Group Members," *Journal of Social Issues* 4 (1948): 41–49; for a good review of role development in groups, see A. P. Hare, "Types of Roles in Small Groups: A Bit of History and a Current Perspective," *Small Group Research* 28 (1994): 433–438; A. J. Salazar, "An Analysis of the Development and Evolution of Roles in the Small Group," *Small Group Research* 27 (1996): 475–503.
35. T. Halfhill, E. Sundstrom, J. Lahner, W. Calderone, and T. M. Nielsen, "Group Personality Composition and Group Effectiveness: An Integrative Review of Empirical Research," *Small Group Research* 36 (2005): 83–105.
36. G. M. Wittenbaum, H. C. Shulman, and M. E. Braz, "Social Ostracism in Task Groups: The Effects of Group Composition," *Small Group Research* 41 (2010): 330–353.
37. R. F. Bales, *Interaction Process Analysis* (Chicago: University of Chicago Press, 1976).
38. Shimanoff, *Communication Rules*.
39. M. E. Scott, "'Communicate through the Roof': A Case Study Analysis of the Communicative Rules and Resources of an Effective Global Virtual Team," *Communication Quarterly* 61 (2013): 301–318.
40. For a discussion of monochronic and polychronic time, see E. T. Hall, *The Silent Language* (New York: Doubleday, 1959).
41. M. J. Waller, M. E. Zellmer-Bruhn, and R. C. Giambatista, "Watching the Clock: Group Pacing Behavior under Dynamic Deadlines," *Academy of Management Journal* 45 (2002): 1046–1055.
42. Hall, *The Silent Language*.
43. M. Shaw, *Group Dynamics: The Psychology of Small Group Behavior* (New York: McGraw-Hill, 1981), 281.
44. J. I. Hurwitz, A. F. Zander, and B. Hymovitch, "Some Effects of Power on the Relations among Group Members," in *Group Dynamics: Research and Theory*, edited by D. Cartwright and A. Zander (New York: Harper & Row, 1953), 483–492; D. C. Barnlund and C. Harland, "Propinquity and Prestige as Determinants of Communication Networks," *Sociometry* 26 (1963): 467–479; G. C. Homans, *The Human Group* (New York: Harcourt Brace and World, 1992); H. H. Kelly, "Communication in Experimentally Created Hierarchies," *Human Relations* 4 (1951): 36–56.
45. C. Anderson, J. S. Beer, J. Chatman, S. Srivastava, and S. E. Spataro, "Knowing Your Place: Self-Perceptions of Status in Face-to-Face Groups," *Journal of Personality and Social Psychology* 91 (2006): 1094–1110.
46. M. R. Singer, *Intercultural Communication: A Perceptual Approach* (Englewood Cliffs, NJ: Prentice Hall, 1987), 118.
47. J. R. P. French and B. H. Raven, "The Bases of Social Power," in *Group Dynamics*, 607–623; B. H. Raven, "A Power Interaction Model of Interpersonal Influence: French and Raven Thirty Years Later," *Journal of Social Behavior and Personality* 7 (1992): 217–244; B. H. Raven "Power, Six Bases of," *Encyclopedia of Leadership* (Thousand Oaks, CA, Sage, 2004): 1242–1249.
48. B. H. Raven, "The Bases of Power and the Power/Interaction Model of Interpersonal Influence," *Analyses of Social Issues and Public Policy* 8 (2008): 1–22; Raven, "A Power Interaction Model of Interpersonal Influence"; Raven, "Power, Six Bases of."
49. A. V. Carron and L. R. Brawley, "Cohesion: Conceptual and Measurement Issues," *Small Group Research* 43 (2012): 726–743; O. Saafein and G. Shaykhian, "Factors Affecting Virtual Team Performance in Telecommunication Support Environment," *Telematics and Informatics* 31 (2014): 459–462.
50. D. Neumann, "Small Group Cohesion and Frequency of Idiom Use," paper presented at the annual meeting of the National Communication Association, Chicago (November 2004); G. Yilmaz, "The Tale of We, You and I: Interpersonal Effects on Pronoun Use in Virtual Teams," *The Florida Communication Journal* 42 (2014).
51. C. R. Evans and K. L. Dion, "Group Cohesion and Performance: A Meta-Analysis," *Small Group Research* 43 (2012): 690–701; S. M. Gully, D. J. Devine, and D. J. Whitney, "A Meta-Analysis of Cohesion and Performance: Effects of Level of Analysis and Task Interdependence" *Small Group Research* 43 (2012): 702–725.
52. M. R. Barrick, B. H. Bradley, A. L. Kristof-Brown, and A. E. Colbert, "The Moderating Role of Top Management Team Interdependence: Implications for Real Teams and Working Groups," *Academy of Management Journal* 50 (2007): 544–557.
53. Adapted from E. G. Bormann and N. C. Bormann, *Effective Small Group Communication* (Minneapolis: Burgess, 1980), 70–72.
54. N. C. Sauer and S. Kauffeld, "Meetings as Networks: Applying Social Network Analysis to Team Interaction," *Communication Methods and Measures* 7 (2013): 26–47; M. Priesemuth, A. Arnaud, and M. Schminke, "Bad Behavior in Groups: The Impact of Overall Justice Climate and Functional Dependence on Counterproductive Work Behavior in Work Units," *Group & Organization Management* 38 (2013): 230–257.
55. C. Savelsbergh, J. M. P. Gevers, B. I. J. M. van der Heijden, and R. F. Poell, "Team Role Stress: Relationships with Team Learning and Performance in Project Teams," *Group & Organization Management* 37 (2012): 67–100.
56. B. Tuckman, "Developmental Sequence in Small Groups," *Psychological Bulletin* 63 (1965): 384–399.
57. B. A. Fisher, "Decision Emergence: Phases in Group Decision Making," *Speech Monographs* 37 (1970): 60.

58. For a discussion of primary tension and group phases, see E. Bormann, *Discussion and Group Methods* (New York: Harper & Row, 1975).
59. S. E. Humphrey, F. Aime, L. Cushenbery, A. D. Hill, J. Fairchild, "Team Conflict Dynamics: Implications of a Dyadic View of Conflict for Team Performance," *Organizational Behavior and Human Decision Processes* 142 (2017): 58–70.
60. P. J. Boyle, D. Hanlon, and J. E. Russo, "The Value of Task Conflict to Group Decisions," *Journal of Behavioral Decision Making* 25 (2012): 217–227; F. R. C. de Wit, K. A. Jehn, and D. Scheepers, "Task Conflict, Information Processing, and Decision-Making: The Damaging Effect of Relationship Conflict," *Organizational Behavior and Human Decision Processes* 122 (2013): 177–189; J. Wombacher and J. Felfe, "The Interplay of Team and Organizational Commitment in Motivating Employees' Interteam Conflict Handling," *Academy of Management Journal* 60.4 (2017): 1554–1581.
61. J. T. Garner and D. L. Iba, "Why Are You Saying That? Increases in Gaze Duration as Responses to Group Member Dissent," *Communication Studies* 68.3 (2017): 353–367.
62. For an examination of the practical role of conflict in jury deliberations, see M. S. Poole and M. Dobosh, "Exploring Conflict Management Processes in Jury Deliberations through Interaction Analysis," *Small Group Research* 41 (2010): 408–426; also see J. Meng, J. Fulk, and Y. C. Yuan, "The Roles and Interplay of Intragroup Conflict and Team Emotion Management on Information Seeking Behaviors in Team Contexts," *Communication Research* 42.5 (2015): 675–700.
63. M. A. Von Glinow, D. Shapiro, and J. Brett, "Can We Talk, and Should We? Managing Emotional Conflict in Multicultural Teams," *Academy of Management Review* 29 (2004): 578–592.
64. M. Janssens and J. M. Brett, "Cultural Intelligence in Global Teams: A Fusion Model of Collaboration," *Group & Organization Management* 31 (2006): 124–153.
65. U. F. Ott and Y. Kimura, " A Set Theoretic Analysis of International Negotiations in Japanese MNEs: Opening the Black Box," *Journal of Business Research*, 69.4 (2016): 1294–1300.
66. G. Lubin, "The Lewis Model Explains Every Culture In The World," *Business Insider*, September 6, 2013, https://www.businessinsider.com/the-lewis-model-2013-9?IR=T.
67. S. A. Wheelan and T. Williams, "Mapping Dynamic Interaction Patterns in Work Groups," *Small Group Research* 34 (2003): 433–467; S. A. Wheelan, B. Davidson, and F. Tilin, "Group Development Across Time: Reality or Illusion?" *Small Group Research* 34 (2003): 223–245.
68. M. S. Poole, "Decision Development in Small Groups: A Multiple Sequence Model of Group Decision Development," *Communication Monographs* 50 (1983): 321–341; also see C. Pavitt and K. Kline Johnson, "Scheidel and Crowell Revisited: A Descriptive Study of Group Proposal Sequencing," *Communication Monographs* 69 (2002): 19–32.

Chapter 10

1. See N. R. F. Maier, "Assets and Liabilities in Group Problem Solving: The Need for an Integrative Function," *Psychological Review* 74 (1967): 239–249; M. Argyle, *Cooperation: The Basis of Sociability* (London: Routledge, 1991); H. A. M. Wilke and R. W. Meertens, *Group Performance* (London: Routledge, 1994); S. Sloman and P. Fernbach, *The Knowledge Illusion: Why We Never Think Alone* (New York: Riverhead Books, 2017); C. R. Chartier and S. Abele, "Groups Outperform Individuals in Tacit Coordination by Using Consensual and Disjunctive Salience," *Organizational Behavior and Human Decision Processes* 141 (2017): 74–81.
2. J. Gonzales, S. Mishra, and R. D. Camp II, "For the Win: Risk-Sensitive Decision-Making in Teams," *Journal of Behavior and Decision Making* 30 (2017): 462–72; S. Mishra, "Decision-Making Under Risk: Integrating Perspectives from Biology, Economics, and Psychology," *Personality and Social Psychology Review* 18 (2014): 280–307; E. Y. Chou and L. F. Norgren, "Safety in Numbers: Why the Mere Physical Presence of Others Affects Risk-taking Behaviors," *Journal of Behavioral Decision Making* 30 (2017): 671–682.
3. Maier, "Assets and Liabilities in Group Problem Solving"; Argyle, *Cooperation*; Wilke and Meertens, *Group Performance*.
4. C. N. DeWall, D. S. Chester, and D. S. White, "Can Acetaminophen Reduce the Pain of Decision-Making?" *Journal of Experimental Social Psychology* 56 (2015): 117–120.
5. For a list of attributes of effective teams, see L. Y. Kim, K. F. Giannitrapani, A. K. Huynh, D. A. Ganz, A. B. Hamilton, E. M. Yano, L. V. Rubenstein, and S. E. Stockdale, "What Makes Team Communication Effective: A Qualitative Analysis of Interprofessional Primary Care Team Members' Perspectives," *Journal of Interprofessional Care* 33 (2019): 836–838.
6. D. F. Crown, "The Use of Group and Groupcentric Individual Goals for Culturally Heterogeneous and Homogeneous Task Groups: An Assessment of European Work Teams," *Small Group Research* 38 (2007): 489–508.
7. C. E. Larson and F. M. J. LaFasto, *Teamwork: What Must Go Right/What Can Go Wrong* (Beverly Hills, CA: Sage, 1989); also see D. D. Chrislip and C. E. Larson, *Collaborative Leadership* (San Francisco: Jossey-Bass, 1994); D. A. Romig, *Breakthrough Teamwork: Outstanding Results Using Structured Teamwork* (Chicago: Irwin, 1996); M. A. Marks, J. E. Mathieu, and S. J. Zaccaro, "A Temporally Based Framework and Taxonomy of Team Processes," *Academy of Management Review* 26 (2001): 356–376; N. Katz, "Sports Teams as a Model for Workplace Teams: Lessons and Liabilities," *Academy of Management Executive* 15 (2001): 56–67.
8. Larson and LaFasto, *Teamwork*; Chrislip and Larson, *Collaborative Leadership*; Romig, *Breakthrough Teamwork*; Y. Gong, T. Y. Kim, D. R. Lee, and J. Zhu, "A Multilevel Model of Team Goal Orientation, Information Exchange, and Creativity," *Academy of Management Journal* 56 (2013): 827–851; A. N. Pieterse, D. van Knippenberg, and D. van Knippenberg, "Cultural Diversity and Team Performance: The Role of Team Member Goal Orientation," *Academy of Management Journal* 56 (2013): 782–804.
9. L. A. DeChurch and C. D. Haas, "Examining Team Planning through an Episodic Lens: Effects of Deliberate, Contingency, and Reactive Planning on Team Effectiveness," *Small Group Research* 39 (2008): 542–568; J. Kotlarsky, B. v. d. Hooff, and L. Houtman, "Are We on the Same Page? Knowledge Boundaries and Transactive Memory System Development in Cross-Functional Teams," *Communication Research* 42.3 (2015): 319–344.
10. Larson and LaFasto, *Teamwork*; N. L. Kerr, "The Most Neglected Moderator in Group Research," *Group Processes & Intergroup Relations* 20.5 (2017): 681–692; also see K. Halvorsen, "Team Decision Making in the Workplace: A Systematic Review of Discourse Analytic Studies," *Journal of Applied Linguistics and Professional Practice* 7.3 (2010): 273–296; M. Schaeffner, H. Huettermann, D. Gerbert, S. Boerner, E. Kearney, and L. J. Song, "Swim or Sink Together: The Potential of Collective Team Identification and Team Member Alignment for Separating Task and Relationship Conflicts," *Group & Organization Management* 40.4 (2015): 467–499.
11. N. A. M. Omar, N. J. Azmi, and N. A. Sani, "Is WhatsApp the Future of Workplace Communication?: Investigating the Use of WhatsApp in Decision-Making Episodes," *Journal of Nusantara Studies* 5 (2020): 414–442.
12. C. M. J. H. Savelsbergh, B. I. J. M. van der Heijden, and R. F. Poell, "The Development and Empirical Validation of a Multidimensional Measurement Instrument for Team Learning Behaviors," *Small Group Research* 40 (2009): 578–607.
13. J. R. Mesmer-Magnus, L. A. DeChurch, M. Jimenez-Rodriguez, and J. Wildman, "A Meta-Analytic Investigation of Virtuality and Information Sharing in Teams," *Organizational Behavior and Human Decision Processes* 115 (2011): 214–225.
14. T. Reimer, A. Reimer, and V. B. Hinsz, "Naive Groups Can Solve the Hidden-Profile Problem," *Human Communication Research* 36

(2010): 443–467; M. S. Eastin, L. A. Kahlor, M. C. Liang, and N. A. Ghannam, "Information-Seeking as a Precaution Behavior: Exploring the Role of Decision-Making Stages," *Human Communication Research* 41 (2015): 603–621.

15. For a review of research about the importance of sharing information to reach a high-quality decision or solution, see J. A. Bonito, M. H. DeCamp, and E. K. Ruppel, "The Process of Information Sharing in Small Groups: Application of a Local Model," *Communication Monographs* 75 (2008): 136–157; W. P. van Ginkel and D. van Knippenberg, "Group Information Elaboration and Group Decision Making: The Role of Shared Task Representations," *Organizational Behavior and Human Decision Processes* 105 (2008): 82–97; T. Reimer, S. Kuendig, U. Hoffrage, E. Park, and V. Hinsz, "Effects of Information Environment on Group Discussions and Decisions in the Hidden-Profile Paradigm," *Communication Monographs* 74 (2007): 1–28; W. P. van Ginkel and D. van Knippenberg, "Knowledge about the Distribution of Information and Group Decision Making: When and Why Does It Work?" *Organizational Behavior and Human Decision Processes* 108 (2009): 218–229.

16. M. Alsharo, "Knowledge Sharing in Virtual Teams: The Impact on Trust, Collaboration, and Team Effectiveness," Unpublished doctoral dissertation, Department of Computer Science and Information Systems, University of Colorado (2013); E. Jones and J. Kelly, "The Psychological Costs of Knowledge Specialization in Groups: Unique Expertise Leaves You Out of the Loop," *Organizational Behavior and Human Decision Processes* 121 (2013): 174–182; H. C. Xie, "The Role of Computer Mediated Communication Competence on Unique Information Pooling and Decision Quality in Virtual Teams," Unpublished M.A. thesis, Michigan State University (2015); C. Garcia and A. Badia, "Information Problem-Solving Skills in Small Virtual Groups and Learning Outcomes," *Journal of Computer Assisted Learning* 33 (2017): 382–392.

17. O. S. Chernyshenko, A. G. Miner, M. R. Baumann, and J. A. Sniezek, "The Impact of Information Distribution, Ownership, and Discussion on Group Member Judgment: The Differential Cue Weighting Model," *Organizational Behavior and Human Decision Processes* 91 (2003): 12–25.

18. D. R. Seibold and R. A. Meyers, "Group Argument: A Structuration Perspective and Research Program," *Small Group Research* 38 (2007): 312–336; M. B. Fornoff and D. D. Henningsen, "Testing the Linear Discrepancy Model in Perceptions of Group Decision-Making," *Western Journal of Communication* 81.4 (2017): 507–521.

19. S. Y. Sung and J. N. Choi, "Effects of Team Knowledge Management on the Creativity and Financial Performance of Organizational Teams," *Organizational Behavior and Human Decision Processes* 118 (2012): 4–13.

20. M. J. W. McLarnon, V. Taras, M. B. L. Donia, T. A. O'Neill, D. Law, P. Steel, "Global Virtual Team Communication, Coordination, and Performance Across Three Peer Feedback Strategies," *Canadian Journal of Behavioural Science* 51 (2019): 207–218.

21. M. Orlirtzky and R. Y. Hirokawa, "To Err Is Human, to Correct for It Divine: A Meta-Analysis of Research Testing the Functional Theory of Group Decision-Making Effectiveness," *Small Group Research* 32.3 (2001): 313–341.

22. Orlitzky and Hirokawa, "To Err Is Human, to Correct for It Divine"; B. L. Smith, "Interpersonal Behaviors That Damage the Productivity of Creative Problem Solving Groups," *Journal of Creative Behavior* 27 (1993): 171–187.

23. H. Ding and X. Ding, "Project Management, Critical Praxis, and Process-Oriented Approach to Teamwork," *Business Communication Quarterly* 71 (2008): 456–471; P. Lofstrand and I. Zakrisson, "Competitive Versus Non-Competitive Goals in Group Decision-Making," *Small Group Research* 45.4 (2014): 451–464.

24. A. Altabbaa, A. Kaba, and T. N. Beran, "Moving on from Structured Communication to Collaboration: A Communication Schema for Interprofessional Teams," *Journal of Communication in Healthcare* 12 (2019): 160–169.

25. A. B. Henley and K. H. Price, "Want a Better Team? Foster a Climate of Fairness," *Academy of Management Executive* 16 (2002): 153–155.

26. J. L. Thompson, "Building Collective Communication Competence in Interdisciplinary Research Teams," *Journal of Applied Communication Research* 37 (2009): 278–297.

27. P. K. Kim, C. D. Cooper, K. T. Dirks, and D. L. Ferrin, "Repairing Trust with Individuals versus Groups," *Organizational Behavior and Human Decision Processes* 120 (2013): 1–14.

28. A. Kane and F. Rink, "When and How Groups Utilize Dissenting Newcomer Knowledge: Newcomers' Future Prospects Condition the Effect of Language-Based Identity Strategies," *Group Processes and Intergroup Relations* (2016): 1–17.

29. A. T. Pescosolido, "Group Efficacy over Time on Group Performance and Development," *Small Group Research* 34 (2003): 20–43.

30. J. S. Prichard and M. J. Ashleigh, "The Effects of Team-Skills Training on Transactive Memory and Performance," *Small Group Research* 38 (2007): 696–726; T. L. Rapp and J. E. Mathieu, "Evaluating an Individually Self-Administered Generic Teamwork Skills Training Program across Time and Levels," *Small Group Communication* 38 (2007): 532–555; S. Asgari and G. D'Alba, "Improving Group Functioning in Solving Realistic Problems," *International Journal for the Scholarship of Teaching & Learning* 5 (2011): 1–14; S. Y. Liaw, S. W. Ooi, K. D. B. Rusli, T. C. Lau, W. W. San Tam, and W. L. Chua, "Nurse-Physician Communication Team Training in Virtual Reality Versus Live Simulations: Randomized Controlled Trial on Team Communication and Teamwork Attitudes," *Journal of Medical Internet Research* 22 (2020): https://ww.jmir.org/2020/4/e17279 (accessed May 27, 2020); A. Hanley, A. A. Kedrowicz, S. Hammond, and E. M. N. Hardie, "Impact of Team Communication Training on Performance and Self-Assessment of Team Functioning During Sophomore Surgery," *Journal of American Association of Veterinary Medical Colleges* 46 (2019): 45–55.

31. S. A. Beebe and J. T. Masterson, *Communicating in Small Groups: Principles and Practices* 12e (Boston: Pearson, 2020); A. B. VanGundy, *Techniques of Structured Problem Solving* 2e (New York: Van Nostrand Reinhold, 1988).

32. J. K. Brilhart and L. M. Jochem, "Effects of Different Patterns on Outcomes of Problem-Solving Discussion," *Journal of Applied Psychology* 48 (1964): 174–179; W. E. Jurma, "Effects of Leader Structuring Style and Task Orientation Characteristics of Group Members," *Communication Monographs* 49 (1979): 282–295; S. Jarboe, "A Comparison of Input-Output, Process-Output, and Input-Process-Output Models of Small Group Problem-Solving Effectiveness," *Communication Monographs* 55 (1988): 121–142; VanGundy, *Techniques of Structured Problem Solving*.

33. S. A. Beebe, "Structure-Interaction Theory: Conceptual, Contextual and Strategic Influences on Human Communication," *Russian Journal of Linguistics Vestnik Rudn: Special Issue: Intercultural Communication Theory and Practice* 19.4 (2015): 7–21; E. Crawford and J. Lepine, "A Configural Theory of Team Processes: Accounting for the Structure of Taskwork and Teamwork," *Academy of Management Review* 38 (2013): 32–48.

34. Y. Liu and P. McLeod, "Individual Preference for Procedural Order and Process Accountability in Group Problem-Solving," *Small Group Research* 45 (2014): 154–175.

35. D. M. Berg, "A Descriptive Analysis of the Distribution and Duration of Themes Discussed by Task-Oriented Small Groups," *Speech Monographs* 34 (1967): 172–175; E. G. Bormann and N. C. Bormann, *Effective Small Group Communication* 2e (Minneapolis: Burgess, 1976), 132; M. S. Poole, "Decision Development in Small Groups III: A Multiple Sequence Model of Group Decision Development," *Communication Monographs* 50 (1983): 321–341; Y. Liu and P. McLeod, "Individual Preference for Procedural Order and Process Accountability in Group Problem-Solving."

36. For an excellent summary of the literature documenting these problems, see Sunwolf and D. R. Seibold, "The Impact of Formal Procedures on Group Processes, Members, and Task Outcomes,"

in *The Handbook of Group Communication Theory and Research*, edited by L. Frey (Thousand Oaks, CA: Sage, 1999), 395–431.
37. J. Dewey, *How We Think* (Boston: D.C. Heath, 1910).
38. For an excellent discussion of how to define and clarify problems including viewing problems as something we want more of or less of, see D. A. Romig, *Breakthrough Teamwork: Outstanding Results Using Breakthrough Teamwork* (Austin, TX: Irwin, 1996).
39. This explanation of the journalists' six questions method is based on a discussion by J. E. Eitington, *The Winning Trainer* (Houston: Gulf Publishing, 1989), 157.
40. Based on the research of K. Lewin, "Frontiers in Group Dynamics," *Human Relations* 1 (1947): 5–42.
41. K. Dijkstra, J. Van Der Pligt, and G. Van Kleef, "Deliberation Versus Intuition: Decomposing the Role of Expertise in Judgement and Decision Making," *Journal of Behavioral Decision Making* 26 (2013): 285–294.
42. M. C. Schilpzand, D. M. Herold, and C. E. Shalley, "Members' Openness to Experience and Teams' Creative Performance," *Small Group Research* 42 (2011): 55–76; S. J. Shin, T. Y. Kim, J. Y. Lee, and L. Bian, "Cognitive Team Diversity and Individual Team Member Creativity: A Cross-Level Interaction," *Academy of Management Journal* 55 (2012): 197–212; P. Alahuhta, E. Nordback, A. Sivunen, and T. Suraka, "Fostering Team Creativity in Virtual Worlds," *Journal of Virtual Worlds Research* 7.3 (2014).
43. See S. Taggar, "Individual Creativity and Group Ability to Utilize Individual Creative Resources: A Multilevel Model," *Academy of Management Journal* 45 (2002): 315–330; C. E. Johnson and M. A. Hackman, *Creative Communication: Principles and Applications* (Prospect Heights, IL: Waveland, 1995).
44. A. F. Osborn, *Applied Imagination* (New York: Scribner's, 1962).
45. A. L. Delbecq, A. H. Van de Ven, and D. H. Gustafson, *Group Techniques for Program Planning: A Guide to Nominal Group and Delphi Processes* (Glenview, IL: Scott, Foresman, 1975), 7–16.
46. O. Goldenberg, J. Larson Jr., and J. Wiley, "Goal Instructions, Response Format, and Idea Generation," *Small Group Research* 44 (2013): 227–256.
47. D. Straker, *Rapid Problem Solving with Post-it Notes* (Tucson: Fisher Books, 1997).
48. D. H. Henningsen and M. Henningsen, "Generating Ideas About the Uses of Brainstorming: Reconsidering the Losses and Gains of Brainstorming Groups Relative to Nominal Groups," *Southern Communication Journal* 78.1 (2013): 42–55.
49. D. H. Henningsen and M. Henningsen, "Generating Ideas About the Uses of Brainstorming."
50. D. H. Henningsen and M. Henningsen, "Generating Ideas About the Uses of Brainstorming."
51. Adapted from Beebe and Masterson, *Communicating in Small Groups*.
52. M. A. Roberto, "Strategic Decision-Making Processes: Beyond the Efficiency-Consensus Trade-Off," *Group & Organizational Management* 29 (2004): 625–658.
53. F. LeFley, "An Exploratory Study of Team Conflict in the Capital Investment Decision-Making Process," *International Journal of Managing Projects in Business* 11 (2018): 960–985; M. P. Healy, T. Vuori, and G. P. Hodgkinson, "When Teams Agree While Disagreeing: Reflexion and Reflection in Shared Cognition," *Academy of Management Review* 40.3 (2015): 399–422; A. A. Kane and F. Rink, "When and How Groups Utilize Dissenting Newcomer Knowledge: Newcomers' Future Prospects Condition the Effect of Language-Based Identity Strategies," *Group Processes & Intergroup Relations* (2016): 1–17.
54. J. S. Rijnbout and B. M. McKimmie, "Deviance in Organizational Group Decision-Making: The Role of Information Processing, Confidence, and Elaboration," *Group Processes & Intergroup Relations* 15 (2012): 813–828.
55. R. Y. Hirokawa, D. S. Gouran, and A. Martz, "Understanding the Sources of Faulty Group Decision Making: A Lesson from the *Challenger* Disaster," *Small Group Behavior* 19 (1988): 411–433.
56. R. K. M. Haurwitz, "Faculty Doubted Bonfire's Stability," *Austin American-Statesman* (December 10, 1999): A1, A2.
57. D. Jehl, "Panel Unanimous: 'Groupthink' Backed Prewar Assumptions, Report Concludes," *New York Times* (July 10, 2004), 1; also see *The 9/11 Commission Report: Final Report of the National Commission on Terrorist Attacks upon the United States* (Washington, DC: National Commission on Terrorist Attacks, 2004).
58. J. F. Veiga, "The Frequency of Self-Limiting Behavior in Groups: A Measure and an Explanation," *Human Relationships* 44 (1991): 877–895.
59. I. L. Janis, *Victims of Groupthink* (Boston: Houghton Mifflin, 1973).
60. R. Y. Hirokawa and D. R. Scheerhorn, "Communication and Faulty Group Decision-Making," in *Communication and Group Decision-Making*, edited by R. Y. Hirokawa, S. Poole, and M. S. Poole (Beverly Hills, CA: Sage, 1996), 63–80.
61. C. M. Mason and M. R. Griffin, "Group Task Satisfaction: The Group's Attitude to Its Task and Work Environment," *Group & Organizational Management* 30 (2005): 625–652; also see K. Parry, M. Cohen, and S. Bhattacharya, "Rise of the Machines: A Critical Consideration of Automated Leadership Decision Making in Organizations," *Group & Organization Management* 41 (2016): 1–24.
62. M. S. Limon and B. H. La France, "Communication Traits and Leadership Emergence: Examining the Impact of Argumentativeness, Communication Apprehension, and Verbal Aggressiveness in Work Groups," *Southern Communication Journal* 70 (2005): 123–133; also see A. M. L. Raes, U. Glunk, M. G. Heijltjes, and R. A. Roe, "Top Management Team and Middle Managers: Making Sense of Leadership," *Small Group Research* 38 (2007): 360–386.
63. See B. M. Bass, *Stogdill's Handbook of Leadership* (New York: Free Press, 1981).
64. A. Srivastava, K. M. Bartol, and E. A. Locke, "Empowering Leadership in Management Teams: Effects of Knowledge Sharing, Efficacy, and Performance," *Academy of Management Journal* 49 (2006): 1239–1251.
65. G. J. Calanes, "In Their Own Words: An Exploratory Study of Bona Fide Group Leaders," *Small Group Research* 34 (2003): 741–770.
66. P. Balkundi and D. Harrison, "Ties, Leaders, and Time in Teams: Strong Inference about Network Structure's Effects on Team Viability and Performance," *Academy of Management Journal* 49 (2006): 49–68.
67. R. White and R. Lippitt, "Leader Behavior and Member Reaction in Three Social Climates," in *Group Dynamics* 3e, edited by D. Cartwright and A. Zander (New York: Harper & Row, 1968), 319.
68. M. Van Vugt, S. F. Jepson, C. M. Hart, and D. De Cremer, "Autocratic Leadership in Social Dilemmas: A Threat to Group Stability," *Journal of Experimental and Social Psychology* 40 (2004): 1–13.
69. S. Halverson, S. E. Murphy, and R. E. Riggio, "Charismatic Leadership in Crisis Situations: A Laboratory Investigation of Stress and Crisis," *Small Group Research* 35 (2004): 495–514.
70. D. S. DeRue, C. M. Barnes, and F. P. Morgeson, "Understanding the Motivational Contingencies of Team Leadership," *Small Group Research* 41 (2010): 621–651.
71. S. S. K. Lam, X. P. Chen, and J. Schaubroeck, "Participative Decision Making and Employee Performance in Different Cultures: The Moderating Effects of Allocentrism/Idiocentrism and Efficacy," *Academy of Management Journal* 45 (2002): 905–914.
72. A. Remmel, "Scientists Want Virtual Meetings to Stay after the COVID Pandemic," *Nature*, March 2, 2021, https://www.nature.com/articles/d41586-021-00513-1.
73. A. Olena, "COVID-19 Ushers in the Future of Conferences," The Scientist, September 28, 2020, https://www.the-scientist.com/news-opinion/covid-19-ushers-in-the-future-of-conferences-67978.
74. B. Frisch and C. Greene, "3 Things Virtual Meetings Offer That In-Person Ones Don't," *Harvard Business Review*, July 23, 2020.

75. T. Richards, "Will COVID-19 Change Conferences for the Better?" July 5, 2020, https://blogs.bmj.com/bmj/2020/06/05/tessa-richards-todays-rapidly-convened-virtual-events-are-pointing-the-way-to-a-greener-more-inclusive-future/.
76. Cavendish Venues, "82% of Meetings Affected by COVID-19, ICCA Research Reveals," October 6, 2020, https://www.cavendishvenues.co.uk/82-of-meetings-affected-by-covid-19-icca-research-reveals/.
77. "Nonverbal Communication Skills: Definition and Examples," November 26, 2020, https://www.indeed.com/career-advice/career-development/nonverbal-communication-skills.
78. D. C. Korten, "Situational Determinants of Leadership Structure," *Journal of Conflict Resolution* 6 (1962): 222–235.
79. P. Hersey, K. Blanchard, and D. Johnson, *Management of Organizational Behavior: Utilizing Human Resources* 9e (Englewood Cliffs, NJ: Prentice–Hall, 2007).
80. For an excellent discussion of transformational leadership applied to teams, see S. D. Dionne, F. J. Yammarino, L. E. Atwater, and W. D. Spangler, "Transformational Leadership and Team Performance," *Journal of Organizational Change Management* 17 (2004): 177–193.
81. R. F. Fiedler, *A Theory of Leadership Effectiveness* (New York: McGraw-Hill, 1967), 144.
82. See K. W. Phillips, G. B. Northcraft, and M. A. Neale, "Surface-Level Diversity Collide: The Effects on Dissenting Group Members," *Organizational Behavior and Human Decision Processes* 9 (2006): 143–160; J. R. Larson, "Deep Diversity and Strong Synergy: Modeling the Impact of Variability in Members' Problem-Solving Strategies on Group Problem-Solving Performance," *Small Group Research* 3 (2007): 413–436.
83. A. Mello and L. Delise, "Cognitive Diversity to Team Outcomes: The Roles of Cohesion and Conflict Management," *Small Group Research* 46.2 (2015): 204–226.
84. R. Rodriguez, "Challenging Demographic Reductionism: A Pilot Study Investigating Diversity in Group Composition," *Small Group Research* 26 (1998): 744–759.
85. Phillips et al., "Surface-Level Diversity Collide."
86. B. M. Bass and M. J. Avolio, "Transformational Leadership and Organizational Culture," *International Journal of Public Administration* 17 (1994): 541–554; also see F. J. Yammarino and A. J. Dubinsky, "Transformational Leadership Theory: Using Levels of Analysis to Determine Boundary Conditions," *Personnel Psychology* 47 (1994): 787–809; J. Cha, Y, Kim, J. Y. Lee, and D. G. Bachrach, "Transformational Leadership and Inter-Team Collaboration: Exploring the Mediating Role of Teamwork Quality and Moderating Role of Team Size," *Group & Organizational Management* 40 (2015): 715–743.
87. For additional research about the efficacy of transformational leadership, see J. McCann, P. Langford, and R. M. Rawlings, "Testing Behling and McFillen's Syncretical Model of Charismatic Transformational Leadership," *Group & Organization Management* 31 (2006): 237–263; R. F. Piccolo and J. Colquitt, "Transformational Leadership and Job Behaviors: The Mediating Role of Core Job Characteristics," *Academy of Management Journal* 49 (2006): 327–340; R. S. Rubin, D. C. Muniz, and W. H. Bommer, "Leading from Within: The Effects of Emotion Recognition and Personality on Transformational Leadership Behavior," *Academy of Management Journal* 48 (2005): 845–858; A. Ergeneli, R. Gohar, and Z. Temirbekova, "Transformational Leadership: Its Relationship to Culture Value Dimensions," *International Journal of Intercultural Relations* 31 (2007): 703–724; B. J. Hoffman, B. H. Bynum, R. F. Piccolo, and A. W. Sutton, "Person-Organization Value Congruence: How Transformational Leaders Influence Work Group Effectiveness," *Academy of Management Journal* 54 (2011): 779–796; J.-W. Huang, "The Effects of Transformational Leadership on the Distinct Aspects Development of Social Identity," *Group Processes & Intergroup Relations* 16 (2013): 87–104; P. Wang, J. C. Rode, K. Shi, Z. Luo, and W. Chen, "A Workgroup Climate Perspective on the Relationships among Transformational Leadership, Workgroup Diversity, and Employee Creativity," *Group & Organizational Management* 38 (2013): 334–360; P. Wang, J. C. Rode, K. Shi, Z. Luo, and W. Chen, "A Workgroup Climate Perspective on the Relationships among Transformational Leadership, Workgroup Diversity, and Employee Creativity," *Group & Organizational Management* 38 (2013): 334–360.
88. P. M. Senge, "The Leader's New Role: Building Learning Organizations," *Sloan Management Review* 32 (1990).
89. M. Zellmer-Bruhn and C. Gibson, "Multinational Organization Context: Implications for Team Learning and Performance," *Academy of Management Journal* 49 (2006): 501–518.
90. D. I. Jung and J. J. Sosik, "Transformational Leadership in Work Groups: The Role of Empowerment, Cohesiveness, and Collective Efficacy on Perceived Group Performance," *Small Group Research* 33 (2002): 313–336; also see T. Dvir, D. Eden, B. J. Avolio, and B. Shamir, "Impact of Transformational Leadership on Follower Development and Performance: A Field Experiment," *Academy of Management Journal* 45 (2002): 735–744; C. L. Hoyt and J. Blascovich, "Transformational and Transactional Leadership in Virtual and Physical Environments," *Small Group Research* 34 (2003): 678–715; S. S. Kahai, R. Huang, and R. J. Jestice, "Interaction Effect of Leadership and Communication Media on Feedback Positivity in Virtual Teams," *Group & Organizational Management* 37 (2012): 716–751; J. Cha, Y. Kim, J. Y. Lee, and D. G. Bachrach, "Transformational Leadership and Inter-Team Collaboration: Exploring the Mediating Role of Teamwork Quality and Moderating Role of Team Size," *Group and Organization Management* 40 (2015): 715–743.
91. V. U. Druskar and J. V. Wheeler, "Managing from the Boundary: The Effective Leadership of Self-Managing Work Teams," *Academy of Management Journal* 46 (2003): 435–457.
92. J. Eisenberg, C. Post, and N. DiTomaso, "Team Dispersion and Performance: The Role of Team Communication and Transformational Leadership," *Small Group Research* 50 (2019): 348–380.
93. J. A. Raelin, "Don't Bother Putting Leadership into People," *Academy of Management Executive* 18 (2004): 131–135; M. W. McCall, "Leadership Development through Experience," *Academy of Management Executive* 18 (2004): 127–130; J. Conger, "Developing Leadership Capability: What's Inside the Black Box?" *Academy of Management Executive* 18 (2004): 136–139; D. Vera and M. Crossan, "Strategic Leadership and Organizational Learning," *Academy of Management Review* 29 (2004): 222–239.
94. D. Barry, *Dave Barry Turns 50* (New York: Ballantine, 1998), 182.
95. T. A. O'Neill and N. J. Allen, "Team Meeting Attitudes: Conceptualization and Investigation of a New Construct," *Small Group Research* 43 (2012): 186–210.
96. S. Kauffeld and N. Lehmann-Willenbrock, "Meetings Matter: Effects of Team Meetings on Team and Organizational Success," *Small Group Research* 43 (2012): 130–158; S. Boerner, M. Schaffner, and D. Gebert, "The Complementarity of Team Meetings and Cross-Functional Communication: Empirical Evidence from New Services Development Teams," *Journal of Leadership & Organizational Studies* 19 (2012): 256–266.
97. R. K. Mosvick and R. B. Nelson, *We've Got to Start Meeting Like This!* (Glenview, IL: Scott, Foresman, 1987).
98. Beebe, "Structure-Interaction Theory."
99. Suggestions about organizing meeting agendas are based on M. Doyle and D. Straus, *How to Make Meetings Work* (New York: Playboy Press, 1976); Mosvick and Nelson, *We've Got to Start Meeting Like This!*; G. Lumsden and D. Lumsden, *Communicating in Groups and Teams: Sharing Leadership* (Belmont, CA: Wadsworth, 1993); D. B. Curtis, J. J. Floyd, and J. L. Winsor, *Business and Professional Communication* (New York: HarperCollins, 1992); Romig, *Breakthrough Teamwork*; T. A. Kayser, *Mining Group Gold* (El Segundo, CA: Serif, 1990); J. E. Tropman and G. Clark Morningstar, *Meetings: How to Make Them Work for You* (New York: Van Nostrand Reinhold, 1985), 56; Beebe and Masterson, *Communicating in Small Groups*.
100. J. E. Tropman, *Making Meetings Work* (Thousand Oaks, CA: Sage, 1996).

101. R. J. Razzante, "Identifying Dominant Group Communication Strategies: A Phenomenological Study," *Communication Studies* 69 (2018): 389–403.
102. J. R. Mesmer-Magnus, L. A. DeChurch, M. Jimenez-Rodriguez, and J. Wildman, "A Meta-Analytic Investigation of Virtuality and Information Sharing in Teams," *Organizational Behavior and Human Decision Processes* 115 (2011): 214–225.
103. See J. A. Bonito, "A Longitudinal Social Relations Analysis of Participation in Small Groups," *Human Communication Research* 32 (2006): 302–321; M. W. Kramer, P. J. Benoit, M. A. Dixon, and J. Benoit-Bryan, "Group Processes in a Teaching Renewal Retreat: Communication Function and Dialectal Tensions," *Southern Communication Journal* 72 (2007): 145–168; J. A. Bonito, M. H. DeCamp, and E. K. Ruppel, "The Process of Information Sharing in Small Groups: Application of a Local Model," *Communication Monographs* 75 (2008): 136–157.
104. See D. S. Gouran, "Variables Related to Consensus in Group Discussions of Questions of Policy," *Speech Monographs* 36 (1969): 385–391; T. J. Knutsun, "An Experimental Study of the Effects of Orientation Behavior on Small Group Consensus," *Speech Monographs* 39 (1972): 159–165; A. Kline, "Orientation and Group Consensus," *Central States Speech Journal* 23 (1972): 44–47.
105. J. Wildman and W. L. Bedwell, "Practicing What We Preach: Teaching Teams Using Validated Team Science," *Small Group Research* 44 (2013): 381–394.
106. S. A. Beebe and J. K. Barge, "Evaluating Group Discussion," in *Small Group Communication: Theory & Practice*, edited by R. Y. Hirokawa, R. S. Cathcart, L. A. Samovar, and L. D. Henman (Los Angeles: Roxbury, 2003); T. Leigh, *Assessing the Reliability and Validity of The Competent Group Communicator Problem Solving Assessment Instrument*. Unpublished M.A. thesis, Texas State University (2009); L. S. Albert, "Using the Competent Small Group Communicator Instrument to Assess Group Performance in the Classroom," ERIC ED472806 (2002) https://eric-ed-gov.libproxy.txstate.edu/contentdelivery/servlet/ERICServlet?accno=ED472806 (accessed May 28, 2020).

Chapter 11

1. "The CASA/GAL Model," National CASA/GAL Association for Children, nationalcasagal.org 2020.
2. The sample speech referenced in this chapter is adapted from D. Reyes, "The Health Risks of Soft Drinks," prepared for Public Speaking at Texas State University, Fall 2016.
3. G. Bodie, "A Racing Heart, Rattling Knees, and Ruminative Thoughts: Defining, Explaining, and Treating Public Speaking Anxiety," *Communication Education* 59 (2010): 70–105.
4. S. Booth-Butterfield, "Instructional Interventions for Reducing Situational Anxiety and Avoidance," *Communication Education* 37 (1988): 214–223.
5. K. Dwyer and M. Davidson, "Is Public Speaking Really More Feared Than Death?" *Communication Research Reports* 29 (2012): 99–107; survey conducted by R. H. Bruskin and Associates, *Spectra* 9 (1973): 4.
6. S. Campbell and J. Larson, "Public Speaking Anxiety: Comparing Face-to-Face and Web-Based Speeches," *Journal of Instructional Pedagogies* 10 (2013): 1–12.
7. L. LeFebre, L. E. LeFebvre, and M. Allen, "Training the Butterflies to Fly in Formation: Cataloguing Student Fears about Public Speaking," *Communication Education* 67 (2018): 348–362; A. Bippus and J. Daly, "What Do People Think Causes Stage Fright? Naïve Attributions About the Reasons for Public-Speaking Anxiety," *Communication Education* 48 (1999): 63–72; G. D. Bodie, "A Racing Heart, Rattling Knees, and Ruminative Thoughts: Defining and Explaining Public Speaking Anxiety," *Communication Education* 59 (2010): 70–105; J. Pearson, L. DeWitt, J. Child, D. Kahl, and V. Dandamudi, "Facing the Fear: An Analysis of Speech-Anxiety Content in Public-Speaking Textbooks," *Communication Research Reports* 24 (2007): 159–168; M. Beatty, J. McCroskey, and A. D. Heisel, "Communication Apprehension as Temperamental Expression: A Communibiological Paradigm," *Communication Monographs* 65 (1998): 197–219; Y. Lin and A. Rancer, "Sex Differences in Intercultural Communication Apprehension, Ethnocentrism, and Intercultural Willingness to Communicate," *Psychological Reports* 92 (2003): 195–200; S. Shimotsu and T. P. Mottet, "The Relationships among Perfectionism, Communication Apprehension, and Temperament," *Communication Research Reports* 26.3 (2009): 188–197.
8. Pearson et al., "Facing the Fear: An Analysis of Speech-Anxiety Content in Public-Speaking Textbooks"; Bodie, "A Racing Heart, Rattling Knees, and Ruminative Thoughts"; see also K. H. White, M. C. Howard, B. Zhong, J. A. Soto, C. R. Perez, E. A. Lee, N. A. Dawson-Andoh, and M. R. Minnick, "The Communication Anxiety Regulation Scale: Development and Initial Validation," *Communication Quarterly* 63 (2015): 23–43.
9. A. Finn, C. Sawyer, and P. Schrodt, "Examining the Effect of Exposure Therapy on Public Speaking State Anxiety," *Communication Education* 58 (2009): 92–109.
10. A. Goberman, S. Hughes, and T. Haydock, "Acoustic Characteristics of Public Speaking: Anxiety and Practice Effects," *Speech Communication* 53 (2011): 875; K. Savitsky and T. Gilovich, "The Illusion of Transparency and the Alleviation of Speech Anxiety," *Journal of Experimental Social Psychology* 39 (2003): 618–625.
11. L. LeFebvre, L. E. LeFebvre, M. Allen, M. M. Buckner, and D. Griffin, "Metamorphosis of Public Speaking Anxiety: Student Fear Transformation Throughout the Introductory Communication Course," *Communication Studies* 71.1 (2020): 98–111; K. Dwyer and D. Fus, "Perceptions of Communication Competence, Self-Efficacy, and Trait Communication Apprehension: Is There an Impact on Basic Course Success?" *Communication Research Reports* 19 (2002): 29–37.
12. C. Berger, "Speechlessness: Causal Attributions, Emotional Features, and Social Consequences," *Journal of Language and Social Psychology* 23 (2004): 147–179; M. Booth-Butterfield, "Stifle or Stimulate? The Effects of Communication Task Structure on Apprehensive and Non-Apprehensive Students," *Communication Education* 35 (1986): 337–348.
13. J. Ayres, "Speech Preparation Processes and Speech Apprehension," *Communication Education* 45 (1996): 228–235.
14. N. Greengold and E. Grodziak, "Making Smart Use of Smart Phones to Improve Public Speaking," *Journal of Technology Integration in the Classroom* 5 (2013): 14.
15. D. Shadinger, J. Katsion, S. Myllykangas, and D. Case, "The Impact of a Positive, Self-Talk Statement on Public Speaking Anxiety," *College Teaching* 68.1 (2020): 5–11; S. McCullough, S. Russell, R. Behnke, C. Sawyer, and P. Witt, "Anticipatory Public Speaking State Anxiety as a Function of Body Sensations and State of Mind," *Communication Quarterly* 54 (2006): 101–109; P. Witt, K. Brown, J. Roberts, J. Weisel, C. Sawyer, and R. Behnke, "Somatic Anxiety Patterns Before, During, and After Giving a Public Speech," *Southern Communication Journal* 71 (2006): 87–100.
16. A. Brooks, "Get Excited: Reappraising Pre-performance Anxiety as Excitement," *Journal of Experimental Psychology* 143 (2014): 1144–1158.
17. K. Macklin, "Speak Easier," *Yoga Journal* 245 (2012): 28.
18. P. Addison, E. Clay, S. Xie, C. Sawyer, and R. Behnke, "Worry as a Function of Public Speaking State Anxiety Type," *Communication Research Reports* 16 (2003): 125–131; D. Duff, T. Levine, M. Beatty, J. Woolbright, and H. Park, "Testing Public Anxiety Treatments Against a Credible Placebo Control," *Communication Education* 56 (2007): 72–88.
19. Addison et al., "Worry as a Function of Public Speaking State Anxiety Type."
20. G. Nash, G. Crimmins, and F. Oprescu, "If First-Year Students Are Afraid of Public Speaking Assessments What Can Teachers Do to Alleviate Such Anxiety?" *Assessment & Evaluation in Higher Education* 41.4 (2016): 586–600; K. Hunter, J. Westwick, and L. Haleta,

"Assessing Success: The Impacts of a Fundamentals of Speech Course on Decreasing Public Speaking Anxiety," *Communication Education* 63 (2014): 124–135.
21. L. Tracy, "Taming Hostile Audiences," *Vital Speeches of the Day* 71.10 (2005).
22. K. Petrova, Untitled, *Winning Orations 2019* (Mankato, MN: Interstate Oratorical Association, 2019): 69.
23. L. Zanteson, "Building a Career Through Public Speaking," *Today's Dietitian* 16.8 (2014): 39.
24. Adapted from J. Boyle, "Spyware Stalking: Time to Take Back the Technology," *Winning Orations 2015* (Mankato, MN: Interstate Oratorical Association, 2015): 32–34.
25. J. Humphrey, "Taking the Stage: How Women Can Achieve a Leadership Presence," *Vital Speeches of the Day* 67.14 (2001).
26. Adapted from C. Chigadza, "The Biggest Healthcare Crisis You've Never Heard Of: World Eyecare," *Winning Orations 2019* (Mankato, MN: Interstate Oratorical Association, 2019): 40–42.
27. "African 'Fairy Circles' May Be by Termites," *Austin American-Statesman*, January 19, 2017, A2.
28. A. Rojas, "Deconstructing the Invisible Prison: Providing an Equitable Educational Experience for Undocumented Students Through the UndocuAlly Program," *Winning Orations 2019* (Mankato, MN: Interstate Oratorical Association, 2019): 10–12.
29. Adapted from S. Begley, "Libraries Without Borders," *Winning Orations 2015* (Mankato, MN: Interstate Oratorical Association, 2015): 67–69.
30. "Refugee Population by Country or Territory of Origin," *World Bank*, 2016, worldbank.org (accessed June 1, 2020); *24/7 Wall Street*, September 21, 2015, 247wallst.com (accessed June 1, 2020).
31. E. Kirk, "Practical Steps in Evaluating Internet Resources," May 7, 2001, www.lehigh.edu (accessed June 1, 2020).
32. T. Buchanan, "Why do People Share Disinformation on Social Media?" Centre for Research and Evidence on Security Threats, September 4, 2020, https://crestresearch.ac.uk/resources/disinformation-on-social-media/.
33. J. Rogalo, "Home *Safe* Home," *Winning Orations 2019* (Mankato, MN: Interstate Oratorical Association, 2019): 79.
34. M. Limon and D. Kazoleas, "A Comparison of Exemplar and Statistical Evidence in Reducing Counter-Arguments and Responses to a Message," *Communication Research Reports* 21 (2004): 291–298.
35. D. Lessing, "On Not Winning the Nobel Prize," *Vital Speeches of the Day* 74.2 (2008).
36. M. Daly, "Beyond Fairness: The Value of an Exclusive Economy," *Vital Speeches of the Day* 85.12 (2019).
37. O. Winfrey, 2020 commencement speech, in N. Bogel-Burroughs, "No Pomp Because of the Circumstances, So Oprah Does Her Thing," *New York Times*, May 16, 2020, A17.
38. G. Whitmer, quoted in A. Sherman, "1918 Pandemic Shows Dangers of Early Letup," April 17, 2020, www.politifact.com (accessed June 1, 2020).
39. S. Malami, "Child Slavery in the Chocolate Industry," *Winning Orations 2019* (Mankato, MN: Interstate Oratorical Association, 2019): 98.
40. R. Walcott, "Dying from Withdrawal: Opioid Related Deaths in U.S. Jails and Prisons," *Winning Orations 2019* (Mankato, MN: Interstate Oratorical Association, 2019): 84.
41. R. Duffield, "Sometimes There Are No Bruises," *Vital Speeches of the Day* 85.2 (2019).
42. K. Winslow, "The Epidemic That Is 3D Printed Guns," *Winning Orations 2019* (Mankato, MN: Interstate Oratorical Association, 2019): 9.
43. M. Rao, "What's the Presidency For?" *Vital Speeches of the Day* 86.4 (2020).
44. E. Trader, "Giving a Voice to Those Not Heard," *Winning Orations 2019* (Mankato, MN: Interstate Oratorical Association, 2019): 35.
45. R. Brown, "Seven Ways of Looking at a Crisis," *Vital Speeches of the Day* 76.6 (2010).
46. L. Miranda, "Your Stories Are Essential," *Vital Speeches of the Day* 82.8 (2016).
47. K. Shofner, "What is Global Language?" United Language Group, https://www.unitedlanguagegroup.com/blog/strategy/what-is-global-english.
48. Adroit Market Research, "English Language Learning Market to grow at 7.1% to hit $54.8 billion by 2025 – Insights on Recent Trends, Size, Share, Growth Opportunities, Key Developments and Future Outlook: Adroit Market Research," July 26, 2019, https://www.globenewswire.com/.
49. F. Pham, "The U.S. Military's Invisible War," prepared for Individual Events/Persuasive Speaking competition, The University of Texas, Spring 2020.

Chapter 12

1. J. Pearson, J. Child, and D. Kahl Jr., "Preparation Meeting Opportunity: How Do College Students Prepare for Public Speeches?" *Communication Quarterly* 54 (2006): 351–366.
2. A. Rynne, "How to Build a Perfectly Published Content Sandwich [Infographic]," *LinkedIn Marketing Solutions Blog*, February 7, 2017, https://business.linkedin.com/marketing-solutions/blog/publishing-on-linkedin/2017/how-to-build-a-perfectly-published-content-sandwich--infographic (accessed June 1, 2020).
3. S. Njapa, "Changing the African Perception," *Winning Orations 2019* (Mankato, MN: Interstate Oratorical Association, 2019): 72–74.
4. Adapted from P. Steiger, "A Closer Look: Three Golden Ages of Journalism?" *Vital Speeches of the Day* 80.8 (2014): 111–114.
5. Adapted from A. Zerull, "Resident Evil: How America's Teaching Hospitals Neglect the Care of Our Caregivers," *Winning Orations 2016* (Mankato, MN: Interstate Oratorical Association, 2016): 161–166.
6. Adapted from R. Walcott, "Dying from Withdrawal: Opioid-Related Deaths in U.S. Jails and Prisons," *Winning Orations 2019* (Mankato, MN: Interstate Oratorical Association, 2019): 84–86.
7. F. Pham, "The U.S. Military's Invisible War," prepared for Individual Events/Persuasive Speaking competition, The University of Texas, Spring 2020.
8. S. A. Gunaratne, "Emerging Global Divides in Media and Communication Theory: European Universalism Versus Non-western Reactions," *Asian Journal of Communication*, 19.4 (2009): 366–383.
9. Martinez-Carter, K. "Culture shock: How to Speak Business Anywhere," BBC online, October 7, 2014, https://www.bbc.com/worklife/article/20141006-talk-shock-youre-doing-it-wrong.
10. K. Morton, "A Howl for Help: The Case for Public and Private Funding of Service Animal Training in Shelters," *Winning Orations 2019* (Mankato, MN: Interstate Oratorical Association, 2019): 96–97.
11. K. Huber, "Things Don't Happen for a Reason. But They Do Often Happen Because Nobody Has Yet Found a Better Way," *Vital Speeches of the Day* 82.8 (2016): 227.
12. A. Kolousek, "Hidden Home School Abuse: Denying Children a Safe Place to Call Home," *Winning Orations 2016* (Mankato, MN: Interstate Oratorical Association, 2016): 35–36.
13. C. Kay, "The U.S. Chamber of Commerce: Commerce or Coerce?" *Winning Orations 2016* (Mankato, MN: Interstate Oratorical Association, 2016): 32.
14. G. Hildebrand, "Cinderella," Texas State University student speech, 2013.
15. R. Shah, "Extend the Reach of Human Dignity to Every Single Person on This Planet," *Vital Speeches of the Day* 85.12 (2019): 331.
16. P. Manning, "You Don't Have to Wonder if I'll Miss It," *Vital Speeches of the Day* 82.5 (2016): 153.
17. R. Reece, "Bees: Buzzing about the Future," prepared for Individual Events/Communication Analysis competition, University of Central Missouri, Spring 2020.

18. N. Modi, "All Our Endeavors Are Centered on 1.3 Billion Indians; But Their Fruits Are for All," *Vital Speeches of the Day* 85.11 (2019): 299.
19. R. Brown, "Mental Illness Is Not a Learning Disability," *Winning Orations 2015* (Mankato, MN: Interstate Oratorical Association, 2015): 41.
20. S. Cohen, "The Kind of World We All Want," *Vital Speeches of the Day* 86.1 (2020): 2.
21. E. McDonnell, untitled speech, *Winning Orations 2019* (Mankato, MN: Interstate Oratorical Association, 2019): 37.
22. K. Winslow, "The Epidemic That Is 3D Printed Guns," *Winning Orations 2019* (Mankato, MN: Interstate Oratorical Association, 2019): 7.
23. C. Newton, untitled speech, prepared for Individual Events/Informative Speaking competition, The University of Texas, Spring 2020.
24. A. Lincoln, "Gettysburg Address," delivered at Gettysburg, PA, November 19, 1863, *Douglass Archives of American Public Address,* August 19, 1998, douglass.speech.nwu.edu/linc_b33.htm (accessed June 1, 2020).
25. D. MacArthur, "Farewell to the Cadets," address delivered at West Point, May 12, 1962, in *Contemporary American Speeches* 7e, edited by R. L. Johannesen, R. R. Allen, and W. A. Linkugel (Dubuque, IA: Kendall/Hunt, 1992), 393.
26. "The Queen's Coronavirus Speech Transcript: 'We Will Succeed and Better Days Will Come,'" April 5, 2020, www.telegraph.co.uk (accessed June 1, 2020).
27. P. Sterman, "The New World Champion of Public Speaking," *Toastmasters* November 2016.
28. M. Reyes, "Body Brokers," prepared for Individual Events/Persuasive Speaking competition, University of Central Missouri, Spring 2020.
29. A. Upshaw, "A Prescription for Addiction," prepared for Individual Events/Persuasive Speaking competition, University of Central Missouri, Spring 2020.
30. The preparation outline and speaking notes in this chapter are adapted from a speech by D. Reyes, "The Health Risks of Soft Drinks," prepared for Public Speaking at Texas State University, Fall 2016.

Chapter 13

1. P. Heinbert, "Relationship of Content and Delivery to General Effectiveness," *Speech Monographs* 30 (1963): 105–107.
2. A. Mehrabian, *Nonverbal Communication* (Hawthorne, NY: Aldine, 1972).
3. J. Detz, "Delivery Plus Content Equals Successful Presentation," *Communication World* 15 (1998): 34.
4. L. Browne, quoted in B. Matthews, "The Script as Friend and Foe," *Toastmaster* 75.8 (2009): 26.
5. P. Begala, "Flying Solo," PBS, *The Clinton Years: Anecdotes,* 2000, www.pbs.org (accessed June 1, 2020).
6. L. White and L. Messer, "An Analysis of Interstate Speeches: Are They Structurally Different?" *National Forensic Journal* 21.2 (2003): 15.
7. G. Orwell, "Politics and the English Language," in *About Language,* edited by W. H. Roberts and G. Turgeson (Boston: Houghton Mifflin, 1986), 282.
8. M. Egkolfopoulou and A. Sebenius, "To Get Around Facebook's Anti-Violence Policies, Groups Turn to a Low-Tech Solution: Coded Language," *Austin American-Statesman,* May 14, 2020, B5–B7.
9. R. Burford-Rice and M. Augoustinos, "'I Didn't Mean That: It Was Just a Slip of the Tongue': Racial Slips and Gaffes in the Public Arena," *British Journal of Social Psychology* 57 (2018): 24.
10. D. Hersman, "I Saw a Woman Today," *Vital Speeches of the Day* 80.5 (2014): 151.
11. M. Klepper, *I'd Rather Die Than Give a Speech* (New York: Carol Publishing Group, 1994), 45.
12. M. McConaughey, in S. O'Neal, "Hollywood, Texas: Matthew McConaughey Has Your Coronavirus Pep Talk," March 20, 2020. www.texasmonthly.com (accessed June 1, 2020); S. Acevedo, "The Future for Girl Scouts in America and Abroad," *Vital Speeches of the Day* 82.10 (2016): 312; K. Burns, "You Are, Whether You Are Yet Aware of It or Not, Charged with Saving Our Union," *Vital Speeches of the Day* 82.8 (2016): 223.
13. B. Moyers, "What Adam Said to Eve," prepared remarks for the annual conference of the Association for Education in Journalism and Mass Communication, Washington, DC, *PBS,* August 8, 2007, www.pbs.org (accessed June 1, 2020).
14. D. Trump, inaugural address, January 20, 2017, www.whitehouse.gov (accessed June 1, 2020).
15. M. Jordan, "Rest in Peace, Little Brother," *Vital Speeches of the Day* 86.4 (2020): 106–107.
16. A. Cuomo, in E. Shapiro, "New York Has Become the Epicenter of the Pandemic," March 27, 2020, abcnews.go.com (accessed June 1, 2020).
17. J. Biden, remarks commemorating the fiftieth anniversary of Kennedy's "Moon Shot" Speech, delivered at the John F. Kennedy Library and Museum, Boston, MA, *White House,* May 25, 2011, www.whitehouse.gov (accessed June 1, 2020).
18. J. Huber, "Things Don't Happen for a Reason. But They Do Often Happen Because Nobody Has Yet Found a Better Way," *Vital Speeches of the Day* 82.8 (2016): 227.
19. S. Malami, "Child Slavery in the Chocolate Industry," *Winning Orations 2019* (Mankato, MN: Interstate Oratorical Association, 2019): 99.
20. L. Fiorella, A. T. Stull, S. Kuhlmann, and R. E. Mayer, "Instructor Presence in Video Lectures: The Role of Dynamic Drawings, Eye Contact, and Instructor Visibility," *Journal of Educational Psychology* 111.7 (2019): 1162–1171; M. Beege, S. Schneider, S. Nebel, and G. D. Rey, "Look Into My Eyes! Exploring the Effect of Addressing in Educational Videos," *Learning and Instruction* 49 (2017) 113–120; S. A. Beebe, "Eye Contact: A Nonverbal Determinant of Speaker Credibility," *Speech Teacher* 23 (1974): 21–25; S. A. Beebe, "Effects of Eye Contact, Posture and Vocal Inflection upon Credibility and Comprehension," *Australian Scan Journal of Nonverbal Communication* 7–8 (1979–1980): 57–70; M. Cobin, "Response to Eye Contact," *Quarterly Journal of Speech* 48 (1963): 415–419.
21. Beebe, "Eye Contact."
22. S. Campbell and J. Larson, "Public Speaking Anxiety: Comparing Face-to-Face and Web-Based Speeches," *Journal of Instructional Pedagogies* 10 (April 2013): 4.
23. E. Adler, "Gestures May Give You a Hand with Speaking," *Austin American-Statesman,* November 25, 1998, E6.
24. J. C. McCroskey, V. P. Richmond, A. Sallinen, J. M. Fayer, and R. A. Barraclough, "A Cross-Cultural and Multi-Behavioral Analysis of the Relationship between Nonverbal Immediacy and Teacher Evaluation," *Communication Education* 44 (1995): 281–290.
25. M. J. Beatty, "Some Effects of Posture on Speaker Credibility," library paper, Central Missouri State University, Warrensburg, MO, 1973.
26. P. Ekman, W. V. Friesen, and S. S. Tomkins, "Facial Affect Scoring Technique: A First Validity Study," *Semiotica* 3 (1971): 37–58.
27. P. Ekman and W. Friesen, *Unmasking the Face* (Englewood Cliffs, NJ: Prentice Hall, 1975).
28. J. Schneider, D. Börner, P. van Rosmalen, and M. Specht, "Presentation Trainer: What Experts and Computers Can Tell About Your Nonverbal Communication," *Journal of Computer Assisted Learning* 33 (2017): 168.
29. M. M. Gill, "Accents and Stereotypes: Their Effect on Perceptions of Teachers and Lecture Comprehension," *Journal of Applied Communication Research* 22 (1994): 348–361.
30. E. Bohn and D. Jabusch, "The Effect of Four Methods of Instruction on the Use of Visual Aids in Speeches," *Western Journal of Speech Communication* 46 (1982): 253–265.

31. Centers for Disease Control and Prevention, "COVID Data Tracker," July 7, 2020, https://www.cdc.gov/covid-data-tracker (accessed July 7, 2020).
32. Centers for Disease Control and Prevention, "COVID Data Tracker."
33. N. Norton, "Beyond Flint: The Poison in Our Pipes," *Winning Orations 2016* (Mankato, MN: Interstate Oratorical Association, 2016): 79.
34. A. Wilson, "In Defense of Rhetoric," *The Toastmaster* 70.2 (2004): 11.
35. Detz, "Delivery plus Content Equals Successful Presentation."
36. S. Cain, "10 Public Speaking Tips for Introverts: Introverts Can Seize the Microphone—and Bring the House Down," July 25, 2011, *psychologytoday.com* (accessed June 1, 2020).
37. T. Smith and A. B. Frymier, "Get 'Real': Does Practicing Speeches before an Audience Improve Performance?" *Communication Quarterly* 54 (2006): 111–125.
38. "Presidential Seal Falls Off Podium as Obama Speaks," *Washington Times*, October 6, 2010, www.washingtontimes.com (accessed June 1, 2020).
39. J. Masterson, S. Beebe, and N. Watson, *Invitation to Effective Speech Communication* (Glenview, IL: Scott, Foresman, 1989), 4.

Chapter 14

1. J. R. Johnson and N. Szczupakiewicz, "The Public Speaking Course: Is It Preparing Students with Work-Related Public Speaking Skills?" *Communication Education* 36 (1987): 131–137.
2. L. Lefever, *The Art of Explanation* (New Jersey: John Wiley & Sons, 2013), 10.
3. For an excellent discussion of teaching someone to perform a skill, especially a social skill, see M. Argyle, *The Psychology of Interpersonal Behavior* (London: Penguin, 1990).
4. G. K. Chesterton, "On Mr. Rudyard Kipling and Making the World Small," *Heretics*, 1905, *Project Gutenberg*, http://www.gutenberg.org/files/470/470-h/470-h.htm#chap03 (accessed June 1, 2020).
5. A. Slagell, "Why Should You Use a Clear Pattern of Organization? Because It Works," *Communication Teacher* 27.4 (2013): 200.
6. For an excellent discussion of strategies for informing others, see K. E. Rowan, "A New Pedagogy for Explanatory Public Speaking: Why Arrangement Should Not Substitute for Invention," *Communication Education* 44 (1995): 236–250.
7. J. Chesebro, "Effects of Teacher Clarity and Nonverbal Immediacy on Student Learning, Receiver Apprehension, and Affect," *Communication Education* 52 (2003): 135–147.
8. J. Zimmer, "Phrases to Avoid on Stage," *Toastmaster* 82.5 (2016): 9.
9. E. Holt, "Gone but Not Forgotten: Desegregation and the Demise of Black-Owned Businesses in San Marcos," lecture delivered at the San Marcos, Texas, Public Library, February 16, 2017.
10. This suggestion is based on an excellent review of the literature found in Rowan, "A New Pedagogy for Explanatory Public Speaking."
11. S. M. Kromka and A. K. Goodboy, "Classroom Storytelling: Using Instructor Narratives to Increase Student Recall, Affect, and Attention," *Communication Education* 68 (2019): 20–43; J. K. Kellas, "Communicated Narrative Sense-Making Theory: Linking Storytelling and Well-Being," in *Engaging Theories in Family Communication: Multiple Perspectives* 2e, edited by D. O. Braithwaite, E. A. Suter, and K. Floyd (New York: Routledge, 2018), 62–73.
12. R. Radice, "How to Put Together a Killer Social Media Presentation," *Sprout Social*, Nov. 2, 2016, https://medium.com/sprout-social (accessed June 1, 2020).
13. K. Morton, "A Howl for Help: The Case for Public and Private Funding of Service Animal Training in Shelters," *Winning Orations 2019* (Mankato, MN: Interstate Oratorical Association, 2019): 96.
14. See, for example, L. Rehling, "Teaching in a High-Tech Conference Room: Academic Adaptations and Workplace Simulations," *Journal of Business and Technical Communication* 19 (2005): 98–113; M. Patterson, D. Dansereau, and D. Newbern, "Effects of Communication Aids and Strategies on Cooperative Teaching," *Journal of Educational Psychology* 84 (1992): 453–461.
15. D. Davis, "Texas Turns to Notable Guest Speakers After the Cancellation of its 2020 Baseball Season," May 22, 2020, www.hookem.com (accessed June 1, 2020).
16. M. Klepper and R. Gunther, *I'd Rather Die Than Give a Speech* (New York: Carol Publishing Group, 1995).
17. Our discussion of using humor is adapted from Klepper and Gunther, *I'd Rather Die Than Give a Speech*.
18. J. Meyer, "Humor as a Double-Edged Sword: Four Functions of Humor in Communication," *Communication Theory* 10 (2000): 311.
19. Klepper and Gunther, *I'd Rather Die Than Give a Speech*.
20. J. Macks, *How to Be Funny* (New York: Simon & Schuster, 2003).
21. S. Beebe, T. Mottet, and K. D. Roach, *Training and Development: Communicating for Success* (Boston: Pearson, 2013); M. Knowles, *The Adult Learner: A Neglected Species* 3e (Houston: Gulf Publishing, 1990).
22. A. Armijo, "Elvis," Texas State University student speech, 2013.

Chapter 15

1. M. Silva, untitled speech, in *Winning Orations 2019* (Mankato, MN: Interstate Oratorical Association, 2019): 31–33.
2. A. Maslow, "A Theory of Human Motivation," in *Motivation and Personality* (New York: Harper & Row, 1954), Chapter 5.
3. See K. L. Higbee, "Fifteen Years of Fear Arousal: Research on Threat Appeals, 1953–1968," *Psychological Bulletin* 72 (1969): 426–444; I. L. Janis and S. Feshback, "Effects of Fear Arousing Communications," *Journal of Abnormal and Social Psychology* 48 (1953): 78–92; P. A. Mongeau, "Another Look at Fear-Arousing Persuasive Appeals," in *Persuasion: Advances through Meta-Analysis*, edited by M. Allen and R. W. Preiss (Cresskill, NJ: Hampton Press, 1998): 65; F. A. Powell and G. R. Miller, "Social Approval and Disapproval Cues in Anxiety Arousing Situations," *Speech Monographs* 34 (1967): 152–159.
4. R. Petty and D. Wegener, "The Elaboration Likelihood Model: Current Status and Controversies," in *Dual Process Theories in Social Psychology*, edited by S. Chaiken and Y. Trope (New York: Guilford, 1999): 41–72; see also R. Petty and J. T. Cacioppo, *Communication and Persuasion: Central and Peripheral Routes to Attitude Change* (New York: Springer-Verlag, 1986).
5. E. McQuarrie and B. Phillips, "Indirect Persuasion in Advertising: How Consumers Process Metaphors Presented in Pictures and Words," *Journal of Advertising* 34.2 (2005): 7–20.
6. T. Chmielewski, "Applying the Elaboration Likelihood Model to Voting," *International Journal of Interdisciplinary Social Sciences* 6.10 (2012): 33–47.
7. Aristotle, *Rhetoric*, translated by L. Cooper (New York: Appleton-Century-Crofts, 1960).
8. For a discussion of the effects of both verbal and nonverbal messages on the persuasiveness of a speech, see N. Jackob, T. Roessing, and T. Petersen, "The Effects of Verbal and Nonverbal Elements in Persuasive Communication: Findings from Two Multi-Method Experiments," *Communications: The European Journal of Communication Research* 36 (2011): 245–271.
9. "Humor Study Finds Britain's Funniest Joke," *RTÉ*, December 20, 2001, www.rte.ie/entertainment/2001 (accessed August 17, 2020).
10. N. Hill, "A Mind is a Terrible Thing to Wait," in *Winning Orations 2019* (Mankato, MN: Interstate Oratorical Association, 2019): 90–92.
11. N. Barton, "The Death of Reading," in *Winning Orations 2004* (Mankato, MN: Interstate Oratorical Association, 2004): 33–35.
12. S. Groom, "Hope for Foster Care," in *Winning Orations 2004*: 60–62.
13. Adapted from L. Ford and S. Smith, "Memorability and Persuasiveness of Organ Donation Message Strategies," *American Behavioral Scientist* 34 (1991): 695.
14. D. Ehninger, B. Gronbeck, R. McKerrow, and A. Monroe, *Principles and Types of Speech Communication* (Glenview, IL: Scott, Foresman, 1986), 15.

15. T. Lorenz, "TikTok Houses as Their Shelter," *New York Times*, May 24, 2020, A1.
16. The illustrations for the steps of the motivated sequence are adapted from S. Agha, "The International Landmine Crisis," prepared for the Interstate Oratorical Association competition, Texas State University, Spring 2011.
17. D. C. Bryant, "Rhetoric: Its Functions and Its Scope," *Quarterly Journal of Speech* 39 (1953): 26.
18. A. Tucker, "No Place to Call Home: Mortgage Discrimination in America," in *Winning Orations 2019* (Mankato, MN: Interstate Oratorical Association, 2019): 25–27.
19. F. Maricchiolo, A. Gnisci, M. Bonaiuto, and G. Ficca, "Effects of Different Types of Hand Gestures in Persuasive Speech on Receivers' Evaluations," *Language and Cognitive Processes* 24 (2009): 239–266.
20. B. Bergeron, "Private Ambulances," prepared for Individual Events/Persuasive Speaking competition, The University of Texas, Spring 2017.

Appendix A

1. R. Bian, F. Sun, Z. Lin, Q. Gao, X. Yuan, and A. Xie, "The Moderating Role of Interviewer's Regulator Focus in the Effectiveness of Impression Management Tactics: Regulatory Fit as a Source of Subjective Value," *The British Psychological Society* 111 (2020): 369–394.
2. J. Bartel, "Teaching Soft Skills for Employability," *TESL Canada Journal* 35 (2018): 78–92.
3. For a review of neuroscience evidence for the phases of an interview, see A. E. Ivey and T. Daniels, *International Journal of Listening* 30 (2016): 99–116.
4. Our discussion of interview questions is based on J. T. Masterson, S. A. Beebe, and N. Watson, *An Invitation to Effective Speech Communication* (Glenview, IL: Scott, Foresman, 1989). We especially acknowledge the contributions of Norm Watson to this discussion.
5. Marshall Brickman originally said this phrase during an interview attributing it to Woody Allen as published in *New York Times*, August, 1977. See: *Quote Investigator*, October 10, 2016, https://quoteinvestigator.com/2013/06/10/showing-up/.
6. *CareerBuilder*, accessed March 21, 2008, www.CareerBuilder.com.
7. N. St. Anthony, "For Job Seekers, In-Person Networking Tops Online Path," *Austin-American Statesman* (January 16, 2017): B5.
8. This resume and our suggestions for developing a resume are based on the 2017 *Texas State University Career Services Manual* (San Marcos, TX: Office of Career Services, 2017).
9. These tips and suggestions are adapted from K. Hansen, "Top 10 Things Job-Seekers Need to Know about Submitting and Posting Your Resume Online," *Quintessential Careers*, accessed September 10, 2014, www.quintcareers.com/e-resumes.html. Also see K. Hansen, "Your E-Resume's File Format Aligns with Its Delivery Method," *Quintessential Careers*, www.quintcareers.com/e-resume_format.html (accessed March 30, 2011).
10. V. Iva and K. Eliska, "Flexible Graduate is Successful Graduate: Key Factors of Successful Job Interview: Results of a Comparative Analysis," *Journal of Competitiveness* 8 (2016): 87–102.
11. V. Iva and K. Eliska, "Flexible Graduate is Successful Graduate."
12. J. L. Winsor, D. B. Curtis, and R. D. Stephens, "National Preferences in Business and Communication Education: A Survey Update," *Journal of the Association for Communication Administration* 3 (1997): 174.
13. D. Dean, "How to Get an On-Site Interview," *Black Collegian*, Second Semester Super Issue (2010): 54.
14. *CareerBuilder*, retrieved March 21, 2008, www.CareerBuilder.com. Suggestions for managing your online persona were taken from A. Simmons, "How to Click and Clean," *Reader's Digest* (April 2008): 154–159.
15. G. Yilmaz and J. M. Q. Johnson, "Tweeting Facts, Facebooking Lives: The Influence of Language Use and Modality on Online Source Credibility," *Communication Research Reports* 33.2 (2016): 137–144.
16. C. Purdy, "The Biggest Lies Job Seekers Tell on Their Resumes—and How They Get Caught," *Monster*. career-advice.monster.com/resumes-cover-letters/resume-writing-tips/the-truth-about-resume-lies-hot-jobs/article.aspx (accessed March 31, 2013).
17. Purdy, "The Biggest Lies Job Seekers Tell on Their Resumes."
18. L. Smith, "70% of Employers Are Snooping Candidates' Social Media Profiles," Careerbuilder (June 15, 2017), www.careerbuilder.com/advice/social-media-survey-2017 (accessed June 6, 2020); A. Klein, "How to Clean Up Your Facebook Before You Apply for a Job or Internship," *Job Advice @Hercampus*, www.hercampus.com/career/job-advice/how-clean-your-facebook-you-apply-job-or-internship (accessed February 17, 2017).
19. K. Kasper, "Jobvite Social Recruiting Survey Finds Over 90% of Employers Will Use Social Recruiting," *Jobvite*, www.jobvite.com/press-releases/2012/jobvite-social-recruiting-survey-finds-90-employers-will-use-social-recruiting-2012 (accessed February 17, 2017).
20. L. Herman, "How to Clean Up Your Social Media During the Job Search," *The Muse*, https://www.themuse.com/advice/how-to-clean-up-your-social-media-during-the-job-search (accessed February 17, 2017).
21. These tips were compiled from: L. Herman, "How to Clean Up Your Social Media During the Job Search," *The Muse*. www.themuse.com/advice/how-to-clean-up-your-social-media-during-the-job-search; The Glassdoor Team, "How to Clean Up Your Social Media Presence and Get a Job," *Glassdoor*, www.glassdoor.com/blog/clean-social-media-presence-job (accessed February 17, 2017); A. Klein, "How to Clean Up Your Facebook Before You Apply for a Job or Internship," *Job Advice @Hercampus*, www.hercampus.com/career/job-advice/how-clean-your-facebook-you-apply-job-or-internship (accessed February 17, 2017); K. Kasper, "Jobvite Social Recruiting Survey Finds Over 90% of Employers Will Use Social Recruiting," *Jobvite*, www.jobvite.com/press-releases/2012/jobvite-social-recruiting-survey-finds-90-employers-will-use-social-recruiting-2012 (accessed February 17, 2017).
22. M. Minto, "The Relative Effects of Content and Vocal Delivery during a Simulated Employment Interview," *Communication Research Reports* 13 (1996): 225–238.
23. R. H. Thompson and J. M. Hart, "Improving the Interviews of College Students Using Behavioral Skills Training," *Journal of Applied Behavior Analysis* 50 (2017): 495–510; R. M. Aysina, Z. A. Maksimenko, and M. V. Nikiforov, "Feasibility and Efficacy of Job Interview Simulation Training for Long-Term Unemployed Individuals," *PsychNology Journal* 14 (2016): 41–60; K. Brazeau, R. A. Rehfeldt, A. Mazo, S. Smalley, S. Krus, and L. Henson, "On the Efficacy of Mindfulness, Defusion, and Behavioral Skills Training on Job Interviewing Skills in Dually-Diagnosed Adults with Developmental Disorders," *Journal of Contextual Behavioral Science* 9 (2017): 145–151; L. K. Barker, J. W. Moore, D. J. Olmi, and K. Rowsey, "A Comparison of Immediate and Post-Session Feedback with Behavioral Skills Training to Improve Interview Skills in College Students," *Journal of Organizational Behavior Management* 39 (2019): 145–163.
24. Adapted from M. S. Hanna and G. Wilson, *Communicating in Business and Professional Settings* (New York: McGraw-Hill, 1991): 263–265.
25. E. Kroll and M. Ziegler, "Discrimination Due to Ethnicity and Gender: How Susceptible Are Video-Based Job Interviews?" *International Journal of Selection and Assessment* 24 (2016): 24–35; F. Dispenza, A. Kumar, J. Standish, S. Norris, and J. Procter, "Disability and Sexual Orientation Disclosure on Employment Interview Ratings: An Analogue Study," *Rehabilitation Counseling Bulletin* 62 (2018): 244–255; A. E. Hoover, T. Hack, A. L. Garcia, W. Goodfriend and M. M. Habashi, "Powerless Men and Agentic Women: Gender Bias in Hiring Decisions," *Sex Roles* 80 (2019): 667–680; D. Grewal, M. C. Ku, S. C. Girod, H. Valantine, "How to

Recognize and Address Unconscious Bias," *The Academic Medicine: A Guide to Achievement and Fulfillment for Academic Faculty* edited by L. W. Roberts (New York: Springer, 2013): 405–412; F. E. Aboud, "The Development of Prejudice in Childhood and Adolescence," *On the Nature of Prejudice* edited by J. F. Dovidio, P. Glick, L. A. Rudman (Malden, MA: Blackwell, 2005): 310–326; A. S. Prestia, "Sabotaging Success: The Role of Unconscious Bias," *Nurse Leader* 17 (2019): 561–564

26. *Texas State University Career Services Manual.*

Appendix B

1. M. Reyes, "Recuperandos," prepared for Individual Events/Informative Speaking competition, University of Central Missouri, Spring 2020.
2. C. Newton, "Queers of the Court," prepared for Individual Events/Persuasive Speaking competition, The University of Texas, Spring 2020.

Credits

Chapter 1   Page 31: Michel de Montaigne, "Of Vanity," in *The Essays of Michel de Montaigne*, translated by Charles Cotton, edited by William Carew Hazlitt, 1877.; **p. 33:** J. C. Humes, *The Sir Winston Method: The Five Secrets of Speaking the Language of Leadership* (New York: William Morrow, 1991).; **p. 33:** J. H. McConnell, *Are You Communicating? You Can't Manage without It* (New York: McGraw-Hill, 1995).; **p. 33:** Schwantes, "Warren Buffett Says"; **p. 33:** Value Investors Portal, "Warren Buffet on Communication Skills," YouTube, December 6, 2010, accessed May 14, 2013, www.youtube.com/watch?v=tpgcEYpLzP0.; **p. 34:** Virginia Satir, *Peoplemaking*, Science and Behavior Books, 1972: 30/304.; **p. 39:** S. B. Shimanoff, *Communication Rules: Theory and Research* (Beverly Hills, CA: Sage, 1980).; **p. 40:** H. Lasswell, "The Structure and Function of Communication in Society," in *The Communication of Ideas*, edited by L. Bryson (New York: Institute for Religious and Social Studies, 1948): 37.; **p. 43:** C. S. Lewis, *The Magician's Nephew* (London: The Bodley Head, 1955): 123.; **p. 45:** Clifford G. Christians, Michael Traber, *Communication Ethics and Universal Values*, Sage Publications, 1997.; **p. 46:** "NCA Credo for Ethical Communication," approved by the NCA Legislative Council, November 1999.; **p. 48:** Sherry Turkle, *Alone Together: Why We Expect More from Technology and Less from Each Other*, Readhowyouwant.com, 2011.; **p. 48:** Broadband Search, *50 Surprising Social Media Statistics in 2020.*; **p. 48:** Broadband Search, *Average Time Spent Daily on Social Media (Latest 2020 Data).*; **p. 48:** M. Osman, *Wild and Interesting Facebook Statistics and Facts (2020)*, accessed May 27, 2020, https://kinsta.com/blog/facebook-statistics/; **pp. 52–53:** Daniel Quinn, *My Ishmael*, (New York: Bantam Books, 1996).; **p. 53:** Robert Fulghum, *All I Really Need to Know I Learned in Kindergarten*, (New York: Ballantine Books, 1988).

Chapter 2   Page 57: Quote by Janis Joplin.; **p. 57:** S. R. Covey, *The Seven Habits of Highly Effective People*, Anniversary Edition (New York: Simon & Schuster, 2013): 74.; **p. 58:** Benjamin Franklin, *Poor Richard's Almanac 1850–52*, J. Doggett Jr., 1849.; **p. 59:** S. E. Wood, E. Green Wood, and D. Boyd, *Mastering the World of Psychology* 6e (Boston: Pearson, 2017): 115.; **p. 59:** P. C. McGraw, *Life Strategies Self-Discovery Journal: Finding What Matters Most for You*, Hyperion Books, 2001.; **p. 60:** Karen Horney, *Neurosis and Human Growth: The Struggle Toward Self-Realization*, Norton, 1991: 17/391.; **p. 64:** G. Steinem, *Revolution from Within: A Book of Self-Esteem* (Boston: Little, Brown, 1993): 26.; **p. 72:** D. T. Kenrick, S. L. Neuberg, and R. B. Cialdini, *Social Psychology: Goals in Interaction* 6e (Boston: Pearson, 2014): 360.; **p. 75:** M. Rosenberg, *Society and the Adolescent Self-Image* rev. ed. (Middletown, CT: Wesleyan University Press, 1989), reprinted with permission, retrieved from www.bsos.umd.edu.

Chapter 3   Page 77: Aldous Huxley.; **p. 81:** *Oxford Desk Dictionary and Thesaurus, American Edition* (New York: Oxford University Press, 2007).; **p. 81:** Quote by Sheila Michaels.; **p. 82:** "A Gender-Neutral Honorific, Mx: Words We're Watching," https://www.merriam-webster.com, accessed June 9, 2020.; **p. 82:** D. K. Ivy, *GenderSpeak: Communicating in a Gendered World* 6e (Dubuque, IA: Kendall Hunt, 2017).; **p. 83:** "Mansplaining," *Merriam-Webster Dictionary*, accessed June 10, 2020, https://www.merriam-webster.com.; **p. 83:** "Introducing 78 More Feelings: Some Scientists Believe We Have Infinite Emotions, So Long as We Can Name Them—and So We Did," *New York* (February 3-16, 2020): 28–39.; **p. 85:** Table based on information from M. Anderson and S. Feinberg, 2000, "Race and Ethnicity and the Controversy over the U.S. Census," *Current Sociology* 48.3: 87–110.; **p. 85:** National Research Council, *Measuring Racial Discrimination* (Washington, DC: National Academies Press, 2004).; **p. 85:** U.S. Census Bureau, 2001, "Population by Race and Hispanic or Latino Origin for All Ages and for 18 Years and Over for the United States: 2000," www.census.gov/PressRelease/www/2001/tables/st00_1.pdf.; **p. 85:** U.S. Census Bureau, 2010, *Questionnaire Reference Book* (Washington, DC: U.S. Department of Commerce, Bureau of the Census, Washington DC), retrieved from 2010census.gov.; **p. 85:** American Community Survey 2020, accessed June 6, 2020, www.census/gov/.; **p. 85:** About #BlackLivesMatter, accessed June 10, 2020, https://blacklivesmatter.com.; **pp. 87–88:** D. K. Ivy, *GenderSpeak: Communicating in a Gendered World* 6e (Dubuque, IA: Kendall Hunt, 2017).; **pp. 90–91:** L. H. Turner, "Message from the President," *Spectra* (November, 2011), accessed February 25, 2017, www.natcom.org.

Chapter 4   Page 96: Marilyn Ferguson.; **p. 109:** Franklin D. Roosevelt, Inaugural Address, March 4, 1933, as published in Samuel Rosenman, ed., *The Public Papers of Franklin D. Roosevelt, Volume Two: The Year of Crisis*, 1933 (New York: Random House, 1938): 11–16.; **p. 112:** P. A. Andersen, *Nonverbal Communication: Forms and Functions* 2e (Long Grove, IL: Waveland, 2008): 168.

Chapter 5   Page 117: Stephen R. Covey, *The Seven Habits of Highly Effective People* (New York: Simon & Schuster, 2013).; **p. 119:** Andre Maurois, *Memoirs 1885–1967* (London: Bodley Head, 1970): 218.; **pp. 119–120:** "Robert Caro on the Fall of New York and Glenn Close on Complicated Characters," New Yorker Radio Hour, WNYC (May 4, 2018), as reported by K. Murphy, *You're Not Listening: What You're Missing and Why It Matters* (New York: Celadon, 2019): 124.; **p. 126:** J. L. Gonzalez-Balado, ed., *Mother Teresa: In My Own Words* (New York: Gramercy Books, 1997).; **p. 138:** H. J. M. Nouwen, "Listening as Spiritual Hospitality," in *Bread for the Journey* (New York: HarperCollins, 1997).

Chapter 6   Page 143: C. S. Lewis.; **p. 151:** B. Allen, *Differences Matter*: 113.; **p. 151:** G. A. Yep, "Toward Thick(er) Intersectionalities: Theorizing, Researching, and Activating the Complexities of Communication and Identities," *Globalizing Intercultural Communication: A Reader* edited by K. Sorrells and S. Sekimoto (Los Angeles, CA: Sage, 2015): 86.; **p. 153:** "One in Three US Residents Member of a Minority Group," *Marketing Charts*, May 21, 2007, accessed September 25, 2014, www.marketingcharts.com/traditional/one-in-three-us-residents-a-member-of-a-minority-group-418.; **p. 154:** C. H. Dodd, *Dynamics of Intercultural Communication* (New York: McGraw-Hill, 1998).;

p. 156: A. S. Waterman, *The Psychology of Individualism* (Santa Barbara, CA: Praeger, 1984): 4–5.; **pp. 156–157:** W. B. Gudykunst, *Bridging Differences: Effective Intergroup Communication* (Newbury Park, CA: Sage, 1998).; **p. 159:** Table adapted with permission from Geert Hofstede, Gert Jan Hofstede, and Michael Minkov, *Cultures and Organizations, Software of the Mind*, Third Revised Edition (New York: McGraw Hill, 2010). ISBN 0-07-166418-1 © Geert Hofstede BV.; **pp. 164:** E. Roosevelt, as cited by Lustig and Koester, *Intercultural Competence*.; **pp. 168–169:** H. J. M. Nouwen, *Bread for the Journey* (New York: HarperCollins, 1997).; **p. 169:** R. H. Farrell, ed., *Off the Record: The Private Papers of Harry S. Truman* (New York: Harper & Row, 1980): **p. 61**.

Chapter 7   Page 174: Quote by Ralph Waldo Emerson.; **p. 177:** A. Cooper, I. P. McLoughlin, and K. M. Campbell, "Sexuality in Cyberspace: Update for the 21st Century," *Cyberpsychology & Behavior* 32 (2000): 521–536.; **p. 177:** L. K. Guerrero, P. A. Andersen, and W. A. Afifi, *Close Encounters: Communicating in Relationships* 5e (Los Angeles: Sage, 2017), 54: 147.; **p. 181:** "Netflix and chill," Wikipedia, accessed March 11, 2017, from https://en.wikipedia.org.; **p. 185:** Harvey and Weber, *Odyssey of the Heart*: 105–106.; **p. 186:** D. Hample, A. S. Richards, and C. Skubisz, "Blurting," *Communication Monographs* 80 (2013): 503–532.

Chapter 8   Page 193: Franklin D. Roosevelt, undelivered address prepared for Jefferson Day, April 13, 1945.; **p. 195:** Miami Herald (July 9, 1982): 12A.; **p. 197:** V. Satir, *The New Peoplemaking* (Mountain View, CA: Science & Behavior Books, 1988), 4.; **p. 198:** M. E. King and A. G. La Valley, "Partner Influence, Emotion, and Relational Outcomes: A Test of Relational Turbulence Theory in Early Dating Relationships," *Southern Communication Journal* 84.5 (2019): 287–300.; **p. 198:** L. K. Knobloch, "The Relational Turbulence Model: Communicating during Times of Transition," in *Engaging Theories in Interpersonal Communication*: 377–385.; **p. 198:** D. Hauani Solomon, K. M. Weber, and K. R. Steuber, "Turbulence in Relational Transitions," in New Directions in Interpersonal Communication Research, edited by S. W. Smith and S. R. Wilson (Los Angeles: Sage, 2010): 115–134.; **p. 198:** R. M. Dailey, R. A. Pfiester, B. Jin, G. Beck, and G. Clark, "On-Again/Off-Again Dating Relationships: How Are They Different from Other Dating Relationships?" *Personal Relationships* 16 (2009): 23–47.; **p. 198:** Adapted from Steven A. Beebe, Susan J. Beebe, and Mark V. Redmond, *Interpersonal Communication: Relating to Others*, 9e. Reprinted and electronically reproduced by permission of Pearson Education, Inc., Hoboken, NJ. Copyright © 2020.Photograph: BJI/Blue Jean Images/Getty Images (top); MIXA/Getty Images (bottom).; **p. 199:** B. L. Lane and C. W. Piercy, "Making Sense of Becoming Facebook Official: Implications for Identity and Time," in *The Impact of Social Media in Modern Romantic Relationships*: 31–45.; **p. 202:** L. Locker Jr., W. D. McIntosh, A. A. Hackney, J. H. Wilson, and K. E. Wiegand, "The Breakup of Romantic Relationships: Situational Predictors of Perception of Recovery," *North American Journal of Psychology* 12 (2010): 565–578.; **p. 202:** D. Cullingston, *Breaking Up Blues: A Guide to Survival* (New York: Routledge, 2008).; **p. 202:** S. P. Banks, D. M. Altendorf, J. O. Greene, and M. Cody, "An Examination of Relationship Disengagement: Perceptions, Breakup Strategies, and Outcomes," *Western Journal of Speech Communication* 51 (1987): 19–41.; **p. 203:** M. Rabbitt, "Is Infidelity Obsolete?" *Women's Health* (July/August 2010): 144.; **p. 203:** P. J. Lannutti and K. A. Cameron, "Beyond the Breakup: Heterosexual and Homosexual Post-Dissolutional Relationships," *Communication Quarterly* 50 (2002): 153–170.; **p. 207:** W. W. Wilmot and J. L. Hocker, *Interpersonal Conflict* 10e (New York: McGraw-Hill, 2017).; **p. 207:** G. R. Miller and M. Steinberg, *Between People: A New Analysis of Interpersonal Communication* (Chicago: Science Research Associates, 1975.; **p. 208:** I. A. Cionea, S. V. Wilson Mumpower, M. A. Bassick, "Serial Argument Goals, Tactics, and Outcomes in Long-Distance and Geographically Close Romantic Relationships," *Southern Communication Journal* 84.1 (2019): 1–16.; **p. 208:** I. A. Cionea, A. J. Johnson, and E. N. Bostwick, "Argument Interdependence: Connections to Serial Argument Goals and Tactics in Romantic Relationships," *Journal of Social and Personal Relationships* 36.7 (2019): 1975–1995.; **p. 208:** T. R. Worley and J. Samp, "Goal Variability and Perceived Resolvability in Serial Argumentation," *Communication Research* 45.3 (2018): 422–442.; **p. 208:** S. Morrison and P. Schrodt, "The Perceived Threat and Resolvability of Serial Arguments as Correlates of Relational Uncertainty in Romantic Relationships," *Communication Studies* 68.1 (2017): 56–71.; **p. 209:** R. Fisher, W. Ury, and B. Patton, *Getting to Yes: Negotiating Agreement without Giving In Revised Edition* (New York: Penguin Books, 2011).; **p. 210:** A. Ellis, A New Guide to Rational Living (North Hollywood, CA: Wilshire Books, 1977).; **p. 211:** J. Roessler, "Thinking, Inner Speech, and Self-Awareness," *Review of Philosophy and Psychology* 7 (2016): 541–557.

Chapter 9   Page 216: M. L. King, Jr. "A Christmas Sermon on Peace, (1967)," *A Testament of Hope: The Essential Writings and Speeches of Martin Luther King*, (Ed.) J. M. Washington (New York: HarperCollins, 1991): 253.; **p. 230:** Adapted from E. G. Bormann and N. C. Bormann, *Effective Small Group Communication* (Minneapolis: Burgess, 1980): 70–72.

Chapter 10   Page 237: Quote by Margaret Mead.; **p. 246:** Adapted from Julius E. Etington, *The Winning Trainer* (Houston: Gulf Publishing, 1989).; **p. 256:** P. M. Senge, "The Leader's New Role: Building Learning Organizations," *Sloan Management Review* 32 (1990).; **p. 257:** Lao Tsu, from the *Tao Te Ching*, 1963: 77.; **p. 257:** D. Barry, *Dave Barry Turns 50* (New York: Ballantine, 1998), 182.

Chapter 11   Page 268: Quote by Franklin D. Roosevelt.; **p. 276:** L. Zanteson, "Building a Career Through Public Speaking," *Today's Dietician* (August 2014), 39.; **p. 278:** Adapted from J. Boyle, "Spyware Stalking: Time to Take Back the Technology," *Winning Orations* 2015 (Manka-to, MN: Interstate Oratorical Association, 2015): 32–34.; **p. 279:** J. Humphrey, "Taking the Stage: How Women Can Achieve a Leadership Presence," *Vital Speeches of the Day* 67.14 (2001).; **p. 281:** "African 'Fairy Circles' May Be by Termites," *Austin American-Statesman*, January 19, 2017, A2.; **p. 282:** A. Rojas, "Deconstructing the Invisible Prison: Providing an Equitable Educational Experience for Undocumented Students Through the UndocuAlly Program, " *Winning Orations 2019* (Mankato, MN: Interstate Oratorical Association, 2019): 10–12.; **p. 282:** Adapted from Samantha Begley, "Libraries Without Borders," *Winning Orations 2015* (Mankato, MN: Interstate Oratorical Association, 2015): 67–69.; **p. 286:** N. Martin, "How Social Media Has Changed How We Consume News," November 30, 2018, accessed June 1, 2020, www.forbes.com.; **p. 287:** J. Rogalo, "Home Safe Home," *Winning Orations 2019* (Mankato, MN: Interstate Oratorical Association, 2019): 79.;

p. 288: D. Lessing, "On Not Winning the Nobel Prize," *Vital Speeches of the Day* 74.2 (2008).; **p. 288:** M. Daly, "Beyond Fairness: The Value of an Exclusive Economy," *Vital Speeches of the Day* 85.12 (2019).; **p. 288:** O. Winfrey, 2020 commencement speech, in N. Bogel-Burroughs, "No Pomp Because of the Circumstances, So Oprah Does Her Thing," *New York Times*, May 16, 2020, A17.; **p. 289:** G. Whitmer, quoted in A. Sherman, "1918 Pandemic Shows Dangers of Early Letup," April 17, 2020, accessed June 1, 2020, www.politifact.com.; **p. 289:** R. Duffield, "Sometimes There Are No Bruises," *Vital Speeches of the Day* 85.2 (2019).; **p. 289:** K. Winslow, "The Epidemic That Is 3D Printed Guns," *Winning Orations* 2019 (Mankato, MN: Interstate Oratorical Association, 2019): 9.; **p. 290:** E. Trader, "Giving a Voice to Those Not Heard," *Winning Orations* 2019 (Mankato, MN: Interstate Oratorical Association, 2019): 35.; **p. 290:** R. Brown, "Seven Ways of Looking at a Crisis," *Vital Speeches of the Day* 76.6 (2010).; **p. 290:** Florynce Kennedy.

Chapter 12   Page 296: A. Rynne, "How to Build a Perfectly Published Content Sandwich [Infographic]," LinkedIn Marketing Solutions Blog, February 7, 2017, accessed June 1, 2020, https://business.linkedin.com/marketing-solutions/blog/publishing-on-linkedin/2017/how-to-build-a-perfectly-published-content-sandwich--infographic.; **p. 297:** S. Njapa, "Changing the African Perception," *Winning Orations* 2019 (Mankato, MN: Interstate Oratorical Association, 2019): 72–74.; **p. 297:** Adapted from P. Steiger, "A Closer Look: Three Golden Ages of Journalism?" *Vital Speeches of the Day* 80.8 (2014): 111–114.; **p. 298:** Adapted from A. Zerull, "Resident Evil: How America's Teaching Hospitals Neglect the Care of Our Caregivers," *Winning Orations* 2016 (Mankato, MN: Interstate Oratorical Association, 2016): 161–166.; **p. 298:** Adapted from R. Walcott, "Dying from Withdrawal: Opioid-Related Deaths in U.S. Jails and Prisons," *Winning Orations* 2019 (Mankato, MN: Interstate Oratorical Association, 2019): 84–86.; **p. 298:** F. Pham, "The U.S. Military's Invisible War," prepared for Individual Events/Persuasive Speaking competition, The University of Texas, Spring 2020.; **p. 300:** K. Morton, "A Howl for Help: The Case for Public and Private Funding of Service Animal Training in Shelters," *Winning Orations* 2019 (Mankato, MN: Interstate Oratorical Association, 2019): 96–97.; **p. 300:** K. Huber, "Things Don't Happen For a Reason. But They Do Often Happen Because Nobody Has Yet Found a Better Way," *Vital Speeches of the Day* 82.8 (2016).; **p. 302:** R. Shah, "Extend the Reach of Human Dignity to Every Single Person on This Planet," *Vital Speeches of the Day* 85.12 (2019): 331.; **p. 303:** P. Manning, "You Don't Have to Wonder if I'll Miss It," *Vital Speeches of the Day* 82.5 (2016).; **p. 303:** R. Reece, "Bees: Buzzing about the Future," prepared for Individual Events/Communication Analysis competition, University of Central Missouri, Spring 2020.; **p. 303:** N. Modi, "All Our Endeavors Are Centered on 1.3 Billion Indians; But Their Fruits Are for All," *Vital Speeches of the Day*, 85.11 (2019): 299.; **p. 304:** R. Brown, "Mental Illness Is Not a Learning Disability," *Winning Orations* 2015 (Mankato, MN: Interstate Oratorical Association, 2015): 41.; **p. 304:** S. Cohen, "The Kind of World We All Want," *Vital Speeches of the Day*, 86.1 (2020): 2.; **p. 304:** E. McDonnell, untitled speech, *Winning Orations* 2019 (Mankato, MN: Interstate Oratorical Association, 2019): 37.; **p. 305:** K. Winslow, "The Epidemic That Is 3D Printed Guns," *Winning Orations* 2019 (Mankato, MN: Interstate Oratorical Association, 2019): 7.; **p. 305:** A. Lincoln, "Gettysburg Address," delivered at Gettysburg, PA, November 19, 1863, Douglass Archives of American Public Address, August 19, 1998, douglass.speech.nwu.edu/linc_b33.htm, pg.; **p. 305:** D. MacArthur, "Farewell to the Cadets," address delivered at West Point, May 12, 1962, in *Contemporary American Speeches* 7e, edited by R. L. Johannesen, R. R. Allen, and W. A. Linkugel (Dubuque, IA: Kendall/Hunt, 1992): 393.; **p. 305:** "The Queen's Coronavirus Speech Transcript: 'We Will Succeed and Better Days Will Come,'" April 5, 2020, accessed June 1, 2020, www.telegraph.co.uk.; **p. 305:** P. Sterman, "The New World Champion of Public Speaking," *Toastmasters November 2016*.

Chapter 13   Page 313: Walt Whitman (1819–1892), U.S. poet. "Calamus: A Song of Joys," *Leaves of Grass* (1855).; **p. 315:** L. Browne, quoted in B. Matthews, "The Script as Friend and Foe," *Toastmaster* 75.8 (2009): 26.; **p. 317:** L. White and L. Messer, "An Analysis of Interstate Speeches: Are They Structurally Different?" *National Forensic Journal* 21.2 (2003): 15.; **p. 317:** G. Orwell, "Politics and the English Language," in *About Language*, edited by W. H. Roberts and G. Turgeson (Boston: Houghton Mifflin, 1986): 282.; **p. 319:** D. Hersman, "I Saw a Woman Today," *Vital Speeches of the Day* 80.5 (2014): 151.; **p. 319:** M. McConaughey, in S. O'Neal, "Hollywood, Texas: Matthew McConaughey Has Your Coronavirus Pep Talk." March 20, 2020, accessed June 1, 2020, www.texasmonthly.com.; **p. 319:** S. Acevedo, "The Future for Girl Scouts in America and Abroad," *Vital Speeches of the Day* 82.10 (2016): 312.; **p. 319:** K. Burns, "You Are, Whether You Are Yet Aware of It or Not, Charged with Saving Our Union," *Vital Speeches of the Day* 82.8 (2016): 223.; **p. 320:** M. Jordan, "Rest in Peace, Little Brother," *Vital Speeches of the Day* 86.4 (2020): 106–107.; **p. 320:** A. Cuomo, in E. Shapiro, "New York Has Become the Epicenter of the Pandemic." March 27, 2020, accessed June 1, 2020, abcnews.go.com.; **p. 320:** J. Biden, remarks commemorating the fiftieth anniversary of Kennedy's "Moon Shot" Speech, delivered at the John F. Kennedy Library and Museum, Boston, MA, White House, May 25, 2011, accessed June 1, 2020, www.whitehouse.gov.; **p. 320:** J. Huber, "Things Don't Happen for a Reason. But They Do Often Happen Because Nobody Has Yet Found a Better Way," *Vital Speeches of the Day* 82.8 (2016): 227.; **p. 323:** J. C. McCroskey, V. P. Richmond, A. Sallinen, J. M. Fayer, and R. A. Barraclough, "A Cross-Cultural and Multi-Behavioral Analysis of the Relationship between Nonverbal Immediacy and Teacher Evaluation," *Communication Education* 44 (1995): 281–290.; **p. 330:** N. Norton, "Beyond Flint: The Poison in Our Pipes," *Winning Orations* 2016 (Mankato, MN: Interstate Oratorical Association, 2016): 79.; **p. 330:** A. Wilson, "In Defense of Rhetoric," *The Toastmaster* 70.2 (2004): 11.; **p. 331:** J. Detz, "Delivery plus Content Equals Successful Presentation,"; **p. 332:** S. Cain, "10 Public Speaking Tips for Introverts: Introverts Can Seize the Microphone—and Bring the House Down," July 25, 2011, accessed June 1, 2020, psychologytoday.com.; **p. 332:** T. Smith and A. B. Frymier, "Get 'Real': Does Practicing Speeches before an Audience Improve Performance?" *Communication Quarterly* 54 (2006): 111–125.; **p. 334:** "Presidential Seal Falls Off Podium as Obama Speaks," Washington Times, October 6, 2010, accessed June 1, 2020, www.washingtontimes.com.; **p. 334:** J. Masterson,

S. Beebe, and N. Watson, *Invitation to Effective Speech Communication* (Glenview, IL: Scott, Foresman, 1989): 4.

Chapter 14   Page 336: Common, 87th Academy Award speech, 2015, quoted in "Common: Grammy, Emmy and Oscar-winning Artist, Actor, Author and Activist," accessed May 27, 2020, www.txstate.edu.; **p. 337:** L. Lefever, *The Art of Explanation* (New Jersey: John Wiley & Sons, 2013): 10.; **p. 340:** G. K. Chesterton, "On Mr. Rudyard Kipling and Making the World Small," *Heretics*, 1905, Project Gutenberg, accessed June 1, 2020, http://www.gutenberg.org/files/470/470-h/470-h.htm#chap03.; **p. 344:** J. Zimmer, "Phrases to Avoid on Stage," *Toastmaster* 82.5 (2016): 9.; **p. 345:** This suggestion is based on an excellent review of the literature found in K. Rowan, "A New Pedagogy for Explanatory Public Speaking: Why Arrangement Should Not Substitute for Invention," *Communication Education* 44 (1995): 236–250.; **p. 347:** M. Klepper and R. Gunther, *I'd Rather Die Than Give a Speech* (New York: Carol Publishing Group, 1995).; **p. 347:** J. Meyer, "Humor as a Double-Edged Sword: Four Functions of Humor in Communication," *Communication Theory* 10 (2000): 311.; **pp. 347–348:** Klepper and Gunther, *I'd Rather Die Than Give a Speech*.; **p. 348:** J. Macks, *How to Be Funny* (New York: Simon & Schuster, 2003).; **p. 348:** S. Beebe, T. Mottet, and K. D. Roach, *Training and Development: Communicating for Success* (Boston: Pearson, 2013).; **p. 348:** M. Knowles, *The Adult Learner: A Neglected Species* 3e (Houston: Gulf Publishing, 1990).; **pp. 350–351:** A. Armijo, "Elvis," Texas State University student speech, 2013.

Chapter 15   Page 354: Joseph Conrad, A personal record, 1912.; **p. 357:** Maslow, Abraham, *Motivation and Personality* (New York: HarperCollins, 1954).; **p. 358:** E. McQuarrie and B. Phillips, "Indirect Persuasion in Advertising: How Consumers Process Metaphors Presented in Pictures and Words," *Journal of Advertising* 34.2 (2005): 7–20.; **p. 361:** Aristotle, Rhetoric, translated by L. Cooper (New York: Appleton-Century-Crofts, 1960).; **p. 364:** "Humor Study Finds Britain's Funniest Joke," RTÉ, Dec. 20, 2001, accessed August 17, 2020, www.rte.ie/entertainment/2001.; **p. 366:** N. Hill, "A Mind is a Terrible Thing to Wait," in *Winning Orations* 2019 (Mankato, MN: Interstate Oratorical Association, 2019): 90–92.; **p. 367:** N. Barton, "The Death of Reading," in *Winning Orations* 2004 (Mankato, MN: Interstate Oratorical Association, 2004): 33–35.; **p. 367:** S. Groom, "Hope for Foster Care," in *Winning Orations* 2004: 60–62.; **p. 368:** Adapted from L. Ford and S. Smith, "Memorability and Persuasiveness of Organ Donation Message Strategies," *American Behavioral Scientist* 34 (1991): 695.; **p. 368:** T. Lorenz, "TikTok Houses as Their Shelter," *New York Times*, May 24, 2020, A1.; **p. 369:** The illustrations for the steps of the motivated sequence are adapted from S. Agha, "The International Landmine Crisis," prepared for the Interstate Oratorical Association competition, Texas State University, Spring 2011.; **p. 372:** A. Tucker, "No Place to Call Home: Mortgage Discrimination in America," in *Winning Orations* 2019 (Mankato, MN: Interstate Oratorical Association, 2019): 25–27.; **p. 373:** G. Ficca, et al., "Effects of Different Types of Hand Gestures in Persuasive Speech on Receivers' Evaluations," *Language and Cognitive Processes* 24 (2009): 239–266.; **pp. 373–376:** B. Bergeron, "Private Ambulances," prepared for Individual Events/Persuasive Speaking competition, The University of Texas, Spring 2017.

Appendix B   Pages 401–402: M. Reyes, "Recuperandos," prepared for Individual Events/Informative Speaking competition, University of Central Missouri, Spring 2020.; **pp. 403–405:** C. Newton, "Queers of the Court," prepared for Individual Events/Persuasive Speaking competition, The University of Texas, Spring 2020.

Index

A

Ability bias, 90
The Abolition of Man (Lewis), 163
Abstract meaning, 81
Academic Search Ultimate, 286
Accountability, of Internet resources, 285
Accuracy, of Internet resources, 285
Acknowledgments, for source material, 291
Actionable intelligence, 274
Action model of communication, 39, 40, 44
Action plans, of groups, 250, 251
Actions
    motivated sequence stage, 369
    words effect on, 83
Active listening, 135
Active strategy, 182
Acton (Lord), 161
Adaptation
    age differences and, 149
    barriers to, 164
    communication principles in, 32, 54, 144, 170
    cultural differences and, 152
    defined, 54, 169
    effective meetings and, 257, 262
    ethical, 169
    in family relations, 197
    in first conversations, 183
    gender and sexual orientation issues in, 147
    goals and strategy choice, 170
    in group communication, 218
    to listening situation, 123
    in nonverbal messages, 100
    principle overview, 54
    in public speaking, 269, 270, 274, 291, 314, 348, 366
    race and ethnicity issues in, 151
    in situational leadership, 254
    strategies for, 170
Adult learning principles, 348
African cultures, 155
Age differences, 149
Age discrimination, 89, 90
Agendas, 258–259, 262
Aggressive communication, 205
AIDS, 84
All-channel network pattern, 230
Allen, Brenda, 151
Alliteration, 320
Allness, 85
Ally training, 147
"Alpha face" expression, 107, 108
Altman, Irwin, 188
Ambiguous communication, 101
Analogies, 288, 290, 363

Analytical listeners, 122
Andersen, Peter, 112
Androgynous, 145
Animals, as presentation aids, 332
Anticipatory communication, 128
Antithesis, 320
Appeal to misplaced authority, 365
Appearance
    in job interviews, 391
    in material self, 60
    as nonverbal code, 104, 105
    of speakers, 326
Appraisal interviews, 381
Appropriateness, in self-disclosure, 187
Arab nations, 154, 155
Aristotle, 50, 194, 355, 361
Arousal, 112
Arroyo, Analisa, 106
Articulation, 326
Artifact, 105
Ascribed identity, 63
Asian cultures
    collectivist, 156
    eye contact preferences in, 321
    high-context, 154, 155
    long-term oriented, 159
Assertive communication, 205
Association for the Protection and Assistance of the Convicted (APAC), 401–403
Attend, in listening process, 120
Attention
    motivated sequence stage, 368, 372
    perception stage, 69
Attention shifts, 127
Attitudes
    defined, 60
    of effective group members, 242
    in job interviews, 395
    in nonverbal messages, 98
    as target of persuasive speech, 360
Attraction, defined, 176. *See also* interpersonal attraction
Attribution, for source material, 291, 292
Audience
    adapting speeches to, 269, 270, 273, 274, 279, 291, 303, 314, 348, 366
    getting attention of, 303, 344–348
    listening skills and, 120
    motivating, 305
    neutral, 371, 372
    public speaking anxiety and, 272, 273
    receptive, 371, 373
    unreceptive, 372
Audience-centered idea, 280
Audience-centered public speaker, 269, 270

Audio presentation aids, 329, 330
Australian culture, 155, 157, 159
Authoritarian leaders, 253, 254
Autonomy versus connection, 204
Avowed identity, 63
Awareness. *See also* self-awareness
    adaptation and, 170
    communication principles in, 32, 51, 58
    in coworker relations, 197
    in developing sensitivity, 241
    effective meetings and, 257, 262
    in emotion management, 126
    in family relations, 195
    in friendships, 194
    in group communication, 218
    in group dynamics, 225
    increasing, 72
    perception as, 69–73
    principle overview, 51
    self-concept as, 59–63
    self-esteem as, 64–69
Ayds, 83

B

Baby boomers, 148, 149
Bafflegab, 92
Baggage (psychological), 69
Bandwagon fallacy, 365
Barbie doll, 65
Bar graphs, 328
Barker, Larry, 123
Barnlund, Dean, 38
Barry, Dave, 257
Baxter, Leslie, 204
Begala, Paul, 316
Behavior as communication, 37
Beliefs
    as self-concept component, 60
    as target of persuasive speech, 360
Benne, Kenneth, 223–225
Berger, Charles, 181
Beverly, Aaron, 305
Bias, in language, 84–90
Biden, Joe, 320
Biographical speeches, 338, 339, 341, 342
Blanchard, Ken, 255
Blockers, in groups, 243
Body (interview phase), 383–386
Body Language (Fast), 103
Body movement, 105, 106, 114
Bolls, Paul, 189
Bonfire disaster (Texas A&M University), 250
Books, as supporting material source, 286
Boolean search, 284
Bradac, James, 182

455

Brainstorming
    in small groups, 248
    for speech topics, 275
Brazil, 159
Breakups (relationship dissolution), 201
Breathing
    for anxiety, 273
    for emotional control, 138
Brewer, Jamie, 89
British culture, 314, 323
Brown, Donald, 162
Brown, Robert, 290
Brunner, Steven, 106
Bryant, Donald C., 371
Brzezinski, Mika, 64
Buffett, Warren, 33
Bullies, in groups, 243
Burgoon, Judee, 101
Bush, George W., 330
Bypassing, 80

C

Cadence, of language, 320
Cain, Susan, 332
Calabrese, Richard, 181
Canadian culture, 159
CareerBuilder, 386, 392
Carell, Steve, 107
Carrell, Lori, 171
Cartoons, using, 347
Causal fallacy, 364
Causal reasoning, 363, 364
Cause and effect organization, 298, 299, 367, 370
Central idea, 280, 304, 305, 360, 361
Centralized power, 157
Certainty (value), 160
Chain interaction pattern, 230
Challenger space shuttle, 249
Chameleon effect, 100
Channels
    defined, 40
    in nonverbal communication, 104
Chaplin, William, 99
Charisma, 362
Charts, as presentation aids, 327, 331
Chesterton, G. K., 340
Children, as presentation aids, 332
Chinese culture, 128, 159, 160, 314
Christians, Clifford, 45
Chronological organization
    informative speeches, 341, 342
    main ideas, 296, 299
    supporting material, 299
Chronological sequence, 283
Clarity
    in informative speeches, 343, 344
    of words, 317
Class bias, 89, 90
Classification, in speeches, 288
Clinton, Bill, 316
Clique, 230
Closedness versus openness, 204
Closed questions, 383

Closure
    perceptual process, 70
    speech conclusion function, 306
Cluster maps, 275
Co-culture, 82, 153
Code switching, 78
Coercion, 355
Coercive power, 229
Cognitive dissonance, 356
Cohesiveness, 229, 230
Collaboration
    with difficult group members, 243
    listening and, 119
    when not to collaborate, 222
Colleagues, 195, 197
Collectivist cultures
    defined, 156, 160
    leadership style preference, 254
    listening styles and, 123
Collett, Peter, 107
Commission, 89
Common values, 162, 163
Communication. *See also specific principles of communication*
    characteristics of, 37
    competence criteria, 44–46
    defensive, 90
    defined, 35
    dishonest, 49
    ethics of, 43, 46
    face-to-face contexts, 49
    failure rates, 33
    group patterns of, 230
    intercultural, 154, 164–171
    interpersonal, 49, 175
    job performance and, 196
    maxims of, 38
    mediated, 46–48, 175, 219, 226, 233
    mediated interpersonal, 181
    models of, 39–44
    principles of, 50–54
    process recap, 41
    reasons for studying, 34
    supportive, 90
    in twenty-first century, 46–49
Communication accommodation theory, 169
Communication competence, 44
Communication Ethics and Universal Values (Christians and Traber), 45
Communication interaction pattern, 230
Communication principles for a lifetime, 196–198
Communication triage, 127
Compacting statistics, 289
Competence, of speakers, 361, 362
Complementarity, 179
Complexity (organization strategy)
    informative speeches, 342
    main ideas, 296, 299
Complexity of communication, 38
Compliments, in conversation, 184, 185
Computer-generated presentation aids, 327
Concentration, in listening, 125
Concept maps, 275

Conclusions
    of interviews, 386
    in speeches, 305–306
Concrete meaning, 81
Concrete words, 317, 319
Confidence, for public speaking, 273
The Confidence Code (Kay, Shipman), 64
Confidential information, in informative speeches, 339
Conflict management, 209–212. *See also* interpersonal conflict
Conflict phase, in group development, 232–234
Conformity pressure, 238
Confrontational style, 209
Connection versus autonomy, 203
Connotative meaning, 81
Consensus, 249
Constructive conflict, 206
Content dimension, 38
Content sandwich, 296
Contexts of communication
    cultural, 155, 167
    defined, 41
    face-to-face, 49, 179, 181, 202
    as listening barriers, 129
    meaning and, 82
    mediated, 46–48, 175, 219, 226, 233
Continuous communication, 103
Control
    of facial expressions, 108
    interpersonal power as, 208
    versus problem-solving, 90, 91
Conversational narcissism (self-absorbed communicator style), 184
Conversations
    asking questions in, 182, 184
    giving compliments in, 184, 185
    initiating, 182, 183
    narcissistic, 184
Cook, Dane, 92
Cooley, Charles Horton, 62
Cooperation, in constructive conflict, 206
Cooperative style, 209
Coordination, in teams, 221
Correct words, 318
Covey, Stephen, 58
Coworkers, 196
Creativity, 238, 246
Credibility, 304, 361, 362
Criteria, in problem solving, 245
Critical/cultural approach to communication, 42
Critical listeners, 123
Criticism
    in group meetings, 248
    as listening barrier, 126
Cronkite, Waler, 339
Cultural contexts, 42, 155, 167
Cultural values
    defined, 154
    types of, 155–160
Culture and cultural differences
    biased language and, 84

co-cultures, 82, 153
communication principles and, 51
defined, 82, 152
forms of, 102
groups and teams and, 234
high-context, 154, 155
intercultural communication, 154
leadership styles and, 254
learning about, 166
listening and, 128
low-context, 154, 155, 166
meaning and, 82
nonverbal delivery of speeches and, 322, 323
nonverbal messages and, 100, 105, 154
norms, 226
in organizational patterns, 299
spatial relations and, 112
speech delivery styles and, 314
time perceptions, 322
Culture shock, 153
Cyber (internet) infidelity, 203
Cyclical relationships, 203
Czech Republic culture, 159

D

Dailey, René, 203
Dangerous information, in informative speeches, 339
Dating
online, 177, 180
versus hanging out, 182
Decentralized power, 157
Deception, in online relationships, 182
Deception detection, 113, 114
Decoding, 40
Deductive reasoning, 363, 364
Deep breathing, for anxiety, 272
Deep-level diversity, 256
Defensive communication, 90
Definitions, in speeches, 288, 290
De-intensification stage, 201
Delivery cues, for speeches, 311
Democratic leaders, 253, 254
Denotative meaning, 81
Derived credibility, 362
Description, in speeches, 288, 290
Destructive conflict, 206
Dewey, John, 244
Dialect, 326
Dialectical perspective, 204
Differences
assumptions of, 162–164
as basis of conflict, 205
strategies for bridging, 146, 164–171
Direct perception checking, 73
Disciplinary interviews, 381
Discrimination, 164
Disfluency, 114
Dishonesty
in digital communication, 49
nonverbal deception cues, 113, 114
Distracted listening, 118
Diversity. *See also* culture and cultural differences
in audience-centered public speaking, 270
deep- and surface-level, 256
forms of, 102, 145–151
in Internet resources, 285
Dodd, Carley, 154
Dominance
in group members, 238, 243
nonverbal cues, 113
Doohan, Eve-Anne, 136
Doorknob disclosure
Drama, in language, 319, 320
Drawings, as presentation aids, 327, 331
Dynamism, 362

E

E-communications. *See* social media
Egocentricism, 167
Ego conflict, 207
Ekman, Paul, 104, 108, 324
Elaboration likelihood model (ELM), 358, 359
Emergence phase, 233, 234
Emoticons, 181
Emotional appeals (pathos), 361, 366, 371
Emotional Intelligence (Goleman), 138
Emotional noise, 126
Emotional (social) support, 136–137, 186
Emotions
in conflict management, 209, 210
management strategies, 126
in nonverbal messages, 37, 98, 107, 108
paraphrasing, 139
in persuasion (pathos), 361, 365, 366, 371
in relationship maintenance, 189
in words, 83, 91
Empathy
defined, 91
in interviews, 396, 397
as listening goal, 132
as other-orientation strategy, 168, 169
in responding, 137–139
Employability, 33–34
Encoding, 40
Engagement of audience, 345
Enjoyment, as listening goal, 132
Entertainment, as speech purpose, 277
Enthusiasm, in job interview, 391
Erzen, Tanya, 402
Ethics
acknowledgments and, 291
in adaptation, 169–170
in communication competence, 45
defined, 45
in persuasion, 355, 357
in recording interviews, 382, 398
as speech evaluation criteria, 334
in world religions, 46
Ethnicity, 150–151
biased language and, 84, 90
defined, 150
versus race, 150
Ethnocentrism, 160, 161
Ethos, 361, 362
European cultures. *See also specific countries*
high- and low-context, 154, 155
monochronic, 226
restrained, 160
Evaluation, as listening goal, 132
Events, speeches about, 339, 340
Evidence, 363
Exclusive (sexist) language, 86
Exit interviews, 381
Expectancy violations theory, 101
Experience
in job interviews, 391
power of words and, 82–84
as supporting material source, 284, 286
Experiential baggage, 69
Expert power, 228, 229
Expert testimony, 289
Explanations, in speeches, 288, 290
Exploration stage, 199, 200
Expression–privacy tension, 204
Extemporaneous speaking, 316
Eye contact
during presentations, 322, 326, 331
listening and, 133
as nonverbal communication, 106

F

Facebook
FBO status, 185, 199
online image and, 392
self-esteem and, 64, 65
usage data, 58
as voter information source, 285
Face-to-face communication
for breakups, 202
contexts of, 49, 50
versus mediated interpersonal, 181
Facial expressions, 107, 108, 324, 326
Fact proposition, 360, 361
Families, 197
Fast, Julius, 103
Fear, of public speaking. *See* public speaking anxiety
Fear appeals, 357, 358
Feedback, defined, 41. *See also* responding skills
Feelings. *See* emotions
Feminine culture, 160
Feminine listening style, 128
Figurative analogies, 289
Figurative language, 319, 320
Filipino culture, 156, 159
Filled pauses, 114
Final summary, 302
First conversations, 182, 183
Fisher, Aubrey, 231
Flay, Bobbie, 341
Flexibility in language, 92
Flirtation cues, 180, 181
Flirtmojis, 181
Focus group, 219
Follow-through, of group members, 243
Force field analysis technique, 246
Forming, 231
Franklin, Benjamin, 58

Frequency of communication, 47, 48
Friendships, 194
Friesen, Wallace, 104, 108
Fuller, Buckminster, 290
Functional approach to leadership, 252, 253, 256
Funnel sequence, 384

G

Gatekeeper skills, 260, 261
Gay. *See* LGBTQ individuals
Gender
    in assumed roles, 63, 64
    biased language and, 84, 90
    defined, 64
    as diversity, 144
    self-esteem and, 64
Gender differences adapting to
    adapting to, 146
    communication approaches, 146
    emotional expression, 190
    listening styles, 123, 128
Gender expression, 145
Gender identity, 88–89, 146, 147
Gender-neutral language, 86
General purpose, 277, 278, 359
Generations, 148–149
Generation X, 148, 149
Generic language, 86
German culture, 154, 155, 168
Gestures
    as kinesics component, 105
    in nonverbal delivery of speeches, 322, 325, 349
    unreceptive audience and, 372
Ghosting, 201
Gibb, Jack, 90
Gide, André, 166
Globalization, 152
Goals
    adaptation strategy and, 170
    in communication competence, 45
    in conflict management, 211
    in groups and teams, 221, 239, 242, 249
    in job interviews, 391
    of listening, 132
Goleman, Daniel, 138
Graphs, as presentation aids, 328, 331
Grave dressing, 201
Gray, John, 145
Great Britain, 314, 323
Grievance interviews, 381
Group associations, 63
Group deviate, 231
Group dynamics
    cohesiveness, 229, 230
    norms, 227
    power, 228–229
    roles, 222
    rules, 225, 226
    status, 227
Groups
    advantages of, 238
    attitudes toward, 217
    defined, 218
    development stages of, 230–234
    difficult members in, 243
    disadvantages of, 238
    effective member attributes, 239–243
    in individualistic versus collectivist cultures, 234
    problem-solving steps in, 243–251
    role classifications, 224–225
    small group communication, 50, 220
    types of, 218
    versus teams, 220
    when not to collaborate, 222
Groupthink, 249, 250
Gudykunst, William, 165
Gunny-sacking, 93

H

Habitual relationships, 203
Habituation, 273
Hall, Edward T., 111, 152, 154
Halo effect, 104
Handouts, 332
Handshakes, 99
Hanging out, versus dating, 182, 183
Hansen, Katherine, 388
Happiness, 159, 160
Haptics, 108
Hard evidence, 300
Harvey, John, 185
Hasty generalization, 365
Health, improving, 35
Health communication, 50
Hearing, 120
Helical Model of Communication, 37
Hersey, Paul, 255
Hersman, Deborah, 319
Heterosexist language, 89
Hierarchy of needs, 356, 357
High-context cultures, 154, 155
Historical context, 42
Hocker, Joyce, 207
Hofstede, Geert, 153, 155
Holmes, Janet, 185
Holmes, Sherlock, 364
Homophobia (term), 88, 148
Homophobic language, 88
Honesty
    in reaching consensus, 249
    in relationships, 68
Hong Kong, 159
Horney, Karen, 60
Howe, Neil, 148
How We Think (Dewey), 244
Huber, Jeff, 300, 320
Human communication
    defined, 35
    model of, 44
    process recap, 41
Humblebrag, 92
Humes, James, 33
Humor, 343, 347, 348
Hypothetical illustration, 287
Hypothetical questions, 383

I

Ideas
    brainstorming, 248
    in group collaboration, 240, 242
    simplifying for clarity, 343, 344
    speeches about, 340
Identification with audience, 371
Illusion of transparency, 272
Illustration, in speeches, 287, 290
Images, as presentation aid, 327
"I" messages, 91, 210, 261
Immediacy
    nonverbal cues, 112, 180
    of twenty-first century communication, 46–47
Impersonal communication, 49, 176
Impromptu speaking, 316
India, 157
Indirect perception checking, 73
Indirect persuasion, 358, 359
Individualistic cultures
    countries with, 159
    defined, 156, 160
    listening styles and, 123
Individualization stage, 200, 201
Individual roles, 223
Indonesia, 157
Inductive reasoning, 363, 364
Indulgent cultures, 159, 160
Inescapability of communication, 37
Inflection, 325
Influence, in interpersonal communication, 175
Information-gathering interviews, 380, 381, 395, 396
Information overload, 127
Information power, 229
Information-processing barriers, 126–129
Information use
    as adaptation strategy, 166, 170
    as goal of meeting, 258
    group collaboration and, 222, 238, 240, 242
Informative speeches
    adapting to audience, 349
    clarity of, 343, 344
    on confidential or dangerous information, 339
    interesting quality of, 344–348
    memorable quality of, 348–349
    organization strategies for, 340–342
    purpose of, 277, 278, 337
    sample speeches, 350, 405
    types of, 337–340
Ingham, Harry, 189
In-group, 227
Initial credibility, 362
Initial previews, 301, 304
Initiation stage, 200
Inner speech, 66
Instagram, 47, 58
Integration–separation tension, 204
Intensification stage, 200
Intention, in communication competence, 44
Interaction model of communication, 40, 42, 43

Interactive strategy, 182
Interactive synchrony, 100
Intercultural communication, 154
Intercultural communication competence, 167
Intercultural conflict, 208
Interesting quality, of informative speeches, 344–348
Internal previews, 301
Internal summary, 302
Internet
    evaluating resources on, 284
    loneliness and, 48
    as speech topic source, 275
    as supporting material source, 284, 286
Interpersonal attraction
    communicating, 181
    defined, 177
    factors in, 177–179
    initiating relationships and, 181–185
Interpersonal communication
    attributes of, 175, 176
    defined, 49, 175
    relationship stages and, 198
Interpersonal conflict
    constructive versus destructive, 206
    defined, 205
    in groups or teams, 222, 231, 234
    managing, 212
    properties of, 209
    types of, 207
Interpersonal inertness, 120
Interpersonal power, defined, 206. *See also* power
Interpretation (perception stage), 71
Interpreters, 343
Intersectionality, 151–152
Interviews
    defined, 380
    information-gathering interviews, 395–396
    job interviews, 386
    phases of, 382–386
    recording, 383
    as supporting material source, 286
    types of, 380–382
Intimacy
    relationship stage, 199
    self-disclosure and, 186
Intimate space, 111
Intractable (irresolvable) conflict, 208
Intrapersonal communication, 51, 66
Introductions
    of speakers, 339
    in speeches, 303, 304, 306, 371
Inversion, 319, 320
Inverted funnel sequence, 384
Irish culture, 156
Irresolvable (intractable) conflict, 208
Irreversibility of communication, 37
"I" statements. *See* "I" messages

J

James, William, 60, 61
Japanese culture, 129, 159, 314
Jargon, 343

Job interviews
    conduct during, 395
    defined, 381, 382
    follow up after, 395
    preparation for, 386, 391
    resumes for, 386
    typical questions asked, 394
Job performance
    communication skills and, 197
    performance reviews, 381
Johari Window, 189
John Paul II (Pope), 362
Johnson, David, 58, 186, 187
Johnson, Lyndon, 101
Jones, Paula, 89, 90
Jourard, Sidney, 186, 190
JSTOR, 286
Jumping on the bandwagon, 365

K

Kale, David, 162
Kay, Katty, 64
Keller, Helen, 90
Kennedy, John F., 109, 320, 339
Kenrick, Douglas, 72
Kenya, 156
Kiesler, Sara, 47
Kim, Young, 165
Kinesics, 105
King, Martin Luther, Jr., 109
Klepper, Michael, 347
Kluckhohn, Clyde, 161
Knapp, Mark, 198
Knowing Your Value (Brzezinski), 64
Knowledge. *See* information use; personal knowledge
Kraut, Robert, 47

L

Laissez-faire leaders, 253, 254
Lamberg, Eric, 106
Language
    bias in, 84–90
    defined, 52, 80
    in effective verbal speeches, 317–320
    gender and sexual orientation issues, 147
    importance of, 79
    rhythm of, 320
    for supportive communication, 90
    texting and, 53, 78
    words and meanings in, 80–84
Lasswell, Harold, 40
Latin American culture, 226
Lay testimony, 290
Leadership
    defined, 251
    functional approach, 252, 253, 256
    power distribution and, 157
    role in groups, 223
    situational approach, 254–256
    styles approach, 253, 254, 256
    trait approach, 252, 256
    transformational, 257

Lean In (Sandberg), 64
Learning
    for cultural communication competence, 166
    as listening goal, 132
Legitimate power, 228, 229
Lesbians. *See* LGBTQ+ individuals
Lessing, Doris, 288
Lewis, C. S., 43, 45, 145, 163
LexisNexis Academic, 286
LGBTQ+ individuals
    cultural sensitivity toward, 146–148
Library holdings, 286
Line graphs, 328
LinkedIn, 34
Lippman, Walter, 232
Listening goals, 132
Listening skills, 130–135
    adaptation and, 170
    barriers to, 125–130, 133
    communication principles in, 32, 54, 118
    in conflict management, 211
    for cultural communication competence, 167
    defined, 120
    in developing sensitivity, 241
    in developing speeches, 291
    distracted listening, 118
    effective meetings and, 257, 262
    elements of, 120
    failure rates, 33
    in family relations, 195
    in friendships, 194
    gender differences in, 123, 128
    of great conversationalists, 182, 184
    in group communication, 218
    importance of, 118–120
    in interviews, 397
    principle overview, 54
    in reaching consensus, 249
    retention rates, 125
    self-awareness and, 123, 125–127, 131
    styles of, 125
Literal analogies, 288
Literary quotations, 290
Logical divisions, 282, 298
Logical fallacies, 364, 365
Logos, 361, 363, 364
Loneliness, and Internet use, 48
Long-term time orientation, 158–160
Lose-lose approach to conflict, 205
Low-context cultures, 154, 155, 166
Luft, Joe, 189

M

Main ideas
    generating, 282
    organizing, 299
Man-linked terminology, 86
Manning, Peyton, 303
Manuscript speaking, 315, 316
Maps, as presentation aids, 327, 331
Masculine-as-generic language, 86
Masculine culture, 159, 160
Masculine listening style, 128

Maslow, Abraham
    hierarchy of needs, 356, 357
    self-awareness framework, 59
Mass communication, 46
Matching hypothesis, 177
Material self, 60
Matures (generation), 148
Maturity, in job interview, 391
McConnell, John H., 33
McGraw, Phil (a.k.a. Dr. Phil), 59
Mead, George Herbert, 62
Mead, Margaret, 220
Meaning
    bypassing in, 80, 81
    co-creation of, 43
    in communication definition, 36
    defined, 80
    in words, 80
Mediated communication
    defined, 46, 175
    virtual groups or teams, 226, 233
Mediated interpersonal communication
    breakups via, 201
    deceptive, 182
    defined, 175
    versus face-to-face, 181
Meetings
    agendas for, 257–259, 262
    goals for, 257, 258
    leading, 259
    managing interaction in, 259–262
    phone use during, 220
    time spent in, 217
Mehrabian, Albert, 98, 113
Memorable quality, of informative speeches, 348–349
Memorized speaking, 315, 316
Men
    communication approach, 145–150
    emotional suppression in, 189–190
    listening style, 128
Men Are from Mars, Women Are from Venus (Gray), 145
Message creation, 42, 43
Message duration, 114
Message exchange, 41, 42
Messages
    in communication definition, 36
    defined, 40
Message transfer, 39, 40
Messer, Lucas, 317
Metadiscussion, 261
Meta-message, 132
Metaphors, 319, 320
Mexican culture, 159
Microphones, 324
Middle Eastern culture, 226
Millennials, 148
Miller, Gerald, 207
Mimicry, 100
Mindfulness
    development, 165–166
    listening and, 131

Minto, Mary, 393
Miranda, Lin-Manuel, 291
Misogynist, 164
Misplaced authority appeal, 365
Models, as presentation aids, 330, 331
Monochronic time perspective, 226
Monroe, Alan, 368
Montgomery, Barbara, 204
Mother Teresa, 126
Motivated sequence, 368
Motivation, 165
    for audience to listen, 345
    speech conclusion function, 305
Movement, during presentations, 323, 325, 349
Moyers, Bill, 320
Mswaka, Walter, 402
Multichanneled communication, 104
Multitasking, 47, 104, 127
Muratori, Lisa, 106
Murray, Henry, 161

N

Name calling, 210
Narcissism, 67, 184
National Communication Association, 46, 90
Nationality, and biased language, 84, 90
Need (motivated sequence stage), 368
Needs hierarchy, 356, 357
Negative visualization, 369
Neologism, 82
Networking, 387
Neutral audience, 372
Neves, Ernani, 402
Newspaper headlines
    misleading, 44
    for speech topic ideas, 275
Newton, Caleb, 403–405
Nigeria, 159
9/11 terrorist attacks, 250
Noise
    defined, 41, 129
    emotional, 126
Nominal group technique (silent brainstorming), 274
Nonconfrontational style, 209, 210
Nonlinguistic communication, 103
Non sequitur, 363
Nonverbal communication, 53
Nonverbal delivery of speeches
    appearance, 326
    eye contact, 322
    facial expressions, 324
    for persuasion, 373
    physical delivery, 322–323
    as reinforcement of key ideas, 349, 350
    vocal delivery, 324–325
Nonverbal messages
    adaptation and, 170
    communication codes of, 104
    communication principles in, 32, 53, 97
    in conflict management, 210

    in coworker relations, 197
    cues to deception, 113–114
    as cultural context, 154
    defined, 97
    in developing sensitivity, 241
    effective meetings and, 257, 262
    as emotional expression, 36, 107
    in family relations, 195
    in friendships, 194–195
    functions of, 100
    in group communication, 218
    interpreting, 112, 113
    listening and, 133
    nature of, 101–104
    in persuasive speeches, 366
    principle overview, 53
    reasons for studying, 98–100
Nonverbal supporting material, 284, 290, 291
Nonverbal transitions, 302
Norming, 231
Norms, 227
North American culture, 154, 155, 157, 166
Note cards, for speaker notes, 310
Nouwen, Henri J. M., 138, 168
Novelty versus predictability, 204
Numerical data, in speeches, 289, 290

O

Obama, Barack, 109, 301, 334
Objectivity, of Internet resources, 285
Objects
    as presentation aids, 330, 331
    speeches about, 337, 340, 341
Occasion, and speech topic, 274
Omission, 89, 319, 320
On-again/off-again relationships, 203
Online databases, 286
Online dating, 45, 177, 180. *See also* mediated interpersonal communication
Online sex, 203
Opening (interview phase), 382
Opening lines, of first conversations, 182
Openness versus closedness, 204
Open questions, 383
Operational definition, 288
Opinions, in speeches, 289, 290
Optimism, in group members, 242
Oral citation, 292
Organization (perception stage), 70, 71
Organizational communication, 50
Organizational patterns
    cultural diversity in, 299
    for informational speeches, 340–342
    for interviews, 380–389
    for persuasive speeches, 366–370
    types of, 296–299
Orientation phase, 231, 234
Orwell, George, 317
Other-oriented communication
    to avoid misunderstandings, 37
    for cultural communication competence, 166, 170

defined, 54, 167
to improve listening, 130
Outlines, for speeches, 306

P

Pacing of speeches, 344
Pakistan, 159
Paralanguage (vocalics), 110
Parallelism, 320
Paraphrasing, 137, 139
Passive approach (self-silencing), 205
Passive strategy (uncertainty reduction), 182
Pathos, 361, 366, 371
Pauses in speech, 114, 349
Peer pressure, in groups, 238
People
    as presentation aids, 330, 331
    speeches about, 337, 339, 341
Perception
    defined, 69
    enhancing, 71–73
    process recap, 70
    stages of, 69–71
    variation in, 71
Perception checking, 73, 102, 211
Performance reviews, 381
Performing, 231
Peripheral persuasion, 358
Personal attacks
    in conflict management, 210
    as logical fallacy, 364
Personal brand, 392
Personality, in job interview, 391
Personal knowledge, as supporting material source, 284, 286
Personal preference, 297
Personal space, 111
Personification, 319, 320
Persuasion
    versus coercion, 355
    defined, 50, 355
    ethics and, 355, 356, 357
    in groupthink, 250
    psychology of, 355–359
    as speech purpose, 277
Persuasion interviews, 381
Persuasive speeches
    adapting to audience, 359, 360, 366, 371–373
    credibility of speaker (ethos), 361, 362
    emotional appeals in (pathos), 361, 366, 371
    evidence and reasoning in (logos), 361, 363, 364
    logical fallacies in, 364, 365
    organization strategies for, 366–370
    propositions in, 360, 361
    purpose of, 359, 360
    sample speeches, 386–388, 418–420
    topics and topic sources, 359
Pew Research Center, 148
Philippines, 157, 159
Photographs, as presentation aids, 327, 331
Physical attraction, 176, 177, 179

Physical attractiveness, 104, 105
Physical context, 42
Physical delivery, 322–323
Physical environments
    as listening barriers, 130
    as nonverbal communication, 110
Physiological needs, 356
Pickup lines, 182
Pie graphs, 328
Piggybacking, in brainstorming, 247
Pitch, of speech, 325, 326
Place, as listening barrier, 130
Plagiarism, 292
Platinum Rule, 139
Polarization, 90
Policy proposition, 361
Polychronic time perspective, 226
Porter, Richard, 162
Positionality, 152
Positive attitudes
    development, 165–166
    as group member, 242
Positive motivation, 357, 358
Positive visualization, 369
Postdissolutional relationship, 203
Post hoc, ergo propter hoc, 364
Post-interaction stage, 201
Posture, 105, 106, 323, 326
Power
    conflict and, 208
    defined, 208, 228
    types of, 228, 229
Power distribution
    cultural values and, 157, 159
    ethnocentrism and, 161
    in groups or teams, 228
Predictability versus novelty, 204
Pre-interaction awareness stage, in relationships, 199
Pre-interaction phase of listening, 130
Prejudice, 164, 166
Preparation, for public speaking, 272
Preparation outline, 306
Presentation aids, 327–332. *See also* visual aids
Presentational communication, 49, 50
Presley, Elvis, 349–351
Prespeaking exercises, 273
Previews, 301, 304
Primacy, 300, 373
Primary groups, 218, 219
Primary tension, 232
Principles of communication, 50. *See also specific principles*
Privacy
    expression–privacy tension, 204
    violations of, 111
Probing questions, 383
Problem–solution organization, 298, 299, 366, 367, 370
Problem solving
    in conflict management, 212
    versus control, 91
    in groups, 243–251

Problem-solving interviews, 381
Procedures, speeches about, 337, 341
Process conflict, 232
Process function, 252, 253
Processing rate, 127
Profanity, 210
Proof, 363
Propositions, 360, 361
Proxemics, 111
Proximity, in interpersonal attraction, 178
Pseudoconflict, 207
Psychological baggage, 68
Psychological context, 42
Public-opinion polls, 381
Public space, 111
Public speaking. *See also* speeches
    audience-centered model, 269, 270
    building confidence for, 270–273
    defined, 269
    listening skills and, 120
    as presentational communication, 49, 50
public speaking anxiety
    defined, 271
    reasons for, 271
    strategies for overcoming, 272, 273
    symptoms of, 272, 273
"Puckered chin" expression, 107, 108
Purpose statement, for speeches, 277–279, 337, 359, 360
Push–pull dynamics, 204

Q

Quality, in interpersonal communication, 176
Questions
    as central idea, 281
    as conversation skill, 183
    for cultural communication competence, 167
    in interviews, 383–385, 393–395, 398
    listening and, 136, 345
    in problem solving, 245
Quiet (Cain), 332
Quinn, Daniel, 52
Quintilian, 361
Quorum, 260

R

Race, 150–151
    biased language and, 84, 90
    term, 149
Racism, 150
Rate of speech, 325, 343
Reading, for speech topic ideas, 275
Reasoning, 363, 364
Reasoning by analogy, 363
Reasons, as main ideas, 282, 298
Receiver, 40
Receiver apprehension, 127
Recency, 300
Receptive audience, 371, 373
Reciprocity, in self-disclosure, 187
Reclaiming Conversation (Turkle), 181
Red herring, 365

Redmond, Mark, 168
Redundancy, in speeches, 348
Reference resources, 286
Referent power, 228, 229
Reflective thinking, 244–251
Reframing, 67
Refutation, 368, 370
Reinforcement, in speeches, 348
Reinforcement phase, 234
Relating to audience, 345
Relational conflict, 232
Relational de-escalation, 201
Relational dialectics, 204
Relational escalation, 200
Relational listeners, 122, 123
Relationship dimension, 38
Relationships. *See also* interpersonal conflict
   as adaptation goal, 170
   attraction in, 176–181
   of choice, 175
   of circumstance, 175
   communication principles applied to, 197
   defined, 175
   development stages, 197
   dissolution of (breakups), 201–203
   FBO (Facebook official), 185, 199
   of group members, 241, 242
   honest, 68
   improving, 34
   initiating, 181–185
   interpersonal communication in, 49, 84
   listening and, 118, 119
   nonverbal messages and, 99
   postdissolutional, 203
   self-concept and, 61
   self-disclosure in, 185–189
   self-esteem and, 68, 69
   supportive, 90–92
   tensions in (push–pull dynamics), 204
Religion
   biased language and, 84, 90
   ethics in, 45
   versus spirituality, 61
Remembering, in listening process, 121
Repetition, 320
Responding skills
   adaptation and, 171
   in developing speeches, 291
   effective meetings and, 257, 262
   in family relations, 195
   in friendships, 194
   in group communication, 218
   improving, 140
   in interviews, 393
   in listening process, 121
Response latency, 114
Responsibilities, in teams, 220, 221
Restrained cultures, 159, 160
Results-driven structure, 239, 242
Retarded (term), 89, 90
Reward power, 228, 229
Rhetoric, 50, 361, 371
Rhetoric (Aristotle), 50, 355
Rhythm of language, 320

Risk, in self-disclosure, 187
Rogers, Carl, 138
Roles
   assumed, 63
   in groups and teams, 221, 222
Roosevelt, Eleanor, 164
Roosevelt, Franklin D., 362
Rules
   defined, 39
   of nonverbal communication, 101, 102
   in teams, 221, 225, 226
   versus norms, 226
Russia, 160
Ryan, Liz, 392

S

Safety needs, 356
Saint-Exupéry, Antoine de, 138
Samovar, Larry, 162
Sandberg, Sheryl, 64
Sapir, Edward, 80
Sapir–Whorf Hypothesis, 80
Sargent, Stephanie, 128
Satir, Virginia, 34
Satisfaction (motivated sequence stage), 368, 369
Scandinavia, 154, 155
Secondary groups, 219
Secondary tension, 232
Second guessing, 123
"Second screen" phenomenon, 104
Selection
   in listening process, 120
   perception stage, 70
Self, 59
Self-absorbed communicator style (conversational narcissism), 184
Self-actualization needs, 357
Self-awareness
   defined, 59
   in group members, 240, 241
   listening and, 125, 127, 131
   Maslow's framework of, 59
   in social media use, 58
   in speech topic selection, 274
   in supporting material, 290
Self barriers, 125–126
Self-concept
   components of, 60–61
   defined, 60
   development of, 61–63
Self-concept clarity, 64
Self-disclosure
   defined, 185
   models of, 186, 188
   properties of, 187, 188
Self-esteem
   compliments and, 184, 185
   constructive conflict and, 206
   enhancing, 66–69
   factors affecting, 64–66
   fluctuations in, 64, 65
Self-esteem needs, 357
Self-expression, in job interview, 391

Self-focus, 125, 130, 138
Self-fulfilling prophecy, 242
Self-labels, 63
Self-reflexiveness, 63
Self-silencing, 205
Self-talk, 66, 138, 165, 211
Senge, Peter, 256
Sense, in communication definition, 36, 37
Sensitivity, in group members, 241, 242
Sensory images, 346
Separation stage, 201
September 11, 2001 terrorist attacks, 250
Serial arguments, 208
The Seven Habits of Highly Effective People (Covey), 58
Sex (biological)
   in assumed roles, 63
   as diversity, 145
Sexist (exclusive) language, 86
Sexual attraction, 177, 179
Sexual harassment, 185
Sexual orientation, 90, 146–218
Shannon, Claude, 40
Sheats, Paul, 223
Shifting attention, 127
Shimanoff, Susan, 39
Shipman, Claire, 64
Short-term time orientation, 158–160
Sign language, 97
Signposts, 300, 302
Silent brainstorming (nominal group technique), 274
Similarity
   assumptions of, 161, 162, 164
   in interpersonal attraction, 178
Similes, 319, 320
Simmons, Andy, 392
Simple conflict, 207
Simple words, 317, 318
Situational approach to leadership, 254–256
Skills development, 167–171
Slang, 343
Slayen, Galia, 65
Small group communication, 50, 220
Smartphones
   nonverbal behavior and, 105
   for speaker notes, 310, 311
   usage data, 46
   using in meetings, 220
Snapchat, 58
Social attraction, 177
Social class, 151
Social comparison, 65
Social decentering, 131, 168
Social groups, 219
Social isolation, 48
Socialization, 151
Social media
   angry responses on, 137
   breakups via, 201
   cyber infidelity, 203
   fitness posts, 106
   intercultural communication and, 154
   language and, 82

online dating, 45, 177
online image, 392
self-awareness and, 58
self-esteem and, 64
social support through, 190
video chats, 196
Social needs, 356
Social penetration model, 188
Social roles, 223, 224
Social self, 61
Social space, 111
Social support, 139–140, 190
Socioeconomic class bias, 90
Soft evidence, 300
Soft-to-hard evidence organization, 300
Source, 40
South American culture, 155, 226
Spanish culture, 159
Spatial organization
  informative speeches, 341, 342
  main ideas, 299
Spatial relations, 100, 102, 111
Speaker anxiety. *See* public speaking anxiety
Speakers, introducing, 339
Speaking notes, 310–311
Specificity (organization strategy), 300
Specific purpose, 278, 279, 360
Specific words, 317, 318
Speech errors, 114
Speeches. *See also* informative speeches; persuasive speeches; public speaking
  adapting to audience, 270, 273, 275, 303, 314
  buying, 277
  central idea for, 280
  conclusions in, 305–306
  as content sandwich, 296
  delivery styles, 314–316
  dress and grooming for, 326
  evaluation criteria, 334
  introductions in, 303, 305, 306
  main ideas in, 282, 296–299
  nonverbal delivery of, 321–326
  organization of, 296–299
  outlining, 311
  parts of, 296
  presentation aids for, 327–332
  public speaking anxiety and, 271–273
  purpose statement for, 277–279
  rehearsing, 331, 332, 333
  speaking notes for, 310–311
  supporting material for, 284–292, 299
  topic selection for, 274–276
  verbal delivery, 320
Spiritual self, 61
Stability–change tension, 204
Stacks (library collections), 286
Stage fright. *See* public speaking anxiety
Stagnation or turmoil stage, 200
Standard outline format, 307, 311
State conversational narcissism, 184
Statistics, in speeches, 289, 290
Status, 227
Steinberg, Mark, 207
Steinem, Gloria, 64

Stereotypes
  as adaptation barrier, 163
  age-based, 148
  avoiding, 73
  defined, 163
Stop, look, listen (listening skills), 130–135
Storming, 231
Strauss, William, 148
Stress management, 34
Structure
  of group discussion, 243, 244
  results-driven, 239, 242
Study groups, 219
Styles approach to leadership, 253, 254, 256
Summaries, 305
Superiority, 92, 93, 160, 164
Supporting material
  acknowledgment of, 291
  attention-getting, 345
  communication principles and, 290, 291
  defined, 284
  sources of, 284–286
  types of, 287–290
Supportive communication, 90
Surface-level diversity, 256
Suspension, 319, 320
Switzerland, 155
Syllogism, 363
Symbolic self-awareness, 59
Symbols
  defined, 36, 80
  in language, 52, 53
Sympathetic listeners, 122
Sympathy, 168
Systemic racism, 150

T

Taiwanese culture, 159
Tannen, Deborah, 145
Tao (C. S. Lewis term), 163
Task conflict, 232
Task function, 252
Task-oriented listeners, 123
Task roles, 223
Taylor, Dalmas, 188
TEACH acronym, 338
Team ground rules, 226
Teams. *See also* groups
  characteristics of, 220
  collectivist cultures, 234
  defined, 220
  development stages of, 231–234
  group dynamics in, 230
  versus groups, 220
  in individualistic versus
  when not to collaborate, 222
Technology
  in communication, 46–49
  millennials, and, 148
  privacy violations and, 112
  role in proximity, 178–179
Tension
  in group development, 232
  in relationships (push–pull dynamics), 204

Terminal credibility, 362
Territoriality, 111
Territorial marker, 111
Texas A&M University bonfire disaster, 250
Texting
  breakups via, 202
  language skills and, 53, 78
  while walking, 105
Textisms, 78
Text presentation aids, 327
Thank You for Being Late (Friedman), 144
Therapy groups, 219
Thesaurus, 317
Thoughts, words effect on, 83
TikTok, 48
Time
  cultural expectations and, 322
  as group collaboration issue, 222, 238
  monitoring in meetings, 261
  monochronic versus polychronic perspective, 226
  short-term versus long-term orientation, 158–160
Timeliness, of Internet resources, 285
Timing
  of feedback, 136
  as listening barrier, 129
Tinder dating app, 177
Tolerate ambiguity, 166
Topical organization, 297
  informative speeches, 340–342
  main ideas, 296, 299
Topics for speeches
  in central idea, 281
  introducing, 303
  selecting and narrowing, 274–276
Touch, 108, 109
Touch ethic, 109
Traber, Michael, 45
Trait approach to leadership, 251, 252, 256
Trait conversational narcissism, 184
Transaction model of communication, 42, 43
Transformational approach to leadership, 257
Transgender
  biased language and, 86, 87
  defined, 87
  voices of, 109–110
Transitions, 301, 302
Transphobia, 88
Transphobic language, 88
Trigger words, 91
Truman, Harry, 169
Trump, Donald, 107, 108, 320
Trustworthiness, 362
Tunnel sequence, 385
Turkle, Sherry, 181
Turmoil or stagnation stage, 200
Turner, Lynn H., 90
Twain, Mark, 164
Tyson, Mike, 110

U

Unbiased words, 318
Uncertainty

communication, 181
cultural tolerance for, 157, 159, 160
managing through communication, 181
Uncertainty-reduction theory, 181
Understanding
as adaptation goal, 169
in communication competence, 44
in conflict management, 211
in listening process, 121
in responding, 135
United States
individualism in, 156, 157
indulgent culture of, 159
time orientation in, 159, 226
Universal values, 162, 163
Unreceptive audience, 372
Usability, of Internet resources, 285

V

Value, in self-esteem, 63
Value proposition, 360, 361
Values (principles)
cultural, 160
defined, 60
as target of persuasive speech, 360
universal, 162, 163
Vangelisti, Anita, 199
Van Ness, Dan, 401
Verbal delivery of speeches, 321, 348
Verbal drama, 319
Verbal messages
adaptation and, 170
biased language, 90
communication principles in, 32, 52, 78
in coworker relations, 197
effective meetings and, 262
in family relations, 195
in friendships, 194–195
in group communication, 218
nonverbal contradictions, 99, 100
in persuasive speeches, 366
principle overview, 52, 53
reasons for studying, 79
for supportive communication, 90
words and meanings in, 80
Verbal supporting material, 284, 291
Verbal transitions, 302
Vertical search engine, 284
Video chats, 196
Video presentation aids, 329, 330
Virtual groups or teams, 219, 226, 233
Visual aids
to explain procedures, 338
guidelines for using, 330–332
in informative speeches, 348–350
for intercultural communication, 301
in persuasive speeches, 366
to present statistics, 291
types of, 284, 327–331
Visual dominance ratio, 106
Visualization, 66, 369
Visual supporting material. *See* visual aids
Vivid words, 318
Vocal delivery, 324–325
Vocalics (paralanguage), 113
Voice, 113
Volume, of speech, 324, 326

W

Walker, Loren, 402
Walking behavior, 105, 106
Waterman, Alan, 156
Watson, John H. (a.k.a. Dr. Watson), 364
Watson, Kitty, 123
Weaver, James, 128
Weaver, Warren, 40
Weber, Ann, 185
Web searches
for speech topics, 275
tools for narrowing, 284
Weger, Harry, 137
Wheel interaction pattern, 231
White, Leah, 317
Whorf, Benjamin Lee, 80
Wiio, Osmo, 38
Wikipedia, 285
Wilmot, William, 207
Wilson, Ruth Gilmore, 401
Win-lose approach to conflict, 205
Win-win approach to conflict, 207, 210
Women
communication approach, 145
discrimination against, 164
emotional expression in, 190
listening style, 123, 128
nonverbal communication, 104, 112
self-esteem, 64, 65
sexist language and, 86
Word pictures, 346
Words
accurate, 318
clarity of, 317
meanings and, 80
power of, 83
for resumes, 389
for supportive communication, 90–92
Word structures, in speech, 320
World Trade Center destruction, 250
Worldview, 154, 161

X

Xenophobia, 161

Y

"You" messages, 91, 261
Young, Whitney, 101

Z

Ziglar, Zig, 395
Zimmer, John, 344